Photo Credits: **Part I opener** Courtesy Paintbrush Diplomacy. **Chapter 1 opener** Courtesy Paintbrush Diplomacy. **8** Photograph by Jeffrey Ploskonka, National Museum of African Art, Eliot Elisofon Archives, Smithsonian Institution. **9** (top right) Photo by Lee Stalsworth. **9** (bottom left) Photograph by Jeffrey Ploskonka, National Museum of African Art, Eliot Elisophon Archives, Smithsonian Institution. **9** (bottom right) Photo by Peter Harholdt. **25** (top) Dixon Ticonderoga Company. **40** Scala/Art Resource, N.Y. **41** Sachio Yoshida, Japan Creators' Association, Illustration Bank. **55** Photographer: Ann Gummerson. **58** Photo by Kay Alexander. **Chapter 4 opener** Courtesy Paintbrush Diplomacy. **105** ''Jane C., Symbolisches Denken in Bildern und Sprach,'' Max Klager, Ernst Reinhardt Verlag, Munchen, Basel, 1978. **113** Baltimore Museum of Art, Department of Education. **116** Photo by Brad Herzog. **126** *Creative and Mental Growth*, rev. ed., Victor Lowenfeld, The Macmillan Co., N.Y., 1952. **Chapter 5 opener** By permission of Foreign Language Press. **133** Lorna Selfe, *Nadia*, Harcourt Brace Jovanovich, 1977. **147** *Winslow Homer: A Portrait* by Jean Gould, Dodd Mead & Co., 1962. **Part III opener** Courtesy Paintbrush Diplomacy. **167** Photo by John Tennant. **168** Photo by Malcom Varon, N.Y. © 1987. **Chapter 7 opener** Photo courtesy Education Development Center, Inc., Newton, MA. **204** Sidney Janis Gallery, New York. **205** (left & right) Photo by Jerry Jacka. **Chapter 9 opener** Courtesy International Business Machines, Incorporated. **Chapter 10 opener** Courtesy Paintbrush Diplomacy. **267** (top) Dr. Arne A. Kollwitz. Used with permission. **277** Jerry N. Uelsmann Fotofolio, Box 661 Canal Sta., N.Y., N.Y. 10013. **286** © Ken Burris, Shelburne, VT, All rights reserved. **293** Photo by Kay Alexander. **305** (bottom) Photograph by Robert E. Mates. **311** (top right) Photograph by Robert E. Mates. **321** Photo by Adam Woolfitt. **Chapter 12 opener** Michelangelo, *Sistine Ceiling*, detail, 1508–1512. Scala/Art Resource, N.Y. **332** Scala/Art Resource, N.Y. **333** Photograph by Jeffrey Ploskonka, National Museum of African Art, Museum Purchase, Smithsonian Institution. **342** Hedrich-Blessing. **350** Rick Stromoski. **352** Photograph by Geoffry Johnson. **Chapter 13 opener** Photo: Reg Morrison/Weldon Trannies. **377** Scala/Art Resource, N.Y. **381** Scala/Art Resource, N.Y. **384** National Museum of American Art/Art Resource, N.Y. **386** (top) Photo by Robert Witanowski. **387** (bottom) Photo by © 1988 Geoffry Clements, Inc., New York. **Chapter 15 opener** Courtesy Paintbrush Diplomacy. **Chapter 16 opener** Winslow Homer, *The Country School*, 1871, 54.3 × 97.5 cm. The Saint Louis Art Museum. Museum purchase. **498** Photo by Roger Graves. **535** Photo by Rick Steadry. **539** Photo by Jack Engeman Studio. **Chapter 18 opener** Richard Hutchings/InfoEdit. **552** Photo by Malcom Varon, N.Y.C. © 1977. **553** Photo by Malcom Varon, N.Y.C. © 1987.

ISBN: 0-15-507295-1

Library of Congress Catalog Card Number: 90-81891

Printed in the United States of America

CHILDREN AND THEIR ART

METHODS FOR THE ELEMENTARY SCHOOL

FIFTH EDITION

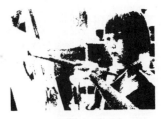

AL HURWITZ

Maryland Institute, College of Art

•

MICHAEL DAY

Brigham Young University

HBJ

HARCOURT BRACE JOVANOVICH COLLEGE PUB

Fort Worth   Philadelphia   San Diego   New York   Orlando   Austin
Toronto   Montreal   London   Sydney   Tokyo

PREFACE

The fifth edition of *Children and Their Art* continues to build on the sound structure of the first edition, authored by Charles Gaitskell in 1958. A glance at the original table of contents will attest to Gaitskell's foresight about the direction that art education would take. Subsequent editions have enlarged the scope of the original by adding new topics, which has kept the content current with contemporary theory and practice. This edition expands upon Gaitskell's intention to give future art teachers a comprehensive introduction to the teaching of art that provides both a theoretical and a practical basis for instruction.

Although the fifth edition reflects many changes, and includes more illustrations and many new topics, the presentation of a comprehensive, up-to-date view of art at the elementary and middle school level is consistent with Gaitskell's original aims. Some concerns emphasized by Gaitskell—such as the developmental aspects of children's artistic behavior and the relationship of art and society—maintain their position in this work, while other topics from the first edition have evolved over the years. For example, the interest in art appreciation has been redefined to include the study of art history, art criticism, and aesthetics, which are now covered in separate chapters. Concern for gifted children and for handicapped and special learners continues to receive attention in this edition.

Advances in media technology—the widespread use of computers, videos, compact discs, and the easy availability of excellent quality art reproductions, filmstrips, slides, and other teaching resources could not be predicted in the late 1950s when the first edition appeared. Recent changes include the search for historical antecedents of art education and a shift from the use of predominantly Western European artworks to the selection of examples from many cultures and eras. The fifth edition includes coverage of the major changes in art education that have occurred since 1958, when art education focused almost exclusively on children's art production itself.

These changes, reflecting advances and shifting concerns in general education as well as in art education, have created an interesting distinction. The title of the book, *Children and Their Art*, now refers not only to what children create and express with art media, but also to their understanding from the broader perspectives of art history, art criticism, and aesthetics presented at levels appropriate for children's abilities. These ideas about art are introduced in an integrated fashion, often centered around art production activities.

This edition includes many changes that we hope will enhance its usefulness for readers. There are more color illustrations, with more examples of children's art and works by adult artists. The book has been reorganized into five parts for easier study and quicker reference. New classroom-tested activities have been added to every chapter. Picture captions have been expanded to provide more information, and bibliographies now appear at the end of each chapter, where they will be easier to use. Lists of art curricula, film, and art reproduction distributors have been revised. A brief history of art education and a listing of major art museums have also been added.

Many individuals, including art teachers and students, assisted the authors as they prepared the fifth edition. Examples of children's artwork come from the highly regarded schools in Dade County, Florida, the Newton schools in Massachusetts, the Metropolitan Separate School Board of Toronto, the Provo, Utah, schools and from the schools in Grosse Pointe, Michigan, and Simsbury, Connecticut. In Newton, the students of Maida Abrams, Lori Schill, Pauline Joseph, Shelly Belsh, Carolyn W. Shapiro, Arlene D. Bandes, Susan Jenkinson, Susan Varga, and Lilli Ann Killeen Rosenberg and Ben Rosenberg made valuable contributions, as did the students of Bonnie Busco in Provo, Cynthia Rehm in Simsbury, and Paula Miriani in Grosse Pointe. Judy Waters of the Roland Park Country School in Baltimore provided the "Living Reproduction," and Ruth Aukerman, also from Maryland, provided examples from her classes at the Maryland Institute, College of Art. Special thanks are also due Yvonne Anderson, Karen Carrol, and Margaret DiBlasio for their helpful comments in specific areas of the manuscript.

We wish also to express our thanks to the Metropolitan Separate School Board of Toronto for submitting a large collection of slides illustrating various aspects of the art production of children and for permitting us to use some of these slides. In particular, we thank Albert St. R. Mallon, assistant superintendent of curriculum (Visual Arts), and the following art consultants and resource teachers: Margaret Adamson, Gabrielle Tutak, Eleanor Copeman-Harris, Susan Ashour, and Taida Supronas. Together, these five collected student work from some 230 schools. Thanks also to the Foster Parents Plan for material from its global education project, "See Me, Share My World: Understanding the Third World Through Children's Art."

The authors are both active members of the International Society for Education Through Art (INSEA), the only worldwide organization for art teachers. It is therefore fitting that the examples of children's work in this edition, gathered during our travels and through personal contacts, continue to reflect our understanding of visual expression as a universal phenomenon and as a unifying factor across cultures.

We are most grateful to the following INSEA members who gave or lent us the work of children in their countries: Mahmoud El-Bassiouny, Qatar University; Mitsui Nagamachi, Japan; Jan Meyer, South Africa; and Jan de Grauw, the Netherlands. Others, who not only contributed artwork but also served as generous and enthusiastic hosts during the author's travels, must be especially noted: Izzika and Jaffa Goan and Ayila Gordon, Israel Museum; Moshe Tamir, Ministry of Education, Israel; Jawad Hakim, Paley Art Centre, Jerusalem,

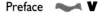

Israel; Ahmad Al Fayyumi, Al-Aasam School, Beersheva, Israel; Valentina Hudoshina, Hermitage Museum, Leningrad, the Soviet Union; Jack Condous, president of the INSEA, Adelaide, Australia; Andrea Karpati, University of Budapest, Hungary; Magda Koltai, Komlo, Hungary; Jane Winney, Auckland, New Zealand; George Luis, Rio de Janeiro, Brazil; Ray Thorburn, Department of Education, New Zealand; Ray Sampson, Head Inspector of Art, Western Australia; Chong-hiok, Hong-Ik University, Seoul, Korea; Chio Duk Hyu, University of Seoul, and Kuo-hsiung Ho, Seoul; Martin Taamsma, Johann Ligtvoet, Pieter Hermans, and Marjo Van Hoorn, the Netherlands; Max Klager, Heidelberg, The Federal Republic of Germany; and E. V. Kvyatkovsky and Vladimir Razumny of the Soviet Union.

Some Americans who made specific contributions in reviewing material are Brent and Marjorie Wilson, The Pennsylvania State University; Donald Brigham, Attleboro schools, Massachusetts; Phyllis Gold Gluck, Brooklyn College; Judith Grunbaum, Newton, Massachusetts; and Virgie Day, Barbra Wardle, and Mark Johnson, Brigham Young University, Provo, Utah. Thanks are due the Department of Art and the College of Fine Arts and Communications, Brigham Young University, for generous encouragement and support, and to David Baker and Kay Alexander for their critiques of the previous editions of this book.

Helen Hurwitz, Christina Demorest, Sharon Heelis, and Kay Hair gave invaluable secretarial assistance in preparing the manuscript, and JoAnn Blackburn spent many hours pursuing library research for this effort.

Finally, the editiorial and production staff at Harcourt Brace Jovanovich, in particular Julia Berrisford, acquisitions editor, and David Watt, manuscript editor, served as models for editor-author relationships. Their concern for detail and their seemingly infinite patience in dealing with two authors, rather than just one, should provide a standard that other publishers might emulate. We also wish to thank Michael Biskup, production editor, Kay Faust, designer, Cindy Robinson, art editor, and Diane Southworth, production manager, for their special contributions.

Al Hurwitz

Michael Day

~CONTENTS~

PART II CHILDREN AS LEARNERS

PART III CONTENT OF ART

INSTRUCTION

CURRICULUM AND EVALUATION

The authors wish to dedicate this edition to Dr. Charles Dudley Gaitskell — administrator, writer, educator.

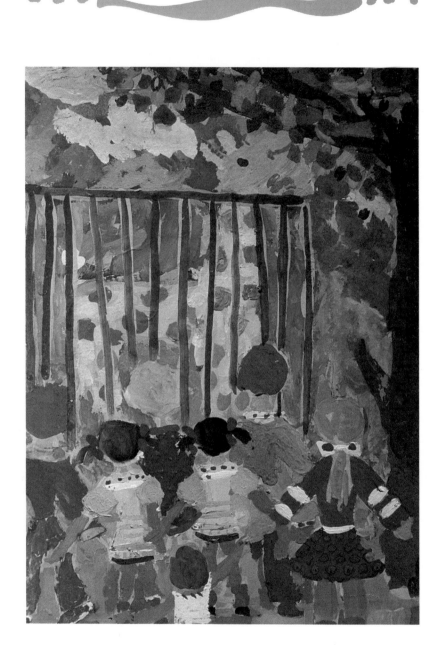

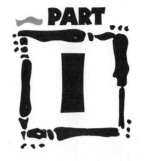

PART I

FOUNDATIONS AND GOALS FOR ART EDUCATION

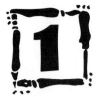

FOUNDATIONS OF ART EDUCATION: CHILDREN, ART, AND SOCIETY

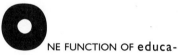

ONE FUNCTION OF education is to maintain the culture — its values, ideals, and patterns of living — through the training of succeeding generations. In art, this maintenance is difficult because the arts have not been generally recognized as central in our culture. We must set up objectives for art education in a society that surrounds itself with art forms, but that is generally unaware of the aesthetic qualities. We must work with many people who have negative feelings about artists and designers, so we cannot derive all our values about art education from the general public.[1]

June King McFee

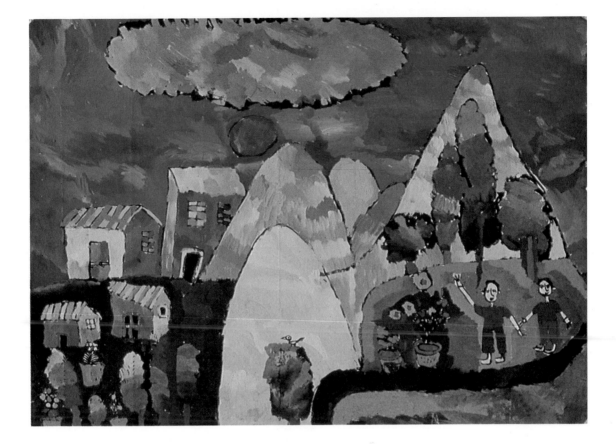

The foundations of art education have been built over the years on increased knowledge and changing beliefs about the nature of the visual arts, conceptions of children and adults as learners, and the values of society as conveyed through educational goals and practices.[2] During this century, the visual arts have gone through rapid shifts in emphasis, far-reaching innovations, and technological advances similar to those in science, social institutions, communications, and transportation. Those who study world cultures understand that changes in the various aspects of human endeavor are often interrelated and interdependent, and that art often reveals aspects of existence common to different societies and eras. Changes in art, which are the content for art education, naturally affect what is taught in educational programs and how it is taught.

Because teaching is an activity that emerges from some conception about how learning occurs, changing views of the learner and of the teaching-learning process affect educational programs probably as much as changes in the content of education. Advances in psychology, as they are applied by educators, have made major contributions to the foundations of art education. Knowledge of the psychological characteristics of learners and their implications for education are essential factors of enlightened art programs.

A third major element in any educational program is the impact of society's values and beliefs. Political, economic, and social changes result in changes in educational institutions and practices. This chapter provides a brief survey of contemporary art education as we review changes in art, in conceptions of the learner, and in the types of education valued by society.

NATURE OF THE VISUAL ARTS

To obtain a basic understanding of art, we might imagine ourselves back in history, before the advent of personal adornment, even before the age of cave paintings. From this vantage we may recognize the importance of one early achievement: the invention of containers. The seemingly simple realization that a hollow space would allow someone to store water or grain must have been one of the wonders of primitive technology. Eventually, someone must have noticed that if greater attention were given to the *shape* of a vessel as well as the thickness of its walls, the container would somehow be more satisfactory. In perfecting the form in order to improve the function, that anonymous fabricator was working on the level of enlightened craftsmanship.

Later, a person making a container, or pot, must have experimented with the *surface* of the vessel, although this had nothing at all to do

Ceramic containers from the Ch'ing dynasty of the K'ang-Hsi period. (National Gallery of Art, Washington, D.C., Widner Collection.)

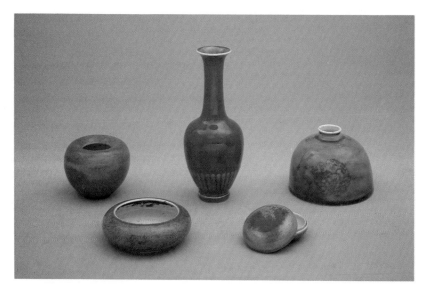

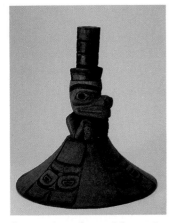

A crest hat of wood from the Haida Indians of British Columbia, worn for ceremonial occasions. In this case, a clan totem is represented. (Courtesy of the National Museum of Natural History, Smithsonian Institution, Washington, D.C.)

with its *function*—that is, with how much the pot can carry or how much wear it can survive. Decoration can only make the handling and the seeing of the object a more *pleasurable* experience. This development of the idea of decoration provided the potter with unlimited options for technique and design. Once the object was formed, shapes could be inscribed or painted in patterns that might include swirls, loops, straight lines, or combinations of any of these.

These early craftspersons probably discovered that decoration could have *meaning,* that signs could stand for ideas. They found that symbols might not only express fears, dreams, and fantasies, but could communicate their states of mind to other people. Cave paintings reflect this function, for in these the animals depicted are more than recognizable shapes taken from the experiences of the group—they probably represent rituals whereby hunters could record concern for survival.[3] Decoration now moved into the more profound sphere of the image as metaphor, and not every member of the tribe was capable of making such a transference. Those who could we now call *artists*.[4]

As art moved beyond utilitarian functions and attention was centered upon appearance as well as use, the notion of *aesthetic* response evolved. A painting or a fine vessel might be valued as an investment or as historical data, but central to its existence as a work of art is the power to provide pleasure or stimulation as distinctive in its way as musical compositions or poetry. When we view art objects from other cultures, we can respond to the aesthetic "vibrations" of the work despite a lack of knowledge of conditions surrounding the creation of the object. When available, historical and cultural information can extend

Fishskin boots from the Nanai Amur River, Siberia. The skin is taken from salmon and is decorated with designs from Chinese mythology. (From the collections of the American Museum of Natural History, New York City, Department of Anthropology, #70-620a,b. Photograph courtesy Smithsonian Institution.)

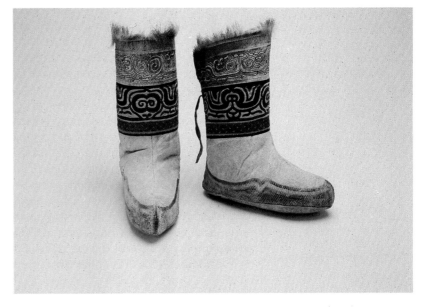

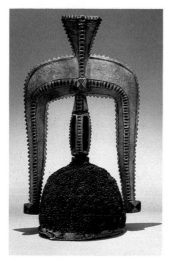

A headdress from the Koro peoples of the Ache group of Nigeria, made of wood, seeds, fiber, and resin. (National Museum of African Art, Washington, D.C.)

and intensify our responses to an artwork and greatly increase our understanding of it.

As we discuss the *visual arts* in this book, we refer to the traditional *fine arts*, such as drawing, painting, printmaking, and sculpture, including more contemporary modes such as photography, video, and computer-generated imagery; the *applied arts* that surround us every day, such as architecture, ceramics, weaving, graphic design, illustration, interior design, and fashion design; and *folk art* that emerges from the creative impulses of untutored artists in many forms, such as painting, carvings, built environments, or objects such as weather vanes, furniture, or quilts, to mention only a few.

As educators concerned with the nature of art, we might consider for study the visual arts of many cultures, including Western European traditions, Egyptian, Oriental, African, pre-Columbian, native American, North and South American, Polynesian, and others. The visual arts ranging from prehistoric to contemporary times are worthy of study, including periods such as ancient, medieval, Renaissance, and modern. Within the ranges of cultures and periods are numerous styles of art such as Chinese T'ang dynasty, archaic Greek, African Benin, Italian baroque, surrealism, pop art, and neoexpressionism that can provide fascinating insights into the nature of art on a worldwide basis.

Over time, as art has become increasingly complex and diverse, professions have grown out of needs to preserve, study, interpret, and judge artworks of today and from the past. A complex system of art museums, galleries, publications, markets, laws, and private and governmental agencies that support and oversee the art community has evolved. This system employs numerous art professionals, such as art educators, gallery directors, art dealers, museum curators, conservators, producers of art reproductions, and many more.

Four art disciplines provide the basic expertise that, in various combinations of emphasis, endow most of the art professionals with knowledge and skills necessary for their specific functions. These are the disciplines practices by artists, art critics, art historians, and aestheticians. Within each of these four disciplines or fields is found wide diversity that reflects many other influences, such as the political, social, philosophical, and psychological.[5]

As they have for centuries, the fine, applied, and folk artists of today continue to create a wide range of art objects that vary in purpose, quality, and influence. Art critics respond to these objects as they perceive, describe, interpret, and judge them for the professional art world and the lay public. Art historians preserve, study, classify, interpret, and write about important art objects from the past. Aestheticians employ philosophical methods of inquiry and discourse to examine fundamental issues about the nature of art, such as its definition,

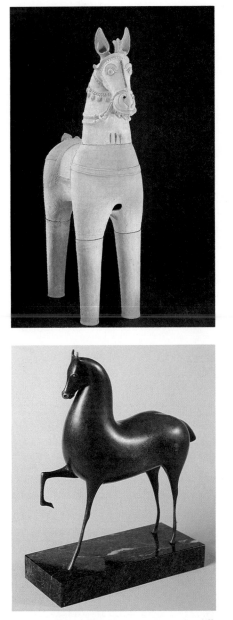

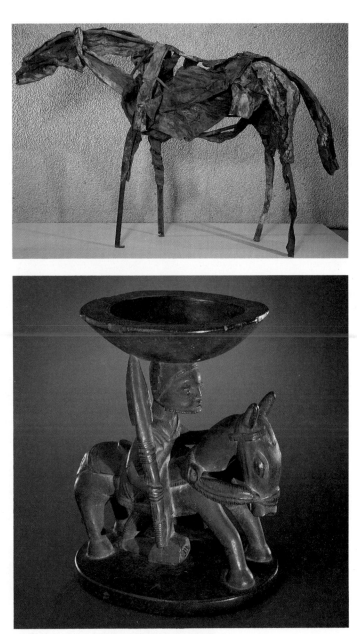

One way to study culture is to note the differences in treatment of the same subject. Compare the differences (clockwise from top left) between a terracotta horse from India (Sackler Gallery, Washington, D.C.); Deborah Butterfield's *Horse*, 1985, constructed of painted and rusted steel (Hirshhorn Museum and Sculpture Garden, Smithsonian Institution, The Thomas M. Evans, Jerome L. Green, Joseph H. Hirshhorn, and Sidney and Francis Lewis Purchase Fund); a divination cup of the Yoruba peoples in Africa (National Museum of African Art © Smithsonian Institution 1988. Museum purchase, 85-1-9); and Elie Nadelman's *Horse*, c. 1914, bronze (Hirshhorn Museum and Sculpture Garden, Smithsonian Institution. Gift of Joseph H. Hirshhorn, 1966).

The traditional distinction between fine and applied art can be discerned in these two works: Alexander Calder's *Obus*, 1972, a steel stabile considered fine art because it is free of any constraint other than those created by the artist (National Gallery of Art, Washington, D.C. Collection of Mr. and Mrs. Paul Mellon 1983.1.49 © NGA); and Michael Hurwitz's elegantly designed wooden rocker (below), which does not fall into a fine art category because its design has limitations placed upon it by its functional character.

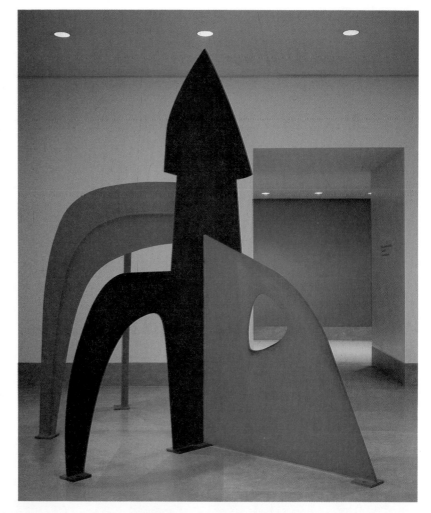

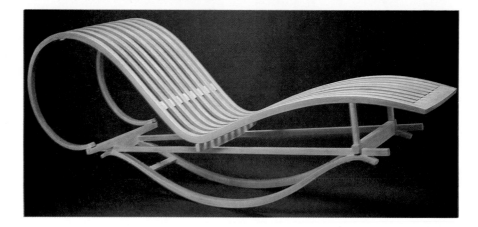

The four art disciplines, their relationships with their academic disciplines, and their relationships with the art professions.

Psychology   Theology   Politics   Anthropology   Economics

Philosophy   Technology   Sociology

Art Production

Art Criticism

Art History

Aesthetics

Historian   Artist   Critic   Aesthetician

Museum Director   Curator   Dealer   Registrar   Conservator

Educator   Curriculum Writer   Publisher

questions of quality and value, and issues of creation and response to art.[6]

This book provides chapters that explicate and explore each of these art disciplines in greater detail (see Chapters 7, 8, 9, 10, and 11).

CONCEPTIONS OF THE LEARNER

Is the mind of a child a blank tablet waiting to receive the imprint of the teacher? Are learners passive receivers, active seekers, or some combination of both? Does learning take place most efficiently through the use of all the senses? Are drill and repetition necessary? Does learning transfer from one task or problem to another? Is learning self-determined or is it the result of influences from the environment? Obviously the views a teacher holds on these and other issues in learning theory will influence educational practice. Whether the various conceptions of learning are developed by individual educators or are implied by psychological investigation, their practical influence cannot be overlooked.

Contemporary education, like modern art, is not a product of the last three or four decades. Many of the basic ideas to be found both in aesthetics and teaching theory today may be traced to ideas held by philosophers and teachers who lived long ago, as well as to psychologists of more recent years.

Contemporary art education, then, is a field fed by the history of art and of general education. The development of current practice in art education is also supported by the investigation of psychologists into learning processes. This discussion of various views of learners will begin with a review of early "intuitive" educators before discussing the contributions of psychology.

Early Educators and Philosophers

An eighteenth-century philosopher whose ideas influenced early childhood education, Jean-Jacques Rousseau, advocated that teaching should be related to childhood interests and that education should be concerned with the everyday life of the child. He emphasized these ideas in his novel *Emile*:

> What must we think of the barbarous education, which sacrifices the present to the uncertain future, which loads a child with chains of every sort, and begins by making him miserable, in order to prepare him, long in advance, for some pretended happiness which it is probable he will never enjoy?[7]

Let children be children, Rousseau advocated, and let them learn through self-initiated activities. On the matter of competition—a question still being debated in education[8]—Rousseau declared that self-competition is preferable to rivalry with other children. Although Rousseau had his own school it must be admitted that he was a theorist and a dreamer and that some of his ideas about teaching were quite impractical. It remained for future teachers to make pedagogical order out of Rousseau's theories. Three teachers—Johann Pestalozzi, Johann Friedrich Herbart, and Friedrich Fröbel—contributed to this process.

Unlike most of his predecessors, the Swiss, Pestalozzi, gave particular emphasis to the idea that education is more than the process of recording sense impressions on a passive mind.[9] Learners must be active participants and must reorganize the experiences that they encounter. As a pioneer and experimenter, Pestalozzi lacked the perspective to systematize his thoughts into a teaching methodology. The task of developing a systematic pedagogy was left to Johann Friedrich Herbart, a German philosopher and educator who gained inspiration to perform his task from Pestalozzi. Herbart developed a systematic way for teachers to develop plans for instruction involving five steps: preparation, presentation of new information, association of new material with previous learning, generalization of rules or principles using the inductive process, and application of learning to specific cases.[10] Although Herbart's methodology might seem overly formal to teachers today, his teachings nevertheless recognized in the learning process the natural capacities, interests, and activities of children.

Fröbel, also a German and something of a mystic, established his first kindergarten in 1837 after visiting Pestalozzi's school. His teaching methods were founded on the naturalism preached by Rousseau and practiced by Pestalozzi. Fröbel used objects that have basic geometric shapes—cubes, spheres, prisms, and so on—to instruct children on the theory that children would gain awareness of universal divine order through constant association with these "perfect" universal forms. Fröbel's strong beliefs that children would be taught from the concrete to the abstract and that a school should be a miniature society are still considered sound. He referred to his task-centered objects as "gifts."

Although the educational theories and practices just described have had their effects on art education, an even stronger influence is to be found in the development of psychological thought. Because a complete and detailed study of the effects of psychology on methodology is not possible here, we shall consider only a few important influences on teaching methods in art. These influences include (1) the *functional* school of psychology, from which developed E. L. Thorndike's stimulus-response theory of learning and much of John Dewey's philosophy; (2) the Gestalt school of psychology; (3) behavioral psychology and the work of B. F. Skinner; (4) humanistic psychology as developed by Carl Rogers and others; (5) cognitive psychology of Jean Piaget and current researchers; and (6) the so-called *split-brain* research on hemispheric functions. Howard Gardner's theory of multiple intelligences will be discussed in Chapter 5.

Functional Psychology

Known as the father of progressive education, the American philosopher John Dewey has had a tremendous influence on education in this country since the early decades of this century, when children's desks were bolted to the classroom floor in straight rows and rote learning was a primary school activity.

Dewey is considered one of the founders of the functional school of psychology and was, in his early years, closely associated with it. As a philosopher, of course, Dewey later ranged far in his ideas, but they were unmistakably colored by functionalism. He was greatly concerned with the relationship of learners to their environment and to the society in which they live. He regarded education as the "continuing re-creation of experience".[11] According to Dewey, experience and education are not synonymous: education involves the direction and control of experience, and a meaningful experience implies active participation and control on the part of learners. Knowledge is not static, Dewey said, nor is it gained in a static environment to be used in a static society. Learning must lead to more learning—the process is never-ending. Dewey's ideas readily lend themselves to the teaching of art. Indeed, he was a philosopher of aesthetics as well as education and produced a classic book on the subject, *Art as Experience*.[12]

John Dewey's ideas were supplemented by the work of G. Stanley Hall in the child study movement during the early part of this century. Hall thought that the selection of all learning activity should proceed from the study of child development, and that a teacher's primary obligation was to study the child rather than the subject. As early as 1901 Hall stated, "The guardians of the young should strive first of all to keep out of nature's way and to prevent harm and should merit the proud title of defenders of the happiness and rights of children."[13] Statements such as that provided the groundwork for the laissez-faire methods of much instruction of the Progressive Era. Referring again to Tyler's three considerations for educational programs, Hall's attention was focused on the learner much more than on subject content or society's goals. Teachers were encouraged to say, "I don't teach art (or math or science), I teach children."[14]

Another psychologist associated with the functional school of thought was E. L. Thorndike who based his educational theories on what is called the *stimulus-response* or S-R theory.[15] According to this theory, learning consists in the establishment of a series of connections, or pathways, in the brain resulting from a specific response to stimulus. Between the nerve endings is a juncture, or synapse, which tends to resist the impulse of the stimulus but which can be bridged by repeated stimuli. These physiological data led Thorndike to believe that learning was a matter of repetitive drill. The most efficient teaching would result from breaking a school subject into minute parts. Drills based on these minute details would then allow the learner to develop "a wonderfully elaborate and intricate system of connections."[16] Although psychological studies have progressed beyond Thorndike's initial thought, it is not difficult to discover curricula based on his notions in today's schools, especially in the areas of reading and mathematics.

Gestalt Psychology

The system of psychology called *Gestalt* has had a strong influence on contemporary art education. In *The Growth of the Mind*[17] Kurt Koffka produced evidence to show that in learning an organism acts as a total entity and does not exercise only certain parts. Wolfgang Köhler, a German psychologist, performed experiments with primates that supported the gestaltist theories. In his experiments, primates showed "insight" in solving problems. On the basis of such evidence, the gestaltists maintained that wholes are primary and parts derive their properties and behavior from them. The learner, in other words, acquires knowledge not by building a system of neurological connections bit by bit, but by achieving "insight"; that is, understanding the relationships among the various aspects of the learning situation.

Rudolf Arnheim, in his book *Art and Visual Perception*,[18] has provided art teachers with the clearest and most completely stated view of Gestalt psychology. He includes material ranging from an analysis of Picasso's *Guernica* to a discussion of the development of children's perception. Gestalt psychology has proved to be useful to many art educators because of the gestalt nature of the visual arts. A painting, for example, can be analyzed part by part, but for it to be perceived aesthetically the entire painting must be viewed. Within works of art each part affects all the others parts simultaneously, so that if one aspect is altered, such as the area or brightness of a color, the entire work is changed. In art and in Gestalt psychology, the whole is more than the sum of its parts.

B. F. Skinner and Behaviorism

The educational literature reflects aspects of these earlier developments as well as the strong influences of two divergent philosophical and psychological viewpoints known as *behaviorism* and *humanism*. The behaviorist orientation, most notably represented in the works of psychologist B. F. Skinner,[19] considers the learner to be a relatively passive organism governed by stimuli supplied by the external environment. Through proper control of environmental stimuli the learner's behavior can be, to a significant extent, predicted. According to this view, human behavior is governed by the same universal laws that govern all natural phenomena and the scientific method is appropriate for the study of the human organism.

Skinner is widely regarded as one of the most influential figures in modern psychology, as well as one of the most controversial.[20] His study of behavior as an objective science has resulted in developments such as programmed instruction and teaching machines, which have made computer instruction a common reality in many schools. The essential and controversial aspect of the behaviorist view has to do with the degree to which behavior can be controlled.

The influence of behavioral psychology on education is immense. In addition to programmed and computer-assisted instruction, educators have gone through phases of emphasis on the writing of behavioral objectives for all aspects of the curriculum. Educational evaluation, measurement, and testing have gained emphasis under this orientation. The so-called accountability movement in education has relied largely on the assessment of observable behaviors.[21]

Humanistic Psychology

The contemporary antithesis to Skinnerian behaviorism has been conveyed by humanistic psychologists such as Rollo May, Abraham Maslow,[22] and especially Carl Rogers.[23] Humanists consider the learner, not the environment, to be the source of all acts. The learner is free to make choices, and behavior is only the observable expression of an essentially private, inner world of being. The individual exists uniquely within a subjective world of feelings, emotions, and perceptions, many of which are not acted out in behavior.

Research in humanistic psychology has followed the direction of clinical work with human subjects, as opposed to the behaviorists' controlled scientific methodology in the laboratory with animals as subjects. Rogers has devoted most of his professional life to clinical work wih individual subjects in an endeavor to provide therapy and gain understanding.[24] He believes that an educational climate must be developed "in which innovation is not at all frightening, in which creative capacities of all concerned are nourished and expressed rather than stifled."[25] The goal of education, according to Rogers, must be the facilitation of learning, for only the person who has learned how to learn, to adapt, and to change is an educated person. The humanistic view of education coincides with the beliefs of many art educators who would emphasize the creative and expressive facets of the human personality.

Piaget and Cognitive Psychology

Through his work over a period of fifty years, Swiss psychologist Jean Piaget became a major influence in cognitive psychology. His work has had an extensive impact on education. It represents one of the most systematic and comprehensive theories of cognitive development.[26] Piaget examined such topics as the evolution of language and thought in children; the child's conceptions of the world, of number, time, and space; and other aspects of a child's intellectual development.

Piaget outlined three major stages or *periods* in the child's cognitive development: the sensorimotor period, the period of concrete operations, and the period of formal operations. He believed that children develop through interaction with the environment rather than exclusively through either heredity or environment. He saw sensorimotor activity as a basis for higher intellectual development and stressed the active use of the senses in learning.[27] According to Piaget, the child neither "flowers," as described by Rousseau, nor is "programmed" in the manner Skinner describes. Rather, the child develops sequentially through Piaget's three stages. An essential notion of his and of developmental psychology in general, is that intellectually a child is quali-tatively different from an adult, and this difference varies according to age and to progress within the three stages. For educators, this implies that knowledge of the learner's characteristics is essential to curricular and instructional decision making.

Current research in cognitive psychology, as it is applied in educa-tion, emphasizes interactions between knowledge and various levels of thinking. Resnick and Klopfer point out that

> Before knowledge becomes truly generative — knowledge that can be used to interpret new situations, to solve problems, to think and reason, and to learn — students must elaborate and question what they are told, examine the new information in relation to other information, and build new knowl-edge structures.[28]

This view recognizes that learners require a certain *amount* of knowl-edge in order to use knowledge flexibly or creatively and that learning is easier once a generative knowledge base has been established. This poses for educators the problem of how to get students started in de-veloping their base of generative knowledge so they can learn more easily and independently.

In art education this view of a "thinking curriculum" correlates well with the use of content and methods of inquiry derived from the four art disciplines. Art teachers can engage students in thinking and rea-soning about art, questioning ideas about art, solving problems through active engagement, and being involved in their own creation, response, and examination of art objects. The art curriculum has the potential, as well, to engage students in several ways: through refined perceptions of aesthetic qualities of artworks; analysis and interpreta-tion of meanings, often metaphorical, embedded in works of art; through inquiry into social, political, and other contexts that give rise to artistic creation; and pondering and discussing important perennial questions about the nature of art, art appreciation, and the creation of art.

Split-brain Research

A discussion of changing conceptions of the learner would not be com-plete without some mention of research[29] into the functions of the two hemispheres of the human brain and the effects of this research on education.[30] For many years, scientists have known that the human brain is composed of two physically equivalent hemispheres and that each half controls movement of the opposite half of the body. Knowl-edge of brain function has increased through careful study of individ-uals with brain damage caused by strokes, accidents, or tumors. Re-cently, brain researchers have devised indirect methods for studying hemisphere functions by presenting competing sounds simultaneously in the right and left ears, by presenting visual information to one eye or the other, and by measuring eye movements of subjects after posing different types of questions. The most dramatic advance in this area of research occurred when physicians developed a surgical technique, which involved severing the nerve fibers joining the two brain hemispheres, to control violent epileptic seizures. The relatively small number of patients who have agreed to submit to this last resort for their debilitating seizures have been the subjects of careful study of right- and left-hemisphere functions.

Results of these split-brain studies have supported the notion that the right- and left brain hemispheres are somewhat specialized in their functions. In a summary of these findings, Howard Gardner explains that

> the left hemisphere has manifested a clear advantage in dealing with language, particularly with consonant sounds and rules of grammar. Processing of vowel sounds and access to the meaning of words seem to reside in both hemispheres. The left hemisphere also assumes a more dominant role than the right in classifying objects into standard, linguistically defined categories; it can ferret out from a set of objects all the large red cones or all the pieces of furniture.
>
> The right hemisphere has no cognitive preferences equivalent in strength to the left hemisphere's for language. Nonetheless, the right hemisphere does seem relatively more important in spatial tasks. We may tend to rely on it in finding our way around an unfamiliar site or in mentally manipulating the image of a two- or three-dimensional form. The right hemisphere also seems crucial in making fine sensory discriminations; these range from the recognition of faces to the detection of unfamiliar tactile patterns.[31]

Less cautious researchers label the left hemisphere as verbal and analytic in function and the right brain as nonverbal and global. Taken further in theory, the left brain becomes analytical, rational, logical, and linear, and the right brain is viewed as nonrational, intuitive, and holistic.[32] The implication for education is that both sides of the brain should be recognized and developed in a balanced educational program. Schools, it would seem, are most effective in educating only half of the human brain.

Whether or not the left- and right-brain hemispheres in normal people function as separately and independently as the above view indicates, split-brain research has focused attention on many of the human capacities that have been largely ignored in school programs. These capacities are often emphasized in the arts, where intuition, holistic viewing, nonrational and nonverbal thought and expression are valued and developed.

It is not necessary for educators to take sides about learning theory, but it is a good idea for all educators to be aware of the major positions and their implications for teaching practice. Knowledge of major orientations will assist the individual in sorting out and evaluating the profusion of ideas, assertions, and programs.

In conclusion, the antecedents of art education which exist apart from art itself may be thought of as follows:

Rousseau was a social philosopher who developed a view of education that was largely *intuitive*. Pestalozzi and Fröbel, also intuitive rather than scientific thinkers, focused their attention more upon the *specifics* of learning, and Thorndike, Skinner, and Piaget supported their psychological theories by using research methodology. The contributions of Rudolph Arnheim and John Dewey reflected not only backgrounds in psychology, but art and philosophy as well.

Although psychologists will continue to provide insights about artistic behavior, art teachers in the next decade also will look to artists, critics, aestheticians, and historians for validation of the content of their programs. As elementary teachers focus their attentions on children in the nursery and pre-school, they will draw heavily upon what psychology has to offer to guide the teaching of art to very young learners.

VALUES OF SOCIETY

Educator's concerns with the nature of art and their conceptions of how young people learn are balanced, in the process of education, by the values of society. In a democracy these values are brought to bear on education by the taxpaying public, usually through community school systems, election of school boards, and hiring of school administrators, faculty, and staff to carry out the wishes of the electorate. Public schools in the United States have been responsive also to the needs and values of the larger society, sometimes on a national level. Changes in education brought about by space exploration, the civil rights movement, the need for safe drivers on our streets and highways, the problems of alcohol and drug abuse, and the threat of AIDS are only a few examples of how the needs and values of society influence what occurs in school classrooms.

Art education in the United States has been influenced no less by societal values than by innovations in art or advances in psychology. The programs of art instruction initiated by Walter Smith, for example, were motivated by the business community's need to design goods that could compete on an international basis. The creativity and self-expression emphasis of Viktor Lowenfeld was based on a particular view of child development. And, current approaches to art education emphasize learning derived from disciplined art content.

The art program is an especially appropriate and effective place in the general school curriculum to deal with social issues, problems, and values. This is precisely because the history of art is replete with the most vivid images of social values, such as Picasso's masterpiece protesting war and violence, *Guernica*, an Indian statue of a contemplative *Buddha*, Judy Chicago's feminist statement, *The Dinner Party*, or a Navajo wedding basket. The art of any cultural or ethnic group often reveals values held by that group. Understanding of art created within a particular culture requires knowledge of the purposes, functions, and meanings of artworks within the context of their creation.

The history of art education includes significant emphasis on democratic values. The freedom necessary for the success of an aesthetic act cannot be separated from the freedom of thought and action that is the prerogative of individuals living in a democracy. Art educators have been among the pioneers in developing a pedagogy compatible with democratic practices.[33] What assisted them as much as anything else was their understanding that art could not be taught successfully unless it was presented in an atmosphere designed to develop individual, and at times possibly nonconformist, expression. It is the emphasis that art education places upon personal decision making that often separates art classes from many others.

As individuals we become involved in interpersonal relationships and in social or political events. As citizens we learn to respect and live with our neighbors in various social contexts. Good citizens often improve the quality of everyone's life by taking appropriate actions to affect the broad social and environmental issues confronting the community at large.[34] These broad social concerns are present as themes in many significant works of art. They become relevant whenever art education extends our view beyond the concerns of individuals to the values of society at large.[35]

Even aesthetic values have become the focus of social issues. Beginning the 1920s, critics expressed serious concern about the general level of aesthetic taste in the United States. Artist and author Roger Fry stated that in aesthetic matters people were "satisfied . . . with grossness, a sheer barbarity and squalor which would have shocked the thirteenth century profoundly."[36] As early as 1934, Dewey asked, "Why is the architecture of our cities so unworthy of a fine civilization? It is not from lack of materials nor lack of technical capacity . . . yet it is not merely slums but the apartments of the well-to-do that are aesthetically repellent."[37]

Statements like these offered a challenge to education, for such condemnation referred indirectly to the masses of people educated in public schools. The inference was that the art education program was not effective in developing the ability to recognize good design from bad. Art educators continue to seriously consider methods of developing critical thinking and aesthetic sensitivity in children. Aesthetic issues continue to be central to the social and environmental needs of society. The impact of the mass media, the changing faces of cities, forms of suburbia, and the pollution of natural resources are factors of modern living in all parts of the world, and need to be brought to the attention of children. How effective art teachers can be in their attempts to create visual sensitivity is still a matter of speculation. One thing is certain: the future designers and planners who share the task of creating environments that humanize and enhance our lives are students in our schools at this very moment.

Public Attitudes Toward Art

The influences of democracy and freedom already discussed are fundamental and have been in operation since the founding of this country. Other values and attitudes toward art perpetuated from early times have not all been beneficial to art education. Unlike Europeans, American pioneers did not grow up in the midst of an artistic and architectural tradition. Aesthetic and artistic concerns often were low in priority, since the tasks of survival and practical living required much time and energy. In place of an aristocracy, the traditional patrons of the arts, our thriving democracy produced business leaders and politicians. Since business and politics are often based in practicality, only when the arts could be viewed as making a profitable contribution were they placed higher in priority. The attitude that art is a frill to be turned to only after the "real work" is done is still quite evident and is largely the reason that art has never achieved a place in the school curriculum comparable to the "three Rs," science, and social studies. Nevertheless, art education has progressed in theory and in professional practice to the point where the most enlightened educators view it as an essential rather than as a peripheral aspect of a balanced curriculum.[38]

These positive attitudes toward art education might well be the result of the dedicated service of thousands of art teachers during the past fifty years. At least the positive change in attitude toward the arts—as verified by attendance records for art museums, theaters, concerts, and so on—directly correlates with the increased attention paid to the teaching of art in the schools.

The quality of art programs varies widely from state to state and from school district to school district according to the values of legislators, school leaders, and communities, and according to varying degrees of financial stability. One effect of this seemingly perpetual adversity is the development of art programs based on well-thought-out rationales.[39] Probably no other group of educators has had to work as diligently as art educators to provide sound educational justifications for their programs.

CHANGE IN ART EDUCATION

The history of art education is a fascinating, ongoing tapestry of interwoven threads that form a complex design. Three of the most prominent threads — the nature of art, conceptions of the learner, and the values of society — have already been discussed. Others represent the works of individual artists, writers, and teachers, and the advances in technology, curriculum projects, and even legislation. It is difficult to gain a clear view of the emerging pattern while the design is still being developed. The following brief discussion is an attempt to identify some of the more prominent threads in the historical development of art education.

In the United States, for example, the origins of art education in the schools are related to the requirements of business and industry, or the goals of society in mid-nineteenth century New England. American business leaders witnessed how the English had raised their standards of industrial design in order to compete favorably with European business in taste, style, and beauty. England's schools of design

Title page of Walter Smith's plan for art education in American schools.

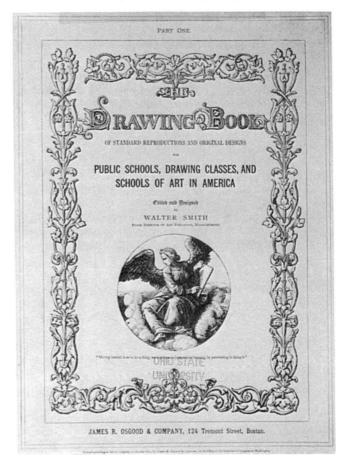

were revitalized in the 1850s, and they produced a corps of skilled designers for industry. In the United States, a few shrewd businessmen noted cause and effect and urged skeptical merchants and manufacturers to see the practical necessity of art education for competition in world trade markets. Following the British example, the Americans recruited Walter Smith,[40] a graduate of England's South Kensington School, and appointed him concurrently director of drawing in the public schools of Boston and state director of art education for Massachusetts. Smith began his monumental task in 1871, just a few months after the Massachusetts legislature passed the first law in the United States making drawing a required subject in the public schools.

Walter Smith approached his work with great vision and vitality and began the development of a sequential curriculum for industrial drawing. Within nine years, he had founded and directed the Massachusetts Normal Art School, the first in the country, and had implemented his curriculum in all Massachusetts primary grades up to high school. In addition, Smith's writings and the teachers trained at the Normal School extended Smith's influence across the country. Smith's publications included a volume entitled *Art Education, Scholastic and Industrial* and many series of drawing books for instructional purposes. In format, the series of drawing books was very similar. Usually the purpose of the series was "the laying of a good foundation for more advanced art training." The following statements about the particular aims of the books are typical:

1. To train the eye in the accurate perception of form, size, and proportion and to exactness in the measurement of distances and angles

2. To train the hand to freedom and rapidity of execution

3. To train the memory to accurate recollection of the forms and arrangements of objects

4. To cultivate and refine the taste by the study, delineation, and recollection of beautiful forms

This beginning of art education was quite different from what we experience today. Smith's instruction led teachers and children through a rather rigid sequence of freehand, model, memory, and geometric and perspective drawing. Rote learning, copying, and repetition were common aspects of the sequential curriculum.

> Smith's method of presenting the content depended upon class instructions and relied heavily upon the use of the blackboard, from which the students copied the problem the teacher drew. Prints and drawings were also copied by the students. Smith justified copy work in two ways: that it was the only rational way to learn, since drawing was essentially copying; and that it was the only practical way to teach, since classes were large and only a very limited amount of time was allotted in the school week to drawing.[41]

Although we would reject this type of art program today, Smith's accomplishments were well ahead of his time. His program broke new ground and gave art education in the United States a firm foundation upon which to build, a status the subject had never before had, and a precedent that could never be ignored.[42]

Cizek and Children's Artistic Expression

Until the advent of expressionism, or emphasis on children's creative art production, art education remained remarkably aloof from artistic tradition. Expressionism first had its effect on art education largely through the work of one outstanding teacher, Franz Cizek. Cizek, an Austrian, went to Vienna in 1865 to study art. In 1904 he accepted the position of chief of the Department of Experimentation and Research at the Vienna School of Applied Arts. His now-famous art classes for children were developed in this department.

Cizek eliminated certain activities from these classes, such as making color charts and photographic drawing of natural objects. Rather, he encouraged children to present, in visual form, their personal reactions to happenings in their lives.[43] In the output produced under his guidance—much of which has been preserved—the children depicted themselves at play and doing the things that naturally engage the attention and interest of the young. Cizek always maintained that it was not his aim to develop artists. Instead, he held as his one goal the development of the creative power that he found in all children and that he felt could blossom in accordance with "natural laws."[44]

Much of the work produced in Cizek's classrooms reveals the charm of expression of which children, under sympathetic teachers, are capable. Some of the output may now seem oversweet, overdirected, and discloses pretty mannerisms, such as a profusion of stars in the sky areas of compositions or a stylized expression of childish innocence in the faces. These mannerisms imply that some of the classes may have been highly structured and that the artistic development of the children was brought about as much by some of Cizek's teachers as by the "natural laws" that Cizek advocated. Nevertheless, Cizek is an important figure in art education, and his work deserves the widespread admiration it has received. The contemporary belief that children, under certain conditions, are capable of expressing themselves in a personal, creative, and acceptable manner derives largely from his demonstrations in Vienna.

The Teachers: Dow and Sargent

Other threads appear in the warp and weft of the history of art education. Great teachers emerged, such as Arthur Wesley Dow of Columbia University, Walter Sargent of the University of Chicago, and Royal B. Farnum of the Rhode Island School of Design.[45] Dow was concerned with analyzing the structure of art and sought to develop a systematic way in which it could be taught. He developed and taught

Examples of artwork by students in Franz Cizek's classes in Vienna include linoleum block prints by a five-year-old child (top) and an older student (bottom).

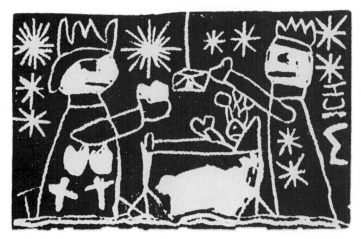

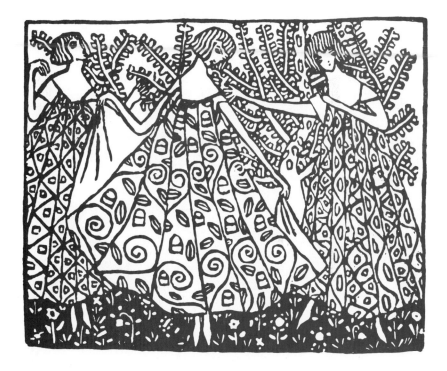

what we know today as the *elements and principles of design*. Within this formalist view, the artist works with line, value, and color, composing these elements to create symmetry, repetition, unity, transition, and subordination, which can be controlled to achieve harmonious relationships. Many contemporary art curricula are still organized purely on the basis of a list of design elements and principles.

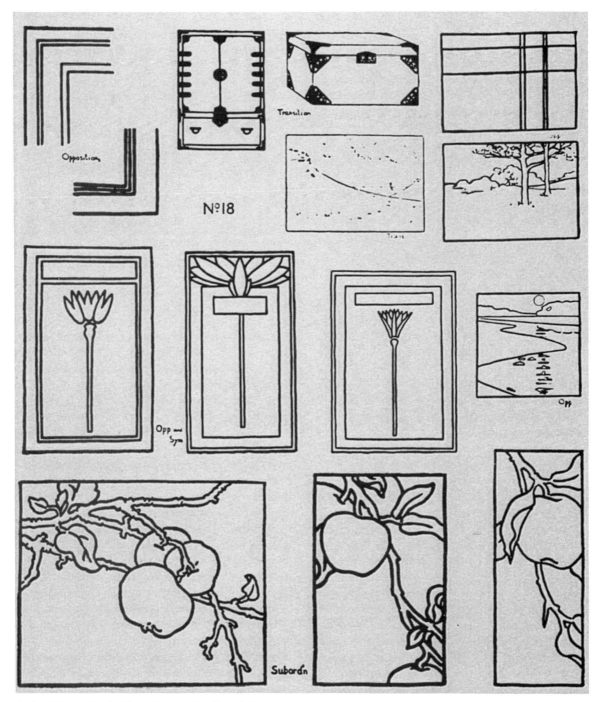

Arthur Wesley Dow's debt to Japanese handling of placement of form in composition is evident in this illustration from his book *Composition*, 1899.

Walter Sargent's contribution to art education came from his focus on the process by which children learn to draw. He described in acceptable terms three factors that he believed influence children's ability to draw. First, children must want to say something, must have some idea or image to express through drawing. Second, children need to work from devices such as three-dimensional models or pictures in making drawings. Finally, children often learn to draw one thing well but not others, so that skill in drawing is specific; a person could be good at drawing houses or boats and not good at drawing horses or cows.

It is a tribute to Sargent that these three points are echoed in recent literature of art education, such as the work of Brent and Marjorie Wilson:

> The process of losing innocence in art involves the acquisition of artistic conventions — this imitative process which has for too long remained hidden . . . this borrowing and working from pre-existing images sometimes began before the age of six.[46]
>
> Our third major observation is that individuals employ a separate program for each object which they depict. . . . In the case of those objects that are well drawn, they have repeatedly played essentially the same program, sharpening their ability to recall the desired configuration easily from memory.[47]

Following Cizek's focus on creative art activity for young children and the values of the progressive education movement inspired by Dewey, art educators in the United States such as Margaret Mathias and Belle Boas were influential in shaping the field of art education through their teaching, writing, and professional activism. Mathias wrote of the natural growth of children's expression through art, and also affirmed her belief in the value of art appreciation, "for understanding the art of others." In this she anticipated the work of Farnum and others who directed attention to the viewing of art by professional artists. At the same time Boas projected the earlier work of Dow as she called attention in her book to development of "good taste" and aesthetic judgement in the lives of children through their study of design principles.[48]

Royal B. Farnum was one of the many art educators involved in the *picture study* movement during the 1920s. When it became possible through advances in printing technology to produce inexpensive color reproductions of paintings, many art educators of that era took the opportunity to present children with lessons in art appreciation. It was characteristic that the pictures chosen for study were not contemporary with the time, presented a narrow standard of "beauty," and often carried a religious or moral message. In his book *Education Through Pictures: The Practical Picture Study Course*,[49] published in 1931, Farnum lists no works of art by Picasso, Dali, Matisse, Cezanne, Van Gogh, or even Monet or Renoir. Instead, the works are chosen from earlier times, with at least fourteen of the total of eighty being pictures on religious themes.

Although it is easy to be critical of early attempts at art appreciation, we must recognize the pioneering nature of this type of art education. Nevertheless, as Elliot Eisner has pointed out, ''Until very recently art education as a field has been quite unresponsive to contemporary developments in the world of art. Art education until as late as the middle of the twentieth century was more a reflection of lay artistic tastes than it was a leader in shaping those tastes and in enabling students to experience the work of the artistic frontiers of their day.''[50]

The Owatonna Project

The Owatonna Art Project in Minnesota was the most successful of several community art projects funded by the federal government in the 1930s. The object of the Owatonna Project was to create art activities based on the aesthetic interests of community members. Rather than import exhibits of avant-garde art, this project promoted ''home decoration, school and public park plantings, [and] visually interesting window displays in commercial areas.''[51] The idea was to apply principles of art in everyday life for a richer experience. The Owatonna Project was a successful cooperative effort that involved many sectors of the community, the local schools, and the University of Minnesota. Unfortunately it was interrupted by the outbreak of World War II and never achieved the impact it might have had under different circumstances.

The Bauhaus

Another influence in the late 1930s was the Bauhaus, a German professional art school committed to integrating the technology of its day into the artist's work. As a result of its influence, modern art materials, photography, and visual investigation involving sensory awareness found their way into the secondary school art program. Interest in the technology of art (notably in the communications media), concern for the elements of design, and an adventurous attitude toward new materials are all consistent with the Bauhaus attitude. The Bauhaus stimulated a growing interest in a multisensory approach to art as well as a tendency to incorporate aesthetic concerns into environmental and industrial design, especially in secondary schools.

Creativity and Art Education

Art educators' interest in the development of creativity is well documented by the titles of prominent books published in the field, especially during the 1940s and 1950s. Victor D'Amico's *Creative Teaching in Art*,[52] Viktor Lowenfeld's *Creative and Mental Growth*,[53] and later, Manuel Barkan's *Through Art to Creativity*[54] were three of the most influential. Long an interest of art educators, creativity was also the focus of considerable attention and study by psychologists. The progressive education movement had laid a groundwork for this interest by relating the free and expressive aspects of art creativity to a theory of personality development.

When the movement declined in the late 1950s, members of the American Psychological Association, acting on the suggestion of their president, J. P. Guilford,[55] assumed leadership in applying more rigorous techniques to problems such as the analysis of creative behavior and the identification of characteristic behaviors of professionals in both the arts and sciences. Within a decade, what had formerly existed on the level of a philosophical mystique was replaced by scientific inquiry.

The research tools of psychologists—tests, measurements, computers, and clinical methods—were brought to bear on the processes of artistic creation. In considering the creative process, psychologists went beyond the visual arts and established commonalities of experience among all types of people involved in solutions to creative problems. Creativity in the schools was no longer the private preserve of the art room. As a result of discovering how the creative process served teachers of other subjects, ideas emerged that would permit art teachers to view their profession with new understanding. Art teachers have long suspected that art, taught under proper conditions, can promote values that transcend the boundaries of the art lesson.

The work of Viktor Lowenfeld emerged as the single most influential force in shaping the field of art education from the early 1950s into the decade of the 1980s. Lowenfeld was head of a large doctoral program in art education at the Pennsylvania State University. Many of the graduates from his program became established in other colleges and universities around the country and in positions at state and school district levels. *Creative and Mental Growth* became the classic work in art education, was translated into other languages, and continued to be published in numerous editions, even after Lowenfeld's death in 1960.

Lowenfeld espoused many of the views of art education that we have noted from the time of Pestalozzi through the era of progressive education. He combined a primary emphasis on the development of creativity with his theory of personality integration through art activities. This involved seven areas of personality growth, such as physical, social, creative, and mental. Almost exclusive emphasis was placed on art production activities, beginning at very early ages and involving a wide range of art materials to encourage children to explore and create. Lowenfeld emphasized the supportive and motivational roles of teachers, with much less emphasis on explicit instruction. Teachers were counseled to beware of imposing adult concepts and views on children, who were encouraged to develop their natural creative powers.

Art as a Body of Knowledge: Towards Art Content

The creativity rationale for art education and the interest in personality development so strongly advocated by Lowenfeld and others dominated the field well into the 1960s, when a new generation of scholars and educators began to question that direction and to suggest, for the first time, that the study of art was worthwhile *per se*. Attention was focused on art considered as a body of knowledge that could be learned by children, as well as a series of developmental activities.[56] Justifications for art in the schools arose from art's value to other areas of concern, such as development of competent industrial designers, development of perception, achievement of general educational goals, or cultural literacy. Content-centered writers justified the study of art on the basis of what functions art performs in society and why those functions are important to understand.[57] This position, as Eisner points out, "emphasizes the kinds of contributions to human experience and understanding that only art can provide; it emphasizes what is indigenous and unique to art."[58]

Contemporary art programs now recognize a body of art knowledge that fosters understanding of art and responding to art as well as activities that result primarily in art production. Students are exposed to the visual arts of the ancient and modern eras through films, slides, and reproductions as well as actual art objects in galleries, studios, and museums, when possible. Awareness of the world of art and of the concepts, language, and approaches used in responding to art not only help students understand and appreciate the art of others but increase students' sensitivity to their own art work.[59]

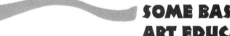

SOME BASIC BELIEFS IN CONTEMPORARY ART EDUCATION

Art education today is still very much a composite of what has gone before. It is not difficult to identify the many threads in the pattern that we have discussed. The development of strong professional associations such as the National Art Education Association (NAEA) in the United States, the CSEA in Canada, the SEA in the United Kingdom, and the INSEA as a world organization; the publication of an impressive body of literature in the field, including a burgeoning research literature; and the emergence of well-founded teacher-education programs in colleges and universities have resulted in an enlightened group of art educators. This increased level of professional communication has not resulted in a narrow unanimity of thought about the goals of art education in contemporary society, although some points are agreed on by most art educators. The following statements of the NAEA can be regarded as basic beliefs on which many current art education programs are founded.

- The earliest evidence of human activity is recorded in visual form. Making and using art to communicate and express ideas, and to convey hopes and feelings has been a basic human activity throughout history; it is a fundamental way humankind has used to give form to imagination, to define the environment, and to express aspirations for the future.
- Art is one of the most revealing of human activities and one of the richest sources for understanding human societies and the motives of those who created them.
- Making art is central in the art education of all students. In the early grades art-making is a primary vehicle through which children can most fluently tell stories, relate experiences, fantasize, convey messages, express feelings, and give ideas concrete form. But at any age or level of sophistication, making art involves more. It is a complex and integrative process through which students learn to observe, recall, find relationships, make choices, accept or reject alternatives, respond, value, and make decisions.
- Art objects are at the center of the study of art and understanding them and their contribution to the human state is what a quality art education is concerned with. Historical inquiry in art, critical judgment about art, and aesthetic response to art all exist because there are art objects that people have made. A quality art education can only be achieved when teachers and students alike explore the object through each of its four components: students need to make art, respond to art, understand its history, and make judgments about it.
- An education of excellence must include a quality art education for all students.[60]

In addition to these general statements about the nature of art and its place in culture and society, many art educators share the belief that all children possess both innate creative and appreciative abilities that can be nurtured through art instruction.

There are, of course, many beliefs held by people engaged in art education that may not be shared by the authors. It is likely, also, that the views expressed in this book are subjects of controversy. Nevertheless, a review of literature in the field will verify that the beliefs and assumptions stated above are quite pervasive. Awareness of them will assist teachers in accepting or rejecting them as experience suggests, or developing and testing new ideas about art education.

◆ NOTES TO THE TEXT

1. June King McFee, *Preparation for Art* (San Francisco: Wadsworth Publishing Co., 1961), p. 170.

2. Ralph Tyler, *Basic Principles of Curriculum and Instruction* (Chicago: University of Chicago Press, 1950).

3. Albert Elsen, *Purposes of Art*, 2nd ed. (New York: Holt, Rinehart & Winston, 1968).

4. Edmund Feldman, *The Artist* (Englewood Cliffs, New Jersey: Prentice-Hall, Inc., 1982).

5. Gilbert Clark, Michael Day, and Dwaine Greer, "Discipline-Based Art Education: Becoming Students of Art," in *Discipline-Based Art Education: Origins, Meaning, and Development*, Ralph Smith, ed. (Urbana: University of Illinois Press, 1989).

6. For discussions of each of these four art disciplines as sources for art curricula, see the essays by Frederick Spratt, Eugene Kleinbauer, Howard Risatti, and Donald Crawford in *Discipline-Based Art Education: Origins, Meaning, and Development*, Ralph Smith, ed., *op. cit.*

7. Jean-Jacques Rousseau, *Emile*, trans. Barbara Foxley. London: J. M. Dent and Sons, LTD 1977.

8. See, for example, the work of David Johnson and Roger Johnson of the University of Minnesota.

9. See Pestalozzi's novel *Leonard and Gertrude* (1781) and his book on education *How Gertrude Teaches Her Children* (1801).

10. Herbart wrote *ABC of Sense Perception* to explain Pestalozzi's views. See Herbart's *Text Book of Psychology* (1816) and *Outlines of Educational Doctrine* (1835).

11. John Dewey, *Philosophy in Civilization* (New York: Minton, Balch & Co., 1931).

12. John Dewey, *Art as Experience* (New York: Capricon Books, G. P. Putnam's Sons, 1934).

13. G. Stanley Hall, *The Forum* 32 (1901-02): 24–25.

14. Current sentiment on this issue in education definitely favors study of the subject, as evidenced by requirements in some states that prospective teachers receive the baccalaureate degree in an academic subject prior to beginning course work for certification to teach. Some universities associated with the Holmes Group (a group of reformers who hold that education degrees and teacher certification should be accomplished in a fifth year of study) have virtually eliminated undergraduate programs in colleges of education. It is likely that this issue, as many in education, will swing like a pendulum back toward more emphasis on the study of learners as a prerequisite for teacher certification.

15. In 1913 and 1914 Thorndike published his three-volume *Educational Psychology*, comprising Vol. I, *The Original Nature of Man*; Vol. II, *The Psychology of Learning*; Vol. III, *Work, Fatigue, and Individual Differences*.

16. E. L. Thorndike, *Educational Psychology: Briefer Course* (New York: Teacher's College, 1914), p. 173.

17. Kurt Koffka, *The Growth of the Mind* (Totowa, N.J.: Littlefield, Adams, 1959).

18. Rudolf Arnheim, *Art and Visual Perception*, 4th ed. (Berkeley: University of California Press, 1964).

19. Examples of B. F. Skinner's writings include: *Walden Two* (New York: Macmillan, 1948), *Science and Human Behavior* (New York: Macmillan, 1953), and *Beyond Freedom and Dignity* (New York: Knopf, 1971).

20. Frank Milhollan and Bill Forisha, *From Skinner to Rogers: Contrasting Approaches to Education* (Lincoln, NE: Professional Educators, 1972), p. 46.

21. See B. F. Skinner, *The Technology of Teaching* (New York: Appleton-Century-Crofts, 1968); Benjamin Bloom, ed., *Taxonomy of Educational Objectives: Cognitive Domain* (New York: David McKay, 1956), and *Affective Domain* (1964); and Robert Mager, *Preparing Instructional Objectives* (Palo Alto: Fearon, 1962).

22. Abraham H. Maslow, "Existential Psychology—What's In It for Us?" in *Existential Psychology*, ed. Rollo May (New York: Random House, 1961).

23. Carl R. Rogers, *Freedom to Learn* (Columbus, OH: Merrill, 1969).

24. Carl R. Rogers, "A Theory of Therapy, Personality, and Inter-Personal Relationships, as Developed in the Client-Centered Framework," in *Psychology: A Study of*

Science, Vol. III, ed. S. Koch (New York: McGraw-Hill, 1959), pp. 200-01.

25. Milhollan and Forisha, p. 116.

26. See, for example, Barbel Inhelder and Jean Piaget, *The Growth of Logical Thinking from Childhood to Adolescence* (New York: Basic Books, 1958) and *The Early Growth of Logic in the Child* (New York: Norton, 1964), and Jean Piaget, *Science of Education and the Psychology of the Child* (New York: Viking, 1971).

27. Kenneth Lansing, "The Research of Jean Piaget and Its Implications for Art Education in the Elementary School," *Studies in Art Education*, Vol. 7, No. 2 (Spring 1966).

28. Lauren B. Resnick and Leopold E. Klopfer, eds. *Toward the Thinking Curriculum: Current Cognitive Research* (Alexandria, VA: Yearbook of the Association for Supervision and Curriculum Development, 1989).

29. For example, see R. W. Sperry, "Hemisphere Disconnection and Unity in Conscious Awareness," *American Psychologist* 23 (1968), pp. 723-33; J. Levy, "Psychobiological Implications of Bilateral Asymmetry," in *Hemisphere Function in the Human Brain*, ed. S. J. Dimond and J. G. Beaumont (New York: Wiley, 1974); and J. Paredes and M. Hepburn, "The Split-Brain and the Culture-Cognition Paradox," *Current Anthropology*, Vol. 17 (March 1976), p. 1.

30. A sample of articles includes: Madeline Hunter, "Right-Brained Kids in Left-Brained Schools," *Today's Education*, November-December 1976; Elliot Eisner, "The Impoverished Mind," *Educational Leadership*, Vol. 35, No. 8 (May 1978); and Evelyn Virsheys, *Right Brain People in a Left Brain World* (Los Angeles: Guild of Tutors, 1978).

31. Howard Gardner, "What We Know (and Don't Know) About the Two Halves of the Brain," *Harvard Magazine*, March-April 1978.

32. Betty Edwards, *Drawing on the Right Side of the Brain* (Los Angeles: Tarcher, 1979), p. 40.

33. Italo De Francesco, *Art Education: Its Means and Ends* (New York: Harper and Row, 1958).

34. June McFee, *Preparation for Art* (Belmont, CA: Wadsworth, 1961).

35. June McFee and Rogena Degge, *Art, Culture, and Environment* (Dubuque, IA: Kendall-Hunt, 1980).

36. Roger Fry, *Vision and Design* (New York: Meridian, 1956), p. 23.

37. Dewey, *Art as Experience*, p. 344.

38. Endorsements of art as an essential component in general education are on record from many professional education groups, such as the Association for Supervision and Curriculum Development, the College Board, the National Endowment for the Arts, the Council for Basic Education, the National Art Education Association, the National Parent and Teachers Association, and the Getty Center for Education in the Arts.

39. Michael Day, "Rationales for Art Education: Thinking Through and Telling Why," *Art Education*, Vol. 25, No. 2 (February 1972), pp. 27-32.

40. Harry Green, "Walter Smith: The Forgotten Man," *Art Education*, Vol. 19, No. 1 (January 1966).

41. Ibid., p. 5.

42. Foster Wygant, *Art in American Schools in the Nineteenth Century* (Cincinnati: Interwood Press, 1983).

43. Peter Smith, "Franz Cizek: The Patriarch," *Art Education*, March 1985.

44. W. Viola, *Child Art and Franz Cizek* (New York: Reynal and Hitchcock, 1936).

45. Stephen Dobbs, "The Paradox of Art Education in the Public Schools: A Brief History of Influences," ERIC Publication ED 049 196 (1971), 48 pp.

46. Brent Wilson and Marjorie Wilson, "An Iconoclastic View of the Imagery Sources in the Drawings of Young People," *Art Education*, January 1977, p. 5.

47. Ibid., p. 9.

48. Frederick M. Logan, *Growth of Art in American Schools* (New York: Harper and Brothers, 1955). See also Logan's "Update '75, Growth in American Art Education," *Studies in Art Education*, Vol. 17, No. 1, 1975.

49. Royal B. Farnum, *Education Through Pictures* (Westport, CT: Art Extension Press, 1931).

50. Elliot Eisner and David Ecker, eds., *Readings in Art Education* (Waltham, MA: Blaisdell, 1966).

51. Dobbs, "The Paradox of Art Education," p. 24.

52. Victor D'Amico, *Creative Teaching in Art* (Scranton, PA: International Textbook, 1942).

53. Viktor Lowenfeld, *Creative and Mental Growth* (New York: Macmillan, 1947).

54. Manuel Barkan, *Through Art to Creativity*, (Boston: Allyn and Bacon, Inc., 1960).

55. J. P. Guilford, ''The Nature of Creative Thinking,'' *American Psychologist*, September 1950.

56. Ronald Silverman, *Learning About Art: A Practical Approach* (Newport Beach, CA. Romar Arts, 1984).

57. For example, see Ralph Smith, ed., *Aesthetics and Criticism in Art Education* (Chicago: Rand McNally, 1966); Edmund Feldman, *Art as Image and Idea* (Englewood Cliffs, N.J.: Prentice-Hall, 1967); and McFee, *Preparation for Art* (Belmont, CA: Wadsworth, 1966).

58. Elliot Eisner, *Educating Artistic Vision* (New York: Macmillan, 1972).

59. Michael Day, ''Child Art, School Art, and the Real World of Art,'' in Dobbs, *Arts Education and Back to Basics*.

60. NAEA, *Quality Art Education: Goals for Schools* (Reston, VA: National Art Education Association, 1986).

◆ ACTIVITIES FOR THE READER

1. Visit an elementary school and observe the instruction and learning activities. From your observations is valid subject content being taught? Is the teacher's conception of children as learners an obvious influence in the classroom? Can you identify any goals that are based on the values of society?

2. As you observe children at work or play, make notes of what you consider to be their creative acts. In what subjects do opportunities for creative behaviors occur most often?

3. Do the children receive regular art instruction? Is the art program balanced with activities that foster a broad understanding of art? Are reproductions of artworks displayed in the room? Is children's art work displayed in the room?

4. As you observe instruction in art and other subject areas, are children involved in higher levels of thinking? In art are they engaged in creative activities that require making judgments about their own art work? Do the children discuss art using appropriate vocabulary? Do they describe and analyze art? Do they attempt interpretations of meaning in works of art? Are they able to defend their observations, interpretations, and judgments?

5. What evidence of instruction in art history can you observe in the classroom and in discussions between the teacher and students?

6. Turn to the historical framework of art education in Appendix A. Add to the framework any events or persons that you think should be included.

7. Teachers should realize that creativity can be developed in all areas of the curriculum. The following signs of creative behavior have been taken from Torrance's observations in his research on creativity. Might any of these items apply to the teaching of art?

Intense absorption in listening, observing, doing

Intense animation and physical involvement

Challenging ideas of authorities

Checking many sources of information

Taking a close look at things

Eagerly telling others about one's discoveries

Continuing a creative activity after the scheduled time for quitting

Showing relationships among apparently unrelated ideas

Following through on ideas set in motion

Manifesting curiosity, wanting to know, digging deeper

Guessing or predicting outcomes and then testing them

Honestly and intensely searching for the truth

Resisting distractions

Losing awareness of time

Penetrating observations and questions

Seeking alternatives and exploring possibilities

◆ SUGGESTED READINGS

Arnheim, Rudolf. *Art and Visual Perception*, 4th ed. Berkeley: University of California Press, 1964. Gestalt psychological view of art, perception, and artistic development.

Chapman, Laura. *Approaches to Art Education*. New York: Harcourt Brace Jovanovich, 1978. Chapters 1, 2, 3, and 6 invite comparison with this text.

Dewey, John. *Art as Experience*. New York: Putnam, 1958. The classic text by the great philosopher of education. Essential for art educators.

Diamondstein, Barbaralee, ed. *The Art World*. New York: Artnews Books, 1977. A fascinating illustrated compilation of highlight articles from seventy-five years of the publication, *ARTNews*.

Dobbs, Stephen, ed. *Arts Education and Back to Basics*. Reston, VA: National Art Education Association, 1979. An anthology of articles by prominent educators on the "back to basics" movement in education.

Eisner, Elliot. *Educating Artistic Vision*. New York: Macmillan, 1972. The views of a prominent art educator on art education.

————, and David Ecker, eds. *Readings in Art Education*. Waltham, MA: Blaisdell, 1966. For a general overview of the field of art education, see Chapter 1, "What is Art Education?"

Efland, Arthur. *History of Art Education: Intellectual and Social Comments*. New York: Teachers' College Press, Columbia University, 1989. Updates Fred Logan's work stressing connections among ideas and movements.

Feldman, Edmund. *Varieties of Visual Experience: Art as Image and Idea*, 2nd ed. Englewood Cliffs, NJ: Prentice-Hall, 1972. A well-illustrated and articulate discussion of art.

Gardner, Helen. *Art Through the Ages*, 9th ed. Rev. by Horst de la Croix and Richard G. Tansey. New York: Harcourt Brace Jovanovich, 1991. A classic general textbook on the history of art.

Kaufman, Irving. *Art Education in Contemporary Culture*. New York: Macmillan, 1966. See Chapter 13, "Popular Culture and Taste," and Chapter 9, "The Visual World Today," for the relationship of art education to society at large.

Logan, Fred M. *Growth of Art in American Schools*. New York: Harper & Row, 1955. The essential book on the history of art education in the United States.

McFee, June, and Rogena Degge. *Art, Culture, and Environment*. Dubuque, IA: Kendall-Hunt, 1980. Sociological and anthropological perspectives on art education.

Smith, Ralph, ed. *Aesthetics and Criticism in Art Education*. Chicago: Rand McNally, 1966. An anthology of writings that helped shape the modern era of art education.

ART EDUCATION IN CONTEMPORARY CLASSROOMS: ISSUES AND PRACTICES

HEN OUR CHILDREN
are unable to "read" the languages of art, or music, or mathematics, or written prose, the content these forms possess
and the experience they provide cannot be known. It is in this
sense that the curriculum of the school is aimed — or should
be aimed — at the development of multiple forms of literacy.[1]

Elliot Eisner

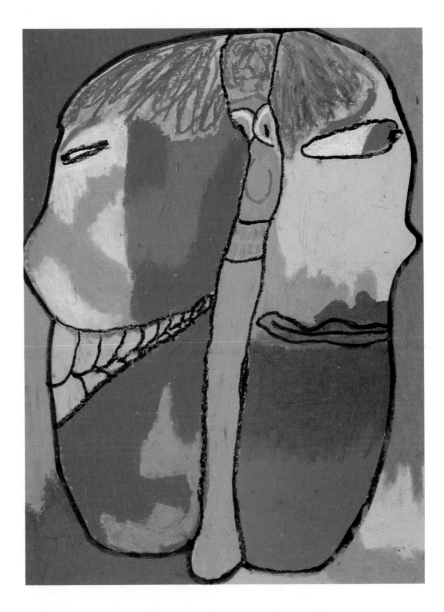

ART IS NECESSARY, NOT JUST "NICE"

Noted philosopher of education Harry S. Broudy has raised and commented eloquently on the question, "What is the role of art in general education?"[2] He pointed out that if art is an essential component for a balanced education, then there should be no question of its inclusion in the regular curriculum of elementary and secondary schools. If art is only something "nice" for the children to have after "serious" school-work, then, says Broudy, it has no place in the curriculum. There are numerous nice experiences for children to have, and any of them will do.[3]

However, if the state or school district board of education promises a quality, balanced education for all students, and if this is to include the aesthetic domain of human experience, then art must be offered if that promise is to be redeemed. Art becomes a basic subject required within any curriculum of excellence.[4]

The history of art education reveals that sometimes too many promises or claims have been made for art as a subject in school. We can note in the literature claims that art will increase creativity, enhance personality development, improve school attendance, enhance reading skills, and stimulate the right side of the brain. Each of these claims has a valid foundation, sometimes based on educational research. None of these claims, however, is unique to the study of art; each can be achieved through other areas of the curriculum as well as through art class.

Contemporary art education recognizes the many benefits that accrue from regular programs of instruction in art. The rationale for art in the schools, however, is based on the essential contributions that come from studying art. Art is taught because, like science, language, and

Art images such as Emmanuel Gottlieb Leutze's *Washington Crossing the Delaware*, 1851, become cultural referents—the prior knowledge that we need in order to understand educated discourse and everyday experience. (The Metropolitan Museum of Art, New York. Gift of John Stewart Kennedy.)

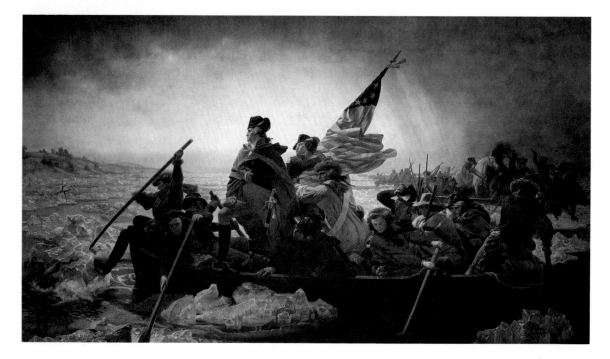

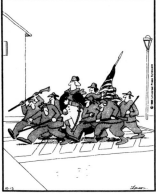

Washington crossing the street

Gary Larson's humorous takeoff on Leutze's serious painting is an example of parody. Without knowledge of the original image we simply would not get the joke. (The Far Side. Copyright © 1986 Universal Press Syndicate. Reprinted with permission. All rights reserved.)

mathematics, the study of art is essential for an educated understanding of the world. Philosopher Nelson Goodman has pointed out that art, like the sciences, provides "ways of understanding and even of constructing our environments."[5] Without basic understandings of science children and adults are not fully educated. For example, we would not be able to comprehend how the TV news can feature a live interview from China if we did not know that the earth is spherical, that satellites revolve around the planet, and that radio waves can be transmitted via communication satellites. Similarly, citizens have no possibility of understanding the threat of AIDS if they have no knowledge of the existence of microorganisms like viruses.

Art as well as science provides a fundamental lens of understanding through which we can view and interpret the world in which we live.[6] Children who do not receive a sound art education are denied a balanced, well-rounded general education and are excluded from much of educated discourse. A person who has never seen the Emanuel Leutze painting, *Washington Crossing the Delaware*, an important event in American history, will not apprehend the humor in Gary Larson's cartoon, *Washington Crossing the Street*. The person simply will not "get" the joke. Without the image in mind of Sandro Botticelli's masterpiece, *The Birth of Venus*, a person will miss the layers of meaning conveyed by Sachio Yoshida's Venus that focuses on humanity's eternal search for youth, beauty, health, and vigor. In this latter instance the search relies on technologies of the present and the future.

The rationale for art as an essential subject in the elementary school is founded on much more than an ability to understand a joke. Broudy,[7] Eisner,[8] Langer,[9] and other writers have convincingly developed the case for art in education. This case will be elaborated and extended throughout this book.

"The arts are an essential element of education, just like reading, writing, and arithmetic. . . . (The arts) are keys that unlock profound human understanding and accomplishment."[10]

William Bennett, U.S. Secretary of Education

"Art is humanity's most essential, most universal language. It is not a frill, but a necessary part of communication. We must give our children knowledge and understanding of civilization's most profound works."[11]

Ernest Boyer, President, Carnegie Foundation for the Advancement of Teaching

"Arts education is a requisite and integrated component of the entire educational process."[12]

Nelson Goodman, Harvard Graduate School of Education

What views might we have, then, of the characteristics and outcomes of sound programs of art education? When art is implemented as a regular part of the basic curriculum, what might we expect as out-

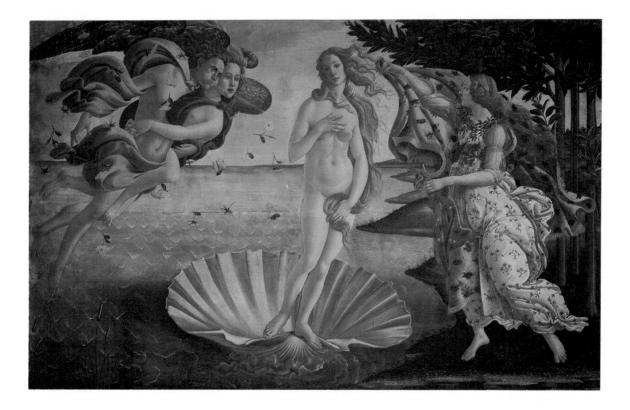

For centuries Botticelli's *Birth of Venus*, 1482, has served to objectify notions of beauty, love, health, and vigor, just as an Indian Buddha sculpture exemplifies contemplation and inner harmony, and Bartholdi's *Statue of Liberty* communicates ideals of freedom. (Galleria degli Uffizi, Florence.)

comes in the lives of the children? What does a sound program of art education look like? How much does it cost? How much time in the school week does it require? How does it relate to the rest of the curriculum? Who should teach art? These questions and more represent issues or threads that make up the constantly changing tapestry of art education. As the threads change color and texture across the years, the design of the tapestry is altered subtly or drastically, according to the times.

As we have learned from the brief history of art education in Chapter 1, there are many views about the contributions of art in education and its implementation in schools. It is not possible, therefore, nor is it desirable, to present single answers to any of the questions posed above. Rather, we present here a view generally well accepted in the field of art education, with expectations that there are many valid variations of that view.

A BALANCED PROGRAM OF ART EDUCATION

The National Art Education Association recommends a "program of art instruction that integrates the study of aesthetics, art criticism, art

Contemporary artist Sachio Yoshida's version of Botticelli's *Birth
of Venus* carries the context of five
hundred years, but is a technological, futuristic image.

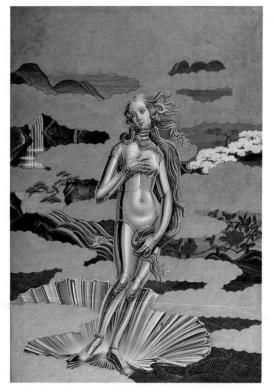

history, and art production."[13] This means that children will be engaged in making art, viewing and discussing art, reading and writing
about art, learning about contexts in which art has been created, and
pondering fundamental questions about art.

This broad view of art education represents a major shift from the
time of Viktor Lowenfeld, when almost exclusive emphasis was placed
on children's art making and the benefits on personality development.
This shift in emphasis means that contemporary art programs look
and feel different from those of the past.

Contemporary art programs are founded on the rationale that art is
an essential and unique component of the complete general education
curriculum. Art is not in the school specifically to serve other subjects,
such as social studies, or to provide released time for classroom teachers, although both of these benefits might be present. The art program
requires regular instructional time and careful attention to curriculum
content organized for cumulative learning. Evaluation of student
progress and program effectiveness are as important as with any other
school subjects.

In a classroom where art is taught we expect to see children's art
work displayed. The work of children reflects the individuality of expression that is fundamental to art, but will also exhibit the results of

instruction. The work of the children becomes more sophisticated with each grade level as they gain the knowledge and skills of art production.

A comprehensive art program also reflects attention to the history of art and the works of adult artists. Good quality art reproductions are used for instruction and displayed in the classroom and in the school. Teachers have access to instructional materials such as art filmstrips, slides, videos, textbooks, and magazines, just as with other school subjects.

A visitor to a contemporary classroom sees children learning ways to discuss and respond to works of art (originals whenever possible), reading and writing about art (sometimes correlated with language instruction), investigating questions about art (through class discussion or library research), as well as making their own art. Students are enthusiastic and interested in all of these learning activities.

Integrating Art with the Elementary Curriculum

Contemporary art instruction relates in many ways to other areas in the curriculum. The history of art relates naturally to *historical topics* usually studied at various grade levels. Most history texts, in fact, are illustrated with works of art, providing a ready means for integration. *Social issues*, as discussed in Chapter 1, are often expressed by means of powerful art images. Artists of many cultures and eras have dealt with virtually every universal social issue and human value, and teachers have access to the images they have produced.

Language instruction can be readily integrated with and enhanced by the art curriculum. Art criticism uses visual concepts and terms (vocabulary) in discussing art. Children learn systematic ways to talk and write about art. Visual art images are intrinsically interesting and provide issues and topics that fascinate children and motivate them to speak and write. Art learning activities derived from art criticism can take children beyond descriptive use of language to formal analysis and interpretation of meaning in art.

A current concern in general education has to do with *levels of thinking* that are fostered within all subjects in the curriculum.[14] Evidently, too much of children's time is spent with lower levels of thinking involving rote memorization, identification, and recall, and too few higher level thinking skills are developed. Some educators are surprised to learn that the art curriculum is one of the easiest and most direct means to engage children in higher levels of thinking. Art criticism involves forming hypotheses for interpretations of meaning in visual works and discussion, debate, and defense of different interpretations based on visual evidence in the work itself.

Children routinely make judgments about the relationships of each element that they introduce in their own art work to the totality of the work. A child's tentative decision to introduce hot reds and yellows in a painting that is composed of cool colors requires the child to make sophisticated perceptions, weigh options, interpret implications, and judge appropriateness in relation to intended expressive qualities. The child must decide, for example, if red and yellow fit with the overall character of the painting. Few subjects in the curriculum, if any, provide such ready means for children to engage in this type of decision making and problem solving.

Each time a new artwork is introduced to children in the classroom an aesthetics issue is introduced. For example, when a teacher shows a slide of a pot by the native American artist, Maria Martinez, the question might arise, "Is a simple clay pot art?" As they are noted to do, children often come up with numerous questions that address fundamental issues, such as, "If this pot is art, does that mean that all pots are art?" When teachers are confronted with these difficult questions and others that inevitably seem to follow, such as, "Why is this pot in the art museum and others are not?" they usually wish to find some way to deal with them in an educationally productive way.

Aesthetics is the philosophical discipline that deals with fundamental questions about art. When questions arise in the classroom that address topics such as the nature of art, how quality is determined, or how one becomes an artist, teachers and students become involved in aesthetics discourses at levels appropriate for the age and understanding of the children. This type of discourse is almost always conducted using *higher levels of thinking* so valued by those concerned with general education.

Outcomes of a Balanced Art Program for Children

Many of the benefits of art education that have been mentioned in conjunction with programs of the past might accrue when students have access to regular instruction in art. Often, children enjoy their overall school experience more because art touches on areas that are not addressed in other classes. Being able to make art is very important to many children and some may attend school more regularly when there is a good art program. When children attend school they do better in all of their classes.

It is often during art instruction that children have opportunities to express ideas, opinions, and judgments (either through their own art production or discussion of other works) that seem to be rare during a typical school day. In art children are often praised for the uniqueness of their work rather than its uniformity to a predetermined standard or response. For example, a math program, spelling assignment, or history quiz might be completed most successfully when all students make identical responses. In art however, each student might successfully complete an assignment based on the concept of "landscape," but each student's landscape painting is unique.

However, it is not upon the benefits of art instruction that we focus when we discuss the hoped for outcomes of a sound art program.

Children are highly motivated to make objects with art materials, and art production is at the center of a good elementary art program. Students should have opportunities to work with a variety of materials, including three-dimensional media such as clay.

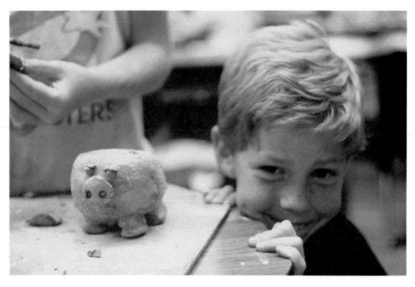

Rather, it is those outcomes that are unique to the study of art: knowledge of art, skills for making and learning about art, and attitudes that will enrich lives through art. It is development of the artistic or aesthetic lens through which to experience and understand the world that is the primary goal of art in general education. Without this lens, this fundamental means for construing meaning in the world, the very lives of children will be diminished.

A young person who has participated in a quality art program throughout the elementary grades will have the following experiences:

1. The student will have created drawings, paintings, and other art work from observation and imagination. The child will have progressed through stages of symbol formation and elaboration, and will have developed relatively sophisticated levels of art-making skills. The child will have developed an understanding of art as a means for expressing ideas, feelings, and ideals, and will have gained abilities to make art far beyond those possible without regular instruction.

2. The student will have had access to a rich store of visual art images, referred to by Broudy as the "imagic store." The child will have seen, during the years from kindergarten through grades six, seven, or eight, literally hundreds of exemplary works of fine, folk, and applied visual arts. This "imagic store" is one of the sources of imagination and provides the prior knowledge and references upon which understanding of educated discourse is based.

3. The student will have gained a basic understanding of the range of the visual arts throughout history and across many cultures. The

Children of all ages enjoy looking at reproductions of art and learning about the artists who created them. Whenever possible, children should also have the opportunity to see actual artworks. Museum and gallery trips and visits by artists are fascinating experiences for children who have been well prepared through art instruction.

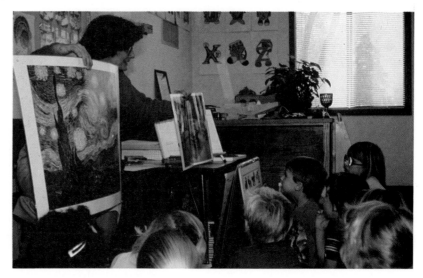

child will be conversant with numerous art terms and concepts from the history of art as well as with many particular landmark works and the artists or cultures that produced them. The child will likely have developed preferences for some types or styles of art and will have learned a significant amount about particular artists or cultures that created favorite works.

4. The student will have discussed and investigated many of the ways that the visual arts are influenced by the contexts of their creation, such as psychological factors in an artist's life, political events, social values, or changes in technology. The child will also gain understandings about how art expresses cultural values and, in turn, influences society.

5. The student will have discussed, read about, and written about many artworks. The child will be comfortable with the prospect of talking about unfamiliar or avant-garde works of art and will not be intimidated by a lack of historical knowledge when doing so. The child will know how to use the library to seek specific information about art and artists.

6. The student will have engaged in many discussions about the very nature of art, including contemporary issues that surround the making, appreciating, displaying, buying and selling, and interpreting works of art. The child will realize that there are several ways of defining what art is and what should count as quality in art, and that each of these viewpoints can be supported with sound, although sometimes incompatible, arguments. The child will also understand that when persons disagree in their assessments of

quality of art, these disagreements might well be the result of judgments based on different aesthetic stances rather than differences in perceptions of art.

The fortunate children who experience a regular program of art instruction and learning such as described here will have exercised their creative abilities in art, thought deeply about art, responded to and learned about art, artists, and their contexts, and will have developed the aesthetic lens of the visual arts that empowers them to view their world with added meaning and significance. They will have taken one of the essential steps toward achieving a well-rounded, balanced general education that is the right of every child in this society and a requirement for an enlightened citizenry.

ISSUES AND TOPICS IN ART EDUCATION

Following are several art education situations taken from real-life circumstances. They illustrate some of the issues that arise within school settings and highlight a few of the many complex issues that attend any serious educational undertaking. Each brief description of an art teaching situation is followed by questions that readers might ponder independently or discuss with fellow students if this reading is associated with a course of study. The solutions or actions that were taken by the educators in each case might or might not agree with your views. You might wish to discuss other ways that the problems or issues might have been addressed with different results.

Teaching All The Students

Issues and topics:

Instructional methods and skills
Mainstreaming of students
Gifted and talented, special students, English as second language (ESL) students
Visual teaching and learning
Educational games

An art teacher was in a quandary because of the wide variations among students in her art classes. She had to teach, in the same classroom, students with high abilities, those with mental or physical handicaps, and a few students recently arrived from other countries who could speak very little English. She wondered how she could accommodate all of these students and their individual needs.

The art teacher had an adequate art classroom and a good curriculum. She also had access to teaching materials such as art prints, slides, and videos as well as regular art supplies such as paints and

Effective teachers work closely with children, providing learning activities and instruction appropriate for their age levels. Instruction is based on sound concepts and methods derived from the art disciplines.

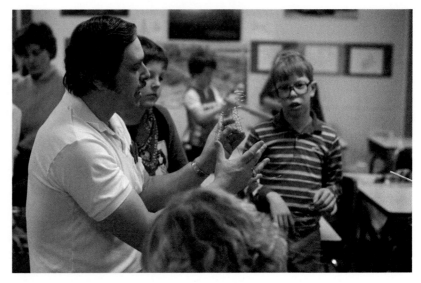

clay Her problem was mainly one of spreading herself too thinly among all of the children who required individual attention.

Questions.

> Is this situation typical in most schools?
> How can art teachers accommodate different learning styles and other needs among their students?
> Is it important for teachers to develop a range of instructional skills?
> How can art teachers get the most from the visual nature of their subject?

What the Art Teacher Did.   This teacher found that she could arrange her classroom and her instructional strategies in ways that allowed her to spend more time with individuals. Careful planning and preparation actually made her job easier and she found that she enjoyed each class period more because she was able to relax and communicate with the children.

The art teacher did several things that helped. First, she organized visual materials, art prints, pictures of artists, information about artists and their art, color charts, etc. and arranged them in displays that she had ready to mount with the corresponding lessons. She made word labels for major concepts, such as "still life," "impressionism," or "architecture," and placed them next to the appropriate visual images. These displays helped focus her lessons and made the concepts that she taught clearly apparent to all of the students. Those with weak English skills were able to learn new vocabulary with available visual referents.

The teacher also organized several learning centers around the classroom. One center contained a collection of art magazines, such as *American Artist*, *School Arts*, *Art and Man*, and *ArtNews*. She arranged a card file with questions typed on index cards. The questions referred to articles in specific issues of the magazines. Students at this center would browse through the card file and the magazines, then would read an article and answer the questions on the card for extra credit.

Another learning center featured a stack of picture postcards of artworks. Here the index cards challenged students to sort and arrange the postcard images according to specific tasks. One card asked the student to "Find three sculptures. List the titles and artists." (For young children with limited reading and writing skills the directions can be simpler and color- or shape-coded). Another card directed, "Find five works by Picasso. List the titles. Which is your favorite? Why?" Another said, "Find three images that convey violence (or love, peace, etc.). List them and tell why you chose each one." The teacher made some cards to challenge the most sophisticated students and others she made very simple.

Another learning center had several art games that students could play by themselves, in pairs, or in small groups. Another center had paper, drawing crayons and pencils, construction paper scraps, magazines for collage materials, and glue. The cards indicated studio art production activities that students could do individually.

The art teacher taught regular art lessons to the entire group and used the learning centers for students who finished early or who, for some reason, might not be able to complete the regular assignment. She also scheduled learning center time, supplementing this with slide shows on art topics and videos for students who preferred not to use the learning centers.

A Happy Compromise

Issues and topics:

  Who teaches art in elementary schools?
  Creative utilization of resources
  Cooperative teaching
  Curriculum integration

A medium-sized suburban school district had an adequate art curriculum and a district art supervisor to oversee the art program. They had a good supply budget and a small number of art teachers, but not enough to meet all of the students on a regular basis. There was a dispute within the district leadership about who should teach art to elementary children.

One side says:

We must have certified art specialists to teach art to all of the children, as the National Art Education Association recommends. Regular classroom teachers just do not have the background of knowledge or the interest to be good art teachers. They are already overburdened with a multitude of preparations and having to teach art only adds to the burden.

The other side says:

We know that teachers are overburdened and have much less preparation to teach art than art specialists. But classroom teachers know their students best and they know what they teach in all of the subjects during the week. The art teachers can't get to know the children because they see so many and don't get around often enough to make art as meaningful as it should be. When art specialists teach art it becomes an isolated subject, unrelated to the rest of the curriculum. The main function of art class under this system is to provide classroom teachers with a preparation period.

Questions.

Which side of the issue would you take? Why?
Is there truth on both sides?
How does this issue change if we consider other subjects such as music? Physical education? Reading? Mathematics?
Can the same arguments apply?

What the District Did. This district decided that they wanted to have their cake and eat it too. They compromised by maintaining what they saw as the best of both sides of the issue. Now all students are taught by art specialists for at least one hour every other week. During this session the art teacher introduces an art lesson, including the most demanding instruction and technical information. Classroom teachers participate and assist with the lesson. When the art teacher moves on, completion of the lesson becomes the responsibility of the classroom teacher, who has not had to take time for another preparation and who can integrate and relate the art content of the lesson with the rest of the curriculum.

Having participated in the lesson introduction, and with further advice from the art teacher, sometimes in the form of handouts or notes, the classroom teacher feels capable of following up and helping each individual to complete the lesson during another regularly scheduled art period.

A Spooky Tale

Issues and topics:

Organizing factors for art curriculum
Valid content for art instruction
Integrating content from the four art disciplines
Cooperative curriculum development

The four elementary art teachers in this district were good friends, as well as conscientious educators and, like many elementary teachers, they had an abundance of energy and liked to improve their programs. As they discussed their art programs over a rare lunch together, each expressed dissatisfaction with what they were doing with respect to the art curriculum and holidays. It seemed that the holidays dominated the art program and, as Halloween was only a few weeks away, they shared their plans for art activities. They discussed the usual projects centered around pumpkins, witches, black cats, and the like that the children were encouraged to make with various materials such as cut paper, crayon-resist, and clay. As they continued to talk and share ideas for change, they became very excited and began making assignments for each of them to carry out to cooperatively develop a Halloween unit.

Questions.

What are the possible drawbacks with an art curriculum centered on holidays?
Why were the art teachers dissatisfied?
Wouldn't it be easier to continue the old way?

What the Art Teachers Did.   A person walking around the elementary schools in the district the last week in October would notice a variety of displays in the hallways. One display featured a quote from Shakespeare about "the very witching hour of night when churchyards yawn and Hell itself breathes out contagion." Reproductions of paintings by Hieronymous Bosch on the theme of Hell, and the dark imaginative works of Francisco Goya reinforced the mood set by the poet. A wide range of student tempera paintings on dire themes completed the display. It was apparent from their handling of color that students had received instruction in color theory that allowed them to lower intensity and value of the paints, which are dispensed as bright and pure pigments.

Another school had a display of wicker masks and pictures of costumes used by various cultures for their versions of the Halloween experience. Students had made their own versions of masks from a variety of materials. Discussion with the art teachers reveals some of the ideas that they generated to initiate their new unit. For grade five (no teacher used all of these ideas):

1. Review the sources of Halloween as we know it. Discover how the celebration is accomplished in other cultures.

2. Arrange a still life of masks, parts of costumes, dried corn husks, gourds, and other objects associated with Halloween. Students will paint or draw the arrangement.

What the District Did. This district had the advantages of persistent leadership and small size so that changes could be made much more readily than in very large districts. They also had a well-developed system for implementing a new curriculum, including time for teacher in-service training and evaluation.

The board authorized the superintendent to send five interested teachers to a graduate course in art curricula at the nearby university. The professor of art education who taught the course allowed the group to work together on the class-required curriculum project. Later, the district hired the professor as a consultant to help with further development of the curriculum. When the curriculum was written in a usable form, the question arose regarding how they would implement it. The classroom teacher who had been assigned half-time to oversee the project did not have the technical expertise, for example, to order paints and brushes, select prints and slides, and give direction for operation of the ceramics kilns. The art specialist was hired full-time to perform these functions and to support the teachers in implementation of the art curriculum.

Community Needs and Resources

Issues and topics:

Local needs, local resources, and local control of curriculum
Responding to local populations
Teaching about art from different ethnic groups
Community and state resources for art education

Sister Margaret taught sixth grade in a Catholic parochial school near the center of a large metropolitan area. Her duties included working with the upper elementary grade teachers in developing a program of art instruction. Since the diocese in which she worked had no art supervisor, she appealed to two agencies for assistance, the state department of education and the department of education of the city in which her school was located. Both agencies responded by sending her the curriculum guides for art that were developed by several school districts in the state.

The Sister and her colleagues studied the guides carefully and came to the conclusion that, although they offered much useful information, none of the guides appeared to be especially appropriate for their student population, made up primarily of black Americans (the issues involved would be similar for groups of Americans with other ethnic origins, such as Hispanic or Southeast Asian). They all seemed to focus more on the interests, attitudes, and backgrounds of suburban white students with little recognition of any ethnic groups.

Questions.

Do most large school districts have written art guides?

How distinct are differences in school populations from district to district?

How can art teachers adapt curriculum in response to the interests and needs of their students and the local community?

Should teachers emphasize art from the various ethnic and cultural backgrounds of their students? Why or why not?

Should all students — regardless of ethnic background — study the art of the Western world? Why or why not?

What the Teachers Did.   Sister Margaret and her colleagues decided that their students would benefit from increased awareness of the African roots of their culture and how contemporary African-American artists have expressed the black experience through their art. They reviewed the resources of their community and found much of interest. The local art museum had a good collection of objects from various African countries and an excellent collection of publications about the art of Africa. They also learned of two artists of African ancestry in the community, one a young man who painted and the other an older woman who was widely known for her fine quilts. Both artists were interested in discussing their art and sharing some of their time with students.

With assistance from the professionals in the art museum and the local artists, the teachers were able to collect magazine articles, books, slides, and other materials about African-American artists. They learned about:

Artists whose subject matter reflected concerns of the black community, such as Romare Bearden, Faith Ringgold, and Jacob Lawrence

Artists who dealt in purely abstract forms based upon African imagery, such as Hale Woodruff

Artists who were untrained "naives" or folk artists, such as Horace Pippin; and others, such as Edward Bannister, whose traditional academic art skills made their work indistinguishable from their white contemporaries

The tradition of quilting as an art form among black women that began very early in the settling of this country and continues to the present

After discovering and collecting these resources, the teachers decided to adopt much of the content of the art guide they considered to be best for their purposes. They then determined how they would adapt the guide to include, in addition to references of Western art, important African and African-American content they had organized. A major task was to devise ways that this content could be presented as activities for their students.

Over the next two years they developed an art program in which attention was paid to history and culture, through the study of varieties of art expression, to criticism through perception and discussion of differences in styles and themes, and to aesthetics through pondering questions about the nature of a black aesthetic or different purposes of art in different cultures. When studio activities included in the guides were used in conjunction with these three areas, Sister Margaret had a balanced program that respected not only the world of her students, but the content of art as well. She planned to expand the approach by looking for applied artists in the community, such as designers or architects, who might contribute to the art program.

There are literally hundreds of possible situations that could be presented here. The reader might be able to add additional interesting examples for discussion. Hopefully the material presented here and in the other chapters in this book will help prepare the reader to recognize and deal with similar educational issues and topics that will face any person who makes a serious attempt to teach art to young people.

This chapter attempted to demonstrate some of the issues and options involved with development of a balanced art program. Each vignette raised questions based on real-life situations with the constant factors of respect for the needs of children and the sources of art. Art, as previously noted, is derived from basic human needs to express ideals and feelings through visual materials, be they paint and brush, clay and fire, or needle and thread. When we arrive at some satisfactory match among three critical elements of the child, community values, and the study of art, we have the beginnings of a curriculum

In a balanced art program, the child can function as critic as well as artist. Here, an eleven year old serves as guide, leading a discussion with a group of adults.

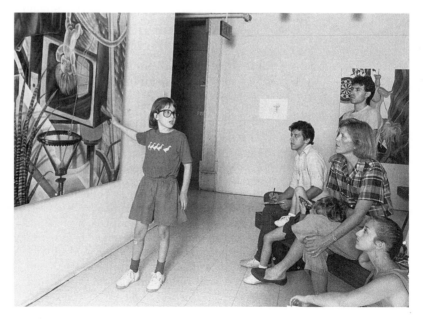

based upon the grass roots of both art and education. Such a view of art education is consistent with the general goals of education, which have been defined by Lawrence Cremin as "the deliberate, systematic, sustained effort to transmit or evoke knowledge, attitudes, values, skills and sensibilities."[16] There is not one condition of Cremin's definition that cannot be fulfilled within a balanced art program.

When we sharpen our powers of observation we develop "skill" and when, in developing such skills we refer to the ways in which the painter Jan Vermeer, a Bambara carver, or the sculptor Louise Nevelson have dealt with similar expressive problems, we extend our knowledge. When we can open ourselves to approaches to art that are not specifically skill oriented or that extend our definition of skill, as in the case of Jackson Pollock, our attitudes become more sophisticated. When our art programs are sequentially planned and implemented our efforts are systematic and sustained. The children who have the opportunity to gain the type of art education envisioned by Cremin are most likely to appreciate the rich contributions of the visual arts throughout their lives and will most likely support art as an essential component of general education for the next generation as well.

◆ NOTES TO THE TEXT

1. Elliot Eisner, *The Role of Discipline-Based Art Education in America's Schools* (Los Angeles: The Getty Center for Education in the Arts, 1986), p. 5.

2. Harry S. Broudy, "Arts Education—Necessary or Just Nice?" *Phi Delta Kappan*, Vol. 60, No. 5 (January 1979), pp. 347-50.

3. Harry S. Broudy, "The Role of Art in General Education" (Los Angeles: The Getty Center for Education in the Arts, videotape of Broudy lecture, 1987).

4. Gilbert Clark, Michael Day, and Dwaine Greer, "Discipline-Based Art Education: Becoming Students of Art," *The Journal of Aesthetic Education*, Summer 1987.

5. Nelson Goodman, "Aims and Claims," in *Art, Mind, and Education*, Howard Gardner and D. N. Perkins, eds. (Urbana: University of Illinois Press, 1989), p. 1.

6. Harry S. Broudy, *The Role of Imagery in Learning* (Los Angeles: The Getty Center for Education in the Arts, 1987).

7. Harry S. Broudy, *Enlightened Cherishing: An Essay on Aesthetic Education* (Urbana: University of Illinois Press, 1972).

8. Elliot Eisner, *Cognition and Curriculum* (New York: Longman, 1982).

9. Susanne Langer, *Mind: An Essay on Human Feeling*, Vol. 1 (Baltimore: Johns Hopkins University Press, 1967).

10. William Bennett, "Why the Arts are Essential," *Educational Leadership*, Vol. 45, No. 4 (January 1988), p. 4.

11. Ernest Boyer, *Toward Civilization: A Report on Arts Education* (National Endowment for the Arts, 1988), p. 14.

12. Nelson Goodman, *op. cit.*

13. National Art Education Association, *Quality Art Education* (Reston, VA: NAEA, 1986).

14. Lauren Resnick and Leopold E. Klopfer, "Toward the Thinking Curriculum: An Overview," in *Toward the Thinking Curriculum: Current Cognitive Research* (Association for Supervision and Curriculum Development, 1989).

◆ ACTIVITIES FOR THE READER

1. Visit an art classroom and observe the teacher instruct several classes. Make a list of the different teaching methods employed by the teacher. Does the teacher employ an appropriate range of teaching methods, such as discussion, demonstration, lecture, group activities, and so on? What visual aids does the teacher use?

2. While visiting an art classroom make a chart of the content that is being taught. What are the students learning about art production, art history, art criticism, aesthetics? How well is the art curriculum balanced? If possible, talk to students and through your conversation learn what kinds of things they know about art. What seem to be the results of the art program as exemplified in the children's conversation about art?

3. While visiting an art classroom do you notice any students who might be in special programs? In what ways does the teacher attempt to accommodate different learning styles and paces? Do you observe any learning centers in the room?

4. In the art room(s) that you visit do you observe visual teaching through bulletin board displays, art prints, or other means? What does the student work on display indicate about the art instruction that students have received? Can you observe the results of instruction in the work of students? Does the work of older students appear more sophisticated and accomplished than the work of younger children?

5. In the school(s) you visit is art taught by elementary classroom teachers, by art specialists, or a combination of both? How many minutes of art do students receive each week, on the average? If art is taught by an art specialist, does the classroom teacher stay in the room to observe or assist? How many pupil contacts does the art specialist have?

6. What is the apparent emphasis on holiday-centered art projects in the school you visit? Ask to see the written curriculum or curriculum guide used in the school. Do you find a balanced curriculum in the written material? Do you observe a balanced art program in action?

7. What is the ethnic makeup of the students you observe? Do you see evidence of art teaching related to the ethnic backgrounds of the students? Do you see evidence that students are learning about art from different cultures, times, and locations?

◆ SUGGESTED READINGS

Harry S. Broudy, *Enlightened Cherishing: An Essay on Aesthetic Education* (Urbana: University of Illinois Press, 1972). A delightful philosophical essay on the benefits of the arts in education.

Michael Day, Elliot Eisner, Robert Stake, Brent Wilson, and Marjorie Wilson, *Art History, Art Criticism, and Art Production: An Examination of Art Education in Selected School Districts*, Vol. II (Santa Monica, CA: The Rand Corporation, 1985). This document describes exemplary art programs in seven school districts of different sizes in seven states from New York to California.

Elliot Eisner, *The Role of Discipline-Based Art Education in America's Schools* (Los Angeles: The Getty Center for Education in the Arts, 1986). An essay that develops a rationale for art in general education.

National Endowment for the Arts, *Toward Civilization: A Report on Arts Education* (Washington, DC: National Education Association, 1988). This important report on the status of the arts in education provides the best statistical view of school art programs with recommendations for improving their status.

Ralph A. Smith, *Excellence in Art Education: Ideas and Initiatives* (Reston, VA: National Art Education Association, 1986). This work was commissioned by the NAEA and contains Smith's views on art in education.

Ralph A. Smith, ed., *Discipline-Based Art Education: Origins, Meaning, and Development* (Urbana: University of Illinois Press, 1989). This broad study contains numerous descriptions of art programs from many different circumstances, including a number of innovative examples.

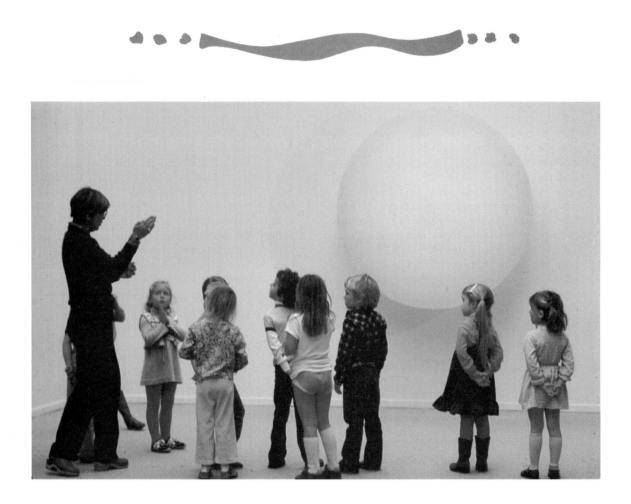
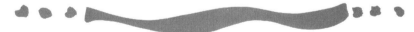

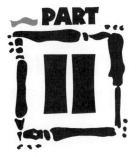

PART II

CHILDREN AS LEARNERS

CHILDREN'S ARTISTIC DEVELOPMENT: HOW CHILDREN GROW AND LEARN

VERY CHILD IS an artist.

The problem is how to remain an artist once he grows up.

Once I drew like Raphael, but it has taken me a whole lifetime to learn to draw like children.[1]

Pablo Picasso

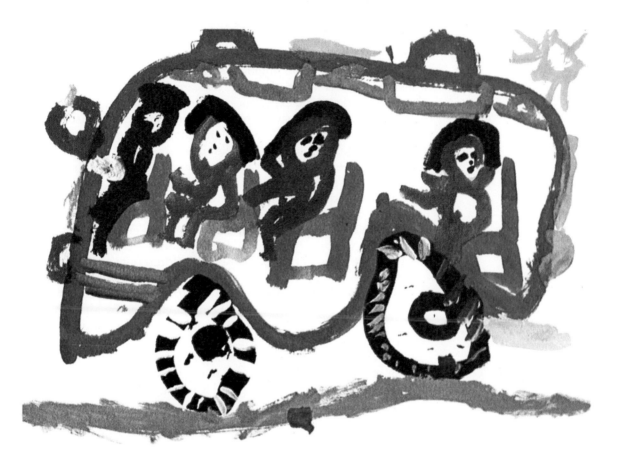

For many years adults have been fascinated with drawings, paintings, and other art objects made by children. Psychologists, educators, parents, and other interested adults have studied children's art from several vantages. Analysis of art products of children has been viewed as a means to look into their young minds and hearts, to learn what they are interested in, what they know, and how they think. Children's art has been studied as an expression of their emotional lives or personality development. Some scholars have viewed the apparent changes in the ways children draw and paint as they grow older as a basis for theories of mental development. More recently, ways that children understand what art is, how it is made by artists, and how it is judged and valued have been studied by researchers. This chapter discusses the emotional, developmental, and cognitive aspects of children's development in art and investigates relationships between children's art products and the works of adult artists.

ART AND PERSONALITY

Each child is an individual with unique potentials and experiences, and each will develop uniquely in art as in other domains of human learning. As art making becomes a means for children to express their emotions, ideas, and experiences, their art production will of necessity be idiosyncratic. However, children of the same age are also similar in many ways. Teachers of specific grade levels come to know how the typical behaviors, capabilities, and interests of a group of fourth graders, for example, will vary from those of a group of first graders. These broad similarities within age groups are observed also in children's art production and in their understanding about art. Even emotional content in children's art, the themes that they choose to represent, the feelings and relationships that they explore through their drawings and paintings, can be seen to change according to age levels.

In what ways does the artwork of children reflect aspects of their personalities? How do children use art expression as a means to deal with emotional situations in their lives? Should teachers attempt to interpret the psychological well-being of children by analyzing their artwork? These questions are difficult to answer definitively because of the obvious difficulty in learning exactly what young children with limited verbal abilities are thinking and feeling. These issues have been studied and observed over many years, however, and insights have been gathered that can guide teaching practice.

Very young children, even prior to age two, evidently enjoy the process of making marks by whatever means are available. The kinesthetic experience of rhythmic movement coupled with the observable results of their actions provides reinforcement for children to engage in very early graphic activities such as drawing and painting. As they grow older and develop their cognitive and psychomotor skills, children are able to express their ideas and feelings in their artwork.

As they develop personal graphic symbol systems, art production becomes a personal language for many children, although much of what they communicate may not be accessible to others. Indeed, because these young artists of ages 2, 3, and 4 are not concerned with producing an art object, as adults perceive art, they often draw or paint directly over one graphic idea with a subsequent image that might in turn suggest a second or third idea. There might be layers of a child's thought and emotion buried within what to many adults might appear to be a scribble or a mess of paint. Researchers who have observed and listened to young children during this process have noted their flexibility in moving from one idea or theme to another, often talking to themselves or singing as they draw or paint.

As children grow older, into the preschool and kindergarten ages, the result of their artwork often becomes more readily discernible and easier to interpret, especially as verbal skills increase so that they can explain their images, interests, and intentions. The development of children's abilities to create graphic symbols that represent persons, animals, and objects extends the range of what they can communicate in their art and increases the likelihood that knowledgeable adults can interpret meaning from their art products.

In the normal course of living prior to formal school experiences, children often relate and explore events in their lives that are emotionally important to them. Relationships with parents, siblings, family pets, or even fantasy characters often are depicted and explored in drawings, paintings, and clay. Children often are able to integrate the worlds of imagination, fantasy, and reality in their artistic creations. Sometimes children's understanding of how parts of the real world function can be seen in their artwork, as when they draw family members engaged in activities, when they draw animals, houses, cars, or airplanes, and when they deal with their personal fears or aspirations.

Because young children often seem to have naive abilities to draw and paint about their emotional lives in very uninhibited ways, adults understandably have been very interested in their artwork. Children at early ages tend to draw and paint the people and events in their lives—both happy and sad—that are meaningful to them. This seems to be a very natural and healthy practice that is exhibited by children from all parts of the world. Knowledgeable teachers of art recognize this and encourage children in their natural interests as they gradually assist children to enlarge their understanding of the world of art.

Some psychologists and educators are especially interested in children's graphic works as a window into their thoughts and feelings, especially for those children who might be emotionally disturbed or who have experienced emotional traumas of some sort. The subject matter of drawings, paintings, and sculptures by such children, ways that they represent themselves and others in their works, and even the manner by which they create with art materials can sometimes provide clues to their emotional lives. This is the area of special concern for art therapists.

An example of this type of revelation can be seen in the drawings and paintings of Hmong children who witnessed the horrors and violence of war in Southeast Asia and later emigrated to North America and entered American and Canadian schools. Similarly, children who experience personal trauma sometimes focus on these topics in their art production and, through the process of dealing with the traumatic event in a safe, nonthreatening medium over which they have control, gain some resolution for themselves. The abilities of children to represent, manipulate, and control their worlds through art, and thus to deal with difficult life situations, is the source of the therapeutic dimension of art. Many art educators emphasize this capacity of art in their educational programs for very young children. Regardless of programmatic emphasis, it would be unwise for teachers to ignore or in any way diminish the spontaneous interest in making art that characterizes children everywhere.

It is not the art teacher's role to attempt to render psychological interpretations of particular children in their classes by analyzing their art products. This chapter discusses some of the normal characteristics in children's drawings and paintings. This knowledge will assist perceptive teachers to note gross variations from the norm on the part of particular children. Very unusual art products can be clues that teachers can share with appropriate school personnel, such as the other teachers, school counselors, or school psychologists. This information, along with records of prodigious or retarded work in other curricular areas such as verbal language, music, or mathematics can be useful in helping school officials to provide the best educational opportunities for each child.

STAGES OF GRAPHIC REPRESENTATION

Experienced teachers who work with children at particular age levels come to know a great deal about how children behave at those levels. A good deal of "teacher talk" or professional shoptalk in faculty lounges is concerned with these behavioral characteristics and with the noticeable gains in maturity as children move from grade to grade. Major proportions of the fields of developmental psychology and cognitive psychology are dedicated to the study of these maturational or developmental changes in children. Educators are concerned with the findings of these studies as they might apply to teaching and learning in the schools, and continuously attempt to make school learning environments more appropriate for the development characteristics of children at different age levels. For example, the organization of learning centers for use by a few children in the classroom while others are working in reading groups or other activities is very different from the nineteenth century when desks were bolted to the floor in rows and all students participated in rote lessons copied from the blackboard. The middle school movement is motivated in large part by recognition of developmental differences of children as they progress from the elementary school years toward the more independent life of high school students.

Children's capacities to make and understand art develop in parallel fashion to changes in the cognitive, emotional, social, and physical dimensions of their lives. The notion that children progress through stages of development in these various areas is central to the field of developmental psychology and the writings of Lowenfeld,[2] Piaget,[3] Gardner,[4] and others. Developmental or stage theory associated with art is based on the assumption of *untutored progression*, accounted for primarily by qualitative differences in the minds of children and results of their life experiences as they grow older.

Although there are problems inherent with these assumptions when we take the position that children should be educated in art, the basic information that is available through study of stages or changes in the ways children make and think about art can be very valuable for teachers. Knowledge of developmental stages in art can provide teachers with insights about what children are attempting in their artwork and ways that appropriate motivation and instruction might be provided.

Children grow and develop in generally predictable ways, with wide variations within an age norm or stage. Just as reading levels vary widely in an average class of twenty-five or thirty children (and the variation increases with each grade level), so abilities in art vary widely as well. This means that teachers can come to know, generally, what to expect and plan for when they are preparing their art programs, but they must be aware of the unique educational needs of each child.

We present a simplified version of stage theory that describes three general stages of children's graphic development, known here as the *manipulative stage (ages 2–5)*, the *symbol-making stage (ages 6–9)*, and the *preadolescent stage (ages 10-13)*. Important differences in artistic development are noted between the stages, which are also quite broad.

The Role of Art Instruction

Some of the characteristics of children's art products are altered when they are given instruction in art production and when they learn more about the adult world of art. Rather than viewing these alterations of the natural as negative, we view them as the normal outcome of education in any area of learning in the school curriculum. When we accept the obligation to provide art education as an essential component in the general education of all children, we accept the fact that education will alter the way children think and act. The moral and ethical requirement for teachers is to assure that changes they bring about in the lives of children are positive, enabling, and life-enhancing.

The first stage is one at which children manipulate materials, initially in an exploratory, random fashion. Later in this stage the manipulation becomes increasingly organized until the children give a title to the marks they make. During the next stage, the children develop a series of distinct symbols that stand for objects in their experience. These symbols are eventually related to an environment within the drawing. Finally comes a preadolescent stage, at which the children become critical of their work and express themselves in a more self-conscious manner. The fact that these stages appear in the work of most children in no way detracts from the unique qualities of each child's work. Indeed, within the framework of the recognized stages of expression, the individuality of children stands out more clearly. *Stages of artistic development are useful norms that can enlighten the teacher, but should not be considered as goals for education.* The effects of a positive, supportive educational environment can be seen in the children's artwork, and their progress can be enriched and accelerated by the efforts of well-prepared and sensitive teachers.

The Manipulative Stage (Ages 2–5, Early Childhood)

Drawing is a natural and virtually universal activity for children around the world. From infancy onward, children mark, scribble, and draw with whatever materials are available. As soon as they can grasp a marking instrument of some sort—a crayon, a pencil, or even a lipstick or piece of charcoal—children make marks and scribbles. Some adults discourage this behavior in their offspring, especially when it occurs on walls, floors, and other surfaces not intended for graphic purposes, and they are relieved when their children outgrow the tendency to engage in scribbling.

These parents, and often teachers, too, do not realize that what we call scribbling can be a worthwhile learning activity for very young children.* By scribbling, an infant literally "makes a mark on the world," in one of the earliest examples of personal causation: Children come to realize in physical and visual terms that they can exercise control over their environment. Before the age of two infants are fascinated by their abilities to make oral noises—babblings, cries, gurgles, and laughs. All of these sounds cease instantly upon completion and leave the child no residue for observation. Graphic marks that the infant makes remain, however, and provide evidence of the marking behavior. The child marks and sees the marks with the dawning awareness that it can alter them and add to them. This is a significant realization for such a tiny person and, as Elliot Eisner explains, is also a source of pleasure:

> The rhythmic movement of the arm and wrist, the stimulation of watching lines appear where none existed before are themselves satisfying and self-justifying. They are intrinsic sources of satisfaction.[5]

*Although the term "scribble" has been accepted by psychologists and art educators in relation to children's drawing, it is in fact a misnomer. Children's scribbles are not the hasty, careless, or meaningless marks defined in the dictionary. The marks that children make are more accurately described as "pre-symbolic graphic investigation." As Judith Burton of Teacher's College, Columbia University, has noted, the word "scribbling" intimates behavior that is not serious or order-seeking, behavior that must be overcome as soon as possible so that the serious business of symbolization can begin. We err when "we mistake the swirls and swooshes and speeds of pre-symbolic action as hurried, mindless and meaningless. Nothing could be further from the truth" (personal correspondence with author).

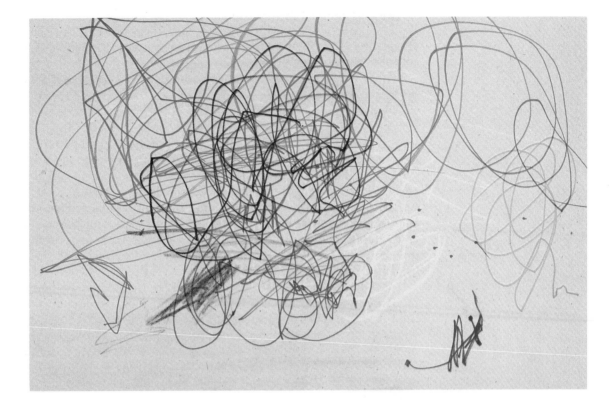

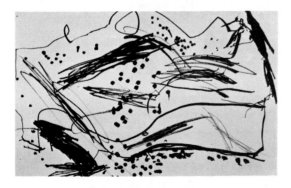

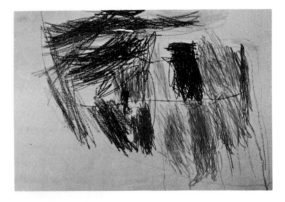

Children who scribble (preschematic investigation) develop a repertoire of lines and marks they will use later. As these examples show, there is considerable development even within this stage from the seemingly random and exploratory (top) to an increased sense of organization (bottom left) to the use of color and a more conscious connection between parts of the whole configuration (bottom right).

Through their preschematic efforts, children aged one through three or four develop a repertoire or vocabulary of graphic marks which they create primarily for the kinesthetic rewards inherent in the manipulation of lines, colors, and textures.

Scribbled marks are precursors to the visual symbol system of drawing that each child develops independently and uses in his or her own way. Children who have the necessary opportunities to scribble develop the ability to produce a wide variety of lines, marks, dots, and shapes during the first two or three years of life. This repertoire of graphic marks is utilized later by the child for the invention of visual symbols in the form of drawings. The child who develops a variety of graphic marks during the scribbling years will manifest this visual vocabulary to produce symbolic drawings that increase in richness and sophistication as the child matures. Children who rarely engage in early graphic activities usually exhibit a narrower vocabulary in their drawings and sometimes require considerable encouragement to continue to develop their drawing abilities.

This initial stage of artistic production is referred to here as the manipulative stage and can last through ages four or five in many children. The manipulative stage is also known as the scribble stage, but whereas the *scribble* implies a distinct early phase of image development, *manipulative* implies a general stage of initial exploration and experimentation with any new materials. Scribbling is the beginning of the manipulative stage and usually lasts until the children are in kindergarten.

Periods of producing what appear to be scribbles depend on the child's muscular development, intelligence, parental encouragement, and the time devoted to practice. As time goes on, these seemingly random drawings are increasingly controlled; they become more purposeful and rhythmic. Eventually, many children tend to resolve their marks into large circular patterns, and they learn to vary their lines so that they are sweeping, rippling, delicate, or bold. When a child can return a moving line to its point of inception, a sense of control is vastly increased, leading to the creation of the mandala.

The great variety of circular patterns, or "mandalas," according to Rhoda Kellogg's[6] analysis of thousands of children's drawings, appears as a final stage between scribbling and representation. The term *mandala* is usually used to describe a circle divided into quarters by two crossed lines. Carl Jung[7] and Rudolf Arnheim[8] both viewed the mandala as a universal, culture-free symbol that evolves out of a physical condition (that is, as a basic property of the nervous system) as well as a psychological need. It is interesting that the mandala, like other manifestations of children's early drawing, can appear as readily among Nigerian children as among children in an American nursery school.

As they experiment with making marks and as they gain experience, normal children progress through the manipulative stage. They

The mandalas at the top served as models for the head and hands of the figures at the bottom. The mandala is one of the rudiments of graphic vocabulary that can be used by children for various purposes.

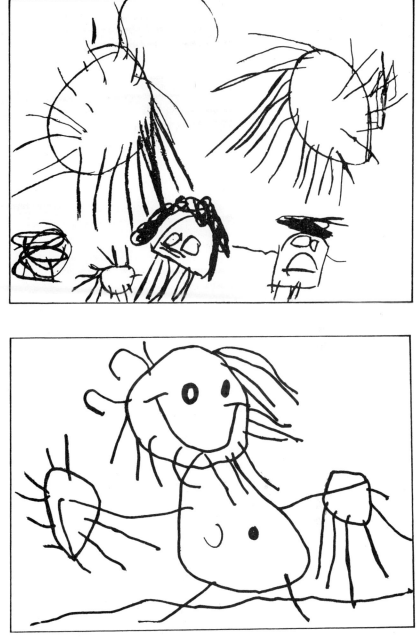

develop a greater variety of marks, and different marks and scribbles are used in varying combinations. Random manipulation becomes more controlled as children invent and repeat patterns and combinations of marks. Lines of all types are used by children in their marking, including vertical, horizontal, diagonal, curved, wavy, and zigzag lines. Some children will attend to drawing intently for periods of thirty minutes or more and will produce a series of a dozen or more drawings within a brief time.

Children aged two to five also begin to learn about qualities of art media. They are fascinated by the materials around them, the multitude of textures, colors, smells, tastes, weights, and other properties. They are interested in art materials because of the intrinsic visual and tactile properties. They can manipulate art materials and can even transform their characteristics. With a brush they can make paint into a line or a shape or various textures. How thrilling it is for the child to learn that colors change when mixed together—and that he or she can be an agent of change. Similarly, the child can make a piece of clay into a coil or pinch it into small flat shapes or scratch it with an object to create an interesting texture. Children experience the same exploratory process with other media such as scraps of wood, cardboard boxes, and so on. After perhaps five or six weeks of work with several art media, most children gain sufficient skill to repeat lines or shapes with paint, clay, boxes, or scraps of materials.

Picture making in general comes naturally to children at a surprisingly early age. Some children will grasp a crayon and make marks with it before they are fifteen months old. Children's bodily movements are overall movements and result in a broad rhythmic action. When very young children paint, they do so from their fingertips to the ends of their toes. Not until they grow older and gain control of the smaller muscles do their muscular actions in art become localized to hand, arm, and shoulder.

As well as exhibiting an ability to design in two dimensions, the preschool child often learns to produce three-dimensional designs. By the time some children have reached the age of three, they have experimented with sand and—sometimes to their parents' horror—mud. They are capable of joining together scraps of wood and cardboard boxes or using building blocks to bring about the semblance of an organized three-dimensional form.

On entering kindergarten at the age of four or five, even those children who have had practice at home with art materials and who have produced pleasing designs tend to regress. The causes of such a condition are not hard to find. In the first place, the children are passing through a period of adjustment to a new social setting. Many of them are away from the protection of their parents and their homes for the first time. Unfamiliar faces and situations surround them, and a new and powerful adult in the form of a teacher must sometimes be placated. Also, many are passing through a new phase of artistic development. From the scribble or manipulative stage they are progressing into the stage of symbols. In the *symbolic* stage marks can no longer be placed at random on a sheet of paper but rather must be set down with greatly increased precision. In their attempt to achieve greater command of symbols, children tend to lose their natural sense of freedom. Not until they feel more at home in their new environment will qualities of spontaneity and directness return. Regressions in ability occur with each child from time to time and may be observed at any level of development. Absence from school, illness, or temporary emotional upsets can be reflected in the design output of any child.

Judith Burton describes three types of conceptual learning accomplished by children in the manipulative stage. When children are able to grasp the outstanding features of lines, shapes, and textures, and when they learn that materials can be organized in many different ways, they have formed *visual concepts*. *Relational concepts* are formed when children can construct relationships of order and comparison, and when they can apply these relationships knowledgeably.

> For example, when organizing a painting, children make careful decisions about the placement of their lines and shapes, whether they are to be close together or far apart, positioned in the middle, top or bottom of the page, or enclosed within each other.[9]

Expressive concepts are formed when children recognize the connections between their actions with art materials, the visual outcomes, and the sensations these actions cause. Children begin to describe lines as "fast" or "wiggly" and shapes as "fat" or "pointy." The fact that the child can control and select the qualities of the elements of design and can organize them in ways that express happiness, bounciness, or tiredness represents significant artistic development. It means that the child has developed a graphic language with which he or she can begin to express and communicate ideas and feelings.

Up to this point children may or may not have established a theme or expression, nor given a title to their work. Since drawing is an emotional as well as cognitive (intellectual) process, children will often accompany their work with appropriate sounds. Eventually, however, children will lift their eyes from their work and say, "It's me," or "It's a window," or even "That's Daddy driving his car." The manipulative process has at last reached the stage at which the product may be given a title. We may assume that, in general, children up to this stage share these characteristics:

1. The work of art is primarily instrumental in nature; in other words, it is an adjunct of another thought process as well as an end in itself.

2. Early drawings are general rather than specific; that is, they deal with dominant impressions as opposed to differentiation. (Noses may be more significant than the roundness of the head.)

3. Each stage of development is usually accompanied by a period of retrenchment, often regression, during which the schema are repeated in a seemingly mechanistic way.[10]

We cannot overemphasize the importance of the "naming of a scribble" in the life and development of a child. Naming—matching a word with an image—can precede the drawing experience when parents read to them from illustrated books. Many parents watch with great anticipation and record the exact age when their child takes the first step; the child's first word is another memorable occasion; but neither is as intellectually significant as the child's own invention of a graphic symbol, for this act places the child far ahead of all other mammals and reveals the tremendous mental potential of human beings.

We have no precise knowledge as to how children arrive at such pictorial-verbal equivalents. On the one hand, it has been suggested that the shapes they produce in their controlled manipulations remind them of objects in their environment. On the other hand, the dawning realization that marks or shapes can convey meaning, together with a newly acquired skill to produce them at will, may prompt them to create their own symbols. Perhaps the symbol appears as a result of both mental processes, varying in degree according to the personality of its author. Whatever the process may be, the ability to produce symbols constitutes an enormous advance in the child's educational history. By the first grade, the child has developed his or her own means of expression and communication that are definitive, personal, flexible, and artistically effective.

The first-named scribble is usually a form of mandala—a circular or generally round shape. The child sees the shape as it appears among random scribbles and marks and learns to repeat the shape at will. The production of symbols demands a relatively high degree of precision because a symbol, unlike most of the results of manipulation, is a precise statement of a fact or event in experience.

The teacher of the primary grades must be prepared to find pupils at many stages of development and to see pupils progress at different rates. In the case of most normal children, however, the teacher might expect satisfactory progress through the three phases of the manipulative period to take about six weeks to two months. At the end of this period most children will be entering, or ready to enter, the symbol stage.

Actually, *no one leaves the manipulative stage entirely*. Confronted with an unfamiliar substance or a new tool, even as adults we are likely to perform some manipulation before we begin to work in earnest. After buying a new pen, for example, we generally scribble a few marks with it before settling down to write a letter. Artists who purchase a new kind of paint will in all likelihood experiment with it before they paint seriously. Indeed, the manipulation of paint was one of the chief characteristics of abstract expressionist painting. Moreover, the painterly surface is one of the hallmarks of all romantic art, much as the repression of painterly effects is a distinguishing characteristic of classicism. Surface manipulation plays the same role in sculpture. The teacher should realize that manipulation is not a waste of educational time and materials; it is a highly educative process. The interaction between ideas and materials that the children gain through manipulation allows them to enter more easily into the symbolic phase of expression.

The Symbol-Making Stage (Ages 6–9, Grades 1–4)

When the normal child makes a connection between image and idea, assigning meaning to a drawn shape, the shape becomes a symbol. Initially, this shape is used to stand for whatever the child chooses. A shape designated as "Mommy" might appear very similar to another shape that the child calls "house." The early symbol is, in the terms of psychologist Rudolf Arnheim, *undifferentiated*.[11] It serves the child by standing for many objects. A parallel use in the verbal symbol system is demonstrated when a young child who has learned to say "doggie" in relation to the family pet points to a sheep, cow, or other furry four-legged animal and says "doggie." Adults correct the child and introduce the appropriate term. The child then has a more differentiated symbol to apply: "doggie" for one kind of animal, "sheep" for another, and so on.

A similar process develops with children's drawings. The initial primitive symbol can stand for whatever the child chooses it to represent. As the child's symbol-making ability progresses, the child produces more sophisticated graphic symbols. This can be seen especially in children's early representations of the human figure. The primitive circular shape stands for "Mommy." Later, a line and two marks inside the shape are "Mommy" with eyes and mouth. The primitive shape is differentiated further by the addition of two lines that represent legs, two lines for arms, and a scribble that stands for hair.

Psychologist Dale Harris relates degrees of differentiation to general intelligence. The ability of a child to exercise memory as a basis for differentiation, as in relating parts of a subject to the same source, can be used as a key to intelligence and potential reading ability. A drawing of a shoe gives the subject one score, but a shoe with a heel and laces increases the score.[12]

It is at this point that a fundamental misunderstanding of children's graphic representation can occur. Most adults, including some experts in children's artistic development, view these early drawings of people as heads with arms and legs protruding. They have been termed "head-persons" or "tadpole" figures because the head apparently dominates. The question is asked, "Why do children draw figures this way?" Those who are experienced with children at this level realize that the children understand human anatomy much differently than their drawings would suggest. They know the parts of the body and

Illustrating a range in children's degrees of differentiation, the top drawing by a four-year-old Australian shows a family as a series of tadpole-like figures emerging at the end of the scribble stage, while the lower drawing by a ten-year-old Brazilian exhibits the stage of realism, around two years in advance of her age level.

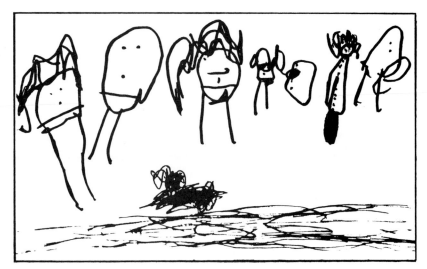

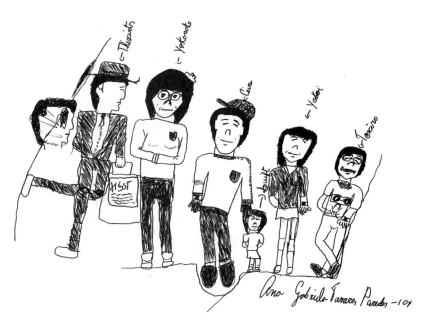

they know that arms do not protrude from the head—they are aware of shoulders, chest, and stomach. Why, then, do these early drawings appear to represent heads with arms and legs and no torso? Arnheim's explanation is eminently logical and useful:

> Representation never produces a replica of the object but its structural equivalent in a given medium. . . . The young child spontaneously discovers and accepts the fact that a visual object on paper can stand for an enormously different one in nature.[13]

This means that the child's primitive symbol, the circular shape, stands for the entire person, not just the head. This is a person with eyes and a mouth, a person with hair. It does not represent only the head of a person with inappropriately placed appendages. This interpretation eliminates the apparent discrepancy between what children draw and paint and their understanding of the world around them, especially the human figure. We must recognize that children's symbols are not replicas of the world and that the materials used by children will influence their symbol making.[14] In other words, *children at this stage draw what they know, not what they see.*

As children grow and develop from this early symbolic behavior into the symbol-making stage, they produce increasingly differentiated representations. The human figure appears with more details, such as feet, hands, fingers, nose, teeth, and perhaps clothing. It is interesting to note again how children create equivalents rather than replicas of their subjects. Hair might be represented by a few lines or by an active scribble. Fingers are often shown as a series of lines protruding from the hands with a "fingerness" quality, but with little regard for exact number.

Eventually a body is drawn with the head attached and with arms and legs in the appropriate location. This more true-to-life figure drawing is usually achieved through a process of experimentation with the medium. Sometimes the space between two long legs becomes the body. Some children add another larger circular shape for the body and draw the head on top. Once the child's representation of the human figure has reached the point where all of the body parts are explicitly included, the symbol can be used and elaborated upon in many significant ways. The child can draw men and women, boys and girls, and people with different costumes and occupations. Most children also develop symbols for other objects in the world, including animals and birds, houses and other buildings, cars, trucks, and other vehicles, and in general anything that interests the child.

Relating Symbols to an Environment.   Whenever pupils produce two or more symbols related in thought within the same composition, they have demonstrated an advance in visual communication, for they have realized that a relationship of objects and events exists in the world. The problems that confront them at this point revolve around a search for a personal means of expressing satisfactory relationships between symbols, ideas, experience, and environment. In striving for such connections they are engaged in the main task of all artists. This development can occur only if educational conditions are right. Unfortunately, during these delicate developmental stages problems may develop if adults view children's art as a crude version of adult work. Children's work up to this point sometimes appears to the eye of the uninitiated

Examples of the results when children draw what they know rather than what they see are shown in these X-ray views (top) of an eight-year-old Australian child's conception of armies using a tunnel, an interior view of a lion by an eight-year-old Korean child (middle), and a gifted nine-year-old's drawing of Noah's ark that accommodates an interest in cartooning (bottom).

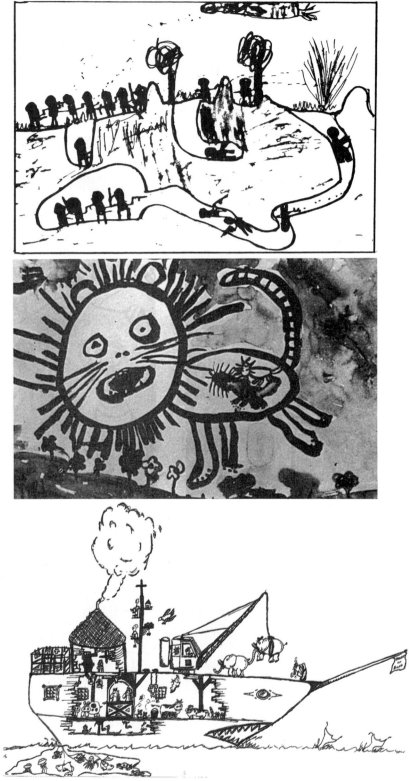

as untidy, disorderly, and often unintelligible. To make children's work neater or clearer, adults sometimes inappropriately use certain "devices" such as outlining objects for them to color or giving them the work of others to copy and trace. The problem with many of these devices is that they are devoid of educational value because they are adult solutions to a child's point of view. Because of this, adult models can discourage some children from developing their own ideas.

Children may begin relating a symbol to its environment by simple means. They may render in paint, clay, or some other suitable medium two similar symbols for human beings, to which they give the title "Me and My Mother." Soon they begin to put together symbols for diverse objects that have a relationship in their thought. Their work may be given such titles as the following:

Our House Has Windows
My Dog Fetching a Stick
I Am Watching Television
Riding to School with Daddy
Throwing the Ball to Maria
Mommy and I Are Cooking

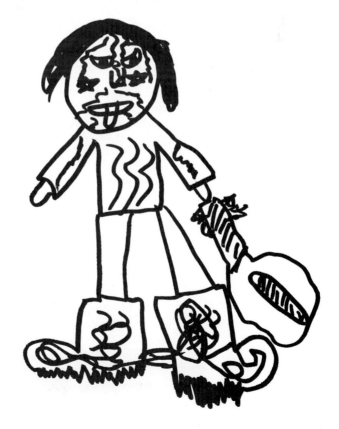

A picture of a rock star by a six-year-old child. The subjective response is reflected through the use of detail: fingers are not as important as the face paint, details of clothing, and the structure of the guitar.

Frequently, children weave into one composition events that occur at different times. In a sense, they may treat the subject of a painting as they do that of a written composition. For example, in a painting entitled *Shopping with Mother*, they may show themselves and their mother driving to a shopping center, making various purchases, and finally unpacking the parcels at home. Here we have, as it were, a story in three paragraphs with all the items placed on one painting surface.

Expression based on vicarious experiences—stories told or read to them, events they have seen on the television or in the movies—may appear in children's art. Brent and Marjorie Wilson have studied the themes of children's drawings and describe the surprisingly broad range of thought and feeling depicted by them. In order to encourage children to draw stories, the Wilsons provided paper divided into frames and made the following request:

> Have you ever drawn pictures to tell stories? Have you ever drawn adventures that you, or heroes, or animals might have? Have you drawn stories about strange creatures in strange worlds? Have you ever drawn stories of battles or machines, even of plants and insects? Have you ever drawn stories about sports or vacations or holiday celebrations? Have you drawn stories about everyday things that happen to people? Please draw a story using boxes to show what first happens in your story, what happens next, and how things finally turn out.[15]

In analyzing many children's graphic narratives (story drawings), the Wilsons found about twenty different themes.

> Children continually draw *quests* ranging from space odysseys to mountain climbing; *trials* depicting tests of strength, courage, and perseverance; and they show *contests* and *conflicts* in which individuals and groups engage in battles, sports contests, and fights. The process of *survival* is a persistent theme, where children depict evasive actions, but here the characters make little effort to fight back. Little fish are eaten by big fish, and people eat the big fish. Children show *bonding*, love or affection between individuals, animals, plants (and even shoes) in any combination. The process of *creation* is shown through all kinds of depictions of constructing and making, such as building a house, arranging a bouquet, or modeling a sculpture. Sometimes creation is followed by *destruction* of plants, animals, and people as well as objects. They are eaten, swallowed, or killed. Quite a number of story drawings deal with *death*. Children are no more immune to contemplations of death than any other group.[16]

Other themes included growth, failure, success, freedom, and daily rhythms; the slice-of-life themes of going to school, going on a picnic and returning, or going to the playground. Although children may first depict nothing but the objects they mention in the titles of their output, when encouraged, they begin to provide a setting or background for objects, and even produce graphic narratives.

These topics are universal themes found in all of the arts from poetry and literature to music and the visual arts. Teachers of art will be able to channel children's innate interests in these themes and ideas toward integrated learning about art, as the children make their own art, view works of art by adult artists based on the same themes, and learn about the history and circumstances that caused artists from many cultures to share the same ideas and feelings. As we will note in Chapter 16 on curriculum, themes provide a very useful means by which to organize art learning for school programs.

Children's Use of Space.   As children's use of symbols broadens and their expression consequently grows in complexity, the task of finding adequate graphic techniques to make their meaning clear becomes increasingly difficult. Their strong desire to express ideas with clarity leads them to adopt many curious artistic conventions. The ingenuity exhibited by children in overcoming their lack of technical skills and in developing expressive devices of their own is fascinating to behold.

Children are confronted with unavoidable spatial problems in their drawings and other two-dimensional work. At first, objects and symbols produced or placed on paper are not related to each other by the child. There is no up or down, or surface on which people or objects are made to stand. For the child, the sheet of paper (picture space) is a place, and all of the objects are together in this place within the edges of the paper. An obvious device utilized by children to make their artistic expression clear is to *vary the relative sizes of the symbols* used in their work. A symbol having emotional or intellectual importance to the pupils may be made larger than others related to it. "Mother," for example, may be depicted as being larger than a house; or perhaps more frequently, children — who are generally egocentric at this stage — will delineate themselves as towering over their associates. The children will employ this device in connection with all the familiar art materials, but it is especially noticeable in their painting. When children paint, they not only give a greater size to the object that appeals most to them, but also may paint it in a favorite color. *Color is often chosen for its emotional appeal* rather than for its resemblance to a natural object. Soon, of course, the children's observation of the world affects their choice of color — sky becomes blue and grass green. When this happens, at about seven years of age, their paintings tend to lose some of their naivete.

Even though young children lack many technical skills to express ideas through visual forms, many are extraordinarily inventive in devising relatively complicated means by which to present their emotional and intellectual reactions to life. Through normal development children become increasingly aware of relationships among the images they create. They want to make objects or people "stand up" or

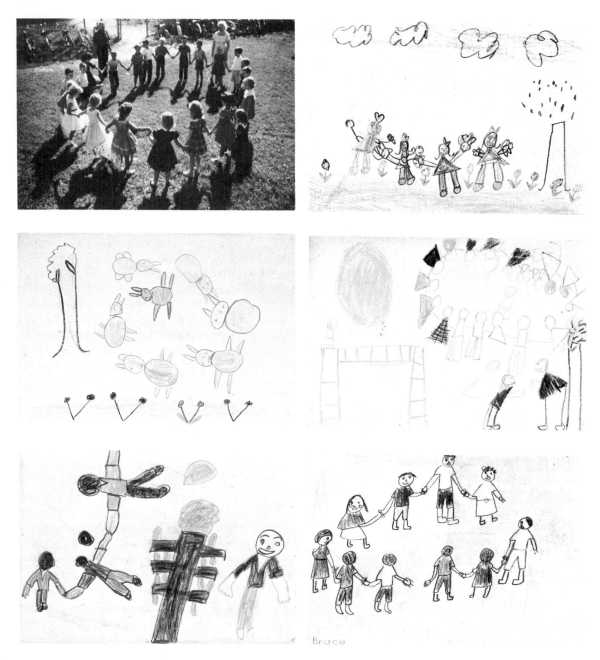

After they played circle games, first graders were asked to draw their favorite games. Note the treatment of people in a circle. Note also the wide range of expression as each child extracted that part of the experience which had the most meaning. To one child, it was a fashion parade; to another, the game Rabbit Run was meant to be taken literally. Another child, evicted from the games for misbehavior, shows himself sulking on the Jungle Jim, while a fourth child, likewise ostracized, was obviously less disturbed by the situation. The fifth child is interested in the problem of shifting views of people standing on the playground. Physical involvement may have destroyed the baseline and expanded the use of space.

stand together, and they seek a place that will serve to support them. The bottom edge of the paper often is chosen to perform this function, and people, houses, and trees are lined up nicely along this initial *baseline*. Before long, other baselines are drawn higher on the paper, usually horizontal to match the bottom edge. Sometimes *multiple baselines* are drawn and objects are lined up on each of them.

The invention of a baseline on which to place objects is an example of what Arnheim terms "representational concepts," which are "the conception of the form by which the perceived structure of the object can be represented with the properties of a given medium."[17] The baseline represents the relationships of objects in the real three-dimensional world, at least for the child at this level of development. It is interesting to note that the baseline, multiple baselines, and virtually all of the other representational concepts found in children's art can also be found in examples of adult art in many cultures.

At the same stage that children develop baselines, it is not unusual for them to place a strip of color or line at the top of the paper to represent the sky. Between the sky and the ground is air, which it is not necessary to represent because it is invisible. Often accompanying the strip of color as sky is a symbol for the sun, which is frequently depicted as a circular shape with radiating lines. Starlike shapes are sometimes added as a further indication of sky. These symbols may persist for years, and the sky does not appear as a solid mass of color touching the earth until the child has developed greater maturity of expression, either as a result of sensitive art instruction or, eventually, because of maturation.

Another spatial problem that must also be dealt with by young symbol makers is *overlap*. Because children realize that two objects cannot occupy the same space at the same time, they typically avoid overlapping objects in their drawings. Because the paper is flat, unlike the real world, overlapping appears to be inconsistent in drawings. Nevertheless, children often represent houses with people inside or show a baby inside the mother's stomach in apparent *X-ray views*. This convention is a logical one to solve a difficult artistic problem—how to represent the interior of a closed object. It is similar to the theater stage where one side of the set is open to allow the audience to look in.

As children become less egocentric and more interested in how the world functions, the subject matter of their art often becomes more complex. They encounter numerous representational problems, such as including many parts of an event or representing a comprehensive view. Children often solve such representational problems by utilizing

Overlapping is dealt with directly in this assignment based upon a crowd scene by an eleven-year-old Icelander.

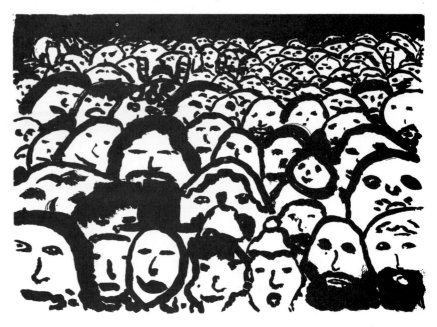

a *bird's-eye view*, a *foldover view*, or *multiple views* in one drawing or painting. For example, in a drawing of a football game, the symbol-making child might draw the field's yardlines striped from a bird's-eye view to depict the space on which the players run. The football players are drawn from a side view, which is more useful for pictorial purposes than the bird's-eye view and is also easier to represent. Even in drawing a single figure, it is not unusual for children to combine profile and front views to best represent the sitting or moving posture of the person.[18]

In a picture of a hockey game or of people seated around a table, some of the participants may appear to be lying flat or to be standing on their heads. The many children who produce compositions of this type usually do so by moving their picture in a circular fashion as they delineate objects or people. Thus, a child may draw a table and place Mother or Father at the head of it. Then, by turning the paper slightly, the child may place Brother in the now upright position. This process continues until all are shown seated at the table. As an alternative to moving the drawing or painting surface, children may walk around the work, drawing as they go.

The foldover view is an interesting phenomenon, seen in the drawings and paintings of numerous children. Again, it is a logical solution to a difficult representational problem. For example, the child wishes to draw a scene including a street, with sidewalks and buildings on both sides. The child draws the street and sidewalks using a bird's-eye view. The buildings on one side of the street are drawn up from the sidewalk and the sky is above the buildings. The child then turns the paper around and draws the buildings and sky on the other side of the street up from the sidewalk. The drawings appears to have half of the buildings right-side up and the other half upside down. There is sky at the top and at the bottom of the picture. The logic of this can be demonstrated by folding the picture on both sides of the street at the base of the buildings and tipping the buildings up vertically. Now the scene is like a diorama, and a person walking down the street could look left or right and see buildings and sky in proper placement.

Adult artists from various times, places, and cultures have all dealt with these problems associated with spatial representation. Egyptian art is typified by a rigid convention for the human figure with particular representations of the eye, the profile head, hair, and so on. Chinese artists developed conventional ways to represent mountains rising from the mist, bamboo plants, and the human figure. Renaissance artists developed the conventions of linear perspective, which is one way artists deal systematically with the problems of representing the three-dimensional world on a two-dimensional surface. Artists of every era learn the artistic conventions of their culture and use them, reject them, or develop new solutions to problems that in turn become another set of artistic conventions. Artists learn the available conventions of their cultures and apply them in unique and expressive ways in their own work. This process of learning conventions, applying them, and innovating with them is useful also for children, especially as they approach adolescence and their critical awareness becomes more acute.

Diagrams on the left show symbols that represent people, trees, and houses, proceeding (left to right) from the simple to the complex. These are the work of kindergarten children.

The drawing (to the right) of a schoolhouse shows a range of ideas in advance of the level of drawing, such as relative sizes of people, an inside-out relationship, subjects connected to each other, filling of the entire space, and the use of smoke to indicate a specific function.

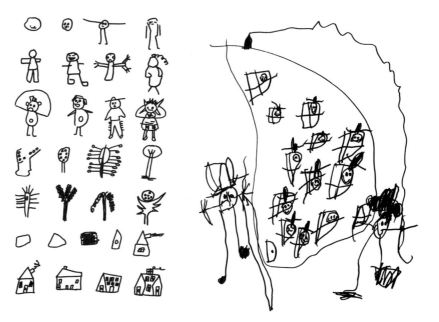

The Schema and the Stereotype.   Symbol-making children develop ways of drawing objects or figures so that they become graphic equivalents of what they represent. A *schema* is a drawing (or painting or clay form) developed by a child that *has a degree of resemblance to an actual object*. The arms of a man, for example, are drawn differently from the branches of a tree. Children use these simple drawings consistently again and again to designate the same objects.[19] To create a schema, ''the child not only has to fashion a graphic equivalent of objects in the world, but also has to design each solution so as to differentiate the marks from others that she makes.''[20] In this sense, schema are a later form of the principle of differentiation.

Children learn to render the petals of a flower or the parts of people and animals in ways that serve their purposes. Children who develop their own schemata naturally understand them and are able to use them in flexible ways. A child who has developed a schema for the figure of a girl, for example, is able to draw girls with different clothing or different hair or different poses. The basic schema for *girl* remains fairly uniform, but the child can accomplish reasonable variations. Sometimes children will alter their schema by leaving parts out or by exaggerating certain parts that are especially significant. Drawings are sometimes left unfinished or some parts are obviously unattended to by the child. These variations should serve to remind adults that children often are more interested in the process of drawing or painting than they are in the result of their efforts as a work of art. The child who draws a picture of his interaction with the neighborhood bully is emotionally more involved with the situation than with the outcome of the drawing as a finished piece. In the child's depiction of the story, it matters little if the fence is not completed — the child knows it is there. The legs that are running and the arm that is throwing are the essential and emotionally significant parts that receive the child's careful attention. Burton reminds us that children's art does not so much make visual statements as make experience visible.[21] The distinction is an important one for understanding children's art.

Children who continue to make art as they progress through the typical symbol-making ages of six, seven, and eight usually precede a number of schemata that change and gain in sophistication and detail as the children's understanding progresses. Some children focus almost exclusively on the human figure; others draw many objects. Because of the time and effort required to develop an advanced schema, most children (and adults) are able to draw some objects much better than others. It depends on what each person has developed during the schematic years.

Children in the primary grades approach art as though it were their own private discovery, working freely and unself-consciously, despite the profusion of visual influences around them. Allowing children in this stage to use a coloring book opens the door to self-doubt, because they are dramatically confronted with the gap between an adult's image and their own. In attempting to draw a clown at a later time, they may recall a "grown-up" clown they had once colored, and either try unsuccessfully to emulate it or suddenly become dissatisfied with their own rendering.

Artistic *stereotypes* are images that children repeat from another source without real understanding. Because children do not understand the stereotypes, they can only repeat them inflexibly, and often incorrectly or inappropriately. A pervasive example is the looped V-shape that represents birds in flight. This was developed by artists to represent birds in the distance, where the details of body, tail, head, and feet are not distinguishable. Watercolor artists who paint coastal scenes with seagulls often make this shorthand image with expressive brushlines but usually vary the position of the wings so that the wings do not appear to flap in unison. Artists also often make visual references to the birds' bodies, and then paint the birds in the foreground in greater detail.

All of these variations of the looped V-shape and the concurrent understandings are not available to children who pick up the stereotype for flying birds and apply it inappropriately. Children demonstrate their lack of understanding of the meaning and origin of the stereotype in drawings where the looped V is upside down and the birds are apparently flapping their wings upward instead of downward. Sometimes the children's marks look more like the letter *M*.

Many stereotypes are available to children through television, advertising, and cartoon strips in newspapers and comic books. Others are passed on from child to child. There are two problems with children's use of stereotypes. First, children cannot utilize stereotypes for the central purposes of their artistic development because the stereotypes are not their own. Second, reliance on copying stereotypes robs children of the confidence required to develop their own schemata. The slick cartoon images created by adult artists often induce young children to believe that their own drawings do not compare favorably and therefore become discouraged with their own production.

The Wilsons have pointed out that children and adults learn to make graphic images by copying, to some degree, the graphic images already in their environment.[22] The pervasiveness of adult graphic images (potential stereotypes) in most children's environment suggests that there is no sure way to protect children from these influences if, indeed, protection is warranted. Children will continue to be influenced by Snoopy, smiley-face buttons, Star Wars characters and the like, regardless of what adults do or say. Yet several observations regarding stereotypes and copying are useful for parents and teachers.

1. Graphic images become stereotypes for children only when they
   are unable to utilize them with flexibility and understanding. A

teacher might lead a child away from the use of stereotypes by suggesting that the child draw a story using the stereotype as a character. The child might learn enough about the graphic image to apply it flexibly, in which case it is no longer a stereotype; or the child might discover that the stereotype has no useful place in the drawing repertoire and abandon it.

2. When copying tends to stultify or intimidate the individual, it is harmful. In dealing with children who are involved with copying, the teacher can help them identify what they might learn from their efforts and how they might apply this learning in their own original artwork.

3. Because it is inevitable that children will be exposed to adult graphic images, many of which may be of low artistic quality, it makes good sense for teachers to expose children to high-quality artworks. Slides, reproductions, films, and books of great art are readily available. Just as in literature, music, or mathematics, children should become aware of the best that the world has to offer in art.

Children are much less likely to rely on stereotypes when they are engaged in a regular program of art that offers a variety of graphic options. Children who develop their own artistic skills are much too interested in their own work to be sidetracked into copying images that are of no expressive value to them.

The Preadolescent Stage (Ages 10–13, Grades 5–8)

The preadolescent stage includes children from approximately the fourth to the seventh grades and even into the eighth grade. It is good to acknowledge again the wide variation in rates of maturity among children. This range can be seen quite obviously in sixth- and seventh-grade classrooms, where girls are usually more physically mature than boys, and in the eighth and ninth grades where some boys have reached puberty and others are still a year or two away from it. Teachers at each higher grade level also must deal with the continuously widening intellectual range among students. For example, the range of reading levels in fourth grade is typically four years while the range is seven years in the seventh grade.

The physical, mental, and social changes that occur during these years set preadolescent children apart from younger children in the symbol-making stage. Although preadolescent children are still naturally inquisitive and creative, they have learned to be more cautious. Younger children work in art with abandon and will often try anything that the teacher suggests in their art. For the younger children practically every art experience is a new one, and they enjoy working on unfamiliar ground. During the years of the preadolescent stage, however, children become more socially aware and sensitive to peer opinion.

The range of topics that interest preadolescent children expands significantly during these years as they become more conceptually sophisticated and more aware of the teen world. Preadolescent boys and girls increasingly turn to the adolescent culture of popular music, interests in television, movies, music videos, ways of dressing and grooming, and even the use of an adolescent language that varies with each new generation. The ways that children in these age groups consider gender differences is in fluctuation as well. Just prior to adolescence, boys and girls tend to stay separated and often pursue separate interests and activities. As they near the onset of puberty and for the remainder of their public or prep school careers, most boys and girls become involved more and more in social interactions between the sexes.

The age range from ten to twelve or thirteen is crucial from the standpoint of art education. It is during these years that most children cease to be significantly involved in making art. Indeed, when asked to make a drawing, the majority of adults will refer back to images that they made before reaching the teen years. Drawings of human figures made by adults are very often difficult to distinguish from the figure drawings of preadolescent children. This is because when individuals give up drawing, their development is virtually arrested at that level. With the development of critical skills at about age eleven, children become critically aware of the qualities of their own art products. If their own drawings and paintings appear to them more closely related to childhood than to the approaching adolescent years, they become self-conscious and dissatisfied with their artwork and tend to produce less or quit altogether. Nine- or ten-year-old children's dissatisfaction with their own best efforts to produce art marks the beginning of a representational stage when children desire to develop technical competencies and expand their repertoire of representational skills.

The solution to the problem of decline in art production prior to the teen years seems relatively clear. The preadolescent years are critical in the artistic development of children. They must make enough progress during this period so that, when they become capable of self-criticism, they will not find their own work too wanting. If children are to continue artistic production during adulthood, they must work with diligence, mastering the technical and expressive conventions of adult art that provide a bridge between the art worlds of the child and the adult. Children readily learn from the multitude of graphic images that are part of the popular culture. Unless instruction is provided, many children will not advance in their own production and appreciation beyond this level. It is the responsibility of art educators to upgrade the level of this visual influence by providing children with examples of the best imagery that the world of art has to offer.

The role of the art teacher changes during students' preadolescent years. Students are more receptive to instruction in competencies of drawing, color and design principles, technical skills in painting, printmaking, sculpture, and other modes of artmaking. Children want to know about ways that artists handle the problems of overlap, size, and placement relationships, and convergence of lines for representing space and depth in drawings and paintings. They are receptive to instruction in many technical aspects of art and are motivated to become skilled in making art that passes their own critical judgment and that of their peers. They are ready to learn more about what artists of the past have created and what contemporary artists are doing and why.

Teachers can draw upon the full range of the visual arts, including instruction derived from applied visual modes such as graphic design, lettering and layout, and illustration. Students become increasingly interested in social, political, and personal influences in art and can respond to themes presented by the teacher that will engage them in discussion as well as production. These years can be tremendously rich and exciting for children and for their teachers as the world of art unfolds before them. The child's gaze is directed toward the teen and adult years, and it is there that much of the content of art as a subject lies. It is the responsibility of art education to foster the transition from enthusiastic and involved child artists entering kindergarten to enthusiastic and involved young people who value art and for whom art is a meaningful and vital part of life.

WHY CHILDREN MAKE ART

The virtually universal participation of children in marking and graphic symbol making strongly suggests that basic reasons exist for these behaviors. Children must gain satisfaction from these activities or they would not engage in them spontaneously. On this topic, however, writers and educators must speculate, because they are unable either to communicate sufficiently well with young children or to recall their own early art experiences. Nevertheless, through lengthy and careful observation of children and through the application of useful psychological theory, it is possible to speculate with some confidence.

For children, art is a means to engage all of their senses for learning and expression. Creating art heightens children's sensitivity to the physical world and fosters a more perceptive appreciation of the environment. Art helps children order their sense impressions and provides a means for them to express imagination and feelings.

The effects of art activity on children's self-concept and general personality development can be very beneficial. Art can provide a means for children to develop their inherent creative abilities and, in the process, to integrate their emotional, social, and aesthetic selves. Children's art is often seen as instrumental in fostering and preserving each individual's identity, uniqueness, self-esteem, and personal accomplishment.

In addition, some educators claim that art activity contributes to cognitive development. More than fifty years ago John Dewey stated:

> To think effectively in terms of relations of qualities is as severe a demand upon thought as to think in terms of symbols, verbal and mathematical. Indeed, since words are easily manipulated in mechanical ways, the production of a work of genuine art probably demands more intelligence than does most of the so-called thinking that goes on among those who pride themselves on being "intellectuals."[23]

Eisner has outlined no fewer than nine things, from symbol formation and symbolic play to the expressive function of visual forms, that children can learn through the act of painting.[24] Children's early graphic behavior—the making, scribbling, and manipulation of materials—appears to be intrinsically pleasurable. As they move into the symbol-making phase, these psychomotor and kinesthetic rewards are reinforced by children's newly developed ability to conceive and convey meanings. This power to use the images that they create as symbols for the world allows children to construct their own knowable world and to convey what they know to others. Eisner writes:

> Children learn that the images and symbols they create can be used to transport them into a fantasy world, that they can create an imaginary world through the use of their own images and through them become a part of other situations in which they can play other roles.
>
> For children the taking of new roles through imagination is an important source of learning. It allows them to practice in the context of play what they cannot actually do in the "real world." It affords them opportunities to empathetically participate in the life of another.[25]

As we watch children draw or paint we are often struck by their concentration and involvement in what they are doing. Children fre-

The four-year-old boy who drew this family group was able to identify and describe the figures.

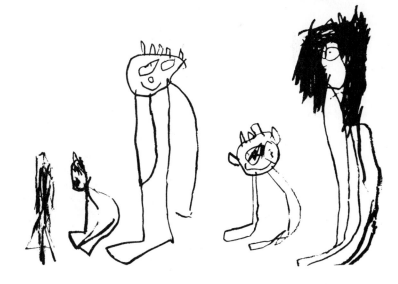

quently talk as they draw, and it is only through close observation that an adult can gain an understanding of what has been created by a particular child. For example, through discussion with her four-year-old boy, a mother learned that his drawing was a picture of the family. The figure on the right (see page 89) with lots of dark hair is the mother; the short figure is the father; next is the child who drew the picture. The small figure next to the boy is his baby sister. When asked by his mother where his brother (a sibling rival) was, the child quickly made the scribble on the left and said, "Here he is, he is hiding behind a bush." In this drawing we see several things:

1. The child is developing symbols for the human figure and can make basic differentiations to represent specific individuals.

2. The child is able not only to represent figures, but also to consider family relationships in his drawing.

3. The emotions of the child are important and obvious in his drawing. Mother is most important in his life and is made prominent in the drawing. His own figure is large. The brother with whom he feels competitive is conveniently left out of the picture. Later he is represented only in a hurried scribble.

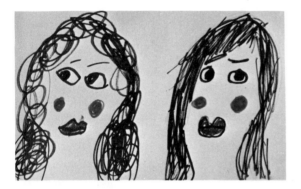
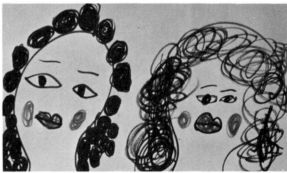

This series of portraits provides a spontaneous narrative of a personal experience by a seven-year-old girl (described on page 91) shows her awareness of social relationships and the level of her ability to tell a story.

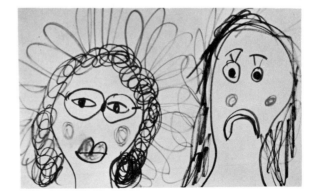

One of the fascinating and charming aspects of children's art is that it can often serve as a window into the minds and emotions of the children. A series of drawings was done by a seven-year-old girl as a response to her experience at school. The first drawing shows the girl admiring a classmate who has pretty curls and is neat and prim. The child artist is an active girl, her hair is stringy, and she is disheveled. Her classmates note these characteristics and comment unfavorably. This motivates the girl to ask her mother to give her a permanent wave. She has the permanent and puts ribbons in her neat hair. After a few hours at school, running and playing, her hair is stringy and the ribbons are untied. The pretty classmate is as neat as ever.

This art product reveals the following:

1. The child is very aware of peer social relationships at school, and she is concerned about her appearance.

2. She is able to reconstruct the series of events in her drawings and to identify her feelings.

3. She is able to tell her story with graphic images in a direct and effective way.

The therapeutic value of making these drawings is not possible to determine. The child was motivated to make them, however, and she did sort out the experience through her art.

In similar ways, children deal with many of life's concerns, joys, and trials through their art products. A child is afraid of fire and paints a picture of someone escaping from a burning building. A child is fascinated with football, invents team players, and draws them in action; the favorite team wins. A child hears a fairy tale and draws a picture illustrating the story. A child visits a grandparent and makes a painting of the experience. The list of possible subjects for child art is as endless as the list of life experiences.

The Wilsons emphasize the narrative dimension of children's drawings. Drawings are produced, they believe, to tell a story, to relate an event, or to tell what some object is like.

> We think that visual narratives are told as part of the process of making personal symbolic models of the world—actually not just *the world*, but *worlds* . . . To understand himself or herself or his or her environment, the child makes drawings that serve as models for how things might be. Thus the drawings provide a means for constructing, testing, and prophesying what can be . . . In their fantasy worlds, children are able to create all the characters, all the settings, and all the rules.[26]

Through their art, children can create worlds and control actions and outcomes as they investigate, in a safe way, concepts, relationships, understandings, and models of behavior.

Children can create fantasies and stories through plays and songs as well as through the visual arts, although drawing seems to be a very

The handling of proportion, detail, composition, imagination, and humor place this five-year-old girl's drawing of a costume party well ahead of her peers.

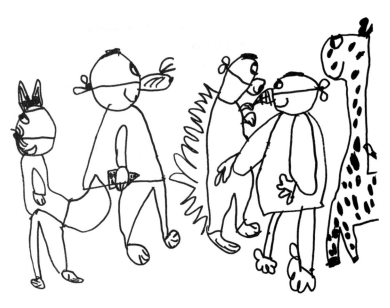

significant medium for such accomplishments. Beyond these functions of art in the lives of children, there are several other aspects of learning that are unique to the visual arts. As children create visual representations, they are required to combine the elements of design into structures with meaning and then to judge the adequacy and quality of their own work. Then they must proceed on the basis of their own judgments. The flexibility of art activity, where even the purpose of the process can change on the basis of the individual's judgment, is very different from other areas of learning that rely on the achievement of stated criteria and the memorizing and recitation of correct answers.

As children enter the preadolescent stage, their interest in art moves from using it solely for personal expression to consciously improving the quality of visual forms. Children become interested in the visual properties of their works—composition, the elements of design—and in the technical aspects of materials and processes. There are very few activities available to people of any age that allow the personal control from initiation to completion that is typical of art activity.

Artistic behavior seen from a broad perspective suggests a reciprocal action between art making and responding to art. The imagination can be as intensely engaged in studying art works as in their creation. The sensory appeal of color as children apply it in a painting can also draw them into a still life by Bonnard, a color field painting by Frankenthaler, or a fourteenth-century Japanese batik. The process of engagement with the world of artworks can be as powerfully absorbing and satisfying as the process of their creation.

The narrative function of art is apparent in this sequence from a major effort by a fourteen-year-old boy. He tells of his traditionally unsuccessful high-school football team triumphing over the opposition. This is an example of world-making through art: characters, story, dialog, action, and composition were all developed by the youngster.

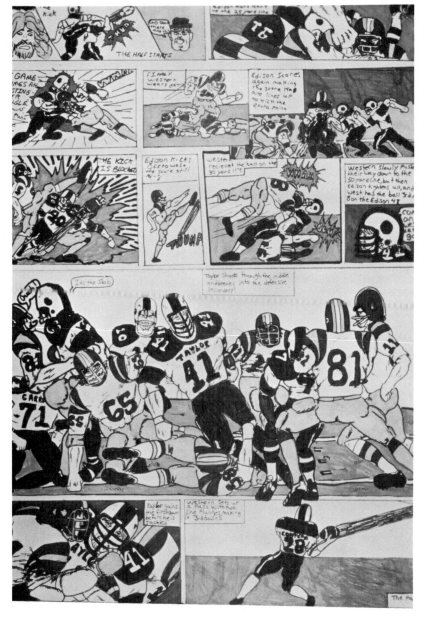

CHILDREN'S CONCEPTUAL DEVELOPMENT IN ART

It is clear that the intellect is involved in the making of art. Psychologists Howard Gardner and D. N. Perkins, for example, believe that art is "usually celebrated as the dominion of the emotions," but is actually

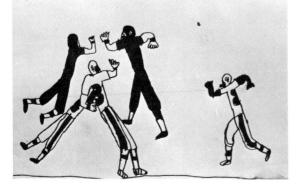

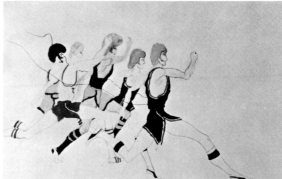

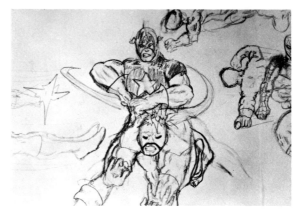

These three drawings by a boy at the ages of nine, twelve, and fifteen document his progress in representing action by the human figure. In the absence of appropriate instruction and encouragement, many young people cease to draw by the age of twelve.

"profoundly cognitive."[27] Richard Pousette-Dart, an artist who paints in the abstract expressionist style, stated that art is "the result of somebody bringing all their faculties to it. Art is a complete realization of one's being, a matter of exquisite focus, awareness, consciousness."[28]

It is also clear that children progress in ways that they are able to understand art, to perceive art and respond to it, to relate art to their own life experiences and to other contexts in the history of art, and to ponder pervasive and fundamental questions about art. Understanding of art in these areas is not necessarily developed simply through art making. Gardner suggests that "there are separate developmental sagas which govern skills of perception, reflection, and critical judgment" in art.[29]

In one study of children's understanding about art, researchers learned that children of different age levels held widely differing views about basic art topics.[30] They interviewed children from ages four through sixteen, showed them reproductions of artworks, and asked them questions about where art comes from, how one becomes an artist, what can count as art, style in art, how one recognizes quality, and who is able to make judgments about art. The researchers discovered, as we might expect, that children gained in their understanding about art and held fewer serious misconceptions as they grew older. This development occurred most likely because of added experience with age and because of normal physical and mental maturation.

They learned, however, that misconceptions about art were common. Some young children, for example, believed that art could be created by animals, or that animals couldn't paint only because they couldn't hold a brush. When questions were asked having to do with how works of art are judged for quality and how they are selected for display in a gallery or museum, different misconceptions emerged, especially among the younger children. Even teenagers, however, exhibited in some cases extremely limited understanding about the basic notions surrounding the creation of, response to, and judgment of art.

This study points out for teachers of art the advisability of learning more about what their students think and understand about art. It is one thing to show students reproductions of paintings or pictures of sculpture, and another to assure that they have basic conceptions about art that will allow them to appreciate what they see. Children who are unaware that "a painting is produced by an individual and that it need not faithfully depict a subject cannot fully appreciate an art museum."[31] The appreciation of art demands understanding which prevents misconstruals and enriches one's experience.

As with other subjects in the school curriculum, those teaching art should carefully consider the conceptual levels of their students. For example, very young children have limited conceptions of time; the notion of a decade or a century might not be within their intellectual grasp. The historical fact that Rembrandt was a sixteenth-century artist, therefore, might not be relevant when a teacher is showing students the artist's drawings or paintings. Most often, errors of aiming too high or too low conceptually can be avoided if teachers engage their students in discussions of what they are seeing and learning about art. Beyond simple factual items, such as the issue of animals making art, there are basic questions about art that can be discussed fruitfully over and over as students progress from grade level to grade level. One such question is, "How is quality in art determined?" This question can be discussed in terms simple enough for a first grader—"Some people (such as art critics or gallery directors) study and devote their lives to judging art"—or for an eighth grade student—"Judgment of quality depends on one's aesthetic stance, or beliefs about the nature of art."

Just as the art production activities for sixth grade students may be more sophisticated than activities for first graders, content derived from art history, criticism, and aesthetics will be taught in ways that are appropriate for children's ages and abilities. Generally, the learning activities will become more difficult and more conceptually sophisticated with each grade level, and teachers will build on learning that has occurred in prior grades.[32]

Teachers should also take care that they do not aim too low in their assessments of what children at particular ages can do. We continue to discover that children can learn and do more than we had anticipated. For example, one study suggested that very young children are able to recognize artistic style, even in response to abstract paintings where subject matter is not a clue.[33] Teachers need to continue to challenge the fastest students in the class in order to keep their interest and involvement, while concurrently accommodating the needs of slower and special learners. Subsequent chapters on the four art disciplines, curriculum and instruction, and evaluation will discuss these issues in greater depth and hopefully will provide useful information for teachers with respect to these issues.

ARTISTS AND CHILDREN'S ART

It has been the goal of many adult artists to capture the freshness, spontaneity, and directness so apparent in the art of children. Examples of artistic conventions commonly used by children can be seen in artworks from many cultures and times. Enlargement of important figures in painting and sculpture is a common device in early Christian art. The placement of mountains and trees as seen in Chinese landscapes is similar in many respects to ways that children manipulate space in their drawings and paintings. The cubist painters consciously depicted multiple views of objects, flattened space, and distorted images, devices that children typically accomplish in the course of their natural development in art. Artists such as Jean Dubuffet, Paul Klee and Karel Appel took great pains to eliminate all vestiges of adult conventions from their works in order to achieve the expressiveness associated with children's art. The worldwide neoexpressionist movement typically exhibits a level of technical proficiency that appears very close to the abilities of middle school children. According to Gardner, it is the child's approach to art, "his preconscious sense of form, his willingness to explore and to solve problems that arise, his capacity to take risks, his affective needs which must be worked out in a symbolic realm," that many adult artists wish to emulate.[34]

Is the art of children, then, to be considered in the same way as the work of mature artists, and in what ways are they different?

In the case of naive painters (sometimes referred to as intuitive, or folk artists) such as Grandma Moses, Horace Pippin, and Henri Rousseau, whose works contain distinctively childlike qualities, similarities with children's work is unplanned. Naive artists, by definition, lack professional training and enjoy an independence from the mainstream of art that places them in a situation similar to children, who have not yet developed adult conventions of art production. Nevertheless, as with the work of children, some naive artists have created charming works of aesthetic merit by utilizing devices such as crude perspective, flat patterning, preoccupation with detail, and arbitrary use of space, almost always accompanied by strong emotional involvement with the subject matter of the works.

These characteristics of children's art are noted also in the works of folk artists from many cultures. As in the carvings of Eskimos or the masks from various African peoples, what initially appears to be child-like directness or simplification upon careful perception is seen to be the work of sophisticated and highly skilled artists.

Some mature artists in the Western tradition actively have sought to achieve a semblance of the spontaneity often found in the works of children. These artists, such as Picasso and the cubists, or Matisse and the fauvists, were well grounded and expert in the standard art techniques of their times, but chose to ignore or reject them in order to achieve their expressive purposes. Others, such as Paul Klee, pursued what is seen by the innocent eye, uncorrupted by a technological society. He left us a body of work noted for its remarkable range — humorous, delicate, and mystical — drawing its strength from the shapes and symbols of the four- to six-year-old child.

Children's art is typified by great pleasure and intense involvement in the making, and young children are willing to disregard what others are doing and to pursue their own ideas to conclusion. As children make art they explore, extend themselves, and solve problems of representation and communication. They are often flexible and open to suggestion as visual accidents occur: dribbles of paint, unintended marks, bleeding, and commingling colors suggest new forms and expressions. All of these characteristics also describe various adult artists.

There are also important differences, however, between the art of children and the art of the professional artist. Small children paint the sky yellow and the tree red because they have not yet developed the conventions of local color, of making objects approximate their appearance, or of controlling the mixing of hues, values, and intensities. The fauvists, who were known for their "wild" use of color, disregarded the conventions of local color with which they were quite familiar, and did so for their own expressive purposes. Although Picasso displayed attributes in his work similar to children's artistic production, we see at work "a host of factors that separate him from the child: his perfected technical facility, his ability to render almost instantly the exact image he desires, the capacity to plan ahead for periods of time and to follow through a project over a great period of time."[35] Picasso also had a tremendous knowledge of the works of other artists and how they were made, and he was very much aware of the techniques, norms, and conventions of art and of the expressive consequences in his own work when he chose to violate them. Beyond this technical and expressive dimension of art, there is also the development of the adult artist's personality that is unavailable to the child because of a lack of experience. Life's events, crises, responsibilities, hardships, and satisfactions are the stuff out of which art is made, and it is the person with the most developed feeling for life who is most likely to create art that will speak with significance.

Given these differences, we can celebrate the art of children as well as the art of adults. We can be charmed and delighted by the work of children and we can see in their art production the crucial seeds of future achievement. The value of children's art varies according to the point of view of the observer. The educator may view it as one route to the development of the aesthetic lens; the psychologist as a key to understanding behavior; and the artist may see it as the child's most direct confrontation with the inner world of sensation and feeling. But educator, psychologist, and artist all view children's artistic development as a unique and essential component of their general education.

◆ NOTES TO THE TEXT

1. Ellen Winner, *Invented Worlds: The Psychology of the Arts* (Cambridge, MA: Harvard University Press, 1982), p. 387.

2. Viktor Lowenfeld and Lambert Brittain, *Creative and Mental Growth*, 8th ed. (New York: Macmillan, 1987).

3. Jean Piaget, *The Origins of Intelligence in Children*, (New York: Norton, 1963).

4. Howard Gardner, *Artful Scribbles: The Significance of Children's Drawings*, (New York: Basic Books, 1980).

5. Elliot Eisner, "What Do Children Learn When They Paint?" *Art Education*, Vol. 31, No. 3 (March 1978), p. 6.

6. Rhoda Kellogg, *Analyzing Children's Art*, (Palo Alto, CA: National Press Books, 1969).

7. Carl Jung, *Psychology and Religion*, (New Haven: Yale University Press, 1960).

8. Rudolf Arnheim, *Art and Visual Perception*, (Berkeley: University of California Press, 1967).

9. Judith Burton, "Beginnings of Artistic Language," *School Arts*, September 1980, p. 9.

10. Helga Eng, *The Psychology of Children's Drawings*, trans. H. Stafford Hatfield (New York: Harcourt Brace Jovanovich, 1931).

11. Rudolf Arnheim, *Art and Visual Perception*.

12. Dale B. Harris, *Children's Drawings as Measures of Intellectual Maturity*, (New York: Harcourt Brace Jovanovich, 1963).

13. Rudolf Arnheim, *Art and Visual Perception*, p. 162.

14. For a careful verification of this principle, see Claire Golomb, *Young Children's Sculpture and Drawing*, (Cambridge, MA: Harvard University Press, 1974).

15. Brent Wilson and Marjorie Wilson, "Drawing Realities: The Themes of Children's Story Drawings," *School Arts*, May 1979, p. 16.

16. Wilson and Wilson, p. 15.

17. Arnheim, p. 163.

18. Judith M. Burton, "Representing Experience from Imagination and Observation," *School Arts*, December, 1980.

19. Betty Lark-Horovitz, Hilda P. Lewis, and Mark Luca, *Understanding Children's Art for Better Teaching*, (Columbus, Ohio: Charles E. Merrill, 1967), p. 7.

20. Howard Gardner, *Artful Scribbles*, p. 67.

21. Judith M. Burton, "Visual Events" *School Arts*, November, 1980, p. 63.

22. Brent Wilson and Marjorie Wilson, "An Iconoclastic View of the Imagery Sources in the Drawings of Young People," *Art Education*, Vol. 30, No. 1 (January 1977).

23. John Dewey, *Art as Experience* (New York: G. P. Putnam's Sons, 1938), p. 46.

24. Eisner, op. cit.

25. Eisner, p. 7.

26. Brent Wilson and Marjorie Wilson, "Children's Story Drawings: Reinventing Worlds," *School Arts*, April 1979, p. 8.

27. D. N. Perkins and Howard Gardner, "A Brief Introduction to Project Zero," *Art, Mind and Education* (Urbana: University of Illinois Press, 1989), p. ix.

28. Catherine Barnett, "The Conundrum of Willem de Kooning," *Art & Antiques*, November, 1989, p. 73.

29. Howard Gardner, "Toward More Effective Arts Education," *Art, Mind and Education* (Urbana: University of Illinois Press, 1989), p. 160.

30. Howard Gardner, Ellen Winner, and Mary Kircher, "Children's Conceptions of the Arts," *The Journal of Aesthetic Education*, July, 1985.

31. Gardner, Winner, and Kircher, p. 61.

32. Michael Parsons, *How We Understand Art: A Cognitive Developmental Account of Aesthetic Experience* (New York: Cambridge University Press, 1987).

33. George W. Hardiman and Theodore Zernich, "Discrimination of Style in Painting: A Developmental Study," *Studies in Art Education*, Vol. 26, No. 3, 1985.

34. Howard Gardner, *Artful Scribbles*, p. 269.

35. Ibid., p. 268.

◆ ACTIVITIES FOR THE READER

1. Collect from a kindergarten and a first grade class a series of drawings and paintings that illustrate the three phases of the manipulative stage.
2. Collect some drawings or paintings by a single child to illustrate the development of a symbol such as that for "person," "toy," or "animal."
3. Collect from several children in the first to third grades a series of drawings and paintings that illustrate developments in symbolic expression.
4. Collect from pupils enrolled in the third to sixth grades drawings and paintings that illustrate some of the major developments in the preadolescent stage.
5. Make one collection of drawings and paintings that is representative of artistic development from kindergarten to the end of sixth grade.
6. Collect work in three-dimensional materials, such as clay or paper, from the pupils in situations identical with, and for purposes similar to, those mentioned in the five activities above.
7. Show children an original painting or a good quality reproduction. Discuss with each child various questions about the origins, creator, and expressive qualities of the artwork.

◆ SUGGESTED READINGS

Gardner, Howard, *Artful Scribbles: The Significance of Children's Drawings*, New York: Basic Books, 1980. A leading psychologist discusses all of the issues mentioned in this chapter, adding case studies, a discussion of Picasso's *Guernica*, and a personal perspective. Gardner's clarity is matched only by his scholarship.

Kellogg, Rhoda, *Analyzing Children's Art*, Palo Alto, CA: National Press Books, 1969. Clearly written and profusely illustrated coverage of the preschool years in art.

Lark-Horovitz, Betty, Hilda P. Lewis, and Mark Luca, *Understanding Children's Art for Better Teaching*, Columbus, Ohio: Charles E. Merrill, 1967. Comprehensive in scope and thoroughly documented by numerous research studies.

Lowenfeld, Viktor, *Creative and Mental Growth*, New York: Macmillan, 1952. The first edition is recommended for this classic work on the nature of artistic development and its role in child development.

4

CHILDREN
WITH
SPECIAL NEEDS:
ART FOR
ALL
CHILDREN

HEY TOOK AWAY what
should have been my eyes,
   (But I remembered Milton's Paradise).
They took away what should have been my ears,
   (Beethoven came and wiped away my tears).
They took away what should have been my tongue,
   (But I had talked with God when I was young).
He would not let them take away my soul —
   Possessing that, I still possess the whole.[1]

Helen Keller

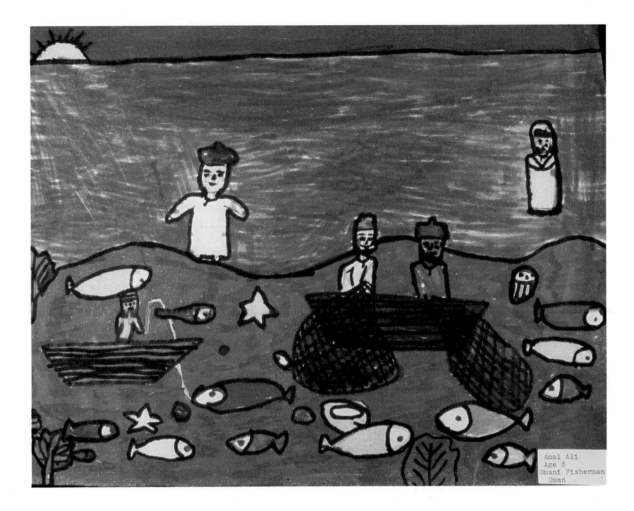

Amal Ali
Age 8
Omani Fisherman
Oman

General education is intended to accommodate the broad range of students who can benefit from regular schooling. This range encompasses the entire spectrum of learning types, including children who, for various reasons, are handicapped or challenged learners. Children who are mentally retarded, physically or emotionally handicapped, or who speak English as a second language (ESL) are often "mainstreamed" in regular classrooms where they associate with all of their peers, rather than exclusively with a limited subgroup related to their particular handicap. The placement of special students in regular classrooms has, in many instances, improved their educational opportunities and broadened their social contacts. At the same time teachers are challenged by the broad range of learners and special learning needs of their students, and must be prepared to educate all children who are assigned to their classes.

When we consider the wide range of learning styles and abilities among so-called normal learners (for example, across four standard deviations on a normal curve of IQ scores), the average class size in elementary and middle school classrooms, the inclusion of one or more special learners in most classrooms, and the charge to regard each child as an individual, we gain some appreciation for the complexity of being an effective teacher. School programs typically employ trained experts who work with special groups of students, such as hearing-impaired, physically handicapped, or mentally retarded. Classroom teachers rely on these experts for support and assistance with special students. All teachers, however, must gain a basic understanding of the needs of special learners and develop ways to adapt their instructional programs to these needs.[2]

The goals of general education are usually appropriate for all learners, regardless of their special status. For example, we attempt to teach all students to read, although some will learn to do so very slowly and with great difficulty. Reading instruction must be adapted for visually impaired learners or for those who do not yet speak English, but the goal to teach reading remains unchanged. The same is true with general education goals for writing, mathematics, social studies, and the arts. The goals and learning activities for art education outlined in Chapters 1 and 2 are valid for nearly all students, but must be adapted according to the levels and abilities of individual special learners.

One of the advances in special education over the past decade is the attitude that encourages special learners of all types to advance as far as their capabilities will allow. An example of this attitude can be seen in the case of Down's syndrome children, many of whom have progressed much further educationally than was previously believed possible.[3] Events for these students such as the Special Olympics and Very Special Arts[4] have sensitized many people to the needs, capabilities, and contributions of persons with disabilities or challenges. Teachers should be in the forefront of those who are dedicated to assisting special learners to enjoy as full and productive life as possible.

CONTRIBUTIONS OF ART FOR SPECIAL LEARNERS

The art program in many schools traditionally has been viewed as a particularly favorable setting for educating special learners, for several good reasons. Children in art are able to manipulate materials such as paint or clay in direct response to their senses of sight, sound, smell, and touch. The materials of art are sensory, concrete, and manipulable in direct ways that are unique within the school curriculum. All of the senses can be brought into interaction, providing opportunities to adapt and substitute art-making activities for students who have some sensory or motor impairment. For example, even totally blind children can form expressive objects with clay. Hearing-impaired children can visually observe a demonstration of color mixing with paint and can try the process with immediately verifiable results. Children with motor difficulties can work with finger paints or with large brushes for painting.

Another reason why art class is often a supportive place for special learners has to do with the tradition of personal expression in art. Even when all students have the same assignment or task, such as painting a landscape, the outcome for each child can be unique. Each can paint their own version of a landscape with a stipulated definition (e.g., an outdoor scene), yet each one can express a different mood or point of view. This opportunity for individuality within an assigned task is readily provided by sound art instruction.

The comprehensive program of art education that we describe in this book is especially adaptable to the needs of special learners (as well as to varying learning styles among all students) because of the wide range of possible art activities. A balanced art program includes the sensory, cognitive, and manipulative activities of art production as well as activities that emphasize visual perception, discussion of artworks, investigation of culture and history, and questioning of fundamental ideas about art. It is unlikely that any student will be able to do all of these activities with equal facility, but it is *likely* that all students, including special learners of all types, will find one or more of these activities that they will be able to do, enjoy, and learn from. The breadth and variety of valid art learning activities is one more characteristic of the art program that makes art education especially valuable for special learners.

Art as Therapy

Participation in art activities can have therapeutic effects for many special learners. Engaging in art production might serve a therapeutic function, in fact, for almost any person.[5] The same might be said for any educational pursuit that requires total involvement, such as a scientific experiment, a cooking activity, or participation in a sports event. However, the aspect of art activity that provides so much therapeutic potential is the creative and expressive dimension. Art, according to Susanne Langer, is "the objectification of human feeling."[6] Verbal language, says Langer, is inadequate for the expression of the life of feeling that all human beings share, but which can be adequately expressed only through the arts.

Art therapists are able to engage their clients or patients in arts activities that encourage free expression of emotions. Acts of artistic expression, such as drawing or painting, can result in communication of feelings that defy verbal expression. Once the art object has been created, once the feelings have been objectified as an artwork, they then can be viewed and discussed. Thus, art activity assists the therapist and client in two ways. First, creation of the art object can be an expressive release for the patient, providing satisfaction. Second, the object becomes a focus for discussion between therapist and patient, often leading to helpful revelations of the person's emotional life. Trained professional art therapists are capable of helping individuals to interpret meanings from their artworks, and use this knowledge to improve patients' mental or emotional health.

The therapeutic aspect of art education can occur in classrooms with regular students, and more particularly with special students who might have fewer or less developed communication skills. Any person with strong emotions and limited ways of expressing them might benefit from artistic expression. There are numerous cases of mentally retarded children, immigrant students with little English capability, children who have experienced traumatic events, and others for whom artistic expression has provided a desperately needed means for expression. The art objects that these children produce often provide sensitive teachers with insights into the mental and emotional lives of the children. *Teachers, however, are not professionally trained art therapists and should not attempt to fulfill that role.* Insights that teachers glean through children's art activities and products should be shared with professional school personnel such as psychologists or therapists. Working together, school teams of counselors, psychologists, administrators, parents, and teachers can best develop and provide the educational opportunities needed for each individual learner.

Legislation in the United States has drawn attention to the need for educational programs for the handicapped. Federal Chapter 766 mandated the "mainstreaming" of children with special needs into integrated situations with "normal" children. The goal is to meet the educational needs of every handicapped student on an individual basis while at the same time integrating (mainstreaming) such students into the normal schoolday's activities, so that each child has as much contact as possible with children who do not share their problems.

The use of all the arts in teaching the handicapped child has also been fostered and developed by the National Committee of Arts for the Handicapped. Through state-run festivals, teacher-training symposiums, and exhibits, the importance of arts programs for children with special needs is gaining public attention. Research by this committee has emphasized the value of arts instruction in special education. Federal and state funding (in Canada, provincial funding) has opened professional opportunities within the public sector in the fields of special education and art, integrated arts, dance, and music therapy. As these approaches become accepted, their balance of visual, manipulative, and kinesthetic expression aid children whose learning styles are visual, manipulative, auditory, and kinesthetic—as well as verbal.

G. Orville Johnson pointed out that art can provide specific skills for the handicapped child: a means of communication, a way to express feelings and emotions, improved observation and awareness, sensory stimulation, and improved motor skills. The ability of many handicapped children to use oral and written language is limited.

> The deaf child cannot hear spoken words, the cerebral palsied child may have difficulty in speaking, the mentally retarded child is limited in his vocabulary, a child with a specific learning disability may be deficient in visual and auditory decoding and encoding, and for the emotionally disturbed child oral communication may be associated with unpleasant and traumatic experiences. The arts can provide many of these children with means of communication that is less dependent upon their areas of disabilities and that is not associated with previous frustrating and failed experiences . . .[7]

The visual arts also provide rich experiences for children with limited physical capabilities but keen perceptual and cognitive abilities.

A distinction is made between exceptional children who receive special schooling and slow-learning children who are capable of functioning within normal school situations. *Slow learners* are those pupils who make considerably lower-than-average scores on intelligence tests and who progress in academic subjects at a pace manifestly slower than that displayed by the majority of their fellow students.[8] As the work of German art educator Max Klager attests, a sensitive teacher can attain remarkable artistic results with slow learners. His longitudinal studies of several mentally retarded individuals demonstrated that the subjects' personalities, as well as the visual quality of their work, showed remarkable progress with proper supervision.[9]

The slow or retarded learner is but one of the many types of special children that the art or classroom teacher is likely to encounter in the course of a usual teaching situation.

The current policy is to move handicapped children out of specialized schools and into regular schools. As a result, all teachers must be prepared to teach handicapped students. Teachers need to examine each subject area in search of more effective means for dealing with the gifted, the emotionally disturbed, the physically impaired, and the mentally retarded.

This chapter focuses on teaching art to slow learners. First, characteristics of the art of slow learners and subject matter they are likely to select will be considered. Then, teaching methods and art activities especially suitable for these children will be discussed. Adaptation of art instruction for this group of special learners is presented as a model for accommodation of the needs of any special learners.

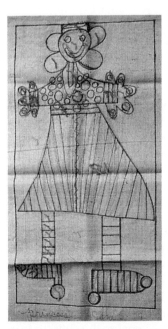

Stitchery by Jane C., a girl with Down's syndrome. The high level of design control suggests that giftedness in art exists regardless of IQ.

THE ART OF SLOW LEARNERS

The causes for retardation should be noted. While some children may indeed be suffering from cerebral or neurological dysfunctions, the deficiency of others may be due to a lack of personal attention (loving, touching, and playing) or to general sensory and environmental deprivation.

Approximately 1 in 800 newborns have mental retardation caused by Down's syndrome (the presence of 47 chromosomes instead of the normal 46). In today's society many Down's syndrome children, usually in the 40 to 70 IQ range, commonly go to regular schools, live in group homes, and work at jobs. With good health care and access to current therapies, 80 percent of the Down's syndrome adults will live past age 55 (in past decades, only 50 percent lived past age 10). The success and visibility of Chris Burke, a Down's syndrome young man who acts in a weekly network television program, has helped to increase the general acceptance and understanding of mentally retarded persons.[10]

Both Donald Uhlin[11] and Zaidee Lindsay[12] view the sensory nature of art experiences as a positive factor in the development of a sense of self in the child. Art experiences, and crafts in particular, can involve the student in learning situations that are tactile, sensory, and stimulating physically as well as mentally. Identifying the causes for retardation are best accomplished through a team approach when the art or classroom teacher has a psychologist, physician, or psychiatrist to consult.

The implementation of what is known as the *core evaluation* by a team including a psychologist, a social worker, a classroom teacher, and various specialists helps to develop the educational plan best suited to the student's learning style. The arts specialists can provide valuable information in developing objectives and learning goals for the child with special needs.

The classification of mental ability by IQ varies according to different systems. Table 4-1 gives some indication of differences suggested by four major agencies. Any child who functions below 70 IQ can be considered a slow learner as dealt with in this chapter.

Slow learners enrolled in a regular classroom begin their artistic career, like normal children, by manipulating art materials rather than by drawing or modeling recognizable objects. They are sometimes slower than normal children to play with the materials given to them and may not initially explore their possibilities fully. However, with patience and encouragement the repetition of skills will enable the child to feel more comfortable with new media. Even so, the child's symbol formation will reflect his developmental level. Thus, a child of chronological age fifteen whose developmental age is four can be expected to create symbols appropriate only to a four-year-old.

TABLE 4-1

Comparative Systems of Classifying Retardation by I.Q.

U.S. President's Panel on Mental Retardation		English System	National Association for Retarded Children and American Association on Mental Deficiency
I.Q.	Classification		
50-70	Mild	ESN (Educationally subnormal)	70-85 mildly retarded
35-49	Moderate	SSN (severely subnormal)	below 70 moderately retarded
20-34	Severe	SSN	
Below 20	Profound	SSN	

Slow learners sometimes continue in the manipulative stage longer than normal children. This painting by a retarded eight-year-old displays considerable spontaneity and improvisation.

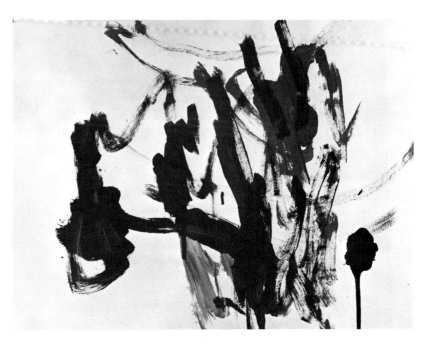

Whereas a normal five-year-old may arrive at the symbol stage within three weeks to six months, the five-year-old slow learner who has an IQ of about 70 may not reach this stage for a year or more. In time, however, slow learners arrive at the symbol stage in a manner resembling that of normal children. Once the symbol stage has been reached, several symbols may appear in their output in quick succession.

Because of their greater chronological age, mentally retarded children often possess physical coordination superior to those of normal children of the same mental age. These physical abilities, of course, help them to master drawing skills more readily and allow them to repeat a recently developed symbol without much practice. Retarded children are as slow to make progress in the stage of symbols as they are to pass through the period of manipulation. Nevertheless, a slow learner, like a normal child, will sometimes surprise a teacher with a burst of progress.

As noted earlier, regression from the symbol stage to that of manipulation will sometimes occur in the work of all children as a result of such factors as fatigue, ill health, temporary emotional disturbances, periods of intense concentration, interruptions of various kinds, absence from school, or faulty teaching methods. Reversion of this kind occurs more frequently with mentally retarded children than with normal children.

Gradually, retarded or slow learners come to spend more time on their work and thus begin to add details to their symbols. Sometimes they learn to relate their symbols to one another. The progress they make depends largely, of course, on the attention they give to their work. Slow learners' attention spans tend to increase with both their chronological age and their mental age.

Slow learners are likely to use stereotypes in their drawings and paintings rather than developing their own schemata. As with all children, slow learners should be encouraged to explore with art materials and to devise their own images rather than rely on stereotypes that have no real meaning in the context of their artwork.

A few observations must be made concerning the general composition and aesthetic qualities of the pictorial output of slow learners. These children often use the usual childlike conventions, such as X rays, series, and foldover pictures, but they adopt these relatively complicated conventions only after much practice.

Many of the conventions, conceptions, and misconceptions that are associated with children's artistic development are discussed in Chapter 3. This discussion applies as well to slow learners with appropriate adjustment for mental ages rather than chronological ages of the children. The differences in mental capabilities of a retarded eleven-year-old, however, along with more extensive life experiences and different interests, will often show up in the child's artwork.

The teacher's attitude in approaching children with special needs is of utmost importance.[13] Patience helps to develop trust. Accepting the children as they are and guiding them to progress at their own rate will enable children to work with confidence. An awareness of the particular learning style of each child will aid the teacher in developing a program of appropriate activities. As the teacher helps the child to expand and broaden a sensory vocabulary the child's ability to grasp abstract concepts can deepen. Art production activities are nurtured by sensory information, so that the stimulation of the visual, auditory, tactile, and olfactory senses will give the child a sharpened ability with which to approach communication and expression in various media.

Many slow learners can benefit from the visual and verbal aspects of a comprehensive art program as well as from participating in art production. A fourth grade teacher introduced her students to art criticism by teaching them to name objects depicted in paintings (using good quality color reproductions). She taught them to name colors, types of lines, shapes, and then introduced visual concepts such as contrast and balance. At a parent's night at the school, a mother approached the teacher and asked what she had done so successfully to stimulate her Down's syndrome daughter's language development. "When Susie comes home after school she loves to open a picture book, point to the pictures, and describe what she sees. We have encouraged this and have noticed much progress in her language abilities."[14]

SUBJECT MATTER SELECTED BY SLOW LEARNERS

As indicated earlier, all children who have the aptitude to do so pass through the normal stages of pictorial expression mentioned in Chapter 3—the manipulation, symbol, and preadolescent stages. The child with a mental age of around three and a chronological age of six will not go beyond manipulating materials; however, the child with the same chronological age and a mental age of four or more may begin to enter the symbol stage. With a mental age of five, the child will even place symbols within their environment.

Once they progress beyond the stage of manipulation, slow learners, like normal children, discover subject matter for expression in their own experiences. Many of the titles they give to their works are little different from those selected by normal children. The titles describe events that occur at home, at school, at play, or in the community. The following are representative:

We Are Working Around the House (Apartment)
Our Class Went to Visit a Farm
I Saw a Big Fire
My Favorite Foods

Titles such as these are usually selected by slow learners in the late symbol or preadolescent stage of expression with the highest IQs. The titles are concise and in most of them the children have identified themselves with their environment. The less able the slow learners, the less inclined they are to relate themselves to the world in which

The artwork of children with behavioral problems—another type of handicap—often reflects their moods, as in this drawing by a nine-year-old Canadian girl from a broken home. She drew people she knew, then in a rage obliterated them with scribbles. After such outbursts, however, her drawings took on firmer and more organized patterns.

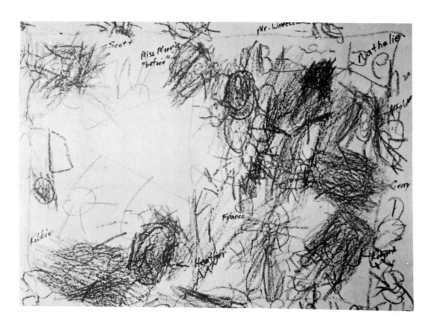

they live. In other words, an ability to identify oneself with the environment seems to vary directly with intelligence.[15]

The themes that many slow learners select are often closely connected with little, intimate events in life. A normal child might overlook them, or, having touched on them once or twice, would then find other interests. Many slow learners, on the other hand, seem to find constant interest in pictures of this nature. Some representative titles are as follows:

> I Sat on Our Steps
> The Birds Are in the Trees
> Our School Bus

Like normal children, mentally retarded children frequently like to depict their reactions to vicarious experience, even though they are more attracted to actual experience. Dramatized versions of familiar stories and events shown on the movie or television screen may excite them to visual expression. However, the teacher should, whenever possible, connect the physical experiences of the children and their drawings. Situations that deal with personal accidents (''falling down,'' ''bumping my head'') make effective sources for drawing, as do activities such as rolling or bouncing balls and using playground equipment.

Adolescent slow learners with an IQ of at least 70, no matter what their grade level, tend to use some of the subject matter found in the artwork of the normal adolescent. Their work often exhibits a growing interest in social events at which both sexes are present. Considerable

Top: The illustration for the story of Noah's ark was drawn by the attendant of a boy who was incapacitated in speech and movement. His nurse developed the picture from whatever sounds the boy conveyed. The boy's desire to contribute personally was so strong that a brush was strapped to his wrist so that he could add his own concluding touches in watercolor — an example of the will to create, which cannot be stifled even under the most limiting circumstances. Bottom: Another version of the Noah story, by a twelve-year-old retarded Hungarian child. His conception of God as well as the idea of each person as victim of his own private thunderstorm is strikingly original.

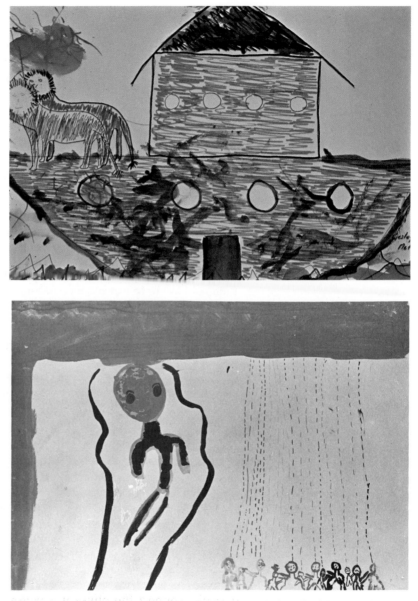

attention is many times given to anatomical detail of human beings shown in the pictures.

METHODS OF TEACHING

To teach slow learners, a teacher must possess a number of commendable personal qualities and professional abilities. The teacher must above all be patient, for these children progress slowly in their work.

The teacher must, furthermore, be able to stimulate these children so that they improve mentally, but at the same time not hurry them into work that is beyond their abilities. Finally, the teacher must treat every slow learner as a unique person. A study of their output in art offers a striking illustration of the fact that the personalities of slow learners differ widely.

Bryant and Schwann were interested in seeing if the design sense of retarded children could be improved, and developed a test to assess sensitivities to five art elements: line, shape, color, value, and texture. Based on these elements, fifteen lessons of a half-hour each were provided over a period of time. Their study suggests that children with substandard IQs (23–80) can learn design concepts through systematic teaching. They discovered that children can

> learn art terminology by direct exposure to concrete objects, which they are able to observe, examine, manipulate, verbalize about, react to, and put together in some artistic way. They can get involved in producing art, which they understand and enjoy. The materials needed in the art lessons do not have to be expensive or elaborate; rather, they can be readily procured from the home, the school supply room, and the local community store.[16]

If in an otherwise normal class the teacher finds one or two particularly slow learners in art who require special attention, this should not create problems. Obviously, the teacher should in no way indicate to other members of the class the deficiencies of their mentally retarded classmates. Since all successful teaching in art demands that the teacher treat all pupils as individuals, the fact that the slow learners are afforded certain special attention should in no sense make them unique in the eyes of their fellows. Every child in the class, whether handicapped, normal, or gifted will require individual treatment. If the teacher is placed in charge of an entire class of slow learners, similar educational principles apply. Although every member of the group may be retarded, no two children will react in an identical manner to art. Here, as elsewhere, every child must be offered an educational program tailored to individual needs and capacities.

Step-by-step teaching practices, while rarely of value to normal pupils because they present little challenge, may often give the slower learner a valuable and necessary sense of achievement. Frequently, this teaching method, if used wisely, may lead slow learners into more creative endeavors.

The approved methods now used with normal children are to a large extent also effective when used with slow learners. The handicapped children, however, require more individual attention than their normal counterparts, and the pace of teaching often has to be slowed. Motivation, classroom arrangements, and appraisal of the effectiveness of the program in progress, nevertheless, require little or no modification in principle when applied to retarded pupils.

Teaching slow learners does not require as much reorientation on the part of the teacher as one might suppose. It does require teaching in sequential concrete terms, hence the importance of demonstrating art processes, of simplifying, of slowing down verbal instructions, of having the patience to repeat directions, and above all of breaking down the learning experience into manageable stages. These few suggestions are also recommended for teaching certain types of emotionally and physically handicapped children.

Using Museums

Innovative approaches, such as taking handicapped children to art museums, have proved valuable in stimulating perceptual awareness and in developing an appreciation of the larger artistic world. A program developed at the Boston Museum of Fine Arts in conjunction with the Newton Public Schools enables students with special needs to participate in an integrated program with normal learners. Activities

Many museums are now devising ways to better accommodate children with special needs. Here, a guide is signing to a group of hearing-impaired children.

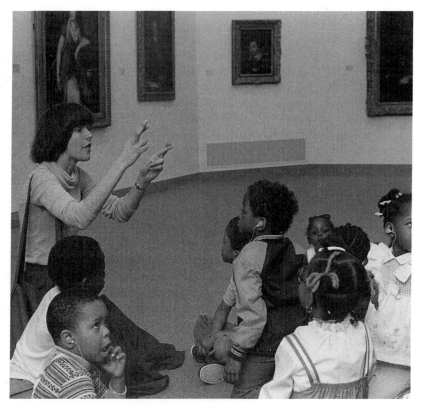

include responding to artwork in the museum and then creating art-work in the museum's education department. Cooperative activities that enable normal and special-needs youngsters to share feelings, thoughts, and group projects bring the qualities common to all human beings — as well as mutual respect and greater understanding — to the surface in a healthy and supportive atmosphere. One teacher describes a typical session of this program as follows:

> During one lesson at the museum, each child in the classroom was handed a color card — theirs for the day. After talking about the color cards, the children watched slides of painting — in this instance abstract painting. The colors were bright and bold and the children were interested. The slides remained on the screen as the children were asked to identify the colors and as they successfully did so, they beamed with pleasure and pride. The lesson was skillfully repetitive and afterwards, the children visited a gallery where they saw the paintings they had just seen on the screen.[17]

In the gallery, the children were asked to look for colors in the paintings as, with their teachers' help, they began to learn the names of colors they saw in the paintings.

Suitable Individual Activities

Having discussed the characteristics of slow learners, as well as methods of teaching them, we may now consider in detail some art activities especially suitable for them. Stimulating a sensory vocabulary in each student is an important step in developing an art program for the handicapped. Children whose cognitive ability is limited to concrete thinking will need more visual, kinesthetic, and manipulative activities to aid them in experiencing the world. As their sensory experience is broadened, their expressive ability and self-confidence in the art-making process will increase.

Most art activities have proved to be sufficiently flexible to be performed by slow learners either in special classes or in regular classrooms. These activities include some types of drawing and painting, some forms of paper and cardboard work, a certain amount of sculpture and pottery, and some types of printmaking. Simple perceptual and verbal activities, such as aesthetic scanning, can be adapted for slow learners, and the children also enjoy learning about the lives and works of artists such as Vincent van Gogh, Georgia O'Keeffe, and others. Little additional comment about teaching these activities will be offered, since the reader may refer to other chapters where teaching methods are discussed at length.

Basic Activities

Media and Techniques. In drawing and painting, slow learners may use the standard tools and equipment recommended for other pupils. Hence, wax crayons, tempera paint, the usual types of brushes and papers, and so on may be employed. Nearly all slow learners are capable of producing creative paper work. Most of these pupils achieve greatest success when cut paper is used as a medium for two-dimensional pictures. Some pupils, however, may begin to build their pictures into three dimensions. Nearly all these children enjoy box sculpture, and many of them seem capable of doing some freestanding paper sculpture. Many slow learners can use molds to make simple masks, and nearly all of them can work successfully with papier-mâché if it is prepared in advance for them.

Carving in wood and other substances is not recommended for most slow learners. The tools required in much of this work are too dangerous for them, and the technique is beyond their ability. Simple forms of modeling and ceramics, however, are recommended. The direct nature of modeling pleases these pupils, and the expressive potential of ceramics makes this craft highly suitable. Vegetable printing is also a useful technique, largely because it is repetitive. Stencil and linoleum work may be too difficult to master.

With all the basic activities mentioned above, the teacher of slow learners must modify classroom techniques to suit the abilities of these pupils. A step-by-step approach becomes necessary not only in the work itself but also in the selection of tools and media. If their IQ scores are below 70, preadolescent slow learners usually experience difficulty when confronted by a wide range of color or by the problems of mixing tints, shades, and even secondary hues. The teacher will

An example of graphic design that combines printmaking, poetry, and typography. This picture is from a publication of the Dr. Francis Perkins School, Lancaster, Massachusetts.

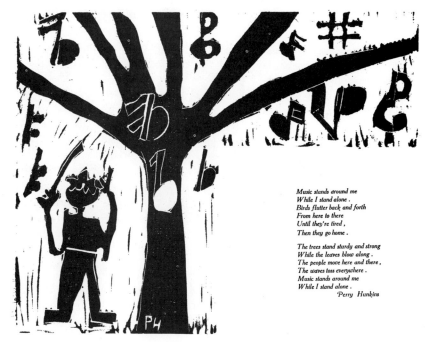

Music stands around me
While I stand alone .
Birds flutter back and forth
From here to there
Until they're tired ,
Then they go home .

The trees stand sturdy and strong
While the leaves blow along .
The people move here and there ,
The waves toss everywhere .
Music stands around me
While I stand alone .
　　　　　Perry Hunkins

often find it useful to supply some colors ready-mixed. Chalk and charcoal might also create difficulties for some slow learners.

When three-dimensional work such as pottery or box sculpture is being taught to slow learners, the teacher would be wise to analyze the process from start to finish in terms of separate operations. Then, before the pupils begin work, they should be shown a finished object, so they know what to expect at the end of their work. After that, however, demonstrations and general teaching should be performed only one operation at a time. The pupils should select the tools only for the one operation, complete the operation, and then return the tools. This process should then be repeated until all the necessary operations have been mastered.

History and Criticism. Slow learners can participate in all types of art activities if they are adapted to their ability levels. For example, postcard images of artworks are readily available from art museums and commercial publishers. Retarded children can sort these images according to simple categories, such as subject matter (trees, animals, persons), art mode (pictures of buildings, pictures of furniture), color (name hues, possibly distinguish warm and cool), mood (happy, frightening), and many others. Color cards can be made using watercolors and paints and sorted, mixed, and matched by the children according to basic color theory.

Slow children can enjoy stories about artists, seeing pictures of them (photographs or self-portraits), hearing stories of their lives and work, and looking at and reading children's books about art. Like nor-

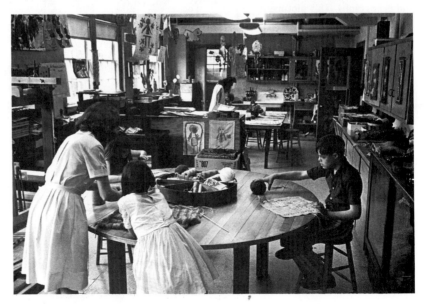

In this well-appointed art classroom, slow learners have ample space to explore weaving, stitchery, and knitting. (Photo by Bradford Herzog.)

mal children, slow learners can enjoy looking at world maps and seeing where particular artworks are from (such as pottery, masks, pyramids, totem poles, etc.), seeing pictures of the people who created them, and learning how they were used in the culture of context. A balanced art program can provide rich opportunities for learning for mentally retarded children as well as for normal and gifted children. The full educational resources — including art reproductions, games, films and videos, slides, books, and magazines — should be brought to bear for the art education of all children.

ADAPTING ART PRODUCTION FOR SLOW LEARNERS

Stitchery The use of fibers and needles to create works of fine art, applied art, and folk art has a long history within many cultures around the world. Ivory-carved figures of the First Dynasty (3400 B.C.) of Egypt indicate that the history of stitched and quilted apparel dates from at least that early in human culture. According to one writer:

> Stitch by stitch, the story of humanity describing the fabric of everyday life has been sewn into countless examples of quilting, patchwork, and appliqué. Memories and milestones have been stitched by queens and commoners to create functional furnishings for home and family. These pieces are art — folk art, reflecting personal images of one's life.[18]

A significant portion of the history of cultures might be revealed through study of the fiber arts of the respective peoples that constitute civilization. The great museums of the world display examples of needlework, such as quilting, embroidery, patchwork, appliqué, and trapunto from all corners of the earth. The fiber arts have gained in prominence within the contemporary art world, resulting in fine examples of wall hangings, graphic pieces, decorative and functional fiber works, and many large, three-dimensional pieces that might be classified as sculpture.

Stitchery, or work with cloth, needle, and fibers is a rich area of study for students in elementary and middle schools. This art mode allows for many creative opportunities within the ability levels of children, presented in conjunction with critical and historical learning about works of fiber arts and their cultural and historical significance. Because stitchery lends itself so readily to the needs and abilities of slow learners, we present it in this section with the understanding that the suggested activities are adapted for slow learners. We recommend the study of fiber arts for all students.

Stitchery need not mean commercially stamped products of questionable merit; it can be as stimulating and original as many other contemporary art forms. In one form or another stitchery is popular with children in all grades. The products of their work can be purely decorative, such as wall hangings, or they can be practical, such as pillow covers, purses, and aprons. The subject matter of the designs may be nonobjective or representational. Appliqué techniques are also possible with stitches. Stitchery is a good activity for a group or for the individual child.

Media and Techniques. To a large extent this activity makes use of scrap materials. Cotton and burlap are very good materials on which to work. If colored burlap is not available, potato or apple sacks will do just as well. Needles may be purchased in almost any department store, as well as embroidery cottons in many colors. Yarns in different weights and colors add variety to the work.

Many kinds of stitches are used in this activity, among them the simple running stitch and the more complicated stitches such as the blanket, buttonhole, chain, daisy, outline, and feather stitches.[19] The design, which can be planned in advance or created on the cloth, is outlined with a simple stitch, and areas are given texture with the more complicated stitches. Buttons, beads, and brightly colored felts may be incorporated into the design for accents. As in any design, too many conflicting patterns in the same piece should be avoided; it is advisable to work for a few balances—line and mass, pattern and solid, large and small. When the work is completed, it may be mounted in a picture frame for display.

Teaching. The most practical way to teach stitchery is to treat it as a form of picture making. With the simple materials mentioned above, even mentally retarded children may immediately set to work. There is no need at first to show them a number of complicated stitches, because what is known as the *running stitch* comes quite naturally to them. The running stitch consists simply of running the needle in and out through the fabric at fairly regular intervals. It is the simplest kind of stitch with which to draw a line or outline a shape, and it can also be used to fill shapes with color. Thus, children may use the needle directly as a means of expression. After selecting their cotton or burlap background material, they may start working without drawing lines. When they have gained experience in the technique, they might later sketch some ideas in pencil before they begin the actual stitchery. After this they may be taught the more complicated stitches, some of which are rather easy to learn.

Slow learners have little difficulty in acquiring the skills needed for stitchery and are generally very creative in this activity. They can experiment with using threads and backgrounds of varying colors, weights, and textures, or explore the potentialities of a newly discovered stitch.

Tapestry weaving is also a quasi-group activity suitable for slow learners. Each child contributes his or her own square of weaving; then all the pieces are sewn together and attached to a frame. Although this tapestry is designed for random arrangement, children should be encouraged to decide where their own portions will be placed.

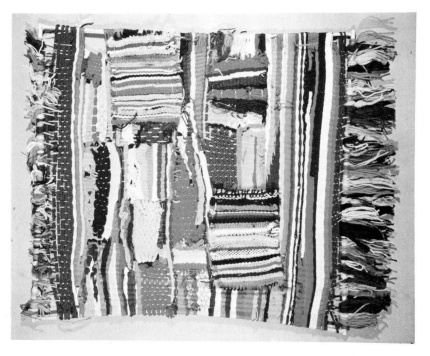

The pedagogical case for weaving and stitchery has been stated by Schill and Abrams in their discussion of the role of manipulation of media in teaching retarded children.

> Various forms of conceptual thinking can be initiated for these children through art. Color, perception, size and shape discrimination and light and dark, over and under, around and through, and numerous others can be integrated into the total art program. However, the retarded child will not develop them unless they are consciously and overtly taught.[20]

Conscious and overt teaching, as has been stated, imply simplification, concrete presentation, and above all, patience.

Bookcraft

Bookcraft has been mentioned as one possibility for group work. But it is also suitable as an individual activity for all children. Most slow learners can learn to make books, which may be used as attractive scrapbooks or notebooks, with decorated covers and endpapers. Much of this work appeals to slow learners because the techniques used to decorate the books can be simple and yet result in quite spectacular designs.

Bookbinding is a craft that is also well represented in cultural history from various parts of the world. From the idea of papyrus scrolls, to the illuminated manuscripts of early Christian times, to the gigantic modern publishing industry, the notion of packaging or binding writ-

In this open-fold book made by a slow learner, yarn holds the spine in place; heavy cloth remnants and a crayon-and-watercolor resist make the cover decoration. Both the picture and the cloth were pasted to heavy cardboard backing with white glue. The book contains prints made by the pupil's classmates.

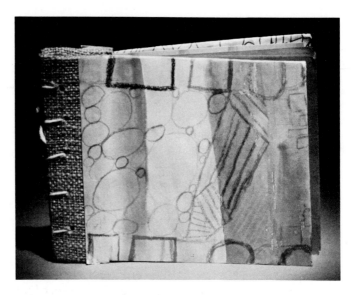

ten and graphic materials for utility and aesthetic pleasure has been universal. The simplest series of drawings, group of poems, recipes for preparing food, or daily personal thoughts are enhanced and lended import by their placement in book form. The applied arts of graphic design, lettering, illustration, and bookbinding can be explored by children as they make book covers for their own collections of words and pictures.

Media and Techniques.   First, the pupil decorates the front and back of the cover paper. This may be done by drawing, stick or vegetable printing, finger painting, or exploration with media. Some of the techniques, depending on experimentation, are as follows:

1. Tempera colors are brushed and spattered over paper that has been dampened with water. The colors will run and blend. After several trials, children will select their favorite work.

2. A few drops of thin oil paint of various colors are placed in a shallow pan of water. By gently blowing on the surface of the water, the pupils develop a swirling pattern of color. Paper should then be slipped into the water at one end of the pan, submerged completely, and then raised gently. The oil paint will adhere to the paper to form a unique pattern. Children can experiment with different color combinations and patterns.

3. A toothbrush loaded with tempera paint is held over a sheet of paper. Using a scraper such as a knife, pupils draw the blade toward themselves over the toothbrush, thereby speckling the paper with paint. Several colors may be used. This technique can be con-

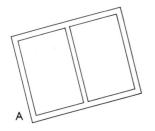

A　B　C　D

Processes in making a simple booklet: (A) placing cardboard on treated cover paper; (B) mitering and folding the cover paper; and (C) sewing the page inserts. The finished booklet is shown in D.

trolled by using a mask, or covering paper, to block off areas where the spray is not desired. Children can explore with different stencil shapes, color combinations, and compositions.

To make the cover of the book, pupils place the prepared cover paper on the desk, with the undecorated side of the cover paper facing them. Next, they cut a sheet of stiff cardboard slightly smaller than the cover sheet. They then cut the cardboard into two pieces of equal size and lay the two pieces side by side over the cover paper, leaving a small gap between them to form the spine of the book. The cardboard and cover paper are pasted together; the corners are carefully folded and, if the pupils are capable of doing so, mitered. The pupils then fold the edges of the cover paper over the cardboard.

To prepare the inside of the book, sheets of paper about one-quarter of an inch smaller than the cover are folded to form pages. These are lightly stitched together with a needle and thread along their spine. The front and back pages of this assembly are then pasted and pressed to the covers. To complete the book, the pupil may shellac the cover.

Teaching.　Although the exact steps of making a book must be taught to slow learners, the teacher can employ a creative approach both in experimentation for decorating paper and to some extent in the actual making of the book. The experimental techniques should be demonstrated one at a time, so that the pupils will not become confused by a multiplicity of materials and ways of using them. Maximum and minimum size limits for the book should be established, but the pupils can decide on the exact dimensions they want to use within those limitations.

Suitable Group Activities

Whether in special classes comprising only slow learners, or in classes in which there are only one or two slow learners, the mentally retarded require thoughtful consideration when group activities take place.

Most retarded pupils have difficulty participating in class or group art activities largely because of considerable differences in the mental and chronological ages of individual members of the group, even among pupils in special classes for the retarded. Group activity presents many difficulties for normal people; for the mentally retarded the group activity must be very carefully chosen and supervised, if it is to succeed.

A highly recommended group activity for slow learners is puppetry. This activity allows children to work both as an individual and as a member of a group. Only the simplest of puppets need be made for a successful group performance. Stick and fist puppets are suitable for most slow learners. The child's subjects, cut in cardboard and tacked to sticks, or doll-like creatures made from old socks or paper bags and manipulated with the fingers, will serve as suitable characters for a play. A large cardboard carton provides a simple stage. The spoken lines and the action of the play may be derived from a well-liked story or based on some experience in the children's lives.

Because mural making demands a high level of group cooperation and organization, this activity as handled in conventional situations is not generally recommended for slow learners. The quasi-group activity, however, in which the general plan is discussed and decided on by a group but in which each child works independently on a section of the display, is more practical for slow learners, as it is for young children. Slow learners may not be able to grasp the design concept of a mural, nor is it important that they do. What they do know is that working on a large scale is a pleasurable experience. Many partly cooperative activities of this type may be carried out in clay or in other modeling or building materials, including empty boxes and odd pieces of wood. A service station, a farm, a village, or a playground are subjects that slow learners might be interested in developing.

When only one or two noticeable-slow learners are found in a class of normal children, the difficulties arising from group work are greater, since these pupils must participate and attempt to hold their own with their classmates. The problem of having these pupils purposefully occupied is not too great when the whole class is engaged in a group activity such as puppetry. That activity involves a variety of tasks, such as assembling the stage or hemming curtains, to which slow learners can contribute if given some guidance. In the more difficult activities involving only a few major tasks, such as, say, mural making, the slow learners' relative lack of ability tends to become conspicuous. Obviously, they cannot be asked to do only such menial jobs as washing brushes or cleaning paint tins. They must be given more important jobs, if they are to retain their self-respect.

Some teachers arrange privately with one of the more intelligent and sympathetic class members who have been chosen as leaders to elect a slow learner to the team. This leader provides the slow learner with some aspect of the drawing and painting, and coaches and supervises the slow learner carefully. The contribution of the slow learner in the mural activity may range from filling in areas of color, outlining areas, creating repeat borders — tasks that can be undertaken with the knowledge that they contribute materially to the activity.

The gains to be derived for slow learners working in art may be summarized by the following seven points:

1. Through art activity, slow learners might create a product that is not noticeably inferior to that of their neighbors. Their efforts need not suffer by comparison.

2. The process of concept-formation through art takes place for slow learners as it does for average and above-average children. Through art, slow learners can present ideas that may otherwise be denied expression because of limited ability in handling language skills.

3. For the trained observer, the drawings of slow learners may provide diagnostic clues to emotional difficulties that sometimes accompany retardation.

4. Art activity can function as therapy, providing a source of satisfaction and stability to children who have a history of failure.

5. Working in art provides vital sensory and motor experiences that involve the total mental and physical capabilities of the children. The integration of physical and mental operations in turn facilitates the union of thought and feeling. In this respect, art serves the same unifying function for children of all abilities.

6. Artistic activity provides slow learners with experience in decision making and problem solving, which are socially useful skills.

7. The art room can provide a nonthreatening atmosphere in which to begin the mainstreaming process of integrating normal children and children with special needs.

Other Kinds of Handicaps

Although this chapter has concentrated on art and retardation, teachers may be faced with other kinds of handicaps, as children with disabilities are moved from special learning situations into the regular classroom. Teachers cannot become instant authorities on the many problems that may confront them, but Table 4-2 provides a guideline for beginning to deal with problems that may arise. This chart was organized by a group of art teachers who were interested in preparing themselves for those handicapped children they might be teaching the following year. The chart, while incomplete, reflects not only their own experience and judgment, but that of others cited in the Suggested Readings at the end of this chapter. It can also provide readers with a format within which to add their own observations and find-

4-2

ties Suggested Teaching Methods for Special Needs

Identification	Characteristics	Appropriate Approach	Suggested Activities
Mentally Retarded	Slower to learn and to perform. Short attention span, impaired self-image. Limited spatial perception. Difficulty in socialization. Poor body awareness. Learns through concrete approaches.	Overteaching and repetition. Specific instruction in specific skills. Regular follow-up imperative. Simplication of concepts and skills in lessons. Gradual addition of steps in sequential order.	Activities relating to emotions. Direct manipulation of materials: finger paint, fabrics, clay, etc. Body sensory awareness through motion and tactile experiences. Simple puppets (paper bag, paper plate, sock). Unconventional media (shaving cream, vanilla pudding, chocolate syrup) on formica surfaces. Painting on a mirror. Self-adornment (costumes, hats, jewelry, body paint). Thickened tempera paint (with soap flakes). Sand casting, Play Dough, simple weaving, papier-mâché. Tactile boards and boxes. Junk and body printing. Constructions, stuffed shapes.
Visually Impaired (blind or partially sighted)	Limited or no visual field. Uncomfortable in unfamiliar physical setting. Difficulty in perceiving total image. Learns through tactile and auditory experiences. Lack of environmental awareness.	Organize materials so child has same place to work each time. Develop familiarity with environment. Develop tactile sense to the fullest. Develop sense of rhythm, patterns, motion sequencing, body awareness, and sense of space.	Tactile experiences. Matching and sorting textures, texture boards, texture walls, aprons with textures. Feely boxes. Clay. Collages of wide range of textures. Sand casting. Construction and junk sculpture. All tactile media as above. Weaving, macramé. Shape-discrimination games.
Perceptually Handicapped (extreme reading disability)	Lack of form discrimination. Lack of spatial orientation. Hyperactive, especially in periods of frustration. Poor	Keep visual distraction to a minimum. Repetition. Develop sense of rhythm, pattern, motion.	Body awareness exercises, calisthenics and movement to music. Sequencing activities. Matching colors, sizes, shapes.

ings. Therapists urge us to view a handicap not so much as a defect but rather as a difference, and so to discover in it the potential for a specific and unique creativity—one through which other sensory modes may even be heightened.

As we opened ourselves to their [blind children's] unique ways of being, we learned to value their otherness, to treasure the ways in which they sensitized us. The children expanded our sensory awareness by referring to "clay that smells like candy," "markers," or "soft paper." They tuned us in

Identification	Characteristics	Appropriate Approach	Suggested Activities
	eye-hand coordination. Impaired visual reception. Poor kinesthetic performance. Distractible. Failure syndrome.		Letter, number, and shape collages. Use of tactile media to develop eye-hand coordination. Construction. Hammer and nail letters. Pencil drawings. Drama, puppetry. Stuffed letters.
Hearing Impaired (deaf or partially deaf)	Limited language. Difficulty in communication. Lack of conceptual language. Limited environmental awareness. Tends to withdraw. Difficult to motivate. Sensitivity to visual world.	Develop nonverbal communication. Instruct through demonstration and illustration of work. Emphasize visual and tactile experiences. Develop sense of rhythm, pattern motion, sequencing, body awareness, and space.	Drawing or painting based on bodily movements. Drawing on blackboard. Any activity based on clear, well-trained demonstration by teacher (clay, sculpture, collage, etc.). Color discrimination. Weaving, sewing. Printing, painting.
Orthopedic Problems (cerebral palsy)	Spastic, rigid, jerky, involuntary movement. Impaired eye-hand coordination, impaired speech and general communication. Lack of muscular control.	Extend art time. Secure materials and sufficient space. Teach through actual manipulation, direct tactile experiences before using tools. Build up handles on tools with plasticene or foam rubber. Attach drawing instruments to wrists.	Large felt-tip pens provide emphatic lines and bright colors. Thickened tempera paint. All tactile media as above. Water play. Any activity that uses the hands and body in a physiotherapeutic manner.
Emotionally Disturbed	Short attention span and easily distracted. Failure syndrome. Lacks self-confidence. Hyperactive. Poor self-image. Egocentric.	Create a code of acceptable behavior. Limits are imperative. Provide security through repetition of activities and single tasks. Experiences should be "open." Encourage expression of feelings.	Stuffing precut shapes. Making media such as Play Dough, papier-mâché pulp. Constructions (glued). Body awareness. Costumes and puppets. Painting with thickened paint. All tactile media as above. Water play. Bookmaking.

to sounds, like Billy, who took intense pleasure in "a marker that squeaks a whole lot . . . that makes a whole lotta noise." Although one would not have chosen a felt-tip marker as the most appropriate tool for a boy with no vision, Billy taught us not to allow our own preconceptions to interfere with what media we might offer a handicapped child.

Through their sensitive use of their hands, those who could see nothing taught us about a kind of "free-floating tactile attention" in their approach to shape, form, and texture . . . They seemed to know where to position their wood-scraps, suggesting a "tactile aesthetic" different from a visual one.[21]

The therapist also tells how a child with limited vision experienced a "kind of 'color shock'" from the intense hues of tempera paint. "And Terry, a deaf-blind child, literally jumped for joy when she accidentally discovered that wet clay pressed on the white paper made a visible mark . . . The art program . . . opened our eyes to the need and capacity for joy . . . The intensity of the children's sensory-motor pleasure in the art experience was inescapable."[22]

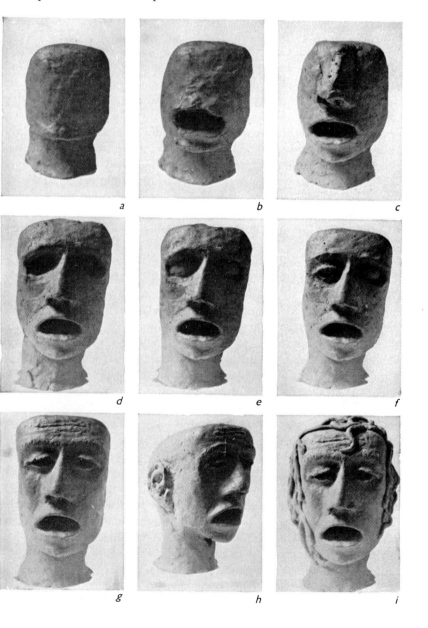

Viktor Lowenfeld documents the development of a portrait in clay by a sixteen-year-old blind girl. The project shown here develops from a general outline (a) to the finished head (i). Although known mostly for his work on artistic development, Lowenfeld began his career working with children and adults with special needs to develop his theory of visual and haptic types. These classifications, which he likened to expressionist and impressionist modes of art, is consistent with both normal and special-needs children.

"Pain." Visual-blind sculpture. Congenitally blind sixteen-year-old girl.
a). General outline
b). Cavity of the mouth is formed
c). Nose is added
d). Eye sockets are hollowed out
e). Eyeballs are put in
f). Lids are pulled over
g). Wrinkles are formed
h). Ears are added
i). The head is finished. All features are incorporated into a unified surface. Typical for the visual type.

Trainable mentally retarded children make advances in behavior, speech, and language through arts programs. Through creative drama, deaf children can shed the fear of using words. Music has helped to develop a rhythmical sense in handicapped children, as well as to aid them in relaxing their muscles. Movement activities can help the blind child gain the freedom to explore space.

In a study by J. Craig Greene and T. S. Hasselbrings, a curriculum was "designed so that the students actually were exposed to language concepts within the process of making art objects. Through a concrete method, abstract verbal concepts were earned and integrated into each student's life." A multisensory approach can foster greater understanding of abstract concepts. "A highly visual curriculum which attempts to unify the total learning experience of the hearing impaired child" can often be achieved through arts activities. Using the visual, tactile, and linguistic modes results in a "greater concept attainment."[23]

◆ NOTES TO THE TEXT

1. Helen Keller, "On Herself," The Faith of Helen Keller, Jack Belck, ed. (Kansas City, MO: Hallmark Editions, 1967).

2. G. Wallace and J. M. Kauffman, *Teaching Students with Learning and Behavior Problems*, 3rd ed. (Columbus, OH: Merrill, 1986).

3. Cindy Yorks, "Moving Up," *USA Weekend*, November 24–26, 1989.

4. For more information write to: *Very Special Arts Newsletter*, Education Office, The John F. Kennedy Center for the Performing Arts, Washington, D.C. 20566.

5. Edith Kramer, "Art Therapy and Art Education: Overlapping Functions," *Art Education*, April 1980.

6. Susanne Langer, *Mind: An Essay on Human Feeling*, Vol. 1 (Baltimore: The Johns Hopkins Press, 1967), p. 87.

7. G. Orville Johnson, "Art and the Special Education Teacher," *Viewpoints: Dialogue in Art Education*, Vol. 3, No. 1 (1976).

8. See, for example, D. P. Hallahan, J. M. Kauffman, and J. W. Lloyd, *Introduction to Learning Disabilities* (Englewood Cliffs, NJ: Prentice-Hall, 1985); James Kauffman, *Characteristics of Children's Behavior Disorders*, 3rd ed., (Columbus, OH: Merrill, 1985); and R. J. Morris and B. Blatt, *Special Education: Research and Trends* (New York: Pergamon, 1990).

9. Max Klager, *Jane C. — Symbolisches Denken in Bildern und Sprache* (Munchen, Basel: Ernst Reinhardt Verlag, 1978).

10. Cindy Yorks, *USA Weekend*.

11. Donald Uhlin, *Art for Exceptional Children* (Dubuque, IA: Wm. C. Brown, 1972), Chapter 3, "The Mentally Deficient Personality in Art."

12. Zaidee Lindsay, *Art and the Handicapped Child* (New York: Van Nostrand Reinhold, 1972), pp. 18-45.

13. Betty Copeland, "Mainstreaming Art for the Handicapped Child: Resources for Teacher Preparation," *Art Education*, November 1984.

14. This anecdote was related in personal conversation with the authors.

15. For more assistance in understanding appropriate activities for special learners, see William Davis, *Resource Guide to Special Education* (New York: Allyn and Bacon, 1986); and James Patton, James Payne, James

Kauffman, Gweneth Brown, and Ruth Payne, *Exceptional Children in Focus*, 4th ed. (Columbus, OH: Charles Merrill, 1989).

16. Antusa P. Bryant and Leroy B. Schwann, "Art and Mentally Retarded Children," *Studies in Art Education*, Vol. 12, No. 3 (Spring 1971), p. 56.

17. Maida Abrams and Lori Schill, "Art in Special Education" (unpublished report).

18. Thelma Newman, *Quilting, Patchwork, Appliqué, and Trapunto* (New York: Crown Publishers, 1974).

19. See for example, David Clark, ed., *Stitchery, Embroidery, Appliqué, Crewel* (Menlo Park, CA: Lane Publishing, 1975); Kay Parker, *Contemporary Quilts* (Tru-mansburg, NY: The Crossing Press, 1981); and Jeane Hutchins, ed., *The Fiberarts Design Book II* (Asheville, NC: Lark Books, 1983).

20. Maida Abrams and Lori Schill, op. cit.

21. Personal conversation with authors.

22. Judith Rubin, "Growing Through Art with the Multiple Handicapped," *Viewpoints: Dialogue in Art Education, 1976*.

23. J. Craig Greene and T. S. Hasselbrings, "The Acquisition of Language Concepts by Hearing Impaired Children Through Selected Aspects of Experimental Core Art Curriculum," *Studies in Art Education*, Vol. 22, No. 2 (1981).

◆ ACTIVITIES FOR THE READER

1. Collect drawings and paintings done by slow learners in various grades and with various IQs. Compare the work of each group of slow learners with that of a group of normal children who (a) are in corresponding grades and (b) have corresponding chronological ages. List the differences between the work of slow learners and that of normal pupils in each instance.

2. Compare the work habits of the slow learners with those of the normal pupils in the instances described in the activity above.

3. From a collection of work by slow learners, select pieces of art having some pleasing aesthetic qualities. How would the number of pieces selected compare with the number obtained from a collection of equal size comprising the work of normal children in corresponding stages? List some of the chief characteristics of the work chosen from the slow learners' collection.

4. Make a list of titles that slow learners give to their drawings and paintings. Can you give any explanations for the titles?

5. Describe the personal characteristics of a teacher of slow learners whom you know well.

6. In preparing to teach a class of slow learning boys and girls (IQ range 50 to 70, chronological age range 11 to 15), analyze the *operation* and *demonstrations* considered necessary for a successful outcome in each of the following activities: (a) making a design in stitchery; (b) making a small clay bowl by the coil method; (c) making a tempera painting.

7. Write a lesson plan strategy for teaching a group of slow learners to view and discuss a large reproduction of a painting. What rules would you establish for discussion? What items would you attend to first? How would you engage the children in the activity?

8. Assume that you have a physically impaired child in a wheelchair in class. This child is unable to work with clay, but can turn pages of books and magazines. What would you prepare for this child while the class is working with ceramic clay?

9. Assume that you have several students who have recently immigrated to this country and speak very little English. You are teaching a lesson on landscape painting, including instruction in color mixing with tempera paints. You plan to show slides of landscape paintings from several cultures. How will you accommodate the ESL students? How can you involve them and help them to learn more English?

10. Observe an art class that has one or two slow learners at work on group activities. Note the techniques used to assist the slow learners. Describe opportunities missed to help the handicapped children. Suggest practical steps that might have been taken to assist them.

◆ SUGGESTED READINGS

Davis, William. *Resource Guide to Special Education* (New York: Allyn and Bacon, 1986). A general guide for teachers of special learners.

Hallahan, D. P., J. M. Kauffman, and J. W. Lloyd, *Introduction to Learning Disabilities* (Englewood Cliffs, NJ: Prentice-Hall, 1985). This book provides general information of value to art teachers.

Lark-Horovitz, Betty, Hilda P. Lewis and Mark Luca, *Understanding Children's Art for Better Teaching* (Columbus, OH: Charles Merrill, 1967). Chapter 6, ''The Exceptional Child,'' discusses children who have disabilities and children who are gifted.

Rubin, Judith. *Child Art Therapy* (New York: Van Nostrand Reinhold, 1978).

Uhlin, Donald. *Art for Exceptional Children* (Dubuque, IA: Wm. C. Brown, 1972). Part II is particularly valuable for definitions, classification, and suggestions for instruction.

Ulman, Elinor, and Penny Dachinger, eds. *Art Therapy in Theory and Practice* (New York: Schocken Books, 1975).

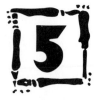

TALENTED CHILDREN: THE NATURE OF ARTISTIC GIFTEDNESS

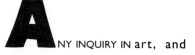

ANY INQUIRY IN art, and especially one concerned with the sources of artistic accomplishment, must necessarily confront the issue of talent — the status of those individuals who, owing to nature, nurture, or some indissoluble blend, possess special gifts.[1]

Howard Gardner

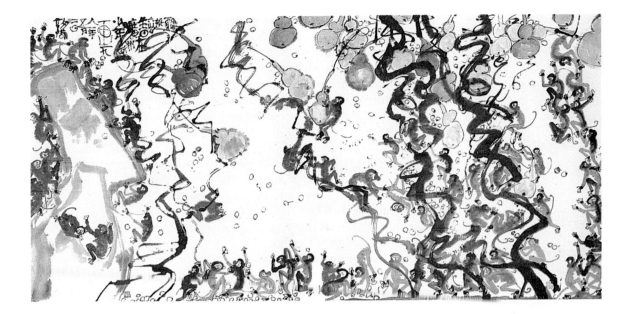

Every child has a profile of mental and physical strengths and weaknesses. Some children are physically well coordinated and others excel in mathematics or learn to read quickly. Some children are musically inclined, or are verbally adept, or have an ability to make others laugh. In the area of art, some children can draw well at early ages and others are especially able to appreciate and understand works of art. Each and every child has a combination of the multitude of human abilities and a profile of interests that makes him or her a unique individual.

In general education we assume that all normal children have the necessary abilities that will allow them to learn to read, write, speak correctly, perform mathematical operations, gather concepts and information, think in sophisticated ways, and accomplish the many other basic activities that are part of the prescribed course of study. As all of the children gain a general education, required for full citizenship in society, some will take these basic abilities and carry them to extraordinary degrees of accomplishment. Every child will learn to write; a few will become poets. Every child will learn basic mathematics and science; a few will become mathematicians and scientists. Every child will learn to draw, paint, and examine and discuss works of art; a few will become artists, critics, and historians. Teachers have the responsibility to help all of the children reach the goals of general education. Teachers also have the responsibility to encourage and support children who, because of their precociousness and interest, will go far beyond the goals of general education in some areas of human learning and performance.

Our education system has in the past been more successful with general education for students in the normal range of abilities than it has in providing for the needs of gifted and talented children.

Neglect of these students cannot be excused on the grounds that gifted children are able to make satisfactory progress without help. On the contrary, there is much evidence that cases of failure, delinquency, apparent laziness, and general maladjustment easily occur among gifted children as a result of educational neglect. A major part of this neglect is the failure of teachers to provide educational challenges that interest fast learners and channel their creative energies in positive directions. The lot of academically gifted children has improved through the addition of special programs, grouping for ability levels, team teaching, and use of paraprofessionals and volunteers. Children who are gifted in art, however, typically have not been as readily identified or as well provided for.

This chapter deals with three main topics: how to identify children gifted in art,[2] what types of educational programs and practices are needed for their support, and how gifted children can be encouraged to continue in their development.

IDENTIFYING GIFTED CHILDREN

It seems to be more difficult to identify artistically talented children than academically gifted students. With the latter, educators can rely to a large extent on pupils' scores on IQ and other standardized tests, along with reports of their interests, activities, and performance in the area of interest. The identification of artistic talent is even more difficult. While the results of some studies suggest that children gifted in art often score high on IQ tests, not every child with high IQ scores possesses artistic talent. Some, indeed, with exceptionally high IQs may appear to be lacking in even normal artistic skills and sensibilities.

One of the greatest difficulties in discovering artistic talent arises from the fact that no reliable measures exist to judge either art production or appreciation. Whatever beliefs we may hold about a particular child's abilities in art are usually based on personal appraisal rather than on data gathered objectively. Most experts hold that subjective appraisals are not so important in reading, spelling, and number work, where fundamental abilities can be measured fairly accurately and, as a consequence, talent can be identified. We might suspect, however, that the expressive and appreciative aspects of even these academic fields are no more amenable to a reliable measurement than they are in art.

Since most teachers depend on subjective means to identify artistically talented youngsters, their estimate of the children's artistic fu-

Nadia, the most celebrated of visually gifted autistic children, drew hundreds of horses. This one was drawn when she was four and one-half years old.

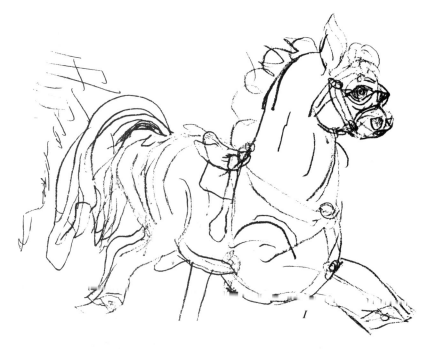

ture can be relied on only with reservations. Nevertheless, the pooled opinion of informed people has frequently led to surprisingly accurate judgments concerning artistic talent.

A U.S. Department of Education publication offers the following official designation of giftedness and talent, which is often referred to by proposal writers:

> Gifted and talented children are those identified by professionally qualified persons who, by virtue of outstanding abilities, are capable of high performance. These are children who require differentiated educational programs in order to realize their contribution to self and society. Children capable of high performance include those with demonstrated achievement and/or potential ability in any of the following areas, singly or in combination:
>
> 1. General intellectual ability
> 2. Specific academic aptitude
> 3. Creative or productive thinking
> 4. Leadership ability
> 5. Visual and performing arts
> 6. Psychomotor ability[3]

Even a definition as simple as this one can be misconstrued, however, and some school districts and other educational agencies in the various states develop their own definitions. Some groups, for example, have added categories for "ethical sensitivity" and "moral responsibility," and others have deleted some of the categories noted above. Phrases in definitions of giftedness, such as "professionally qualified persons" and "high performance" are always subject to interpretation and debate. As a result of the inevitable ambiguity associated with identifying children who are gifted and talented in any category, but especially in art, many school districts have developed their own systems.

One school district, typical of many others, has developed procedures for admitting children to gifted programs that combine teacher nominations, test scores, examples of work, interviews, and other means. In contrast, one large district administers a gifted and talented elementary school populated with children whose parents and teachers have nominated them. No tests, reviews, grades, portfolios, or requirements are utilized. Their belief is that children who are ready for a fast-paced and enriched school program will fit in well at this school, and children who are not ready will prefer a regular school. Sometimes a system for identifying gifted children is criticized for bias in selecting only certain types of children and eliminating others, possibly from particular ethnic or socioeconomic groups. In some cases resources for gifted programs are limited and parents are anxious to have their children identified in this category, leading to a competitive atmosphere and potential hard feelings. For these reasons and others, the best systems for identifying students who might benefit from special programs for the gifted and talented are usually developed on the local levels in response to local needs and resources.

Characteristics of Gifted Children

Several authorities have made the study of artistically gifted children a special concern. One of the earliest efforts to characterize the special capacity for art was made by Norman Meier, a psychologist whose interest in the subject led him to design tests to assess the degree and kind of artistic talent among children. Meier claimed that gifted children derive their artistic ability from superior manual skill, energy, aesthetic intelligence, perceptual facility, and creative imagination. His study of gifted and average children led him to conclude that, since youngsters with the greatest artistic aptitude had a greater number of artists in their family histories, the genetic factor played a major role in determining artistic abilities.

The lists of characteristics of gifted children varies from one writer to another. Using points on which there is greatest consensus, we might construct a profile of a gifted child as follows. A child gifted in art observes acutely and has a vivid memory, is adept at handling problems requiring imagination, and is open to new experiences, yet can delve deeply into a limited area. The child takes art seriously and derives great personal satisfaction from the work. The child is per-

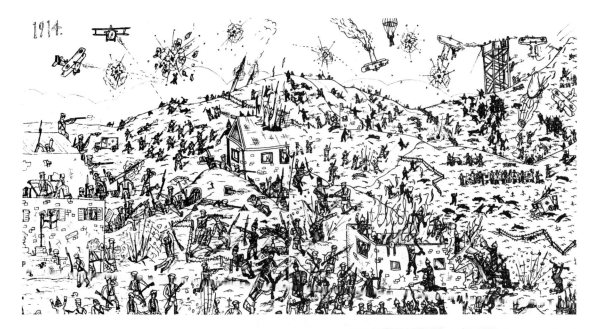

The rich variety of forms, ideas, and uses of the human figure in this drawing by a sixth grader shows a gifted child's range of interest and conceptualization. It also demonstrates the child's narrative sense, patience, and ability to depict a strong emotional experience. Nothing in the composition is static; everything is in a state of turmoil and change.

sistent and spends much time making and learning about art. Indeed, the gifted child may sometimes be obsessive or compulsive about artwork, neglecting other areas of study for it.[4]

Thus stated, this composite of the qualities of a gifted child suggests a list of acceptable goals for any art program. If this is so, can we not assume that the character and behavior of the gifted child provides us with very definite clues as to the nature of an art program for average students? This is mentioned as more hypothesis than recommendation, yet the idea seems worth pursuing.

As special programs for artistically gifted children have grown in number in both schools and museums, teachers have come to realize that many traits of creative behavior are shared by average or nonartistic as well as gifted children. Attitudes toward art such as self-direction and commitment merit attention and are best noted through observation. The following list of characteristics, both general and artistic, has been dividend into categories of behavior relevant to artistic talent.[5]

GENERAL CHARACTERISTICS

Precocity. Children who are gifted in art usually begin at an early age—in many cases before starting school and often as early as age three. A classic example is Yani's monkeys at the beginning of this chapter. Yani, a Chinese child, was six years old when she painted this.

Emergence Through Drawing. Giftedness first evinces itself through drawing, and for the most part will remain in this realm of

Pennsylvania, drawn from memory by a fifth grader a year after he moved away. He later attended art school and is now a successful furniture designer. Like most artists, he began by drawing far more frequently and intensely than his classmates did. For this drawing, the child's memory fueled his sense of structure and ability to create patterns from nature.

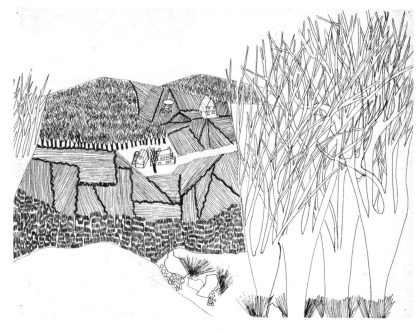

expression until the child tries other forms of expression or becomes bored with drawing. Drawing dominates not only because it is accessible, but because it fulfills the need for rendering detail.

Rapidity of Development. All children progress through certain stages of visual development. The gifted child may traverse such stages at an accelerated pace, often condensing a year's progress into months or weeks.

Extended Concentration. Visually gifted children stay with an artistic problem longer than others, because they both derive greater pleasure from it and see more possibilities in it.

Self-directedness. Gifted children are highly self-motivated and have the drive to work on their own.

Possible Inconsistency with Creative Behavior. The behavior of the artistically gifted is not necessarily consistent with characteristics usually associated with creativity; in many cases the opposite may be true. The success won through long hours of practice is not easily relinquished in favor of journeys into the unknown. Young people's reluctance to make fools of themselves, to appear ridiculous, or to lose face before their peers tends to instill attitudes of extreme caution when confronting new problems.

Art as an Escape. The gifted child may use art as a retreat from responsibility and spend more than a normal amount of time drawing. This is often accompanied by the kind of fantasizing reflected in the artwork. No talent, however impressive, is beneficial if used as an escape from other realities, and precocity in and of itself should not absolve a child from fulfilling the same responsibilities required of others.

CHARACTERISTICS OF WORK

Verisimilitude, Being True to Life. Although most children develop the desire to depict people and other subjects from their environment in the upper elementary years, gifted children develop both the skills and the inclination at an earlier age.

Visual Fluency. Perhaps the most significant of all, this characteristic is most similar to that of the trained artist. Visually fluent children may have more ideas than they have time to depict. Asked to draw a still life, they will include details missed by others; given a story to illustrate, they present many episodes rather than just one. They draw as spontaneously as most people talk, because through drawing they maintain a dialogue with the world.

Complexity and Elaboration. In their drawings, most children create "schemas" that are adequate to their needs; the gifted child goes beyond these and elaborates upon them, sometimes as an adjunct of storytelling or fantasizing, and sometimes for the sheer fun of adding details of clothes, body parts, or objects related to the

Visual fluency is a marked characteristic of this nine-year-old Russian emigre child. As a caricature, this work shows humor without relying upon the context of cartoons. For this child, drawing is a means to an end rather than an end in itself.

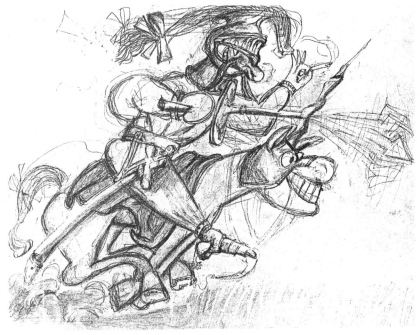

schema. Wholes are related to parts as powers of recollection are tested and transformed into a growing repertoire of images.

Sensitivity to Art Media. Since one of the characteristics of gifted-ness is immersion, it is logical to assume that through hours of prac-tice the child will master any media of particular interest. Where most fourth graders are content to use a color straight out of the box or tube, a gifted one may become quickly bored with packaged color and combine several colors to achieve desired effects. A child may be instinctively sensitive to what a particular medium can do, or may consciously try to attain mastery through practice. Older chil-dren (ages 10 to 12) are more apt to do this than are younger ones.

Random Improvisation. Gifted children often doodle — they impro-vise with lines, shapes, and patterns, and seem conscious of nega-tive areas or spaces between the lines, and are absorbed with the effects of lines. They transfer this interest to subjects such as the human face; like cartoonists, they experiment with the influence of minute changes on facial expression, noting the differences that the slightest shift in the direction of a line can make.

Some psychologists, such as Howard Gardner, believe that educa-tors have accepted a view of intelligence that is limited and neglects the importance of other mental capacities. Gardner's's theory of multi-ple intelligences includes "logical," "mathematical," and "language" as traits (from which most conventional ideas of intelligence are drawn). Gardner also includes "musical" and "personal" abilities.[6] "Spatial" intelligence relates to artistic ability. When a teacher engages in a discussion of aesthetics, or asks a child to write or talk about art, they extend not only the subject matter of art, but exercise other modes of intelligence. Artistic or spatial intelligence can also be distributed or divided into categories of artistic intelligence, some of which draw upon other modes mentioned by Gardner. As an example, an art direc-tor may begin as an artist (spatial), but call upon abilities which relate to mathematical, language, and personal skills, for without these abili-ties it would be impossible to give a client a cost estimate, write copy, or work as part of a planning team. While certain kinds of intelligence are genetic or inherited, all can be strengthened if the desire for im-provement is sufficiently strong.

Table 5-1 is an attempt to place artistic intelligence in an appropriate context. Using three categories — cognitive, artistic, and creative — it indicates the manifestation of each type in the child's behavior, the tests that identify each, and the artistic career suitable to each type.

Since all three areas reflect forms of intelligence, intelligence can be regarded not as a single characteristic but as a phenomenon that con-tains multiple ways of dealing with knowledge. Throughout the pri-mary grades, the child is holistic and makes no distinctions between the three categories. Task commitment is an overriding cluster of at-tributes without which none of the other three kinds of intelligence

~~~ **TABLE 5-1**

Defining Artistic Intelligence

Task Commitment: An Overriding Attitudinal Factor		
Personal traits such as Desire to succeed Goal orientation Persistence Extended concentration Positive self-image Independent action		

General Pool of Artistic Intelligence

Cognitive Characteristics	Artistic Characteristics	Creative Characteristics
(Convergent Thinking)	(Convergent and Divergent Thinking)	(Divergent Thinking)
Verbal facility Abstract reasoning skills Synthesizing ability	Sensory attunement Imaging impulse Visual fluency Fluency of ideas Perceptual awareness Skills related to memory, spatial relationships, etc.	Problem-solving skills Imagination Originality Risk-taking Elaboration Flexibility

Examples of Instruments for Identification†

Cognitive Characteristics	Artistic Characteristics	Creative Characteristics
Perceptual Acuity Test Differential Aptitude (verbal, abstract, spatial, mechanical skills) Barron Symbol Equivalents Stanford-Binet Test Iowa Tests of Basic Skills (cognitive abilities) Otis Lennon Mental Ability Rutgers Drawing Test* Goodenough-Harris "Draw-a-Man" Test*	Child's Aesthetic Judgment Test Hall Mosaic Construction Test Welsh Figure Preference Test Tests in Fundamental Abilities of Visual Arts (Lewerenz)	Barron Threshold Test Torrance Tests for Creative Thinking Purdue Creativity Tests Southern California Tests of Divergent Production

Emergence of talent through drawing; branching into arts areas

Professional Levels

Draws on all modes of intelligence as required		
Art director Art critic Art historian Teacher	Craftsperson Fine artist Teacher	Architect Industrial designer Film, video, special effects technician Teacher

*Can have implications for artistic assessment.
†A full listing of tests is published by The Psychological Corporation, 757 Third Avenue, New York, N.Y. 10017.

The class cartoonist may have more wit, inventiveness, and persistence than the "serious" artist. The ten-year-old boy who made this drawing had been interested in cartoons since the age of six. His drawing shows a keen observation of people, places, and events.

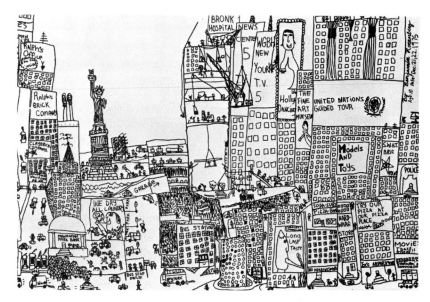

can reach fruition. It should be noted, moreover, that all three realms may interact as they are influenced by three factors: environment, genetics, and personality. The last two factors, however, are less open to change than the first.

Case History of Two Students

Strong indications of the nature of talent may sometimes be found in case histories of artistically gifted people, but it is often difficult to unearth actual evidence of their early work. A child's art is usually lost, and both parents and teachers are generally unable to recall accurately the child's early behavior. For some cases, however, there are reasonably detailed and apparently accurate data.

Among these cases are the histories of two girls of the same age from upper-middle-class homes, Susan McF and Mary M. These girls showed promise of talent in art very early in their lives. A study of their work shows that both of them began manipulating media just before they were a year old and that they had passed beyond the stage of manipulation before their second birthdays. Around fifteen months Susan was naming the marks she was producing in crayon. Mary did the same when she was sixteen months old. Around this age Mary began to use some spoken words clearly, but Susan was slower to learn to speak and instead was producing sounds such as "rrr," which consistently stood for "automobile," and "goong" for "duck." When she depicted such objects in her paintings by the use of symbols, she named them in this vocabulary. When twenty-five months old, Susan produced an attractive montage with sticky tape and colored paper. Around twenty-seven months of age, both girls could delineate many different symbols and give them some relationship in the same composition.

Both children led normal, active lives and during warm weather neglected their art for outdoor games. A study of their work (which their parents carefully dated) reveals, however, that inactivity in art did not seem to interfere with their continuous development. By the time both children were three years old they were overlapping objects in their drawings and paintings, and at four Mary seemed to recognize texture as an expressive element of design. By six, they were skilled in a variety of techniques—toning colors, devising textural effects, and inventing outstanding compositions. Before she was seven, Mary even gave hints of linear perspective in her work. It is important to note that both girls attended elementary schools that apparently provided progressive and highly commendable art programs.

By the time Susan was ten years old and Mary ten years and eight months, their work had lost most of its childlike qualities. Each girl passed through a realistic stage in which objects were rendered rather photographically. Then Susan's work became distinctly mannered in its rhythms, and Mary's output became reminiscent of that of several artists. In quick succession, she went through an Aubrey Beardsley period, followed by one reflecting the influence of Degas and later Matisse. When they were twelve years old, the girls met and became friends. They attended the same art classes in high school and produced paintings in a style obviously derived from that of the impressionists.

Fortunately, their secondary school art program proved almost as effective as that of the elementary school. After a time their work became noticeably more personal. Eventually both girls attended special classes for children with artistic talent, where they remained for four years. Here they produced paintings and sculpture in forms that continued to be recognizably personal. Both girls went on to attend a college of art where, according to their teachers, they gave evidence of outstanding artistic ability.

There seems to be little doubt that Mary and Susan were talented. What characteristics common to both might identify them as such? First, an almost lifelong preoccupation with art. Although their interest in art was at times intermittent, their production of art forms was for the most part uninterrupted. Second, both girls came from cultured homes in which the parents enjoyed artistic interests. Both environment and biological inheritance often contribute to talent. Children of artistic parents have the double advantage of artistic "nature" and artistic "nurture" often denied the children of parents who lack these interests and abilities.[7]

Third, the progress of Mary and Susan throughout the phases of their childlike expression was both richer and more rapid than normal. Although both girls developed a skill in handling tools and materials that was obviously above average, neither allowed her skill to assume paramount importance in her output. Again, at one period the girls' artwork apparently was dominated by technique, and the work of other artists whom they admired strongly influenced their output. Fortunately, however, their insight into artistic processes and their personal integrity, intellectual vigor, and vision were sufficient to overcome these powerful influences, which can be very seductive to the gifted young person who seeks a satisfying means of artistic expression.

Artists Examining Their Past

Another form of case history may be gathered from listening to the earliest memories of adult artists. When asked to reflect on their earliest artistic experiences, artists seem to have remarkable powers of recall. Much of what they describe, however, may on first reading appear to have little to do with conventional views of art. This is evidenced by the following reminiscence by a professor, art historian, and critic.[8]

> Let me emphasize at the outset that neither the concepts to which I refer, nor the vocabulary used to express them, were available in the milieu in which I grew up. Ideas like creativity, imagination, originality, and self-expression simply were not elements of the conceptual framework of my family, my friends, or my teachers until I entered high school. For example: I have been told by my parents that at the age of nine or ten months I would play with buttons for long periods of time, grouping them by size, shape, and color, and various combinations of these characteristics, as well as by the patterns and designs that I could form on the tray of my high chair. I could distinguish very subtle differences in color.
>
> We were a poor immigrant working-class family. My father was a cutter in a garment sweatshop. I had very few toys and preferred to play with household objects and spools of thread that my father brought from the factory.
>
> I do remember that already at age two I was scribbling frantically and constantly on every available surface. I tore open grocery bags to make larger surfaces. At this age I remember being scolded for drawing on the sidewalk, the front stoop, and all over the steel-gray surface of the porch. I liked the light chalk lines on the dark background.
>
> At about age 5 or 6 I made my own greeting cards, and as I learned to read and write, I combined pictures with words in many different ways. Magazine pictures, fabrics, candy wrappers, and other textures were added to my designs, although of course I had never heard of collage. I made my own comic books and I experimented with three-dimensional ideas such as pop-ups . . .
>
> I was acknowledged as the "artist" of the school where, as with my family, the criterion for judging my work as good was my ability to draw and paint realistically. Consequently, this recognition was a kind of exploitation . . . I spent very little time in the classroom. I was released from

classes to paint hall murals, Christmas murals, stage sets, and posters. There were no art books in the school. When I was about nine years old, I started to copy paintings from art books in the public library and soon commenced to make composite copies of the great masters. At about this time, the librarian refused to let me borrow books on Greek sculpture. "I know why you want them," she said. "You want to look at the dirty pictures."

Burt Silverman, a well-known illustrator, recalls his childhood in art as follows.[9]

I was born in Brooklyn in 1928. Compared to many kids born during the Depression, I had a comfortable childhood. But by current middle-class standards, my cultural life was really rather deprived. No puppet shows, children's theaters, museum tours, or marvelously illustrated children's books. Yet something *was* different for me. I could draw very well. I also had parents who recognized that painting pictures *could* be a valid substitute for the Stradivarius. I'm sure that they were also encouraged by the fact that my talents were clearly recognized by others. Special attention at school — a sense of being better at art than the other kids — made up for the fact that I was a rotten third baseman on the stickball team.

I drew and painted that special world of daydreams and fantasies that is so much a part of a child's life. My pictures were images of faraway places and exotic people — sunset landscapes, sailing ships, and ancient Roman soldiers. (Indeed, these were the characteristic elements of the romantic paintings of the nineteenth century; years later I discovered Turner and Constable with a sense of immediate recognition.) I was fascinated by illustrations in romantic adventure stories for kids. I lay in wait lustfully for N. C. Wyeth's and Howard Pyle's books in the local library. Beset by boyhood reveries, I drew pictures to give them substance, and I attempted to draw them as realistically as possible.

My efforts were reinforced by the admiration of my peers and adults alike. And so at the age of nine, I got thirty-five cents every Saturday morning for the subway ride (and a malted) to Pratt Institute's children's classes.

I was also given my first art book at this time. It was a history of Northern European Renaissance artists like Van Eyck and Van der Weyden — strange names and forbiddingly austere paintings of people in long cloaks. I began to learn of a whole new world of great art. Other books followed. One in particular, called *Modern American Painting*, was a favorite. It was a pictorial survey of American art from the Colonial period up to the late 1930s, with marvelous full-page reproductions of Homer, Whistler, Ryder, and Sargent. I was nine or ten years old when I painted my first oil, a copy of Hopper's *Lighthouse*, from this book. But curiously enough, I had never seen an original painting, nor even the *outside* of a museum or gallery. In those days a kid from Brooklyn went to Manhattan only to see a specialist.

The World's Fair

That was all to change, however, with the arrival of the first New York World's Fair in 1939. For with it came a mammoth exhibition of the world's great masterpieces. The show was dazzling in its scope and quality, covering 500 years of Western art including all the giants — Caravaggio, Rembrandt, Velázquez, Tintoretto, Veronese, Titian, and on and on. I wandered awestruck through the three vast pavilions. I felt a surge of excitement that was to transform me. I'd had no prior experience to prepare me for the impact of these paintings. The size and color—the *aliveness* of the work— hit me almost like a physical blow. But it was the more naturalistic painters who were especially absorbing. The paintings of Eakins, Homer, and Sargent were breathtaking. I couldn't believe that it was possible for anyone to *really* paint these pictures. Even now, I can recall the feeling: a childlike gasp, almost an unwillingness to look too long, lest it somehow be "used up."

I came from that show forever stamped a realist. I wasn't aware then of any movements in art history or even of the concept of realism. But the paintings suddenly brought into focus all my aspirations about art. I wanted to paint the world as beautifully—and as accurately—as those great artists did. To this moment, I can say that some of that original feeling still persists—that thirsting for the world made more real through paint.

Other artists have certain memories in common—parents who were ignorant of art yet sympathetic to their children's interests; an impulse to copy; and an affinity for realism. Their first experiences with museums were definitely positive, and, as with many writers and actors, their childhoods were particularly rich in fantasy, daydreams, and love of stories.

THE EVALUATION OF TALENT

The teacher who suspects a child of possessing unusual artistic talent might be wise to enlist the opinions of others, including artists and art teachers. Opinions of such well-informed people, furthermore, might be sought over a relatively long period of time. A sudden appearance of talent may later prove to be merely a remarkable but temporary development of skill. Again, what appears to be artistic talent in early years may disappear as the child develops other interests into which energies and abilities are channeled.

When teachers want information on a particular aspect of talent, they can devise certain tasks to reveal particular skills. Characteristics to be studied in the area of art might include observational ability; color sensitivity; ability to fuse drawing and imagination; emotional expressiveness; memory; handling of space; and sensitivity to media.

Teachers might also notice the interest that children have for looking at art, especially original art in galleries and museums and reading about art and artists. They might note, as well, children who seem to be adept at discussing works of art, making interesting interpretations of meaning, relating to other artworks, and generally appearing knowledgeable and comfortable in the presence of art and talk about art.

The problem of assessing giftedness continues throughout a child's school career. Those who are most concerned with its identification are the admissions personnel of art schools. While the traditional means of admission rests on the applicant's portfolio (which reflects the child's capabilities in drawing, color, or design), many art schools have for sometime used other criteria for admission, such as problem-solving abilities, evidence of creative thinking, and personality traits that are assessed through personal interviews. In other words, an alert student with a flexible and inventive mind may now have an advantage over an applicant whose main talent lies in skillful watercolors.

The system of identification that is based on both time and the opinions of several specialists seems to function with reasonable efficiency. Pupils are selected for advanced art instruction by peer and teacher recommendations based on apparent art production abilities, interest, and general school success. Students might move into or out of the advanced class according to their self-evaluations and observations of progress by the art teacher.

In some special art classes offered to children, a major criterion for admission was commitment to art rather than talent as such. These special classes demonstrated that skill does indeed improve in many instances, once children work in an environment of peers who share their enthusiasm. The classes were specifically designed for those whose hunger for art was simply not satisfied by the amount of activity the normal school could allow. In other words, it is possible to hunger for art without the ability to produce artwork of outstanding quality.

SPECIAL ARRANGEMENTS IN ART FOR GIFTED CHILDREN

When gifted children have been identified, the problem concerning suitable educational treatment for them arises. An "enriched" program may be offered by the classroom teacher or art consultant, whereby the pupil is assigned advanced work, given special materials, and allowed to take time from other obligations to work in art. The danger here is that the classroom teacher might not be equipped to provide special help, or that excusing the child from nonart activities to work in art might arouse adverse reactions from the rest of the class. We also must bear in mind the negative attitudes that many teachers take toward children who are particularly nonconformist in their creative behavior.

Another arrangement for helping the gifted is the "special class" in which only talented children are enrolled. Such classes may be offered

A ten-year-old girl in the special art classes at the Pioneer Youth Palace in Moscow. Children in these classes are encouraged to work large in clay modeling and to combine animal and human forms into fantastic figures.

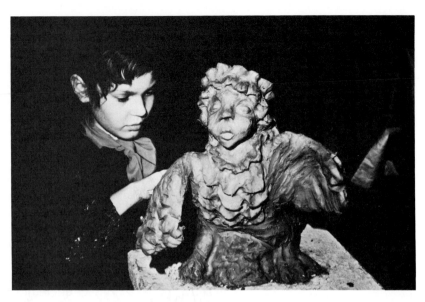

during school hours, after school, or on Saturday mornings. Many educators believe these classes provide the best solution to the problem of meeting the needs of the gifted. Teachers can be engaged who possess capabilities in special artistic fields. Much as a sympathetic teacher of general education may help a gifted child in art, a specialist can provide even more assistance. In the special classes the need to provide for individual differences will be even more apparent. According to David Manzella:

> These classes should be taught by producing and exhibiting art educators or by professional artists. They should be real studio experiences with a real aura of art about them—not ersatz . . . fabrications. These would not be general art classes in which a little of this and a little of that was presented, and a ceramist taught painting, and a painter, weaving. My recommendation would be to secure the services of good artists who love to teach and are sympathetic with and have an understanding of children and young people. And I would have these artists teach in whatever medium and in whatever way they found most satisfactory. . . . The nature of the particular medium is not important. A youngster's abilities can be challenged and nurtured by good teaching in all forms of the visual arts.[10]

Whatever special arrangements are made for the child with artistic talent, two considerations of paramount importance to the child's future development must be kept in mind. In the first place, on no account should the child's artistic development be unduly hastened into adult forms of expression. In the elementary school, the talented youngster is still a youngster, and artistic growth must occur with due respect for this fact. Even so, in the second place, every talented child must be provided with sufficient challenge to work to capacity. Unless this condition prevails, the gifted pupil may lose interest in the work, and considerable energies and abilities may be dissipated in less worthwhile ways.

Under what circumstances will talent flourish? To begin with, the home should, at best, encourage an interest in art and, at worst, not discourage it. While it may be true in some cases that, no matter what the circumstances, "genius will out," a sympathetic home environment is extremely stimulating. The home that provides suitable art media, a collection of art books, and a convenient place to work, together with loving and intelligent parents to admire the work being produced and to encourage further production will aid substantially in fostering talent. Next, the elementary and secondary schools that the gifted pupil attends should provide a sufficiently stimulating and challenging art program. Finally, somewhere along the line of artistic prog-

Winslow Homer drew *Beetle 'n Wedge* at age 11. Note the four structural studies at the bottom of the page, a member of the Wyeth family among them. (From *Winslow Homer: A Portrait* by Jean Gould. Dodd, Mead and Company, 1962.)

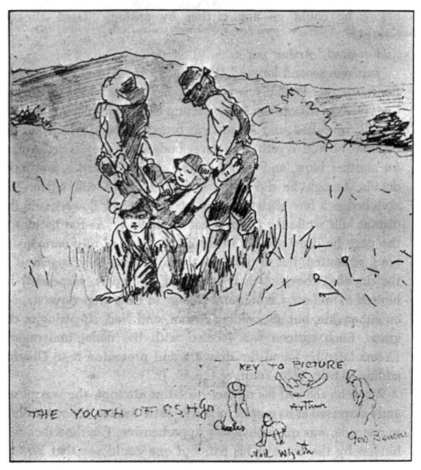

ress, the gifted pupil should be afforded special opportunities for the cultivation of talent and should have the opportunity to encounter a supportive teacher who is sensitive to any capabilities that set the gifted child apart from other pupils. Some questions teachers and administrators might ask themselves when identifying and planning for gifted children are the following:

Have I notified the parents that their child has special talents that deserve support?

In dealing with gifted children, am I being overly solicitous — giving more attention than needed?

Am I adding an appreciative or critical dimension to the activities by showing and discussing artworks that are related to studio activities?

Have I investigated any sources of additional help from the community, such as special classes in museums?

Do I have rapport with the children? Do they respect my opinions?

Has their ability in self-appraisal improved?

Do I know how to deal with and interpret the extreme attitudes sometimes displayed by gifted children?

SUGGESTED ART ACTIVITIES

It is unwise to offer the gifted a curriculum that is oriented primarily toward media. The talented child can be challenged by ideas as well as by materials in special classes. Moreover, there should be opportunities for students to work in one area in depth. A conceptual approach to art activities begins with an idea and then asks the child to use materials merely as a means of solving a problem. The problem may be stated as follows: "One characteristic of human beings is that they design their environment for pleasure and for aesthetic purposes as well as for function and utility. In creating your own environment, take into consideration purpose, scale, and materials." Stating the problem in this manner opens up a number of choices for the student and encourages decision making that is different from the kind that results when the child is given such directions as: "On the table you will find cardboard, pins, knives, and rulers. These are the materials to be used in making a scale model of a vacation home."

The teacher of the special class or the art consultant teaching in an after-school program should take an inventory of art activities offered prior to the special class in order to better plan the new program. Thus, a child who is interested in sculpture but has worked only in clay might try a large scale plaster or wood carving. In printmaking, a child who has worked only in linoleum may try a woodcut, or one who has handled both of these could attempt a multicolor silkscreen or any other problem beyond the capabilities of the other children. These activities extend the range of the child's experience and serve to compensate for the relatively limited exposure to art in the regular school program.

Gifted children are especially ready to learn from the lives and works of exemplary artists. A child interested in making a wood or clay sculpture, for example, should have access to books, filmstrips, videos, or slides that show how different artists approach this process. They might learn how some artists make pencil sketches of their ideas for a sculpture, selecting the most promising idea, and then assembling the materials needed to carry out the idea. They might learn that other artists make sketches, usually in small scale, from the same materials used for the final sculpture. Gifted boys and girls should learn that there are fine men and women sculptors who devote their lives to this art form. They should become familiar with sculptural pieces from their own country and time, done by living artists, as well as the heritage of sculpture from other times and places. They should learn that sculpture can be representational or abstract or nonobjective, depending on the expressive purposes of artists. Gifted children should have experiences that help them to understand that artists make sculptures that express meaning and feeling, and they should gain skills in reading meaning from art.

General Activities

Gifted children demonstrate a number of peculiarities in their selection of art activities. Their interests in such basic types of artwork as cartooning, portraiture, and sculpture develop early, and they appear to find greater challenge and deeper satisfaction in these than they do in some of the crafts, such as weaving a paper construction. While they may occasionally turn to crafts for their novelty, they generally return with renewed interest to what might be described as the more classic or traditional art forms, possibly because these art forms afford an opportunity to display the children's special brand of precocity.

Gifted children usually prefer to work at art by themselves rather than participate in group endeavors. Although as a group the gifted are socially inclined, they seem to recognize in art a subject that demands individual deliberation and effort. They are not entirely adverse to participating in puppet shows, mural making, and other art forms requiring a pooled effort, but most are happiest when they are submerged as individuals in artistic problems.

Painting in Oils

Painting in oils is a good example of a special activity suitable for the gifted. It offers the student an effective means of identifying with "real artists." The oils are rich and sensual in color and are far more versatile

This painting by a ten-year-old gypsy girl in rural Hungary shows an affinity for design enriched by detail. The ability to fill space in an interesting way is in advance of the level of drawing for her age.

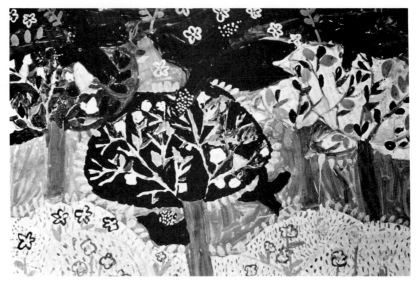

than most water-based paints. The slow-drying quality of oil paint makes it suitable for art projects undertaken over a period of time. By the time they reach preadolescence, gifted children should have had an opportunity to work with it. However, not even the most gifted children can use it effectively until they have had experience with many other types of paint.

Other Media for Drawing and Painting

Gifted pupils in the preadolescent stage will find several other challenging media that may not be available in the regular art program. Some of the more expensive colored drawing inks, for example, might be used in conjunction with India ink or in some of the mixed media techniques previously mentioned. Work with felt pens and pointed brushes might be explored. Charcoal pastels, and conté crayon in black and brown can also be used fairly extensively, either in quick sketching or in more deliberate drawing. Some of this line drawing might lead to a consideration of more advanced graphic processes like serigraphy and lithography.

Some gifted children in the preadolescent stage become proficient in the use of various types of watercolor. In the opinion of many painters, transparent watercolor is one of the most subtle and difficult of media. It must be used with precision and speed, and its "wetness," or watery character, should be reflected in the finished work. Good watercolor paints, brushes, and especially papers are relatively expensive. The pigments in tubes are more convenient to use than those in cake form. When gifted pupils begin to paint seriously in watercolors, they should be provided with materials of a higher quality than is usually found in the school art program. The many acrylic paints on the market offer colors as intense as oils, as well as quick-drying properties. Gouache is an opaque watercolor similar in handling to oils and acrylic paints; it dries quickly and, unlike tempera, is both water soluble and, when dry, waterproof. The use of these media may require demonstrations, which specialists are usually more capable of handling than classroom teachers.

It would be a mistake, however, to be preoccupied with adding more kinds of media. Instead, the emphasis should be upon the nature of the art problem (more challenging) and the instruction (more specific, where needed), and upon the creation of additional time, preferably in a peer group. Teachers should require more of gifted children, set higher standards of work, and be more directive when the occasion demands it. Instruction, therefore, differs as much in intensity as in kind.

TEACHING THE GIFTED CHILD

The young gifted child will, of course, make use of the usual materials and perform the basic activities mentioned in earlier chapters in connection with the general art program for normal children. Since the gifted can be recognized only over a period of time, they must obviously take part in the art program designed for all until their talent is discovered. When it is clear that individuals possess gifts above the ordinary, the teacher can help the children to progress at their optimum level of accomplishment. This may be done through any art form. In drawing and painting, it means more drawing and painting; in sculpture, more three-dimensional activities. Progress in art occurs when the worker keeps producing art. Mere quantity of production or repetition of forms previously created is not progress, but production that leads to improved skill, more penetrating insight, and greater mastery of media will help to develop a child's talent.

The principle of teaching in response to the needs of the learner is emphasized throughout this book. The preceding chapter observed that, in order to profit from art at all, some slow learners need to be subjected to a step-by-step method of instruction. With the gifted the reverse is necessary. Here the teacher is faced with the necessity for what might be described as "under-teaching." Every attempt must be made to challenge the greater abilities of gifted children. Whenever they can learn a fact or a technique for themselves, they should do so. Assistance must in general be withheld until the children have explored their own avenues for solutions to their problems. Gifted pupils who are given this type of educational treatment thrive on it, and so does their art.

Although artistically gifted children are normally motivated to express themselves with drawing and painting media, they should always have access to fine works of art in the media of their choice or, failing the actual works, good reproductions of them. The teacher should suggest certain outstanding works for them to study at art galleries and museums. Talented children can be assumed to be capable of extending their passion for creating works of art to the appreciation or criticism of art. Artworks should be discussed—both for their own sake and for the problems they pose as regards the work currently in progress.

The teacher will have to make special efforts with gifted pupils from underprivileged homes to encourage them to see the best art and to read good books on art. Gifted children from well-endowed homes generally have opportunities to add to their knowledge of art. Underprivileged children enjoy few, if any, such opportunities. Indeed, their gift must often be an especially vital one if it is to survive. In their case, the teacher's duty is to supply the inspiration and sources of knowledge that their home environment has denied them.

As one authority has noted:

> Art teachers should recognize that gifted education in art, whether it be for the academically or the artistically gifted—or both—must be as rich in ideas as it is in studio experiences. Likewise, the experiences should emphasize looking at and responding to works of art as well as creating images and objects. What is clearly apparent from practice is that bright students respond quickly and adeptly to art instruction. On the other hand, those with artistic gifts often need to be challenged to use their image-making abilities to think about and explore the world of ideas which reside in the history of art and in the realm of aesthetics.[11]

◆ NOTES TO THE TEXT

1. Howard Gardner, *Artful Scribbles* (New York: Basic Books, 1980), p. 17.

2. In much educational writing *gifted* refers to children with a high general intelligence, while *talented* refers to a special capability in one field of endeavor. This differentiation of meaning is by no means universal and has not been adopted here. In this chapter the words are used interchangeably.

3. U.S. Department of Education, *Education of the Gifted and Talented: Report to Congress* (Washington, D.C.: U.S. Government Printing Office, 1972).

4. Joseph Renzulli, "What Makes Giftedness: A Redefinition," *Phi Delta Kappan* 60, No. 3 (November 1978).

5. Al Hurwitz, *The Gifted and Talented in Art: A Guide to Program Planning* (Worchester, MA: Davis Publications, 1983).

6. Howard Gardner, *Frames of Mind: The Theory of Multiple Intelligences* (New York: Basic Books, 1984).

7. Because each girl had highly educated parents who are especially interested in art, records of their art were preserved. The parents systematically filed the children's work after writing comments about each piece on its reverse side. Both children eventually enrolled in classes for gifted children, at which time the parents disclosed the girls' records. The girls' IQ scores were: Mary, 120; Susan, 130.

8. Dr. Phyllis Gold Gluck, Brooklyn College, N.Y. Used by permission.

9. Burt Silverman, *Painting People* (New York: Watson-Guptill, 1977), p. 10.

10. David Manzella, *Educationists and the Evisceration of the Visual Arts* (Scranton, PA: International Textbook, 1963), pp. 91–92.

11. Karen Lee Carroll, *Towards a Fuller Conception of Giftedness: Art in Gifted Education and the Gifted in Art Education* (Teachers College, Columbia University: Unpublished doctoral dissertation, 1987).

◆ ACTIVITIES FOR THE READER

1. Study some children considered to be artistically gifted. Make a note of their outstanding personal qualities and work habits, and their attitudes toward their contemporaries.
2. Make a collection of drawings and paintings by artistically gifted children. Analyze the work for its subject matter, design, and technique. Compare this collection with one composed of the work of normal children of the same chronological ages as those in the gifted group.
3. Study the home environment of several artistically gifted pupils. How does this environment rate culturally and economically?
4. Set up a still-life arrangement and sketch it on paper in pencil or ink. Then outline the general composition in thin paint on canvas and begin to paint with oils or acrylics. It is wise to keep to a few pigments at first — say, one bright one, like yellow, and umber, black, and white. Paint bold strokes with medium-thick paint on the areas having middle light values. Later, add highlights in thicker paint, using a palette knife if desired. Paint the shadow areas in thinner paint.
5. Paint a landscape or portrait in oils, but continue to keep the number of colors restricted.
6. Contact some artists and request that they lend you a drawing from their schooldays, if one still exists. Talk to several artists and ask them to recall their earliest recollections of interest in art.

◆ SUGGESTED READINGS

Baker, Catherine. *The Innocent Artists*. Pool, England: Blandford Press, 1980. A personal record of an art teacher's experiences in Papua, New Guinea. Vivid evidence that exceptional visual sensitivity exists as a phenomenon in all cultures.

Cane, Florence. *The Artist in Each of Us*. New York: Pantheon, 1951. Contains a number of valuable case studies of artistic children.

Clark, Gilbert A., and Zimmerman, Enid. *Resources for Educating Artistically Talented Students*. Syracuse, N.Y.: Syracuse University Press, 1987. A thorough record of what exists, where to go for help, and how to go about establishing programs for the gifted. A unique source book of information.

Gardner, Howard. *Artful Scribbles: The Significance of Children's Drawings*. New York: Basic Books, 1980. See "Portraits of an Adolescent Artist" and the account of Nadia for one of the few references to the subject of artistic talent.

Hurwitz, Al. *The Gifted and Talented in Art*. Worchester, MA: Davis, 1983. Descriptions of programs for the gifted from local to national levels. Includes suggestions for activities. Profusely illustrated.

Case Studies

Bond, Constance. "A Child Prodigy from China Wields a Magical Brush." *Smithsonian Magazine* (September 1989).

Fein, Sylvia. *Heidi's Horse*. Pleasant Hill, CA: Exelrod Press, 1976.

Paine, Shiela. *Six Children Draw*. New York: Academic Press, 1981.

Selfe, Lorna. *Nadia: A Case of Extraordinary Ability in an Autistic Child*. New York: Harcourt Brace Jovanovich, 1977.

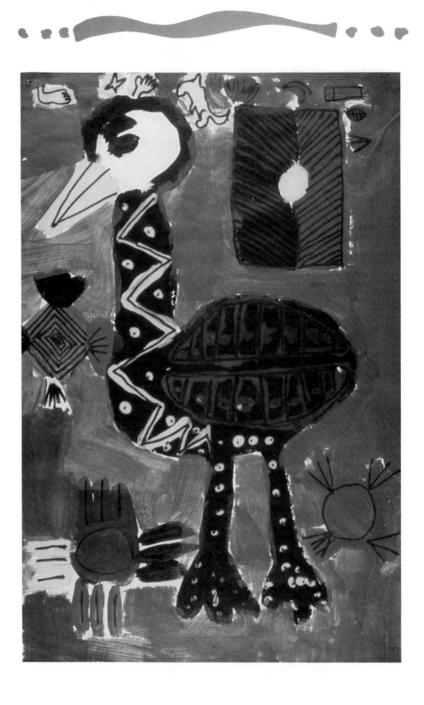

PART III

CONTENT OF ART

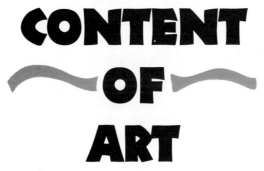

DRAWING AND PAINTING: AT THE HEART OF THE STUDIO EXPERIENCE

EACH GENERATION IN-
vents new functions for drawing and resurrects old ones . . .
some modern artists use drawing to create an expressive division of space, to build spatial relationships; for others it
serves as a compositional search for the unknown. In fact,
drawing can be all these things and more. The vision of each
artist determines the function of his drawing and the direction it will take.[1]

Bernard Chaet

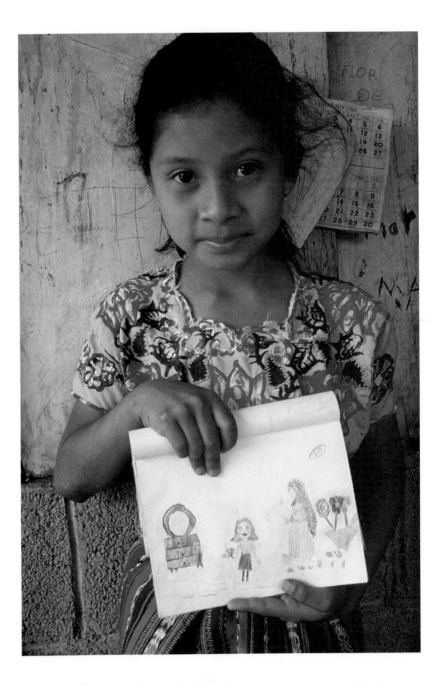

Drawing and painting are probably the most pervasive of all art activities engaged in by children. Through these two modes of art production children participate in the exploration of media, the creation of symbols, the development of narrative themes, and the solving of visual problems using the elements and principles of design. The emphasis in contemporary art education is on the expressive aspects of both responsive and creative experience, with support and instruction by the teacher appropriate for the levels of development of the children.

Children produce drawings and paintings that say something about their reactions to experience or heighten their abilities to observe. Certainly, when taught effectively, drawing and painting activities are universally enjoyed and provide a very flexible and practical means of expression for the young at all stages of artistic development.

This chapter will describe the tools and materials for drawing and painting and comment on their use at various developmental levels. We will also refer to certain problems related to the teaching of drawing and painting, such as dealing with spatial relationships; working with color; producing figure, landscape, portrait, and still-life compositions; using mixed media; and improving pictorial composition. Included in our discussions of all modes of art production are comments that refer to the historical, critical, and aesthetic dimensions of art.

The chief purposes in encouraging preschool children to draw and paint are, first, to allow them to become familiar with the materials associated with picture making, and second, to help them develop their own ideas more readily when they reach the symbol stage. As previously noted in the chapter on artistic development, children draw and paint for several reasons, and these reasons change as children grow and mature. From the manipulation of materials to the creation of symbols to an emerging interest in aesthetic qualities and meaning in works of art, children make and respond to art in dynamic ways. Very young children require little or no external motivation to engage in art activities, but as they grow older and are more aware of their capacities, and more critical of their abilities, children can benefit increasingly from the guidance of a knowledgeable and sensitive instructor. Numerous suggestions are provided in this chapter to help teachers foster artistic growth in their students.

THE MANIPULATIVE STAGE

Media and Techniques

Ages 2-5

In selecting media for children who are in the manipulative stage, the teacher must keep in mind the children's working methods and their natural inclination to work quickly and spontaneously. Paints or crayons should be easy to handle and should yield a rich and satisfying sweep of color when applied to a surface. For beginners, soft chalk and charcoal are too dusty and tend to smear and break too easily. These media are more acceptable when the child has progressed well into the symbol stage, in about the second grade.[2]

Young children who are beginning to draw seem to prefer felt-tip pens and wax crayons to other media. A box of crayons contains a wide variety of colors. The crayons should be firm enough not to break but soft enough for the color to adhere to the paper without undue pressure. Felt-tip pens are especially popular because of their vivid colors and ease of handling. They are available in a variety of sizes, colors, and prices and can be very stimulating for all age groups. Even very young children will sometimes draw in great detail with fine-point pens, even though the details are marks and scribbles.

Teachers must be careful when selecting pens for school use. Use of nontoxic pens prevents health hazards. Teachers should avoid using pens with fruit aromas or flavors, particularly with young children who will tend to taste the ink. Crayon-pastels combine the soft, richly colored qualities of pastels (colored chalks) with the dustless quality of crayons. These are usually more expensive than crayons but are well received as art media by all age groups.

There is a wide variety of papers appropriate for drawing, and a range of sizes and shapes of paper provides interesting alternatives for young artists. Regular 9-by-12-inch white drawing paper is a standard. Manila paper is inexpensive and has sufficient "tooth" for crayon. Newsprint is also suitable, but although it is cheaper than manila paper, it's texture is too smooth and it tears easily. It is often possible to find discarded papers, such as computer printout or the back of obsolete forms which cost virtually nothing. Teachers should vary the size of the paper and be aware of the relationship between the size of the pencil or brush and that of the paper.

Children in kindergarten should learn to work with paint, an exciting medium that they find attractive. The most suitable paint for the beginner is an opaque medium usually called *tempera*, which may be purchased in several forms, the most usual being liquid or powder. The powdered variety is somewhat less expensive than the liquid but must be mixed with water before it is used. (With beginning pupils, the teacher must mix all the paint.) Powdered tempera has one advantage over liquid tempera: its textural qualities can be varied as desired. The liquid paint tends to go on with a uniform smoothness, whereas the powdered variety can be applied with varying degrees of roughness or smoothness depending on how much water is mixed with it. School-quality acrylic paints are also available.

The broad, muscular fashion in which young children naturally work is even more noticeable with paint than with crayon. Large sheets of paper (18 by 24 inches) allow for young painters' large strokes and exuberant movements. The teacher should use a variety of paper and brush sizes so that the children can explore different ways of controlling the paint. Newsprint and manila paper are both suitable, as are the thicker papers such as bogus and kraft. The children can also use newspapers and colored poster paper.

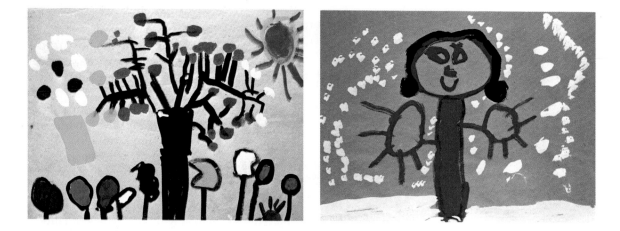

These illustrations by kindergarten and first-grade pupils show children's early linear orientation as well as the broad, muscular fashion and fairly large area in which they work.

Paintbrushes are usually flat or round, and the coarseness of the bristles varies from very stiff to very soft. Cost is always a factor in purchasing art materials for schools, but it is inconsiderate to ask children to express themselves with materials that even an experienced adult could not control. The poorest-quality brushes, although usually the least expensive, might not be the best value. Cheap brushes often have uneven shapes and are difficult to control, thus frustrating the painter. Bristles can fall out in the process of painting and during vigorous cleaning. It is better to invest in decent-quality paintbrushes for better service and less frequent replacement. Purchase a variety of brushes, particularly large bristle brushes (10-inch handle, ½-inch flat bristles) for young children. After use, wash brushes in water and store in jars with the bristles up to avoid permanent creases.

Very young children are usually anxious to experiment with media and will use whatever crayons, paint, and paper they find within reach. Their attention span is short, however, so within five minutes they may exhaust their interest in one kind of work and seek a new activity. The more children experiment with art media the longer their attention span becomes, and some children remain involved in art activities for extended periods of time.

When children first use paint, it is a wise practice to offer them only one color. When they have gained some familiarity with the manipulation of the paint, the teacher can give them two colors, then three, then four. By providing children with the primary hues—red, yellow, and blue—plus black and white paints, the teacher can encourage them to discover the basics of color mixing at a very early age. Colors will mix at first by accident (the red and yellow miraculously turning orange can be quite exciting).

The paint should be distributed in small containers such as glass jars, coffee cans, milk cartons, or orange juice cans. Place these containers firmly in a wire basket or a cardboard or wooden box to prevent accidents. Very young children should have one brush for each color because they cannot at first be expected to wash their equipment between changes of color. The attentive teacher can give simple instructions on how to clean brushes in water and how to mix or lighten colors.

From the beginning of the children's experience with paint, the teacher should attempt to enlarge their color vocabulary. This can occur naturally by naming colors as they are used. The use of "coloring drills," often seen in some kindergartens, seems unnatural and should be avoided. Children learn about color most effectively by using it, talking about it, and identifying color terms in artworks.

Because many children come to school with a linear orientation to picture-making, their first experiments in painting during both the manipulative and symbolic stages are likely to be brush drawings. Picture making in its early stages is generally a matter of enclosing images with lines rather than the more sophisticated work of placing areas of color next to each other. Even if they begin as painters, children will often complete their work by going over it with black lines to lend greater clarity to the shapes. At first the teacher should accept whatever strategies the children happen to use, but should keep an eye on their work habits and handling of materials and should get them to talk about their work during the evaluation period.

When the children are familiar with crayons, paints, and brushes, the teacher may try a few simple teaching methods to encourage them and perhaps to help them improve their technique. Sometimes background music helps children improve the rhythm of their lines or color areas. When certain children in the group make discoveries, such as stipple or dry-brush effects, the teacher might draw the attention of the entire class to these discoveries. The teacher should also, in a general way, praise each child's industry or some other broad aspect of the child's endeavor.

When children reach the phase of named manipulation, that is, the creation of a symbol, the teacher should encourage them to talk about the subject matter of their painting. In so doing, the pupils tend to clarify their ideas and thus progress into further stages of development. The relation between ideas, language, and images is very intense at this age and should be encouraged. Whatever learning takes place at the stage of manipulation, however, depends largely on the children. A pleasant working environment and one in which suitable materials are readily at hand are the main ingredients of a successful program during this stage of expression. The teacher must give much thought to preparing and distributing supplies and equipment and must work out satisfactory procedures for collecting work and cleaning up after each session.

Paintings by two six-year-olds, one from the United States, the other from France. Children in the primary grades normally do not fill the pictorial space as completely as they have here. For children at this age, art largely is a graphic — that is, drawing — process. Paintings first emerge as brush drawings, which then may be filled in with areas of color. The teachers of these children have made a conscious attempt to direct attention to certain "painterly" approaches, such as color against color, color and moving line, and forms that cover the complete surface of the paper.

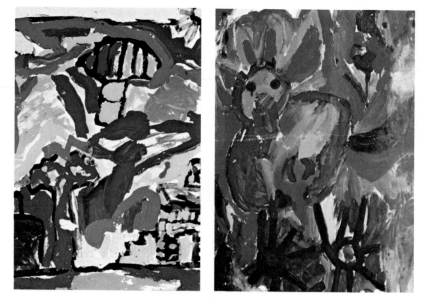

THE SYMBOL-MAKING STAGE

Media and Techniques

In earlier art sessions little or no chalk is used, but in the symbol-making stage, with their newly acquired skills, children will probably be ready to use soft chalk, or "pastels," as they are sometimes called, which may be purchased in sets of ten to twelve colors. "Dustless" chalk, while lacking in color potency, leaves less residue on children's clothing. Charcoal is another medium that might be used. Pressed charcoal in hard sticks is better than the "willow vine" variety, which breaks easily. Chalk and charcoal can be used conveniently on manila and some newsprint papers, which should be large, about 12 by 18 inches. Use spray fixative to seal the chalk or charcoal and avoid smudging. Always be sure to use any spray materials in a well-ventilated space or under an exhaust hood. If prolonged use is required, use a filter mask. The crayon-pastels mentioned earlier are appropriate also for school-age children and require no fixative.

It is possible to use transparent watercolor for painting, but the teacher must realize that it is more difficult to control than tempera and proceed accordingly. Watercolors require more instruction and more structured supervision for children to use them successfully. Some teachers prefer to wait until children are older before introducing watercolor painting.

Teaching

In the symbol-making stage, drawings and paintings represent subject matter derived directly from the children's experiences in life. The teacher may thus from time to time assist the children in recalling the important facts and features of the depicted objects. For example, for those children developing symbols for "man" or "woman," the teacher could draw attention to such activities as running, jumping, climbing, brushing teeth, wearing shoes, combing hair, and washing hands. If the children act out these activities, the concept inherent in the symbol is expressed more completely. Judicious questioning by the teacher concerning both the appearance of the symbol in the children's work and its actual appearance as observed by the children in their environment might also be effective. These teaching methods, it should be noted, are not suggested for the purpose of producing "realistic" work, but rather to help the children concentrate on an item of experience so that their statements concerning it may grow more complete.

When the children relate their symbols to their settings, their chief difficulty often arises from an inability to make the symbol sufficiently distinct from the background of a picture. The following dialog between a teacher and a third grade pupil relates to such a problem.

TEACHER: Mark, it looks as if you're about finished. What do you think?

MARK: I don't like it.

TEACHER: What's the matter with it?

MARK: I don't know.

TEACHER: You know, there comes a time when every artist has to stop and look at his work. You notice things you don't see up close. *(Tacks painting on easel.)* Now look at it hard.

MARK: You can't see it too clear—

TEACHER: You mean the tent?

MARK: It doesn't show up.

TEACHER: What we need is a way to make the subject—that is, the tent—stand out. What can you do? I can think of something right off.

MARK: I know—paint stripes on it.

TEACHER: Try it and see what happens. You can paint over it if you don't like it.

There could have been other solutions, such as using an outline or increasing the size of the tent. The important point of this dialog is that the teacher got Mark to discover his own solution without requiring him to give a single correct answer. The problem of developing contrasts between figure and ground, especially in color, light and shade, and sometimes texture, is an important one that the pupil should be helped to solve at this time.

THE PREADOLESCENT STAGE

Preadolescent children are ready to develop real competencies in drawing[3] and painting activities. By the time children reach the fourth and fifth grades, they will probably have had considerable experience with art media and will have developed many skills in their use. A brush or crayon should now do what the child wants it to do.

Media and Techniques

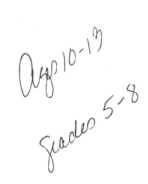

age 10-13
grades 5-8

The teacher should provide a wide variety of brushes, ranging from about size 4 to size 10 of the soft, pointed type made of sable or camel hair. The teacher should also make available the bristle-type brush in long flat, short flat, and round types and in all sizes from ⅛ inch to 1 inch in width. Since children at this stage will sooner or later use tints and shades of color, it is sometimes a good idea to provide a neutral-toned paper to make the tonalities of paint more effective. Pupils in the preadolescent stage will require not only the standard opaque and transparent paints but also inks, crayons, oil crayons, pressed charcoal, pastels, and drawing pencils of reasonably good quality. Crayon can have a range of some twenty colors. Soft lead pencils range in weight from 3B to 8B.

The discussion that follows will focus on several important techniques that preadolescents are expected to develop at this stage—techniques involving facility in use of color, understanding of space, skills in drawing from observation, and ability to mix media. Because the teacher's role is central to the process of developing these techniques, comments on how to teach them are incorporated into this discussion rather than set forth in a separate section.

Developing "Color Awareness." In the early preadolescent stage, children are concerned with the relationship of background to foreground. This concern, together with their interest in the effects of light and shade, involves them in problems related to the tonalities of color. By learning more about mixing colors, children increase their choices, thereby using a wider range of colors. They also learn how to lower color intensity by adding small amounts of the complementary color and how to lighten color by adding white.[4]

Once it is decided that pupils will mix colors themselves, the physical arrangements in the classroom for the distribution of pigments must be carefully planned. The "cafeteria" system allows the pupils to select their colors from jars of powdered or liquid tempera. Using a spoon or wooden paddle, they place the desired quantity of each color in a muffin tin. The mixing of paint and water and mixing of colors can be done directly in the tins. Because children sometimes waste paint, the teacher should tell them to take only enough pigment for their painting. They should be cautioned not to mix too large a quantity. By adding colors, such as blue to yellow to make green, or red to white to make pink, they can save paint.

There are a variety of ways to alter the standard hues. Mixing black with a standard tempera color creates a shade, while adding white to a color produces a tint. If watercolor is used, adding black creates a shade, but the white paper showing through the watered-down pigment creates the tint. Light areas must be carefully planned in advance. The ability to mix tints and shades and thus arrive at different values greatly broadens pupils' ability to use color. Preadolescent children can also alter hues without undue difficulty by mixing the standard hue with its complement. Hence, when green is added to red the character of red is altered; the more green added, the greater the change in the red, until finally it turns a brownish gray. Grays achieved this way have a varied character and are different from those achieved by mixing black and white. When used in a composition, these grays give dramatic emphasis to the areas of bright color.

By the time the children have gained some ability in mixing colors, they should have a reasonably broad range of standard hues, including red, yellow, blue, green, violet, orange, magenta, turquoise, and brown. Because the choice of colors is so wide, however, the teacher may find it necessary from time to time to caution pupils against using too broad a palette. Children often attempt to use too many colors; in fact, they sometimes try to use every available color in one painting. They then find it difficult to build a unified composition.

Children in the upper elementary-school grades are capable not only of looking analytically at how color behaves, as in the color wheel, but also of using what they learn about color in their paintings. This is not as true of children who have not yet reached the preadolescent stage, since young children tend to work intuitively; the works of first graders often exhibit exciting, "painterly" qualities. But the upper grader, being more cautious and less spontaneous in expression, requires stronger and more specific motivation. Color activities built around problems posed by the teacher enable the student to learn more about the interaction of color as well as to arrive at a more personal, expressive use of color.

Here are some suggestions to develop general color awareness.

1. Questions about sensitivity to color in the environment:
   How many colors can you see in this room?
   Would everyone who is wearing red please stand together?
   Name the colors you see outside the window. Can you grade them according to brightness or dullness?

2. Problems relating to color investigation:
   First make a painting with just three primary colors—red, yellow, and blue. Mix them any way you like. In a second painting,

add black and white to the three colors.

Compare the brown in the bottle with a brown of your own, made by mixing black and red. Which do you like better?

Mix your own orange and compare it with the prepared orange in the bottle. Which do you prefer?

3. Problems relating to the nature of pigment:

   What happens when you use color on wet paper?

   What happens when you use color on black paper?

   What happens when you combine painting and collage? Notice how a separation of color and texture appears. How can you bring the painted part and the collage section together?

4. Problems relating to the emotive power of color:

   Mix a group of colors suitable for a painting about a hurricane, a picnic, a carnival.

   Prepare little "families" or related groups of color around specific ideas and see how close you can get to what you are trying to express. For example, for a blazing house, you might group red, black, and orange; for an autumn scene, yellow, red, brown, and orange.

5. Color days:

   Colors may differ according to their relation to other colors. For a homework assignment, have everyone bring in anything that they think is red. All examples should be no larger than the palm of their hands. Paste all contributions randomly, making certain the selections touch each other. Assign a different color each day or session and ask teams of students to prepare them instead of the teacher. When the color blue is assigned, have a reproduction of one of Picasso's blue period works and ask the class to point out the tones that match most closely. The exercise, when completed, will be an attractive introduction to the possibilities of abstract art and collage. If mounted behind a circular opening, it will improve the appearance of the presentation.

6. To make color mixing more dramatic, fill jars half with water and add color inks or tempera. When the teacher pours one jar of colored water into another, the effect of the art teacher as "mad chemist" will not soon be forgotten.

7. Give each student a small section (two by two inches) of a reproduction and see how close they can come to matching the colors on a larger (one by one inch) scale. Use a color-centered work from the fauvist, expressionist, or Blau Reiter schools. The effect, when assembled, will be striking.

8. Relate color theory to subjects with interesting divisions of space, such as the history of costume. Keep paintings consistent in size

Frank Stella, *Darabjerd III*, 1967. Fluorescent acrylic is applied in flat, hard-edged shapes on canvas, a good example of vivid bright color that can be used in learning the vocabulary of color. (Hirschhorn Museum and Sculpture Garden, Smithsonian Institution. Gift of Joseph H. Hirschhorn, 1972.)

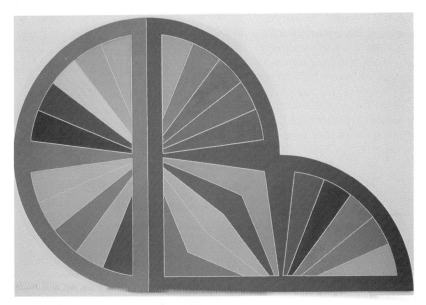

and mount them as a parade, with monochromatic Elizabethans preceding analogous Victorian ladies, and so on.

9. Ask the students to select one of their contour line drawings and to fill in separate areas with hues taken from their color vocabulary.

Color and Art History. Another way to study color is by using works of art as a frame of reference or as an organizing factor. There is *symbolic* use of color as in the case of red and blue used for Madonna figures of the Renaissance, *realistic* color use based upon the actual color of the subject (blue skies, green grass, etc.), *flat* application of color as in minimal or hard-edged painting, and there is color directed at specific *moods* as in the case of theatre set designs. Color can be bold, bright, and painterly as in the case of the *expressionists*, linked to light as in the work of the *impressionists*, or limited and restrained as in the early work of the *cubists*. When discussions of such differences are drawn for examples, students should be able to identify works by different artists, art movements, and cultures in examples that are new to them.

By the third grade children can easily master color vocabulary—especially if some imagination is used in reinforcing the terms. The following exercise requires a student to mix colors within an interesting context based upon the history of costume design.

1. Ask the students to select a costume from history (it might be European, Oriental, native American, or contemporary American, etc.). The costume should have at least six clearly separated areas, such as hat, cape or shawl, and so forth.

Georgia O'Keeffe, *Oriental Poppies*, 1928. The brilliant use of limited color unfolds in this close-up of a flower. By bringing the viewer close to the flowers, the artist can fill the canvas with the vibrant color of the petals. Blowing up a detail such as this can be used as a drawing assignment in several contexts.

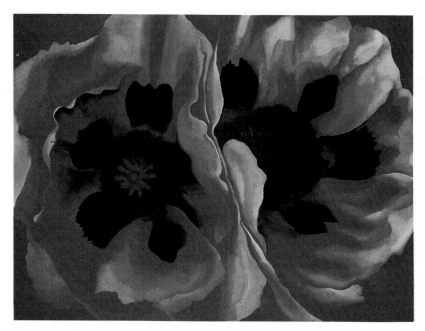

2. Working from the costume or picture of a costume, ask students to make a contour line drawing of the subject.

3. In each outlined area students are to write a number.

4. On the chalkboard write numbers followed by the color terms you have been studying, such as primary, complementary, analogous, warm, cool, etc.

5. The students' task is to fill in each numbered area with the corresponding color concept listed on the chalkboard. If paint is used, students can blend from one area to another, such as "warm" into "cool" colors.

Such problems may be viewed as ends unto themselves or as preliminary stages to more complete picture making. They lead into the area of art appreciation when the children are asked to relate their class activities to the solutions developed by artists. Thus, in conjunction with exercises in the emotive power of color, the teacher may refer to El Greco's *View of Toledo*, O'Keeffe's *Red Poppy*, Bearden's *Patchwork Quilt*, and many of Picasso's blue period paintings.

Perspective

Masses and Shapes in Space. The problem of rendering space often frustrates the older child, who will require the help of the teacher. Teaching perspective is similar to teaching sensitivity to color in that in neither case does an *intellectual* approach assure that personally expressive use will follow. Children can have their attention directed to the fact that distance may be achieved through overlapping, diminution of size, consistency of vertical edges, atmospheric perspective or neutralization of receding color, and convergence of lines. This knowledge, however, has only limited value if the children are not able to see the many ways in which perspective may be used; indeed, effective pictorial expression may occur without recourse to linear perspective. The works of such painters as Van Gogh, Picasso, Cassatt, and Hockney as well as traditional paintings from China should be studied as examples of ways that artists have distorted, adjusted, and exaggerated the principles of perspective for particular artistic ends. The teacher should have on hand art reproductions (from books, magazines, or other sources) that demonstrate different ways that space has been treated by artists. Such examples might show:

1. The Oriental placement of objects, which usually disregards the deep, penetrating space of Western art

2. The Renaissance use of linear perspective, with its vanishing points and diminishing verticals and horizontals

3. Cubist dissolution of Renaissance-type space, with its substitution of multiple views, shifting planes, and disregard of "local" or realistic color

4. Photographic techniques using aerial views, linear perspective, and unusual points of view in landscape subjects

5. Disregard for the principles of perspective by the abstract expressionists, who returned to the integrity of the picture plane and rejected the depiction of three dimensions on a two-dimensional surface

6. Renewed interest in spatial relationships by contemporary realists such as Richard Estes, who applies the rules of perspective to city scenes, and David Hockney, who continues to investigate ideas first seen in the works of the cubists

Space may also be studied by examining color in nonobjective paintings where there are no familiar associations to come between the viewer and the painting. Children can describe which colors seem to come forward and which recede, which ones "fight" with each other and which are harmonious. Abstract painter Hans Hofmann referred to the tensions of color as a process of "push and pull."

In teaching perspective, as in teaching about color, the teacher should keep in mind that children may produce successful work without using linear perspective. Linear perspective is a system developed during the Renaissance which provides a set of rules or guidelines for rendering objects and buildings with an appearance of three dimensions. There are many guides that provide the accepted diagrams that art students have traditionally used, and children, while eager and able to copy such guides, rarely understand the connection between what they copy and what they see in the real world.

Students in the lower grades will accept their handling of space, but around the middle grades, some will become dissatisfied with their efforts. When this happens, children are ready for instruction that deals with basic problems of perspective. Following are five conventions of perspective that children can begin to use very early and can gain in competency as they grow and progress:

1. *Overlapping* causes one object to appear to be in front of another in space. Draw anything that involves a grouping of objects. You can begin with pieces of fruit or any scene where objects overlap.

2. *Diminishing size* of objects gives them the appearance of being farther from the viewer. Draw the same subject as in #1, making the objects in front larger and the objects that are overlapped smaller.

3. *Placement* of objects on the picture space implies distance. For objects on the ground (or floor, table, etc.), closest objects are near the bottom of the picture space. As the object is moved upwards it appears to recede in the distance. Combined with diminishing size, this convention is very effective.

4. If we stand directly in front of a building, the sides will not be visible. When we move to the right or left, the sides begin to appear and the top edges of the sides of the building *appear to slope downward*. This is actually a manifestation of diminishing size. Ask students to test this concept at home or in the neighborhood, or at school. A culminating activity for these four principles might be to trace evidence of each directly on a photograph (old architectural or home magazines are good sources), or paint directly on the window of the room if buildings are seen.

5. Although *colors appear less intense* with distance, don't expect to see this unless great distance is involved. The edges and colors of close subjects, such as the backyard, are clearer than the mountains on the horizon, or the distant view of a city. Have students plan a painting of overlapping city forms such as skyscrapers, applying color concepts such as *tint* and *shade* to achieve a sense of distance.

Any instruction beyond this point should require a more formal application of the conventions of linear perspective using *horizon lines, vanishing points,* and *guide lines* for constructing the illusion of three dimensions on a two-dimensional surface. Students who are ready for this advanced level of instruction and investigation should observe their environment as well as the works of artists who apply the rules of perspective.

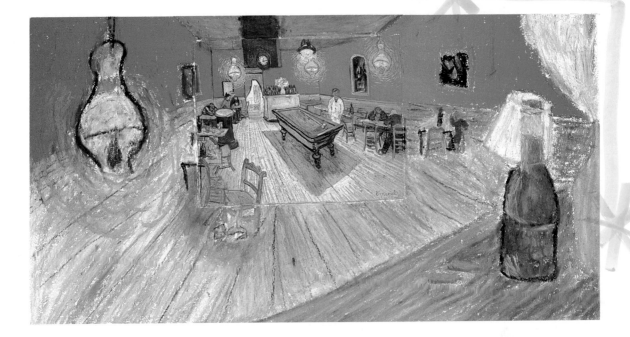

By placing a postcard of an artwork or fragment of a photograph in the center of a piece of drawing paper and using the image for cues to fill the entire page by extending the artwork, students can develop a better understanding of perspective. In this case, a sixth grader extended Vincent van Gogh's *The Night Cafe*, 1888. (Yale University Art Gallery. Bequest of Stephen Carlton Clark, B.A. 1903.)

Developing Skills in Drawing from Observation. Most art educators now make a distinction between three categories of activity: *self-expression*, *observation*, and *appreciation*. In terms of child development, self-expression has greater implications for the lower elementary grades, and observation is more relevant to the capabilities of elementary school children in the upper graders. Although art educators are still divided as to when drawing from observation should begin, a growing number feel that directed perception satisfies a strong desire among older children to depict subject matter.[5]

We need to ask the question: Is "realistic" drawing necessarily "good" or "bad" drawing? The issue of good or bad exists apart from any particular style, for values in drawing, as in painting, reside chiefly in form rather than in the degree of realistic representation. In an attempt to find a place in art for realistic drawing, "the painter may . . . imitate what he sees," says L. A. Reid, "but he imitates what he sees, because what he sees fulfills and satisfies his needs."[6] Good drawing necessarily occurs, then, when the artists select, interpret, and present in a personal, aesthetically coherent composition those items of experience that move them, regardless of whether or not the presentation is realistic. Weak drawing occurs when the forms used are drawn merely to fill gaps in the pictorial surface, without regard for the unity of the composition. In accomplishing the feat of organization, an artist may purposely depart from nature to varying degrees in the interest of design.

There is not enough time and little merit in encouraging children of any age to draw with photographic accuracy. But a distinction must be made between requiring children to work for realism in drawing and using certain drawing techniques to heighten their visual acuity. Few teachers who use nature as a model or have the class work with contour line really believe that they are forcing their students to conform to photographic realism. In the first place this kind of professional faculty is impossible to achieve on the elementary level, and secondly, there would be very little point to such a goal, even if it were possible to attain. The argument that working from nature is inhibiting to children is no longer accepted by most art educators.

The question a teacher must inevitably ask is, ''What can the child learn from drawing activities?'' Drawing activities can serve to fulfill the following goals:

1. Provide pleasurable art activity that allows children to attain a degree of success

2. Direct children away from stereotypes towards their personal means of expression

3. Provide children with usable skills that may be employed in other art activities

4. Offer an opportunity to study works of outstanding professional artists

5. To see freshly through close observation

6. To exercise imaginative powers

7. To develop skills of concentration

8. To exercise memory

Sources of Observation.   Good drawing depends in no small measure on the producer's experience of the things drawn. Such experience, it should be noted, depends not only on the eye, but on a total reaction of the artist, involving, ideally, all the senses. Often in the fifth and sixth grades, good drawing may be developed through the use of some time-honored subjects that demand a comprehensive reaction to experience. Using sources grounded in experience, the child may produce drawings of the human face and figure, landscapes, and still-life subjects. According to what subjects, materials, visual references, and motivating forces the teacher selects, drawing can be an exciting and pleasurable activity, or an academic and inhibiting one. Table 6-1 compares two approaches to teaching drawing activities for a sixth grade class.

As far as is practicable, the children should be responsible for arranging their sources of observation. For example, they should have some control in posing the model for life drawing. The teacher, of

～ TABLE 6-1

Two Approaches to Teaching Drawing

	Subject	Materials	Instructions for Visual Reference	Motivation and Historial References
Negative Instruction	**Still life:** A wine bottle, a tennis ball, and a plate on a table at the front of the room.	Hard pencil on newsprint, 8 by 10 inches, flat desk tops used as work surface.	"Draw everything you see — light and dark, lines, and so on."	None.
	Human figure: A girl posed sitting in a chair, which is on the floor.	Ballpoint pens on newsprint, 18 by 24 inches.	"Make the drawing as real as you can; make the folds really stand out."	None.
Positive Instruction	**Still life:** Four still-life centers, each composed of large shapes of interesting objects — pieces of machinery, drapery, and so on.	Dustless chalk on black construction paper, 12 by 18 inches; drawing boards used as work surface.	"Concentrate just on contour. Use a different color chalk for each object and let the lines for the shapes flow through one another."	Contour drawing clearly demonstrated. Line drawings by Matisse, Picasso, or good commercial illustrations shown.
	Human figure: A boy and a girl, one sitting, one standing, dressed in odd bits of costume and holding musical instruments; placed above eye level.	Black crayon and watercolor wash on 40-pound white paper (size optional).	"Balance light washes of watercolor against line. Lay in the broad directions of the figures in wash, and when it dries, work the lines over the wash."	Demonstration given: wash and line drawings by Rembrandt, Tiepolo, and Daumier shown. Lesson related to previous experiences in drawing.

course, will have to oversee the lighting and the setting of reasonable time limits for poses. Artificial lighting by one or more spotlights can be used, and these lights must be moved until anatomical details are clearly revealed and an interesting pattern of the elements, especially line and light and shade, is visible. Models must not be asked to pose for too long (usually for a preadolescent youngster, ten minutes is a lifetime). However, if the pose is too brief for a complete drawing to be made, the teacher merely needs to remind the model to memorize the position in order to return to it after a rest. The teacher, of course, should also remember the pose in case the pupil forgets it. Chalk marks to indicate the position of the feet often help the model to resume the pose.

In producing life drawings and portraits, older pupils will be assisted by an elementary study both of pertinent relationships among parts of the body and of approximate sizes of parts of the figure. The pupil who is maturing physiologically often shows an interest in the human body by drawing certain anatomical details in a rather pronounced manner. Any emphasis beyond the requirements of aesthetics may be counteracted to some degree by a study of the human body. The teacher should point out the nature of the mechanically independent body blocks—the head, the torso, and the pelvic girdle.

The human figure lends itself to interpretation. Once the children have closely examined the figure, they might be asked to interpret it in terms of fantasy or qualities of mood—joy, doom, strength, violence. Such subjects can be drawn from observation as well as imagination, for students can be posed displaying these moods.

In still-life work, the pupils should not only arrange their own groups of objects, but they should also be given the opportunity to become thoroughly familiar with each item. By handling the objects

This illustration from a Japanese curriculum guide for the fourth grade shows ten and eleven year olds' capabilities in using the contour approach with both pencil and brush.

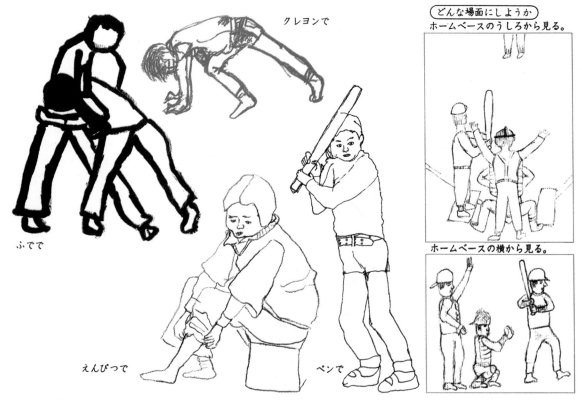

・同じ場面でも見るいちによって感じがちがってくる。何をかくか決めたら，どのいちから見たようにとらえるか
を考える。・人物の動作やとくちょうをスケッチし，感じをこめて下絵をかく。

4

they may make note of differences in textures and degrees of hardness and softness. Sole dependence on the eye in artwork limits unnecessarily the experience of the creator.

Selection of still-life material is another instance of the need for the teacher to plan a program with the pupils' preferences in mind. The teacher must, of course, ensure the adequacy of still-life arrangements. They must have a challenging variety of objects, in which there are various types of contrasting surfaces, such as the textures found in glass, fur, metal, cloth, and wood. Contrast in the shapes of objects must also be arresting. The other elements — line, space, light and shade, texture, and color — should also be considered for the variety they can bring to a still-life arrangement. As the objects are assembled, however, they should be brought together into a unified composition.

Once the objects of the still life have been selected and arranged, the teacher must establish some visual points of reference with which the pupils can work. These might include getting them to use objects that have inherent interest (masks, dolls, toys) and that have simple shapes.

1. Search for size relationships among various objects.

2. Concentrate on the edges of objects (contour drawing).

3. Use crayon to indicate shadows.

4. Use one object (an ink bottle, a wine bottle, a hammer) to arrange repeated shapes, overlapping portions of the object to obtain a pleasing flow.

5. Concentrate only on shape by drawing the forms, each on a different color paper, cutting them out, and pasting them on neutral-toned paper in overlapping planes.

6. Relate the objects to the size and shape of the paper. Students will find they can work on rectangular surfaces (12 by 18 inches), on squares, and even on circular shapes; they can draw small objects many times their size and reduce large objects to paper size.

In general, landscapes selected for outdoor painting or for preliminary studies to be finished in the classroom should have a reasonable number of objects in them that can be used as a basis for composition. Hence a scene with a barn, some animals, a silo, and some farm machinery is preferable to a sky and a wheatfield, or a lake and a distant shore. By having many objects before them, the pupils may select items that they think will make an interesting composition. The wheatfield or the lake may not give them enough material to draw. Children can be sent outside the classroom to bring back sketches of the environment for their classmates to identify. A simple homework assignment is to have the students bring in drawings of their homes that show the surrounding landscape.

The work in these activities need not be of long duration. Some pupils, however, may wish to produce a more finished work and, of course, should be encouraged to do so.

Contour Drawing as a Basis for Observation.   Contour-line drawing, which can be applied to landscape, figures, or objects, is considered by many educators to be a sound basis of perception. The contour approach

Self-portraits have a strong intrinsic appeal to students. Mirrors should be on the list of requests that teachers send to parents. This example is the work of a ten-year-old Chinese child.

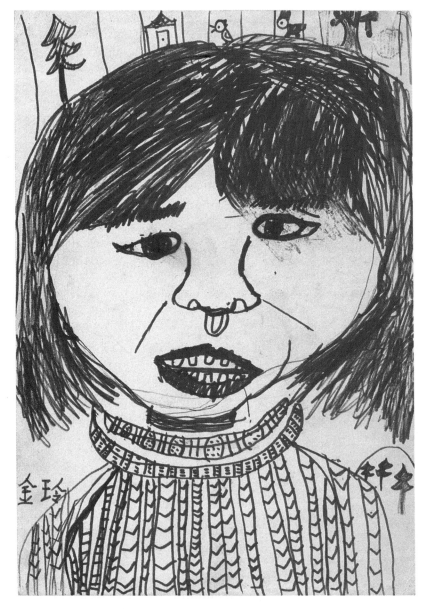

requires the children to focus their visual attention on the edges of a form and to note detail and structure; they are thus encouraged to move away from visual clichés to a fresh regard for subjects they may have lived with but never truly examined. The following teaching session demonstrates how one teacher went about introducing this method of drawing.

TEACHER: . . . I need someone . . . to pose. Michael, how about you? *(Michael is chosen because he is the tallest boy with the tightest pants. He will do very well for the purpose of the lesson. The teacher has him sit above eye level in a chair placed on a table.)* Now listen carefully. First, is there anyone here who is not able to draw a picture of Michael in the air by following the edge of his body with his finger? . . . Then let's try it. *(The teacher closes his right eye and slowly follows the outer edge of the subject in the air. The class follows, feeling fairly certain of success, at least at this stage.)* Very good. That wasn't too bad, was it?

PAUL: But that's not drawing.

TEACHER: Let's wait and see. Now, suppose I had a pane of glass hanging from the ceiling and some white paint. Couldn't you *trace* the lines in Michael's body right on the glass? *(They think about this for a moment.)* After all, it's the next thing to drawing a line in the air, isn't it?

ALICE: We don't have any glass.

TEACHER: True. I wish we did. But if we did you could do it, couldn't you? *(All agree they could.)* O.K. — then if you can follow the lines through the glass, you can *see* them. If I ask you to put them on your paper instead, what will your problem be?

ANDY: How can we look at Michael and at our paper at the same time?

TEACHER: Andy is right. We can't do it, so we just won't look at our paper. . . . May I show you what I mean? *(The class heartily approves of this. The teacher goes to the blackboard.)* Now, I'm not going to look at the blackboard because I'm more interested in training my eye than in making a pretty picture. I'm going to concentrate just on following the edge. Do you know what the word *concentrate* means? Who knows?

ALICE: To think very hard about something.

TEACHER: Exactly. So I'm going to think very hard — to concentrate — on the outside edges of Michael. We call this *contour-line drawing. (Writes it on blackboard.)* Contours are edges of shapes. You don't see *lines* in nature as a rule. . . . What you see mostly are dark shapes against light shapes, and where they meet you have *lines.* Who can see some in this room? *(Among those mentioned are where walls meet the ceiling, where books touch one another, and where the dark silhouette of the plants meets the light sky.)* Very good, you get the idea.

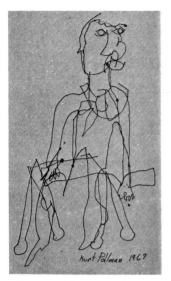

One type of contour drawing is this continuous contour of a figure by a fifth grader.

We start with edges — or contours — then. Another example is my arm. *(He puts it up against the blackboard.)* If I ask you to draw my arm from *memory*, you might come up with something that looks like this *(draws several schematic arms — a sausage shape, a stick arm, a segmented form divided into fingers, hand, forearm and upper arm divisions, and so on. The class is visibly amused).* Now, watch this carefully and see what happens when I concentrate on the contour of my arm. *(With his right hand he follows the top contour and the underside of his arm. As he removes his arm from the blackboard the class is delighted to see a line drawing of the teacher's arm remain on the board.)*

VERNON: I used to draw around my fingers that way.

TEACHER: Well, it's kind of hard to trace around every object you'll ever want to draw, and even if you could, would that teach you how to look?

VERNON: But you just did it on the blackboard.

TEACHER: What was I trying to show you?

ALICE: You were trying to show what the *eye* is supposed to do.

TEACHER: Exactly. I showed you what the eye must do *without* a subject to feel. What did the eye show me about my arm? *(The class notes wrinkles, the separation of shirtsleeve and wristwatch and hand.)* I'll bet you didn't realize there were so many dips and squiggles in just one arm, even without shading — that is, without dark and light. Once a contour drawing is finished, the eye fills *in between* the lines. Now, let me try Michael. *(As he draws he describes what is happening.)* Now, I'm starting at the top of his head, working down to his toe, I'm going up over the ear, down to the neck, and on to the collar. Now I move away, along the shoulder, and here the line turns down the arm. *(He continues in this manner until the line reaches the foot of the model and starts the process over again, moving the line down the opposite side of the figure.)*

The discussion points made by the teacher in the dialog were arrived at after careful study of the kinds of problems children face when attempting contour-line drawing. Their confusion arises in part from the necessity to coordinate eye and hand in analytic drawing skills. Because the contour-line drawing focuses on only one aspect of form — that of the edges of the subject — it cannot be expected that the relationship of parts will follow. This problem should be taken up as a second stage in the activity of contour-line drawing.

Developing Methods of Mixing Media. Children can mix media from an early age, so that by the time they reach the higher elementary grades they may achieve some outstandingly successful results by this means. The use of resist techniques, for example, is practical for preadolescents and tends to maintain their interest in their work. Scratchboard techniques may also be handled effectively by older pupils.

The technique of using resists relies on the fact that waxy media will shed liquid color if the color has been sufficiently thinned with water. A reasonably heavy paper or cardboard having a mat, or nonshiny, surface is required. Ordinary wax crayons are suitable and may be used with watercolor, thinned tempera paint, or colored inks. The last are particularly pleasant to use with this technique. In producing a picture, the pupil first makes a drawing with wax crayon and then lays down a wash of color or colors. To provide accents in the work, thicker paint or India ink may be used. The ink may be applied with either a pen or a brush, or with both tools.

In using a scratchboard, the pupil scratches away an overall dark coating to expose selected parts of an undersurface. Scratchboard may be either purchased or made by the pupils. If it is to be made, bristol board is probably the most desirable to use. The surface is prepared by covering the bristol board, or other glazed cardboard, with a heavy coat of wax crayons in light colors. A coating of tempera paint or India ink sufficiently thick to cover the wax should then be applied and left to dry. Later, the drawing may be made with a variety of tools, including pen points, bobby pins, scissors, and so on. A careful handling of black, white, and textured areas has highly dramatic effects.

The techniques described above are basic and may be expanded in several ways. For example, white wax crayon may be used in the resist painting, with paint providing color. Another resist technique is to "paint" the design with rubber cement and then float tempera or watercolor over the surface. The next day, the cement can be peeled off, revealing broken white areas against the color ground.

Lines in dark ink or tempera work well over collages of colored tissues, and rich effects can be obtained by covering thick tempera paintings with India ink and washing the ink away under a faucet. The danger of mixing media lies in a tendency toward gimmickry, but often the use of combined materials can solve special design problems. We should not consider these techniques as merely child's play. Many reputable artists have used them to produce significant drawings and paintings. Some of Henry Moore's sketches, for example, produced with wax and watercolor in the London air-raid shelters during World War II, are particularly noteworthy.[7]

Other forms of mixed media are as follows:

India ink and watercolor. The child may draw in ink first, then add color or reverse the procedure.

Watercolor washes over crayon drawings. This is a way of increasing an awareness of "negative space" or background areas.

Black tempera or India ink over crayon or colored chalk. Here the black paint settles in the unpainted areas. The student can wash away the paint, controlling the amount left on the surface of the colored areas.

THE DEVELOPMENT OF PICTORIAL COMPOSITION

Some assistance in pictorial composition must occasionally be offered if the children are to realize their goals of expression. This means that children should be helped toward an understanding of the meaning of design and a feeling for it, largely in connection with their general picture making. As they gain experience with the elements of design, children should be praised for any discoveries they make, and any obvious advances might be discussed informally by the class. Professional work emphasizing certain elements of design can be brought to the attention of even those pupils who are still in the early symbol stage. The works of Picasso, Matisse, Johns, Wyeth, Frankenthaler, and others may be viewed by children with much pleasure and considerable profit if related to their own acts of expression. The teacher should also use slides and originals of work by the children to demonstrate the possibilities of design on their own level for interaction between studio experience and critical skill.

As they grow older, children tend to become more concerned with certain elements of design than others. Somewhere around the fifth grade, preadolescents begin to incorporate shading in their pictures and to pay some attention to background details. It is then that they require more direct instruction in arriving at tonalities.

Form and Idea

Questions directed at the children are valuable for yielding visual information that can lead to more satisfactory picture making. When this technique is used, the teacher should try to establish the connection between *ideas* and *pictorial form*. This can begin when the children are at an early age by playing a *memory game*. Here the teacher simply draws a large rectangle on the chalkboard and asks someone in the class to draw a subject in the center, say a turtle. The teacher then draws a second rectangle next to the first and puts the same subject in it. What then follows is a series of questions about the turtle. The children answer the questions by coming up and adding details to the turtle in the second rectangle. As shapes, ideas, and forms are added, the picture becomes enriched and the space *around* the turtle is filled as a result of the information acquired. When the picture is finished the first one looks quite barren by comparison. The questions surrounding the subject might be posed as follows:

Q. Where does a turtle live?
A. In and around the water.
Q. How will we know it's water?
A. Water has waves and fishes.

Q. How will we know there is land next to the water?
A. There is grass, rocks, and trees.
Q. What does a turtle eat? Wheaties? Canned pineapple? Peanut but-
ter? What does he eat?
A. He eats insects, bugs.
A. He can eat his food from a can, too.
Q. Think hard now: Where are there interesting designs on a turtle?
A. On his shell. . . .

Composition is thus approached through the grouping and arranging of forms and ideas. As each answer provides additional visual information, the picture takes on a life of its own by the relation of
memory to drawing. The teacher can play this simple game with third
graders, and it can provide a way of thinking about picture making.

Another important task for the teacher is the development of a vocabulary of design terms. In all other subject areas, attention is paid to
the exact meanings of words. This has not always been the case in art
education, partly because the vocabulary of art in general has tended,
at times, to be nebulous, and partly because teachers have not always
used authoritative sources for a precise vocabulary of art terms.

Some teachers have been eminently successful in assisting children
to use words about design with precise meaning. They have done so,
of course, with due regard for the fact that art learning should not be
primarily verbal, but should consist of a balance of visual, cognitive,
and tactile experiences. These teachers have made sure that, if not at
first, then eventually the terms are used with understanding and precision. Thus, although the teacher might at first compliment a child on
the rhythmic flow of lines in a composition by saying that the quality of
line was like the "blowing of the wind," later the teacher would use the
word *rhythm*. In this incidental but natural manner the vocabulary of
even the youngest child can be developed.

If continual attention has been paid to vocabulary building, pupils
may develop a reasonably adequate command of art terms that will
enable them to participate in a more formal program of composition
and art appreciation. It is necessary for pupils to have a working vocabulary in art prior to the time they reach adolescence. At that period
in their development, they are often ready and eager to approach design in a more intellectual manner. Without a basic art vocabulary,
they will have difficulty engaging in the type of art activities their stage
of development requires. Memory, as the retention of form, is the ability to store experience and plays a much more important role in the
arts than most people realize.

Memory and Drawing

Actors must memorize their lines, musicians their notes, and orches-
tral conductors a complex array of instrumentation. Writers rely on

memory of their own personal histories, dancers display choreographic memory, and artists develop a kind of visual encyclopedia of images and forms that they have encountered. Most of us do this casually — on the run, so to speak — but the memory of an artist is trained as conscientiously as a pianist practices the scales. It is important that children become aware of the powers of their own memories in order to depict them later and to gain the insight that memory can give to their own sense of self. The process of "becoming" is more fulfilling if we retain some sense of continuity with former states of being.

If asked to work in the abstract, children rely on visual judgment, both conscious and intuitive. When asked to deal with a subject from their own lives, such as a visit to the doctor, they must deal not only with the memory of form but also with its surrounding knowledge. Preschool children are content with graphic symbols, but older children are often frustrated by their inability to capture memory and match it with form as they know it. To be able to recall the shape of a tractor and to describe it is one thing, but to find the right lines and shapes to depict it does not come as easily. Here are some suggestions to help children utilize their memories.

1. Divide the class into pairs, and have the children study their partners closely for two minutes. Everyone then turns around and makes some change or adjustment in clothing, hair, facial expression, and so on. Turning back to each other, the partners are asked to note the changes.

2. Before going on a field trip, discuss things to look for; call attention to shapes, patterns, colors; and tell the class before leaving that they will be expected to draw what they have seen. This will sharpen their perceptions.

3. Have each child in the class draw a scene from his or her neighborhood to send to a class in a foreign country. Remind the children that those receiving the collection may not read English and that art, as a universal language, will have to tell the story of life in their country.

4. Prepare a still life of contrasting shapes and have the class draw it from observation, putting in as many details as they can. Take the still life away and ask the children to draw it from memory. Check these drawings against the original. What was not included?

5. Ask the children to draw a picture of their very first memory of school. Again, they are to put in as many details as possible. How early can memory be pushed back? What details remain?

6. Take the class outside to study a tree or house. Discuss the characteristics that make the object special. Return to the classroom and draw the object from memory.

7. Have the children close their eyes. Describe a scene with which the class is familiar. Be precise with large things such as buildings and streets, and do not worry about details. Ask the children to build up the picture in their minds as it is described and then draw it or paint it.

8. Show a slide of a painting—one with a strong composition that is not too complex. Let the class study it for three minutes, then turn on the lights and ask them to draw it. Do this several times with pictures of increasing complexity of design.

9. Ask the children to pretend they are on the back of a giant bird who will fly them to school. How many street corners, stores, streets, and the like will they see from the air? Have them draw a diagram of the aerial view just as they would walk it.

10. To demonstrate how conscious a process memorization can be, have the children draw the entrance to their house, extending the doorway and its surroundings to both sides of the paper. Then ask the children to either draw the same subject from observation or to study it consciously with an eye for another memory drawing the following day.

WORKING WITH NARRATIVES: STORY TELLING

Another approach is exemplified in the studies by Wilson, Hurwitz, and Wilson.[8] Their emphasis is on narrative drawing, graphic storytelling, and the creation of new and exciting worlds by children. Their ideas have centered on the ways children learn to draw from the graphic models of other children, of adults, and of the media, and on the way children use their drawings to tell stories; stories that motivate them to depict people and action and events.

This five-frame story drawing collected by the Wilsons is an example of the influence of stories and images derived from the entertainment media. In response to a request to tell a story with drawings within the frame format, this sixth grader chose to represent a simple vignette based on a television commercial for a fast-food chain. Quite simply, the story deals with the typical advertising theme of initial deprivation and ultimate acquisition—the character in the story is suffering a "Big Mac attack." He breaks through the wall of the restaurant in his haste to obtain and eventually bite into the desired hamburger sandwich. Television has also taught the young boy the sophisticated devices of the closeup—witness the lusciously drippy, well-packed sandwich in the second frame—and the long shot—in the next frame—as well as the ability to zoom in and out of the action.

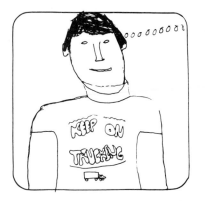

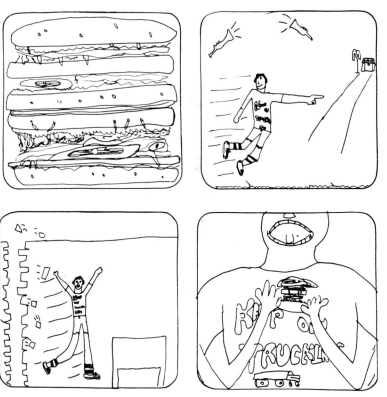

Children like to tell as well as listen to stories. Narrative art encourages both visual and ideational fluency. One picture becomes a beginning for an entire scenario rather than an end in itself, as one image and event set the stage for succeeding ones.

The writers have developed several methods for encouraging children to develop graphic skills. These skills are viewed as a graphic vocabulary and grammar, and they assist the child in producing drawings that are satisfying and meaningful. Following are several of the exercises:

1. Ask children to draw as many versions of a single object as possible. Examples might be different types of people, shoes, cars, trees, insects, and so on.

2. Ask children to think of a person, such as a dancer, acrobat, sports player, or superhero, who goes through lots of motions. On a long strip of paper, show the figure going through its action as it moves from side to side across the paper.

3. Ask the children to think about excesses and then to draw people who are very tall, very thin, situations that are too bad, too weird, and so on.

4. Using the concept of metamorphosis, ask children to start with one object, such as a car, and to gradually change it in a series of steps until it looks like something else, perhaps an elephant.

5. Ask children to draw a face, and then to draw the same face with a series of expressions, such as sad, happy, excited, or frightened.

◆ NOTES TO THE TEXT

1. Bernard Chaet, *The Art of Drawing* (New York: Holt, Rinehart & Winston, 1978).

2. In the use of all art materials and processes, teachers must take care to select safe materials for student use and to explicitly teach safe methods with appropriate health precautions.

3. See drawing books such as Janet Allen, *Drawing* (New York: Van Nostrand Reinhold, 1980); Bert Dodson, *Keys to Drawing* (Cincinnati: North Light Publishers, 1985); and Nathan Goldstein, *The Art of Responsive Drawing*, 3rd ed. (Englewood Cliffs, NJ: Prentice-Hall, 1984).

4. For a concise review of painting materials and techniques, see Jonathan Stephenson, *The Materials and Techniques of Painting* (New York: Watson-Guptill, 1989).

5. Pearl Greenberg recommends the use of models, still life, and landscape as early as the second grade in *Children's Experiences in Art* (New York: Reinhold, 1977).

6. L. A. Reid, *A Study in Aesthetics* (New York: Macmillan, 1931), p. 236.

7. See Henry Moore, *Shelter Sketch Book* (New York: Wittenborn, 1946).

8. Brent Wilson, Al Hurwitz, and Marjorie Wilson, *Teaching Drawing From Art* (Worcester, MA: Davis Publications, 1987), see Chapter 13.

◆ ACTIVITIES FOR THE READER

Teachers should be thoroughly familiar with the tools, media, and techniques they will use in the classroom. The following activities are suggested to help them gain this familiarity. Because knowledge of the processes of art, in this instance, is more important than the art produced, teachers should not feel hampered by technical inabilities. Experience with art media is what counts at this stage.

1. Using a large-bristle brush for broad work, paint in tempera an interesting arrangement of color areas on a sheet of dark paper. Try to develop varied textural effects over these areas in the following ways:

   a. *By using dry-brush*: Dip the brush in paint and rub it nearly dry on a piece of scrap paper. Then ''dry-brush'' an area where the new color will show.

   b. *By stippling*: Holding a nearly dry brush upright so that the bristles strike the paper vertically, stamp it lightly so that a stipple pattern of paint shows.

   c. *By brush drawing*: Select a sable brush and load it with paint. Paint a pattern over a color area with wavy or crisscrossed lines, small circles, or some other marks to give a rougher-looking texture than is found in surrounding areas.

   d. *By using powdered paint*: Apply liberal amounts of powdered paint mixed with very little water to your composition to obtain some rough areas (add sawdust or sand to liquid tempera if you have no powdered tempera).

   e. *By using a sponge*: Paint the surface of the sponge or dip it into the paint and rub the sponge on your composition.

   f. *By using a brayer*: Roll the brayer in paint and pull it over cut-paper forms. Experiment with the roller by using the edge or by wrapping string around it. Place small pools of color next to each other and pull the brayer over them, changing directions until you have blocks of broken color that lock into each other.

2. Select some objects you think are interesting and use them to make a still-life arrangement. Sketch the arrangement with wax crayons, using light, bright color where you see the highlights at their brightest, and using dark-colored crayons where you see the darkest shadows.

3. Using heavy drawing pencil, try to draw the following subjects in a strictly accurate, photographically correct manner. (Remember that lines below the horizon line rise to this level; lines above fall to this level; all lines meet at the horizon line.)

   a. A sidewalk or passageway as though you were standing in the center.

   b. A cup and saucer on a table below your eye level.

   c. A chimney stack, silo, or gas storage tank, the top of which is above your eye level.

   d. A group of various-sized boxes piled on a table or on the floor. (It is easier to draw if you first paint the boxes one unifying color, such as gray or white.)

4. Sketch a house or a collection of houses or other objects with crayon or heavy pencil, following the rules of linear perspective. In another drawing, rearrange the areas you drew to change the patterns of masses and spaces. Carry the lines through each other, taking liberties with the spaces between the lines. Notice how this freedom gives your picture more variety.

5. Have a friend pose for you. On manila or newsprint measuring at least 12 by 18 inches, make contour drawings in conté crayon or heavy pencil. Draw quickly, taking no longer than three to five minutes for each sketch. Do not erase mistakes—simply draw new lines. Make many drawings of this type based on standing, sitting, and reclining poses.

   Now begin to draw more carefully, thinking of places where bones are close to the surface and where flesh is thicker. Heavy pressure with the drawing medium will indicate shadows; the reverse will indicate light areas. Think also of the torso, the head, and the pelvic region as moving somewhat independently of each other. Begin to check body proportions.

Later make drawings with ink and a sable brush. Always work quickly and fearlessly. Try using some of the suggested visual references for drawing listed in the section "Sources of Observation."

6. Place yourself before a mirror for a self-portrait. Study the different flat areas, or planes, of your face. Notice the position of prominent features (especially eyes, which are about halfway between the top of your head and the bottom of your chin). Quickly draw a life-size head in charcoal, crayon, or chalk. When your features have become more familiar to you, try some other media, such as ink or paint. Try a self-portrait that is many times larger than life-size.

7. The formal exercises listed below express nothing and are valueless for children, but they can help you develop technique.

   a. Draw about a dozen 2-by-2-inch squares, one below the other. Paint the top square a standard hue; leave the bottom one white. Make a gradation of color areas ranging from the standard hue to white by progressively adding white to the standard hue. The "jumps" between areas should appear even.

   b. Repeat a, using some other hues. Use transparent watercolor as well as tempera for some exercises, adding water instead of white paint to the watercolor pigment.

   c. Repeat, this time adding the complementary color to the first one chosen. Now the gradations will go from standard to gray rather than to white.

   d. Add black progressively to a standard hue to obtain twelve "jumps" from standard to black.

   e. Try shading about six 3-inch-square areas with conté crayon, charcoal, or heavy pencil so that you progress from very light gray to very dark gray.

   f. Draw textures in four 3-inch-square areas so that each square appears "rougher" than the next. Crisscrossed lines, wavy lines, circles, dots, and crosses are some devices to use. India ink and a writing pen are useful tools in this exercise.

   g. Using the side of a crayon, take a series of "rubbings" from such surfaces as wood, sidewalks, rough walls, and so on. Create a design using the rubbings you have collected.

◆ SUGGESTED READINGS

Chaet, Bernard. *An Artist's Notebook*. New York: Holt, Rinehart & Winston, 1979. Discussion of materials and techniques for drawing and painting, beautifully illustrated with reproductions of the works of many great artists.

————. *The Art of Drawing*. New York: Holt, Rinehart & Winston. A course in drawing with projects and exercises for teaching, profusely illustrated with drawings by professional artists and students.

Dobin, Jay. *Perspective: A New System for Designers*. New York: Hill and Wang, 1957. The fundamentals of linear perspectives.

Edwards, Betty. *Drawing on the Right Side of the Brain*. Los Angeles: J. P. Tarcher, 1979. This book illustrates a number of time-tested drawing exercises for beginning and intermediate students.

Goldsmith, Lawrence C. *Watercolor Bold and Free*. New York: Watson-Guptill, 1980. Beautifully illustrated in color, this book presents paintings by many watercolorists in a variety of styles. Each painting exemplifies a different painting lesson explained in the text.

McFee, June King, and Degge, Rogena M. *Art, Culture, and Environment*. Belmont, CA: Wadsworth, 1977. Part I, "Seeing to Draw and Drawing to See."

Nicolaides, Kimon. *The Natural Way to Draw*. Boston: Houghton Mifflin, 1941. The classic drawing text that presents the author's sound and successful approach to drawing instruction.

Wilson, Brent, Al Hurwitz and Marjorie Wilson. *Teaching Drawing from Art*. Worcester, MA: Davis Publications, 1987.

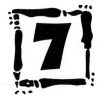

SCULPTURE
AND
CERAMICS:
ART IN
THREE
DIMENSIONS

CREATING WORKS OF art in three dimensions is of particular significance. Human beings experience the world in three dimensions. Men, women, and children establish scale in accordance with their own bodies. Each of us is three dimensional in a three-dimensional world.[1]

Wayne Higby

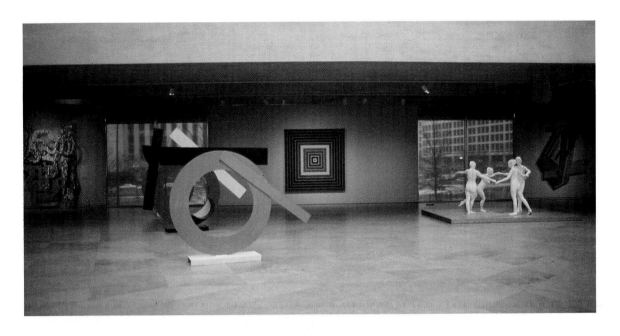

Drawing and painting, as previously examined in Chapter 6, are accomplished primarily on two-dimensional surfaces, usually paper, canvas, or board. Art that extends into the third dimension includes sculpture and ceramics, which in some ways overlap as art modes. Some sculpture, for example, is made of fired clay and can be considered as ceramic sculpture. Ceramics includes pottery made of fired clay and even in this area there is overlap with sculpture, as some pots exhibit fine sculptural qualities, some are purposely nonfunctional, and sometimes pots are used as components in sculpture. Ceramic pottery is an ancient art mode and also one of the most universal, as pots are found that were created far back in time and in all parts of the world. Sculpture is discussed first in this chapter, with attention paid to media and methods for its creation and suggestions for teaching children and young people about sculpture. Discussion of ceramics follows, with special attention to the area of pottery, and including references to historical and critical learning that accompany the making of ceramics.

SCULPTURE: MODELING, CARVING, AND CONSTRUCTING

When we consider the beginnings of sculpture we think of very ancient, even prehistoric, examples that were created before the great sculptures from Egypt that date back nearly six thousand years. Yet the art of sculpture continues today as one of the most highly respected and dynamic of the art modes. Sculpture is often classified as either free-standing or relief. Free-standing sculpture, or sculpture in the round, is the type that can be viewed from many angles, such as a statue of a person or animal that a person might walk around. Relief sculpture is usually viewed from the front, like a painting, and is often seen on walls or other surfaces that cannot be viewed from behind.

As is the case with all significant works of art, sculptures reflect ideas, values, and practices of the artists who created them and the societies and cultures to which the artists belong. Ancient Egyptian

This stone sculpture is nearly 4,500 years old. The larger figure represents an Egyptian king and the smaller one an Egyptian deity, juxtaposing political authority and religious beliefs in one artwork. Children can learn about such cultural contexts and the purposes of artworks in order to better understand and appreciate them. (The Metropolitan Museum of Art, New York.)

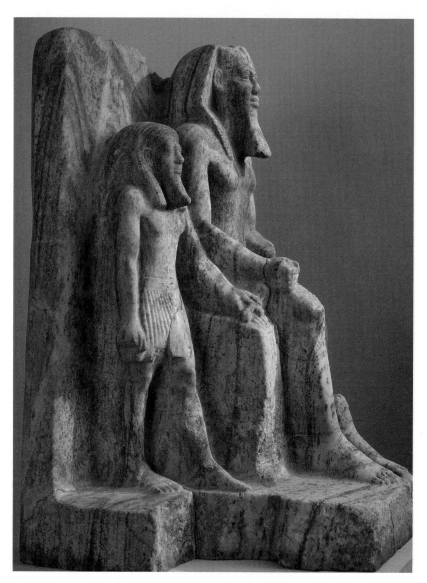

art, for example, was commissioned by the powerful rulers of the time and served purposes profoundly influenced by the religious beliefs of the culture. In contrast, contemporary art is influenced by the individuality of artists. Yet even the highly individual work of today's sculptors reflects the society in which they live. These relationships can be seen in the carved wooden figures of the Yoruba peoples of Nigeria, the bronze sculptures of sacred bulls from India, and the mobiles (moving sculptures) of Calder that, incidently, add another category to sculpture — that which moves while the viewer remains stationary.

Modeling, carving, and construction are typical processes involved in making sculpture. Modeling involves building up a form from material, such as clay, and then adding and shaping the material. For example, when modeling a head in clay, the basic form is modeled and then more clay is added and shaped to develop the nose, hair, ears, and other features. *Modeling*, then, is usually an additive process. *Carving* is typically a subtractive process in which the material, such as wood or plaster, is carved or chipped away until the desired sculptural form emerges. Sculpture also involves a process of *constructing*, in which the materials are cut or shaped or found, and bound together with appropriate materials. Welded metal, nailed or glued wood, and a limitless array of materials, from sheet plastic and glass to driftwood and junk, can all be used to construct sculpture. Constructing is usually an additive process.

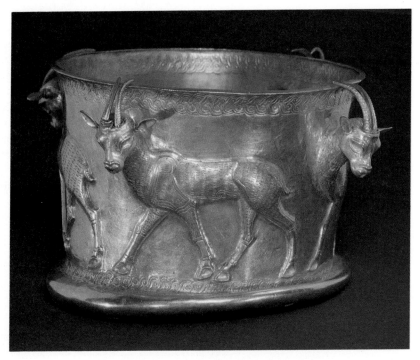

This very old and beautiful gold cup, made in Iran about 3,000 years ago, is an example of relief sculpture. The gazelles can be seen only from one side, although their heads and horns are actually "in the round." The cup is also an example of a utilitarian object that has been raised to the level of fine art by its decorative and sculptural work. (The Metropolitan Museum of Art, New York.)

Today's art requires a rather broad definition of sculpture, one that takes into account the mixed-media approach and the interrelation of art and technology. "Shaped canvases" can be viewed as painted sculpture or as painting that moves into space. In assemblage, artists create unusual contexts for mundane "found objects." The pop artist Marisol combines whimsical and traditional drawing with carved and geometric forms. Jean Tinguely animates his constructions with intricate mechanical devices; other artists experiment with sound and light as components of the total sculptural experience. Because children respond positively to many of the concepts inherent in sculpture today, problems of both a traditional and a contemporary nature should be considered when planning activities that are built around forming, shaping, and constructing.

In the traditional sense, carving and modeling are activities in which raw materials from the earth and the forest are directly manipulated by the artist. In modeling, artists may approach clay with few tools other than their bare hands, while in carving wood and other media, a tool as primitive as a knife allows artists to pit their skill against the material. If the artist shows respect for it, the primary characteristics of the original material remain in the finished product. Wood remains wood, clay remains clay, and each substance clearly demonstrates its influence on the art form into which it was fashioned.

Children in all stages of development can work successfully in modeling clay and in one or another form of wood sculpture. Only older preadolescents, however, are able to carve wood and plaster of paris, since the skills involved are beyond the ability of younger children and some of the tools required are too dangerous for them to use. It is important when considering the appropriateness of art activities for various grade levels to make a distinction between *media* and *techniques*. Instead of arbitrarily relegating any one type of material to a particular grade level, the teacher should examine the material in terms of the specific problem to be explored. While it is true that the range of manual control varies with the age of the children, there are some techniques associated with a particular medium that are within the children's capability on every grade level. For instance, even elementary school children engaged in making animal figures can be encouraged to "pull out the shapes" and to "piece the figure together so that the parts don't fall off." They can practice maintaining uniform thickness of the side of a pinch pot and can press patterns of found objects into clay tiles. These ideas might be presented to the children with such remarks as:

"There are many ways of making sculpture. As all artists do, choose the one that is most comfortable for you."

"Some kinds of modeling (or sculpture) require practice, just like learning a musical instrument or handling a ball. It may be difficult at first, but practice will help you to make something that you will want to keep."

"Even a flat piece of sculpture (relief) can be made to catch light. Then it will make interesting surface patterns."

"There is an animal form trapped in this piece of clay. Can you help it come out, so we can see what it is?"

Sculpture has a universal appeal, and the problems of creating forms in space and of welding materials and processes to ideas engages the interest of people of all age groups. Indeed, the ideas discussed in this chapter are as useful to senior high school or even college students as they are to elementary school students. The children who make their first papier-mâché masks and the team of teenagers involved in carving totemic figures out of discarded telephone poles can benefit equally from the practical suggestions found here.

Sculpture can be taught using simple materials, such as paper or boxes or wood blocks, to more sophisticated and difficult materials and techniques, such as those required for wood carving. Ceramic clay methods can be taught to all age groups.

SCULPTURE WITH PAPER

Paper is one of the most accessible, least expensive, and versatile materials for the making of art. Not only is paper used as a surface on which to draw, paint, print, and make collage, but it is an art medium in its own right. Paper can be cut into intricate patterns, built into sturdy and detailed sculptures; it can be cut, folded, expanded, curled, twisted, torn, rolled, laminated, creped, and scored. The art world has undergone a resurgence in the use of paper as a medium of artistic expression. Prominent artists such as Louise Nevelson, Frank Stella, and Sam Gilliam have produced works of art from handmade paper.[2]

Because paper has so many uses as a medium of art expression, there are no firm rules about when paper work should be offered in the art program. Paper can be used in sculpture or as part of a mixed media process. The teacher should encourage children to test paper and to get some sense of its special qualities of strength, tension, and resilience. Children should learn that if they tear paper, it offers little resistance; yet if they pull it, another kind of force is involved. The many different types of paper, from heavy cardboard to delicate rice paper, and its numerous forms, such as boxes, cans, cups, and cartons, make paper an ideal medium for experimentation by children. More sophisticated paper projects continue to interest children even into their adolescent years. The fact that mature artists use paper as a medium lends validity and integrity to its use in the school art program.

Box Sculpture

Media and Techniques. Probably the simplest type of sculpture for very young children is that made with paper or cardboard boxes. The only supplies necessary are an assortment of small cardboard containers, masking tape or other sticky paper tape, and possibly white glue. Tempera paint and suitable brushes can also be supplied. The containers should vary in shape and range in size from, say, about one inch to one foot on each side. If possible, cardboard tubes of different diameters and lengths and perhaps a few empty thread spools should also be provided.

The beginning of this activity is very much like building with blocks. Young children are able to innovate and learn as they stack the boxes and watch them tumble down. Then the children can use masking tape to secure the paper containers and build a permanent structure. For a more stable sculpture, children can glue the boxes and secure them with tape until the glue dries.

Young children delight in gluing containers together to build shapes at random, and later they like to paint them. As might be expected, they first build without apparent plan or subject matter in mind. Very quickly, however, children begin to name their constructions. "This is a bridge," says five-year-old Peter to his classmates, describing an object that faintly resembles such a structure. "This is my dad's factory," says Arthur, who has placed a chimneylike object on top of a box. "I guess it's a castle," says Mary, describing a gaily painted construction. This parallels the naming stage in drawing that occurs at an earlier age. Soon children begin to make plans before starting their work. One child might decide to make a boat; another, to construct a house, paint it red, and build a garden around it. Thus, when working in sculpture, children tend to progress through the usual stages of manipulation and symbolic expression.

Teaching. For children in the manipulative stage, little teaching is required apart from the usual general encouragement and an attempt to keep the children free of glue and paint. In the symbol stage, the children should have ample opportunity to discuss their symbols with the teacher and with one another. In this way their work will grow in clarity and completeness. The teacher should encourage children in this stage to add significant details in cut paper and in paint.

Older children, in the preadolescent stage, construct marvelous sculptural forms using paper containers. These sculptures can become quite large—taller than the young artists—and still remain lightweight and easy to move. The teacher can provide motivation by showing pictures or slides of sculpture. Modern, nonobjective, or abstract sculptures interest children and, at the same time, expose them to the real world of art. The sculptural forms of other cultures can be studied; for example, the monumental sculpture of ancient Egypt or the abstract forms of African carvings. The following text describes how to implement a paper sculpture project based on the totem poles of the Indians of North America.

The teacher might begin by asking students what they know about totem poles; where they are found, how large they are, what they are made of, and what their purposes are. The teacher can supply information that is not forthcoming in the discussion or can assign individuals or groups of students to investigate and report. Pictures of totem poles can be shown, studied, and discussed. When the children have become sufficiently knowledgeable about totem poles to understand a related project, the teacher suggests that they make totem poles out of paper and cardboard containers. Depending on the ages of the group and the level of detail desired by the teacher, the children might begin planning totem poles based on ideas learned through their studies of Northwest coast Indians. They might give symbolic meaning to each figure and a definite order for the figures from bottom to top just as real totems have. In such a project, it is often desirable to encourage the children to work in groups of three or four.

The students begin construction by gathering a variety of rectangular, round, and unusually shaped containers and stacking them to create a pole-like form. Flexible cardboard can be cut and shaped into tubes, triangular forms, and so on, according to need. The pieces are taped together as the pole takes shape. At this point the class should decide what holes and notches to cut with a knife or scissors to make facial features, and what shapes to add to make wings, arms, headpieces, fabricated from paper and taped onto the pole.

When the basic pole is completed, surface decorations of cut colored paper can be glued on or tempera paint applied. The entire construction and decoration can follow a traditional Indian theme or can be a contemporary example of the totem concept. The results are often striking and impressive in their size and visual presence. In this type of project, children learn not only about an art medium, design, and technique, but also about the art of another culture.

Other Freestanding Forms

Children in the upper elementary grades find other freestanding forms of paper sculpture challenging. The supplies required for such sculpture include the usual scissors, knife, construction paper, and cardboard; odds and ends of colored paper, tape, and glue; and a vast array of miscellaneous articles such as drinking straws, toothpicks, and pins with colored heads.

The chief problem in developing freestanding forms in paper lies in the necessity to develop a shape that will support the completed object. A tentlike form is perhaps the first such shape children will devise. Later they may fashion a paper tube or cone strong enough to

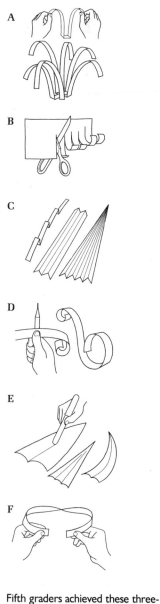

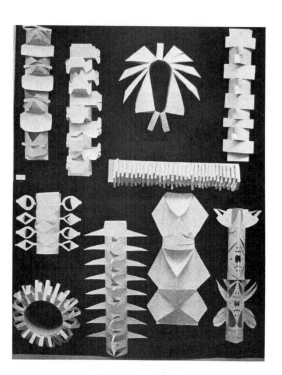

Fifth graders achieved these three-dimensional effects by cutting, scoring, and folding. (Photo by Rick Steadry). Above are some ways of developing three-dimensional forms in paper: (A) folding and bending, (B) frilling, (C) pleating, (D) stretching, (E) scoring, and (F) twisting.

support whatever details they plan to add. In constructing a figure, for example, the children might make a cylinder of paper for the head, body, and legs. The arms might be cut from flat paper and glued to the sides of the cylinder. A hat could be made in a conical shape from more paper. Details of features and clothing might then be added with either paint or more paper.

Media and Techniques. For preadolescent children, it is practical to use rolled paper to construct objects. Old newspapers may be used together with glue, tape, and sometimes wire. Children who begin this work obviously must possess some ability to make plans in advance of production. Their plans must include an idea of the nature and size of the object to be fashioned. What will be its general shape? When this is decided, the underlying structure is easily developed. When making a human figure, for example, arms, legs, body, and head may all be produced from rolled newspapers. A chief component, say, the body, should be taped at several places and other components taped to it. Should one part of the creation tend to be flimsy because of extreme length, it can be reinforced by wire or strips of cardboard or wood.

When the main structure is complete, it is strengthened by carefully wrapping one-inch-wide strips of newspaper, dipped in art paste, around all parts of the object—until it looks like an Egyptian mummy. While it is still wet, the children can add details, such as eyes, ears, and

Sculpture with boxes and bags turns into costume as these eleven-year-olds turn themselves into robots for a school play. The simple processes of pasting, joining, painting, and collage can be used to create sculpture, stage properties, or costumes.

nose made of other objects. When dry, the creation may be painted and covered with shellac or varnish. Wheat paste is not recommended because of possible allergic reactions, the difficulty in storing the wheat paste and water solution, and its attraction for insect and animal pests. The vinyl wallpaper pastes are generally superior to wheat paste.

Teaching. The teacher will often find it necessary to resort to demonstrations of the techniques involved in general freestanding paper sculpture and rolled-paper sculpture. *It is important that teachers always try art projects themselves before introducing them to students.* This is the best way to anticipate problems and the need for demonstrations. As a project progresses, teachers should observe each pupil and be ready to make suggestions, so that an otherwise impractical improvisation in a paper technique can be successfully altered.

As the pupils gain experience, the teacher must emphasize the necessity of making reasonably detailed plans in advance. The pupils might make sketches of the basic shape of a figure so that it can be accurately cut out. Even a sketch of a rolled-paper figure in which some indication of proportions and reinforcement points is given is occasionally helpful. In fact, the pupils and teacher together might well go through all stages of using a medium in advance of individual construction.

Papier-Mâché. Papier-mâché, or mashed paper, has been used as a modeling medium for centuries. Chinese soldiers of antiquity are said

Because paper is both versatile and inexpensive, papier-mâché can be used to create large forms. Papier-mâché can be draped or pressed on any surface, from balloons to modeled clay. It can also be squeezed into soft pulp and modeled very much like clay. When dry, it can be lifted off the base and painted.

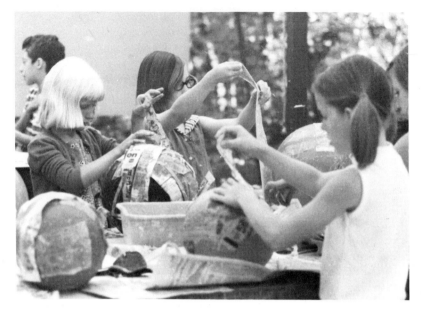

to have made their armor with this material. Mashed paper is strong and may be put to many uses in an art class. To prepare this claylike medium, tear newsprint into small pieces. (Do not use magazine paper with a glazed surface, because fibers do not break down as readily into a mash.) Leave the torn paper to soak overnight in water. It is possible to use an electric blender to mash the paper in water, but is not necessary. Instead, mash the paper in a strainer to remove the water, or wring it in a cotton cloth. Four sheets of newspaper shredded will need four tablespoons of white glue as a binder. Stir until the pulp has a claylike consistency. If desired, a spoonful of linseed oil can be added for smoothness and a few drops of oil of cloves or wintergreen as a preservative. This mixture can be wrapped in plastic and stored in the refrigerator. The teacher can also purchase commercially prepared mixtures of papier-mâché that require only the addition of water.

Children in the manipulative stage can roll papier-mâché and pummel it; in the symbol stage they can produce three-dimensional forms with it — shapes of different fruits, for example. Preadolescent children can learn to control the medium further and model sculptured pieces. After the mashed paper has dried — a process that takes about a week — it can be worked with hand tools. The dried papier-mâché forms can be sandpapered; holes can be bored in it; it can be carved and painted. Acrylic paint is particularly useful both for its brilliant color and its protective qualities. Objects painted with other types of paint should be shellacked if possible.

SCULPTURE IN WOOD

Using Scraps of Wood

Children can handle wood in many ways. Odd shapes can be glued into structures just as they are, or they can be adjusted by carving, sawing, and planing. The surface of the wood in turn can be left as is, or it can be painted or stained. Surfaces can also be sanded smooth or "pebbled" with carving tools; edges can be rounded with a file or plane. The options for design in wood, as in painting, are many, the only limitations being the child's manual control and the tools available.

Media and Techniques. If access to an industrial arts shop in a nearby secondary school is available, the teacher may obtain scraps of wood varying in shape and size. These scraps should be inspected to see that they have no dangerous splinters. In addition to scraps of wood the children might be supplied with tongue depressors, swab sticks, and wooden spools. To fix pieces of wood together, use a particularly strong glue such as white vinyl, which can be purchased at any hardware store. *As with all materials used to make art, care should be exercised for the health and safety of students and teachers.* Avoid glues that might have toxic fumes, and be wary of fast-sticking glues that can stick fingers or objects together.

Children in the manipulative and symbol stages put together pieces of wood much as they put together the boxes and tubes in box sculpture. They select two pieces of wood, smear both with glue along the edges to be stuck, and then press them firmly together. If hammers and nails are available, children can nail together the pieces of wood to make a strong, permanent bond. The process is continued until several pieces of wood form one solid structure. A swab stick or a tongue depressor can be used to apply the glue. After assembling the pieces, children often like to paint their structures. A complex piece, composed of eight or nine wood scraps varying in size and shape, can be given unity through the addition of a single color or through color patterns that correspond to sharply articulated planes. Whereas older children may use paint and sculpture to solve a problem in design, younger children may color surfaces only for decoration. Relating the activity to the works of adult sculptors can help the children understand the significance of making sculpture.

Sculpture in the Round

Media and Techniques. Only older preadolescent children, usually in about the fifth and sixth grades, will be able to produce wood sculpture in the traditional manner. Traditional wood sculpture consists of carving bumps and hollows in a suitable piece of wood. Very hard woods like oak are not suitable for children's work since they may demand more strength than children possess, and offer more opportunities for accidents.

Wherever possible, woods from the local environment should be selected. By using local wood, children explore their immediate environment and capitalize on their own resources. Wood from poplars, pines, birches, and many other trees, when seasoned, has excellent qualities for sculpture. Lumber yards often sell suitable scraps of these woods. If the wood is damp, it should be stacked under cover outdoors until it dries. Wind dries the wood, and stacking prevents it from warping.

Sets of carving tools may be bought that allow children to produce a wide variety of cuts. These tools are obtainable in a number of shapes, such as straight-edged knives, V-gouges, and U-gouges. All tools should be kept sharp. In addition, some files, rasps, and sandpaper, from coarse to fine grain, may be required.

Wood can be cut on a piece of plywood placed over a school desk, but wood sculpture is best performed on an industrial arts (carpenter's) bench. These benches usually are fitted with vises that allow the student to place both hands on the cutting tools. (Without a vise, the student must hold the wood with one hand and carve with the other. Unless great care is exercised injuries can occur.) In general, the wood should be cut in the direction away from the body. Rough two-by-four strips bolted to the side of the work table will provide a protective surface against which pupils who work without a vise can carve. This permits students to sit while carving.

The method of working with wood recommended here is that of "roughing out" the subject from all sides. The student holds the wood in one hand and presses it against the bench, or places it in the vise, if one is available, while applying the carving tool along the grain. Turning the piece and cutting, the student gets rid of excess wood until the desired shape begins to be formed. Rasps—very coarse files—may be used at the close of the roughing-out process if the vise is used. The

This wood sculpture by Louise Nevelson, *Case With Five Balusters*, 1959, demonstrates the rhythmic possibilities of wood as a medium. (Courtesy of The Pace Gallery, New York.)

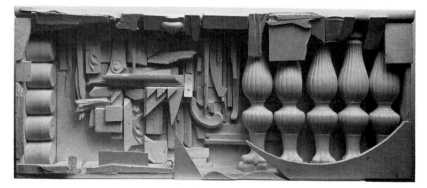

sculpting-in-the-round approach allows the student to create a solid, chunky piece of sculpture that is attractive in its "woodiness." Soap may be used as a preliminary activity to acquaint students with the idea of "roughing out" the basic shape.

The piece must be finished with some care, so that neither the design nor the inherent quality of the wood is spoiled. For a smooth finish, the student can use a rasp followed by a file and later by sandpaper on the surface. Wood usually requires the application of a preservative; perhaps the most acceptable is wax. A thin coat of solidified wax can be applied with a cloth and then polished vigorously. Successive coats should follow until the wood glows. A thin oil stain might occasionally be employed to enhance the wood, but this preservative should be used with caution. For one thing, it is often difficult to maintain a desired uniformity of tone because of the effect of the grain of the wood. Also, a bright stain may distort the natural appearance of the wood. Too often, a fine white wood can be spoiled by the application of a "mahogany" stain. Other than wax, perhaps the safest and most satisfactory finishes for wood are clear varnish and colorless shellac, both of which may be applied with a brush. In short, unless the wood is to be painted, nothing is better than the quality of wood itself.

Teaching. Sculpture in wood affords many opportunities for effective teaching; in particular it calls for discussion, demonstration, and reference to the history of sculpture. Wood is a medium with many excellent qualities that must not be destroyed through clumsy and inappropriate working techniques. The teacher's first task is to discuss with the class the fine qualities of wood—its color; its grain; its various surface qualities enhanced by different finishes, including sanding, waxing, and painting. Studies might be made of the various uses to which wood may be put and of how people have often relied on it to develop civilization. It is always useful to show children examples of good quality art done by adult artists and to discuss the works with them. This is especially true if pieces can be found that exemplify and illustrate the goals set by the teacher, such as respecting the natural properties of the material and allowing the material to contribute to the total expressiveness of the sculpture. Viewing and discussing art can also assist children to clarify the artistic purposes in their own work. The teacher will also find it necessary to discuss the subject matter suitable for wood sculpture. Making references to sculpture in wood, from medieval German sculptors to moderns such as Louise Nevelson, will teach students that sculpture is a form of expression as personal as painting. In addition to suggesting expression based on representational themes such as animals, the teacher might encourage students to do some nonobjective work such as the "feelies" shown on page 202.

Wood scultpure made by sixth graders. These objects are similar to the "feelies" of the Bauhaus school. They provide a basic lesson in the various stages of wood sculpture—shaping, filing, sanding, and staining. "Feelies" can also be made of clay or soap. (Photo by Royal Studio.)

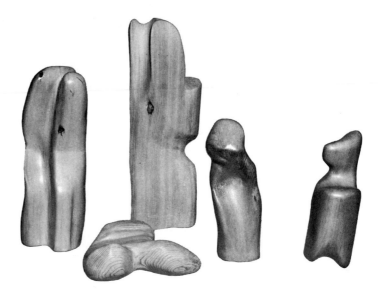

Because most tools for working with wood are dangerous, the teacher should demonstrate the correct ways of handling them and discuss safety in using tools. The teacher should give lessons concerning the sharpening and care of tools, emphasizing the pride good artisans have in their tools. A class trip to a sculptor's studio would be very worthwhile. A suitable project as this point might be the making of "feelies," small, highly polished carved objects designed to feel good in the hand.[3] Before working with wood itself, it might be a good idea for children to experiment with clay and soap to find out how material can relate to the hand. Because the "feelie" is hand-sized, the student has no difficulty giving the wood a high finish by sawing, filing, sanding, polishing, and waxing.

As the children work in wood, they should be taught that the bumps, hollows, and textures they have carved must be studied for the patterns of light and shade they produce. By holding a child's sculpture in a reasonably strong light coming from one source, the teacher can demonstrate how to study the highlights and shadows. As in other art forms, it is far more important for children to learn to judge the quality of sculpture from the point of view of design than to judge it for its "realistic" appearance.

As in painting, teachers should use a reference to an artist when stressing a concept. For example, Henry Moore's works can be used to clarify the relationship between art and nature. The hollows and protuberances of Moore's work are three-dimensional treatments of the positive and negative spaces used by painters.

SCULPTURE IN PLASTER OF PARIS

For most children in the preadolescent stage, a suitable medium for sculpture is plaster of paris. A child who is capable of using any kind of cutting tool safely can use this material successfully. Plaster of paris can produce sculpted pieces displaying satisfying qualities either in relief or in the round.

Media and Techniques.   The plaster is usually bought in sacks. It should be mixed by sifting handfuls of the plaster into a pail of water until the plaster reaches the water level. The mixture should then be activated by sliding the hand under the plaster and moving the fingers around the bottom of the pail. This attains a creamy consistency without lumps. Waterproof gloves or other protection prevents possible skin reactions to the plaster. If the plaster tends to dry too quickly, the rate of drying may be slowed by adding about a teaspoonful of salt for every two cups of plaster.

After it is mixed with water, the plaster must be poured quickly into a mold to dry and harden. Small cardboard containers such as milk cartons make suitable molds. (Children may also create their own molds by taping sections of heavy cardboard together.) The container is selected according to the type of work intended; a shoe box, for example, might have the right length and height for a plaque on which a relief sculpture could be carved, and a carton that held a large tube of toothpaste would serve as a mold for plaster to be carved in the round. When the plaster dries, which it does with extraordinary rapidity, it contracts slightly so that the cardboard is easily peeled away.

Plaster may be combined with other materials, thus allowing for a choice in the degree of density. Students can mix, in various proportions, plaster, vermiculite, sawdust, dirt, and sand. Samples of these aggregates might be prepared and records kept of the degrees of hardness, kinds of texture, and so on that are obtainable with different proportions. Students might want to add some tempera for color and thus create truly personalized carving media.

The techniques used in cutting plaster are somewhat less difficult for children than those used with wood. Almost any cutting tool may be used on plaster—pocketknives, woodworking tools, or linoleum cutters. Even worn-out dentist's tools can be used. No special accommodation is necessary for this work; the cutting can be done on an old drawing board. When cutting is satisfactorily completed, the plaster should be lightly rubbed with fine sandpaper to obtain smooth surfaces where they are desired.

Another method of working with plaster is to dip surgical bandages or strips of cloth into plaster and drape them over armatures or other substructures. Rolls of plaster-infused gauze used for medical casts are excellent for this method. The sculptor George Segal has been responsible for a whole new direction in art with his plaster body-castings placed in complete environments.

Plaster is one of the most versatile and least expensive of all art media. It does require more preparation and cleanup than many other activities, but it lends itself to working outdoors. Considerable care must be taken to keep the classroom floor clean, preferably with a damp cloth or mop to avoid making dust. If plaster bits are walked on they are ground into powder and, when stirred up by activity, can cause an unhealthy breathing environment. Students leaving an untidy room after working with plaster can be identified by the trail of white footprints. Plaster and wood are in themselves two very good reasons for separate art rooms in all schools.

Teaching. Because this medium is easier to cut than wood, demonstration need occupy relatively little time. Students often require more assistance in preparing the plaster than they do in working with it. The teacher should be sure that the children know what their subject matter and technique will be before they mold their plaster. Low relief requires a flat slab, while sculpture in the round requires a block of plaster. Obviously, once the plaster is molded the children are committed to work that suits the shape of the material. As for carving, the suggestions made earlier about wood carving are generally applicable to the problems that arise in working with plaster of paris.

Girl Putting on Her Shoe, 1968, one of George Segal's plaster body-castings placed in its own environment. Since it appears to be an exact replica, the teacher may have to justify it as art. Segal's pieces, like all sculpture, are transformations, not replicas—they bring about distinctive changes in their surrounding area. (Collection of Mr. and Mrs. William Paley, New York. Courtesy, Sidney Janis Gallery, New York.)

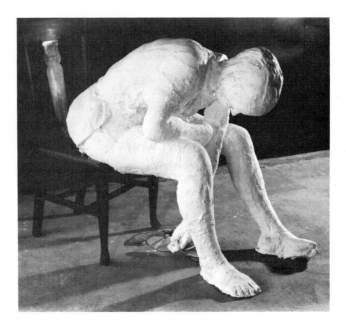

CERAMICS: ART FROM EARTH AND FIRE

The field of ceramics is very broad, including the ancient pottery of many cultures, ceramic sculpture, and contemporary commercial, industrial, and studio pottery. The ceramics industry influences our lives on a daily basis through production of many items from ordinary cups and plates to fine china and industrial items such as insulators and tiles that are used for space vehicles. However, it is the part of the ceramics industry that involves artistic expression that interests us here. Contemporary ceramic artists work with clay to produce sculptures and studio potters make a wide range of hand-built and wheel-thrown utilitarian items.

Taking clay from the earth, shaping it, decorating it, and firing it is a very old and very basic profession that is often passed down as a legacy within families. Well-known Pueblo Indian potter Margaret Gutierrez explained how she learned the ceramic art.

> Our great-great-grandfather, Ta-Key-Sane, was the one who created or started this kind of pottery, a long time ago. When my great grandfather passed away, my grandfather took over except this time my grandmother was making the pottery and my grandfather did the designing. By this time my father, Van, was old enough to travel with my grandfather into the hills and mountains hunting game for food, but at the same time they would be hunting for clay of different colors; and also for flowers and roots for paints which would turn into different colors when fired. By the time my father was ten years of age, he was helping to design pottery, but he could also make pottery.[4]

Margaret and her brother Luther learned the secrets of this style of pottery from their father and continue to develop their tradition and

These dynamically designed pots are handmade by native Americans at the Acoma pueblo in New Mexico. The technique and style of potterymaking is passed down within the families for generations. Design terms that apply here are contrast, rhythm, and pattern.

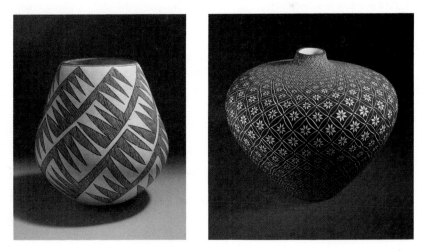

pass it on to the next generation. The work of Pueblo potters is highly prized as a relatively pure cultural expression and as finely crafted, beautifully expressive works of art. They are collected and displayed by museums of art and other serious art collectors.

As children make ceramics objects, either sculptural or utilitarian, they will also learn about contemporary ceramic artists and about ceramics from other cultures past and present. They will also have opportunities to discuss their own clay work and the work of professional artists. According to Edmund Feldman, the art of critical examination is essential for full understanding of clay objects because "we have to find out how they work practically, expressively, and symbolically in our lives."[5]

MODELING WITH CLAY

Modeling is an activity in which children in all stages of development may participate. Clay has been a standard modeling medium in the schools for many years because it is inexpensive and easily manipulated.

Media and Techniques.   Clay may be purchased or it may be found in the ground in some localities, especially along lakes, bays, or small creeks. Any slippery, soapy earth having a red, blue, or whitish tinge and adhering tenaciously to the hands is probably clay. Working with the earth, however, will soon reveal whether or not it is suitable for modeling.[6] Natural clay must usually be refined before it can be used as a

Clay is a popular medium for elementary art because it lends itself to table projects like the modeling these primary grade children are doing.

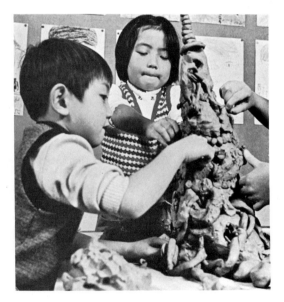

modeling medium. If dry, it should be powdered and put through a sieve to remove lumps, pebbles, and other foreign matter. If wet, it must be rolled and kneaded on a *bat*, a porous slab, and any lumps or foreign substances removed by hand as they come to the surface. A suitable porous bat can be made of plaster of paris. If clay is too wet, it can be dried relatively quickly by placing it on a plaster bat and turning it over every thirty minutes or so. The plaster tends to draw moisture from the clay.

When purchased, standard dry clay (always cheaper than prepared clay) is usually packaged in 50- or 100-pound bags. In preparation for use, water should be poured over about half a pail of clay and mixed in with a spoon. It takes about 5 quarts of warm water to thoroughly soak 25 pounds of dry clay. A tablespoon of vinegar added to the water will neutralize any alkaline content and make it easier on the hands. After the clay has settled overnight, any excess water can be poured off. Clay also comes in a plastic state, usually in 25- to 100-pound bags. It is more expensive than dry clay because of the shipping charge for the added water content, but it is still relatively inexpensive. One pound of clay makes a ball the size of an adult's fist, and this is a good average amount for a child to work with.

Before modeling can be successfully performed, the refined and dampened clay should be kneaded and rolled on the porous surface until it is almost rubbery. When a coil of it can be twisted and bent so that it neither breaks readily nor adheres unpleasantly to the hands, it is ready for modeling. To assist in working with clay to the necessary condition, an apparatus called a *wedging table* is useful. The wedging table consists merely of two boards about ½-inch thick, on 5-ply wood, fixed at right angles to each other with screws. Brackets strengthen this assembly. The measurements of each board should be at least 18 by 24 inches. A length of fine but strong wire should be attached from the top center of the upright board to the outside center of the lower board. *Wedging* makes the clay uniformly moist and free of air bubbles. A lump of clay is cut by pressing it into the wire. The resulting two pieces are then thrown with force onto the surface of the wedging table or slapped together. If the slapping of clay gets out of hand, the children should be encouraged to *knead* the clay from a standing position. This entails folding the clay back into itself, without trapping any air in the folds, until it has the proper rubbery texture. This process is continued until no tiny bubble holes are to be seen in the clay when cut with a wire tool.

A reasonably large quantity of clay for modeling may be prepared in advance and stored for a short time in airtight tins or earthenware containers. Indeed, this storing tends to make it more workable. Small pieces of clay for each pupil may subsequently be cut away by means of a wire. Used clay can often be reclaimed by soaking it in water for about forty-eight hours and then placing it on a plaster bat to dry to a workable consistency.

Before the children work with clay or other modeling materials, the working surfaces should be protected with newspapers, cardboard sheets, clear plastic, or oilcloth. The children will find it convenient to model the clay on a board placed on the protective covering. While working, the children can turn the board to view the sculpture from all sides. Plaster bats provide both a working and a kneading surface.

Modeling in clay and other materials is essentially an activity for the hands, and requires few tools. Sets of tools are available to assist more experienced children in producing details in their pieces. Tools can be made easily from wide tongue depressors broken lengthwise and sanded with sandpaper or shaped with a knife or file. Pointed or round-ended tools can be made from dowels. A damp sponge or cloth is useful to moisten the fingers and partially clean them at the close of the activity. The teacher should not use the sponge to smooth out objects. The surface of the clay is a record of the children's individuality, as is the texture of their crayons or the marks of their brushes and, as such, should be preserved as part of their total response.

The child's stage of development in pictorial work is reflected in the output in clay. The youngest and most inexperienced children are satisfied with a short period of manipulation, after which the clay is left in a shape resembling nothing in particular. Later, the children may give a name to shapes of this kind. Still later, the symbols associated with drawing and painting may appear in the clay in three-dimensional form. Finally, preadolescents refine their symbols, aiming at greater detail and realistic proportion. Younger children are less concerned about the permanence of their objects than are older ones, who want to see their pieces fired and carried to completion through the use of glazes.

There is no one technique recommended for modeling. Children begin to model naturally with considerable energy, enthusiasm, and, generally, dexterity. Given a piece of clay weighing from half a pound for kindergarten and first grade pupils to 2 pounds for those in higher grades, children will squeeze, stroke, pinch, and pat it to get a satisfactory result. Whereas younger children may pull out their subject from a central mass of clay, they seldom draw this way, preferring to assemble objects out of separate parts. When demonstrating, it is recommended that both additive and modeling from a central mass of clay be offered as options.

The finished product in clay must be a solid, compact composition. As they gain confidence in the medium, children attempt to form slender protuberances. These usually fall off, and children quickly learn not to draw out the clay too far from the central mass. They may add little pellets of clay for, say, eyes and buttons, but even these must be kept reasonably flat if they are to adhere to the main body of the clay. It is important to understand that clay shrinks as it dries, so that if a wet piece is adhered to a drier piece, the wet one will shrink more in drying and will break off. Pieces to be joined must be similar in moisture content. The use of watery clay, or *slip*, may help children fix these extra pieces. Slip is prepared by mixing some of the clay used in the modeling with water until the mixture has the consistency of thick cream. The child *scores*, or roughens, the two surfaces to be stuck together with the teeth of a comb, a knitting needle, or a pointed stick, and then paints or dabs on the slip with the fingers before pressing the pieces together.

If worked on too long, clay becomes too dry to manipulate. In order for it to be kept sufficiently moist from one day to the next, it should be wrapped in a damp cloth over which is wrapped a plastic sheet, and, if possible, the whole should be placed in a covered tin until it is to be worked again. When the work is finished and left on a shelf to dry, it should be dampened from time to time with water applied with a paintbrush. The small protuberances will thus be prevented from cracking or dropping off before the main body of the work has dried.

Teaching. The teacher must be concerned with the preparation of the clay, the physical arrangements for handling it in the classroom, and the subject matter selected by the children.

For the youngest children the teacher must prepare the clay. For the older children, step-by-step instructions and then careful supervision of their preparation of the medium are needed. The clay must be prepared correctly if the work is to be successful. The room and its furnishings must be adequately protected from clay dust and particles. The teacher should ask each child to spread newspaper on the floor under the work area. Desks or tables on which the work is performed should be covered with oilcloth, rubber, or plastic sheeting, or with more paper. Many cleaning cloths dampened with water should be readily at hand, and the pupils should be taught to use them both when the work is in progress and when it is finished. The pupils must also learn to pick up the protective coverings carefully so that clay particles are not left on the desks or floor.

Good teachers will see that adequate shelves are provided for storing clay work. Teachers should carefully supervise as each child stores the work and make sure that the products are in no way damaged during the storage process.

Subject matter for modeling in clay is somewhat restricted. Usually it involves one person or thing, or at the most two persons or things resolved into a closely knit composition. Only objects or shapes that are chunky and solid can be successfully rendered. Thus the human figure and certain animals such as owls, squirrels, or pigs, which can be successfully stylized into a solid form, are more suitable subjects than naturally spindly creatures such as giraffes, spiders, and flamingos. Students should discuss and select a subject in keeping with the nature of clay before they begin work.

Working from a posed figure can be a desirable activity for more experienced children. Positioning the human body and interpreting its general proportions can be exciting art experiences when carried through in both the flat and in-the-round approaches. The upper grade child can establish a basic standing figure without too much difficulty, but to make the figure sit, crawl, sleep, and perform other such activities often requires a posed model.

Modeling in clay can be used to reinforce other learning in art. If fifth and sixth graders sketch the human figure, they can sculpt it as well, working either for heightened observation or for purposes of personal expression. If they are examining texture through collage, children can study texture further by impressing found objects—bark, string, burlap, and the like—into the responsive surface of clay. Plaster casts can be made of such exercises and when combined, make attractive wall panels.

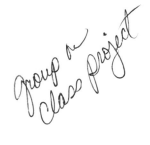

Long-Range Planning in Clay

The following activities provide examples of a sequence of activities based upon broad age levels.

Early Grades.

> Make a flat slab of clay with the palms of the hands.
> Roll the clay into a thick coil, a thin coil, a big clay ball, and several small clay balls. How closely to a ball can you shape your clay? A square?
> "Pull" a bird out of one lump of clay using a particular texture for feathers.
> Make a pinch pot out of one small ball of clay, striving for even wall thickness.

Middle Grades.

> Join two pieces of clay together.
> Show a film, slides, or books illustrating the clay process and finished clay objects. (Degas's ballerinas, Jacob Epstein's portraits, Barye's animals, etc.)
> Make a mother and child sculpture of one kind of animal.
> Make a prehistoric creature, embellishing it with natural textures by imprinting objects such as leaves or fir cones.
> Make a clay figure showing a particular emotional state.
> Make a clay figure showing some action, such as found in pre-Columbian village sculpture.
> Make a fantasy clay world or an imaginary environment.

Allow a small group of the most advanced students to be responsible for firing clay objects under the supervision of the teacher.

Upper Grades.

Make a large coil pot.

Make a clay container. Decorate it with a pattern consisting of either an incised texture or added bits of clay.

Make a three-dimensional version of a drawing or painting as the subject matter.

Make a ceramic slab wall hanging as a group project.

Make a portrait, using the back or shoulders as a solid base.

MAKING POTTERY

As previously mentioned, containers from ancient cultures in China, Greece, South America, and many other parts of the world still exist in museums and private collections. Archeologists learn much about ancient peoples from their artifacts, which in many cases rival or exceed in quality of design and construction the best work that we are able to produce today.

Media and Techniques. The two most basic hand-forming pottery techniques are the pinch and coil methods. Each of these methods has varying levels of sophistication and they are often used together by an innovative potter. In the symbol stage, children can make pots by hollowing a solid lump of clay. Preadolescents are capable of what are called the *coil* and *slab* methods. A simple pinch pot is a good project on which to start a child at any age. Children may begin by shaping the clay into a ball and working the thumb of one hand into the center. They then rotate the ball slowly in the palm of one hand, gently pressing the clay between the thumb and the fingers of the other hand to expand the wall. The wall should be thick and the pot periodically tapped on the table to maintain a flat base. If the walls are thick enough, they may subsequently be decorated by incising lines or pressing hard-edged objects into the surface.

It is useful for children to know and apply a few basic concepts and terms as they make pottery. We have already mentioned that clay shrinks as it dries, so that a bowl, cup, or other object should be made about 25 percent larger than the desired size for the finished piece. Children should be reminded to join pieces of clay that have about the same moisture content and will therefore shrink together about the same amount. Clay that is allowed to dry until it loses most of its elasticity is called *leather hard*. Clay in the leather-hard state is very easy to work with. It is nearly rigid, but not brittle. It is strong and can be carved or scraped easily. As the clay continues to dry it becomes *bone*

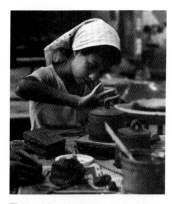

This student is making a pinch pot. The pot and brush contain slip for engobe decoration. Sponges are used to smooth contours of the finished pot; lids and handles have also been dealt with. A well-equipped ceramic workshop can thus provide children with a wide range of experience not normally available.

The coil method of potterymaking: (A) trimming the base, (B) rolling the coil, (C) applying the coil, (D) smoothing the coil, and (E) trimming the lip. This technique can also be combined with sections of slabs on flat areas.

dry. This is the stage when pieces are extremely brittle and fragile. Bone-dry pieces should not be handled unnecessarily, since this is when most breakage occurs. Pots broken at this stage are very difficult to repair satisfactorily.

When the pottery or clay sculpture pieces are completely dry they will not feel as cool to the touch as pieces that still contain moisture, since the evaporation of water from a clay piece actually cools it. Only bone-dry pieces should be placed (stacked) in the kiln for firing. Pieces that are very thick, that have air bubbles in the clay, or that are not completely dry very often will explode during firing. A slow firing is best to minimize explosions and fractures. Slow cooling helps to avoid breakage caused by uneven contraction between thick and thin parts of a piece of pottery.

Clay that has not been fired is called *greenware,* not because of its color, but because of its immaturity. The firing of greenware is called the *bisque firing* and the fired pieces are labeled *bisqueware.* After firing, the bisqueware is fused and hard and will no longer dissolve when water is applied. It is ready for glazing or other surface decoration. The firing of glazed bisqueware is called the *glaze firing.*

In producing coil pottery, children will find it convenient to work on a small board or plaster bat. A ball of clay is flattened on the bat until it is about half an inch thick. Then it is trimmed with a knife to the desired size, usually about 3 to 5 inches in diameter. Next, a coil of clay about half an inch in diameter is produced by rolling the clay. The coil is then applied to the edge of the base, which should be scored and dampened with slip so that adhesion is assured. The coil should then be pinched to the base. A second coil is built on the first in the same way. No more than four or five coils should be made in one day, lest the assembly collapse under its own weight. After allowing the clay to dry for a day to become leather hard, the pupil may add another four or five coils. The top coil is covered with plastic and kept damp so that it will adhere well to the additional coils. This process is repeated until the bowl or pot has reached the desired height and shape.

The position of the coils determines the shape of the bowl. Placing a coil slightly on the outside of the one beneath it will flare the bowl; placing it toward the inside will diminish the bowl in diameter. Although a perfectly uniform bowl is not expected, nor indeed altogether desirable, it is necessary to examine the rising edges from all angles to see that the shape of the object is reasonably symmetrical. A *template,* or contour, cut in cardboard may be applied to the side of the bowl, but this shaping technique is frowned on by some teachers for the good reason that it is mechanical and rather extraneous to the process of coil pottery.

When the outlines of the bowl are formed, pupils should either smooth both the inside and the outside with their fingers or smooth

The slab method of making pottery: (A) preparing the clay, (B) placing the supporting coil, (C) applying the sides, and (D) smoothing the sides with sponge and sandpaper.

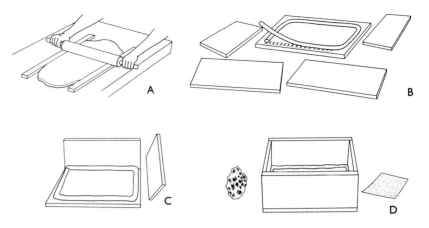

just the inside for support and allow the exterior coil texture to show. Dipping the fingers in slip facilitates the smoothing process. The lip of the bowl should be flattened or tapered and perhaps trimmed with a wire tool or knife. The bowl should then be cut away from the slab with a wire. Its edges may then be gently smoothed with the fingers.

FINISHING PROCESSES

Media and Techniques.   Several techniques may be used to decorate objects made of clay. These include glazing, incising, painting with engobe (colored slip), pressing with various objects, and a technique of incising through engobe known as sgraffito.

The successful glazing of clay requires skill and experience. First, the raw clay must be very carefully wedged to remove air bubbles. Next, after the modeling is done, the object must be dried thoroughly. Then a kiln or oven must be stacked with the pieces for preliminary or bisque firing. When the first firing has been successfully completed, the glazes (of which there are at least five distinct types) must be applied, the kiln stacked in such a way as to prevent the glazes on one object from touching another, and the second process of firing and cooling completed. Although it produces lovely results, glazing is a complicated process, and few people learn to do it merely by reading a book on the subject. Always check a prepared glaze to be certain it does not contain lead.

Incising involves scoring the clay with various objects. The clay must be partly dry before incising can be done. Any one of a number of objects, ranging from nails and knitting needles to keys and pieces of comb, can be repeatedly pressed into fairly moist clay to make an interesting pattern.

Engobe, or colored slip, is underglaze pigment. Commercially prepared engobe is available from school supply houses. The engobe is painted on nearly dry (leather hard) clay with a sable brush. When the painted clay is dry, it must be fired as described earlier. A second firing is required if transparent glaze is applied over the bisque-fired engobe.

Sgraffito combines both incising and painting with engobe. Engobe is painted onto the partially dried object. In order to get thorough coverage and avoid streaks, two coats should be applied, the first by brushing consistently in one direction, the second by brushing consistently in another direction. When the engobe coats have almost dried, lines are incised through them — usually with a stick — to the clay before firing the object.

Following the lead of some professional potters, a number of teachers are experimenting with new approaches to surface decoration, which may include polymer acrylics or even tempera paint. In the latter case, when the paint is dry it may be left mat (nonglossy) or covered with a protective coating of shellac. The new polymer paints, unlike tempera, will not come off when the object is handled. Shoe polish gives a pleasing surface tone and may be used in place of paint; it comes in a surprising range of colors. In all cases the clay should be bisque fired before a coating is applied.

Teaching. Finishing clay objects produced by elementary school children places the teacher in an educational and artistic dilemma. Glazing is the most acceptable finish for clay. Although clay will take paint, which may in turn be covered with shellac or varnish or give it a shine, such a finish is not suited to clay and tends to make even the best work look cheap and tawdry. On the other hand, children can paint clay easily enough, but most of them cannot successfully fire it without help from the teacher. So much help is required, in fact, that the children must usually surrender their control of this activity to an adult.

Teachers have attempted to solve the dilemma arising from the finishing of clay products in several ways. Some tell the children that it is impossible for them to fire and glaze their work at the present time, but that they might instead try pressing or incising a design into it. The decorated object is then preserved in its natural form. Often teachers glaze for each child one or two products finished in engobe, sgraffito, or another technique that the teacher has demonstrated. Others show the children how to coat the work with shellac and explain that this is merely a makeshift process. Still other teachers, having explained that not all the steps in glazing can be performed by the children themselves, go ahead with glazing but take every opportunity to let the children do whatever lies within their competence. Thus, a young child might at first only paint a bowl with engobe but later might help to stack the kiln. None of these alternatives is wholly satisfactory, but perhaps the last provides the children with the most insight into and experience with the craft of pottery.

THE EMERGENCE OF NEW FORMS IN SCULPTURE AND CERAMICS

The art teacher will occasionally be unable to relate sculpture and ceramic activities in an elementary program to the work of professionals. Materials and methods are difficult to duplicate in fields where contemporary artists work with such diverse means as synthetics, electricity, and control of the atmosphere. In general, teachers should be cautioned against concentrating on any extreme approach for the sake of living out their own personal interests. A teacher's indiscriminate pursuit of the avant-garde may have as little meaning to fifth graders as a stubborn reverence for traditional forms.

Sculpture and ceramics, like any art form, should challenge a child within the boundaries of enthusiasm and capability, providing experience in depth and breadth. There is a time to work from observation and a time to work from one's imagination; a time for ideas that move quickly and a time for sequential approaches. Children may carve and model as artists have done for ages or they may combine assembled constructions with light and motion, as is currently practiced. They may also take a functional form—such as a container—and endow it with some human attribute. When an idea becomes as important as a form, then pottery moves closer to sculpture. In a broad sense, sculpture in particular may be said to encompass many kinds of volumes and masses organized within a spatial context. It can be created with boxes or junk, papier-mâché, clay, or plaster. During the course of six or seven years in an elementary school, a child should have the pleasure of working with many approaches.

Although a conscientious teacher plans for most of the activities, a portion of the program should be left open for the unexpected. A windfall of unusual materials, a trip to a gallery, a magazine article, or acquaintance with a great artist could capture the interest of both students and teacher in a new activity.

◆ NOTES TO THE TEXT

1. Wayne Higby, "Viewing the Launching Pad: The Arts, Clay, and Education," in Gerry Williams, ed., *The Case for Clay in Art Education*, symposium report in *Studio Potter*, Vol. 16. No. 2 (1988).

2. Jules Heller, *Papermaking* (New York: Watson-Guptill, 1978), p. 11.

3. The Bauhaus included such exercises in its design course. The artists began by rolling the wood over and over again in their hands until a certain shape began to suggest itself. This experimentation often led to the solution of such varied industrial problems as developing handles for gun stocks and designing refrigerator doors.

4. Maxwell Museum of Anthropology, *Seven Families in Pueblo Pottery* (Albuquerque, NM: University of New Mexico Press, 1974), p. 43.

5. Edmund Feldman, ''Clay: Arguments For and With,'' in Gerry Williams, ed., *The Case for Clay in Art Education*, symposium report in *Studio Potter*, Vol. 16. No. 2 (1988).

6. See Michael Casson, *The Craft of the Potter* (Woodbury, NY: Barron's Educational Series, 1979).

◆ ACTIVITIES FOR THE READER

1. Survey the district around your school for materials suitable for sculpture and pottery. Is there any clay, wood, or wire to be had? Test the materials according to the suggestions found earlier in this chapter under the subheadings ''Media and Techniques.''

2. Seek out an efficient industrial arts teacher who should be only too happy to talk about wood. Ask questions about the types of woods and their various properties, seasoning wood, hand and power tools for woodworking, the care of tools (including sharpening), and finishes for wood. Ask for demonstrations of some of the processes associated with woodworking. Seek advice about brands of tools and types of sharpening stones. Exchange a picture you have made for scraps of wood (sanded ones, if possible).

3. Go to a good furniture store and make a note of the different types of finishes. Speak to an industrial arts teacher in one of your secondary schools if you do not understand how some of the finishes are obtained.

4. Glue scraps of wood together to form a piece of sculpture. Smooth the surfaces of the sculpture with medium and then fine sandpaper. Wax the sculpture and polish it with a soft cloth until it glows. Ordinary solid floor wax is suitable.

5. Experiment with various kinds of woods by cutting them with a heavy pocketknife. (Keep the knife sharp by rubbing it gently over a fine oilstone.) When you find wood that you like to cut, plan, either in your mind's eye or in a pencil sketch first on paper and then on the wood, a nonobjective design that you intend to cut. Start cutting, turning the wood from time to time so that you cut from all angles. Cut away from you and keep your other hand behind the cutting edge. Study the developing design for unity and variety of the elements. If you would like to put some holes in the wood to get three-dimensional effects, you will have to use a large drill or brace-and-bit. When the carving more or less satisfies you, put it gently in a vise and start filing it smooth. Sometimes sculptors protect their work from the jaws of the vise by placing pieces of wood between the sculpture and the jaws. Let the file ''bite'' by pushing it away from you. Finish with medium and fine sandpaper and, finally, polish with about a dozen coats of wax.

6. Cast a plaque about 6 by 9 inches in plaster of paris. Carve a nonobjective design in the plaque based on overlapping oblongs and squares. In some areas devise textural effects by cutting or gouging.

7. Cast a block of plaster of paris about 2 by 2 by 8 inches. Plan a representational subject (a torso is excellent) and carve it out of the block.

8. Model a nonobjective shape in clay; model a representational form in clay.

9. Try a self-portrait in clay. Imagine yourself in an unusual role—a king, a slave, a dreamer, or a prophet. Use a soda bottle filled with sand as an armature to control the weight of the clay.

10. Roll a slab of clay big enough to wrap around an oatmeal box. Press rows of designs into the clay with hard-edged objects such as seed pods, coins, tools, wood ends, and the like. Keep a balance of large and small shapes and deep and shallow marks. Wrap the slab around the oatmeal box and seal the joined edges by pinching them. Remove the oatmeal box. Add a clay base and fire the object. You will have a unique container. Cut a rectangle measuring at least 18 by 20 inches from a half-inch-thick slab of clay. With a nail file, begin cutting out a family of shapes, both curved and angular. Use some linear shapes as links in your design. As you cut out the shapes, place them on a

board covered with sand, dirt, or dried clay. (This will keep your forms from sticking.) Make sure that the forms overlap or touch one another. After sprinkling the design with more sand or dried clay, place a second board on top of the pieces and press down hard. (You can even jump up and down on it.) Lift up the board and notice the subtle play of edges and the unifying surface quality attained by the pressure of the board. You can cut the design into sections and begin all over again.

11. Make freestanding figures of animals or people based on each of the following basic forms: (a) a tent made with one simple fold; (b) a cylinder; (c) a cone that may be cut to shape after twisting and gluing. Heads and legs should be devised by cutting and shaping paper and gluing it in place. Add features and details of clothing by gluing cut-paper pieces to the basic shape.

12. Make an object out of rolled newspaper. Roll the newspaper into a tight cylinder for the body and tie it with string in three or four places. For arms and legs, make thinner cylinders of newspaper tied with string as above. Tie the arms and legs to the body. Next the neck and head should either be modeled separately and attached to the body or be bent under as an extension of the body cylinder. Dip strips of newspaper or paper toweling about 1 inch wide into paste and wrap them around the figure. When the object is dry add details with colored paper, scraps of fur, and so on. Finish with paint and shellac.

13. Identify the terms listed in the caption of the Egyptian sculpture of "Sahura and a Deity" near the beginning of this chapter.

◆ SUGGESTED READINGS

Casson, Michael. *The Craft of the Potter.* Woodbury, NY: Barron's Educational Series, 1979. A relatively inexpensive yet comprehensive book that covers hand-building, throwing, decorating, glazing, and firing. It is well illustrated.

Heller, Jules. *Papermaking.* New York: Watson-Guptill, 1978. An articulate text on the topic with excellent illustrations and beautiful color reproductions of paper works by contemporary artists.

Kraus, William and Toni Sikes. *The Guild: A Sourcebook of American Craft Artists.* New York: Kraus Sikes, 1987. This book has hundreds of color photographs of contemporary sculpture, ceramics, and crafts.

Nelson, Glenn C. *Ceramics*, 4th ed. New York: Holt, Rinehart and Winston, 1978. A classic text for anyone working in ceramics, this book has a great deal of technical information and includes many excellent color as well as black-and-white illustrations of ceramic pieces from around the world.

Newman, Thelma, J. Newman, and L. Newman. *Paper as Art and Craft.* New York: Crown, 1973. A helpful book on the use of paper as an art form.

Rathus, Lois Fichner. *Understanding Art*, 2nd ed. Englewood Cliffs, NJ: Prentice-Hall, 1989. See especially Chapter 6, "Sculpture," and Chapter 9, "The Art of Everyday Living: Crafts and Design."

Roettger, Ernst. *Creative Clay Design.* New York: Van Nostrand Reinhold, 1972. Another of Roettger's series of books that apply design principles to various media. This book provides a wealth of ideas for surface decoration in clay.

Toulouse, Betty. *Pueblo Pottery of the New Mexico Indians: Ever Constant, Ever Changing.* Sante Fe: Museum of New Mexico Press, 1977. An historical treatment of the modern era of native American pottery.

Williams, Gerry, ed. "The Case for Clay in Art Education," Symposium report in *Studio Potter*, Vol. 16, No. 2 (1988).

Verhelst, Wilbert. *Sculpture: Tools, Materials, and Techniques*, 2nd ed. Englewood Cliffs, NJ: Prentice-Hall, 1988. A thorough guide to advanced sculpture methods of use in teaching children about how professional artists create sculpture.

PRINTMAKING: MULTIPLE ART IMAGES

A FINE PRINT may be produced lovingly and patiently, or violently and impetuously — dependent upon the "climate" of the printmaker. From a fleeting idea wrested from the complex of human experience, worked through to the final visual image on paper, the print is employed as a medium in its own right. It is utilized by the printmaker for what it alone can accomplish in serving his particular needs. This precious sheet of paper bears the autographic trace of the printmaker on its surface; in his own "handwriting," then, we read the record of his dreams, his hopes, aspirations, play, loves, and fears.[1]

Jules Heller

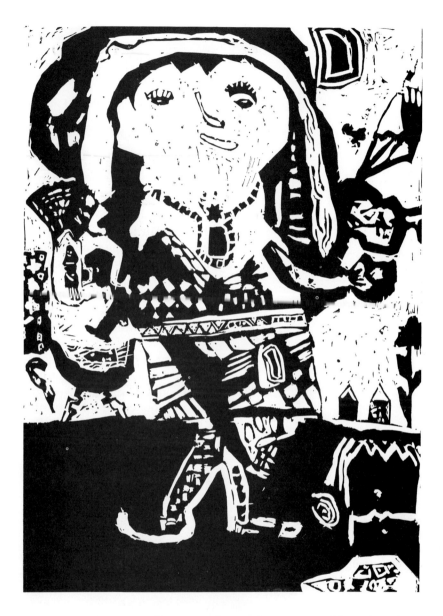

Drawing, printing, sculpture, and ceramics are very old modes of art, as previously discussed, with origins prior to historical records. Printmaking might have occurred during these early times when our distant ancestors colored the palms of their hands with pigments and pressed them against cave walls. However, the art of printmaking as we know it today required a technological innovation that is less than two thousand years old. This innovation was the invention of paper, which is required for the making of prints. Paper, not to be confused

Paper

with the much older Egyptian material, *papyrus*, was invented in A.D. 105 by a Chinese eunuch, Ts'ai Lun, in the court of Ho Ti. One of Ts'ai Lun's duties was to salvage scraps of silk from cuttings of material in the emperor's court:

> Ts'ai Lun hit upon so simple and ingenious a system for recycling the silk scraps that his idea remains at the core of papermaking to this day. The strips were soaked in water and hand-beaten into a pulp. This pulp was then spread evenly over a bamboo screen so that excess water would drain off through the openings between the bamboo strips. When the remaining pulp was sun-dried, the material solidified into *paper*.[2]

The Chinese also invented the oldest form of printmaking, the woodcut. Wood-block pictures and texts existed in China hundreds of years before the first prints appeared in fifteenth-century Europe. The earliest known printed page is a woodcut drawing with Chinese writing dated A.D. 686, discovered in the Cave of the Thousand Buddhas in eastern Turkestan. Papermaking and the art of printmaking on paper didn't reach Europe until the twelfth century, and by the fourteenth century paper mills existed throughout Europe. The first paper mill in England began operation in 1657, followed by America's first paper mill in 1690.

The advent of printmaking was a wonderful innovation for artists and for appreciators of art. Now artists could create *multiples* of their work which could be sold at lower prices to collectors. After carefully preparing the woodcut or other printing surface, artists are now able to make dozens or even hundreds of signed original artworks instead

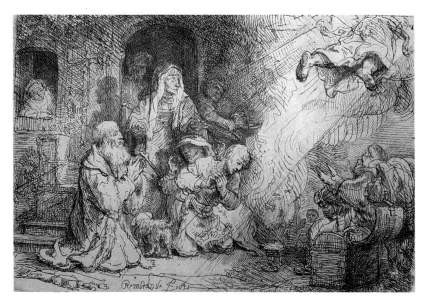

Rembrandt van Rijn, *The Angel Departing from the Family of Tobias*, 1641. This etching is an example of how the artist can achieve fine shading, dramatic contrast of dark and light, and active motion purely through the use of massed line. Rembrandt had a lifelong interest in Biblical themes as sources for his drawings, prints, and paintings. (Courtesy of the Museum of Fine Arts, Brigham Young University.)

of only one, as is usually the case with drawing, painting, and sculpture. Because of the lower costs of prints many more people can afford to collect and enjoy original art.

The technologies of printmaking have advanced greatly during the twentieth century so that it is sometimes difficult even for a serious print collector to identify the process or processes used to produce contemporary prints. There are, however, four traditional processes that continue to be used, sometimes in combination. Each of these processes is used by printmakers in many variations. They are:

relief process: Woodcut, linoleum cut, stamps, rubbings, etc. The design area stands out and receives the ink. The rest of the block is cut away so that it will not print when the surface is inked.

surface process: Lithography. The image is drawn directly on the stone (or metal) surface with a greasy crayon or ink. After treatment with turpentine and water, ink is applied to the surface, adhering to the greasy drawing, and a print is made.

intaglio process: Etching, aquatint, engraving, drypoint, etc. Used in many variations, intaglio is basically cutting or scratching into a surface (usually metal) with tools or acid. The cut areas receive and hold the ink for printing.

stencil process: Silk screen (serigraph), photographic silk screen, paper stencil, etc. A stencil is adhered to a fine silk screen, allowing the ink to pass through the open areas onto the paper or other surface. Use of photosensitive stencil material allows artists to integrate photographic images in their prints.[3]

Suzuki Harunobu, *Woman with Mirror*, ca. 1770. This beautiful print is a woodblock with colored ink on paper. Notice the flat colored areas and the delicate lines possible with the woodcut process. Compare the theme of this print with Picasso's *Girl Before a Mirror* on page 355. Which work was created first? Do you think the later artist was aware of the other's work? How are the two works similar? How are they different? Can you detect the cultural origins of each work? (Courtesy of the Freer Gallery of Art, Smithsonian Institution, Washington, D.C.) Compare this also to Mary Cassatt, *The Bath*, 1891. An American Impressionist, Cassatt was influenced by the printmaking techniques and style of the Japanese. Notice the ways this print is similar to Harunobu's *Woman with Mirror*. How are the compositions similar? Note Cassatt's use of line, flat color, and pattern in relation to the Japanese print. *The Bath*, however, is not a woodcut, but is made with several intaglio techniques: drypoint, etching, and aquatint. Other artists influenced by the Japanese include Edgar Degas and Toulouse-Lautrec. (The National Museum of Women in the Arts. Gift of Wallace and Wilhelmina Holladay.)

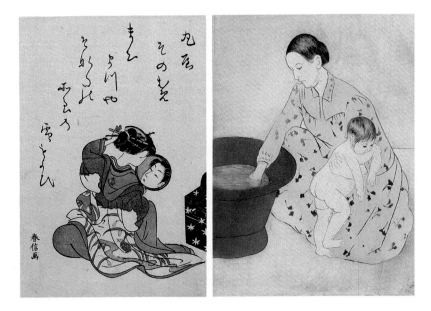

This chapter discusses variations of these printmaking processes that are within the capabilities of children and the resources of most schools. In all printmaking activities in school classrooms, teachers can relate the process to those used by mature artists, using visual examples of the best works. Also, teachers should educate children about printmaking in their everyday lives. These same processes are seen in commercial publications, illustrations, advertising, and on almost every T-shirt with a graphic image.

From preschool children to teenagers, printmaking is a source of fascination and challenge. In contrast to drawing and painting, paper work, and sculpture and pottery, which are largely direct activities, printing is an indirect process; something is done to one substance in order to produce an effect on another substance. Between the child and the finished print, in other words, lies a whole series of moves with intermediary materials that must be completed successfully before the final image itself appears.

It is this emphasis on process that intrigues preadolescents so that they often lose their self-consciousness about the quality of the end product. Why worry about accuracy of shape when it is so much fun to gouge the wood, roll on the ink, and transfer the image? Because printing processes exert especially strong influences on the final product, the treatment of subject matter often requires considerable modification to suit the technique. Children will soon discover that details and shading are more appropriate to drawing than to printmaking and that a successful print makes a strong impact through simplication and contrast.

This chapter includes suggested activities for children related to all four of the printmaking processes mentioned above. Experimental printmaking with such unorthodox materials as corrugated cardboard, collographs, collage, and clay is also discussed. The search for new solutions to traditional problems is as much a part of contemporary printmaking as of painting, and every public school art program should provide for some degree of experimentation in basic art forms.

RUBBINGS

One way to begin printmaking at any level is by transferring a ready-made surface; that is, by making a rubbing. This is an effective way to draw attention to unusual surfaces that may go unnoticed. A gravestone, a coin, a cracked part of the sidewalk, a manhole cover, or a section of grating all have a presence that is waiting to be revealed by rubbing the side of a crayon on a sheet of paper placed on the subject. Colors can be changed for different sections of the image, and the paper moved from time to time to create new patterns. Rubbings are

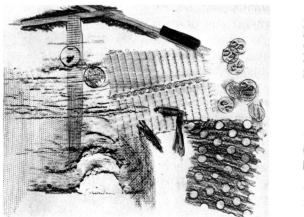
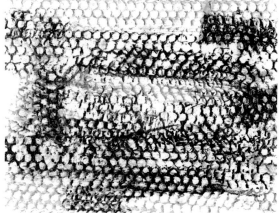

Crayon rubbings of various objects may be used to investigate surface textures. Objects can also be glued to a hard surface and inked to make collage prints. The exploratory stages are usually unplanned, but students can work for some sense of order as they control the overall design of their experiments.

not only a way of sensitizing children to the realm of texture, but also a means of attuning them to the "skin" of the environment.

The paper should be lightweight so that it does not tear easily, and white enough to provide high contrast. (Ordinary typing paper is adequate for small objects). When they use crayons, students should be encouraged to blend colors. Large primary color crayons are fine for this activity, but if the budget will allow, Japanese rice paper and crayon pastels offer the handsomest results. In taking rubbings of raised type—as on manhole covers—students can improvise with the image by rearranging the pattern of form, repeating it, or turning the paper.

～ MONOPRINTING

The printing technique most closely allied to drawing and painting, and to which any child may transfer some picture-making ability, is called monoprinting. Although not as well known as other print forms, monoprinting has a stronger historical background than most teachers realize. Giovanni Castiglione first used the process and Rembrandt used a monoprint technique in making his copper plates. By the mid-1890s, Degas was a leader in this technique. Monoprinting has enjoyed a recent revival of interest among printmakers, some of whom wipe away color from a surface (subtractive method) and some who prefer to add color to the plate (additive).

Media and Techniques. The supplies required include a sheet of glass with the edges taped so the children cannot cut their hands. Instead of glass, a piece of linoleum may be used, measuring about 6 by 8 inches and preferably glued to a slab of wood. In the lower elementary grades, finger paint or tempera may be used directly on the table, since it is easily cleaned with a damp cloth or sponge. Brayers, brushes, pieces of stiff cardboard, or fingers may all be used, depending on the desired effect. Water-soluble ink and paint in a wide range of colors are available, as are newsprint and other reasonably absorbent papers.

To begin the process, the ink is squeezed from the tube onto the surface of the glass or linoleum and then rolled evenly over the surface. More than one color may be used if desired. If two colors are used, for example, they may be dabbed onto the glass and then blended with the brayer. Another method is to mix the colors lightly with a palette knife before rolling. Each technique produces its own effect.

A drawing can be produced with almost any implement that can make a strong mark directly into the ink. The eraser end of a pencil, a piece of cardboard, and a broad pen point are but a few of the suitable tools. The drawing, which is made directly in the ink, must be kept bold because the inked surfaces do not show fine details. Only the ink that is left on the surface will be recorded in the final printing.

For the printing, a sheet of paper should be placed gently over the prepared inky surface and pressed to it with the tips of the fingers. A clean brayer rolled evenly over the paper also produces a good print. The completed print may then be gently peeled away. Sometimes two or three impressions may be taken from one drawing. By using papers with varying textures an interesting variety of prints can be obtained. Although newsprint is recommended because it is cheap and absorbent, other papers should be tried also, such as colored tissue, construction and poster papers, and even the coated stock found in magazine advertisements.

In another method of monoprinting, the glass is covered with ink in the usual manner. The paper is then placed gently over the inked

Arrangements for making a monoprint.

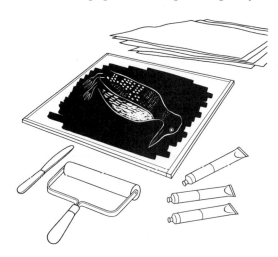

glass. Next the pupil draws with a pencil on the upper side of the paper, taking care not to drag the side of the hand on the paper. The resulting print is a composition of dark lines with some imprint of ink on the background areas. Since children have a tendency to over-ink the plate, they should try a test mark on the corner and lift the paper to see if the line is visible.

Drawing in monoprint creates an arresting line quality — soft, rich, and slightly blurred. Because of this, it is particularly appropriate as an adjunct of contour-line drawing in the upper grades.

Another variation of monoprinting is the *paper stop out* method. Paper forms are cut or torn and then placed in a desired pattern on the inked plate. The impression is made by putting fresh paper on the arrangement and rolling it with the brayer. The cut-paper forms beneath serve to "stop out" the ink, and the areas they cover will appear as a negative pattern (that is, as the color of the paper) in the finished print.

Teaching.   Four main tasks confront the teacher of monoprinting. The first is to arrange tools and supplies so that printing may be done conveniently; the second is to see that the ink does not get all over the children; and third is to give stimulating demonstrations and continued encouragement; and the fourth is to make certain that there is a cleared area for wet prints to hang or otherwise be stored until dry.

Printing should be done on a long table covered with newspapers or oilcloth. At one end or at several points on the table the teacher should arrange the glass, brayers, and inks. Because it would be uneconomical for each pupil to have a separate set of printing tools, the pupils should be given an order in which to work. Those who are not printing should know what other activities are available. As each print is completed the child should place it carefully on the remaining table space. When all the children have finished, the teacher should encourage them to select the prints they consider most interesting. When wet, the prints can be hung with clothespins on an improvised clothesline and then, when dry, pressed between the leaves of a heavy book such as an almanac or a telephone book. When possible, clear a wall on which to mount new prints for drying.

As can be imagined, a large amount of ink comes off on the children's hands. The teacher should make sure that the children either wash their hands often or at least wipe them on a damp cloth. Unless the classroom has a sink, the teacher must provide pails of water, soap, and towels or damp cloths.

The teacher should demonstrate efficiently all methods of monoprinting. Although the techniques are simple enough, it would be wise to practice before the lesson; monoprinting can be very messy unless the teacher has had some previous experience with the work. If the teacher appears clumsy during the demonstration there may be a very inky classroom once the children begin to experiment.

Pupils find monoprinting challenging and stimulating. Once they know how to begin they are eager to discover all the possibilities of this technique. It is a valuable activity not only because it permits spontaneous work but also because it gives children a reasonably accurate idea of the printmaking process in general. Any form of printmaking works well for small groups, especially when they try it for the first time.

VEGETABLE AND STICK PRINTING

All children can produce work in vegetable printing, and nearly every child in the primary grades can print with sticks.

Media and Techniques. For vegetable printing, children should select pieces of vegetable with a hard consistency such as cabbage, carrot, potato, or celery. The pieces should be large enough for the children to grasp easily and should be cut flat on one side or end. All the children need do is dip the flat side of the vegetable into watercolor, tempera paint, or colored ink and then dab it on a sheet of newsprint. The child in kindergarten at first dabs at random but later controls the pattern and develops a rhythmic order of units. Scraps of sponge may also be used in this type of printing.

The next step is to control the design by cutting into the end of the vegetable. The best vegetable for this purpose is a crisp potato, but carrots are also suitable. The potato should be sliced in half and the design cut into the flat side with a knife. If a design of a different shape is wanted, the printing surface can be trimmed into a square. Tempera may then be painted over the designed end, after which printing on paper may begin.

In addition to vegetables, interesting shapes may be obtained by using a variety of wood scraps. If the wood is soaked in water for an hour or so, the grain swells and creates circular patterns. The wood scraps may then be dipped in paint and applied to the printing surface. In such cases, the design rests on the arrangement of odd shapes and colors rather than on the broken surface of one piece of wood. The two techniques might be combined.

An easily manipulated material to use instead of vegetables or sticks is the square soap eraser. The surface is soft enough to be cut by a pin, yet the edges can hold up for dozens of impressions. The six available sides also allow for a variety of imprints. When the class is finished with the project, the teacher can glue all the used erasers to a board, run a brayer of paint over the group, make an impression on paper, and thus have an interesting wall piece for the room.

Stick or soap-eraser printing in two colors by a fifth grader. Cuts were made in the stick with a knife after careful directions were given. Patterning can provide an interesting entree into tesselation (the combining of single units to create larger figurations), like that found in Islamic tile patterns.

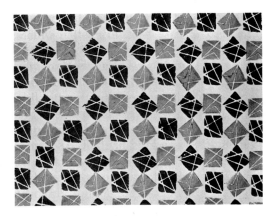

Teaching.   Because the techniques involved in vegetable and stick printing are appealing in themselves, the teacher should have no problem motivating the children. The chief task is to encourage every child to explore the numerous possibilities of the process. The children should be encouraged to find and use many kinds of vegetables and other objects suitable for printing. When controlled cutting is used the teacher could suggest that not merely a knife, but forks, fingernail files, and other implements may also be used to cut the ends of vegetables so that different designs may result. The teacher should also suggest that background papers for these types of printing can be specially prepared by laying down thin color with a wide brush. Also, the teacher should note that backgrounds may be prepared with a large vegetable, such as a cabbage sliced in half, over which a potato or a smaller vegetable with the controlled cut may be used for printing in a contrasting color.

Square soap eraser printing can be made equally challenging. The pupils can use all six sides of an eraser with different designs on each printing surface. Also, combinations of colors should be tested. Backgrounds can also be painted with thin watercolor.

Few, if any, problems will arise over subject matter. Only nonobjective or highly abstract patterns can result from this work, and the techniques lend themselves to repeated patterns rather than to picture making.

STYROFOAM, LINOLEUM, AND WOODCUT PRINTING

A good introduction to the relatively complex method of linoleum and woodcuts is the styrofoam print. Styrofoam is a soft, inexpensive material that can often be obtained by trimming the sides of food containers. All children need is a pencil to press lines onto the soft surface. The lines will remain incised and the ink can be rolled over the surface before applying paper for printing. After children make such a print, they understand the process on which more difficult techniques are built.

Media and Techniques.   When the linoleum or wood has pieces cut out of it, is inked, and, finally, is pressed to a suitably absorbent surface, a linoleum or woodcut print results. The raised parts of the surface create the pattern. The technique requires sharp tools, some physical strength (particularly in the fingers), and an ability to perform several operations of a relatively delicate nature. Only the more mature students in the upper grades will be capable of this work.

The usual heavy floor linoleum with burlap backing is suitable for cutting. It may be purchased from furniture and hardware stores or from firms that lay floor covering. Linoleum comes in large sizes, but scraps of it can often be obtained at a discount. Small pieces may be cut from a larger piece by scoring the linoleum with a knife and then bending it.[4] The linoleum snaps apart where it is scored, and then only the burlap remains to be cut through with a knife. Linoleum can be bought already affixed to wood blocks, but it is quite expensive.

The teacher shares with the student the delight and sense of excitement that only the first print can bring. Changes may have to be made from this point on, but no subsequent printing can offer this sense of surprise when the first print is pulled.

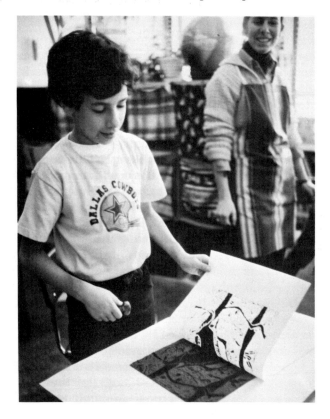

Sets of linoleum cutters and short holders for them are needed. These sets consist of straight knives, V-shaped tools, and U-gouges of varying sizes. The knives and gouges are perhaps the most effective tools, although the V-tool is capable of producing some highly sensitive lines and interesting textural effects. It is especially important to keep the tools sharp, and for this purpose a specially shaped oilstone may be bought.

The same tools are necessary for woodcutting. The best woods to use are maple, pine, and apple.

For receiving the impressions, almost any reasonably absorbent paper is suitable, from inexpensive newsprint to the costly but delightful Japanese rice paper. Generally, paper that is thinner than newsprint tends to stick to the block, and paper heavier than 40-pound bond or construction paper does not have enough resilience to pick up all the details of tool marks. Many textiles, including cottons, linens, and silks, will be found practical for printing if their textures are not rough. For printing on textiles, an oil-based or printer's ink is necessary to obtain a lasting color; otherwise, a water-based ink may be used. A few other supplies are also necessary — rubber brayers, and a sheet of plate glass to be used as a palette.

In cutting the linoleum, many people use the V-tool to make a preliminary outline of the main areas of the composition. When using this tool, it is often more convenient to move the block against the tool than the reverse. After the outlines have been inscribed the white areas in the design may be cleared away with the gouges. If any textural effects are desired in these areas, the linoleum should be gouged so that some ridges are left. If, however, the worker wishes the areas to

An eleven-year-old is cutting his design on a large piece of linoleum. Although basic space, shape, and linear decisions should be made in advance, the scale of the print makes it possible to embellish and enrich the surface. (Note the position of the cutting hand in relation to the supporting hand. Safety precautions are vital whenever sharp instruments are involved.)

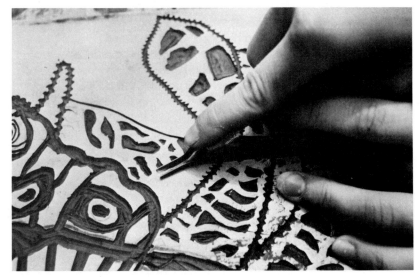

print pure white, the linoleum should be gouged out almost to the burlap backing. Various kinds of textured areas may be made by cutting parallel lines, crosshatching lines, or removing "pecks" of linoleum with the V-tool.

Cutting in wood calls for greater manual control and sharper tools. A woodcut generally does not allow for as much detail as a linoleum cut. To make up for these limitations, it offers a grained surface for dark areas. If the stark black-and-white qualities are combined with a surface of a good grain (complete with knots), a more powerful print can be obtained than with linoleum. During cutting the block should be steadied with a vise or cutting board and turned frequently for curved cuts. Naturally, the softer the wood, the easier it is to cut; pine is ideal for this task. Students should learn how to take care of the tools and keep them sharp. However, even the sharpest gouge may require the use of a hammer to move it along the surface, since wood offers much greater resistance than linoleum.

Children generally will find it helpful to take rubbings of their work from time to time to appraise their progress. To do this, they should place a thin sheet of paper over the working surface and, holding it firmly, rub soft pencil or crayon across the paper.

Although no formula can be offered for making a successful cut, it may be observed that a composition displaying a balance between lines, white, black, and textured areas will prove to be particularly interesting. Blockprints are distinguished by the distribution of light and dark masses across the surface. Because of the relative difficulty in producing detail, these masses tend to be more prominent than in other forms of the plastic arts. Evidence of tool marks lends great vitality to the surface and gives the print the look and feel of the material. A print from a linoleum cut or woodcut should not be mistaken for a pen-and-ink drawing.

When the children find the cut satisfactory, they are ready to pull an impression of it. Before printing on paper it is wise to dampen all but the softest tissue types of paper with a sponge. After the paper has been dampened, it should be placed between pieces of blotting paper to remove any excess moisture. Then the children coat the brayer by rolling it evenly in water-soluble ink on the glass palette. Next, working in several directions with long sweeps of the brayer, they coat the linoleum or wood evenly with ink. The dampened paper (or dry tissue) should then be placed over the block and in turn covered with a sheet of blotting paper. This covering should be pressed and rubbed gently with the hands until enough contact between the block and the paper has been made to make an impression. In order to pull ink up from the block onto the paper a considerable amount of pressure has to be applied. This is usually done by a press or by prolonged rubbing with the back of a large wooden spoon. The spoon must be used with

A linoleum-block print by a group of fourth graders. Water-base ink was used on a discarded cotton sheet (which then served as a window curtain). Permanent, washable inks with an oil base may also be used. This is an effective way to utilize an entire class effort for a practicial purpose, to establish the relation between fine art (the individual's effort) and applied art (the curtain). Every child's print can be used, since pattern and repetition, by their vary nature, will flatter any single unit of the design.

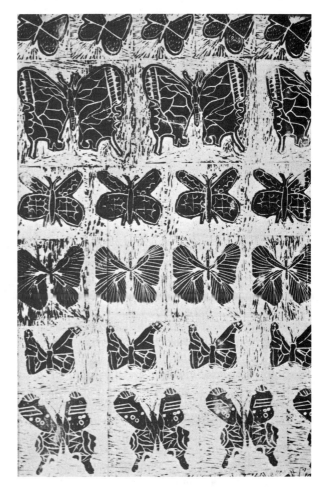

great care lest the paper tear or crinkle. The print may then be peeled away from the block. To prevent it from wrinkling it should be tacked to a drawing board and allowed to dry before it is removed and perhaps mounted.

For exhibition purposes a mount for the print may be constructed by folding in half a sheet of paper of appropriate size and color and then cutting a "window" in one of the halves through which to display the print. The print may then be fixed in place behind the window by means of rubber cement or tape. If the paper on which the print is taken is translucent, as in the case of certain tissues, an interesting effect may be obtained by fixing colored papers behind it. The "window" approach may also be used without the backing and is as satisfactory with heavy white or black paper as with mat board.

When printing is to be done on textiles, the cloth should be spread over felt or newspapers. The block should be inked in the manner just described for paper, except that, as mentioned previously, an oil-based ink should be used to obtain permanent color. The ink may be thinned with turpentine. Printing can be done with the hands, although much pressure must be exerted. A small wooden mallet is the most effective tool for this job. The block should be tapped sharply, first in the center and then on each corner. Each time the block is used it should be freshly and uniformly inked.

Teaching.   The chief problems in teaching wood- and linoleum-cutting and printing concern the development of skill in cutting and the treatment of subject matter. Organization of the classroom is similar to that required of stick printing.

Linoleum- and wood-cutting have often given rise to some unfortunate teaching methods concerning the selection of subject matter. Even teachers who have emphasized the importance of developing original subject matter in the direct processes have allowed pupils to copy designs for their work in linoleum and wood so that they may concentrate on technique. Such a teaching practice, however, proves in the long run to be as ineffective when applied to cutting as it does when applied to other types of art. No matter what the art form being produced, design and technique must develop in close relationship to each other. At first, children should work directly with the material. Rather than attempting to follow a drawing, they should explore ways of cutting. After becoming acquainted with the cutting methods, they can follow the teacher's suggestion of making some preliminary sketches with India ink and a brush. By that time they will have insight into the limitations of the medium and will realize to what extent a plan may help them in their work.

In printing, sketches can also be transferred to the plate with carbon paper or by covering the back of the sketch with an even tone from a soft lead pencil. Children should be encouraged to think in terms of print qualities rather than characteristics associated with drawing and painting. Because the children are working in media that do not permit a great amount of detail or halftones, their preliminary sketches and planning should be done in a single tempera or ink tone rather than pencil or crayon.

Linoleum- and wood-cutting lend themselves to picture making as well as pattern making, so that the problems arising from the selection and treatment of subject matter are varied. The teacher must, of course, help the children to select suitable subjects from their experience and observations. Beyond that, the work produced is modified both by the children's artistic level and by the technique itself. The children's output in using these media, while related to painting and drawing, is not identical to those processes because of differences in the media and tools. Often a display of the entire process of making a cut is helpful in

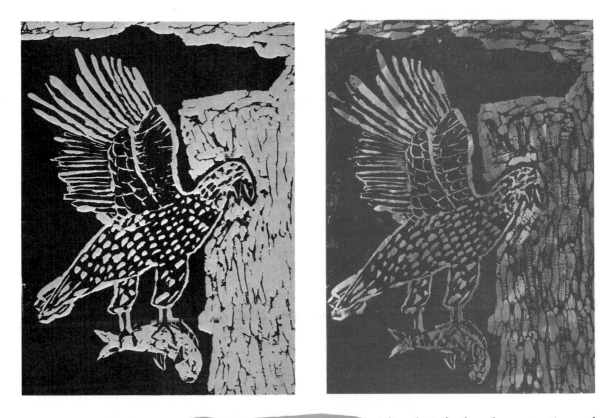

A black-and-white linoleum print compared with the same print on a surface prepared with water-color washes. Sixth grade.

starting the children to work. After that, further demonstrations of technique may be necessary from time to time. These, however, should be kept to a minimum so that children can develop their own methods of working. Linoleum in particular, unlike some other substances, is a medium that allows many variations of approach to be discovered through experience.

The possibilities for exploration of block cutting and printing are endless. The various types of cuts, the selection of different papers, the use of two or more colors on the same block, the placing of units on the textile, and, for sixth grade pupils, even the use of two or more blocks to form a pattern may all be challenging work in this art form.

The preparation of the print surface is an art project in itself. Consider how the following backgrounds will alter a black-and-white print:

Collage of magazine clippings
A page from a telephone book
Mingling pools of tempera
   paint on wet paper
Marbleized paper

Handmade paper
Collage of colored tissue
   paper
Pages from Sunday news-
   paper comics

These backgrounds may be used for random effects, or they may be planned with the design of the print in mind.

Some artists whose work in linoleum and wood the children will enjoy are Antonio Frasconi, Pablo Picasso, Leonard Baskin, Sidney Chafetz, Antonio Posada, and several of the German expressionists. Mexican folk art and medieval and Japanese woodcuts are also rich background sources for appreciation of printmaking.

The Reduction Process

Another variation of the linoleum method is the *reduction* or *subtractive* print. In this method children can begin by printing "an edition" (a dozen or more impressions) in one color. Another section of the plate is carved or "reduced" away, and a second color is added and printed over the first "reduced" position. When this is repeated a third or fourth time, a very rich surface develops, in addition to the added factor of a multicolored print. The original plate is destroyed in the process, of course, but another print form has been created.

Collography and Cardboard

The making of collographs involves cutting shapes out of cardboard, gluing them to another board for backing, inking the entire surface, and printing. The collography permits the worker to obtain interesting light areas around the edges of the raised surfaces, where the brayer cannot reach.

Prints may also be produced by arranging objects such as string, a piece of wire screen, burlap, or scraps of rough-textured cardboard on a clean glass. Newsprint is placed over the arrangement and an inked brayer is run over the paper to obtain a print. These techniques may be used as a preliminary for collage prints, which are made by gluing objects to a cardboard base and coating the assembly with shellac. Literally dozens of prints can be rolled off on such a plate. (The shellac keeps soft materials such as yarn and burlap from shedding onto the brayer and paper.) Variations of the same print can be obtained by pulling a second impression that is slightly off register.

Corrugated cardboard allows children to work on a large scale, since this material can be obtained in sizes as large as refrigerator cartons. It provides three surface areas to print: (1) the flat exterior surface; (2) the striated pattern of corrugation, which is between the surface "skins," and (3) the negative areas — sections of the cardboard completely cut away to reveal the paper on which the print is transferred.

Stenciling

Stenciling allows children to print repeated units of design with considerable control. The activity demands a reasonably high degree of skill and an ability to plan in detail before production. For these reasons, it should be performed only by more experienced preadolescents. In stenciling, shapes are cut out of paper; this paper is placed over a surface and paint applied. Only where holes (negative areas) have been cut will paint appear on the undersurface, and thus a controlled design established. The pieces removed by cutting may also be used as "masks" in the stencil process.

Media and Techniques. Strong waterproof or special stenciling paper as well as oaktag file folders should be used. Knives are required for cutting the stencil paper, and although a sharp pocketknife or single-edged razor blade will serve, for more detailed work special knives made for the purpose should be bought. Hog bristle brushes may be used to apply the paint, but inexpensive stencil brushes are obtainable. If stenciling is done on paper, tempera and watercolor are suitable; for stenciling on textiles, ordinary oil colors in tubes may be used. Special stencil paints, however, are available and are very satisfactory to use. Almost any surface, provided it is not too rough, will receive a stenciled pattern. Evenly woven cotton cloth is perhaps the most suitable textile for children to use, and most types of paper for drawing and painting are serviceable.

The paper being cut for the final stencils should be laid over a glass plate or a piece of hard building board. Care must be taken to be exact in cutting, so that a cut stops where it is supposed to stop and joins exactly with another cut. The worker must leave "ties," or narrow bands of paper, to hold parts of the design together. Hence the design must be simple.

When paper is being stenciled, it should be pinned to a drawing board. Textile, on the other hand, must be stretched tightly over news-

Fifth graders used cans of spray paint in this stencil mural based on a class study of jungle life. The shapes were cut and pinned into place before spraying. The forms were then moved around for a second and third spraying. (The teacher should always check for proper ventilation for spraying.) If spray paint is not available stencils can be painted by dipping a toothbrush in tempera paint and brushing it against a stiff wire-mesh surface. Stencil work povides a graduation of tone and clarity of edge that cannot be obtained through conventional painting techniques.

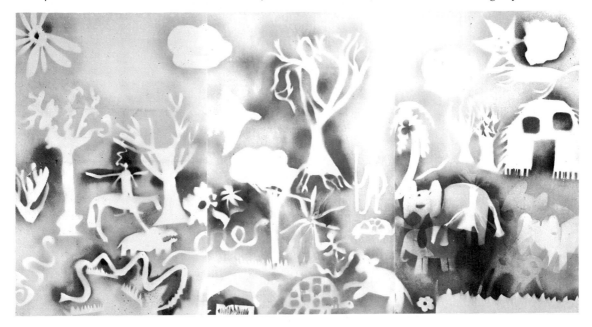

print or blotting paper and then pinned firmly in place. The paper underneath the textile will absorb any excess paint that might otherwise run and spoil the work.

Paint should be thick enough not to run, yet no so thick as to form an unpleasantly heavy coating on the painted surface. Tempera paint for printing on paper can be placed in a muffin tin. After being dipped into the paint the brush should be scrubbed slightly on scrap paper to rid it of excess paint. The amount of paint picked up by the brush can be controlled by gently dabbing the brush on the palette.

This colorful print is a lithograph by the contemporary American artist Robert Rauschenberg. He integrates photographic images with his own brushwork and drawing to create powerful works of art. You can also see evidence of collage techniques and expressive use of color. How does this print compare to the work of Rembrandt? Can you detect differences that place the works in time and location? Do artists continue to work in the manner of Rembrandt? How does the work of artists relate to their times and the societies in which they live? (Courtesy of The Museum of Modern Art, New York.)

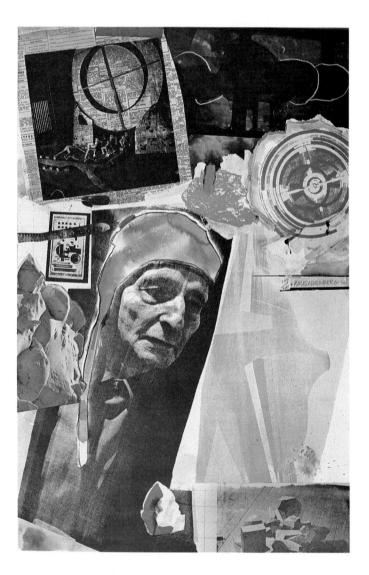

Paint should be applied to the holes in the stencil with some care: if the brush is used too vigorously, the stencil may be damaged. For an even spread of color over the entire cut out area the paint should be applied with a dabbing motion. Stroking from the edge of the stencil into the cut out area will give a shaded effect.

Teaching.   Clean equipment is necessary if smooth work is to result. The brushes in particular should be kept scrupulously clean. While cool water will suffice to wash brushes used with tempera paint and water-soluble ink, turpentine is the solvent for oil-based colors. Brushes that have been cleaned in turpentine should be washed again with soap and cool water. After the brushes have been washed they should be placed in a container with the bristles up. Students should, of course, be taught to clean their palettes after using them. Should students wish to preserve the stencils from one day to another, they should wash the stencils carefully with water or turpentine, depending on the type of paint used, after which the stencils can be suspended from a line strung in a storage cupboard for the purpose.

Finally, the teacher should encourage experimentation, for which stenciling provides many opportunities. Various colors may be used both separately and blended. A good effect is achieved if the stencil is moved slightly when a second color is used. Furthermore, two or more stencils may be used on the same surface.

◆ NOTES TO THE TEXT

1. Heller, Jules, *Print Making Today* (New York: Holt, Rinehart & Winston, 1958), p. xiv.

2. Rosen, Randy, *Prints: The Facts and Fun of Collecting* (New York: Dutton, 1978), p. 185.

3. Rosen, ibid.

4. For beginners, pieces measuring 5 by 6 inches are satisfactory; later, pieces as large as 10 by 12 inches can be used; and for sixth graders, pieces can be even larger. In 1518 Durer made a woodcut print that was 10 by 11 feet.

◆ ACTIVITIES FOR THE READER

1. Produce a monoprint contour-line drawing by using one color and drawing directly in the color after you have applied it to a sheet of glass. Repeat, using two colors lightly blended with the brayer.

2. Produce a monoprint contour-line drawing by drawing on the paper after it has been laid down over the inky glass. Experiment by using several colors of ink at the same time.

3. Produce a nonobjective design in monoprint by laying down an arrangement of string, burlap, and cut cardboard on the inky surface before applying the paper for the impression.

4. Experiment with a number of vegetables, suitably cut, to produce various printed textural effects on paper. Over these effects print an orderly design with a potato or carrot into which you have cut a pattern with a knife.

5. **a.** Experiment with a potato, scoring it not only with a knife but also with a fork or a spoon. Try printing a sheet of paper with an overall pattern that repeats the unit exactly.

   b. Prepare two soap erasers with different designs ("a" and "b") and print the units as follows:

   a, b, a, b, a
   a, b, a, b, a
   a, b, a, b, a
   a, b, a, b, a, etc.

   c. Now print as follows on black paper:

   a, b, b, a
   b, a, a, b
   a, b, b, a
   b, a, a, b, etc.

   d. Print, turning "a" or "b" upside down.

   e. Print, overlapping "a" and "b."

   f. Print with varying space between the "a'''s and "b'''s:

   a a a
   　b b
   a a a

   g. Create some different arrangements, perhaps eventually using three and four motifs, or units. In all cases, the pattern should be repeated exactly.

   h. Combine some of your printed arrangements with interesting backgrounds prepared experimentally.

6. Use an example of Islamic tesselation (tile patterns) as a historical source for creating sequences of patterns.

7. Experiment with a piece of linoleum, making a nonobjective design to obtain many different types of textures. Take several rubbings of your work as you progress. Finally, print it on paper.

8. Cut a 2-inch square of linoleum and glue it to a block. Cut a nonobjective unit of design in this piece of linoleum. Print the design on paper in repeated patterns in the manner indicated in 5a–h, above.

9. From a landscape, still life, life drawing, or some other representational work you have produced, plan a picture to be cut in linoleum. Make an India ink drawing the exact size you intend your cut to be, say 5 by 8 inches. Cover the linoleum with a thin coat of white tempera paint and then redraw your sketch on the linoleum. Start cutting, taking as many rubbings as you require, and later make some test prints to give you an idea of your progress. When the design is ready, print it in several single colors. Then try printing with two colors simultaneously.

10. Take a plank of wood and make a print of the grain. Use light colors and overlap the grain or turn the wood to create patterns. If the pattern of the grain suggests anything to you, cut away a few sections of the wood to make the movement of the pattern even stronger.

11. Make a collograph by cutting out cardboard shapes, gluing them to a base, inking the surface, and taking a print. The thicker the cardboard, the greater the play of light around the edges of your shapes in the print.

12. Make a corrugated print at least 18 by 24 inches. Try one print on a surface that is covered with a colored tissue collage.

13. Cut a stencil, using a nonobjective design no smaller than 3 inches square and print it on paper. Experiment on paper as indicated in 5a–h, above.

14. Obtain a styrofoam meat tray from the local supermarket. Using a ballpoint pen or blunt pencil, draw on the tray. Then, using a brayer, ink the drawn area and print the image on paper cut to fit the tray.

15. Decide how you would explain the differences among other graphic techniques such as intaglio, lithography, photography, and silkscreen.

◆ SUGGESTED READINGS

Andrews, Michael. *Creative Printmaking*. Englewood Cliffs: Prentice-Hall, 1963.

Feldman, Edmund Burke. *Thinking About Art*. Englewood Cliffs, NJ: Prentice-Hall, 1985.

Romano, Clare, and John Ross. *The Complete Printmaker*. New York: Macmillan, 1972. Updates contemporary print processes, many of which are useable in public schools.

Rosen, Randy. *Prints: The Facts and Fun of Collecting*. New York: E. P. Dutton, 1978.

Weiss, Harvey. *Paper, Ink and Roller*. New York: William Scott, 1978.

NEWER MEDIA: IDEAS AND EARTHWORKS — COMPUTERS TO LASERS

THE TRADITIONAL WORK of art will exist as long as walls are solid and contain areas of emptiness. One can detect in the emergence of budding art movements, however, new and embracing attitudes for un-conventional elements and materials in the formation of art objects — earth, water, fire, to name a few, and in particular light.[1]

Lloyd Schultz

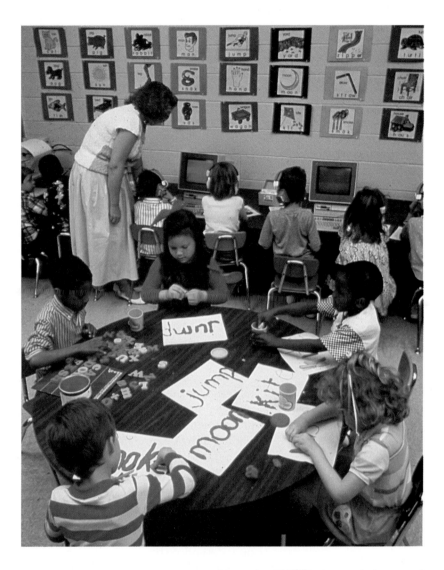

The invention of oil paint in the fifteenth century changed the art of painting forever. Before that time artists had to paint on fast-drying plaster (fresco) or use tempera pigments mixed with water or egg yolk. With the new slow-drying oil paints artists could take time to blend colors carefully and develop images more deliberately. And, if properly applied, the oils improved the longevity of paintings.

Many other technical advances have greatly influenced what artists attempt and what they are able to accomplish. We have mentioned previously the invention of lithography and the making of paper as technical advances in the art of printmaking. During the past century technical advances have occurred at a startling and accelerating rate.

Artists today have a range of art media that their predecessors a hundred years ago never dreamed of. Contemporary artists also use materials in new and unusual ways that would not have been accepted or understood in the past. In this chapter we will sample a few of the newer ideas and media that mark the current art scene, and we will suggest ways that elementary school children might learn about art beyond the traditions of drawing and painting.

NEW IDEAS, NEW MEDIA

The invention of photography in the nineteenth century made a tremendous impact on the visual arts that continues to the present. At first artists moved away from realistic representation because the camera could accomplish that quickly and accurately. Instead, artists developed ideas that the camera could not accomplish. The impressionists developed a painterly style, emphasizing their medium and creating images that expressed mood without great detail. The cubists moved in another direction with greater abstraction, using the real visual world only as a starting point and manipulating the concept of reality in art. The fauvists rejected the notion of local or realistic color and painted in ways that the camera could not duplicate.

Later, other artists began using photographic images as reference material for their drawings, paintings, prints, and sculptures. Instead of rejecting the photographic image and moving as far from it as possible, some artists began to use the camera to assist them. Gradually, photography became more than a technical process and photographers entered the realm of art. Photographers found ways to distort images, alter colors at will, print double or triple images, and generally be as expressive as painters. Currently the lines between photography and painting or printmaking are blurred as artists often combine media. For example, instead of painting, drawing, or sculpting a portrait of the art collector Ethel Scull, Andy Warhol asked her to sit in a coin-operated photo booth and pose for a large number of pictures. He then used a selection of the photographs to make a photoserigraph showing Mrs. Scull in a variety of views and moods, creating a much more revealing portrait of her than any single view could.

From the beginning days of photography we have moved ahead to the technologies of cinema, video, and computer-generated images. Each of these technologies has become an artistic medium and, as with photography, new modes of making art have come into being. The entire movie industry has resulted from that invention and many films are considered works of fine art, and are collected and screened in museums of art. Films are made not only by Hollywood studios, but also by a growing coterie of serious private filmmakers worldwide.

Andy Warhol, *Ethel Scull 36 Times*, 1963. From what you can see in this portrait, what do you suppose the subject is like? Does the work exhibit any plan for color selection and balance? (Collection of Whitney Museum of American Art. Gift of Ethel Redner Scull.)

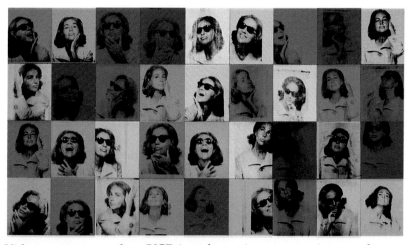

Video cassette recorders (VCRs) are becoming common in many households around the world, creating a large market for video cassettes. Many individuals now use video camcorders to make the equivalent of home movies that were common during the previous generation. Not yet as common or accessible, but developing at a rapid rate, is the technology of computer-generated images. Even personal computer users can purchase programs for "drawing" and "painting" on the computer. A new group of artists have chosen the computer as their art medium. Many college art departments offer courses that teach students to create expressive art images with the computer. In the commercial art fields computer art is well established. Many of the images in television advertising are computer generated, as are an increasing number of movies, such as the pioneering feature film, *Tron*, and numerous animated films. Technology is advancing rapidly in the computer area and it is safe to say that the computer will become increasingly significant as a tool for generating art images.

Virtually every innovation in technology makes an impact in the art area as artists appropriate new media to create images that were previously not feasible. In the area of metals, for example, we are seeing sculptures cast from stainless steel, welded with cor-ten steel, constructed of lightweight expanded aluminum, and suspended with high tensile strength wire cable. Artists have created laser light shows, using colored beams of laser light on a large scale at night, often in conjunction with architectural forms. Others, perhaps after a visit to Las Vegas, have made sculpture from neon tubing of different colors and sizes. An entire range of kinetic sculpture has been developed, including sculptures that are moved by energy produced by water, wind, electricity, gasoline engines, magnets, etc.

Perhaps as important as new technologies are the new ideas that artists continually develop. During the second half of the twentieth century we have witnessed the initiation of conceptual art, environmental art, and art performances. All of these new ideas have resulted in an expansion of acceptable materials for art, such as the 24-mile-long *Running Fence* created by Christo in California of 18-foot-high white nylon material hung from steel poles and more than 100 miles of steel cable.[2] The fence was in existence only two weeks, after which it was dismantled as planned and the materials given to the ranchers on whose lands the fence was constructed. *Running Fence* was an example of conceptual art, in that the idea of a fence uniting the land that had been divided by state jurisdictions, county boundaries, and individual landowners was central to the project. It was environmental art because of its scope and the importance of the environment to its success. In some ways it was also performance art, as an excellent documentary film was made of the project. The film will remain for years after the fence itself has ceased to exist.

Some artists have taken that most basic and ancient of environments, the earth itself, as an art medium. One artist (Walter de Maria) filled a gallery in Munich with rich dark soil to a depth of three feet. This piece was probably much more significant to urban dwellers than farmers who experience soil in large quantities on a daily basis. Another artist (Robert Smithson) created a spiral of rock and dirt that extended into the Great Salt Lake in Utah. As the *Spiral Jetty* remained in place over the months and years the colors of the water changed around the spiral as communication with the lake, water depths, and temperatures differed, allowing different types of marine life and chemicals to accrue. The jetty was later submerged completely as the lake level rose.[3] One motivation for artists who create transitory or temporary works is avoidance of the art market, which some believe is a corrupting influence on creative expression. Also, it is a commentary about the lack of control artists have over their works once they are sold and become, in many cases, market commodities.

An example of the use of interior environments is the work of Sandy Skoglund, who creates unusual settings in rooms.[4] In one piece she painted the entire room, walls, ceiling, and floor with a flat gray paint. A small table, two chairs, refrigerator, and all other items in the room are painted the same gray. An elderly couple (living models, not sculptures) are posed in the room, the man sitting on a chair and the woman in front of the open refrigerator door; both are dressed completely in the same flat gray, making their skin tones stand out in contrast. Also in the room are many bright yellow-green cats (sculptures), each in a different pose. Here is what a critic wrote about this environment, which Skoglund titled *Radioactive Cats*:

> In this humorous and horrific scene, an aging couple in a grimly impoverished interior is inundated by mutant green cats, whose lurid coloration reverberates against the neutralized environment. These voracious animals

Sandy Skogland, *Neo-Auto: The Lost and Found*, © 1986 by Sandy Skogland. Why did the artist use the straight-lined, sharp-cornered shapes on the walls and ceiling? What do these shapes suggest next to the wrecked car? Why are the two persons looking to one side? What effect does Skogland's selection of complementary colors express?

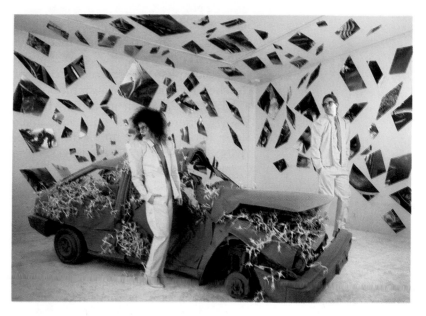

infest every surface in a quest for nonexistent food. This science-fiction fantasy is rendered believable by the veristic nature of photography, which simply records "the truth." Skoglund sculpted the plaster cats herself and readied the set by painting everything in the tiny room a mottled gray. The artist also prepared a version of the tableau as a separate installation, allowing her audience to see both the photography and a portion of the thing photographed.[5]

The artist poses living models in her environments and takes photographs which become the works of art. The actual environments are sometimes displayed in museums and galleries, usually without the living models.

Children are aware of many of these art forms in their everyday lives. Films, videos, computer-generated images in television ads, and, for many, music videos are commonly seen. In many ways children are more "media literate" than their parents and teachers. We will suggest ways that children can participate in art activities based on some of the newer media and ideas. We also suggest that it is worthwhile for children to learn about what contemporary artists are doing and creating and why they are changing the art world. It is unlikely that many elementary schools will be teaching computer graphics as part of the art curriculum in the near future, but it is worthwhile for children to know that this art form is all around them and, in fact, might be influential in their lives. One goal of a balanced art program is to foster in children the ability to be discriminating about the quality, significance, and interpretation of the art of their own time as well as the art of the past.

NEWER MEDIA IN THE CLASSROOM

Although many of these art media are beyond what is available in school art programs, there are some classroom activities that children can accomplish under the direction of an interested and energetic teacher. Here are some examples:

Cindy Sherman is an artist who dresses herself in different costumes, often complete with wigs, makeup, glasses, etc., that transform her apparently into a different person. She then photographs herself (self-portrait) as the other person in an actual indoor or outdoor setting. Some of the portraits are humorous, others are tragic, frightening, beautiful, puzzling, ambivalent, and so on.

> In the color work that Sherman began in 1980, she enlarged the scale, backlit the settings, and increased the subtlety of her female characterizations. As her photographs evolved from costumed melodramas into evocative studies of contemporary women, she explored the edge between art and commerce. It was only a matter of time before Sherman was approached by dress designers who requested her to use their wares in her staged situations. She began shooting the group that includes *Untitled* as an advertising assignment for the French *Vogue*, but early on felt a friction between the manufacturer's expectations of ''cute funny pictures'' and her own creative interests: ''I really started to make fun of, not really of the clothes, but much more of fashion.''[6]

Creating a Gallery of Self-Portraits

Like many children, Cindy Sherman spent a fair portion of her childhood watching TV, drawing, and playing ''dress-up.'' With the use of a camera children in school classrooms can identify characters they would like to represent, assemble the necessary clothes, select the settings, and take the pictures. They can display a gallery of portraits that they have created. Copies can be made for the children and the gallery can be saved by the teacher and added to from year to year.

Ask children to collect photographs of interesting faces that they see in magazines and newspapers. Discuss the moods and feelings that the faces convey. Ask if any of the photographs should be classified as art, or if they belong in the category of ordinary candid shots that anyone can take. What are the differences between the pictures that students believe should qualify as art?

Polaroid Photography as an Art Medium

The prominent British artist David Hockney has explored the polaroid camera as a tool for making art.[7] He is also interested in the cubism of Picasso and Braque, in which multiple views of the same subject are presented in a single painting, producing distortions, but also revealing more information than is possible with only one view (note the similarity with Warhol's idea for the Ethel Scull portrait). Hockney has taken this idea and applied it with unusual results using the polaroid camera.

David Hockney, *Stephen Spender, Mas St. Jerome II*, 1985. © David Hockney 1990. The artist has photographed his subject from several vantage points and distances and combined the images to create a revealing portrait.

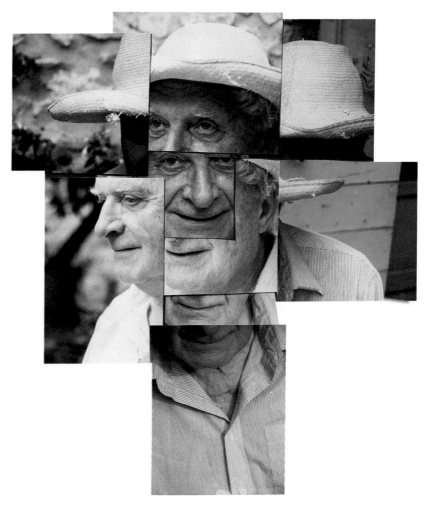

Polaroid cameras are very common and, if the school doesn't have one, one can usually be obtained for temporary use from parents or friends of the school. Ask children to select a scene that they like for some reason, such as their own classroom, a local park, or an interesting building. Working in teams according to how many cameras you have or by taking turns with one camera, have the children take pictures of the selected subject from different points of view. When all the pictures are completed, ask the children to select the ones that are most interesting and best express what they feel about the subject. Then they can assemble the pictures and mount them on a firm surface such as poster board. If they work in teams they might make several polaroid works.

When you display the polaroid "collages" you might include the work of Hockney, along with some information about his life and work.

You might even relate the work to the idea of cubism. Statements by the children about what they were trying to capture and communicate in the photographs would add greatly to the display.

Working in a similar way the children might take pictures of a person (maybe the principal) and assemble a portrait similar to Warhol's approach. They might add drawings or paintings of the person to achieve another dimension of insight and interest to their portrait.

Art from Everything

It is the attitude of artists that determines what materials they will use to create art. This attitude has changed recently to allow virtually any (safe) materials to be used in the creation of works of art. One artist who uses items from the everyday environment is Kenny Scharf, who assembled and painted a variety of materials, including a television set, to create the sculpture *Extravaganza Televisione*.[8]

Ask children to collect many items that they no longer want or need, such as old toys, dishes, plastic items, even small appliances or lamps that are no longer in use. Supplement what they bring with a trip to a local surplus warehouse or thrift store and purchase (or ask for the donation of) interesting items. Collect wood scraps from the high school wood shop, local lumber yard, or from parents who do woodwork. It is possible to collect one or more television sets that still work, although sometimes not very well, among the items.

Tell the children that they are going to work together to make a sculpture out of the collected materials. They can discuss what mood they might want to express: funny, frightening, exciting, beautiful, and so on. Then they can begin selecting objects and try them together to see if they "work" in interesting ways. You will also need to decide at the appropriate time what colors will be best for expressing the mood you have chosen. Individual items will need to be painted prior to combining them with other objects.

One major problem is how to combine the objects so they don't fall apart. You might need hammer and nails, good quality glue, screws and screwdriver, clamps, and whatever other means that you can devise. Decide in advance if you want the sculpture to actually have working parts, such as Scharf's television set. When the sculpture is assembled and stabilized so it won't fall apart, decide what colors would be most appropriate for the final painting. When the work is completed you will have a contemporary sculpture and, if you have included anything electrical that works, you can turn it on and admire the sight, movement, and sound of your work.

Copy Technology for Learning About Art

Most schools have photocopy machines and some school districts have access to color copy machines. There are many uses for such machines that are not very expensive. For example, after discussing and analyzing Van Gogh's *Starry Night*, the teacher can make a copy of the reproduction for every child. Children are then asked to respond to tasks such as, "Use your red crayon to outline the shapes of the trees" or "With your black crayon show the swirling lines in the sky, the trees, and the foreground" or "With your blue crayon make an X on the spots the artist has made most interesting to look at (centers of interest)." This idea can be used for any types of responses you would like children to make as they study and understand a particular work of art.

Artists are beginning to use color copy machines as another addition to printmaking technology. These machines can enlarge, reduce, distort, change color emphasis, and other interesting operations, giving the artist immediate results and ideas for more changes. When the artist has created the final image it can be duplicated on the machine for whatever edition is wanted. Color slides can also be duplicated on color copy machines, making it possible to print from slides and then to alter the print with crayons, paints, or inks, then print the results of that process.

Using the regular copy machine, children can make drawings that can be duplicated and colored or painted on in different ways without destroying the original. The drawing can be enlarged or reduced and several versions can be cut and pasted together, like Hockney does with polaroid shots, to create a collage of multiple versions of a single image drawn by the child. Children can learn about the fluency afforded artists with modern technology as they experiment with the copy machine. They can also learn to manipulate their own ideas in ways that would not be possible without the copy machine.

MEDIA FOR INSTRUCTION

The hardware of media are considerably more than mechanical gadgets for presenting information; they are linked to the very shape and structure of the content being imparted, and thus represent different modes of learning. Let us consider for a moment the many ways by which instructional media are able to extend students' perceptions of a subject such as painting:

A *film* about a particular artist can show something of the process of change and maturation in an individual.

A *comparison of slides* of works of art can lead to a group discussion of likenesses and differences in style and content of art objects.

Packets of small *reproductions* allow students to investigate at their own pace the visual components of a series of paintings.

A *filmstrip* can provide an inexpensive collection of slides centered on a single idea. For commentary there is usually an accompanying record or lecture notes; students can also work from their own impressions.

A *live television lesson* can bring a professional artist to the class for a single performance.

A *portable video tape machine* can play back a demonstration by a visiting artist for future reference or for classes that could not attend the original performance.

A *tape recording* of an interview with a local art critic can be stored for future reference.

A *computer* with color monitor and compact disk can be used to retrieve color images of any artist, style, or work and present them on the screen. A single disk can hold thousands of art images.

It is improbable that any teacher would have access to all of the above modes of instruction, but with time, knowledge, and equipment, teachers can significantly extend their own style of teaching, the pupils' scope of learning, and the range of subject matter. In all modes of media, limitations are offset by the advantages.

Environmental Influences

Children today are both eager and prepared to engage in media activity. The factors that stand in the way of such activity are the teacher's ignorance of media and unwillingness to recognize them as a valid basis for art instruction. The children, unaware of their teacher's reservations, continue to develop in their own environment. Their visual sense is oriented to motion because of early exposure to television and films. They accept condensed time-space concepts because they view live coverage of news events, and they have never doubted, for instance, that they could breakfast in one part of the world and lunch in another.

The art teacher who is truly sensitive to what is happening outside the classroom will give serious thought to incorporating newer media into the art program, realizing that there is no inherent contradiction in goals or philosophy between creating in either the new or the traditional media. Both kinds of materials provide excitement and challenge in the areas of design, including color, and drawing; both elicit original solutions on the part of the child and call for a high level of creative ingenuity. Newer media have simply added such increasingly relevant ingredients as time, motion, and light to the elements of color, space, mass, line, texture, and shade. Teachers will be shortsighted indeed should they fail to capitalize on the built-in motivations provided by the excitement of matching sound to light or image to movement. They will also deprive themselves of a logical means of combining other arts such as music, dance, and choral reading.

The activities described in this chapter have been tested in elementary schools. They range from simple projects that can be carried out in one learning session to more complex operations requiring several sessions. In most cases, the amount of time spent on the project depends on how deeply the teacher wants to probe the subject.

Projected Images

The creation of designs on slides that can be projected gives the child an opportunity to experiment with light. The materials are not expensive, and the activity can be correlated with music and language arts.

Media and Techniques.   The slides should be 2 inches square and made of glass or heavy acetate. These provide the base, or *ground*, for the transparent materials that carry the design. As for these materials, any that permit the passage of light are acceptable—colored cellophane, crystallizing lacquers, theatrical gelatins, colored lacquers, nail polish, and so on. Or the slides may be covered with India ink or tempera paint and sections scratched away to allow passage of light. Applying the color is a simple matter. Nail polish, crystallizing lacquers, and colored lacquers can be painted on with cotton swabs or detail brushes. Colored cellophane and theatrical gelatins can be applied to the slide with white plastic glue that has been thinned out with five parts water to one part glue.

The children can design both sides of the slide; one side might be used for solid color and the other for linear effects with India ink. In such a case the design problem would be to combine the elements of mass and line into a satisfactory whole. Another variant might be to design soft shapes on one side and hard-edged forms on the other. If children want to make a two-slide image, they have not only four sides to plan but also the area between the slides. Here, they may choose to add such "stop outs" as sand, ashes, and thread to create silhouette effects. The edges of the plates should be taped to keep the center of the "sandwich" in place (see illustration). Because of the limited size of the slides, an abstract design is a more appropriate subject than a realistic image. Slides of artworks, landscapes, buildings, and family groups (provided the owners have decided to discard them) can make interesting raw material for photocollages.

The slides can be projected through a standard school projector. Two projectors allow for overlapping of images. It is safe to say that the more projectors going at once, the larger the image, and the darker the room, the more exciting the possibilities. The projects are often as effective when the images are diffused as when they are sharply in focus. A musical selection that the class enjoys might be used as an accompaniment for the designing of the projections. When the slides are run on two projectors in conjunction with the music the class has a novel program for a school assembly or a PTA meeting.

Teaching.   One way to begin instruction is to let the class manipulate color and light on an overhead projector. If time is limited, the teacher

A *A single slide.*

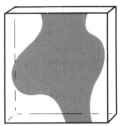

Front side: flowing image (paint, ink, lacquer).

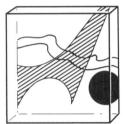

Back side: linear and hard-edged images (ink, cellophane, gelatinate).

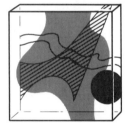

Combined image: hard and soft forms.

Various ways of treating glass slides.

B *A two-slide image.*

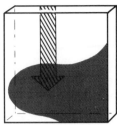

Combined image, slide 1.

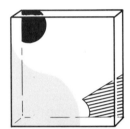

Combined image, slide 2.

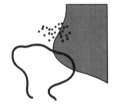

Center section: string, ashes, and cut gelatin.

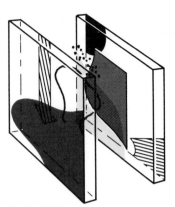

Both slides plus "sandwich" before taping.

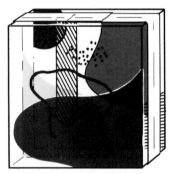

Finished, taped slide showing combined image composed of five patterns.

can move about colored cellophane on a sheet of acetate while the class discusses how such movements affect the image. This activity may be followed by some wet mingling of colored lacquers on the acetate. The discussion may then focus on how such activities can be transferred to the smaller confines of a glass slide. The class might list materials that block the passage of light and those that permit light to pass through. If the teacher has any finished slides on hand, the class can look at them and speculate on how the effects were achieved. By this time the class will be more than ready to begin their own slides. The teacher might want to select music for the class to listen to as they work and, later, help organize a light show to project the finished slides.

Film Animation Without a Camera

There are several techniques with which to create cinematic effects and moving images without actually using a camera. The simplest way to acquaint children with the principles of animation is to gather together as many old telephone books as are available and have the students make marks on the margin. By flipping the edge of the book, the images will dance randomly about. Ask the class how to control the motion, and someone will soon suggest a progression. Once a sequential progression is maintained, the flow of images can be controlled. At this point, the class can move on to the next step and draw directly on film.

Media and Techniques.   Film animation without a camera is accomplished by painting or drawing directly on the actual segments of film. Thus the basic materials for this activity are strips of 16mm film — clear leader or black with an emulsion side — and inks or paint to apply to the film. White leader may also be used; it offers a soft gray background for color. It is also possible to purchase transparent colored leader film.

The most elementary technique is to draw a black line on the clear film. India ink may be used, but it has a tendency to flake off while being used in the projector. The best ink for this technique is Pelikan (K) black, a plastic ink that adheres permanently to the acetate of the film. When black emulsion-type leader film is used, the design consists of white line on a black ground. The white line is produced by scratching through the emulsion with a needlelike tool. Simple etching tools can be made by fixing sewing needles in pencils or sticks. Because it is rather difficult to see the scratched lines, it is advisable to work over a sheet of white paper or on windowpanes. Care should be taken that the lines are not etched too deeply, for the film can be weakened in this way. Another variation of the scratching technique is to punch out a series of holes in varying sizes, thus creating a pattern of flashing lights when the film is projected. Rotating leather punches, which have six or eight sizes of holes, are good to use for this purpose.

Colored lines may be drawn with felt-tip pens. These pens can also be used to make free nonobjective color patterns to serve as background for more controlled black-line exercises. If the student wants to work with color materials of a more plastic nature, two that give excellent results are transparent lacquer and transparent acetate ink. Some fingernail polishes are also transparent and can be used. Transparent lacquer is a thick liquid, so it must be applied to the film with a small brush rather than a pen. Because it has a penetrating odor it should be used only in rooms with proper ventilation. Perhaps the best color medium is acetate ink. It has the brilliant color qualities of transparent lacquer without its offensive fumes, and it can be applied to the film with a pen.

The student should experiment with a variety of pen points or brushes. If the ink resists flowing onto the film, it is possible that the surface is greasy. The film can be cleaned quickly with a rag dampened with alcohol. Sufficient drying time should be allowed before running the film through an editing machine or projector.

The length of the filmstrips need not pose problems as to where to work. The children may work standing up, hanging their strips vertically on the wall or blackboard; they may tape segments of film to cateferia-type tables; or they may move the film along their desks. It is recommended that white paper be used as a backing for the section of film being worked on.

Teaching. Before the actual creative work on the film begins the teacher should explain how motion is achieved in filmmaking. The student should understand that twenty-four frames will pass through the projecting lens in one second at "sound" speed.[9] Since twenty-four frames comes to about 7 inches of film, about 2 feet of film per child will allow three seconds of animation.

Because most students have difficulty understanding the frame and time relationship, it is advisable to present them first with some simple activities exploring fundamental paths of motion—horizontal, vertical, and spatial. One basic activity is to have the student develop a series of dots, circles, stars, crosses, or some other objects that advance or recede. To advance, the objects should begin very small and gradually increase in size until they take up most of the frame. The objects seem to recede when they gradually diminish in size. At least six frames for each stage of growth should be allowed, for it takes this long for the eye to accommodate a distinct unit of motion. In order to have a shape travel horizontally from left to right, the student draws the forward part of the object on the left-hand side of the frame for a six-frame segment. Every time the object is advanced toward the right of the frame the position should be held for six frames, until finally only the last portion of the object is visible from the right-hand edge of the frame.

Anything that can be moved can be animated. These illustrations are two examples. Below, twelve-year-olds change the shape of a pile of sand so that when it is photographed, one shape will "flow" easily into another. The illustration to the right shows a basic setup for clay animation. The background is a mural project; the figures are plasticene; and the police wagon is a painted cereal box. Two lights on either side and a 16- or 8mm film camera in the center complete this mini-studio. Working from a storyboard, the animators can enjoy improvising by reshaping the clay and repositioning the objects.

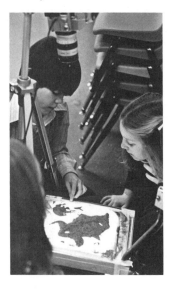

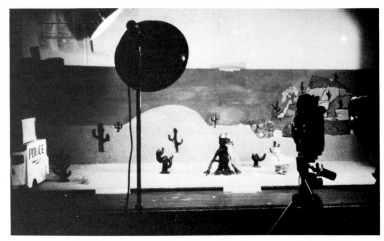

Another activity develops the ability to make a shape grow or change into another shape. This task requires that the student think of the finished product first and then break the design process down into manageable segments that develop logically out of each other. In order to make a line draw itself into a square, for instance, the student might first draw a horizontal line, repeat it for six frames, next draw a connecting vertical line in another six frames, and thus continue until the four sides of the square are completed. This method can be applied to drawing a triangle or even a face.

Ideally, the children should have access to a film-editing machine so that they can view their work immediately. With such a machine, the child can see clearly that each frame is a single discrete image. The flow of one image to the next is controlled in much the same way one controls the movement of "flip books" — by speeding up or retarding the controlling mechanism (see activity 5 at the end of this chapter). By observing how their films work in this machine the students can understand how the movies they see function.

Unless the whole class works in shifts on one large segment of film, it will be necessary to purchase a film splicer to join the segments. There are usually two or three mechanically inclined children in most fifth and sixth grade classes who can be taught to use the splicer. At least five feet of leader should be reserved for splicing at the beginning and at the end of the completed film; this amount is needed to get the film into the projector.

Film animation with a camera is too complex to adequately describe here, but there are excellent books that explain the process in simple, clear terms. If the teacher has a tripod, an 8- or 16mm movie camera with a stop-action mechanism, and two strong lights, the class can animate anything, from people (*pixillation*), to sand, to pictures. Film animation is valuable because it teaches patience, satisfies the desire to learn purely technical processes, and develops narrative skill. An animated film begins when drawing or painting is completed. It allows a child to move very directly into the world of Walt Disney and Ralph Bakshi. After making their own film, children will never look at professional work in quite the same way.

Experiences With a Camera

If a camera is available, whether handmade or on loan from friend or family, it can be used as an instrument for observation and personal commentary. The treatment of one subject in two or more greatly contrasted media (as in sculpture, painting, and photography) is an effective way of attuning children to the possibilities and limitations of art media. Bartow mentions seven tasks for the beginning photographer which are also worth trying in drawing (and writing).

Make a "living comic strip." Tell a story in a series of pictures using real people.

Photograph an autobiography. Tell about yourself by taking pictures of your favorite things, your family, where you live, yourself.

Document your neighborhood. Take pictures of people at work and play, people of different ages, buildings where you and others live, work, spend their time.

Define a word/feeling with a picture or series of pictures. (Happiness, sadness, cold, hot, hard, soft.)

Pretend you're a bug or a giant. Photograph the world through their eyes.

Illustrate a song or a poem or a short story with your own photos.

Film look-alikes. Take a picture of something that looks like an owl but isn't an owl. Does the front of a car look like a smiling face? The branch of a tree like an arm?

Look for patterns. Find repeated designs in the environment, like picket fences, railroad tracks, or bricks.[10]

The Storyboard

The storyboard is a transdisciplinary activity that draws in varying degrees on narrative skill, the linking of image to story, and the use of drawing. It can also prepare children to better understand how filmmakers, animators, and even writers of commercials think on paper.

A storyboard is a sequence of pictures that tells a story or relates to a given problem. Some students may choose to draw their sequences; others may compile them or paste them up from news or magazine photos. The storyboard can be used to plan an 8mm film or can be an activity in itself. Specific homework assignments can be made. For example, children in the upper elementary grades are capable of studying a one-minute television commercial by reducing it to a sequence of storyboard frames, thereby recording the timing of shots, distinguishing between tight shots (very close), long shots (at a distance), close-ups, and so on. In making a storyboard, students can apply the basic vocabulary of film and video to extend their own picture making. Storyboards are the middle ground between the realm of the communications media and the traditional forms of picture making.

MULTIMEDIA: THE LIGHT SHOW

The light show uses media for both its communicative and its creative potential. In addition, the light show allows children to combine many forms of media. For example, consider how a class might treat a holiday or celebration. The class not only has available the traditional performing arts (readings, songs, period music, dramatic scenes), but it also has fresh visual opportunities supplied by the medium of the light show: projection of "fireworks" drawn on clear film, slides of heroes or patriots flashed against a background of moving patterns of stars or flags.

Given a range of basic visual aid equipment to explore, children will engage in manipulative activities very similar to their first reaction to clay or any other new art material. During this initial stage, the children should be encouraged to experiment freely with the tools of light and motion; they should be allowed to combine fixed and moving images, blend sounds, and work light with color in a random fashion. However, to abandon the challenge of ultimately obtaining some sort of content and meaning in their work would be like cutting off the painting experience after a session or two of dripping and splashing. Ideally, the light show should be planned with some degree of structure around a central idea. If children can be taught to plan a light show with as much care and thought as they bring to the creation of a puppet show or mural, their range of learning can be considerably extended.

No single successful way to prepare a light show can be set forth. Much depends on the equipment to which the class has access. The teacher should first take an inventory of the audiovisual equipment in the school. The following items allow students a wide range of effects to work with:

1. *35mm slide projector*: for use with prepared and original projections.[11]

2. *16mm film projector*: for use with both commercially prepared films and drawings and paintings on clear or black leader film.

3. *Overhead projectors*: may be used to manipulate transparent colored theatrical gels and cellophane, or paper cutouts and grease drawings on acetate, which are placed over the colored transparencies. Interesting effects are obtained by connecting segments of cellophane and pulling them slowly under and over the light. Pieces of colored glass or plastic in a bowl of water, when placed under the light source and stirred, project shifting patterns of color. Similar effects may be had with colored varnish, oil, and water mixed in a bowl or pan; these patterns vary with the ways in which the ingredients are combined. Water prisms, "magic reflectors,"[12] and convex and concave lenses moved in front of the light source project dancing light images.

4. *Record players*: the tendency today is to use mostly rock music to accompany a light show, but other varieties of music should be investigated — and at decibel levels that are kind to the human eardrum. Of the classical composers, Bach is a favorite. Music poses a problem: the degree to which its style and mood should be accommodated to the visual images. A natural means of achieving consistency of sound and image is to have the children draw or paint to music, take colored slides of the results, and incorporate them as part of the projections.

5. *Tape recorders*: the students can create their own sound effects by collecting the sounds of the street, birds, traffic, playground, and the like on a battery-powered recorder. They can blow into bottles, snap their fingers, or run a block of wood over a series of objects to produce special sounds. Even within the four walls of their classroom there are surfaces such as glass, metal, and wood that yield interesting aural patterns when combined in varying rhythms. The music teacher might be prevailed on to serve as consultant for such investigations in developing awareness of sound.

Before preparing a light show, the teacher should check with the principal or custodian to determine the maximum carrying power of the source of electricity. For best results the room in which the show is projected should be blacked out as completely as possible, and there should be three basic areas of projection. Because a class will rarely have access to more than one large screen, the children should improvise other screens with sheets or large sections of cardboard that have been painted white. When the surfaces of the improvised screens are covered with paper that is rumpled, scored, bent, or curved, the sculptural effects thus derived can add greater variety to the projection. Parachutes and white sheets may be added to the "hard" shapes so that further variety within the images may be obtained. Certain images are even more interesting when taken off the conventional projection screen — the ceiling and the audience itself can be exciting projection surfaces.

Video

The portable video cassette recorder (VCR) and camcorder are gaining popularity in the schools at a rapid rate. However, the VCR has still to gain wide acceptance as part of the art program, and its position at this time is similar to that of the camera a generation ago. If we examine the creative possibilities of the VCR dispassionately, we must admit that it is a truly revolutionary instrument. To children, it means that they can, in a sense, control the very machine that for so many years has dominated their leisure hours. The tables are suddenly turned, and they as viewers are in command, becoming producer, director, or actor. Their new domain is a television studio in miniature, consisting of camera, television monitor, and tape deck for sound and storage of video tape. It is now possible for formerly passive observers to control the camera, create the image, and get immediate feedback on the monitor. Nor do they have to limit their activities to the school; they can extend their control to the playground, the neighborhood — anywhere the VCR can be carried.

The operation of the VCR is far too complex to describe within the limits of this chapter. As with photography, its technical aspects are best learned in a workshop. It is, however, worth noting some of the ways one art teacher with special training went about building a se-

Nam June Paik, *Family of Robots: Baby*, 1986. In this artwork, the artist combines multimonitor VCRs in a sculptural piece. Some of his other works display banks of color television sets that are programmed independently, but in conjunction with all the others, providing the viewer with an ever-changing total image of color and movement. The viewer can see the entire display as a unified work or concentrate on each screen individually. (Courtesy of Carl Solway Gallery.)

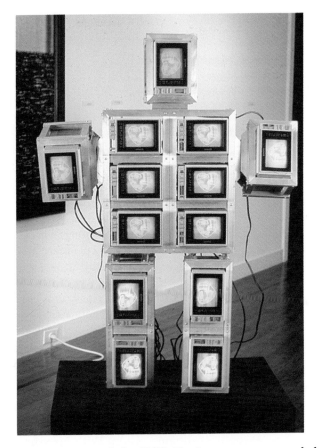

quence of activities around the VCR. During a summer workshop the children, working in rotating groups, did the following:

Designed and presented their own commercials. This involved designing the package, writing copy, and delivering the "message," as well as recording the entire experience on tape.

Designed and assembled several settings for short plays, which were developed from a series of improvisations. Sets were constructed of large sheets of cardboard and included cast-off furniture.

Studied the effects of light and change of scale by examining miniature sets on camera.

Critiqued commercial programming viewed on the monitor.

Role-played various social situations derived from their school and home experiences.

Acted as television art teachers by demonstrating a simple process such as potato printing, stenciling, or collography.

Took turns as cameraman, director, performer, switcher, designer, and producer. They also learned the basic operation and nomenclature of the equipment.[13]

A number of roles related to video production are in evidence here: actors, camera crew, director, and studio audience. Writer and sound technicians are less evident. During the course of a production, students will change roles.

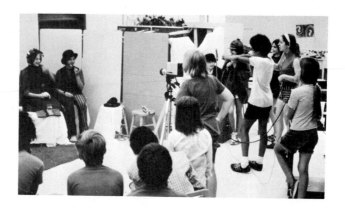

The use of television in the art program remains a relatively unexplored area. A review of the activities listed above must surely make a curious teacher speculate about the many possibilities offered by the VCR and camcorder as a means of extending the children's visual awareness. The use of new technology is available; the problem is to get it into the classroom — or to get the students to the machinery. Several types of computers are capable of programmed animation, and sixth graders can certainly understand basic principles of computer operation, particularly if taught in the context of a math lesson. Xerography — the use of a photocopying machine — in both black and white and color predicts an array of new images. Teachers should bear in mind, however, that new technology is always possible if not easily accessible, and that if Leonardo Da Vinci were alive today, he certainly would have used any means at his disposal capable of extending his unique vision. With his voracious curiosity he would have embraced every means of expression available to him through the advance of technology.

◆ NOTES TO THE TEXT

1. Hurwitz, Al, *Programs of Promise: Art in the Schools* (New York: Harcourt Brace Jovanovich, 1972), p. 145. See "Light Media" quotation by Lloyd Schultz.

2. For a picture and an account of the *Running Fence*, see McCarter, William, and Rita Gilbert, *Living with Art* (New York: Alfred A. Knopf, 1985), p. 284.

3. For a picture and an account of the *Spiral Jetty*, see Fichner-Rathus, Lois, *Understanding Art*, 2nd ed. (Englewood Cliffs, NJ: Prentice-Hall, 1989), p. 143.

4. A picture of *Radioactive Cats* and information about the artist appear in Rosen, Randy, Catherine Brawer, et. al, *Making Their Mark: Women Artists Move into the Mainstream, 1970-1985* (New York: Abbeville Press, 1989), p. 86.

5. Ibid., p. 84.

6. Ibid, p. 138.

7. For more about Hockney's use of the Polaroid image, see Hoy, Anne, "David Hockney's Photo-Mosaics,"

ARTnews, October 1986, pp. 91-96.

8. For more about Scharf's work, see Marzorati, Gerald, "Kenny Schart's Fun-House Big Bang," *ARTnews*, September 1985, pp. 73-81.

9. "Silent" speed slows the film down to sixteen frames per second. But it is recommended that sound speed be used as the basis for designing the film sequence, in case the final result is worthy of having a sound track added.

10. Bartow, Ellie Waterston, *Children Are Centers for Understanding Media* (Washington, DC: ASCD).

11. The various carousel models offer flexibility in timing.

12. Available from Creative Playthings, Princeton, NJ.

13. This special workshop for fifth and sixth graders was offered by the Newton Creative Arts Summer Program, Newton, MA.

◆ ACTIVITIES FOR THE READER

The chapter itself describes many activities to try with the instruments of light and motion. Included here are some more activities of that type.

1. Run two films simultaneously but eliminate the sound of one and the image of the other. Now try to create connections between the image of the one film and the sound track of the other.
2. Using an overhead projector, improvise a series of shifting color patterns by manipulating colored gels and string. Draw on clear acetate with a grease crayon; note how the scale seems to change when the drawing is projected on the screen.
3. For immediate feedback of projected movement, work directly on those parts of the film that are exposed to view while in the projector. With felt-tip pens or hole punchers, work on a section, advance the film, and work on another part; then watch the results by reversing and advancing the film.
4. Obtain films that have outlived their usefulness and are about to be discarded. Work over the images with marking pens or with watercolor mixed with liquid soap, dyes, and inks. Parts of the image can be scratched away with a razor blade or knife. The work may be done randomly (without regard to content) or with some structure (by relating changes to the content of the film). Old film can be made clear by soaking it overnight in half-strength bleach.
5. Any series of still pictures will give the illusion of motion when viewed in sequence. Create a sequence of "flip cards" by working on one side of a group of index cards. By slightly changing the position of the image from card to card, it is possible to create the illusion of a ball flying off the page, a ship sinking into the sea, a smile appearing on a face, or Dr. Jekyll turning into Mr. Hyde.
6. Experiment with methods of correlating music and media. Select some music and create abstract images on glass slides in any manner suggested by the music. Such elements as line, color, and mass should all reflect the mood of the music. The slides can be grouped according to their relation to the changes in the mood and pace of the music. A roughly synchronized slide production can be made if two projectors are used and the image of one is faded into the image of the other by adjusting the focusing mechanism of the projectors.

◆ SUGGESTED READINGS

Doing the Media: A Portfolio of Activities and Resources. New York: Center for Understanding Media, 1973.

Hurwitz, Al. "Redefining the Media of Art." In *Programs of Promise: Art in the Schools.* New York: Harcourt Brace Jovanovich, 1972.

McCarter, William, and Rita Gilbert, *Living with Art* (New York: Alfred A. Knopf, 1985). See especially the sections on Art of the Seventies and Eighties.

Rosen, Randy, Catherine Brawer, et. al, *Making Their Mark: Women Artists Move into the Mainstream, 1970-1985* (New York: Abbeville Press, 1989). This book reviews works by contemporary women artists, many of whom use newer media.

For up-to-date commentary on contemporary artists with photographs of their work, see periodicals such as *Contemporanea*, *ARTnews*, and *Art in America*.

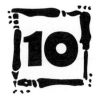

DESIGN: ART LANGUAGE AND APPLICATION

TO CREATE IN any field one must understand that field's essential, basic components. In housing construction, for example, brick, lumber, mortar and nails are the basic materials. Plans are necessary to form these materials into a finished house. The basic ingredients are quite different in music, dance, literature, or art; each discipline requires analysis and dissection to penetrate surface appearances and to grasp the underlying elements comprising the structure.

Jack Stoops and Jerry Samuelson[1]

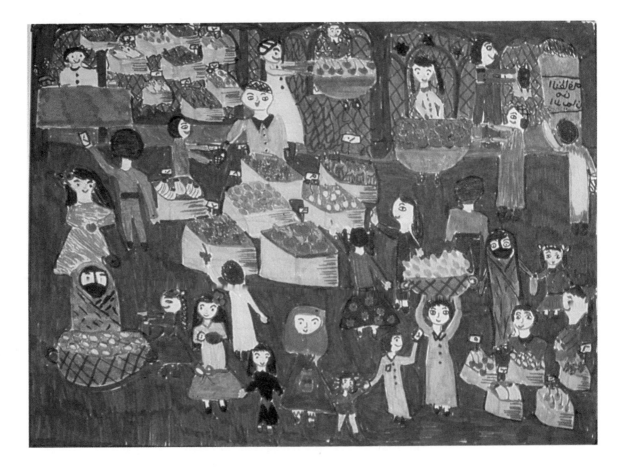

Design is not a separate and distinct area of art; it is an integral part of any art form. The message a creative person wishes to convey is made apparent by the formal organization produced. In any work of art, whether by a child or an adult, design is automatically included in the production. A piece of clay sculpture by a child in the first grade, a Chinese stoneware vase, a painting by Cezanne, a symphony by Beethoven, or a play by Arthur Miller all involve design, structure, and the relation of component elements to a unified whole. Design, therefore, is presented in all art forms and may be intuitively achieved or consciously dealt with. One function of art education is to develop a child's awareness of design. In this chapter we will discuss design as it applies to visual forms of expression, including an analysis of the parts, or elements, that make up design, and an outline of the methods employed by artists to use these elements coherently. The teacher without a knowledge of design is handicapped when the need arises to instruct and assist children with their own artwork and in their understanding of the work of others. The information in this chapter is presented as professional background knowledge with suggestions for practical classroom applications.

THE ELEMENTS OF DESIGN

Design is the organization of parts into a coherent whole. As stated by M. E. Bevlin, "In visual terms, design is the organization of *materials* and *forms* in such a way as to fulfill a specific *purpose*."[2] The designs of accomplished artists should convey the feeling that nothing in the designs could be changed without violating their structure. All the elements of design in use should make a complete, and, as far as can be judged, harmonious whole.

The act of designing is common to all human beings. Early peoples brought order and coherence to their environments while constructing their villages. Homemakers follow the desire for order in rearranging furniture in their living rooms; lawmakers bring order to a legislative session and gardeners bring order to their gardens. Because the desire for order is universal, artistic acts—which demand that a form, composition, or design be achieved—have potential significance for us all.

A distinction can be made between designers who begin with practical functions and use the principles and elements of visual organization to make their solutions as aesthetically pleasing as possible, and artists who use the same elements in nonfunctional ways for purely aesthetic purposes.

Although an artwork can be fully understood only in terms of itself and not its parts, the partial knowledge acquired may be helpful later when considering the object in its entirety.

Those who have attempted to isolate the elements of design have reached only partial agreement. Nevertheless, nearly all agree that the elements of design include *line, shape* (or *mass*), *color, texture,* and *space.* Design in three dimensions includes the element of *mass,* which is analogous to two-dimensional *shape.* The term *form* has two major meanings in art and design. Form is:

1. The underlying structure or *composition* in a work of art.
2. The shape or outline of something.

These elements of art are, in effect, the building blocks of all visual art; they are all that the artist has to work with. The elements will be discussed individually so that teachers may not only acquire some insight into design as it appears in the work of children, but also develop a vocabulary for this segment of art education. Even a rudimentary knowledge of the vocabulary of design can provide the teacher with a basis for discussing works of art.

Each element discussed can be seen in both nature and art. It is the teacher's task to assemble the sources for recognition of the elements and principles and reinforce the understanding of students with art activities that are derived from them.

Contemporary artists, particularly the abstract expressionists, have worked against what they feel are static effects such as symmetry, balance, and classic proportion. Instead, they have placed a premium on accident, stridency, and deliberate avoidance of a "closed" image. Despite this change in the concept of design, the elements exist in all styles, and for purposes of elementary instruction we can use design vocabulary in referring to both the child's work and the work of professionals. The language of design provides a basis for discussing the work of students, which can begin as soon as a child understands—through use and recognition—the meaning of the vocabulary.

Design also has another meaning that is worth noting. Design as a verb can refer to the planning of useful or decorative objects, such as fabrics, appliances, automobiles, or interiors. We can therefore design a container or create a painting wherein elements and principles of design operate effectively. The *principles* of design use the elements but differ from them in that *principles* refer to generalizations regarding the structure of forms, be they from fine arts or commercial design. When elements interact they make up *principles*. Edmund Feldman lists *unity, balance, rhythm,* and *proportion* as the major design principles.[3] Since it is important to convey to young children the meaning of the elements (line, shape, color, texture, and space) as well as the principles, this chapter will discuss both sets of terms. The danger in planning activities related to the design elements is that too often teachers neglect a second, vital stage in making the connections between principles and elements. The ultimate goal of design education is to become aware of this important interaction, in both the children's work and that of professional artists the children study. Teacher and pupil must share some common language, and the terminology of design constitutes the beginning of a mode of discourse that can be referred to during the entire span of the elementary art program.

Line

Line, the path traced by a moving point, is perhaps the most flexible and revealing element of design. If we are angry and doodle a line, our anger is clearly revealed in the marks we make. If we are placid, calm, or pleased, our line takes on a different character. Artists readily express their feelings by means of line. In communicating hatred of war and brutality in general, an artist may use slashing, angular, abrupt lines; presenting feelings about the beauty of a summer landscape, the artist's lines might be gently undulating and flowing.

Line may be used strongly and directly. Kathe Kollwitz used line as a primary means to achieve her end; the strong, powerful line supports both her rage at society and her compassion for its victims. Leonard Baskin creates an uneasy image with sharp cross-hatched lines depicting figure, bird, and barbed wire. The quality of line is in-

Leonard Baskin, *Man of Peace*, 1952. The artist employs a range of lines for this woodcut: heavy and thin, curved and straight, long and short, and the use of cross-hatched shading to create this unsettling image. (Courtesy of the Museum of Modern Art, New York. Gift of the artist.)

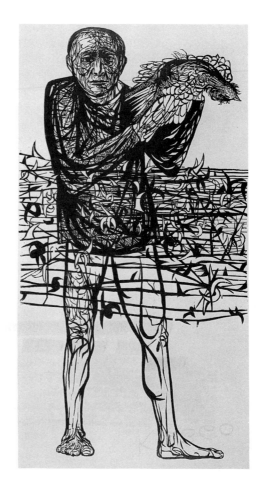

tegral to the meaning of both works. Artists may also imply line — that is, convey it indirectly — by forming edges of contrasting tones that move from one part of a painting to another. Notice the implied line used by Cezanne in his painting of the *Card Players*. Implied lines create directions and are more difficult to discern than isolated lines. In the line diagram, we can see how the linear movement begins over the back of the cardplayer on the right, then swings down over his arm, only to be caught up by the line across the back of the center player. Swirling around this center cardplayer's hat, it moves up over the arm and around the back of the standing man and, falling across the shoulders of the player on the left, ends in the sweep of the chair. Folds in the draperies and shadows in the background augment the sweep of Cezanne's expressive line.

Line has sometimes been called the "nervous system" of a work of art. For most of us, linear experience is our first contact with art — if only because of the availability of pencil, pen, or crayon. The study of

Käthe Kollwitz, *Germany's Children Are Starving*, 1924. Kollwitz's use of bold emphatic lines for the lithograph reinforce the tragic content of her subject.

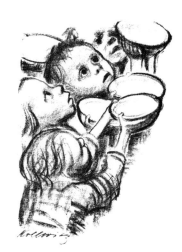

line is particularly effective with elementary school children because they usually have experienced a number of ways of drawing lines with a variety of tools, such as pencils, crayons, and felt-tipped pens. Children will often find their own words to distinguish among the "scratchy" lines of Ben Shahn, the "funny" lines of Paul Klee, or the "squiggly" character of Oriental calligraphy. This sort of discussion provides a basis on which to build the vocabulary of art. The study of

Paul Cezanne, *Card Players*, c. 1892. This painting employs a significant organization of the elements of design. (The Metropolitan Museum of Art, New York. Bequest of Stephen C. Clark, 1960). Below: A diagrammatic indication of the movement of the lines in the *Card Players*.

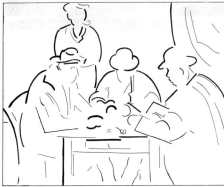

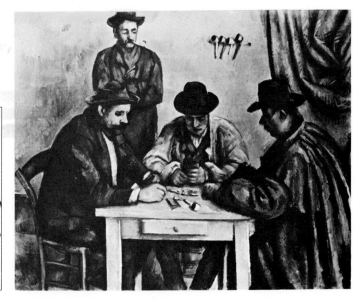

A diagrammatic indication of the distribution of shapes and spaces in the *Card Players*.

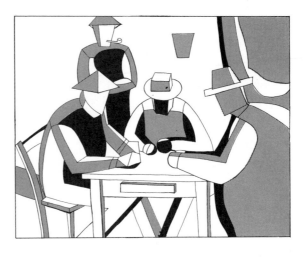

line need not be limited to drawing or painting, for line can be observed and enjoyed in architecture and sculpture as well as in nature, when we observe cracks in a sidewalk or branches against a sky.

Shape

The term *shape* refers to the general outline of something. Shapes can be drawn with lines, painted, or cut out of paper or other two-dimensional materials. They can be categorized as geometric or natural. Geometric shapes include squares, rectangles, circles, and triangles, whereas natural shapes are those found in nature, such as rocks, trees, clouds, and the organic shapes of animal and plant life. Geometric shapes are also found in nature, as in honeycomb, some seashells, and cellular structures. Artists such as Jean Arp or Henry Moore, for example, use the natural biomorphic shapes which suggest natural forms without making specific reference to shapes that occur in nature.

Mass, as discussed earlier, is the three-dimensional equivalent of shape, although it may be found in artworks that give an illusion of mass, such as Michelangelo's paintings in the Sistine Chapel. The cube, pyramid, and sphere are the three-dimensional equivalents of the geometric square, triangle, and circle. Mass refers to the volume or bulk of objects in a work of art, and *space* refers to the areas that surround mass. The aesthetic effect of mass is most readily grasped in architecture and sculpture. The great mass of an office building and the delicate mass of a church spire have the power to move us in different ways. In sculpture, we can be affected by the weight, shape, and balance of the masses created by the sculptor.

Color

Because of the complexity of *color*, both artists and scientists have for years tried to arrive at a theoretical basis for its use. Feldman has noted:

Color theory provides speculative answers to questions which are not often asked in the course of examining works of art. Some color systems seem related to the physiology of perception more than to the aesthetics or psychology of perception. Others may have evolved from industrial needs for the classification and description of dyes, pigments and colored objects. At any rate, artists work with color—pigment, to be exact—more on an intuitive than a scientific basis.[4]

In teaching children about the nature of color, the teacher may vary the methods, using intuitive approaches in the primary grades and gradually teaching color terminology and its application in the middle and upper grades. (Chapter 6 on drawing and painting discusses the properties and definitions of color that provide the basis for more effective color activities and picture making.)

Color is a powerful element, and it serves to emphasize the extent to which all the elements are interdependent. Although the elements have been discussed here separately, in reality they cannot be dissociated. The moment we make a mark on paper with a black crayon, light and shade are involved. If paint has been applied, color is present. As soon as a shape is drawn, it interacts with the space around it. Only for the sake of convenience have we treated these elements as separate entities.

Color functions on two levels. On the cognitive level, color conveys information in purely descriptive terms, as when leaves change color in the fall, and in symbolic terms, as in flags or traffic signals. On the level of feeling (or affective level) color evokes psychological associations and thereby creates moods and feelings. As any industrial design consultant or theatre designer is aware, color affects us emotionally as well as psychologically and can be discussed in terms of the wavelengths of light as legitimately as in terms of the interaction of pig-

These paintings by children reflect an awareness of the possibilities of color that are on the warm side and those that are on the cool. The structure of composition as well as the manner of handling paint make an interesting comparison.

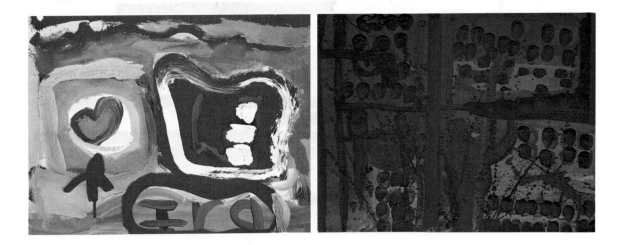

ments. Indeed, so pervasive are color's effects that the vocabulary of color theory can be used metaphorically in a wide variety of contexts — such as in music, when we refer to tone color, or in writing, when we speak of "purple prose."[5]

Color also has been used symbolically within and sometimes across cultures from early Renaissance painters to Navajo weavers. As with texture, color can be based upon real events (green leaves and blue skies) or expressively, as used by the German Brucke and Blau Reiter schools.

The Language of Color. Scientists may define color as an effect of physical forces on our nervous system through impact on the retina. To painters, however, color is far more complex: it is a vital element that is closely related to all the other design elements at their disposal. The sensitivity with which painters use color can convey a personal style and the meaning of a particular work. Ultimately it can influence the varied responses of viewers to a work of art.

The painter's color terminology also differs from the physicist's, whose primary reference is light rather than pigment. In art, a consistent terminology has come to be accepted as a means of discussing and using color, both in looking at works of art and in producing them. The following definitions provide some guidelines for instruction in painting, design, and the appreciation of art.

Hue is another word for color, as in the phrase "the varied hues of the spectrum." Scientifically, a hue is determined by the wavelength of light reflected from an object. As the wavelengths change we note those distinct qualities that we call hues. Hues, therefore, are identifiable segments of light waves.

To the scientist working with light, the primary colors are green, yellow, and red, since these are the irreducible hues from which all other colors can be derived. To the painter working with pigment, on the other hand, the primaries are red, yellow, and blue. Most children can recognize and work with the painter's primaries as well as violet, green, and orange, known as secondary colors because they can be created by mixing the primaries. The tertiary colors result from mixing primary and secondary colors and may be more difficult for children to achieve, since they require a greater control of paint. The tertiaries are also called *grays* and provide richer hues than the simple mixing of black and white will yield.

Value, or *tone*, refers to the degree of darkness or lightness of a hue. The lighter a color, the higher its value; the darker the color, the lower its value. Hence, if white is added, the value is heightened; if black is added, the value is lowered. Hues also may be changed by the use of a *glaze*, or a veil of thin transparent color, which is brushed over the hue. This method of changing a color was much favored during the Renaissance but is currently used less frequently.

Chiaroscuro is the technique used in drawing and painting "to create the effects of light and shadow in the natural world." This entails shading objects from light to dark to give the appearance of three dimensions. In Rembrandt's work, the light appears to glow from within the subject. Monet bathes his haystacks in light, and Orozco and Caravaggio use dark-light contrasts for powerful emotional effects. Children enjoy the dramatic interaction that only opposites can provide. Children are capable not only of identifying value effects but also of applying chiaroscuro in their own work.

Architects and sculptors control the light and dark composition of their work, not by mixing pigments as painters or shading with pencil or crayon as in drawings, but by planning the way that light and shadow interact. A building may be designed with deep recesses to produce shadows in contrast to a facade that catches the light, and sculptors take great pains to control the "hollows" (negative areas) and "bumps" (positive areas) they make so that light and shade are used to their best advantage. A portrait sculptor, for example, in order to achieve the very dark center of the human eye makes a deep recess that becomes dark shadow.

Intensity indicates the freedom from admixture with another color — in other words, the ultimate purity of a color. Any hue that has not been mixed with another color is considered to be at its maximum intensity, although the purity of color can be enhanced or neutralized by adjacent colors in a painting. Although a color can be made more intense by the addition of another color (as in the addition of some oranges to some reds), the original color may lose its distinctive identity as mixing is carried beyond a certain point.

Complementary is a term that refers to the relationship between primary and secondary colors on a color wheel. On the wheel, these col-

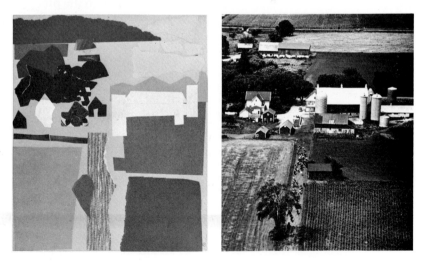

In an example of perceiving and selecting, the cut-paper collage shows how a sixth grader differentiated the light and dark areas in the accompanying photograph. (Photograph by Margaret Bourke-White, *Life Magazine*, © Time Warner, Inc.)

ors are in opposition to one another, as red to green, blue to orange, and yellow to violet. The complementaries are antagonistic in the sense that neither color in a pair possesses any property in common with the other. Complementary pairs, however, are complete in the sense that together they contain all three primaries. For example, the complement of red is green, which is made of yellow and blue. Browns and blacks are obtained by mixing the three primaries in some ratio. Mixing two complementary hues has the same effect as mixing the primaries. Artists make great use of the fact that complementary pairs neutralize each other, creating a wide range of grays, which, as noted earlier, are potentially more interesting than grays composed of black and white.

Analogous colors are intermediate hues on the color wheel and may be explained to children in terms of families of color. Analogous colors can be likened to a family in which a red man and a blue woman produce a violet child. Analogous colors always get along; it is the complementary colors that often disagree.

Warm and *cool* refer to the psychological properties of certain colors. We normally call reds, yellows, and oranges warm colors, which we generally perceive as coming forward, or "advancing," in a field of color. Blues and greens are usually identified as cool and "receding" colors. The movement forward or backward of any color, however, depends entirely on its relationship to the surrounding hues. A red with a touch of blue can appear even cooler than it would by itself when placed next to an intense orange, and may well recede behind it, while yellow with a touch of green, normally warm, will seem very cool when placed next to red-orange, which will advance. Experimentation with recession and advancement of color is of special interest to the hard edge and color field painters.

Color wheels, referred to in the preceding definitions, are chiefly useful as guides to understanding the terminology of color relationships. Teachers should not restrict pupils to the schematized set of relationships shown on the wheel. If color wheels have any virtue, it is to enlarge the options available to pupils rather than narrow them.

Many art forms are produced in which color is lacking—black-and-white films, most forms of sculpture, many of the etching processes, drawings in which black-and-white media are used. Color, then, is a complex element—at once dependent, powerful, and very moving in its sensual appeal. As for the interests of children, teachers will discover that color has an appeal far in excess of the other elements of design.

Texture

Texture is the degree of roughness or smoothness of surface. Every surface has a texture; a pebble on the seashore, a veined leaf, the wrinkled face of an old man, a brick wall, and a sheet of glass all display varying kinds and degrees of texture. We derive a sensuous enjoyment from texture. We like to run our hands lightly over the surface of a tweed jacket or a fur coat; we enjoy holding a smooth stone lightly in our hands or gently stroking a baby's hair. We enjoy textures visually, too, through the sense of touch. Architects plan surface textures for visual contrast, variety, and unity as well as for practical concerns.

Texture appeals to people for both aesthetic and sensuous reasons, although it is doubtful if the two can be entirely separated. The texture that artists use may be actual or simulated. Paper for watercolor paintings is carefully chosen for its textural qualities. Some painters create effects with gesso on a surface before painting on it with tempera or oils. The paint itself may be applied with careful regard for its textural effects. Paint applied thickly has a degree of roughness, but it can also be put on with silky smoothness. In drawing and painting, artists represent textures as well as employ them with roughened painting surfaces or impasto. Richard Estes is known for the photorealistic quality of his city scenes in which he represents concrete buildings, plate glass windows with reflective surfaces, asphalt pavement, shiny automobiles, brick facades and natural textures such as foliage and grass. Sculptors work directly with textures inherent in the materials of their art. Deborah Butterfield has created a series of horses in materials from plaster and bronze to sticks, mud, and wire. The materials that she selects often determine the textures of the sculptures and the moods that they express.

Children delight in surface qualities in drawing, painting, sculpture, and collage activities. Teachers can assist children to explore the possibilities of expression through the use of textures in their own artwork. And, teachers can help children develop visual and tactile sensitivity by discussing the treatment of texture and surface in objects such as a Japanese tea bowl, a monumental Egyptian sculpture, a native American woven basket, a modern automobile, and paintings by Hans Hofmann (textured surface) and William Harnett (realistic illusion of textured objects).

Space

In art there are two types of space: actual space and pictorial space. *Actual space* is two-dimensional, as in drawings, paintings, or prints produced on flat surfaces; or it is three-dimensional as in sculpture, architecture, or ceramics. Artists have learned to be as sensitive to the organization of space as they are to line and shape. As soon as a line or a shape is placed on paper or canvas it sets up a dynamic with the surrounding space. When a second line or shape is added to the composition other spatial relationships are created. Two shapes can be close together or far apart, above and below, side by side, or crowded in a corner. The possibilities multiply as each new shape or line is added to the composition.

Sculpture is three-dimensional and exists in actual space — taking up space and relating to surrounding areas. The sculptor is aware of these relationships and makes purposeful decisions to pierce space with sculptural forms and to cause forms to move in space — as with mobiles or kinetic sculpture.

Pictorial space is the flat surface of the paper, canvas, or other material, and is known also as the *picture plane*. On this surface artists often create the illusion of three-dimensional space. For example, a landscape picture often has a *foreground* of objects that appear near to the viewer, a *middle ground* farther away, and a *background* such as the sky or distant hills that are behind most of the objects in the picture. To achieve this illusion, the artist can overlap objects in the background smaller than similar objects in the foreground.

Linear perspective is a system developed by artists of the Renaissance that approximates the visual phenomenon of apparently diminishing size of objects as their distance from the viewer increases. This system, which utilizes a horizon line and one or more vanishing points, is rarely learned spontaneously and usually requires instruction and practice for mastery. Pictorial space is not limited to linear perspectives and can also be created in a totally abstract and nonobjective painting through the use of shapes and colors that recede or advance.

Whatever line or shape is placed on the picture plane immediately creates a *figure-ground relationship* in which the mark or shape is the "figure" and the surrounding area is the "ground." With three-dimensional works of art, the object is the figure and the space behind or around it is the background, or just the ground. The placement of any figure in a pictorial space shapes the ground according to its position. Every shape and mass is surrounded by the element of space. As an example of the use of space in architecture, consider the courtyards separating the buildings in a modern housing development. Here the architect has carefully planned the amount of space that should be provided between one building and another. If the space had been planned smaller, the buildings might appear to be huddled together; wider, the buildings might not appear to belong to a coherent plan.

The artist working in two dimensions must also regulate the spaces between shapes. In an Andrew Wyeth painting, for example, the intervals between the shapes have their own qualities, ranging from confined to open areas. Children can learn to appreciate these qualities when they create designs by pasting pieces of dark paper on a white background.

Children should be made aware of the action that takes place among all elements of a picture, and one way to call their attention to it is by showing them how artists deal with the problem of shape and space. The illustration on page 268 is a diagram of the shapes and spaces in Cezanne's *Card Players*. The masses formed by the players, the table, and the draperies are presented in a sculptural unity relieved by variations in light and shade, texture, and color. The simplicity of the spaces offers a significant contrast to the detail of the shapes.

THE PRINCIPLES OF DESIGN

It would be convenient to offer a formula for the production of satisfactory designs, but of course, if designs were subject to rules and regulations, art would cease to exist. Every good design is different from every other good design, and all artists have unique ways of using the elements and principles of art. We will now discuss individually those principles mentioned earlier: *unity, rhythm, proportion,* and *balance*.

Unity

We have already mentioned the integrated nature of design. We described design in terms of order and coherence, and we considered it analogous to a world of stability. These are the most obvious characteristics that result from a successful art form, whether musical, dramatic, literary, or graphic. Each element is so arranged that it contributes to a desirable oneness or wholeness. In a drawing, a line ripples across a certain area to be caught up elsewhere; shapes and spaces set up beats and measures in a kind of visual music. Colors, textures, and areas of light and shade all contribute to the orchestration of the visual pattern. This oneness or wholeness we call *unity*.

Without oversimplifying or intellectualizing a process that is largely one of feeling, we may analyze to some extent how unity is achieved in a visual design. Three aspects of design that contribute to the unity of a work of art are the rhythms, the balances, and the centers of interest established.

Rhythm

The controlled movements that are to be found in all good designs are called *rhythms*. They may be established through the use of any of the elements of design—lines, areas of light and shade, spots of color, repetitions of shapes and spaces, or textured surfaces. For example, in a particular work of art a line may ripple in one direction, then undulate in another. This movement may be momentarily halted by an obstructive, brightly colored shape before it darts away elsewhere along a pathway formed by areas of light and shade. Rhythm is used by artists to give movement to the manner in which our eyes move over a work of art and to control the pace at which our gaze travels.

There appear to be at least two main types of rhythm in works of art. The first has the character of a flow, and is usually achieved either by lines or the elongation of forms. (The work of El Greco is an outstanding example.) The second type has the character of a beat. An element may be used in one area of a work and repeated elsewhere, either as an exact duplication of the original theme or motif or only as an echo of it. In traditional paintings we are more likely to find reminiscences of an original motif than duplications. The undulating stripe paintings of Bridget Riley are examples of visual rhythm and visual beat. In many crafts such as weaving or tole ware repetition is used purely for decorative purposes.

Proportion

The size relationships within a composition refer to its *proportion*. Proportion often involves an ideal relationship that the artist strives for. Things that are "out of proportion" are often awkward or disturbing, such as an oversized sofa in a small room, a tiny painting hung alone on a broad expanse of wall, or a part of a figure or other object that is too large or small for the other parts. The ancient Greeks developed an elaborate system of proportion by which they built temples and other edifices.

> The proportions of a classical Greek temple, for example, were rigidly prescribed in a formula that can be stated mathematically as $a:b = b:(a+b)$. Thus, if a is the width of a temple and b the length, the relationship between the two sides becomes apparent. Similar rules governed the height of the temple, the distance between columns, and so forth. When we look at a Greek temple today, even without being aware of the formula, we sense that its proportions are somehow supremely "right," totally satisfying. The same mean rectangle that determined the floor plan of the temple has been found to circumscribe Greek vases and sculpture as well.[6]

Some artists adhere to systems of proportion to achieve their expressive aims. Others convey ideas and feelings by distorting proportion or controlling it in other ways. To children proportion is largely a matter of appropriate size relationships.

Balance

Closely related to the aspect of proportion in design is *balance*. When the eye is attracted equally to the various imaginary axes of a composition, the design is considered to be in balance.

Many writers, particularly those associated with the post-impressionist movement, attempted to explain balance in terms of physics, usually referring to the figure of a seesaw. Unfortunately, the concept is not quite accurate, since physical balance and aesthetic balance, while possibly related, are not synonymous. Balance in aesthetics should be considered as attraction to the eye, or visual interest, rather than as simple gravitational pull. Aesthetic balance refers to all parts of a picture — the top and bottom — and not only to the sides, as the seesaw analogy suggests. Size of the shapes, moreover, while having some influence on aesthetic balance, may easily be compensated, and indeed outweighed, by a strong contrast of elements. A small, bright spot of color, for example, has great visual weight in a gray area as does an area of deep shade next to a highlight.

In many books on art there is still discussion about "formal" versus "informal" balance. The arrangement of a composition with one well-defined figure placed centrally and with balancing elements placed on either side of this center, as in Fra Angelico's *Coronation of the Virgin,* is called *formal* or *symmetrical* balance. All other arrangements are called *informal* or *asymmetrical.*

Attraction to one kind of balance or another seems to be dictated by the ebb and flow of artistic fashion. The history of art shows us that most civilizations (including the Hindu, Aztec, and Japanese) have gone through a symmetrical design phase. The high Renaissance prized symmetry and was followed by the mannerists, who rejected the limitations of two-point perspective. The dadaists of the 1920s and abstract expressionists of the 1950s discarded all semblance of conventional visual order; yet during the 1960s, many hard edge painters and pop artists revived it for the simplicity and directness of its impact on the viewer. Neo-expressionist artists currently opt for more dynamic, informal compositions.

Centers of Interest

Many works of art—perhaps the majority—are arranged so that one center of interest has paramount importance. Just as any of the elements may be used in the development of rhythms, they may be used

Jerry Uelsmann, *Apocalypse II,* 1967. Line, value, and contrast are employed in dramatic fashion in this photograph. The upper part is symmetrical and the lower section departs subtly with the diagonal lines of the beach and the groups of two and three persons. Photographers can manipulate images as readily as painters for their expressive purposes.

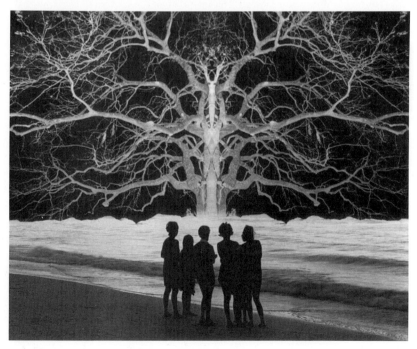

in the establishment of centers of interest. A large shape centrally placed, a bright color area, a sharp contrast between light and shade, an area more heavily textured than its surroundings, a series of lines leading to a certain place — these are some of the means at the disposal of the artist to attract and hold the observer's attention. Even though many artists disregard issues related to balance and centers of interest they remain good focal points for capturing the attention of children when discussing artwork.

Variety of Design

Martin Johnson Heade, *The Coming Storm*, 1859. The artist uses contrast to focus attention on the sail, the man, and the white fabric (lower left). He creates the mood of the coming storm by darkness contrasted with the light on these objects. (The Metropolitan Museum of Art. Gift of Erving Wolf Foundation and Mr. and Mrs. Erving Wolf, 1975.)

The elements of design, then, must be unified if the resulting work is to be successful. It is possible, however, to produce a design that has all the attributes of unity but is neither interesting nor distinguished. A checkerboard, for example, has a rhythmic beat, a series of centers of interest, and a balance, but as a design it is unsatisfactory because it is monotonous and lacks tension. Likewise, a picket fence, a line of identical telephone poles, and a railway track are as uninteresting as the ticking of a clock. A stone wall, however, might have great design interest because of the variety of its units. Even in a brick wall, in which shapes are similar, people generally prefer the random colors, tones, and textures found in old, used brick.

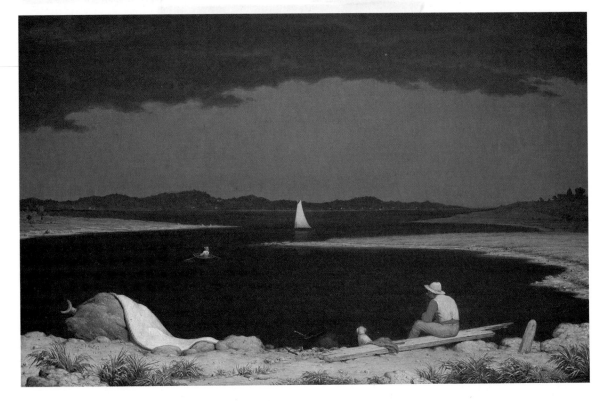

Although painters like Edward Hopper and Stuart Davis have used house gables, telephone poles, and railway tracks as subject matter for their work, they have introduced variations into the delineation of these objects. Pieter Mondrian has even gone so far as to use a single basic shape, the rectangle, as the foundation for his post-cubist compositions. He has, however, varied the size, color, and relationships of this shape sufficiently to generate considerable visual interest.

While the perceptual process, as we have noted, seeks closure, or completeness, educated vision demands that in art, at least, a degree of complexity be attained if our attention is to be held. Every element, therefore, must be employed to bring about a desirable variety within unity.

This variety within unity is, in fact, an expression of life. Philosophers have postulated that design, or form, is a manifestation of people's deepest and most moving experiences. In the designs they produce, people are said to express their relationship to the universe. In *Art as Experience*, Dewey mentioned the mighty rhythms of nature — the course of the seasons and the cycle of lunar changes — together with those movements and phases of the human body, including the pulsing of the blood, appetite and satiety, and birth and death, as basic human experiences from which design may arise.

Sir Herbert Read, commenting on Platonic doctrine, tells us that

> the universality of the aesthetic principle is Plato's philosophy: the fact that it pervades not only man-made things in so far as these are beautiful, but also living bodies and all plants, nature and the universe itself. It is because the harmony is all pervading, the very principle of coherence in the universe, that this principle should be the basis of education.[7]

Dewey, Plato, and Read would, then, seem to assert that the search for order, which the design impulse seeks to fulfill, is important not only for an individual's artwork, but also as a reflection of that person's larger integrative relationship with life itself and can indeed be viewed as a metaphor for life.

THE ATTITUDES AND CREATIVE PROCESSES OF THE ARTIST

What do artists think and feel when they create? How do they know when their work is "right?" There are divergent views on this subject. Some artists feel that the act of designing is a feat of intellect; some hold that it is an emotional adventure. The Gestalt psychologists point out, however, that the human organism acts in totality: when people are occupied with an act of artistic expression, both their feelings (impulses) and intellect (ideas) are involved.

It is true that creative people in different art careers tend to have particular orientations: architects and industrial designers lean toward an intellectual approach to design, whereas painters and poets generally lean toward imaginative and intuitive approaches. Nevertheless, both intellectually and intuitively inclined artists apparently alternate between feeling and thinking. "I feel that this should be done" is followed by "I think that this is right," or vice versa. Thus, emotion enlivens an artistic statement and intellect tempers it. Exactly when intellect is the dominant force in artistic acts, or precisely when feeling replaces intellect, is difficult to detect. Often, creative people themselves are unable to analyze their approach.

In producing a design for functional purposes, such as a design for a building, a piece of pottery, or an item of furniture, some consideration for practical requirements is needed. In such a case, designers' decisions are governed by an honest respect not only for the materials used but also for the purpose to which they are put. Efficiency cannot, of course, always be identical with aesthetic quality, since extreme functionalism, as required in airplanes, must place limitations upon the personal choices that are necessary to artistic acts.

Thus, one important difference between "fine" artists and industrial or commercial designers is the amount of autonomy enjoyed by the former. Unless their work is commissioned, fine artists answer only to themselves; they are members of no team, responsible to no board of directors, and subject to no limitations of time or budget imposed by others. The blessings of freedom, needless to say, place other burdens on them, but it is only through this state of freedom that artists periodically produce works that are unique, authentic, and innovative.

Changing Attitudes Toward Design

Art does not lend itself readily to rules and regulations, and any statement concerning principles must be outlined with caution. Should learners come to rely on the principles they have developed from their experiences to such an extent that they cease to look for new, deeper truths in art, their thinking will become stale. Whatever universal beliefs we may hold about art must, it seems, be subject to continued revision and further inquiry. General truths about art, in short, must always be regarded in a pragmatic light. A principle may not be adequate when we have enjoyed new experiences and gained new insights into design.

The attitude toward honesty in the use of materials reflects this idea. If we are to hold to the idea that artists must respect the integrity of their materials and work from the accepted definitions of painting and sculpture, what are we to say of George Sugarman, who paints his sculpture, or of Marisol, who includes drawing and painting in her sculptures? Should we adhere to the "rules" and reject their work, or should we keep ourselves open to the element of surprise and amusement when confronted with such combinations? Obviously, today's children should be prepared for the art of their time, and there is no reason why there cannot be room in their life for both the "integrity" of a fresco by Michelangelo and the multimedia combines of Robert Rauschenberg. (We must bear in mind that in the opinion of many of his contemporaries, Michelangelo violated the integrity of the human figure by distorting human proportions.)

Each learner arrives at a personal statement of principles that reflects personal experience and its resulting insights.

THE USES OF DESIGN

The language of design as discussed in this chapter provides us with a vocabulary to talk about art more effectively. When used as a verb, as in "design a house," the term implies using the principles and elements for practical purposes (we do not say to a painter, "design a painting"). Design, in its broadest sense, deals with the process of organization of the elements of art for functional purposes. In the "living" or "applied" arts, design shows us its practical side. This can be better understood by studying the diagram that follows, which likens design functions to a concentric scheme with the individual at the center and the community at its outermost layer.

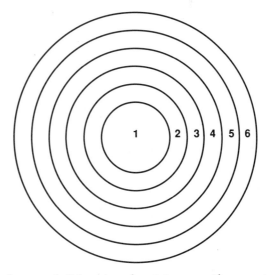

1. Individual uses: clothing, jewelry, tatoos, uniforms, etc.
2. Objects used by individuals: appliances, automobiles, tools.
3. The interiors we live in: furniture, fabrics, wall coverings, etc.
4. Dwellings: apartments to houses.

5. Neighborhoods: from established urban areas to housing developments.

6. New towns and cities: Columbia, Maryland to Brazilia.

Environmental design such as landscaping has its own parameters and extends through circles 4, 5, and 6.

Although the concerns of this book lie mostly with the personally expressive side of art—that is, art that exists only for what it can provide by way of pleasure or intellectual stimulation—we must keep in mind that art for most people exists in ways in which it is used to serve human needs. There is something basic to our nature that makes us designers. An object as simple as a toothpick has undergone so many changes that an example from the turn of the century looks quite different from one purchased today.

To be human means to constantly strive to improve the conditions which can enhance the process of living. The love of the beautiful, the role of technology in manufacturing, the influence of ideas from the fine arts, and the implications of class and prestige all impinge upon the ways in which the principles and elements of design will be used to alter (hopefully to improve) our toothpicks, sports cars, toasters, television sets, etc.

Of course, there are interesting crossovers from one function to another, as in one-of-a-kind buildings, articles of clothing, or furniture or jewelry that not only serve practical needs, but are cherished for their high aesthetic value. When a museum prefers to add a table by George Nakashima to its collection rather than the dozens of paintings and sculptures that have been offered, then the line which traditionally separates useful from fine art has been blurred.

A wide range of applications of design exists, much too broad to discuss here. The following (partial) listing of careers in the applied arts will provide a hint of the extent of these fields:[8]

architecture
interior and display design
graphic design
industrial design
fashion design
film and television
theater and state design
editorial design and illustration
photography
crafts design

Keep in mind that each of these fields of design has numerous parts and permutations involving many other careers. For example, under graphic design we will find, among others:

advertising designer
corporate art director
graphic designer
computer graphics designer
layout and paste-up artists
letterer, calligrapher, type designer
outdoor advertising designer
record jacket designer

We will briefly discuss the fields of graphic design, design for entertainment and architecture; the latter will be the subject of suggested classroom applications.

Graphic Design: Art for Communication and Persuasion

The means used to persuade consumers to use one product over another involve every sort of printed media from handbills to posters, and from newspapers to billboards. Sometimes graphic designers also produce public symbols promoting civic responsibility, as in the case of traffic and safety hazard signs. Two goals are uppermost in the minds of the graphic designer: to communicate quickly and to find the proper match between word and image—hence, the importance of typography. Of the careers mentioned, the one that connects most closely to the task of the art teacher is that of the poster designer. The teacher must be wary that the art program will end up as a service pursuit, producing posters for PTAs, community causes, national campaigns, and school functions. One thing is clear: As long as methods of reproduction on a mass scale are available, there will be graphic designers producing for a mass market. The more underdeveloped the society, the lesser the need of the graphic designer.

When we consider the extent to which children as well as adults are exposed to the influence of graphic design, and the general pervasiveness of the applied arts in our lives, we can gain an appreciation of the importance of including design fundamentals in a comprehensive school art program. When young people become familiar with the principles, practices, and motives behind much of graphic design, they will, hopefully, become more selective rather than be subject to such influences.

Design in the Entertainment Media

Artists and designers in the electronic media occupy a category of their own. The role played in our lives by television alone is as influential as that of graphic design. Artists in film, video, and stage design usually work in concert with other artists and technicians. In live theater, set designers, lighting designers, and makeup and costume designers work with writers, directors, musicians, and actors to create the final presentation. In television, advertising designers often include visual graphics, music, drama, and dance in a thirty-second commercial.

The field of music videos is another example of collaboration, of how hazy the line is between the fine and applied arts. Many music videos are artworks in their own right and might become a contemporary version of the type of collaborations that are inherent in opera, which some label as the ultimate art form.

The applied arts, including the design areas, are often considered in different categories from the fine arts. In the Soviet Union, for example, it would be unlikely to hold an art exhibit on a national level without including the works of theatrical, film, and book designers. In this country it is less likely that the work of such artists would appear in a similar situation. Illustrators and graphic designers have their own recognition and award systems that often result in yearbook publications of the best works in the various fields. The design fields that are located within the entertainment and advertising industries each have their own cultural histories and, since such works can be examined for their social and philosophical contexts, they have a legitimate place in a balanced art program. In order to include areas other than drawing, painting, and sculpture in the art program, teachers require access to visual resources along with an adequate background of understanding of the applied arts.

Architecture as One Example of the Uses of Design

Architecture not only has the best coverage from a design point of view in the books and slides that are available, but has, in addition, a powerful human function that can be studied in every society and in every historical epoch. In order to include architecture in the curriculum, one begins by defining it. One good working definition is that architecture is the art and science of enclosing space for human needs. Architecture has an aesthetic as well as a practical dimension and in some cases achieves a symbolic significance. In order to expand our understanding of the term, we must search for concepts related to architecture that can suggest activities, historic examples, and points of emphasis when introducing activities. Examples of some basic architectural concepts follow.

Function and Form.   Architectural design starts with the needs of the user. Architects do not begin with a set of columns or windows, but with such questions as "Who will use it?" "What functions must the building perform?" and "What are the constraints of cost?" Structures from toolsheds to museums begin on this level. This is known as form following function.

Environment.   Architects capitalize upon the setting and environment of the structure, such as the weather and the local materials of the setting. Designers in Florida will therefore be more likely to use coral and concrete block rather than wood, which is a material more congenial to the Pacific Northwest.

Engineering. Architects must be familiar with the engineering or structural demands of the building. (The medieval designers whose cathedrals collapsed after decades of work learned the hard way that flying buttresses were needed to support the desired height.) Similarly, architects who work in earthquake zones need to know more about building stabilization engineering than most of their colleagues.

In addition to architectural concepts accepted by practitioners in the field, teachers will have to plan activities which reinforce such ideas. Here are some suggestions for activities, some of which are related to the concepts listed.

Space. The architect must be something of a psychologist since sensitivity to the effect of space upon the individual is critical. The effects of space must be considered in the choices architects make when dealing with such issues as height, isolating or joining living areas, and utilizing the space that surrounds the structure.

Frank Lloyd Wright, Living Room from the Francis W. Little House, 1915. This living room by the great American architect expresses the artist's concern for unity within as well as outside the building. He designed the room, windows, and furniture in order to achieve a total unified environment. (The Metropolitan Museum of Art. Purchase, bequest of Emily Crane Chadbourne, 1972. Installation through the generosity of Saul P. Steinberg and Reliance Group Holdings, Inc.)

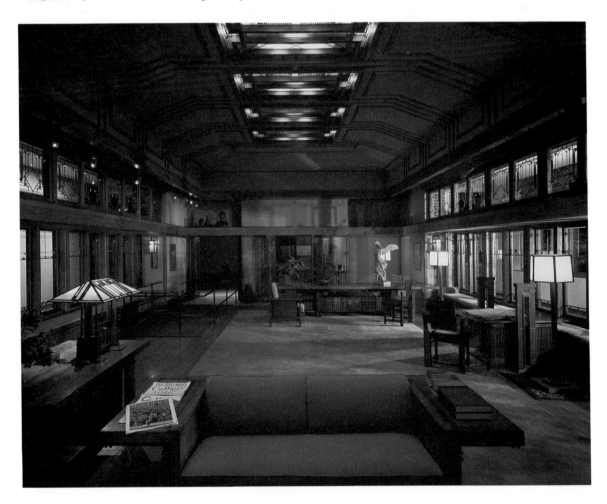

These simple box or container forms have been painted as architectural subjects and will be grouped to create a community. The children are six years old. At this stage, environmental education need not be separated from art-centered activities.

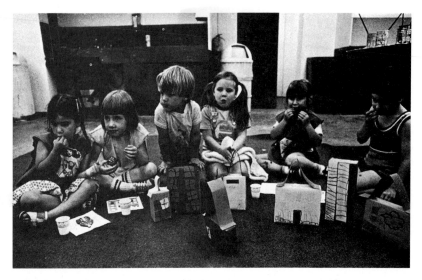

Elements of Design. Architects may consciously utilize the vocabulary of basic design. Paintings use line, texture, repetition, rhythm, light, color, symmetry, shape, and volume for different purposes. Architects can and do find ways of using such elements in the design of a building, always considering the practical implication of their use.

Group Planning. If an assignment is complex, as in the case of an arts center, architects, unlike painters, will plan as a group, brainstorming and sharing their special areas of expertise.

Careers. The architect may begin working with a drafter and later may call upon specialists such as model makers or landscape architects. They also require the services of such specialists as electrical, heating, and plumbing engineers. There is a wide range of careers in architecture that require an understanding of applied design, such as:

city planner/environmental designer
landscape architect
marine architect
playground designer
theme park designer
and others

Teaching Children about Architecture

Following are suggested activities that will introduce children to concepts, practices, and problems associated with the field of architecture.

Materials Investigation: Structure. Students can test materials by making structures of clay or paper, exploring the possibilities of the medium.

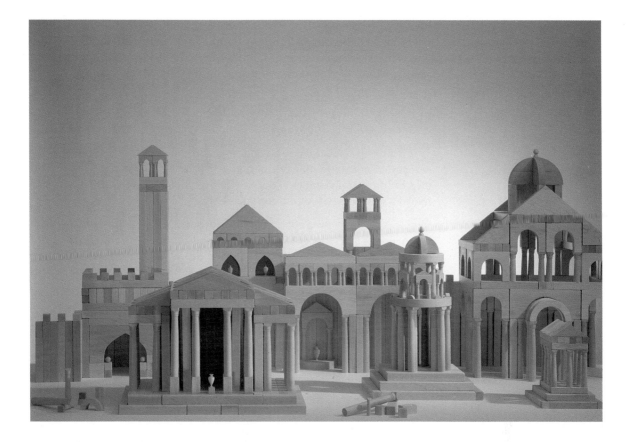

This example of an architectural "toy" shows how far designers have come since building blocks were introduced. Archiblocks shown above encourage improvisation of form and instill an awareness of the history of architecture.

For example, when paper is torn, it has little strength; when it is pulled, it has great tensile strength. Problem: What would be required to turn one 12 × 10 sheet of 60 lb. paper into a bridge that spans two tables to hold a 5 lb. weight?

Brainstorming through Schematic Drawing: Group Planning.   Divide the class into groups and give each a large sheet of paper. Assign an architectural design problem to each group (a special kind of school, an airport, a store) and ask them to role-play architects by engaging in visual brainstorming, listing and transposing human needs into a flow chart of symbols such as bubbles, squares, arrows, etc. Motivation: The teacher can translate the class suggestions onto the blackboard.

Scale Models (careers).   If there is a school of architecture or architectural firm nearby, ask them to save for you any scale models that may be discarded after their use. These can be an introduction to the use of scale and the variety of materials used in models, such as sandpaper (roofs and driveways), dyed bits of sponge (trees and bushes), balsa wood (walls), etc.

Homework (historical).   Copy a facade of a building from another country or historic period and mount them above the blackboard on a time line. Or, ask students for small drawings and mount them along the side of a map of the world with arrows leading to the point of origin.

Street Making (brainstorming).   Have everyone bring in one box to be turned into a house. (Changes or additions to the basic rectangle may be added.) Group them together and see what it would take to turn it into a neighborhood.

Reconstruction through Memory.   Ask the students to suppose they are a bird flying from home to school. What would the earth look like? How many streets can they remember?

Form Analysis (developing critical skills).   Show an architectural slide that is out of focus and ask the students to use the sides of small pieces of crayon to indicate the shadow areas of the volumes of form. Increase the focus two more times and ask them to use the point of the crayon.

◆ NOTES TO THE TEXT

1. Jack Stoops and Jerry Samuelson, *Design Dialogue* (Worcester, MA: Davis, 1983), p. 33.

2. Marjorie Elliott Bevlin, *Design Through Discovery* (New York, NY: Holt, Rinehart, and Winston, 1977), p. 10.

3. Edmund B. Feldman, *Art as Image and Idea* (Englewood Cliffs, NJ: Prentice-Hall, 1967), Chapter 9.

4. Ibid., p. 248.

5. For a discussion of interrelationships between art and music, see Milo Wold and Edmund Cykler, *Music and Art in the Western World*, 7th ed. (Dubuque, IA: Wm. C. Brown, 1983).

6. Bevlin, p. 130.

7. Read, Herbert, *Education Through Art*, rev. ed. (New York, NY: Pantheon, 1958), p. 64.

8. For a more complete discussion of careers, see Gerald Brommer and Joseph Gatto, *Careers in Art: An Illustrated Guide* (Worcester, MA: Davis, 1984).

◆ ACTIVITIES FOR THE READER

Activities Emphasizing Line

1. Select black chalk and a sheet of inexpensive paper, such as newsprint, measuring about 18 by 24 inches and having a natural color. Play some stimulating music and begin to draw a line, not to depict an object but rather to develop a nonobjective arrangement. Draw the line freely, without attempting to

produce a particular effect. Repeat the operation, but in this second case consider the variety of the line. See that it swoops and glides, ripples and pauses. Repeat again, this time thinking of the unity of the composition produced. Play music of a completely different mood and produce some further compositions in line.

2. Cover your hand with cloth or paper. With a short pencil draw an object under observation, such as a park bench, a person, or a flower. Blind contour drawing of this type tends to place more emphasis on line than on any other element. Analyze your handling of edges and do not worry about the relationship of parts. After doing several such drawings, select the most successful and draw it again, referring this time to your paper to connect parts to wholes. Continue this exercise, progressing to more complex forms—fruit to houses, boxes to people, stools to bicycles.

3. Study the paintings and sculpture of such recognized masters as Picasso, Rembrandt, and Barbara Hepworth. Make a line analysis of one of the works. Such an analysis should emphasize the main flows of line in the composition without copying the objects themselves. Pen and ink, soft lead pencil, and crayon are suitable media.

4. Take a subject that is small, such as a piece of popcorn, a bit of crumpled paper, or some nuts and bolts. Using a brush, try to blow the detail up on a sheet of mural paper that measures at least 3 by 4 feet. Consider the space between the lines and how the figure (the object) relates to the ground (the surrounding space). Enlarge a cauliflower bud using several pounds of clay.

Activities Emphasizing Shape, Mass, and Space

1. Cut some rectangular shapes from paper of various tones but generally neutral in color. Move these shapes on a piece of white cardboard until a satisfactory arrangement of the shapes and spaces has been found, then glue them in place. Take similar shapes and drop them from above the cardboard so that they fall in an accidental pattern. Continue this procedure until you come upon an arrangement that pleases you. Compare the "found" design with the planned one. Which do you prefer and why? Does the accident offer an element of surprise that the planned design seems to need?

2. Take toothpicks or balsa strips and glue them together to form a nonobjective three-dimensional construction having interesting internal space relationships.

3. Using pieces of cardboard or wood scraps, make the same type of construction described in Activity 2. Concentrate on the way flat planes work with internal relationships—confirming them, allowing one space to flow into another, and so on. If this sculptural approach to mass and space has caught your interest, try combining the lines of the balsa strips with the planes of the cardboard. You can further articulate your space by connecting one area to another with string and by cutting the cardboard for a colored glass or cellophane insert.

4. Work a mass of clay (of about 8 lbs.) into a block. With simple tools, scoop out sections of the clay and then note how light and shade can be manipulated. When you have established a relationship between shallow and deep areas and the surface of the clay, take a flashlight and study how the character of your work changes with the light source. Think of this in relation to architecture as well as to sculpture. Notice how this problem overlaps with the category below, light and shade.

5. To investigate line and space, try the "exploding" design. Divide a sheet of dark paper into sections and place the sections on white background. Observe how pulling the sections apart creates everything from a thin white line to a dominant segment of white. Do this also with curving lines that bisect the paper.

Activities Emphasizing Light and Shade

1. Paint six or seven containers found around the house (cereal boxes, tea tins, cigar boxes, soup cans) a single unifying tone of white. Group these before you on a table, and draw them with black chalk on gray paper, using white chalk for highlights. Let the color of the paper play through for middle tones and reserve the white and black for the extreme values. Try one view with the flat side of your chalk and another with the point, carefully building your tones by massing strokes and lines.

2. Place the three pieces of sculpture produced to illustrate problems of mass and space in the path of a strong light. Manipulate them until the shadows and highlights on the objects themselves, together

with the shadows cast from one object to another, form an acceptable unity. Observe the pattern of the shadows behind the sculpture.

3. Project a slide of a group of buildings on a sheet of light paper. Forget that you are dealing with buildings and fill in the image with dark and light patterns. As a follow-up, take your sketch outdoors and see if this exercise in concentration on pattern and mass and light and shade has aided you in seeing (and drawing) an actual building.

Activities Emphasizing Texture

1. Cut pieces from printed pages that utilize various kinds and arrangements of type. Paste the pieces on cardboard or paper so that an interesting textural arrangement is developed.

2. Roll out a slab of clay and cut it into various shapes — square, round, rectangular, triangular. Create textural patterns on the surface by pressing found objects (coins, scissors, nuts, wood scraps) into the clay. With softer materials such as sponge, burlap, combs, and string, make patterns even closer to the surface. Use your imagination to think of items other than the ones suggested above.

3. Crumple a piece of paper and spray it with black paint from one angle only. Let the paper dry and press it flat. Notice the startling dimensional quality of the texture.

4. Create a collage that changes texturally in one direction from glassy smoothness to extreme roughness. Feel it with your eyes closed and compare it with those of your classmates. Vary the feel by adjusting the size and location of your textural samples.

Activities Emphasizing Color

1. Paint freely with a large brush, noting the apparent changes in hues as one color is placed next to another. How do the adjacent colors affect each other? Cut out various-sized windows in black paper and move them about your painting, noticing the variety of compositions and color interactions that are possible.

2. Dampen a sheet of heavy white drawing paper and drip tempera paint or watercolors so that different hues run and blend. Note the new colors so formed.

3. Join the class in bringing in a swatch of color you think is red. When placed next to one another, the swatches of paper, paint, and cloth will produce a surprising range of tone and value in a subtly modulated monochromatic collage. Try other colors as well, including black and white. Notice in each case how the surface texture contributes to the effect of the color.

4. Cut out six squares of any single color and paste on them circles of six different colors. Notice how each of the circular background colors changes the nature of the constant foreground color. Is color a fixed entity or does it have relative characteristics?

Activities Emphasizing Function and Adequate Use of Materials

1. Collect your study pictures of families of similar objects such as automobiles, chairs, yachts, and kitchen equipment. Compare one brand with another from the point of view of function. How does a Porsche, for example, compare with a Cadillac or a Datsun in this respect? What concessions have the manufacturers made to style at the expense of function? Why have they done so? To what extent are they justified in doing so? Start a scrapbook that concentrates on the most poorly designed products.

2. Find a number of objects in which a certain material has been processed to resemble another, such as cardboard to resemble leather, or plastic to look like woven cloth. Why has the manufacturer resorted to such practices? What are the opinions of designers and critics about them?

Other Activities

1. Emphasizing analogies: Take a photo of an actual familiar object, and draw another object that the first one appears to resemble. For instance, a fence may remind you of teeth, a fireplug of a robot, and a rock of a loaf of bread.

2. Emphasizing positive and negative patterns of dark and light: Draw an overall pattern using the shape of a common object like scissors, tableware, or an ink bottle. Where the forms overlap, switch back and forth from black to white, so that the objects are fragmented and the viewer becomes engaged in reestablishing the form of the object.

3. Emphasizing variety within a single form: Select any geometric shape as a working module. Using any medium you like, create an arrangement based on your shape, obtaining variety in the design by adjustment of the size or color of the shape, by overlapping, and other effects.

4. Gather as many images as you can from the media that can indicate the design categories discussed. What examples are the most difficult to obtain? Industrial design? Illustration? Theatre design?
5. After watching the credits at the conclusion of a film, make a list of every participant you feel is art-related.

6. Watch any situation comedy (including commercials) and list every art-related career. Eliminate these from the show and try to imagine how it would appear.

Activities for Studying Architecture

Exercising Preference and Judgement What is the least attractive building in the community? The most attractive? Is there a very ugly building in your town? What makes a building very ugly?

Guests Most cities have a branch of the AIA (American Institute of Architects). Branches often have an educational committee with volunteers who will come and talk to a class that requests them.

Aesthetic Decision Making Suppose you had a certain amount of money to open an arts center. If you started from scratch, you'd have everything you need. If you restored an old factory, you might have to make some compromises in parking, flow of visitor traffic, or desirability of location. What factors would influence your decision?

Imagining

♦ Design a tree house for a private hideaway.
♦ Plan a children's center so attractive in appearance and function that no one can resist attending it.
♦ A room of your own is being added to your apartment or home. What will it offer in the way of convenience of work or leisure, hobbies, etc.? What will it look like? Draw each wall separately on cardboard, then stand them vertically on a clay base.
♦ Design a doghouse or a birdhouse using an historical period or culture as a model: classical, Victorian, or thatched hut.

♦ SUGGESTED READINGS

Brommer, Gerald, and Joseph Gatto, *Careers in Art: An Illustrated Guide* (Worcester, MA: Davis Publication, 1984).

Feldman, Edmund B., *Thinking about Art* (Englewood Cliffs, NJ: Prentice-Hall, 1985), Chapter 8.

Rawson, Philip, *Creative Design: A New Look at Design Principles* (London: Macdonald, 1987).

Art Education: The Journal of the NAEA, Vol. 42, No. 5 (September 1989).

For information regarding special projects, write to Project Archi-Teacher, 315 S. State St., Champagne, IL 61821.

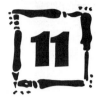

ART CRITICISM: FROM CLASSROOM TO MUSEUM

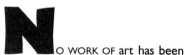O WORK OF ART has been created with such finality that you need contribute nothing to it. You must recreate the work for yourself—it cannot be presented to you ready-made. You cannot look at a picture and find it beautiful by a merely passive act of seeing. The internal relations that make it beautiful to you have to be discovered and in some way have to be put in by you. The artist provides a skeleton; he provides guiding lines; he provides enough to engage your interest and to touch you emotionally. But there is no picture and no poem unless you yourself enter it and fill it out.[1]

Jacob Bronowski

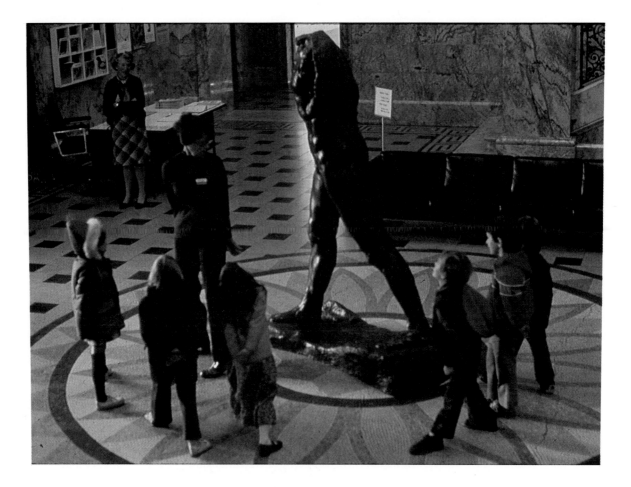

Up to this point, we have considered problems arising from creating art forms. We must now turn to another aspect of art education, that of developing the pupils' appreciation of art through the development of critical skills.

THE NATURE OF ART APPRECIATION AND CRITICISM

Art appreciation, although an outmoded term associated with the picture study movement of the early 1920s, still has some validity. Then, as now, the word "appreciate" means "valuing" or having a sense of an object's worth through the familiarity one gains by sustained, guided study. Appreciation also involves the acquisition of knowledge related to the object, the artist, the materials used, the historical and stylistic setting, and the development of a critical sense. If we accept the fact that critics as well as artists can be models for artistic study, we must think about how critics operate. There are journalistic critics who write for the general public and who avoid the more profound levels of writing, and there are critics who work for art journals who are knowledgeable in history and aesthetics and use language in such a way that criticism itself becomes an art form. The goal of all critics is the same — to provide the reader with information regarding an artist or an exhibit and beyond that, to help the readers to increase their understanding by viewing art through the informed eye that good critics are assumed to possess.

If we study excerpts from the following review, we can gain a clearer idea of the kinds of content that occupy critics.[2] The painting under discussion is Vincent Van Gogh's *Starry Night*. Key phrases have been selected from the review to distinguish four phases of discussion: descriptive, analytical, interpretative, and historical. The judgment about the work's quality is implicit in the critic's choice of this painting. We begin with a statement by the artist, which provides historical context.

> *Historical*: "I devour nature ceaselessly. I exaggerate, sometimes I make changes in the subject, but still I don't invent the whole picture, on the contrary I find it already there; it is a question of picking out what one wants from nature."[3]

In a discussion of the painting, we find illustration of the other three modes of critical approach to the artwork.

> *Descriptive*: "Look at Van Gogh's painting, *The Starry Night*. You can easily recognize village, trees, moon, stars; but clearly this is not the point."
> *Analytical*: "We can point to certain qualities of the brushwork and relate them to the impact of the total work. The individual strokes are 'rough', they vary, although they hold to a definite scale or size . . . These patterns are in themselves dynamic and they are insistently repeated.
> *Interpretative*: ". . . you are at once impressed by a grand, almost hypnotic rhythm which binds all the representational elements together into a kind of cosmic unity . . . Van Gogh lays bare his very act of painting and it is partly through the suggestion of his physical activity that we share his emotion."[4]

When we create a knowledge base in art, we deal with information surrounding a work (names, dates, places) as well as facts concerning physical details taken from the work itself (subject matter, media, colors). Knowledge also includes those concepts of design, technique, and style that the teacher feels can enable the student to "read" a painting. Being able to recognize these factors in an artwork begins in our natural, untrained powers of perception, but requires guided experience in order to make them operable.[5]

Appreciation can begin in a spontaneous, intuitive reaction, but it does not end there. One way to arrive at a deeper level of response is to understand the difference between looking and seeing and in order to do this, we can utilize a process used by professional art critics, as illustrated in the review cited above. The end goal of the critical phase of the appreciative process is to be able to respond more fully to an artwork and to defend one's opinion regarding it.

To accept knowledge about art as a vital component of art appreciation is not to preclude those highly personal reactions to art that come so naturally to all of us. Although we can be drawn to a cathedral because of its sense of grandeur and its use of light (an intuitive response), knowing that the use of the exterior flying buttresses is what creates the passage of light through stained glass windows or being aware that lives have been lost as churches collapsed before buttresses were conceived, is historical knowledge that can enhance our appreciation and heighten our initial intuitive response. The role that historical information and other forms of knowledge play in our responses is also an authentic issue, and is dealt with more fully in the chapter which follows.

Criticism as part of the larger issue of appreciation focuses our attention more intensely upon knowledge that can be obtained from the object itself as the main event rather than upon the circumstances that surround it. There is probably much truth in the old saw about "a picture judging a person" rather than the reverse. What a person is, emotionally, intellectually, and socially will determine the nature of one's appreciation. Although this ability seems to be built around innate qualities, so that some of us are able to acquire it more quickly than others, as teachers we must assume that art appreciation can also be the result of education.

One German literary critic sums it up as follows:

> "Criticism ranges from journalism to scholarship, and in rare moments of glory, it becomes literature in its own right. Above all, the task of criticism is to *mediate*. The critic stands between author (artist) and reader (viewer), mediating between art and society. In this regard his function is primarily educational. The objection often made in regard to the critic—that he has a touch of the schoolmaster—is absolutely justified. Whom do critics wish to instruct? . . . The critic wants to instruct the readers, to point out to them what is good and why it is so. By the same token this means that a critic is obliged to point out what is bad and why."[6]

TEACHING METHODS TO DEVELOP CRITICAL SKILLS

There are a number of viewpoints concerning the teaching of criticism and appreciation in the elementary school. Some feel that there should be no formal teaching, because children are not mature enough to benefit from it; instead, the teacher should encourage the pupils to freely express themselves and then "stand over them in a kind of protective awe."[7] Others feel that appreciative skills should be taught when such teaching appears to be expedient and when the need for it is clearly apparent. This view implies that the logical time for critical activity should arise during studio experience with materials which can be directly related to the kinds of knowledge needed to extend the pupil's power of appreciation. Another viewpoint, already touched on, is that special efforts should make children so aware of critical processes that they can bring some order to their perceptions and apply what they have learned when confronted with artworks of any culture and period.

Few teachers who have ever taught for appreciation and listened to the insights that children bring to viewing would ever take the first position. The freshness, honesty, and directness that characterize the artwork of primary pupils, and the imaginative and intuitive capabilities of most children on the elementary level, combine to provide a positive learning climate for their critical-appreciative activities. The increased verbal skill of children in the upper elementary grades can also compensate to a large degree for the self-consciousness some may feel in certain studio activities, and can often provide highly verbal children with an opportunity to excel in activities that are not studio oriented.

When we ask children to verbalize, to use linguistic as well as visual forms of expression, we are using skills developed in the language arts program for our own ends. Where children may engage in art activities for an hour a week, they will have had two hours of reading and writing on a daily basis since grade one. *Critical activities are the meeting ground between art and language arts and it is due to the students' familiarity with the latter that they take so readily to applying language to the understanding of artworks.*

The second point of view had more advocates twenty-five years ago than today. An extraordinary amount of nonsense has been perpetrated in many classrooms through formal lessons in art appreciation, in which irrelevant questions are asked about certain works of art. Sir Joshua Reynolds's *The Age of Innocence*, for example, may be the picture chosen for study. Even when the questions may seem pertinent to the picture being studied — "Why is the little girl placed where she is in the picture?" or "What colors has the artist used to make us look at her?" — there is some doubt as to the value of the teaching procedure. But when the questions become artistically remote from the work and include sentimental or literary ideas–"Isn't she a pretty little girl?" or "Do you think she is happy" or "Why isn't she wearing shoes? Will it rain?" — critical understanding can never occur. Such questions simply lead the children away from the essence, the inner life of the work into directions that are irrelevant and distracting.

〰 **TABLE 11-1**

A Comparison of Past and Present Methods of Developing Appreciation Through Critical Skill

Past	Present
Rarely went beyond immediate reactions to a work of art.	Defers judgment until the art object has been examined.
Instruction was primarily verbal and teacher-centered.	Instruction may be based on verbalization, perceptual investigation, studio activity, or combinations of these.
Relied primarily on reproductions.	Utilizes a wide range of instructional media — slides, books, reproductions, films, and most important, original works of art, visits to museums and galleries, and visits from local artists.
Based primarily on painting, because of its "storytelling" qualities.	May encompass the complete range of visual form from fine arts (painting, sculpture) to applied arts (industrial design, architecture, and crafts). May also include print media, television, advertising, films, and magazine layouts.
Used literary and sentimental associations as basis for discussion. Concentrated on such elements as beauty and morality to the exclusion of formal qualities.	Bases discussion on the formal qualities of the artwork. Recognizes beauty and other sensuously gratifying qualities as only one part of the aesthetic experience, but also recognizes abrasive and shocking images as legitimate expressions of psychological and political motives.
Neglected the contributions of women artists and representatives of growing minority populations such as black, Hispanic, and Asian.	Utilizes references to the past; shows respect for artistic efforts of all epochs.
Spent much time in anecdotal accounts of artist's life.	Minimizes the life story of the artist and concentrates instead on the work.
Concentrated upon a "great works" approach, to the exclusion of lesser works which have a special contribution to make.	Adopts a broader view of art objects, and can include craft, illustration, media, industrial arts, and comic books, as well as fine arts.

Studio Involvement

Critical skills can also be developed in close relationship to art activities. According to this method a teacher seizes every practical opportunity to introduce the subject of appreciation, not only drawing and painting, but also three-dimensional work such as sculpture, pottery, and architecture. This studio- or activity-centered method is based on the belief that one should not divorce expression from appreciation. After working with a medium, we become conscious of the problems, needs, and goals that have influenced our own expressive acts.

In commenting on the reciprocity between the creative and critical processes in television art instruction, Manuel Barkan and Laura Chapman stated:

> . . . the most sensitive making of art cannot lead to rich comprehension if it is not accompanied by observation of works of art and reflective thought about them. Neither can observation and reflection alone call for the nuances of feeling nor develop the commitment that can result from personal involvement in making works of art. The reciprocal relationship between learning to make art and learning to recognize, attend to, and understand art should guide the planning of art instruction.[8]

The Phased Approach to the Critical Act

The method which follows is a form of analysis related to the distinctions critics make in writing about art. Awareness of formal structure requires children to be acquainted with the components of artworks and the teacher to be sensitive to children's perceptual, linguistic, and creative capabilities. It includes processes whereby students may engage in studio, historical, and critical activities, gaining relevant information while discussing works of art, and suggests deferring judgment and interpretation until the work has been examined and discussed.

One of the goals of critical activity is the development and use of an expanding art vocabulary. Children will not compare a photorealist work and a Van Gogh in terms of "painterly" textures unless this term has been pointed out to them. Even fourth graders are capable of such distinctions if their attention has been directed specifically to nuances of surface, or if they have been brought to discover it for themselves. Consistent use of examples should be selected for those art terms that you expect children to learn. The discussion of the phases of criticism should be studied in reference to the review quoted at the beginning of this chapter.

Description. Although the descriptive level focuses on aspects we generally perceive in ways that are common to most of us, it can also lead to some heated discussions, since what you see as red, your neighbor may see as orange; one person may see square shapes, another trapezoidal. In any case, it is through description that we make language more precise.

From the middle grades on, the teacher should make a distinction between *objective* description, items with which no one will disagree (such as a house, two people walking, a sky that takes up over half the space, etc.), and *personalized* or *evocative* description ("sloppily" painted; may be described by someone else as "loosely" painted and the color red may appear as more orange to another). A scientist may describe a horse by Delacroix as a four-legged quadruped; a critic or a poet may note its "noble bearing" or observe that it "moves like the wind." Evocative description usually involves adjectives. It can be imaginative in nature and although it should be encouraged, students should be made aware of the difference between the two approaches.

Formal Analysis.　Although formal analysis also has a perceptual basis, it takes the descriptive stage a step further by requiring the child to analyze the structure or composition of an artwork. The child who can distinguish between symmetry and asymmetry, identify the artist's media, and be sensitive to the qualities of color and line can discuss the form of an artwork or how it is put together. This is the stage in which the teacher discovers whether the children can use the language of design discussed in the chapter on this subject.

The discussions initiated at both descriptive and formal-analytic stages bring about that intense, sustained visual concentration that is necessary for the critical act. They also set the stage for the development of more informed opinions about art and set the foundation for the interpretation which follows. Description and analysis does not accept premature judgments, requiring, instead, that the student defer certain opinions until they can be handled with that degree of detachment we call "distancing." When we "distance," we put a temporary hold on our emotions and our judgments.

Interpretation.　In the interpretative stage, the student moves to more imaginative levels and is invited to speculate about the meaning embodied in a work or the purpose the artist may have had in mind. To do this, the child is asked to establish some connection between the structure that can be discerned and the direction in which the artist is taking him or her. For example, if the class has agreed that Orozco in his *Zapatistas* used sharp contrasts of dark and light and strong directional forces, the question that follows is, "To what end?". Would the mean-

To sharpen students' analytical skills, the author (left) demonstrates principles by working on an overlay of a reproduction. Students (right) take turns drawing structural lines on slides projected on the blackboard. The students then select a reproduction from the picture wall to develop individual analysis.

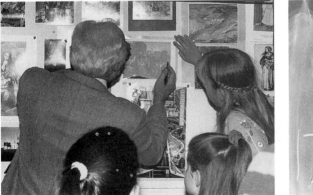
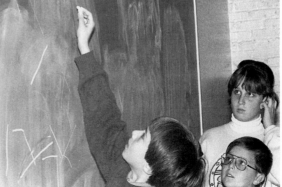

ing have been as clear had the artist used the more delicate colors of impressionism? At this point, the class is getting at the painter's use of compositional elements for a specific end—in the work cited above, compositional elements reinforce Orozco's attitude toward the revolution in Mexico. How does Renoir's sensuous and pleasing color relate to *his* feelings regarding motherhood and courtship? How do de Kooning's fragmented shapes and strident colors tie in with his attitudes regarding certain types of women? Such questions characterize discussion in the interpretative stage, which is open—a time and place without right or wrong answers.

Judgment and Informed Preference.   The critical process normally ends with a judgment, that is, a conclusion regarding the success or failure of an artwork and its ranking with other artworks. Judgment, in this sense, will not be discussed because it is more the province of professional critics and connoisseurs than elementary teachers. Judgment, in the mind of a child, is synonymous with preference. A child's opinion regarding the position of Dürer's etchings in the canon of graphic art would not be terribly enlightening, but the same child's defense of personal acceptance or rejection of Dürer's work is possible and should be encouraged, providing such opinions are open to discussion. It is in the final stage that the teacher can determine to what degree students can use critical and design vocabulary to articulate their views.

It is useful to recognize the distinction between preference and judgment in response to works of art. Preferences are not subject to correction by authority or persuasion since one's personal liking or disliking of an artwork is an aspect of one's individuality. Reactions such as "like/dislike," "it stinks," and "wow" are psychological reactions and by their very nature discourage further discussion. Judgment, however, is subject to argumentation and persuasion. For example, a person might be convinced, on the basis of nutritional evidence, that asparagus is a fine food, but still dislikes asparagus. Instantaneous preference or rejection and judgment may be regarded as the difference between a closed and an open mind.

When someone makes a statement such as, "That is a very strong painting" or "That is a poor example of raku pottery," it is reasonable for someone else to ask, "Why do you say that?" and request some justification for the judgment. If the justification is weak or controversial, then the floor is open to discussion. One goal of critical activity is to move students from closed to open minds, from instantaneous preference to a state of deferred judgment.

It is perfectly reasonable to say, "I know that this drawing is not of high quality, but I like it nevertheless." Conversely, it is appropriate to remark, "I know that this is an excellent sculpture, but I really don't like it." In most instances, however, we are more apt to like a work of art if we understand it and have spent some time with it. In most cases we prefer those works that we judge to be of high quality to those that we judge to be of low quality. Another goal of art appreciation is accepting the fact that preference and judgment are not finite; that they can change over time. Even the greatest critics maintain their personal likes and dislikes. We find, however, as we learn more about art, that our tastes change and expand as our acceptance of artworks increase.

Informed preference is the culminating and most demanding stage. Although it invites students to render their opinions regarding the worth of an object, their opinions must be based on what they have learned in the previous stages. Such questions as the following are asked: "Are you moved by this work of art?" "How do you feel about it?" "Would you like to own it or hang it in your room?" "Does it leave you cold?" "Do you dislike it?" "Why?" Most viewers instinctively begin at the level of preference: what the process of criticism as set forth here attempts to do is to *defer preference until the matter has been given sustained thought and attention.*

Children view criticism as a visual-verbal game and will participate with enthusiasm if the discussions are not too lengthy (a half-hour seems to be an outside limit), and if the artworks under discussion are selected with care. Works with strong color, interesting subject matter, and a clear compositional structure seem to elicit the most positive responses.

In essence, the four stages are related to four basic questions:

"What do you see?" (description)
"How are things put together?" (formal analysis)
"What is the artist trying to say?" (interpretation)
"What do you think of the work, and why?" (informed preference)

In the beginning stages, the phases of criticism should be used in the order described, but when students are familiar with the process, one can begin critical activity at any stage. The roles of studio activity and historical information will depend upon the teacher's knowledge and sense of timing.

The critical approach just described is not the only way to deepen our understanding of art.[9] Another approach is the scanning method suggested by Broudy, who stresses the identification of artistic properties rather than a particular order in recognizing and identifying them.[10] Broudy claims that attention should be directed towards *sensory* properties (shapes, colors, textures), formal properties (balance, unity, repetition, dominance of one factor over another), *expressive* properties (feelings, moods, conflicts), and *technical* properties, which deal with the way art media has been used in its relation to other properties. Broudy also accepts the use of historical settings, the artist's intent, and the application of criteria in making a judgment on an artwork. In both approaches, specific artworks consistently are the primary source of learning. The authors of this book take the position that activities with art media can be used to reinforce and clarify those qualities that are studied in works of art.

A Historian Takes a Critical Approach With Sixth Graders

The following segment of a teaching session demonstrates how a renowned art historian, Dr. James Ackerman, conducted a session on using critical skills.[11] Dr. Ackerman began by making the point that the basic task of the class was to talk about what was seen as well as to look, and that looking would come naturally to the children, since they lived in a visually oriented society with constant exposure to television, films, and mass-printed media. Dr. Ackerman then listed on the blackboard four terms he felt were needed to discuss the paintings shown.

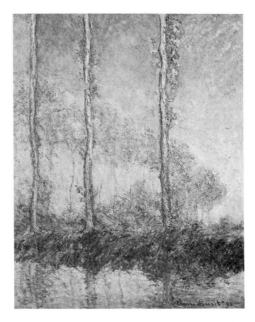

Two views of water discussed in the comparison exercises. Claude Monet, *Poplars*, c. 1891. (Philadelphia Museum of Art. Gift of Chester Dale. Egyptian fresco, XII Dynasty. (The Metropolitan Museum of Art, New York.)

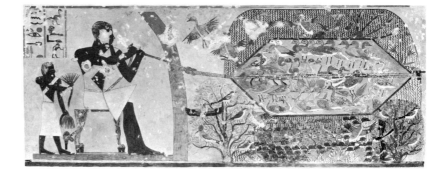

Technique: the way in which artists use materials.

Form: the structure and interaction of components of an artwork.

Meaning: the intention; the ultimate significance of an artwork. Because the children had some difficulty absorbing this concept, Dr. Ackerman accepted the term *subject* in its place.

Feeling: the emotive power that is elicited from a work.

Dr. Ackerman used the comparative method to develop the class discussion. On one screen he showed a slide of an impressionist oil painting of poplars, and next to it an Egyptian wall fresco showing trees framing a pool of fish and ducks. What follows is a selection from the discussion that transpired

DR. A: Who would like to try to describe the painting techniques of these two paintings?

STUDENT: The trees are watercolor . . .

STUDENT: I think they're oil.

DR. A: You're right; that is an oil painting. How about the other . . . ? [A lot of whispering but no volunteers.] Take a guess.

STUDENT: Watercolor — maybe tempera?

DR. A: Why do you say that?

STUDENT: It's flat and bright, not shaded like oils.

DR. A: Very good — flat is a good word, except that in this case the effect is due to a fresco technique. Anyone know what fresco is? [Silence.] Well, it was used by the Egyptians as a way of making painting part of a wall. They did this by using tempera paint on fresh plaster mixed with water and lime. Now back to your "flatness." If you've ever painted on plaster you know it gets soaked up and dries quickly. That doesn't allow for much shading or roundness of forms and instead gets the painter to work in clear, flat areas of color. How did this artist make his shapes seem clearer?

STUDENT: He put lines around them.

DR. A: Very good. Would you care to point to one part of the painting to show what you mean? [Student points to outline of pool.] Now, let's look at the subject. Can we say that one of these paintings is more true to life than the other? Let's take a vote. How many say the poplar trees are more "true to life?" [The class votes as a group in favor of this one.] Why is that?

STUDENT: Well, it doesn't look exactly like a photograph, but it almost could be one.

DR. A: Which do you like better? [The class votes for the impressionist.] Let's see how the painter looks at his subject . . . anyone care to comment?

STUDENT: Well, it's more like real life in the poplars.

STUDENT: The ducks are real life.

STUDENT: But it's mixed up in the fresco.

DR. A: I think you are trying to say that there are two points of view in the Egyptian's. Who can go to the screen and point to one point of view? [One student volunteers and points to the bird's-eye view of the pool.] Where are we standing when we look at the pool?

STUDENT: Above—we're above it.

DR. A: How about the ducks?

STUDENT: You're in front of them.

DR. A: Good. Then we might say that in one way the Egyptian artist used his space and subjects with a lot more freedom than the other artists. But what does the impressionist painting offer us instead of different points of view in the same picture?

STUDENT: You can see more . . . more details . . . more real . . .

DR. A: Would you agree with me that there are many ways of being "true"; that the Egyptian painting shows us the way we know things to be and the impressionist more the way we are likely to react?

Applying A Discovery Method

In the teacher's follow-up on the lesson above, Dr. Ackerman's ideas were used to lead the children to discover a basis for criticism for themselves. The children were shown four reproductions and asked to name the differences they could detect among the works. The paintings were Raphael's *Madonna and Child*, Kollwitz's *Killed in Action*, de Kooning's *Marilyn Monroe*, and Kandinsky's *Improvisation*. The children began by agreeing that the four pictures had easily definable differences. As these were noted, the teacher wrote them on the blackboard in columns, according to whether they related to materials, subject, meaning, form, or style. When the children's powers of observation were apparently exhausted, the teacher wrote the category headings above the columns, pointing out that what the class had really done was create its own critical system or categories of discussion (see Table 11-2, page 306). Such an ordering of concepts demonstrated to the children that there were many ways to discuss works of art. Instead of providing them with answers *prior* to the discussion, the teacher sought to elicit responses by posing questions that centered on a single conceptual problem—the ways in which artists differ in their work. In order to deal with such a problem, the children had to engage in such processes as ordering, comparing, classifying, and making generalizations.[12]

During this discovery discussion, the teacher translated the naive vocabulary of the class into an art-centered vocabulary, adding important characteristics that were missed. This discussion laid the groundwork for lessons which followed. The "materials" column provided the background for a visiting artist to demonstrate the difference between oil and watercolors; the "meaning" classification prepared the class for a lesson in comparison of styles, in which they were shown a

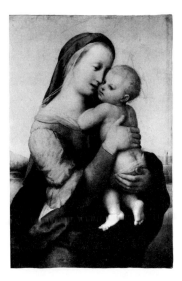

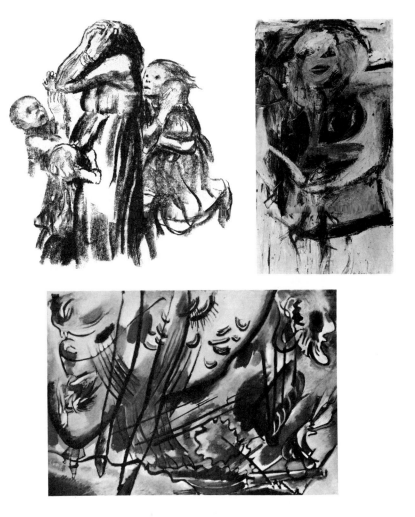

Paintings used in the discovery exercise: Raphael, *Madonna and Child*, 1508. (Scala: New York, Florence. Alte Pinakothek, Munich.) Käthe Kollwitz, *Killed in Action*, 1921, lithograph. Willem de Kooning, *Marilyn Monroe*, 1954. (Scala: New York, Florence. Neuberger Museum, State University of New York at Purchase.) Wassily Kandinsky, *Improvisation 28* (Second Version), 1912. (The Solomon R. Guggenheim Museum, New York. © ADAGP 1990.)

variety of paintings, each with a difference stylistic approach to the same theme. Let us now note other activities that can develop art appreciation.

ESTABLISHING A LANGUAGE BASE

Begin by listing art terms that are to be learned: by lesson, by unit, and by year. Do not use any word unless it has a clear equivalent in an artwork. This can be accomplished with students at any age, as long as the concepts can be clearly illustrated in an artwork. Once having learned a word, students should be expected to use it from then on whenever it is exemplified in work under discussion.

~~ **TABLE 11-2**

Results of the Follow-Up Discovery Discussion

Object: To create content categories that may serve as a basis for building subsequent sessions in art appreciation

Materials (What We Work With)	Subject (What We Paint)	Meaning (Why We Paint)	Form (How a Painting Is Composed)	Style (What Makes Paintings Look Different from One Another)
"Kollwitz uses crayons; it's more a drawing." (Teacher explains difference between drawing and lithography.) "The Raphael must be oil." "The de Kooning could be tempera or house paint." "The Kandinsky painting is thin, it could be watercolor." (Teacher explains that if oil paint is thinned with enough turpentine, it can have the transparency of watercolor.)	"Kollwitz has a sad mother and hungry children." "Raphael has a happy mother and child." "The de Kooning is called *Marilyn Monroe*, but it takes you a long time to see her." "I can't recognize anything in the Kandinsky like I can in the others." (Teacher defines "non-objective" and "abstract.")	"Kollwitz's mother is worried about how she will feed her children." "Kandinsky's has no meaning; it's just shapes, lines, and colors that go all over the place." "I can't tell you what the Kandinsky and de Kooning are all about." "The Raphael is a religious picture."	"I see a triangle in the Raphael and up-and-down forms painted really sloppy in the de Kooning." (Teacher: "We call this painterly, not sloppy.") "The Raphael is quiet. The Kandinsky is loud." (Teacher: What makes one picture "loud" and another "quiet"?) "Kandinsky makes you look in different 'directions': up, over, and around."	"The Raphael looks so real you could walk into it." "The Kollwitz is real too but in a different way." (Teacher defines "selective realism.") Raphael "smooth" "like a photograph" "done carefully" de Kooning "sloppy" "done really fast" "more wild" "messy" Kandinsky "wild" "like a third grader's picture of space"

New critical language also provides the teacher with a way to evaluate learning. The following words suggest three levels of complexity. Terms may overlap categories and can include form qualities, subjects, media, and even emotional states or qualities of feeling.

Level I: Lower Elementary

portrait	shape	contrast	sketch
still life	color	paint	sculpture
landscape	line	art	contour
cartoon			

Level II: Middle Elementary

abstract	watercolor	assemblage	composition
realism	pastel	collage	shading
nonobjective	print	contour	texture
modeling	repetition		

Level III: Upper Elementary and Middle School

style	agitated	technical	symbols
proportion	balance	expressive	theme
perspective	dominance	emphasis	genre
crosshatch	subject	gradation	fantasy
pattern	formal	variation	painterly

Teachers can construct their own lists of terms, suggesting increasing complexity, sequenced instruction, and cumulative learning. Having learned a word on one level, it is then added to the ones on the next. This also opens the door to making variations of key words. As an example, the author showed a group of seventh graders a reproduction of a painting by Jackson Pollock and asked someone to point to the presence of lines. The immediate reaction was to deny the existence of lines. The class was urged to keep looking until the use of line was detected. Within a few minutes, it was discovered that Pollock used several ways of creating lines; he dripped, he brushed, and he painted them. Pollock's method was then related to his general approach to painting which, in turn, emerged as a key to understanding the movement known as abstract expressionism. One term — "line" — thus provided an entry into a major style of this century, or to put it another way, the *microcosmic* opened the door to the *macrocosmic*.

Word Matching

Number every word on the vocabulary list on a piece of cardboard with one side cut like an arrowhead. Hand each student a vocabulary card and have him or her place it on or close to the matching section of a large reproduction. (Use velcro or felt backing or tack to keep it in place.) Or, place the reproduction on the lip of the chalkboard and have students write the new terms on the board, using color-coded chalk to keep categories separate. (Red for formal elements, blue for principles of design, white for expressive characteristics and so on.)

∿ **TABLE 11-3**

Sample Questions Utilizing the Terminology of Art

Terminology	Painting	Question
Social Criticism	The Senate (William Gropper)	After a visit to the United States Senate the artist painted his idea of what he saw. In *your* opinion, this artist seemed to feel that: A. The only things senators did were read papers, sit around, or make speeches that no one cared about. B. All senators are not the dedicated public servants we think they are. C. Most senators read papers in order to know what was happening in different parts of the country.
Depth	The Last Supper (Leonardo da Vinci)	In this wall painting, what gives you the feeling of depth? A. The direction of the lines in the construction of the room. B. The strong and bright colors. C. Both A and B.
Paint Quality (Technique)	Lady with a Parasol (Auguste Renoir)	The edges of the objects in this painting are *mostly:* A. Unclear and fuzzy. B. Sharp and exact. C. Both A and B.

José Clemente Orozco, *Zapatistas*, 1931. The striking contrasts of light and dark in this work can be a starting point for a discussion of ends in painting. Related terms for the students to learn here are *contrast, repetition, diagonal, stylize, selective realism*, and *rhythm*. (Collection, The Museum of Modern Art, New York. Given anonymously.)

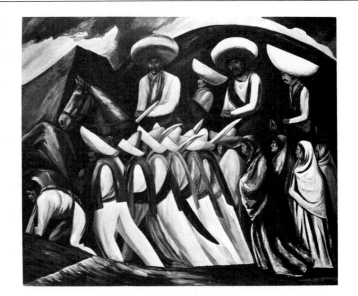

Terminology	Painting	Question
Line Quality	*Killed in Action* (Käthe Kollwitz)	We can describe the line in this print as: A. Delicate and soft. B. Strong and bold. C. Both A and B.
Meaning	*Killed in Action* (Käthe Kollwitz)	Which statement *best* describes what is going on in this print? A. A mother is resting with her children. B. A mother is expressing misery in front of her children. C. A mother is playing with her children.
Style	*Zapatistas* (José Orozco)	The style (the artist's own way of painting) of this picture is called: A. Realism (looks lifelike). B. Selective realism (partly real). C. Abstract (unrecognizable shapes).
Composition	*Poplars* (Claude Monet)	The trees dominate this painting. Monet makes it stand out by: A. Emphasizing the texture of the trees. B. Making the trees large and placing them centrally in the picture. C. Focusing attention on strong vertical shapes.

Visualizing Words Relating to Feelings

Write three words from the following group on cards and distribute them randomly: sad, cheerful, relaxed, bold, angry, nervous, quiet, tranquil, and joyous. Each student then creates a drawing, painting, or piece of sculpture that conveys the essence of the word. Upon completion, display them and ask the class if they can recognize the words. If the words are sufficiently varied, this should be simple.

The next question is: What do the "quiet" words show us that "angry" words do not? The final task is to see how the mood of the word is reflected in art. (The teacher can select the words from the reproductions that happen to be on hand.)

FURTHER SUGGESTIONS FOR STUDY

The Artist of the Week

A lesson need not take up the full art period. An effective learning situation can occur in five to ten minutes. Each art class could begin with an introduction to the "Artist of the Week," the teacher provid-

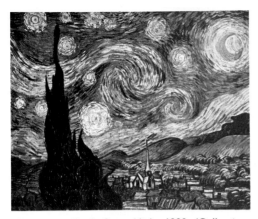

Vincent van Gogh, *Starry Night*, 1889. (Collection, The Museum of Modern Art, New York. Acquired through the Lillie P. Bliss Bequest.)

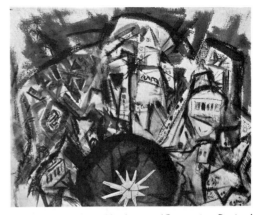

John Marin, *Lower Manhattan (Composing Derived from Top of Woolworth)*, 1922. (Collection, The Museum of Modern Art, New York. Acquired through the Lillie P. Bliss Bequest.)

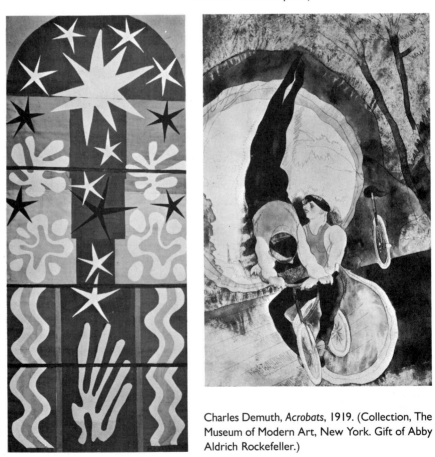

Henri Matisse, *Nuit de Noël*, 1952. Maquette for stained glass window commissioned by *Life* magazine, 1952. (Collection, The Museum of Modern Art, New York. Gift of Time, Inc.

Charles Demuth, *Acrobats*, 1919. (Collection, The Museum of Modern Art, New York. Gift of Abby Aldrich Rockefeller.)

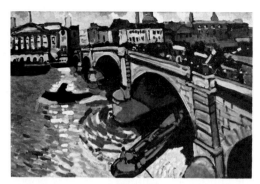

André Derain, *London Bridge*, 1906. (Collection, The Museum of Modern Art, New York. Gift of Mr. and Mrs. Charles Zadok. © ADAGP 1990.)

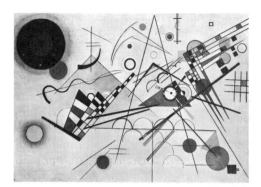

Wassily Kandinsky, *Composition 8*, 1923. (The Solomon R. Guggenheim Museum, New York City. © ADAGP 1990.)

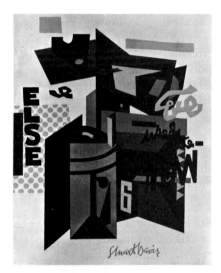

Stuart Davis, *Owh! In San Pao*, 1951. (Collection of the Whitney Museum of American Art, New York.)

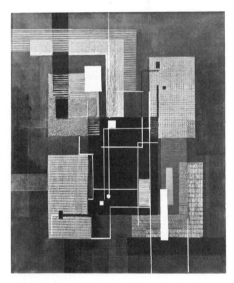

Irene Rice Pereira, *White Lines*, 1942. (Collection, The Museum of Modern Art, New York. Gift of Edgar Kaufmann, Jr.)

Illustrations for a picture wall. Children can become acquainted with the art terms that are italicized in the activities below by matching certain paintings from a basic collection. The terms progress from simple, usually descriptive, to more complex, dealing with qualities in art.

1. Four pictures use the *circle* as an important shape in the composition. (Answer: Van Gogh, Marin, Demuth, Kandinsky)
2. Two are painted in *watercolor*. (Answer: Marin, Demuth)
3. The effectiveness of four paintings rests on the use of colored objects that are *flat* and *hard-edged*. (Answer: Davis, Pereira, Kandinsky, Matisse)
4. Two paintings share a quality of *violence*. (Answer: Van Gogh, Marin)
5. Two of the paintings show obvious uses of *broken color*. (Answer: Van Gogh, Derain)
6. Three paintings use *line* as an important factor. (Answer: Marin, Davis, Kandinsky)

ing some interesting information about the artist and his work, posing some questions of a descriptive, analytical, or interpretative nature, and displaying the picture as part of an expanding exhibit.

Thematic Displays

Teachers can teach critical skills visually as well as verbally by displaying works that relate to each other in some way. For example, three photographs of sculptures of women are placed on the bulletin board: one, the head of an Egyptian; one, an African; and one, an Aztec. After the pictures have been on display for a few days, the teacher asks, "What have you learned by looking at these sculpture heads?" Discussion might include concepts of sculpture, the idea of portraiture, differences in style, similarities, speculation regarding interpretations, and so on.

Connecting with Studio Activity

As previously mentioned, whenever possible, teaching for art appreciation should take place in conjunction with studio art projects. When students are working on a visual or technical problem in their own art, they are more receptive to learning from other artists who have confronted similar problems. For example, children are working on a collage and several are using pictures and fragments of pictures from magazines. Aware of their apparent interest in fantasy, the teacher shows the children pictures of works by artists who specialize in fantasy, such as Dali, Magritte, Klee, Fuselli, or Blake, and discusses the works with them. Children can thus gain empathy by explicitly trying what artists have tried. In another example, the teacher's goal is to help the children understand why the impressionists are called "painters of light," that is, why and how they captured so much sunlight in their work and why their colors are "broken" rather than "solid." The teacher takes the students outdoors on a sunny day to do landscape pictures with craypas. The children are encouraged to capture the colors that they see in sunlit areas. When they return to the classroom, they discuss how working outdoors is different from working in the classroom. Then they view and discuss the impressionists' works a second time and share insights.

WORKING FOR TOTAL GROUP INVOLVEMENT

Instruments of Engagement and Evaluation

Teaching for the critical phase of appreciation, however, poses distinct problems. The role of dialogue has already been mentioned; although verbalizing about art is central to criticism, nonverbal activities must also be considered. Since children vary in their inclinations and abilities to speak about art, class discussions are too often dominated by the articulate students. Moreover, since there is rarely enough time for each member of the class to give his or her opinion, several verbal and nonverbal instruments are described that suggest how to achieve total class involvement. Each task sheet should be related to what may reasonably be expected of children in the area of art appreciation, and each of the instruments attempts to reach one of four goals:

1. To enable the children to discuss artworks with a knowledge of art terminology and to be able to identify the design, meaning, and media as these elements function in particular works of art.
2. To extend the students' range of preference or acceptance of artworks.
3. To sharpen or refine the students' powers of perception of visual elements in artworks.
4. To develop the students' ability to speculate, to imagine, and to form a hypothesis based upon what has been observed.

Statement Matching

One way a teacher can involve a full class in working toward the first goal is to have them respond to multiple-choice questions while they progress through a series of slides or reproductions. The questions should be based on the terminology and concepts the teacher deems valuable. Notice that some questions are purposely more open-ended than others to permit more extended discussion after the test. Thus, as the children see their first Wyeth painting, the teacher may want to emphasize the uses of composition and placement of objects:

> This painting is called *Christina's World*. You notice that the artist has used a high rather than a low horizon line (point to line). Now study it carefully. If you think he did it because the house just happened to be located there, put down A. If you think he did it because it allows for more space between the girl and the house, put down B. If you think he did it because it would look that way if the scene were photographed by a camera, put down C. All right, how many put down A? B? C? How many put down more than one reason? Paul, I notice you didn't raise your hand at all—can't you decide? Mary, you voted for B. How about trying to convince Paul why you voted that way?

Formal Analysis

Another way to involve the whole class in identifying components of design is to give each child a reproduction or photocopy of the same painting and a sheet of tracing paper. The paper is placed over the reproduction and the class is asked to seek out and define such compositional devices as balance, center of interest, directional movement, and "hidden" structure. This method of searching for what lies beneath the form of a subject or composition will be most effective if first demonstrated on an overhead projector.

Andrew Wyeth, *Christina's World*, 1948. Interpretative questions the teacher might pose: What is Christina's relationship to the house? Does it mean something special to her? Does her position on the ground or her infirmity bear on these questions? (The Museum of Modern Art, New York. Purchase.)

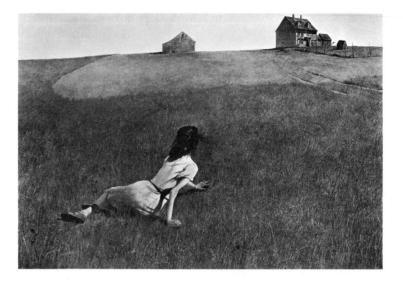

A variation of this method is to project a slide of an artwork on mural paper or on the chalkboard. The teacher beings by chalking a directional line directly on the projected image. Every child must then come up and add their own "invisible" line, such as a triangular shape of a mountain in a Chinese landscape or a Madonna and child (colored chalks may be used to make the final effect more vivid). When the lights are turned on the class is confronted with the skeleton, or substructure, of the work, which has been reduced to an abstract.

If one traces around a subject, they "lose" and must return to their seat to wait for the next round. The final result will show the relationship between the abstract structure that is hidden from view and realistic forms that are first seen. Related to the problem of abstraction is the rearrangement of any set of preliminary drawings. If the illustration shown earlier of Matisse's *Nuit de Noël* is photocopied and randomly cut up, teams of students can attempt to reconstruct the artist's path to abstraction.

A Pre- and Post-Preference Instrument

In order to assess the degree and nature of change in preference, the teacher can use a simple test based on all the slides and reproductions to be used during the course of the year. This is a simple questionnaire that requires children merely to check off the phrase that best describes their reactions to the artworks placed before them. Using the children's style of speech, the responses to be checked might run as follows:

1. I like this painting and wouldn't mind hanging it in my own room.
2. This painting doesn't affect me one way or the other.

3. I don't like this painting.

4. This painting bothers me; as a matter of fact, I really dislike it.

Initially, most children will gravitate toward the familiar, that is, to realistic treatments of subjects that appeal to them. By consistently exposing children throughout the year to works that range across cultures and from the representational to the nonobjective, a competent teacher can open their eyes to a wider range of art. This does not place a premium on any one particular style, but aims at noting changes in taste from whatever point the child begins. If the preference test is given at the beginning and at the end of the course, the teacher should be able to determine how the class has progressed—both as a group and as individuals.

Sorting and Matching

Another way to develop the children's critical skills is to have them work from examples that are used by every class member.[13] The preparation of materials for comparative study might cause the teacher some difficulty, since each participant should have the same set of reproductions. The sets may be compiled from inexpensive museum reproductions, which come in manageable sizes (postcards as a rule are too small). Six reproductions seems to be a number that children can handle; more than this tends to be overwhelming, and there may be occasions when only two or three are appropriate. Whatever the number of pictures, children should examine them and make certain decisions. Such study also allows children to proceed at their own rate and find the viewing distance most convenient for them. Spreading the pictures out on the floor or a table is preferable to flipping through them—the pictures are more easily compared when seen simultaneously. Each collection a student uses should be accompanied by a set of questions designed to focus attention on a particular subject, idea, or term.

The Picture Wall

It is surprising how available art reproductions are once we being looking for them. They now appear in popular magazines, calendars, posters, and of course in museums and card shops. As your collection grows, carry them with you in a large envelope or find a place on the wall of the classroom, including contributions from friends and students as these are added. The picture wall will provide easy access to a variety of instructional aids, since each image will reflect categories of words (mood words, style words, words of formal analysis, identification for subjects, artists, and historical periods). The picture wall, since it is not encumbered by size or frames, is flexible; sections of it are meant to be shifted about; differentiation by selection encourages fluid thinking. One child selects some that deal only with landscape, another selects sculpture, another chooses only nonobjective works, another the work of Louise Nevelson, and so on. The picture wall offers a work and style assessment that can be presented in a spelling bee or other game format.

Physical Identification Another way to approach art appreciation is to get students to empathize with a work by taking on the characteristics of a work with their bodies — their actual selves. They can do this by assuming the pose of a figure or the expressions on the face of a portrait, or even the structure of an abstract work. ("Does your body move the same way to an O'Keeffe as to a Stella?") The teacher can then ask: What is happening inside you? Have you changed in any way? The teacher can show a slide or reproduction of Rodin's *Burghers of Calais*, for example, and have a group of students adopt the same positions as the figures in the sculpture. This will prepare them to make empathetic interpretations of Rodin's work and will raise their receptivity to learning more about the artist and the story behind the sculpture. As well, interesting compositional structures in nonrepresentational paintings can be shown and students asked to change their body positions to reflect the directional forces within the work; to literally project themselves into a work.

TEACHING AIDS FOR DEVELOPING APPRECIATION

Among the teaching aids required in any program of art appreciation are prints, videotapes, films, filmstrips, and slides dealing with a variety of art topics as well as some actual works of art in two and three dimensions. No matter what field of art may be engaging the child's attention — pottery, textiles, drawing, or painting — it will be necessary to have on hand suitable works for reference and study that illustrate as many aspects of art as possible: contemporary, historical, national and foreign, and in particular, art that reflects the ethnic background of the students.

The selection of the images is crucial. The teacher must not only consider the appropriateness of the artwork to the goals of instruction, but reflect sensitivity to the natural preferences of children. The teacher may avoid frustration at the beginning of the year by noting the following points when selecting visual material:

1. Children generally value subject matter more than elements of form and prefer realistically portrayed content to abstract or nonobjective work.

2. As a rule, children prefer clearly stated compositional relationships and well-defined form to diffuse or ambiguous ones.

3. Next to realistically rendered content, color appeals to children most. To this attraction they bring strong emotional associations.

4. Older students are capable of recognizing design as a harmonious entity composed of interactions of parts; this recognition comes at a relatively sophisticated level of appreciation.

5. Young children prefer simple composition; older students are able to appreciate some degree of complexity.

Films, Videos, Filmstrips, and Slides

Each year sees worthwhile additions to a growing library of acceptable art films for the young.[14] These films are designed to fulfill various purposes. Many of them are intended both to stimulate children to produce art and to assist them in mastering various techniques. Some films, such as those from the field of science, are not produced specifically as art films, but prove highly effective in the classroom in both the production and the appreciation of art.

The teacher who uses films in the art programs must understand what constitutes a good film. Before using a film with the class, the teacher obviously must preview it and then decide how effective it may be. What criteria should be used in selecting films or videos to be shown to young children?

1. The film or video should be of high technical and artistic quality. Young children see expertly made films in theaters and on television. Similar high-quality work by producers of children's movies should be standard.

2. The film must be suitable to the children's vocabulary, understanding, and level of maturity.

3. The film should be closely related to the children's content of curriculum. No matter how excellent a film may be in itself, it tends to be a poor educational device when shown out of context.

4. When a film is of the "how-to-do-it" variety, it must not only stimulate the children but also leave some room for them to use their own initiative. Try to use films that attempt to stimulate production, focus attention on design, and give a few basic hints about technique; the content of the films should stop there, however, and the child should be left with challenges to solve independently.

5. Teachers should feel free to turn down the sound and make their own comments, since they know the language level of their particular class.

6. Interactive video can be very valuable, but as of this writing, none exists for the elementary level.

Through a prior acquaintance with the film, the teacher can better time its introduction during the art sessions, as an introduction to a topic, as an aid in teaching a topic, or as a summary for a series of experiences with a topic. Sometimes the teacher may need to comment on the film to the class before it is shown; on other occasions a discussion might take place afterward. Since obtaining a film for a specific art class is often difficult, the projector and a screen as well as the film must be scheduled, sometimes weeks in advance. Therefore, as much advance planning as possible must be done so that the film will suit the type of art activity in progress.

Filmstrips are an excellent value: they take up little space, are usually accompanied by lecture notes (of varying usefulness), and are flexible with regard to timing. They are inflexible, however, in that the images are set in a fixed order. Slides come in a wide range of prices, with the best values to purchased from the major museums. The cheaper slides should be avoided since their colors often are not of a high quality. Subjects such as drawing, architecture, or sculpture, which do not require color fidelity, may be of service even in the inexpensive lines. Also, slides may be arranged any way the teacher desires and can be used with double or multiple projectors for purposes of comparison.

Poster-sized reproductions of design elements, architecture, and sculpture are most useful, but are unfortunately in very short supply.

USING ART MUSEUMS AND GALLERIES

Although we may obtain a reasonably accurate idea about many works of art by consulting reproductions, nothing can actually replace the work itself. How often we feel we know a work of art through a study of reproductions, only to be overwhelmed on first seeing the original! Colors, brushstrokes, textures, and sometimes the scale of the work are never adequately conveyed by a reproduction. It is most desirable, therefore, for children to have the opportunity from time to time to observe original works of art, no matter how familiar they may be with reproductions. The most obvious sources of originals are galleries and museums,[15] local artists, and collectors. Schools situated near art institutions would be remiss indeed not to make use of them. Even if a relatively long journey is necessary, the time and effort required may be considered well spent if children are properly prepared for the experience.

Before a class pays a visit to a museum or gallery, however, the teacher should take the trip alone in order to become acquainted not only with the building and the collections, but also with such mundane but important matters as the location of washrooms for the children and the special rules and regulations of the institution, especially

Working with objects: These students are comparing a wooden comb from the upper Ivory Coast of Africa with a contemporary plastic one. They are fortunate in having a teacher who uses his personal collection as a teaching resource.

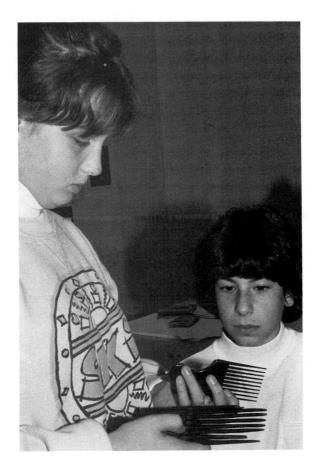

concerning younger visitors. At the same time, the teacher can make any special arrangements with museum officials concerning the program for the children's visit and the length of time it will take.

Activities in Museums

Museums, according to one dictionary, are institutions devoted to the procurement, care, study, and display of objects of lasting interest or value. The museum staffs also engage in scholarly work, ranging from creating a definitive catalogue on a neglected artist to sponsoring an archaeological dig. Museums originated as collections of art assembled by wealthy individuals; today, the thousands of museums that dot our country have gone beyond the arts into such areas as farming, street cars, electricity, and so on. To the art teacher, museums are places where teachers can introduce aesthetic experience in a way that is impossible in the school.

Remember that museums are unnatural settings for art in that they display works out of context, stripped of their original function. As André Malraux has written, "A Romanesque Crucifix was not regarded by its contemporaries as a work of sculpture, nor Cimabue's *Madonna*, a picture. Even Phidias' *Discobolus* was not primarily a statue."[16] Remind students that the African mask they are admiring was meant to be actually worn by someone under certain conditions; that a particular portrait was meant to be hung in a certain kind of house, commissioned by a merchant who sought the approval of posterity through its purchase. Objects should be placed in context whenever possible.

Making youngsters feel at home in museums can be a very practical form of life preparation. Even more people will travel in the future than do at present, and this suggests that the tourist of the future should get more out of the art and architecture of new places than do travelers of this generation. Your students should not be among those who feel they must plod dutifully through galleries or museums. They should, instead, welcome the experience as a result of being in an effective art program.

Here are some suggestions for you and your students to get the most out of your museum visit.

General Guidelines

♦ Prepare for your visit. Build up suspense and anticipation by specific activities such as timing the visit to coordinate with a particular part of your curriculum. Pay particular attention to those factors that can't be appreciated in a slide or reproduction, such as size, and other subtleties that don't register in slides or reproductions.

♦ If you want to teach your class in a museum setting, be sure to get permission in advance. Do not assume that officials will routinely welcome your intentions. (The Museum of Modern Art in New York, for instance, has a policy against unannounced group visits.) If you are not allowed to use the artworks yourself, request the services of a guide to help you with a particular problem; for example, if you want such terms as allegory, symbol, or metaphor explained in terms of specific works. Since you may be requesting a service outside the normal duties of the staff, state the reasons for your requests.

♦ Time the viewing. Have you ever thought about the amount of time given to viewing? Using one gallery, ask students to time viewing patterns among museum-goers. What is the shortest length? The longest? Average? What work receives the most viewing time?

♦ If you have a choice, why not select a neglected museum? Crowds can be avoided this way and you may have a warmer welcome from museum officials. Find out what days and hours are better than others to avoid crowds.

♦ As you walk through a museum, try to see its contents as sources for your curriculum. Dogon masks, cylinder seals of Assyria, the village figures of pre-Columbian societies, and dozens of other subjects all have high interest value for children and teenagers.

♦ Be sensitive to "museumitis" and plan for breaks. When children are tired and hungry, very little appreciation will take place.

♦ Be sensitive to viewing habits. Team viewing does have its advantages. It is good to work in pairs since four eyes may see more than two. On the other hand, nearby responses by others may get in the way of one's own response. Students should be encouraged to determine their own pace and to find their own space. (For example, how close, how far should one be from an object?)

♦ Catalogues often mean more *after* a visit than before, since it is then that we know what the writers are discussing.

♦ Guided tours have their value, but they do pose one problem, especially for younger students—the distracting nature of what the

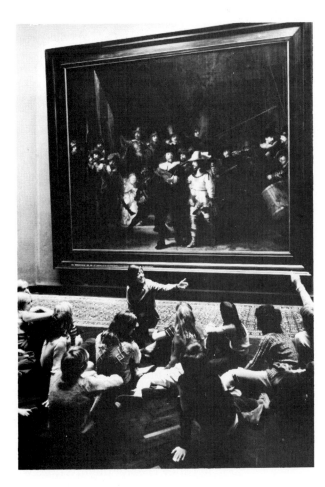

During a museum visit, a teacher discusses Rembrandt's *Night Watch* with her class. Using museums calls for a teacher skilled in leading group discussion. And children usually need experience with art appreciation before they can spend an extended period of time with a single work. (Photo by Adam Woolfitt.)

viewers see peripherally. Why is it that the next gallery so often seems more tempting than what is under discussion?

♦ Some subjects invite very close scrutiny. For such cases, magnifying or even opera glasses will come in handy.

Suggested Learning Tasks

♦ One way to prepare for a new work is to "play along with the artist." Describe the picture in advance and ask the class to draw it and bring their renderings with them to the museum. Have them compare their conception of the subject with that of the artist.

♦ Think of artworks as aesthetic magnets. Since all artworks can't and won't "speak" to each individual, encourage them to go on to the ones that have holding power, that draw them into their presence. They should stand in the center of a gallery and slowly take in its contents, allowing the images to "talk" to them, responding by moving to the ones that have something to say to them. Artworks are like books — there are more to consume than one will ever have time for, so encourage them to give in to their first impressions, bearing in mind that aesthetic response is cumulative, a lifelong process, and the more they look, the more they will understand and enjoy.

♦ One of the many ways to help focus attention is to ask students to concentrate upon one item as rendered in a number of works, such as hands, background, portraits, handling of light sources, etc. Many times just one work can provide enough information for study. For example, Flemish tapestries have a great variety of types of clothing that can be copied, counted, and compared. Although such inventorying is considered a lower order of learning, while students are involved they will note other parts of the work.

♦ Ask everyone to bring a sketchbook and assign one or two exercises based upon work done in class. If you have taught action drawing, ask students to draw a complex composition in a free, loose, gestural style. In the case of sculpture in the round, draw it from three different points of view. If you intend to incorporate the study of mythology in your program, have students make careful studies of armor to be used later in their version of *St. George and the Dragon.*

♦ Try to have enough funds to purchase for each student one postcard at the end of the visit that they have selected for themselves. This will put them in the position of thinking before selecting. Ask them to look at their postcard just before going to bed and to make it the first thing they see upon awaking. After a week, ask them to draw it from memory.

♦ While remaining as unobtrusive as they can, have students take note of comments that people make in their viewing. How would they classify them? Those who have some knowledge of art; those who lack any background? Those who lack background, yet have open minds? Those who have closed minds? Gather their comments and create categories after you have assembled them.

- ◆ Ask the students to suppose there were a fire. Which work(s) would each one save? Why? Suppose you had a choice of saving that work or the life of a vandal who had slashed and smashed artworks just before the flames engulfed the gallery, which would you save and why?
- ◆ Prepare a study sheet or visual "treasure hunt" based upon the example shown below and give each student a copy to work on independently.

A "treasure hunt" or study sheet that students can use to independently observe artworks in a gallery or musuem.

Museum Treasure Hunt

The Impressionists
Rooms 7 and 8

CAN YOU FIND IT?
Can you find each of these in the paintings of the impressionist artists in Rooms 7 and 8 of the museum?
As you find each one, write the name of the artist and the title of the painting in which it appears.

1   A black top hat _____

2   A yellow flower _____

3   A lighthouse _____

4   A newspaper _____

5   A green parasol _____

6   A sky full of stars _____

7   A hat with fluffy blue feathers _____

8   A broom _____

9   Water lilies _____

10   A mandolin hanging on the wall _____

- Select a painting that suggests a narrative (some element of storytelling) and ask the students: "What happened after this particular moment?"

- Have students pretend they are describing a work to someone who is blind. Have the rest of the class turn their backs to the work or blindfold them. What happens when a visual experience is transformed into a verbal record? Do this at least three times and note how the descriptive process gains in acuteness.

- Ask the children to imagine what the portraits say to each other at night when the lights go out and the guards depart?

- Encourage the students to create a narrative connection out of any three works. Try a random sampling and one that is planned.

- Visit the museum in advance of the class visit and learn one story (usually from mythology or history) related to a particular work; tell the story to the class later in the presence of the painting. This advance visit should also include information of historical interest. ("The object Mercury is holding is what we call an 'attribute', something artists traditionally included to identify him or her." Or, "Do you see any Madonna whose costume is not blue?")

- Employ word associations by placing a pile of words lettered in large (6 by 12) pieces of paper in the middle of the floor. Have each student pick up two or three and place them on the floor by the work that they feel is the most appropriate. Use words such as realistic, abstract, nonobjective, hot, cold, active, quiet, etc. Base words selected upon vocabulary studied in class.

- Find out the estimated value of one of the museum's most valued works. Ask students why they think it costs so much. What would this amount buy in the non-art world? A Porsche can cost $60,000. How does that relate to the $17 million that Jasper Johns' work brought in 1989?

- Have students study the gallery for a few minutes and at the teacher's signal, move to the one work they have selected as a gift from the museum director. What was the reason for the selection? Now move to the work they would least like to live with. If there are any works that share both decisions, have the "judges" stand by the works and try to convince each other of the wisdom of their choice.[17]

As museum attendance grows, museums must rely more on individual task sheets rather than upon the use of guides, particularly on weekends when guides may not be available. In order to help children, museums develop interesting guides that invite young museum-goers to discover art on their own.

◆ NOTES TO THE TEXT

1. Jacob Bronowski, *The Visionary Eye* (Cambridge, MA: MIT Press, 1978), p. 13.

2. Eleanor Heartney, *ARTnews*, May 1988.

3. John Rewald, Post-Impressionism from Van Gogh to Gauguin (New York: Museum of Modern Art, 1956), p. 218.

4. Leonard Freedman, ed., *Looking at Modern Painting* (New York: W. W. Norton, 1961), p. 17.

5. For an excellent book of art criticism essays, see Theodore Wolff, *The Many Masks of Modern Art* (Boston: The Christian Science Monitor, 1989).

6. Marcel Reoch-Ranicki, in an interview for Lufthansa's *Germany* magazine, Vol. 33 (February 1988), p. 26.

7. Herbert Read, *Education Through Art*, rev. ed. (New York: Pantheon, 1958), p. 209.

8. Manuel Barkan and Laura Chapman, *Guidelines for Art Instruction Through Television for Elementary Schools* (Bloomington, IN: National Center for School and College Television, 1967), p. 7.

9. Edmund Feldman, *Varieties of Visual Experience: Art as Image and Idea*, 2nd ed. (Englewood Cliffs, NJ: Prentice-Hall, 1981).

10. Harry Broudy, *Enlightened Cherishing* (Urbana: University of Illinois Press, 1972).

11. Dr. James Ackerman is former chairman of the department of fine arts, Harvard University. Because of the length of the tape, excerpts have been interspersed with descriptions of what occurred. This discussion emphasizes the point that art critical skills are employed by many art professionals including, in this case, an art historian.

12. As mentioned in Chapter 1, educators are seeking ways to engage children in higher levels of thinking. Critical and philosophical discussions about works of art are occasions for such thinking. See, for example, D. N. Perkins, "Art as an Occasion of Intelligence." *Educational Leadership*, Vol. 45, No. 4 (January 1988).

13. For a useful guide, see Hermine Feinstein, "The Art Response Guide: How to Read Art for Meaning, A Primer for Art Criticism." *Art Education*, Vol. 42, No. 3 (1989).

14. See Appendix B at the end of this book for a listing of addresses of companies that produce films, videos, and other art teaching resources.

15. For a discussion of art museums and art education, see Danielle Rice, "The Role of the Museum in Discipline-Based Art Education," *Roundtable Series II, Proceedings Report* (Los Angeles: The Getty Center for Education in the Arts, 1988).

16. André Malraux, *The Voices of Silence* (Princeton, NJ: Princeton University Press, 1978), p. 13.

17. For an account of an innovative art museum/school collaboration, see Michael Day, "Diversity and Innovation: Art Education in the Milwaukee Public Schools," *Art History, Art Criticism, and Art Production: An Examination of Art Education in Selected School Districts* (Los Angeles: Rand Corporation, 1984).

◆ ACTIVITIES FOR THE READER

1. Clip an example of art criticism from the newspaper and paste it on a sheet of paper allowing at least three-inch margins. Indicate in the margins the various ways the critic deals with the subject, such as historical, descriptive, analytic, interpretative, judgmental, formal, etc.

2. Describe any occasion on which you gained insight into an artist's work that had previously puzzled you. Can you account for that flash of insight?

3. Describe two paintings that deal with the same subject, and compare them for style, point of view, etc.

4. Outline some teaching procedures for helping fifth grade children to appreciate each of the following: (a) a mural by a well-known painter; (b) the design of a frying pan; (c) the design of living room curtains; (d) a wood sculpture by a well-known artist.

5. Create a visual reduction game by collecting about twenty reproductions and dividing them into subcategories. Directions for such a game might read as follows:
   a. Divide this group of reproductions into two piles, one nonobjective and one realistic.
   b. Now divide the nonobjective pile into two more piles, one emphasizing line and the other solid masses.
   c. Divide the realistic group into two sets, one sentimental in nature and the other aesthetic.

6. In Emile Zola's *L-Assommoir*, the author describes the first visit to the Louvre by a group of working-class Parisians in 1875. Art critic Linda Nochlin, in discussing this passage, intersperses Zola's writing with her own comments.[18] (The italics are from Zola.) "The little group, an amusing spectacle for the artists and regular museum-goers, *trailing all the hand-me-downs of poor people's fashions*, trouped dutifully through the endless halls of the great palace of art. They were somewhat taken aback by the Assyrian Gallery and thought the statues very ugly: nowadays a good stonecarver could do a lot better job than that. . . . *It was with great respect, walking as softly as they could, that they entered the French Gallery*. In the Gallery of Apollo, they were amazed at the sheen of the floor, as shiny as a mirror; in the Salon Carré . . . some of the less-mannerly wedding guests tittered at the naked women, especially impressed by the thighs of Antiope . . . *a jumble of people and things in glaring colors began to give them a headache. . . . Centuries of art passed before their bewildered ignorance, the fine rigidity of the early Italians, the splendor of the Venetians, the sleek and sunny life of the Dutchman. But what interested them the most were the copyists, with their easels set up in the midst of the people, painting away undisturbed. . . . Little by little, the new visitors began to lose their enthusiasm. . . . The wedding party, tired out and losing their respect for things, dragged their hobnailed shoes along, clattering over the sounding floor with the noise of a herd in confusion . . .* For relief, their guide led them to Rubens' *Kermesse*, before which the women screamed and blushed and the men pointed out the dirty details . . . At last, in complete rout, lost and terrified, they found a doorkeeper to *take them in charge and show them the way to one of the doors. Once in the courtyard of the Louvre . . . they breathed again. . . . All the party affected to be very much pleased to have seen it all.*" Questions for consideration: Could this passage be used in a school curriculum, and if so, in what way? If you wanted to see how consistent the reactions and behaviors of Zola's viewers were with those of today, how would you go about comparing the two groups?

◆ SUGGESTED READINGS

Day, Michael. "Seeing, Knowing, and Doing," *School Arts* (February–, March, April 1975). A series of articles that provides examples of instruction for art appreciation.

Dewey, John. *Art as Experience* (New York: Capricorn, 1934). A classic work which deals with the nature of the aesthetic transaction between object and viewer.

Feinstein, Hermine. "The Art Response Guide: How to Read Art for Meaning, A Primer for Art Criticism." *Art Education*, Vol. 42, No. 3 (May 1989).

Feldman, Edmund. *Varieties of Visual Experience: Art as Image and Idea*, 2nd ed. (Englewood Cliffs, NJ: Prentice-Hall, 1972). A comprehensive view of art style, the critical act and modes of artistic expression.

———. *Becoming Human Through Art*. Englewood Cliffs, NJ: Prentice-Hall, 1970. Chapter 11, "Studying Varieties of Language," and Chapter 12, "Mastering the Techniques of Art Criticism."

Hamblen, Karen. "The Feldman Approach: A Catalyst for Examining Issues in Art Criticism Instruction." *The Bulletin of the Caucus on Social Theory and Art Education*, Vol. 6 (1986).

Hurwitz, Al and Stanley Madeja. *The Joyous Vision: A Source Book for Elementary Art Appreciation* (Englewood Cliffs, NJ: Prentice-Hall, 1977). Concentrates upon methods of teaching art criticism and examples of units of instruction.

Mittler, Gene A., *Art in Focus* (Encina, CA: Glencoe Publishing Co., 1986). The critical stage method used in a historical context. Studio experiences are suggested. Well-illustrated.

Ragans, Rosalind. *Art Talk* (Encina, CA: Glencoe Publishing Co., 1988). The critical stage method used without the elements and principles of art design. Well-illustrated. Similar to Mittler's *Art in Focus*, but simpler in style.

Risatti, Howard. "Art Criticism in Discipline-Based Art Education," in Ralph Smith, ed. *Discipline-Based Art Education: Origins, Meaning, and Development* (Urbana: University of Illinois Press, 1989).

Taylor, Rod. *Education for Art* (London: Longman Group, 1986). A British approach to teaching critical responses, citing in-depth studies of students' interactions with artworks.

Wolff, Theodore. *The Many Masks of Modern Art* (Boston: The Christian Science Monitor, 1989). A compilation of critical commentaries by an award winning New York critic.

For a discussion of questioning approaches for art criticism see Karen Hamblen, "An Art Criticism Questioning Strategy within the Framework of Bloom's Taxonomy," *Studies in Art Education*, Vol. 25, No. 3 (1984).

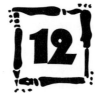

ART HISTORY: OTHER TIMES AND PLACES

A TRUE AND thorough study of art and its historical development necessarily calls for an examination of the artist and his work from many points of view. Beginning with the work itself and taking account of all the available relevant information, the student of art should recognize that an intelligent appreciation of creative activity must proceed from varied sources: biographical data, knowledge of the historical situation and social context, philosophical and esthetic premises of the time, and particular considerations such as working methods, patronage systems, and immediate purposes.

Albert Elsen[1]

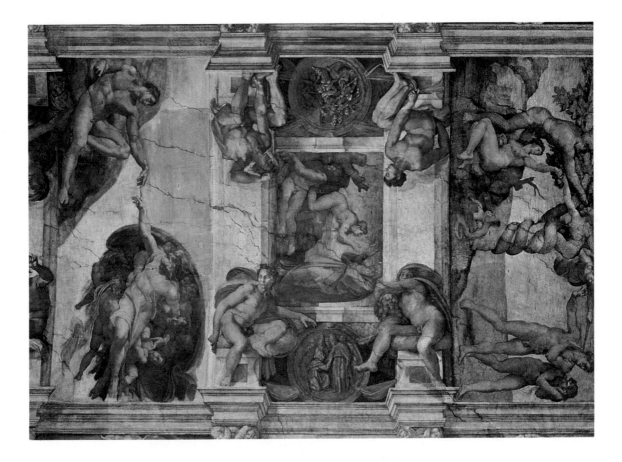

The first account of art history, at least in the Western world, was written by the Florentine architect and painter Giorgio Vasari, whose contemporaries included the great Italian artists Raphael, Andrea del Sarto, Leonardo da Vinci, and Michelangelo, with whom he was well acquainted as a friend. Vasari tells the story of how he happened to undertake the task of writing *Lives of the Artists*. He was involved with a painting commission for the church in Rome under the patronage of Cardinal Farnese. In the evenings he would often join the cardinal for dinner and conversation with other men of arts and letters, including Paolo Giovio, who collected portraits of famous men. During these evenings the idea was initiated that a catalogue of all of the artists and their works would be a marvelous possession of great interest, and it was suggested that Vasari, who had for years filled his notebooks with drawings of great art and notes about the artists, undertake the project. Vasari wrote:

> This I readily promised to do, as best I could, though I knew it was really beyond my powers. And so I started to look through my memoranda and

notes, which I had been gathering on this subject since my childhood as a pastime and because of the affection I bore towards the memory of our artists, every scrap of information about whom was precious to me.[2]

With this book Vasari began a tradition that has been multiplied in importance, complexity, and participation by thousands of professional art historians, many of whom share Vasari's love of art and affection for the memory of great artists. As we can see from the quote at the heading of this chapter, the contemporary field of art history ranges far beyond the scope of Vasari's relatively simple beginning. Art historians today employ technical tools from the physical sciences and methods of inquiry from the social sciences that were unknown in the sixteenth century.

Vasari wrote of the lives of Italian painters, sculptors, and architects from Cimabue, born 1240, to Michelangelo, who died in 1564. Art historians today study art and artists from all continents of the world, a multitude of cultures, and a range of art modes including printmaking, ceramics, decorative arts (including furniture design), and photography, cinema, and video, which have emerged only during the past century.

ART HISTORY CONTENT: A BRIEF SURVEY OF WORLD ART

The intent of art history, especially as we approach it in art education, is to provide information and insights that will enlighten our understanding and appreciation of artworks and their significance and meaning. Often this means learning about the peoples and cultures from which the artworks came and the purposes of the art within those cultures. Art historians have studied the art of the world created not only since Vasari's time, but back into pre-history and the several thousands of years from early Sumerian and Egyptian culture to the present. One of the contributions of art historians has been their categorization of art into styles and historical periods, providing us with conceptual handles to grasp meaning and significance in the art we see. We find art history organized in numerous ways, each of which presents a different emphasis and provides a different insight. For example, art historians have studied and written about art according to periods (the Middle Ages, the age of baroque), styles (romanticism, cubism), cultures (Egyptian, native American), religions (Christian, Islamic), locations or countries (royal Benin art, art of the Andes), themes (the figure, nature), purposes (images of authority, imaginative art), and other categories. Educators can follow and benefit from this range of approaches and should adapt different approaches for different educational goals.

The following very brief survey of world art is only a suggestion of the vast and rich content for the study of art. It is necessarily incomplete and simplified and is included here to demonstrate the range of content for systematic art study appropriate for children in a regular art program. This brief survey will be referred to in a later chapter that discusses organizing content for instruction. The emphasis on European art is partly because visual resources are more readily available in this area and partly because the art of Europe and America is the art of our culture. As African or Russian students would be expected to stress their own visual histories, American students should know about their own art. Some teachers go even further and believe that art history should begin in their own communities, with the buildings and monuments that exist in the immediate world of the student.

This survey has been organized according to historical periods often used by art historians: the ancient world, the classical world, the Middle Ages, renaissance and baroque, the modern world, and contemporary art. Because of the great complexity of art and its relationship to culture, this system of organization, like any other, has certain limitations. For example, the arts of China cross many of these chronological periods, while Byzantine art resides within a narrower time frame. Teachers will need to make educational decisions regarding the terms and concepts their students will be able to understand.

The Ancient World

Prehistoric Art. The earliest art provides the major part of our knowledge of humans who lived before written records. Although the artifacts that have survived are extremely old, some dating back 14,000 years B.C., some are surprisingly sophisticated and aesthetically sensitive. *Paleolithic art* is the art of the last ice age, the time when massive glaciers covered much of Europe and North America. Cave paintings of animals and humans have survived in France and Spain, as have small stone sculptures of female figures, such as the well-known *Venus of Willendorf*. The great stone monument at Stonehenge in England was created primarily during the *Neolithic* period, which ranged from 1800 to 1400 B.C.

The Art of Egypt. When we think of the art and culture of Egypt it is usually in the context of very ancient times. Indeed, in discussing Egyptian art we speak in terms of many centuries, going back nearly five thousand years from the present. Early wall paintings date back to 3500 B.C., and the latest (New Kingdom) period lasted until nearly 1000 B.C., a span of 2,500 years of clearly recognizable Egyptian artistic style. When we consider the pace of contemporary life, with amazing events occurring in all parts of the world, scientific advances that significantly influence our lives within a generation, and political events that drastically alter systems of government for entire continents, all of which becomes known to us almost instantaneously via television, it is difficult for us to *comprehend* the continuity of Egyptian culture. When we compare this continuity to stylistic changes in more recent periods, such as impressionism, which began less than 150 years ago, or pop art, which emerged less than fifty years ago, we gain some perspective about the relative contributions of later art styles to the overall history of art. Life in Egypt evidently changed very slowly and time was a plentiful commodity for Egyptian leaders, who envisioned grand accomplishments that took decades to complete.

The familiar monuments of Egyptian art, the great pyramids at Giza, the Great Sphinx, the magnificent life-size sculptures of royalty, the monumental sculptures of Ramses, the beautiful head of Queen Nefertiti, and the amazing gold coffin cover of Tutankhamen all must be considered and understood in the light of religious beliefs and polit-

This painted limestone sculpture of Queen Nefertiti typifies the simplified form of Egyptian sculpture. (Florence Museum Archeologico.)

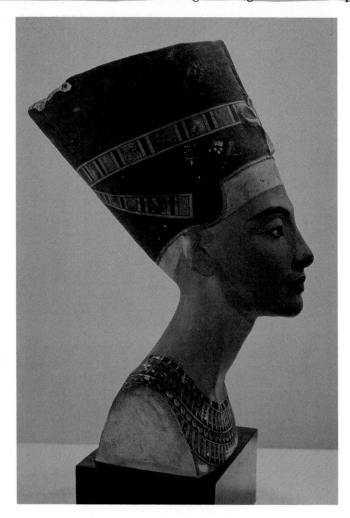

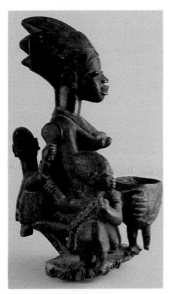

This carved wood sculpture was created in Nigeria, West Africa. The theme of mother and child is universal across cultures and time. Compare this image with other artworks based on the same theme. (National Museum of African Art. Smithsonian Institution, Washington, D.C.)

ical practices of the culture. Virtually all Egyptian art is religious in nature, relating to beliefs about life after death, especially for the pharaoh, his family, and retinue. The pyramids were actually tombs and monuments, and the sculptures and paintings had religious purposes related to the afterlife. Because the pharaoh was considered to be a god as well as a king, the political and religious aspects of art were interrelated.

The Near East. The Mesopotamian region, in the valley between the Tigris and Euphrates rivers, developed civilizations with writing and arts almost concurrently with Egyptian advances. The very early arts of the Sumerians (2800 to 1720 B.C.) include impressive examples of architecture and sculpture, much of which was motivated by religious beliefs.[3] The Sumerians built impressive temples atop their ziggurats, massive stepped platforms that rose like mountains above the flat plains. Some of the small ziggurats are probably older than the Egyptian pyramids.

The Assyrians (1760 to 612 B.C.) followed the Sumerians as rulers of the region and creators of great art. They left behind marvelous examples of fresco paintings, sculpture (especially graceful relief sculptures), and architecture, including elaborate walled cities. They were followed by the Babylonians for a relatively brief period before the region was ruled by the Persians (539 to 465 B.C.). The Persians worshipped in the open air and thus developed almost no religious architecture, but did construct huge and impressive palaces. For example, the audience hall of King Darius had a wooden ceiling supported by 36 columns 40 feet tall.[4]

Art of Africa. Many scientists believe that human life began in Africa, where the oldest human remains have been discovered in southern Rhodesia. The continent of Africa is three times as large as the United States, with nearly a thousand different languages spoken among its peoples. Many distinctive styles of art have developed in Africa, some with traditions that have persisted for a thousand years.[5]

The art of Africa, like the art of China, crosses chronological categories from ancient times, the Middle Ages, and into this century. For example, in West Africa the kingdoms of Yoruba and Benin have existed since the twelfth century and have produced impressive works of architecture, sculpture, personal adornment, costume, and religious objects. Royal Benin sculptural pieces of bronze, cast copper alloy, iron, and ivory are examples of a particular African artistic style among the many styles created by the peoples of the continent.

As in most traditional societies, art in Africa plays an integral role in the daily lives of the people:

African art is pottery for carrying water; it is textiles, leatherwork, and jewelry for wearing; it is sculpture for use in ceremonies and rituals. An African object viewed in isolation, compelling as it may be, loses some of its meaning and visual impact. An African mask, for example, is worn as part of an entire costume that covers the wearer from head to foot. The wearer of the mask participates in a performance that could include music, dance, song, and storytelling.[6]

Much of the history of African art is unknown, as the peoples of past centuries left no written records. African art history is reconstructed by studying oral traditions, European and Arabic documents, languages, and archaeological discoveries. African art influenced European artists near the turn of this century and is a strong factor in American art today, as well as continuing on the African continent.

The Art of Asia. Civilization flourished along the Indus River in India as early as 3000 B.C. Like much of world art, the art of India was motivated and directed to a large extent by religious beliefs. The Buddhist religion emerged in the sixth century B.C., and much of the architecture and sculpture were created in honor of Buddha. Over the centuries many Buddhists came to believe that Buddha was divine. They built cave temples and carved freestanding statues showing him teaching or in meditation:

> His gentle smile and halo suggest saintliness. His long ear lobes show how attentively he listens to the secrets of the cosmos and are a symbolic reflection of his pre-Nirvana existence, when he wore the heavy jewelry of a prince . . . The figure is serene, far beyond sensual pleasure and other attachments.[7]

As Buddhism spread to Southeast Asia and north to Tibet, China, and Japan, painters and sculptors adapted this Indian concept of the Buddha with their own modifications in local imagery.

Buddhism became a major world religion, but did not persist as strongly in India, where the Hindu religion gained prominence. Hindu art and architecture developed into magnificent forms, with structures often completely covered with miles of relief sculpture "of intertwining human, animal, and floral motifs expressing the rhythm of life."[8]

Chinese art maintained a pattern of characteristic forms for nearly four thousand years, developing fine traditions of architecture, pottery, ceramic and bronze sculpture, jade carving, painting, and printmaking.[9] Although art in China began in very ancient times, the study of Chinese art takes the scholar across time periods, through the Middle Ages and into modern times. Art historians have studied the different developments and emphases in Chinese art across the several reigns or dynasties (e.g., Shang dynasty (1766–1045 B.C.), Zhou dynasty (1044 B.C.–A.D. 256), Tang dynasty (A.D. 618–907), Song dynasty (960–1274), Ming dynasty (1368–1644), and the Qing dynasty (1645–1912).

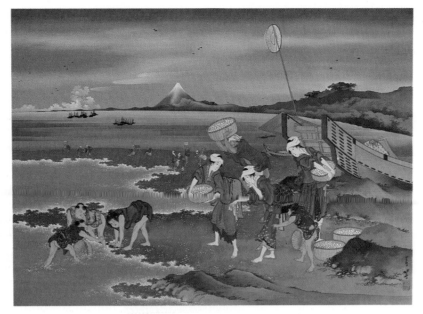

Hokusai, *Clam-gatherers on the Shore*, Edo period. Hokusai painted and made prints in Japan until his death in 1849. This scene of clam-gatherers features families of workers, boats on the shore and in the bay, and a beautifully composed seascape with Mount Fuji in the background. Note Hokusai's use of perspective, especially the diminishing size of figures with distance. Can you separate the ways of depicting space that are Western in nature and those which do not reflect the rules of perspective developed in the Renaissance? (Courtesy of the Freer Gallery of Art, Smithsonian Institution, Washington, D.C.)

Japanese art also ranges from prehistoric periods to contemporary times. Following the evolution of art in China, Japanese art is similar yet distinctive, with many masterworks worthy of note. For example, the Japanese excelled in the areas of landscape design, gardening with plants and natural materials, and they achieved greatness in the areas of pottery and wood-block printing, to name only a few accomplishments. Highlights include the great figure sculptures of Unkei from the Kamakura period (A.D. 1185–1333) and the wonderful polychrome woodblock prints of Hokusai from the Edo period (A.D. 1615–1867).[10]

The Classical World

The traditions of art most influential and best known in contemporary North America come from Western Europe, beginning with the art of Greece (800–100 B.C.). The monuments and masterpieces of European art are much too numerous to mention in this brief survey. We are especially aware of Greek architecture and sculpture, with the Greek temple known as the Parthenon heading the list. The *Discobolos* (discus thrower), *Venus de Milo*, *Nike of Samothrace*, and *Horsemen* from the frieze of the Parthenon, and the *Laocoön Group* (now thought to be a Roman work done in a Greek style) are among the best-known sculptures. The Greeks developed red clay pottery to a high level with distinctive forms for specific purposes (to hold water, wine, oil and so on) and painted with black figures on a natural red background or red figures on a black ground. Much of Greek art depicts gods and goddesses, mythological figures and events, and athletes and leaders with idealized versions of the human figure. According to one author:

> No other culture has had as far-reaching or lasting an influence on art and civilization than that of ancient Greece. . . . Unlike some other cultures which flourished, died, and left barely an imprint on the pages of history, that of Greece has asserted itself time and again over the 3,000 years since its birth. During the fifteenth century, there was a revival of Greek art and culture called the *Renaissance*, and on the eve of the French Revolution of 1789, artists of the *neoclassical* period again turned to the style and subjects of ancient Greece. Our forefathers looked to Greek architectural styles for the building of our nation's capital, and nearly every small town in America has a bank, post office, or library constructed in the Greek Revival style.[11]

Rome conquered Greece and most of the Western world beginning about 30 B.C. and maintained the Roman Empire until nearly A.D. 500. Roman art followed closely the traditions of Greek art, but related more to the political and military aspects of the culture than to religious beliefs. Architecture on a grand scale produced the Colosseum, the Pantheon, the Arch of Constantine, and many beautifully proportioned Roman villas. Roman sculptures of human figures were often startlingly realistic, rather than idealized as the Greek figures. Roman portrait sculptures provide accurate records of a number of leaders of the time:

> Although much Roman art is derived in style from that of Greece, its portrait sculpture originated in a tradition that was wholly Italian. It is in this sculpture that we witness Rome's unique contribution to the arts—that of *realism*.[12]

The Middle Ages

Christian Art. Dominating Europe for centuries, it began especially during the fourth century. Early *Byzantine* art blended influences from the Roman traditions with eastern conventions from Constantinople (Byzantium or modern Istanbul). One of the monuments of the Byzantine era (400–1453) is the church of San Vitale in Ravenna, Italy. This spacious and well-lit church was built on an octagonal plan different from most European cathedrals and is noted for the beautiful mosaics that decorate the walls and ceilings of the edifice.

Romanesque architecture emerged as an important style "quite suddenly when a medieval prophecy foretelling the end of the world in 1000 failed to come true."[13] Christians set out to show their gratitude by building churches across Europe in Italy, Spain, Germany, and France. The Romanesque style was a revival of Roman forms of architecture, as churches were built with a central nave and side aisles. Because of the need to build strong walls to support the broad vaults, the churches were quite dark, with few small windows. *Gothic* cathedrals were then built with even higher walls and arches. Exterior buttresses to support the high walls made large stained glass windows possible and led to the exquisite development of this art form. The Notre Dame Cathedral in Paris and the Chartres Cathedral are two prime examples of the glories of Gothic architecture still in existence today.

Islamic Art. Art by the followers of Mohammed (beginning early in the seventh century), crosses boundaries between Asia, Africa, and Europe. Throughout the Islamic world the Muslims built mosques as houses of worship. From the minarets, or towers, the faithful were called to pray five times daily. Because Muslim tradition forbids representation of the human figure, sculpture, though not unknown, did not develop as in other cultures and religions. Islamic art is magnificent, however, in the development of nonrepresentational decoration using geometric and natural forms as motifs. One of the best-known examples of Islamic architecture is the *Taj Mahal* in Agra, India.

The aesthetic attitudes developed in Asia and the forms and conventions of Eastern artistic creation differed significantly from those common in Western art. Eastern and African art influenced European artists greatly in the late nineteenth and twentieth centuries.

The Art of Oceania. This diverse category includes Australia, New Zealand, New Guinea, and major Pacific island groups. Because warfare among the island peoples was traditionally prominent, many groups devised distinctive war clubs made of wood, stone, and sea shells. Many of the decorated objects relate to religious ceremonies, including masks, costumes, and body decoration used in conjunction with dancing. The Maori people of New Zealand created a distinctive style of the sculpted human figure with linear designs and overall patterns. Intricate carvings and decorations are found on huts, canoes, coffins, staffs, and other artifacts.

The famous monoliths of volcanic stone on Easter Island in Polynesia remain a puzzle. These large, brooding sculptures, originally set on ceremonial stone platforms, were discovered on an Easter Sunday by nineteenth century missionaries. More than 600 of these huge heads and half-length figures survive, some of which are up to 60 feet tall. Because the people who created these sculptures left no records, archeologists speculate that they symbolized the spiritual and political power that chieftains were thought to derive from the gods.

Pre-Columbian Art. The native Americans of Mexico, Central America, and South America shared knowledge needed to cultivate maize, cotton, and tobacco; they used irrigation systems in agriculture and developed weaponry, metalwork, featherwork, basketry, and textiles. Several groups became proficient in astronomy and developed the calendar, mathematics, metallurgy, hieroglyphic writing, amazingly precise architecture, and painting and sculpture. There is evidence that some peoples accomplished surgery. The Mayan peoples, the Incas, and the Aztecs were three major cultures that left behind a wealth of marvelous art objects, including their extensive cities and magnificent temples. As with many early cultures, a major impetus for pre-Columbian art was religious belief.

The plentiful availability of gold and silver, which eventually contributed to the decline of these peoples at the hands of Spanish conquerors, is evident in many pre-Columbian objects. Following is a commentary about a tapestry tunic with golden spangles from the Chimu culture, woven about 1200:

> It may seem unnecessary to our eyes to have added the gold to this tawny-toned tapestry tunic, such is the charm of the tapestry design itself, but perhaps the gold carries status which no textile design could equal. The representation is a row of trees with monkeys in the limbs above plucking fruit for the aide below who holds the bag. . . . The technique of the textile is slit tapestry with alpaca weft and cotton warp, with the golden-toned autumn colors which are characteristic of the fabrics from the north coast of Peru.[14]

It is apparent that very sophisticated and accomplished cultures have disappeared in the jungles of Mexico, and Central and South America, leaving behind intriguing evidences of their thought and customs. Excavations on a number of sites are being conducted currently in hopes of learning more about the arts and sciences of these early civilizations.

Native North American art is similar in many ways to that of Central and South America except that most natives in the northern continent were nomads and did not build permanent cities. One exception to this is the Hopi mesas in Arizona, which are among the oldest continuously inhabited dwellings on the continent. They were inhabited before Europeans came to this land. Also in Arizona, in the Canyon de Chelly and other locations, are the ruins of cliff dwellings built in small communities high in the steep canyon walls by the Anasazi, the "ancient ones." Petroglyphs painted and carved by very old native American cultures, and similar in some ways to the pre-historic cave paintings of Europe, are still found in many isolated canyons in Arizona, Colorado, and Utah.

Many of the points made in the discussion of African peoples apply as well to native American arts and culture. This is a large continent and the various tribes lived in very different climatic, political, and social conditions. The Navajos and Hopis of the Southwest lived in a hot, dry, and in many ways inhospitable climate; the Sioux, plains Indians of the Dakotas and Nebraska, roamed on horses, taking their dwellings with them to follow the buffalo; the Tlingits of the Northwest Coast lived in a humid, wet, coastal environment and depended a great deal on the sea and their skill with boats; and, the Algonquin,

Cree, and Ojibwa peoples of Alaska, Canada, and northern United States lived at the opposite extreme of the Navajos, in the frigid north. Different conditions and lifestyles among the more than 150 major Indian tribes in North America have resulted in a wide range of art forms.

The Northwest Coast native Americans, for example, carved beautifully designed wooden utensils for everyday use, and developed the idea of totem poles into a unique type of sculpture. Navajos are noted for exquisitely designed and woven wool blankets, and silver and turquoise jewelry. The Pueblo peoples have developed highly prized pottery that is collected and exhibited in art museums. Sioux tribes created beautiful clothing, including wedding garments, from tanned and decorated leathers. Unfortunately, much of the best art of native Americans has been lost over the years and many of the craft forms are not being continued within tribal groups. However, the good news is that in some areas, notably the Southwest, traditional art and craft forms are maintained with vital and creative results, such as the woven blankets, pottery, and silver jewelry of the Hopis and Navajos.[15] Recently the Congress of the United States passed legislation to establish a national museum of native American art under the aegis of the Smithsonian Institution in Washington, D.C.

Renaissance and Baroque

The *Renaissance* began in Europe about 1400 and continued for two hundred years. This period marked an increased interest in classical learning, philosophy, and art, hearkening back to the thought of Greece and Rome. With beginnings in Italy, the spirit of the Renaissance moved throughout Europe with notable effects in the Netherlands and Flanders. The pantheon of great artists associated with the Renaissance and the list of masterpieces of art from this period are extensive, including works by Michelangelo (the ceiling of the Sistine Chapel, *Pieta, David*), da Vinci (*The Last Supper, Mona Lisa*), Botticelli (*Birth of Venus*), van Eyck (*Giovanni Arnolfini and His Bride*), Raphael (*The School of Athens*), Pieter Brueghel (*Peasant Wedding*), Dürer (*Adam and Eve*), Altdorfer (*The Battle of Issus*), and many others. Numerous artworks during the Renaissance employed symbolism, often expres-

View of an Ideal City, Central Italian School, 1400–1495. This painting (artist unknown) shows Renaissance knowledge about the use of perspective. To use this in a class discussion of perspective: (A) extend the picture by completing the unfinished buildings; or, (B) with tracing paper, diagram all converging lines to a central vanishing point. This can also be done by projecting the image on a blackboard. (C) Envision the plaza as it might appear today with fast-food restaurants, cafes, pedestrians, a city skyline, traffic, etc. (Walters Art Gallery, Baltimore.)

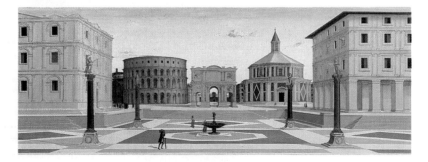

Jan van Eyck, *Giovanni Arnolfini and His Bride*, 1434. This unique portrait was commissioned by an Italian businessman to serve as a record of the couple's marriage and as a kind of wedding contract. It is often discussed by art historians as an example of Christian symbolism in painting. (Reproduced by courtesy of the Trustees, The National Gallery, London.)

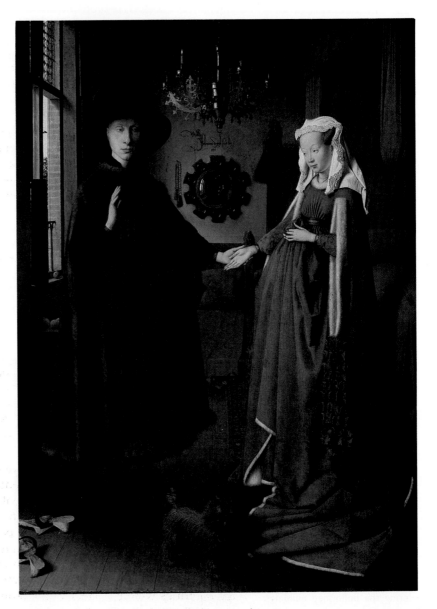

sing Christian concepts or beliefs. For example, van Eyck's painting of the Arnolfini wedding portrays the Italian silk merchant and his shy Flemish bride in a room surrounding by objects with subtle symbolic meanings. The couple standing with shoes off signifies that they stand on sacred ground (the sacred institution of marriage). The dog signifies fidelity; miniature figures of Adam and Eve, the first couple, are carved in the bench; the single candle burning in the chandelier represents the light of Christ; and the convex mirror, symbolic of the all-seeing eye of God, reflects the entire scene.

The small medallions set into the mirror's frame show tiny scenes from the Passion of Christ and represent van Eyck's ever-present promise of salvation for the figures reflected on the mirror's convex surface. These figures include not only the principals, Arnolfini and his wife, but two persons who look into the room through the door. One of these must be the artist himself, since the florid inscription above the mirror, *Johannes de Eyck fuit hic*, announces that he was present.[16]

Following the Renaissance, during the seventeenth and eighteenth centuries, came the age of *baroque art*, with painting and sculpture featuring dark and light contrasts, exaggerated emotions, and dynamic movement in composition. Artists such as Caravaggio (*David with the Head of Goliath*) and Rembrandt (*The Night Watch*) extended the use of light and chiaroscuro for dramatic effect to the same high degree that perspective was earlier developed during the Renaissance. Later, French artists created the intimate *rococo* style with a profusion of curved ornamentation and intricate decoration. The rococo, as the baroque, was manifest in painting, sculpture, architecture, interior design, and in the crafts areas of furniture, tapestry, porcelain, and silver.

The Modern World

Rococo art was replaced in popularity by the *neoclassical* movement, which emphasized straight lines and classical ornamentation in architecture, and balanced formalism, precise linear drawing, and classical subjects such as David's *The Death of Socrates*, and Ingres's *Oedipus and the Sphinx*. Neoclassicism became entrenched in the French Academy and was the style against which the impressionist painters rebelled late in the nineteenth century.

The nineteenth century in Europe was a period of many artistic styles, beginning with the subjective orientation of *romanticism*, which suggested a personal, intensely emotional style. In France, Delacroix (*Liberty Leading the People*) and Géricault (*Raft of the Medusa*) exemplified the romantic movement. The landscape painters of England, Constable (*The Hay Wain*) and Turner (*The Burning of the Houses of Parliament*) expressed the fascination of romanticism with untamed nature, country folk in natural settings, and the picturesque or exotic. Turner's huge paintings were prophetic of the monumental nonobjective canvases of abstract expressionism. The following excerpt from a book about Turner demonstrates how art historical research and writing can enlighten us with respect to an artist's expression.

The old man's [Turner] request was a strange one. Aboard the steamboat *Ariel*, out of Harwich, preparations were afoot for a bad storm that was brewing. The passenger was persistent. Others might want to go below; he wanted to be lashed to a spar on deck. He was a little man, almost gnomelike, and plainly battered by time. But his sharp gray eyes were impelling, and the crew, in the English tradition of tolerance of eccentricity, complied with his wish. Tied to his perilous post for four hours, Joseph Mallord William Turner, England's leading painter, absorbed and observed the onslaught of the elements.[17]

It is certain that this storm, experienced by the artist in all its force and fury, provided the raw material for one of his bombastic paintings of nature's power, such as: *Shade and Darkness: The Evening of the Deluge; Rain, Steam, and Speed;* and *Snowstorm: Hannibal and His Army Crossing the Alps.*

During the second half of the century *realism* and social protest followed the French and American revolutions. Artists depicted social themes, the dignity of working people, and the unfairness of some social institutions and practices. Millet (*The Gleaners*), Daumier (*Third Class Carriage*), and Courbet (*Burial at Ornans*) painted ordinary people with a stark realism that was quite different, both in presentation of subject and paint application, from the neoclassical style of Jacques-Louis David and Ingres.

Art and architecture in the United States during the colonial period and westward expansion largely reflected European styles and tastes. Government and public buildings and the homes of the wealthy were built according to a series of revival architectural styles. Near the turn of the twentieth century, American architect Louis Sullivan expressed ideas (e.g. "form follows function") that were the foundations for design of the American skyscraper. Sullivan's student, Frank Lloyd

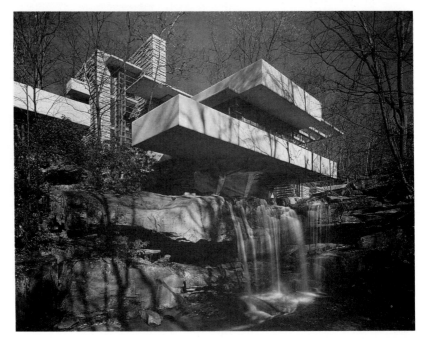

Frank Lloyd Wright, Kaufman House ("Falling Water"), 1936–1939. To design this house in Bear Run, PA, the architect utilized a cantilever construction to place part of the house over the natural waterfall, an example of Wright's approach that wedded structure to environment.

Wright, developed an architectural philosophy and form that became intrinsically American. Wright gained worldwide attention for his blending of nature and modern architectural form in a series of homes built in several states around the country, notably the Robie House in Chicago and the Kaufman House, *Falling Water*, built over a waterfall in Bear Run, Pennsylvania.

Early American painting and sculpture reached points of excellence, but contributed little to the avant-garde development on an international level. Artists such as Bierstadt painted magnificent landscapes of the Rocky Mountains, Yosemite Valley, and the great American West, motivating even more westward migration. Charles Russell and Frederick Remington chronicled the taming of the "Wild West" with their paintings of cowboys, Indians, cavalry, and life on the frontier. George Catlin focused his attention on the life and culture

Frederic Remington, *On Southern Plains*, 1907. Compare this painting of the American West with Picasso's landmark Cubist painting, *Les Demoiselles D'Avignon*, painted the same year. The extreme differences in subject and style explain why the New York Armory Show of 1913, that displayed modern European art for the first time in the United States, was such a controversial event. Remington was one of the excellent artists who recorded the American "Wild West." (The Metropolitan Museum of Art. Gift of Several Gentlemen, 1911.)

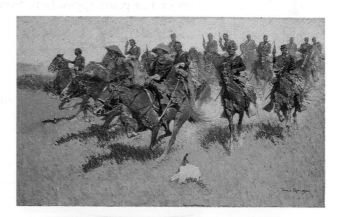

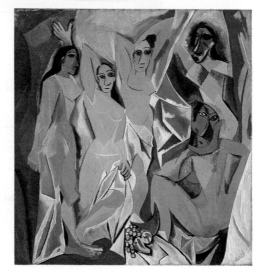

Pablo Picasso, *Les Demoiselles d'Avignon*, 1907. (Museum of Modern Art, New York. Bequest of Lillie P. Bliss.)

of native Americans and painted many authentic portraits and group pictures. The list of great early American artists is a long one that includes Whistler, Cassatt, Homer, Eakins, Church, and many others.

After the advent of *impressionism*, later in the nineteenth century, the pace of new art styles in Europe increased, leading to the development of cubism, fauvism, surrealism, and others in rapid succession. Many innovations or movements in the modern era began in revolutions against accepted artistic tradition or, in many instances, academic dogma. So it was that a group of French painters, including Manet, Monet, Renoir, and others, rejected the narrow aesthetic views of the state academy of artists and developed new purposes and images in painting.[18] These artists, dubbed *impressionists* as the result of a remark by a sarcastic critic, responded to the invention of the camera as a recording device that surpassed the painter in accuracy and to the new scientific knowledge of optics. They began to concentrate on the creation of images that the camera could not achieve as they emphasized mood and visual impression.

The traditional hierarchical organization of subject matter was abandoned in favor of a relatively modern preoccupation with light and color. Flat tones and clear edges were avoided in favor of small strokes of color and indefinite contours, both of which tended to convey a sense of diffuse and often sparkling light. Artists moved their studios outdoors, and painters such as Monet found themselves doing multiple studies of a particular subject as they focused on the light of early morning, high noon, and twilight in relation to a cathedral, a bridge, or a haystack. One might say the impressionists were primarily interested in the effects of light on objects in contrast to their successors, the *post-impressionists*, who were interested primarily in problems of theme, technique, and personal expression.

The more immediate forebears of twentieth-century art were a group of painters known as the *post-impressionists* because of their close relationship to the earlier impressionist movement. The most significant of these artists were Vincent van Gogh, Paul Cézanne, Paul Gauguin, and Georges Seurat.[19] These four men, all highly individualistic, contributed their own distinctive perception of art to those who were to follow. The vivid, emotionally charged works of van Gogh left their mark on the expressionists; the broad, flat tones of Gauguin were to find their echoes in the work of Henri Matisse; and the construction of forms in terms of planes undertaken by Paul Cézanne opened the door to cubism, perhaps the most revolutionary of twentieth-century styles. Cézanne refused to limit his vision to the forms given by the tradition of painting and thus examined the structure beneath the outward aspects of objects. He invited the viewer to study his pictorial subjects from multiple points of view, and he made the space between objects as meaningful as the objects themselves. Cézanne rejected the hazy softness of impressionism and applied his paint in clearly articulated flat strokes of color, which appeared literally to build his paintings as one small passage led to larger areas. This method of organizing the structure of a painting served to unify the entire work into a "fused, crystallized unit, within which the shapes and colors work together."[20]

Fauvism and *expressionism* can be considered together, since they are closely related to one another. Expressionism, although difficult to define because it took numerous forms, was clearly the outgrowth of certain features in post-impressionism, most notably those found in Van Gogh's work but also to some degree those found in Gauguin's as well. Some scholars have claimed that the main feature of this movement was the expression of the artists' feelings rather than their ideas. Others have stated that the movement relied chiefly on design used very abstractly to achieve an order and a rhythm that had greater significance than could be found in art that relied on nature as a basis for expression. In general, expressionism celebrates the artist's individual expressive statement and allows for nearly unbounded abstraction and experimentation.

The *fauvists* may be represented by Henri Matisse and André Derain. Matisse was the leader of this group of painters in France who extended the new use of color created by Gauguin and Van Gogh, carrying it to the point where the group earned the critically derisive term *fauves*, or wild beasts. The art-viewing public at the turn of the century, having just begun to accept the radical innovations of the post-impressionists, could not cope with the fauvists' strident use of pure color, their free-flowing arabesques, purely decorative line, and total disregard of local color (the specific color of a natural object). They were trying to paint according to Derain's clarion call of 1906: "We must, at all costs, break out of the fold in which the realists have imprisoned us."[21] The fauvists were creating their own reality, and they conceived of painting as a vehicle for expression that was totally autonomous, wholly independent of the viewer's perception of the world.

Expressionism, generally speaking, may be said to place emphasis on emotions, sensations, or ideas rather than on the appearance of objects. Expressionist artists present their reactions in a form that is almost invariably a pronounced distortion of the camera view of the environment. Expressionism, in its narrower sense, was a development of early twentieth-century German art in response to the aesthetic furor taking place in France at the same time. We can think of the expressionist artists of Germany, Scandinavia, and Austria as merging the color and design theories of the post-impressionists of France with attitudes toward subject matter that were uniquely Germanic in origin. This merger gave German expressionism its distinguishing charac-

The history of modern art reflects a varied approach to the problems of design and expressiveness. Henri Matisse's *Red Room (Harmony in Red)*, 1908–1909, is an example of fauvism (State Hermitage Museum, Leningrad), while Georges Rouault's *The Old King*, 1916–1938, is an example of expressionism, which also carries forward the traditions of medieval stained glass windows. (The Carnegie Museum of Art, Pittsburgh; Patrons Art Fund, 1940.)

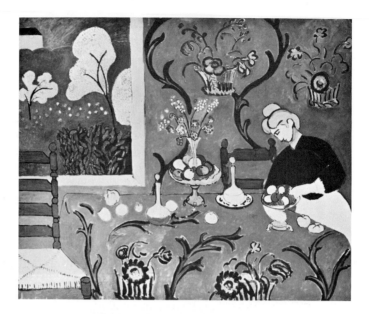

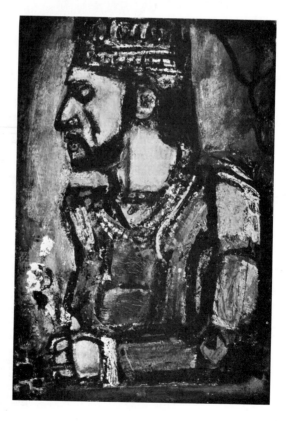

Early in this century, some artists turned from representational art and became solely concerned with pure relations among the design elements. A major figure in this movement was Piet Mondrian, whose *Composition in White, Black and Red*, 1936 (below, left), is a prime example of pure abstraction. (Collection, The Museum of Modern Art, New York. Gift of the Advisory Committee.) The cubists, with a new consciousness of relativity, offered a flexible visual experience by presenting, simultaneously, different views of objects. See below, right: Juan Gris, *Breakfast*, 1914. (Collection, The Museum of Modern Art, New York. Acquired through the Lillie P. Bliss Bequest. © ADAGP 1990.)

teristics: a heightened use of color, an extreme simplification of form and distortion of representational conventions for emotive reasons, a preoccupation with hallucinatory religious experience, and the investment of conventional or "public" subjects, such as landscapes and human figures, with private visionary or mythic meanings. Considerably influenced by the fauvists, the German expressionists in turn affected French painters such as Rouault, especially in terms of the ideological substructure of art. Eventually, the artistic manners and attitudes of the German expressionists were to have a wide influence and to assume the more generalized characteristics described previously.

It was in 1907, when he painted *Les Demoiselles d'Avignon*, that Pablo Picasso took Cézanne's ideas one step further toward what is now known as cubism. *Les Demoiselles* combined the simultaneous perspective of Cézanne with the simple, monumental shapes and sharply faceted surfaces of African and primitive Iberian art. As Picasso developed his ideas along with Georges Braque, the forms of cubism became more complex. By 1911, cubist compositions grew in complexity as planes overlapped, interpenetrated, and moved into areas of total abstraction. Space and form were now handled with a minimum of color, in contrast to the rich hues of fauvism and expressionism. Their spontaneity and painterly qualities, born of their own emotionalism,

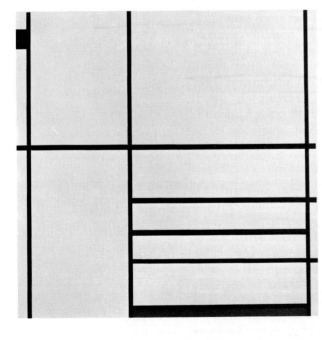

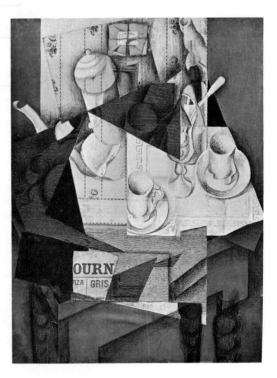

were superseded by a more intellectual concern for order. As Werner Haftmann describes it:

> Cubism embraces all the aspects of the object simultaneously and is more complete than the optical view. From the information and signs conveyed on the rhythmically moving surface, the imagination can reassemble the object in its entirety. . . . Cubism corresponds to that new modern conception of reality which it has been the aim of the whole pictorial effort of the 20th Century to express in visual terms.[23]

Within cubism can be found many of the central concepts of modern art: manipulation and rejection of Renaissance perspective, abstraction to the point of nonobjectivity, emphasis on the integrity of the picture plane, introduction of manufactured elements in collage, and experimentation with different conceptions of reality.

The precursors of *surrealism* were artists such as Paul Klee, Giorgio di Chirico, and Marc Chagall, all of whom dealt with fantasy, dreams, and other states of mind. We may add to these influences the dada movement, whose anti-art theatrics and demonstrations challenged the most basic assumptions about art.[24] André Breton, a poet, first used the term *surrealist* in his own publication, thus reflecting the close connection between an art movement and a literary one, a common situation in the history of art. The artists who were ultimately to be identified with the movement—Salvador Dalí, Joan Miró, Yves Tanguy—all shared Breton's interest in Freud's ideas regarding

Max Ernst, *Eye of Silence*, 1943–1944. This example of surrealism, with its rich body of images drawn from dreams, juxtapositions of dissociated forms, and unorthodox uses of materials, has an unfailing appeal for children. (Washington University Gallery of Art, St. Louis.)

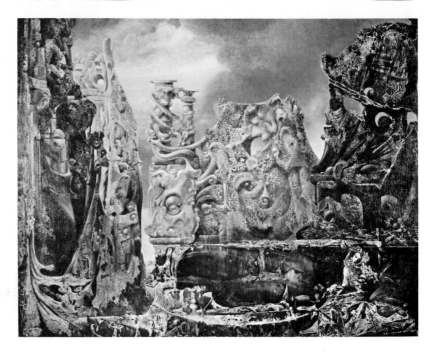

dreams, psychoanalysis, and the relation of conscious and sub-conscious experience as the subject matter for art. They strove to divorce themselves from rational and logical approaches to art. In searching for a definition of surrealism that would apply equally to literature and art, Breton wrote, "Surrealism: the dictation of thought free from any control of reason, independent of any aesthetic or moral preoccupation . . . rests upon a belief in the superior reality of certain forms of association hitherto neglected, in the omnipotence of the dream, in the disinterested play of thought."[25] Influences of surrealism are especially evident in many contemporary music videos.

One of the most revolutionary developments in European art of the early twentieth century was the shift toward what was at first called *nonobjective art*. Wassily Kandinsky, a Russian who lived in Germany and France, is considered the father of nonobjective painting.[26] The concepts subsumed under this term are now usually referred to as nonrepresentational and cover a much wider range of styles than originally. Nonrepresentational art now refers to many of the artistic styles that developed in the United States after World War II, when the center of the avant-garde in art shifted from Paris, which had been occupied during the war, to New York City. The Armory Show of avant-garde European art in New York City in 1913 was a landmark event for American art. This exhibit brought cubist, fauvist, and other newly developed twentieth century art styles to American audiences for the first time. Although many traditional American artists and critics openly derided the abstract forms of modern art, the show was extremely popular, attracting large crowds, and sales of the European art were excellent. The impact of the Armory show is difficult to assess, but there is no doubt that it initiated change in American art.

Contemporary Art

The other event that contributed most significantly to change in American art, and to the eventual preeminence of New York City as the center of world art, was World War II. Because of the impending war a number of influential European artists emigrated to America, including Hans Hofmann, Willem de Kooning, Joseph Albers, Walter Gropius, and others. Paris had been the magnet for artists until the war, but because it was devastated and occupied, most artists fled to other countries. The United States emerged after the war as the most powerful country in the world and New York City acquired the same drawing power for artists that Paris, Rome, and Florence had enjoyed in the past. During the 1940s, 1950s, and 1960s, art styles in America followed the pace established in France during the first half of the century.

Jackson Pollock, Willem de Kooning, Hans Hofmann, and other artists created *abstract expressionism*, the first unique American art style. This style became the most dominant, monolithic art movement in

Suggested activity: How would Mrs. Boswell appear if she were suffering from expressionism or futurism?

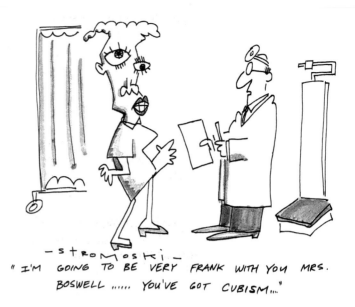

— s t r o M o s k i —

"I'M GOING TO BE VERY FRANK WITH YOU MRS. BOSWELL ...... YOU'VE GOT CUBISM..."

history. Following the direction of earlier artists that moved toward abstraction in art, the abstract expressionists or "action painters" developed a visual art that approached the abstract purity of music. This art is nonobjective, meaning that it does not attempt to represent objects that exist in the real world. It is "presentational" rather than representational. The source of content for painting existed within the sensibility of the artist.

The *pop art* style followed relatively soon after abstract expressionism and also became influential on an international scale. Younger artists such as Andy Warhol, Jasper Johns, and Roy Lichtenstein, who received their art education during the heyday of abstract expressionism, predictably rebelled against the strict prescriptions that attended the supposedly most creative style. Rather than search their own inner emotional states for expression in painting, the newer generation of artists insisted that the modern world of urban living, mass media, and commercial imagery was the real subject for art. They painted the banal and mundane aspects of contemporary life. The pop artists seemed to challenge the viewer, who was uneasy about accepting an art style that celebrated soup cans and soap boxes, by stating boldly: "This is your world! Don't blame the artist if you don't like what you see."

The development of *op art* in England and the U.S. was also a response against the spontaneous, painterly, personalized application of paint by the abstract expressionists. Op artists, such as Richard Anuszkiewicz and Bridget Riley, stayed with the nonobjective approach, but celebrated the geometric precision characteristic of a highly technological society.[27] They used knowledge of human optics to produce images that forced viewers to respond on an autonomic level. For example, the human eye is incapable of focusing on large and small shapes simultaneously. By painting high-contrast lines graduated from large to very small, the artists created artworks that no one can view completely at a single moment. The cool, depersonalized precise forms of op art are responses against the "expressive brush-strokes" of abstract expressionism as well as expressions of a society preoccupied with science and technology.

Realism is one of the oldest and most enduring styles of art. *Photo-realism*, the most recent manifestation of our love for the realistic-appearing image, is appropriately associated with photography. Not only do artists in this stylistic group, such as Chuck Close, Janet Fish, and Richard Estes, use photographic technology for production of their works, but the images themselves could be obtained only through photography. Common photographic conventions, such as cropping, unusual angles, and soft focus caused by shallow depth of field, are consciously included in the paintings. It is accurate also to view the return to realism, this intensified photo-realism where the camera reveals more than the natural eye, as yet another incident in the rejection of total abstraction in art.

Neo-expressionism is another manifestation of the basic expression-istic approach seen earlier in German expressionism during the 1920s and abstract expressionism during the 1950s. It signals, perhaps, a re-turn of initiative in avant-garde art to Europe, although a strong con-tingent of proponents practice in this country. Neo-expressionism is typified by crudity of rendering, violent and cynical themes, and a nihilistic point of view. It is currently the most pervasive and influen-tial world art movement.

Today the influences of world art are intermingled because of the ready availability of good quality art reproductions and the improve-ment of communications in general. Much credit for the availability of information about the arts of world cultures must be given to the many art historians who have laboriously and carefully researched, cate-gorized, analyzed, interpreted, and written about art.

The Changing Face of Art History

Art history, as we have seen, has its origins in Western thought and has changed in its scope and emphasis since the time of Vasari. The discipline continues to change as new scholars with different points of view criticize the field and suggest, even demand, improvements. One needed adjustment in art is an overdue *recognition of the contributions of women artists*. When someone says that they don't know about signifi-cant women artists, or that there were none, they are usually reflecting the information that has come to them through the major art history

String, pieced by Rosie Lee Tompkins; quilted by Willia Etta Graham, 1985. This quilt calls into question many assumptions about the nature of art history. It represents non-Western influences in American art, and serves as an example of art by women artists, by black Americans, is an example of applied arts, and is a collaboration rather than the work of an individual. (Publication: *Who'd A Thought It: Improvisation in African-American Quiltmaking*. San Francisco Craft and Folk Art Museum, San Francisco.)

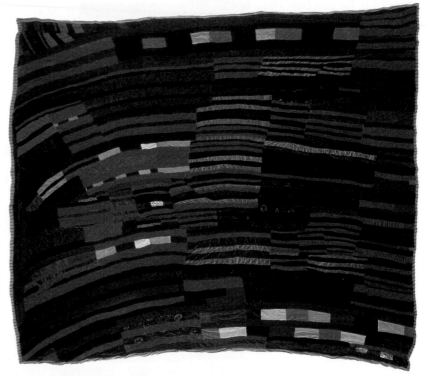

textbooks, whose authors have most often been men. Fortunately, this oversight is being corrected through scholarly research and publication of books such as *A History of Women Artists*,[28] *Making Their Mark: Women Artists Move into the Mainstream*,[29] *Women Artists*,[30] and *National Museum of Women in the Arts*.[31] Women are now in the mainstream of drawing, painting, and sculpture; and forms of expression that have been developed primarily by women, such as quilting, are being recognized for their contributions to traditional and contemporary art. Art periodicals such as *ARTnews* recognize, present, and discuss art by women artists on a regular basis.[32] We are seeing exhibitions of art by women in museums and galleries more frequently, providing more of the equity that has been absent for so long.

Another area that art historians and other art professionals are attending to increasingly is *recognition of non-Western art*. The Western tradition in art has always been the primary focus of art historians, probably because of the discipline's origins and the European heritage of many scholars in this field. Educators in the public schools are especially concerned about the Western emphasis in art programs because of the non-Western ethnic heritage of so many school children. The concern of educators and community leaders with respect to all of Western culture and thought is that students might gain the impres-

Frida Kahlo, *The Little Deer*, 1946. The autobiographical nature of Kahlo's painting requires historical knowledge on the part of the teacher. Children will enjoy speculating as to the reason for the artist's face on the body of a deer and the presence of arrows, but at some point the teacher should inform the class of the bizarre circumstances of the accident that literally drove a piece of metal through the artist's body, leading to innumerable operations and testifying to Kahlo's tenacity for life and devotion to painting. Mention of her marriage to Diego Rivera, although of secondary importance, is also an important historical footnote. (Photo courtesy of Mary-Anne Martin/Fine Art, New York.)

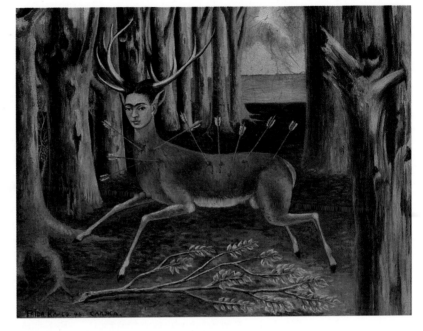

sion that this is the dominant, preeminent, highest culture and that others are less worthy of attention and recognition. When nearly all of the art exemplars used in school art programs are works by males of European heritage, this misconception is perpetuated.

Americans of Hispanic, native, and black heritage have contributed significantly to contemporary art and continue to do so. Jacob Lawrence, Romare Bearden, and Faith Ringgold are well-known today and will be included in future art histories. During recent times, Mexican artists Diego Rivera, Frida Kahlo, David Siqueiros, and Jose Orozco have attracted worldwide acclaim for their large murals and passionate depictions of social and political themes. Contemporary artists from South America, among them Venezuelan-French sculptor Marisol Escobar, are making their marks on the art world. And, native American artists, such as R. C. Gorman, Maria Martinez, and Fritz Scholder have successfully entered the arena of contemporary art.

Art historians are also correcting what some have viewed as an *overemphasis on the formalist tradition* of art. All art disciplines have changed during recent years in the direction of broader applications of perspectives from fields such as psychology, politics, sociology, and anthropology. We can read the writings of critics and historians who apply perspectives of psychoanalysis, feminism, Marxism, and cultural anthropology. Formal analysis of artworks for many is decidedly secondary to psychological and social issues that surround art. These perspectives influence judgments made about entire styles of art, with formalistic styles such as abstract expressionism and op art sliding down the scale and art with social content, such as neo-expressionism gaining respect. For art education in the schools, an overemphasis on formalism can be seen when curricula fail to go beyond superficial teaching of the elements of principles of art, when the social significance of artworks is ignored, and when functions of objects, such as African masks or native American totem poles, are ignored as they are viewed exclusively for their aesthetic properties.

Another current issue in art history and art education is a perceived *overemphasis on the fine arts* to the exclusion of crafts and decorative arts, folk arts, and applied arts, especially commercial applications. The very old debate that centers on distinctions between art and craft, the elitist view that finds little significance in applied arts, and the lack of recognition of art in everyday experience are attitudes that are losing prominence. One scholar, calling for serious consideration of African-American quilts as an art form, speaks to several of the issues mentioned above:

> In the near future, let us hope, sophisticated museum directors will award such treasure special rooms, special curators, just as they now do with European prints or drawings . . . Resistance to the recognition of all this brilliance reflects the heavy weighting which most Americans assign the grand European tradition. The received wisdom is easy to ascertain: there is *one* art history and *one* form of progress and both, of course, derive from western Europe.
>
> In point of fact, there are many art histories in the United States.[33]

SOME METHODS FOR TEACHING ART HISTORY

Children are fascinated with the content of art history and the art images, when teachers can engage them at levels appropriate for their abilities and interests. The traditional method often used by university art history instructors, projecting slides and lecturing, will not be appropriate for most elementary classes. Showing slides and providing information is appropriate in brief sessions, though rarely effective for no more than ten or fifteen minutes. Children often learn more and perceive more carefully when they are engaged in active tasks that relate to the art being studied.

Organizing Art Images

A visual time line and a world map provide useful reference points for art history. Although young children do not have sufficient concepts of lengthy time periods to comprehend units such as centuries and decades, they can understand the implications of relative differences in distance from "now" on the timeline. Similarly, many primary children are not able to conceptualize the distances involved in world geography and cultures, but can see different locations on a globe or world map, and their understandings will progress with their maturity and through what is learned in social studies.

Show children postcards or larger reproductions of artworks that are culturally distinctive, such as an Egyptian sculpture, an African mask, or a Rembrandt painting and ask them to identify where each artwork belongs on the world map and on the timeline. Display the art reproduction on the bulletin board and string a length of yarn from the picture to the correct world location and point on the timeline. Repeat this process as you teach about different periods and styles of art. Eventually the children will be able to associate differences in art styles with different cultures and their locations.

To increase their understanding of modes, write the terms for art modes, such as drawing, painting, sculpture, ceramics, and so forth, on strips of cardboard and place them at the heads of columns on the bulletin board. Using reproductions collected from magazines, or on postcards, etc., ask the children to categorize the art objects according

Pablo Picasso, *Girl Before a Mirror*, 1932. (Collection, The Museum of Modern Art, New York. Gift of Mrs. Simon Guggenheim. Teaching children to recognize important elements in a work of art can enhance their appreciation of the work. A fifth grader's version of the painting (right) illustrates how children also bring their own responses to a work.

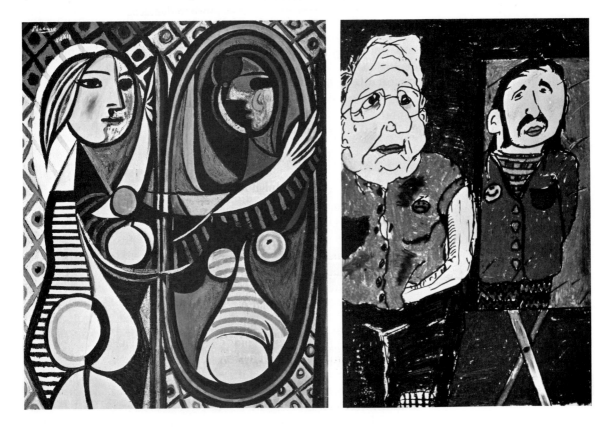

to mode. They can include examples of their own work as well, placing their artwork in the correct columns. This categorization activity can continue to whatever level of sophistication the age group can achieve; for example, sculptures can be grouped according to materials (wood, bronze, stone, and so on), and landscape paintings can be grouped according to artist (Van Gogh, Bierstadt, Monet, etc.). Postcards with a wide range of art reproductions can be purchased at nearly every art museum and can also be ordered from many museums. Some museums publish books of postcards for very reasonable prices. A collection of postcard art images can be one of the art teacher's most versatile resources. Small reproductions of art images can also be collected very inexpensively by cutting pictures of art from art magazines. A magazine that costs five dollars might yield well over a hundred good-quality art reproductions, most in color, appropriate for teaching.

In another exercise, design a bulletin board display of a different artist (Mary Cassatt), culture (African masks), style (Gothic architecture), or other art topic every month or more often. Use good-quality reproductions, pictures of artists if available, titles, concepts, names, dates, and whatever information is appropriate for the age levels and interests of the children and your art curriculum. With all of these display strategies for teaching art history, provide the information that you want children to receive according to your teaching goals. Engage students with questions and discussions about the visual displays, the artists, and the historical contexts. You will note that many will absorb much information and ask for more. They will become able to discuss art with levels of knowledge and understanding that many adults will envy.

Integrating Art History with Criticism, Aesthetics, and Production

Following is a sampling of suggested activities that focus on art history, often integrated with criticism, aesthetics, and art production.

Purposes of Art: Organize the children in small groups of three or four, seated together preferably at tables. Display four or five art reproductions or photographs of objects at the front of the room where all can see, or provide smaller reproductions for each group. Ask each group to decide what the purpose of the object was when it was created. You might include a Greek vessel for holding water, a painting of a king in full royal regalia, a Navajo silver and jade necklace, a cathedral, and so forth. The difficulty and complexity of the tasks should be adapted to the abilities of the grade level. This activity can lead naturally into as much historical content as you wish, as well as art criticism and aesthetics. The idea that there are different purposes to art is a simple but important idea basic to aesthetics.

Sharing Study Sheets. Collect articles, books, pictures, filmstrips, and other materials on a topic such as native American totem poles. Organize a folder with such materials on as many topics as you choose (you

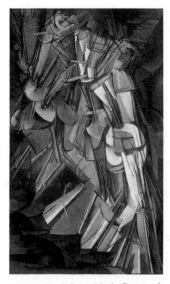

Marcel Duchamp, *Nude Descending a Staircase, No. 2*, 1912. Although derided by some critics ("An explosion in a shingle factory!"), Duchamp exemplifies one goal of the futurist movement: to convey motion on a flat surface. (Philadelphia Museum of Art, Louise and Walter Arensberg Collection.)

can add one or two each year to your files). Divide your class into groups of four or five (this will work best with upper elementary or middle school students). Provide each group with a file, access to whatever audiovisual equipment is needed, and a study sheet asking pertinent questions such as: "Who were the people who created totem poles?", "Where did they live?", "What materials and tools did they use to make the totems, and why?", "When did they begin doing this? When did they stop, if ever?", "Why did they make totem poles? What did the poles mean to the people?", and "How could we make totem poles in art class?"

After appropriate class time (and homework?), ask each group of students to briefly report to the class on their topic. When reports have been given (and perhaps displays mounted), let the class vote on which of the reports they would like to pursue with a production activity. If they choose totem poles, expand the discussion of how this might be done, what materials will be needed, how students might help to collect materials, and what they might learn from making totem poles. In this case, each group might design, construct, and paint their own totem poles and display them with descriptions of the meanings and symbols that they used in their creations. This type of activity is obviously an in-depth project requiring a number of class periods to complete. The results in students' learning and enthusiasm can make the time spent very worthwhile.

Understanding Through Studio Activities. Children often become much more interested in art historical topics when they are involved with related studio activities. If students are working with the idea of forms in motion, they will likely be very interested to see what the futurists accomplished with the concept. A child struggling with the notion of distortion for expressive purpose can become quite involved in reading about Modigliani and looking at his works. Students who are struggling with composition in their paintings are usually very receptive to a five-minute viewing of slides showing masterworks of composition. In all of these situations the art historical content can be purposefully emphasized by the teacher, or it can emerge naturally in the course of discussions and conversations with individual students, and later shared with all class members.

FUNCTIONS OF ART HISTORY AND METHODS OF INQUIRY

Noted art historian Heinrich Wölfflin relates the story of a young artist who, with three of his friends,

> set out to paint part of the landscape, all four firmly resolved not to deviate from nature by a hair's-breadth; and although the subject was the same,

and each quite creditably reproduced what his eyes had seen, the result was four totally different pictures, as different from each other as the personalities of the four painters. Whence the narrator drew the conclusion that there is no such thing as objective vision, and that form and color are always apprehended differently according to temperament.[34]

For the art historian, there is nothing surprising in this observation.

Wölfflin made the point that among artists there is no such thing as objective vision. In recent years we have come to realize that the same thing might be said about historians in general, and art historians in particular. Art historians have at their disposal today such a range of methods of inquiry that they are able to provide us with many points of view about particular artworks, artists, styles, and periods. We are much richer for this diversity.

Contemporary art historian Eugene Kleinbauer discusses two primary modes of art historical inquiry, the *intrinsic* and the *extrinsic*.[35] Using intrinsic methods, art historians focus upon the artwork itself, identifying materials and techniques, establishing authenticity and attribution, dating and provenance, style, stylistic influences, iconography, subject matter, themes, and functions. In order to perform these operations art historians must learn a great deal about the artwork and its context, and they must develop the eye of a connoisseur in order to make extremely fine distinctions. A number of scientific tools are employed by art professionals that reveal important facts to assist art historians.

Extrinsic methods of inquiry involve studies of conditions and influences associated with the creation of the artwork, including artistic

In a memory exercise, a group of upper elementary students observed the *Mona Lisa* for one minute and were then asked to draw the Da Vinci painting from memory.

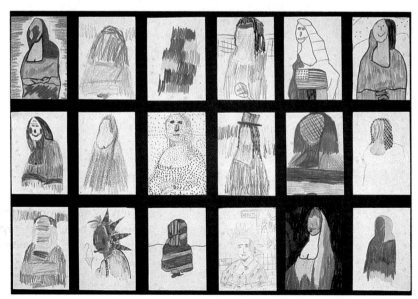

biography, patronage, and the history of the period. Art historians also apply methods derived from psychology and psychoanalysis, and other approaches to learn more about religious, social, philosophical, cultural, and intellectual determinants of the work.

Here is an example of some questions and problems that art historians face: A Rembrandt painting is made available for sale at a reputable New York City auction firm. A museum of art is looking to purchase a Rembrandt painting, which very rarely become available, and this work is exactly what the museum director has in mind. There is a question, however, of the authenticity of the painting. Some authorities suggest that it is by a student of Rembrandt, done in the master's studio under his direction, but it is not of the hand of Rembrandt. Should the museum purchase the painting? How can they establish the painting's authenticity and attribution to Rembrandt? If the issue is not clearly resolved, how will doubt influence the price to be offered for its purchase?

All of the skills and methods of art historians are brought to bear on such questions, often resulting in definitive information that makes answers to these questions obvious. For example, upon investigation of the provenance, or history of ownership of the painting, a scholar discovers a gap of fifty years when the painting was apparently lost. The circumstances of its recent rediscovery suggest that it might be a forgery. The art history scholar, an expert on Dutch painting and Rembrandt in particular, closely analyzes the details of the painting, noting brushstrokes and other painting techniques that are subtly different from Rembrandt's. Scientific analysis of the paint reveals an element that was not available in oil paint until a century after Rembrandt's death. The experts who have examined this painting are able to determine that it is not of the hand of Rembrandt or from his studio, but it is rather a copy from a later date or a forgery created with intent to defraud. Methods such as these are applied by art historians not only in conjunction with the art market, but in the process of their research and writing and for the purpose of improving our understanding of art and the meaning and significance of artworks.

Methods of Art Historical Inquiry as a Basis for Teaching

Teachers can organize classroom art activities based on art historians' methods of inquiry. Following are some examples.

Attribution. Using postcard reproductions (or images from magazines), place about ten paintings on the display board or arrange them on a table. Place a number beside each reproduction. Tell the students that six of the paintings are by the same artist and four are by other artists. (You might use six landscapes by Van Gogh and other landscapes by Gauguin, Monet, and so on. To make the activity easier, select the four to be very different, such as a Japanese landscape, a cubist landscape, or a Grandma Moses landscape). Ask the children to identify which ones are by the same artist and which are not. Can they recognize and name the artist who created the six? Can they identify the artist(s) who painted the other four? How did they know? Older children can respond with pencil and paper. All ages can enjoy discussing the results and justifying their answers.

Viewing Themes in Art Historically. Using available art reproductions— from books, slides, postcards, and so on—organize a series of artworks on a theme such as animals in art, or people working. Ask children to group the reproductions and identify the theme. For example, with the theme of animals in art the works might include such items as a Rauschenberg sculpture with a stuffed chicken on top, a Marino Marini bronze sculpture of a horse, a Chinese carved jade dragon, a Japanese woodblock print of kittens, and a Charles Russell watercolor of a cattle drive. (There are thousands of artworks on this theme; other themes include mother and child, flowers, portraits of authority, etc.).

Depending on the age level of the children, you might ask them to:

1. Determine if possible the materials and processes of each artwork.
2. Determine each artwork's origin and artist.
3. Determine where the artwork was created and where it is now located.
4. Determine who owns the work now.
5. Discuss for what purpose the work was created.
6. Interpret the meaning or expressive properties of the artwork.
7. Compare the artworks according to dates of creation.

Very often some of this information is available on the back of a postcard or in written materials that accompany reproductions. If children can read and use an art dictionary and library resources, the activities can move in that direction. Art historians spend a great portion of their research time looking at works of art, reading about art, and discussing art with other knowledgeable people. Children of all age levels can look at art and discuss their observations, and older children can participate in reading activities as well.

Which Artwork Came First? Again using an array of art reproductions (possibly a selection of six slides projected on a screen), ask children to speculate which artwork was created first in time, which one was created next, and so on. You can control the difficulty of this activity by your selection of artworks. Even very young children can place a Rembrandt portrait earlier in time than a Warhol portrait of Marilyn Monroe. This activity is related to the dating processes of art historians.

Archeological Puzzles.   Some art historians use archeological techniques to learn more about art objects from very old cultures, such as Egyptian or native American. They sometimes find artifacts of artistic merit through digs and they become skilled in piecing broken objects together. For this activity, obtain pictures of three or four Pueblo Indian pots, cut the pictures in pieces with a scissors or blade, and place the pieces together in a bowl or box. A small group of children can work together to arrange the pieces, restoring the pictures of the pots. Ask the children how they knew which pieces fit together (according to color, pattern, size, texture, etc.). Provide information about the pots for the children after they have completed the puzzles. Relate this activity to the work done by art historians who study the arts of very old cultures

Reading about Art History.   Reading is a very important activity for virtually all art historians. There are increasing numbers of good-quality books about art history written for children. School librarians should be encouraged to purchase books about art as well as other subjects in the curriculum. There is a wide range of art magazines available, many of which would be appropriate for elementary school classrooms. Teachers might wish to peruse art magazines prior to making them available to children, checking for items that might be offensive according to the standards of the local school system and community. Older children can do library research on art historical topics and can write essays on topics in art history. Much can be learned through this traditional approach, which is similar to research done by art historians. Older elementary students can also participate in firsthand research. For example, newspapers, news magazines, and television news programs report on art events such as Christo's Surrounded Islands project, or the controversy of the Helga drawings and paintings by Andrew Wyeth. Children can collect clippings of similar art events as sources for reports.

The In-Depth Experience

Spending a prolonged time with a single artwork or artist offers children an opportunity to get at the heart of a work through extended probing below the surface. This requires teachers to become authorities through their own research so that information about the period, the artist, and the general cultural setting can be added to the stages of criticism described earlier. Some ideas can emerge through questioning while others, such as the meaning of symbols or autobiographical references, must be provided by the discussion leader.[36] When in-depth approaches go beyond a single work and are applied to an artist, a movement, a style or a subject, a basis for a unit exists.[37]

One elementary school organized a "Georges Seurat Week" during which all grades studied the life and works of Seurat. Bulletin board

Pavel Tchelitchew, *Hide-and-Seek (Cache-cache)*, 1940–1942. Complex works such as this are good sources for in-depth approaches to the study of art. The rich color, the profusion of embedded images that seem to change as one studies them, the ambiguity of the tree-foot-hand image, the girl disappearing in the center, and the presence of embryos and infants all provide a rich source of speculation about the artist's intent. (Collection, Museum of Modern Art, New York. Mrs. Simon Guggenheim Fund.)

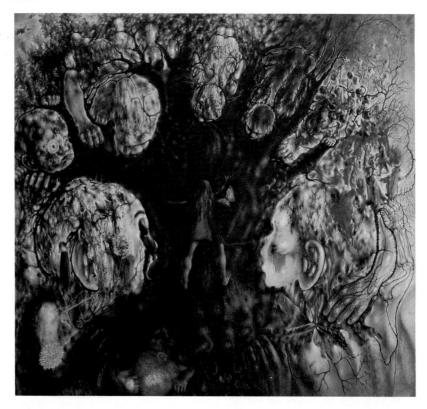

displays about Seurat and his art were placed around the school; children learned about pointillism and painted pictures using that technique (or approximations of the technique). One teacher wrote lyrics about Seurat to be sung to a popular tune. The culminating activity was a school assembly to watch a local theater group perform part of the play *An Afternoon in the Park with Georges*, which they were presenting in a local theater at the time. Then everyone sang the Seurat song, to the enjoyment of all.

Dramatizing Art History. Children can often relate better to historical art concepts through dramatization activities. They can collect clothes and props for costumes, scenes, and sets to portray an artist or art event. For example, have children choose an artist, dress in a costume appropriate for the artist, and then have the class try to guess what artist they are representing. This can be elaborated by using a "20 questions" approach, where the child dressed as the artist will answer students questions about the artist's life and art. This means that the students portraying the artists will have to familiarize themselves with this material.

Here are more dramatization activities:

- The letters of Van Gogh when read aloud and supported by slides of his artwork can be an exciting source for a dramatic reading for an assembly, a PTA meeting or parents' night.
- In 1573, Paolo Veronese was accused of heresy for his painting *Feast in the House of Simon*. The accusations seem utterly groundless today. They included such issues as the reasons for painting someone picking his teeth, as well as objections to portrayals of buffoons, parrots, and even Germans. A staging of excerpts from the transcript of Veronese's trial would interest upper grades and provide opportunity for many roles.[38]
- The following segment of a bombastic futurist manifesto can make an exciting adjunct to the study of this art movement. Simply divide the following passage between alternating groups and have them read it as they work together for a rousing crescendo.

This "living reproduction" of Amigoni Giacomo's *Adoration of the Shepherds* is a contemporary treatment of traditional tableaux. Such "reproductions" are part of an annual event at a middle school, and in this case also served as a Christmas card.

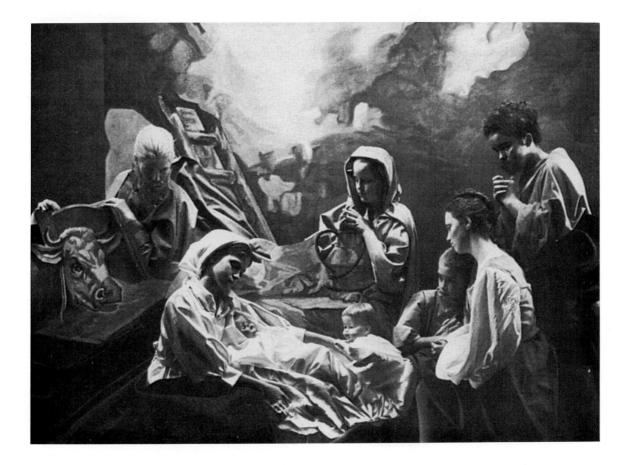

Come, then, the good incendiaries, with their charred fingers! . . . Set fire to the shelves of the libraries! Deviate the course of canals to flood the cellars of the museums! . . . Seize pick-axes and hammers! Sap the foundations of the venerable cities! The oldest among us are thirty; we have, therefore, ten years at least to accomplish our task. When we are forty, let others, younger and more valiant, throw us into the wastepaper basket like useless manuscripts . . . And Injustice, strong and healthy, will burst forth radiantly in their eyes. For art can be nought but violence, cruelty and injustice.[39]

Using a Historical Theory to Bridge Criticism and Art History

In the critical processes, the stage of formal analysis requires the viewer to focus upon the ways in which the elements and/or the principles of art have been employed. An example of this is noting how certain geometric shapes provide the structure for the composition of the work. (Rubens used S-shapes, circles, and "lozenges" or ovoid shapes; Renaissance painters often used the triangle, etc.)

Higher-level analysis involves comparing stylistic differences among two or more historical periods. Heinrich Wölfflin, a well-known Swiss art historian, attempted to set up some guidelines for comparing major styles of art, in this case, the Renaissance and the baroque.[40] He developed the idea of "intuitive forms" — that is, changes of style that occur according to their own inner laws independent of social or historic forces which lie apart from art. When we can recognize such differences, then we can apply them to other periods of art. This is important because through their changes of style, artists often anticipate breakthroughs in the use of formal elements and continue to use them until they are either built upon by succeeding artists or abandoned.

While Wölfflin's guidelines for comparison between Renaissance and baroque painting apply to sculpture and architecture as well as painting, they are most readily recognized in painting. The four concepts of change described below can be identified in the two examples shown.

Linear/Painterly. The contours of linear forms are clearer in the Renaissance than the softer and more uneven edges in baroque work. Since these distinctions are not absolute, they may also appear in the same period in different parts of the country. Although Botticelli's *Primavera* is an example of linear painting in northern Italy, Titian, who worked in the south, preferred softer contours, anticipating the work of baroque painters such as Rubens who appeared much later.

Closed and Open Composition. Renaissance forms were "closed" — that is, they were balanced carefully within the edges of the canvas, where baroque painters extended their subjects *beyond* the confines of the canvas into infinite space.

Giovanni Bellini's *Madonna with Saints Peter and Paul, and Donors*, c. 1510 (Walters Art Gallery, Baltimore) and Anthony van Dyck's *Rinaldo and Armida*, 1629 (Baltimore Museum of Art, Jacob Epstein Collection) are examples of artworks that can be used to clarify a theory of change in style. In this case, the historian responsible is Heinrich Wölfflin. To extend the comparisons, one could add a third example — an earlier work such as one by Giotto and another that follows the Baroque.

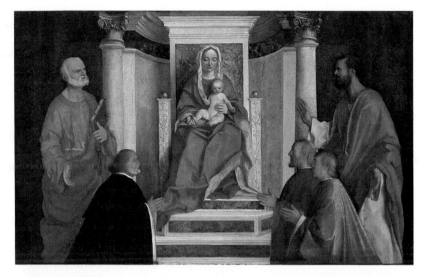

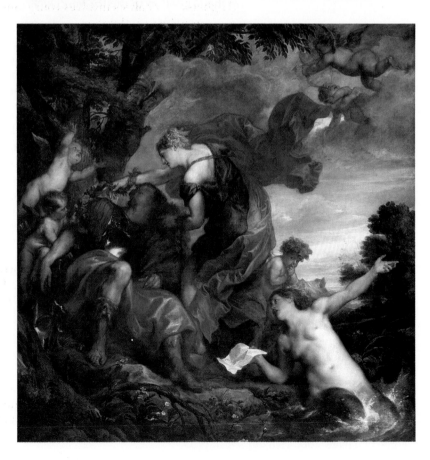

Color. Renaissance painting confined color to the nature of the subjects, particularly clothing. Baroque painting used color not only to describe a part of a subject, but dispersed it throughout the painting. One reason for the Renaissance painter's use of restricted color lay in the accepted convention of the symbolic nature of color, as in the use of the color blue for the Virgin Mary's clothing.

Light. Light was evenly dispersed in the Renaissance, but as in the case of color, was used by baroque painters for the opportunities it offered to create mood and drama.

The Van Dyck and Bellini paintings clarify the concepts described above. One way to present Wölfflin's distinctions is for the teacher to identify key points of difference and then to show the class examples of styles which they are expected to identify based on the teacher's descriptions. Another way is to mount a dozen or so reproductions on the wall and ask students to separate them by Wölfflin's distinctions. Here are some key words and phrases to bear in mind when comparing the (a) Bellini to the (b) Van Dyck.

receding forms	dramatic
dispersed light	active
soft edges	static
symmetrical	even lighting
dynamic	dispersed color

Wölfflin's distinctions place greater demands upon the viewer's powers of concentration, and require higher levels of perceptual development. Where students in lower elementary grades should be able to discern such differences as handling of edges, dramatic use of light, painterliness, and symmetry of composition, they may have greater difficulty in pointing to such factors as recessive space and planar differences. One question to pose to students to help them to discern these differences is: What would you have to do to a baroque painting to make it look more like an early Renaissance work or vice versa?

◆ NOTES TO THE TEXT

1. Albert Elsen, *Purposes of Art*, 2nd ed. (New York: Holt, Rinehart and Winston, 1967), p. 3.

2. Giorgio Vasari, *Lives of the Artists* [1555], trans. George Bull (New York: Penguin, 1981), p. 13.

3. Dates of artistic periods vary according to different published sources. Such differences sometimes occur as scholars select different historical events to mark the beginnings and endings of periods. Estimates of

dates associated with historical periods of art have been taken from several sources, including the very clear chronology in Rita Gilbert and William McCarter, *Living with Art*, 2nd ed. (New York: Alfred A. Knopf, 1989).

4. H. W. Janson, *History of Art* (New York: Harry N. Abrams, 1963), p. 65.

5. For a brief general survey of world art, including the art of Africa, see Stella Pandell Russell, *Art in the World*, 3rd ed. (Chicago: Holt, Rinehart and Winston, 1989).

6. National Museum of African Art, *The Art of West African Kingdoms* (Washington, D.C.: Smithsonian Institution Press, 1987), p. 5.

7. Russell, *op. cit.*, p. 221.

8. *Ibid.*

9. Mary Tregear, *Chinese Art* (New York: Oxford University Press, 1980).

10. Joan Stanley Baker, Japanese Art (London: Thames and Hudson, 1984).

11. Lois Fichner-Rathus, *Understanding Art*, 2nd ed. (Englewood Cliffs, NJ: Prentice-Hall, 1989), p. 260.

12. Fichner-Rathus, *op. cit.*, p. 281.

13. Russell, *op. cit.*, p. 266.

14. Henry La Farge, ed., Museums of the Andes (New York: Newsweek, Inc., 1981), p. 147.

15. Detailed information about native American crafts is available in sources such as Sandra Corrie Newman, *Indian Basket Weaving* (Flagstaff, AZ: Northland Press, 1974), and Louise Lincoln, ed., *Southwest Indian Silver from the Doneghy Collection* (Austin, TX: University of Texas Press, 1982). More art museums in the Southwest and other regions of North America are taking an active role in preserving and documenting this precious art.

16. Horst de la Croix and Richard Tansey, *Gardner's Art Through The Ages*, 7th ed. (New York: Harcourt Brace Jovanovich, 1980), p. 592.

17. Diana Hirsh, *The World of Turner* (New York: Time-Life Books, 1969), p. 7.

18. See Robert Herbert, *Impressionism: Art, Leisure, and Parisian Society* (New York: Yale, 1988).

19. See John Rewald, *Post-Impressionism from Van Gogh to Gauguin*, 3rd ed. (New York: Museum of Modern Art, 1978).

20. Burton Wasserman, *Modern Painting* (Worcester, MA: Davis, 1970), p. 36.

21. Quoted in Werner Haftmann, *Painting in the Twentieth Century* (New York: Praeger, 1965), p. 36.

22. Robert Rosenblum, *Cubism and Twentieth Century Art* (New York: Abrams, 1960).

23. Haftmann, *op. cit.*, p. 80.

24. Hans Richter, *Dada, Art, and Anti-Art* (New York: McGraw-Hill, 1965).

25. Herbert Read, *A Concise History of Modern Painting* (New York: Praeger, 1959), p. 132.

26. For an account of his ideas, see Wassily Kandinsky, *Concerning the Spiritual in Art and Painting in Particular* (New York: Wittenborn, 1964).

27. For an excellent up-to-date and comprehensive reference on artists, art styles, and art terms, see Harold Osborne, ed., *The Oxford Companion to Twentieth-Century Art* (New York: Oxford University Press, 1988).

28. Hugo Munsterberg, *A History of Women Artists* (New York: Clarkson N. Potter, 1975).

29. Nancy Grubb, ed., *Making Their Mark: Women Artists Move in the Mainstream*, 1970-1985 (New York: Abbeville Press, 1989).

30. Nancy G. Heller, *Women Artists: An Illustrated History* (New York: Abbeville Press, 1987).

31. Margaret B. Rennolds, ed., *National Museum of Women in the Arts* (New York: Harry N. Abrams, 1987).

32. See, for example, *ARTnews* cover articles about contemporary women artists, such as "Alice Neel and the Human Comedy," October 1984; "Diversionary (Syn)tactics," about Barbara Kruger, February 1987; and "April Gornik's Stormy Weather," May 1989.

33. Robert Farris Thompson, "From the First to the Final Thunder: African-American Quilts, Monuments of Cultural Assertion," in Leon, Eli, *Who'd A Thought It: Improvisation in African-American Quiltmaking* (San Francisco: San Francisco Craft & Folk Art Museum, 1988), pp. 12, 17.

34. Heinrich Wölfflin, *Principles of Art History [1915, Germany]*, 7th ed., trans. M. D. Hottinger (New York: Dover, 1950), p. 1.

35. Eugene Kleinbauer, "Art History in Discipline-Based Art Education," in Ralph Smith, ed., *Discipline-Based Art Education* (Urbana: University of Illinois Press, 1989).

36. For two examples of in-depth approaches, see Chapter II in Al Hurwitz and Stanley S. Madeja, *The*

Joyous Vision (New York: Prentice-Hall, 1977), the series by Ernest Goldstein (see Suggested Readings), and on a more advanced level, the *Art in Context* series, ed. John Fleming and Hugh Honour (New York: Viking Press, 1972).

37. An exception to this is Jennifer Pazienza's doctoral dissertation (Pennsylvania State University) which describes an entire program based upon a single painting, Velasquez's *Los Meninas*.

38. Elizabeth Gilmore Holt, *Literary Sources of Art History* (Princeton: Princeton University Press, 1947). See also Margaret Battlin et al., *Puzzles about Art: An Aesthetics Casebook* (New York: St. Martins, 1989).

39. Jane Rye, *Futurism*, (New York: Studio Vista Duttom Pictureback, 1972), p. 9.

40. Heinrich Wölfflin, *Principles of Art History* (New York: Dover Books, 1950).

◆ ACTIVITIES FOR THE READER

1. Review the brief introduction to art history in this chapter. Note that, due to the necessary brevity, there was no mention of many important artists, styles, and periods. Where do each of the following names and terms along in this art historical outline?

Etruscan art	Neel
American impressionism	Hudson River school
	Ash Can school
Aegean art	Hellenistic art
Carolingian art	mannerism
Brunelleschi	Mantegna
El Greco	Goya
Caravaggio	Valesquez
Rubens	Vigee-Lebrun
Morisot	Marin
Bonheur	Rodin
Cole	Frankenthaler

2. Make a list of other important names, styles, and periods that you believe should be included in the brief survey of art history.

3. Consult several art history texts, most of which will include a photograph and discussion of van Eyck's *Giovanni Arnolfini and His Bride*. Compare each interpretation of symbols in the painting. Do all the accounts agree, or do interpretations differ? Which interpretation do you believe is most authoritative (accurate)? What did the historian write to convince you of that interpretation?

4. Select any art style or genre from the history of art, such as Japanese landscape, Pueblo pottery, the sculpture of Rodin, or cubist painting. Analyze the topic you have selected with the goal of developing a teaching unit for children. What would you like for children to know about the topic, the artist(s), major artworks, and cultural influences? Analyze the formal properties of the art. What are the major stylistic characteristics, media, processes for creation, themes? Decide which important points, artists, works, and ideas you would like children to learn about. Decide what classroom learning activities will help children to learn about and experience this art form.

5. Consult several art history textbooks. Using the table of contents of each book, compare the categories that author(s) have used to organize art historical content. How do these outlines differ? How are they the same? Do all of the texts cover the same periods, styles, and artists? Compare the ways several texts or encyclopedias treat the same artist or movement.

6. Choose a topic in non-Western art, such as the architecture of India, or Japanese pottery. Using the library, see how many books are available on the topic. Browse through the books to familiarize yourself with the range and depth of content on this topic.

7. Become an authority on a single painting. (There are at least three books written on Picasso's *Guernica*.)

8. Visit two museums if they are available, and compare the kinds of information that are on artwork labels. Do labels represent a philosophy on the part of the museum regarding the nature and degree of communication between the museum and the public?

9. If there is a museum in your vicinity, visit its bookstore and make a list of the art books you think would be interesting to children. (See Suggested Readings.)

10. Rule-governed art

   A. Art and worship

Create a contemporary icon. Include such traditional requirements as the following:

1. Subject must face front.
2. Subject must be a person deserving of hommage.
3. Background must be painted in gold.
4. Subject must wear appropriate garb.

B. The art of the academy

Pretend you are a student of the Academy des Beaux Arts in the nineteenth century. Your examination project is to paint a landscape that includes the following:

1. A grouping of figures such as fauns, satyrs, wood nymphs, shepherds.
2. A group of buildings in the distance.
3. Groups of trees five times the size of the figures.
4. Foreground, middle ground, background.
5. A shaft of light in the middle ground.

The best way to deal with rule-governed art is to assemble at least three examples of style and ask the class to note the factors they have in common.

◆ SUGGESTED READINGS

Beardsley, John, and Jane Livingston. *Hispanic Art in the United States*. New York: Abbeville Press, 1987.

Deighton, Elizabeth, ed. *Looking into Paintings*. London: Faber and Faber, 1985.

De la Croix, Horst, and Richard Tansey. *Gardner's Art Through the Ages*, 9th ed. San Diego: Harcourt Brace Jovanovich, 1991.

Feldman, Edmund B. *The Artist*. Englewood Cliffs, NJ: Prentice-Hall, 1982.

Fichner-Rathus, Lois. *Understanding Art*, 2nd ed. Prentice-Hall, Englewood Cliffs, NJ: 1988.

Gilbert, Rita, and William McCarter. *Living with Art*, 2nd ed. New York: Alfred A. Knopf, 1989.

Goldstein, Ernest, Robert Saunders, Joe Kowalchuck, and Theodore Katz. *Understanding and Creating Art*. Dallas: Garrard Publishing Company, 1986.

Grubb, Nancy, ed. *Making Their Art: Women Artists Move in the Mainstream, 1970-1985*. New York: Abbeville Press, 1989.

Kinney, Jean and Cle. *Varieties of Ethnic Art*. New York: Atheneum, 1976.

National Museum of African Art. *The Art of West African Kingdoms*. Washington, D.C.: Smithsonian Institution Press, 1987.

Pelfrey, Robert, and Mary Hall-Pelfrey. *Art and Mass Media*. New York: Harper and Row, 1985.

Pierce, James Smith. *From Abacus to Zeus: A Handbook of Art History*. Englewood Cliffs, NJ: Prentice-Hall, 1968.

Pointon, Marcia. *History of Art: A Student's Handbook*, 2nd ed. Allen and Unwin, 1986.

Rodriguez, Susan. *Art Smart*. Englewood Cliffs, NJ: Prentice-Hall, 1988.

Russell, Stella Pandell. *Art in the World*, 3rd ed. Chicago: Holt, Rinehart and Winston, 1989.

Ventura, Piero. *Great Painters*. New York: G. Putnam and Sons, 1984.

Wilkins, David, and Bernard Schultz. *Art Past, Art Present*. New York: Harry N. Abrams, 1990.

Woodford, Susan. *Looking at Pictures*. Cambridge: Cambridge University Press, 1983.

Art History Books for Children and Preadolescents

Brown, Osa. *The Metropolitan Museum of Art Activity Book*. New York: Metropolitan Museum of Art, 1983.

Goldstein, Ernest. *Washington Crossing the Delaware*, from the series *Let's Get Lost in Painting*. Champaign, IL: Garrard Publishing Company, 1983.

Glubok, Shirley. *Art of Lands in the Bible*. New York: Atheneum, 1963.

Proddow, Penelope. *Art Tells a Story: Greek and Roman Myths*. Garden City, NY: Doubleday and Company, 1979.

Roboff, Ernest. *Art for Children*. New York: Doubleday and Company, n.d.

Strika, Susan. *The Anti-Coloring Book* series. New York: Holt, Rinehart and Winston, 1978-1983.

Walking, Christine. *Let's Look at Pictures*. London: Medici Society, Ltd., 1976.

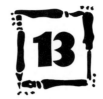

AESTHETICS: PHILOSOPHY IN THE ART ROOM

I DID NOT intend to become a doctor of philosophy by studying philosophy . . . nor did I, by any means, intend originally to qualify for a professorship by a dissertation on philosophy. To decide to become a philosopher seemed as foolish to me as to decide to become a poet. Since my school days, however, I was guided by philosophical questions.

Karl Jaspers[1]

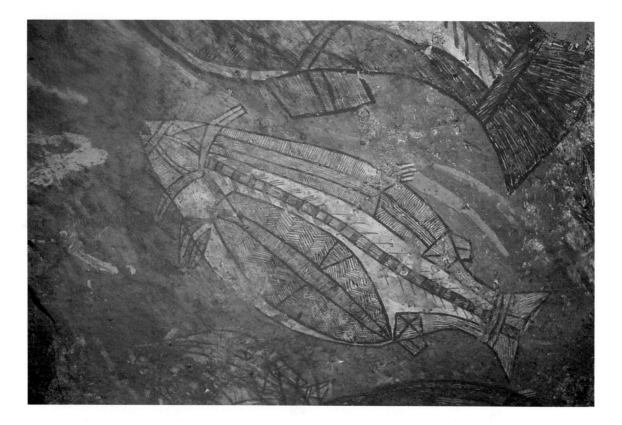

Aesthetics, that branch of philosophy which deals with basic questions surrounding art, is the newest area of interest to those wishing to broaden the base of their art program. Some art teachers question this contemplative study in a traditionally activity-centered subject. Others claim, however, that to attain a fuller understanding of art, one must appreciate the works that artists (and students) create in a broader context. This may require attention to questions about ways an artwork relates to a style, a political issue, or a particular view of what constitutes beauty.

Aesthetics is also a body of writing by philosophers that poses such recurring questions as, ''What is a work of art?'' and ''How does it differ from other objects?'' ''What purposes does art serve?'' ''Can art be judged, and if so, how?'' ''What responsibility does the artist have to society?'' ''Can *nature* be art?'' ''What makes an experience aesthetic?'' ''Can a mass-produced object be a work of art?'' ''How do institutional settings such as museums, galleries, and art magazines define art?'' ''What is the relation between emotion and aesthetic experience?'' ''Why are some artworks labeled masterpieces?'' These questions are not uncommon, even among children who, during an art museum visit, might ask, "Who decides what to put in the museum?" "Is everything in this museum art?" "Why is that chair art?" "Is it better than the chairs at school or at home?" "Why?" Such questions are inevitable from lively children in a stimulating environment and they require thoughtful responses from teachers at levels appropriate for children's capacities of comprehension.

An effective introduction to aesthetics is an essay by the Russian novelist Leo Tolstoy, the title of which poses the most basic question of all, *What Is Art?*[2] In the following section, Tolstoy states his position on the nature of art as suggested by its function.

> Artists who produce art will not be as now, only those rare people, selected from a small part of the whole nation, from the rich classes or those close to them, but all those gifted people of the whole nation, who show themselves able and willing for artistic activities.
>
> Artistic activity will then be accessible to the whole people. And this activity will be accessible to individuals from the whole people, because, in the first place, in the art of the future not only will there be no demand for that complex technical skill which disfigures the art of our times, and demands intense effort and great expenditure of time, but on the contrary there will be a demand for clearness, simplicity and brevity, conditions which are gained not by mechanical effort, but by education of taste. In the second place, artistic activity will become accessible to the whole people, because instead of the present professional schools, accessible only to the few, every one in the preparatory national schools will learn music and painting (singing and drawing) on equal terms with reading, so that every one receiving the first foundations of painting and musical knowledge, and feeling an ability and calling for any of the arts, may be able to perfect himself in it.[3]

It is interesting that Tolstoy, in his discourse about the nature of art, deems it important to discuss art education, which he places at the center of the school curriculum. He continues:

> So completely different from what is now considered art, both in substance and form, will the art of the future be. The subject matter of the art of the future will be only feelings drawing people to unity, or really uniting them; another form of art will be such as to be accessible to everybody. And therefore the ideal of perfection of the future will not be exclusiveness of feeling, accessible only to some, but on the contrary, its universality. And not crowdedness, obscurity, and complexity of form, as it is now held to be, but on the contrary, brevity, clearness, and simplicity of expression. And only when art is like this will it no longer merely amuse and corrupt people, as it does now, demanding the expenditure of their best forces on this, but it will be what it ought to be, an instrument for the transfer of the Christian religious consciousness from the region of intellect and reason to the region of feeling, thus bringing people in reality, in life itself, to that perfection and unity which the religious consciousness points out to them.[4]

If the reader felt intimidated by the thought of dealing directly with aesthetic source material, he or she was doubtless relieved to discover that a philosopher can present a case with simplicity and clarity. Although Tolstoy's views are now considered passé, he poses questions that are still worth pondering. There are enough issues in this brief statement alone to fill a year's agenda of discussion. For example, when Tolstoy says that art should be *accessible* to all, does he mean *available* to all people or *understandable* to all, and if he means understandable to everyone, does this mean that the viewer has no obligation to bring anything to the viewing experience other than an intuitive, spontaneous reaction? If this is true, then is there any point in acquiring a knowledge base for the art that one is likely to encounter in a museum or art gallery? If popular art forms used in advertisements, illustrations, and other sorts of graphic design are understood more readily than a work by Picasso or other fine artists, does that mean that popular art is best? At what point does fine art or high art cease to become serious and turn commercial? Are serious artists, whose works are appreciated by very few, fulfilling their role to society, and does an artist have an obligation to the community in which he or she lives? The Mexican muralists certainly believed the latter. Others, however, feel an artist's sole obligation is to him/herself.

Aesthetics can be described as a question-centered subject where we delve beneath the surface of long-held assumptions. Aesthetics asks us to withhold opinions as the search for answers goes on; where the process of probing is as valuable as the conclusions reached. In this respect, aesthetics questioning is similar to the critical process which asks us to defer judgment of an artwork until we have studied the evidence. As the common phrase puts it, "When the answers are all in, the philosophers get going."

As a subject for study, aesthetics is a noun.[5] When it is used as an adjective—as in *aesthetic education*—it is used to qualify or describe something else. Thus, *aesthetic response* refers to the nature of our reactions to art, and *aesthetic education* to a multi-art curriculum. When aesthetics is seen as a way of uncovering the essence of a problem through discussion and questioning, it is referred to as *aesthetic inquiry*.[6] Aesthetic inquiry in turn may follow a systematic, logical structure known as the *Socratic method*, or it may be more in the nature of a freewheeling discussion.[7]

In this chapter we discuss several traditional, but persistent issues centered on the relationships between art and beauty, art and nature, and art and knowledge. As we will see, each of these larger issues relates to numerous more specific, sometimes even practical questions.

Next, we present three well-established theories of art or *aesthetic stances* that we use as the foundation for making judgments of value and quality with respect to art. These stances, known as mimesis, expressionism, and formalism, provide us with insights for judging art and for understanding how others value art.

Then we move on to discuss some of the questions and issues having to do with art and society, art and money, art and censorship, forgery of art, and other social and political aspects of art. Through this discussion we reiterate that aesthetics questions are not merely esoteric exercises, but are raised in everyday life and are often both urgent and controversial. They are almost always complicated, requiring the type of reasoned thought and communication that the discipline of aesthetics is known to employ.

Finally we present suggestions for integrating aesthetics into art teaching in ways that are interesting for students and teachers alike. Several cases or "puzzles" about art are provided and discussed along with suggested resources and instructional methods of practical use for teachers.

AESTHETICS AND THEORIES ABOUT ART

When aestheticians, critics, artists, and historians attempt to account for the purposes that art serves, how art is judged, how it is received and so on, they create theories — carefully reasoned arguments in support of a particular point of view. Since this book is neither an anthology of theoretical writings or a textbook solely on aesthetics, the following section will only review those theories about art that hold promise for the classroom. Some of these ideas have held the attention of writers since classical times; others could have arisen only in the twentieth century. We will begin by examining one question in depth — What do we mean by the word "beautiful?"

Art and Beauty   When aesthetics first appeared as a separate area of study by Alexander Baumgarten in the middle of the eighteenth century, generations of philosophers had already pondered the concept of the beautiful. The view that art in general must be identified with concepts of beauty has little relevance to aestheticians and artists today.

In ancient Greece, the chief aim of art was the portrayal of an ideal of humanity, one that gave great emphasis to physical beauty. The Byzantine ideal, on the other hand, was the representation of the divine rather than the human; the tribal ideal was the control of awesome forces through powerful images; and the Oriental ideal was the expression of abstract metaphysical concepts. It would be difficult to bring beauty into the service of all the artistic expressions of these concepts of the ideal.

Despite the fact that many Western artists have relied on beauty as a basis for expression, it is merely one of many possible approaches. Goya, for example, found inspiration in the *lack* of beauty, in the horrors of war; Daumier found themes for expression in political revolution; Toulouse-Lautrec, in the degradation of the body and soul. Art, in fact, embraces all of life, not only that small segment of it that may be considered ideally beautiful.

Beauty, to the uninitiated in art, is most often identified with execution as well as subject matter. Thus, in the world of the art academies of the nineteenth century, nobility and virtue were associated with technical virtuosity; later, high-blown sentiment was associated with "realistic" rendering, particularly in Victorian times.

So powerful is the Greek-Roman-Renaissance influence on Western civilization that even today the concept of ideal beauty as a primary concern of art still exerts a major influence on professional art and, hence, on art education in the schools. Nevertheless, to impose such a limiting concept on children, as some teachers have done, is to deny them the opportunity of exploring the rich variety of themes that artistic expression traditionally includes.

Beauty is a good place to begin a discussion on aesthetics if only because of the implications that the idea of the beautiful possesses for the arousal of pleasure. The fact that other interests have superseded the issue of beauty and that it has undergone revision in no way invalidates our interest in the ideal of the beautiful, usually defined as something possessing characteristics with the capacity to excite and stimulate pleasure in the viewer. There are two traditional points of view regarding the nature of the phenomena of pleasure engendered by beauty.

A *relativist* position states that conceptions of the beautiful will vary from person to person for any number of reasons, the major one residing in the nature of the respondents—their shared values and their make up as individuals within a culture. This may explain why critics, however knowledgeable, are still conditioned by their own time and have often failed to appreciate art forms which were in advance of existing styles. The *relativist* view of beauty respects the varieties and shifts of tastes during one's own lifetime regarding a particular work and takes into account the influence of one's culture. Beauty, then, exists not so much in the object as in the beholder.

Does this mean that no standards exist in attempting to determine the conditions of a work of beauty? Not at all, say the *objectivists*, whose roots lie in classical Greek thought. Writers such as Alberti, the Renaissance scholar, have regarded beauty in terms of canons or standards of perfectibility, using criteria such as connectedness and harmonious treatment of principles of design such as rhythm, color, hue, and balance. Beauty, they say, is *in* the artwork and is available to the perceptions of the beholder. In our time, greater attention is paid to the *content* of the work—that is, the *ideas* that forms convey—than to the forms themselves. Children will have very limited comprehension of what objective standards of beauty mean unless they can be shown specific examples. Six and seven year olds, for example, can learn to identify balance, line, and contrast, but have greater difficulties with rhythm, tension, and harmony, which are more advanced attributes. Children are also very quick to make judgments based upon personal associations and are likely to think that a poor rendering of ice cream is more beautiful than a still life containing a dead fish that may be more beautifully rendered.

When a teacher reads a dictionary definition after a class discussion, children will quickly see how limited is the authority of books. Consider the following, taken from the American Heritage Dictionary. ''Beauty: a pleasing quality associated with harmony of form or color.''[8] Such a definition does well by the impressionist painter, but falls short when applied to Goya's *Disasters of War*, a series of etchings which consciously avoid grace and charm, while at the same time gratifying our aesthetic sense. If we accept ''gratify'' as the key condition, then we can be moved by both the sensuousness of a Renoir portrait or the human testimony in a pair of worker's shoes by Van Gogh—far from beautiful in the traditional objectivist sense, but highly gratifying from another point of view.[9]

Teaching for the Issue of Beauty

The following is an edited transcript of a lesson unit on beauty taught by an art teacher to a class of fifth grade students.[10] In this case, a slide of a painting was shown as a reference point during the discussion. The following section is limited to the *interpretative* phase of the critical process. Domenico Ghirlandaio's *Portrait of an Old Man with a Young Boy* was selected as the focal point for an introduction to the relativist point of view toward beauty.

TEACHER: This picture was painted about the time that Columbus discovered America. Let's just take a few moments to look at it. Before you tell me what you *think* of it, see if you can tell me what's happening. Suppose you had to describe the subject to someone who couldn't see—what would you say?

MARK: It's a picture of a boy looking at his father—or grandfather.

TEACHER: That's right! As you read the title you know that this is an Italian man and his grandson. I think the artist is pretty clear about how the man feels about the boy. What do you think?

SARAH: I think he loves him. He is looking at the boy and holding him on his lap.

TEACHER: And how does the boy feel about his grandfather?

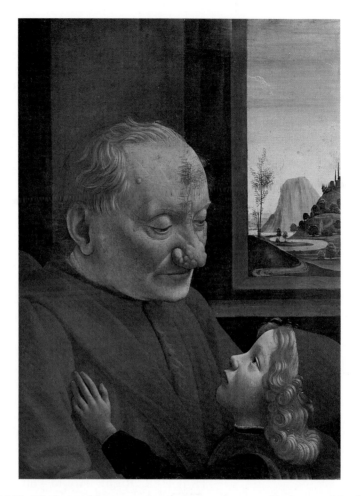

Domenico Ghirlandaio, *Portrait of an Old Man with a Young Boy*, 1480. The subject matter of this painting is so powerful that it is difficult to maintain aesthetic distance. When we learn that the man is the boy's grandfather, the poignancy of the work increases. (Louvre, Paris.)

SARAH: He loves him too—he is facing the grandfather and he has his arm on his shoulder.

TEACHER: Do you all agree to this? (Murmurs of assent.) We began with a description of the painting and now we're talking about the relationship between the two. We could also talk about their clothes and about the scene behind them, or, a doctor might be interested in the medical term for the man's nose—but that's not really what the painting is about. What is it really about? What? (Silence.) Come on—you already said it, Sarah.

SARAH: Love.

TEACHER: Of course; it's about love. Love between young and old, between family members. What other kinds of love are there?

PAUL: My dog loves me—

TEACHER: Right—animals—what else?

SUE: My mother loves to walk.

TEACHER: We can also love things, as well as people, although I think "like" is probably a better word. Love is a stronger word and since people are the most important, I use "love" for people. You know you haven't mentioned one very important part of this painting. (Silence.) I know you can see it—do you feel uncomfortable talking about it?

LORI: His nose—

TEACHER: What about his nose?

LORI: It's gross.

TEACHER: Any other way to describe it?

PAUL: It's ugly—it looks like a cartoon. It's like it has bumps and pimples . . .

TEACHER: Of course today someone with a nose like that could go to a doctor—a plastic surgeon and have it fixed. Tell me, could you love someone with a nose like that? (General discussion—pro and con.)

LORI: I couldn't look at it . . .

TEACHER: Let's suppose someone saved your life, was very generous to you, loved you very much, suppose it was someone you loved *now*, would it make that much difference?

MARK: If it was my father or mother, it would be different. I wouldn't marry someone like that . . .

TEACHER: The nose would still be ugly, but that wouldn't make your parent ugly as a person—do you see the difference? Let's look at it from an opposite direction, can you think of someone who is nice looking on the outside, but ugly on the inside?

SUE: The woman on *Dynasty*—Alexis, the mean one.

LORI: Joan Collins—

TEACHER: Right. Would you agree that there are two kinds of beauty, the beauty we see, and . . . come on . . . you know.

MARK: What's inside. What a person is really like.

TEACHER: There's an old saying—"All that glitters is not gold." There's another saying—"What you see is what you get."—true? Not true? You're right about Joan Collins—that is, the character she plays. Remember, she's an actress; she isn't really that way. She glitters, all right, but don't let that fool you. How does this discussion relate to art? Why do you suppose the artist painted this man?

ALLISON: Maybe the man paid him to paint the picture. Maybe he did it for the money.

TEACHER: Yes, that's very likely, as we have discussed earlier. When the artist saw the man's nose, what do you suppose he thought? That he was being asked to paint an ugly picture?

JUAN: He might not have liked that. But the picture didn't turn out ugly anyway, so it doesn't matter.

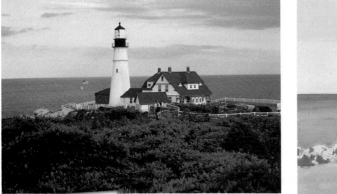

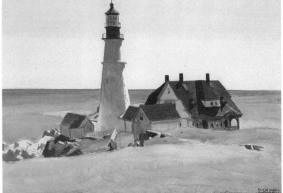

Edward Hopper, *Lighthouse and Building*, Portland Head, Cape Elizabeth, Maine, 1972. Comparing the photograph showing the source of the artist's subject to the watercolor itself, one can see how the artist transformed nature. (Bequest of John T. Spaulding. Courtesy, Museum of Fine Arts, Boston.)

ALLISON: I think the artist might not have liked the nose, but he could see how the man and boy loved each other, so he painted that.
TEACHER: And what does all this tell us about art and beauty?

From this point the class discussed art and beauty and, with guidance from the teacher, viewed artworks from other cultures and compared different conceptions of beauty expressed by the works.

This discussion took about ten minutes of class time. It included writing Ghirlandaio's name on the board and learning how to pronounce it. The teacher also pointed out that it was painted in oils on a wooden panel, and in reply to one question gave the value of around a million dollars. It was also mentioned that the painting was commissioned, that is, painted and paid for by the subject, Sr. Fasettei, "the man with the nose," as the student thereafter referred to him.

Art and Nature: Differences, Similarities, and Fallacies

The language of art can be applied to natural as well as created forms; indeed, the best way to alert children to line, texture, colors, etc. is to begin with parallel references between art and the natural world:

- Lines exist in naked branches seen against the sky as well as in drawings.
- Varieties of green can be discerned in spring foliage as well as in a woodland scene by Neil Welliver.
- Contrast exists between foliage set against white buildings as well as in the paintings of Georgia O'Keeffe.
- Broad rhythms can be seen in the overlapping of mountain ranges and patterns in freshly ploughed fields.

When artists rely upon these to reinforce their subjects, as in a Grant Wood landscape, the connections are easiest to make. The same elements, however, also exist in purely abstract works. If we are moved by and derive pleasure from the existence of design in both art and nature, then why make an aesthetic distinction between the two? Isn't a real lighthouse as significant as one by Edward Hopper? If Hopper has added nothing to the subject of lighthouses, then the answer is yes, but since Hopper goes beyond natural phenomena by endowing it with the stamp of his personal vision, then the difference between the artist's eye and the subject of the artist's attention (the lighthouse) is so critical that comparing one with the other is like using apples as a standard for judging an orange. See if you can discover such an aesthetic fallacy in the following lines from Joyce Kilmer's famous poem "Trees":

> I think that I shall never see
> A poem as lovely as a tree . . .
> Poems are made by fools like me
> But only God can make a tree.[11]

Art and Knowledge: How Much Does One Need to Know?

Study Sandro Botticelli's *Primavera*. Without taking the time to describe or analyze its structure, think about your intuitive response to it. If you are like most people, your reactions will be positive; this is one of the most reproduced, hence most popular, images of Western European art. As one writer states:

> Its complete meaning is as elusive as the remote and wistful elegance of the almost transcendental scene which Botticelli sets before our eyes. This is a picture with layers of meaning, layers that shimmer like the diaphanous veils of its dancing figures.[12]

In this bit of evocative description, the writer has already taken a stand on the relative importance of knowledge and appreciation. In order to sense "wistful elegance" and shimmering "diaphanous veils" we do not need knowledge, but if we are to probe the painting's layers of meaning we are going to need some historical facts that have little or no relation to the realm of intuition. Here are just a few to consider:

- Sandro Botticelli represents a late rather than early Renaissance style of painting. His teachers were Fra Filippo Lippi and the painter-sculptor Andrea Verocchio. The painting is executed on wood, rather than canvas, and bears no signature or title.
- Over forty different plants can be identified in the painting, all of which have a reason for their placement.
- The setting is in a sacred grove, known to everyone who is familiar with Dante's *Divine Comedy* as the boundary between heaven and purgatory.
- Each figure in the painting has its own identity. They are known by their attributes or objects with which they are associated: Cupid with his bow, the myrtle bush with its aphrodisiacal powers with

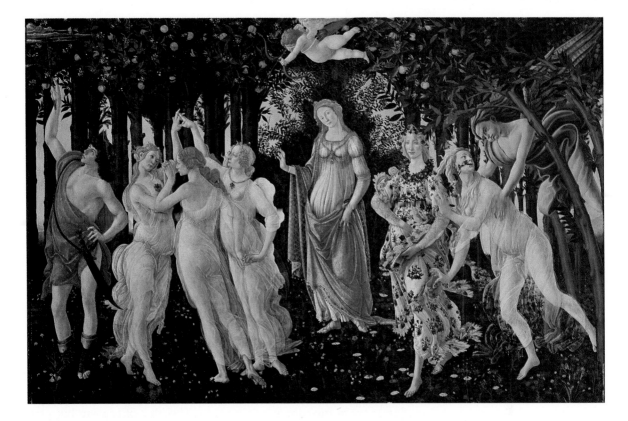

Sandro Botticelli, *Primavera*, 1477. This painting serves to show that a viewer can have both an intuitive as well as knowledge-based appreciation of an artwork, both of which are unique and valid reactions to viewing the painting. (Galleria degli Uffizi, Florence.)

Venus, Mercury with winged heels, and so on. There is less agreement on the meaning of the main figures. Some say one group represents chastity, beauty, and love; others see them as splendor, youth, and happiness.

◆ The *Primavera* also possesses a clear musical analogy to many. The concept of harmony in human affairs is embodied in the mathematical basis of the use of intervals and in the ratios of smaller to larger units of harmonic relationships. "The figures string out across the painting like the notes of an octave. Mercury and Zephyr are the tonic notes. All those in harmony with them face the same way while the discords, the second and seventh notes turn the other way."[13]

The writers from whom this brief listing of facts were taken spent a year in Florence studying five paintings, among them the *Primavera*. This dedication to deciphering the layers of a work is what distinguishes historians from aestheticians. The aesthetic question which is posed by the work of historians is "How much must one know in order to fully appreciate a work of art? Has the knowledge gained by reading about the *Primavera* in any way affected your relation to it, and if so, how?" Of the thousands of visitors who yearly come to the Uffizi to see the *Primavera*, many seek information about the work and the artist, and others do not feel they need anything beyond what they bring to the work.

A work of art, as demonstrated by the *Primavera*, can reach us on several levels. The first level is accessible to anyone with an open eye and mind, but to reach succeeding levels or layers of appreciation, we may have to call upon the insights of art historians, general historians, or anyone who can shed light upon the work from the perspective of their disciplines.

THREE AESTHETIC STANCES: MIMESIS, EXPRESSIONISM, AND FORMALISM

Mimesis: Art as Imitation or Representation of Things as Seen

Must art match what we see? Plato argues that it didn't matter how skillful artists were in portraying the physical world, they could never render the true reality — the essence of objects. Artists were therefore imitators or mimics and because of this, were inherently inferior to poets and musicians. In the beginnings of Western art, people admired the skill that it took to create visual equivalents of the world they knew. The notion of art as imitation or representation of life becomes more complicated as one studies it and discovers related movements and theories, such as the realism of Courbet in his reaction against neoclassic art in the nineteenth century. The idea of realism has also taken the form of *social realism*, which dealt with particular social-consciousness subject matter (the working class); *naturalism*, which overlapped into literature; and *trompe l'oeil* painting, where meticulous handling of detail could deceive the eye. Techniques for imitating nature range from the *illusionistic* devices in perspective developed in the Renaissance and used by both scene designers and painters, to the contemporary photorealists' reliance on photographic veracity. Behind all variations of "art as imitation" lies the assumption that art is most meaningful when it can provide some sort of match between the personal experience of the viewer and the work of the artists. As in all aesthetic theories, the question that inevitably arises is, "Is that all there is to art, and if not, what are the alternatives?"

The major alternative approach to the imitation or *mimesis* theory is the expressionist view.

Art as Expression: Emphasis upon Feeling and Emotion

The idea that expression can be considered as a major function of art creates a distinction between what we *feel* about something and what we *know* about it. Tolstoy believed that the expressive power of art reached its highest form only when an artwork could successfully communicate its meaning to the *viewer*. The emotive power of art was one of the main ideas behind the movement of *expressionism* which began in Germany during the early decades of the twentieth century. The term has since been applied to any movement or artist whose work puts a high priority upon feeling and emotion and has also come to be associated with the formal *means* used by the artist to achieve it, such as spontaneity of execution, heavily applied paint, the use of accidents and, as in the cases of Van Gogh and Jackson Pollack, even to certain kinds of brushes and implements for applying paint. The key element is transmission of feeling—the assumption that to be effective, the viewer must receive the feelings of the artists. As Tolstoy described it, "Art is a human activity that one man consciously . . . hands on to others . . . feelings he has lived through so that other people are infected by them and also experience them."[14] This is also related to *empathy*, which we will discuss later.

It is of course possible to transmit deep feeling and emotional conviction *without* stressing the formal aspects listed above; indeed, realists such as Winslow Homer also direct our emotions through subject matter as well as specific painting techniques. Picasso's *Guernica* is an example of how abstraction treated with a minimal use of color and surface manipulation can also arouse our feelings. Regardless of where one throws one's allegiance, arousing and conveying emotion in the spectator must be taken as a universal condition of the expressive function of art. The current worldwide neoexpressionist movement in art demonstrates again the relevance of this aesthetic stance.

Formalism: The Importance of Structure

Formalist aesthetics asserts that the value of an artwork lies not in its relation to real life or to subject matter—as in a landscape or portrait—but in its use of color, space, rhythm, harmony, and so on. To ask of any artwork that it remind the viewer of something in his/her life rather than the work itself, say the formalists, is to place a limitation on the work. A love of nature, for example, can only partially prepare us to appreciate a Chinese landscape, a Tiffany scene in stained glass, or an Inuit carving. We must be able to respond to the sensory and formal properties of art as well as to subject matter. The critics who developed the formalist theory thought that a picture representing a subject in a recognizable way is essentially an arrangement of colors and forms and must be judged on this basis.

The formalist artist or critic looks for unity and internal consistency in artworks. Whether the object is a painting, pot, or chair, all parts must relate in a unified way to every other part. In terms of balance, emphasis, and variation, to mention only a few principles, the art object must express the artist's intelligent decisions. When a work is lacking in some aspect, the informed viewer or critic can point to the

Which of these was painted by an African-American artist? The answer: all three were painted by William H. Johnson, demonstrating that Western artists who are not folk or naive artists undergo periods of change as new problems are presented. The academic *Still Life* was painted in 1921, the expressionist *Young Pastry Cook*, inspired by Chaim Soutine, in 1927, and *Swing Low Sweet Chariot* in 1939.

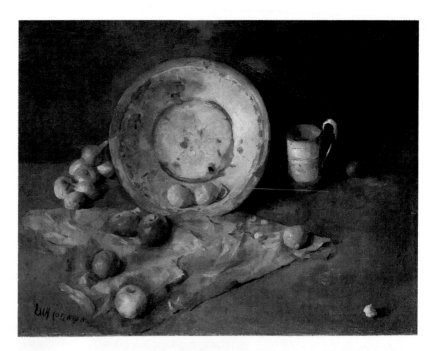

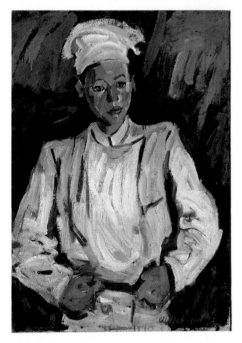

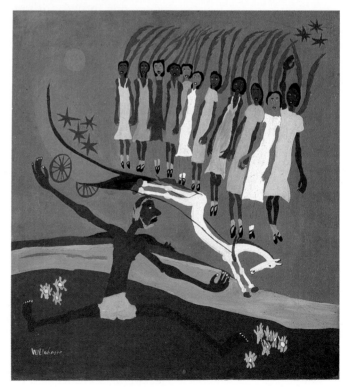

weakness because it is apparent in its lack of consistency with the expression of the complete work. The notion of craftsmanship, artistic skill, or competency in technique is often included within the formalistic viewpoint. The formalist keeps his/her eye on this arrangement, while the expressionist is interested in the feelings or emotions the artist wants to convey through that order.

The Intentional Fallacy

The fallacy of artistic intention is interesting because of the sharp division it has created among critics, philosophers, and artists. Everyone seems to agree that any artist has some purpose in mind when beginning a work, but from this limited consensus point on, opinions diverge. The intentionalist critics say that if the goal of the artist is not taken into consideration, we may be looking for the wrong things or expecting more than the artist can deliver.

Others argue that we must deal only with what we see since the artist might not be around to question and even if he or she were present, artists are not always articulate with respect to their work. The fallacy lies in the belief that it is necessary to know the artist's intention before we can appreciate his/her work. As an example, although cultural differences may stand in the way of completely understanding some art forms, we can still appreciate and enjoy Haida masks or totem poles without knowing the artists' original intentions. When an intentionalist points to an artist such as Jackson Pollack, whose decision to rely on accidents precludes a clear intention, the opposing side will say that when Pollack decided *not* to plan ahead, that decision in itself is a statement of intent. Both sides would have to admit that in most cases, there is always some element of surprise or discovery even when the artist's intentions are formulated in advance. Artists will often comment upon the things that people see in their work which have little to do with what they had in mind. Tom Stoppard, the British playwright, likens it to going to a foreign country. The customs officer asks you to describe what you have in your suitcase and you list such items as clothing, toilet articles, and books, but the customs officer upon investigating says, "That's odd, I don't see any clothing. I see candy, stuffed animals, and jewelry." The more poetic, personal, or imaginative a style of criticism, the less attention will be paid to the original intent of the artists. When children role play the critic, they should be aware of these two approaches: interpretation that is derived from the goals of the artist; and interpretation that inspires imaginative or purely literary responses.

Some artists are offended when asked to explain the meaning of their work. They take the position that if they could explain the meaning there would be no reason to create the artwork; that the work must speak for itself. Other artists are not articulate and have no interest in

Which of these were painted by women artists? The answer: all four of them. This poses a question — Is there a feminine aesthetic, and if so, how is it expressed? Through subject matter, as in mother and child themes; through a particular medium, such as quilts or fabric sculpture? If there are recognizable factors which exist apart from media and content, what are they? These same questions can be applied to the aesthetics of any group, racial, ethnic, religious, cultural, etc. On this page, these works are: Pat Renick, *Life Boats: Boat about Life*; Grace Hartigan, *Shinnecock Canal*, 1957 (Museum of Modern Art, New York. Gift of James Thrall Soby); next page, Niki de Saint Phalle, *Yellow Peril*, (Collection Robert and Jane Meyerhoff); Lee Bontecou, *Untitled*, 1961 (Collection of Whitney Museum of American Art, New York).

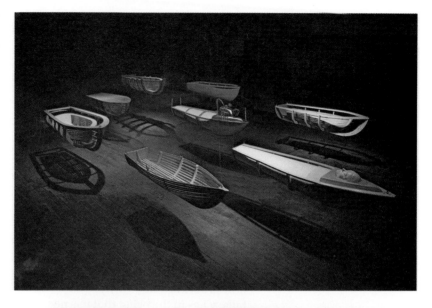

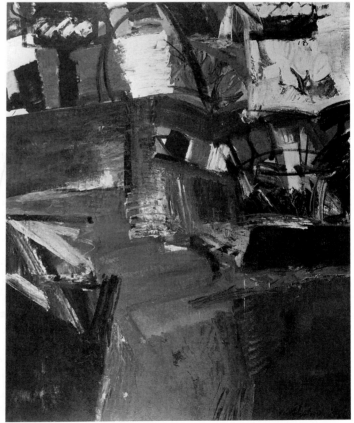

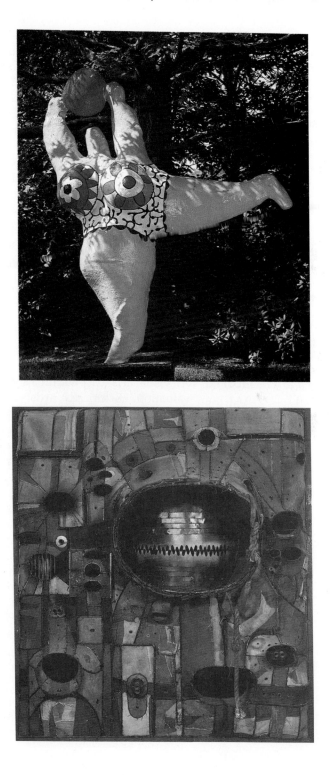

speaking and writing about their art or the work of other artists. They feel that they should not be burdened with interpreting their own work. Probably all artists are, to some extent at least, culture-bound, in that they are unable to detach themselves from the influences and conventions of the society in which they live. The idea that only the artist can provide the real meaning of a work of art is, basically, impractical for these reasons and because most artists are no longer living and able to answer our questions.

Art critics are the professionals that have the greatest responsibility to explain, interpret, and assess works of art. This is not to suggest that the written or spoken ideas of artists about their own work, their motivations and influences, or their personal lives is of no worth. Art historians spend much time and effort searching for such material from artists of the past, and good critics are sensitive to the entire body of work of contemporary artists. Intentionalists and non-intentionalists differ primarily in the emphasis each places on artists' interpretations of their own work.

ART AND SOCIETY

Art and Material Values

All visual arts exist within a social setting that includes an economy of valuation. Historically, artists have been supported by political rulers, church leaders, wealthy gentry, and business leaders. Much of our legacy of great art was created by artists who were entirely supported or commissioned by one of these powerful groups. Unless they are independently wealthy or supported by family money, many artists today are individual entrepreneurs who make their living from selling their work. Commercial artists, designers of all types, architects, and others work within the business community and are paid for their creative production. A large number of artists support themselves by teaching art to others, a noble tradition that goes back many centuries. The relationships between art and material values are many and complex, including the amounts of money that artists receive for their work.

A week rarely goes by without some transaction involving an enormous sum of money being paid for an artwork. In November 1987, Van Gogh's *Irises* was purchased by an Australian collector for a record $53.9 million. This is for a work by an artist who sold only one painting during his lifetime for a very small sum. The question that immediately comes to mind is, how can any single artwork be worth that much? This same query raised considerable heat some years ago when Australian tax money was expended (only $13 million in this case for Jackson Pollack's *Blue Poles*). People may only shake their heads in disbelief when a private party spends his or her own money, but will become vociferous in their objections when public funds are involved. In any case, we cannot deal with the question of dollar value without considering the value of an artwork as a unique, one-of-a-kind phenomenon for which there can be no exact counterpart. Questions that often arise are, "How does one arrive at the monetary value of a work of art?" "Who sets the standard, what are the criteria and how do we go about getting such information?" A question for students could be, "What could you do with $53 million to support art in your community?" One might discover that a whole museum could be built for that sum; another, a community art center; and another may discover that six minor Van Gogh's can be purchased for this same price. Whatever the solution, it will require some research on the part of students demonstrating differing philosophies. Dealing with implications of a news item leads us to the bridge that connects theory and speculation to the real world of tomorrow's headlines.

Aesthetics: Politics and Real Life

Aesthetic problems posed by *headline aesthetics* (current news items that pose aesthetics questions) may come from any number of traditional concerns, such as the question of beauty or the artist's responsibility to society. We can also call this *practical aesthetics* since it can involve us on a personal level, such as the expenditure of public tax monies. Newspapers and magazines, the main source of "headline aesthetics," also possess an aura of authenticity that is more compelling than any textbook. Following are some typical examples of the controversy that occurs when aesthetic ambiguity meets the American public:

- Richard Serra sues the General Services Administration when it decides to move his sculpture, *Tilted Arc*, to a site other than the one for which it was designed because of public hostility to the work.
- A mural in Aberdeen, Maryland is cut up and reassembled. The artist, William Smith, charges the Marriott Corporation with lowering the monetary value as well as violating the artistic integrity of the painting.
- Sculptor David Smith disowns one of his works whose paint has been stripped away by a collector. The practice continues even after his death and the executors of his estate are involved in litigations.
- A Pittsburgh man changes the color of an Alexander Calder mobile from black to green and gold since these are the county colors.
- An art supervisor is asked by the secretaries' association to take down an exhibition of teachers' work because drawings of nudes are found offensive. This brings us to the most pervasive controversy of all, the problem of censorship.

Censorship and Art: A Problem For Aesthetics

Upper-grade students will have no problem in responding to the following item that appeared in the *Smithsonian* magazine.

> A bitter and still-spreading controversy in the arts was recently precipitated when the Corcoran Gallery of Art in Washington, D.C. canceled its plans to exhibit the photographic works of the late Robert Mapplethorpe. The cancellation of the show — characterized by some as including depictions of sado-masochism, homoeroticism, disturbing images of children and portrayals of sex acts beyond the limits of public tolerance — led to two opposing forms of protest. One was an immediate invitation from the Washington Project for the Arts, less susceptible than the Corcoran to public and offical pressure, to transfer the exhibit to its smaller galleries. The other was the passage by the U.S. Senate of a measure introduced by Senator Jesse Helms, which would prohibit federal funding not only of work of this character but of material denigrating "a person, group or class of citizens on the basis of race, creed, sex, handicap, age or national origin.[15]

Censorship of art by persons with questionable art expertise, exemplified by this incident, is certainly not new to art educators, particularly to supervisors whose job it is to schedule exhibits of various kinds in public places.

Is the aesthetic issue at stake here the freedom of the artist? Censorship is as much a problem today as it was to Plato, who recommended censoring poets (and doubtless artists as well) because of the potential conflict between artistic freedom and the good of society. Some typical questions which emerge from the Mapplethorpe controversy are as follows:

- How legitimate are the measures introduced by Senator Helms? If justified, should the director of the Corcoran have deleted questionable photographs? Would this have been an "honorable" compromise?
- Is the issue one of spending public funds on art, or is it an issue of art judgments being made by persons not qualified as art critics? Should politicians, with the dual responsibilities to promote and support the arts and to spend public monies wisely, have the option to judge the quality and significance of the art they support? Can politicians perform the functions of art critics, or should they commission professional critics to make such decisions?
- What problems arise when politicians or other bureaucrats take upon themselves the function of judging the quality and significance of art? Is this practice consistent with the freedom of speech guaranteed in the Constitution of the United States? Are there historical precedents for this practice? What can we learn from these precedents?
- When works of art supported by public funds are vulgar, disrespectful of some group or institution, or beyond standards of decency held by most people, do public officials have an obligation to display those works? Are standards of community morality and decency

separate from standards of artistic quality? If they are separate, which standards take precedence in the Mapplethorpe case? Should the photographs continue to be displayed because of their artistic excellence attested to by knowledgeable art professionals, or should the photographs be removed because they offend a large number of viewers, including politicians?

As with many problems in life, there are no easy answers to these aesthetic issues. It seems that each question raises even more questions. Nevertheless, these are real issues that must be resolved in real life, one way or the other. In some ways the study of aesthetics is one of the most useful things that we can ask students to do, because it gives them valuable experience in thinking carefully and logically about very "messy" real-life problems and learning to evaluate different points of view, each of which might have some merit. Yet, they are not exposed to any risk in discussing problems about art. Following are some additional cases related to censorship of art.

Other Examples of The Censorship Issue.

- Cartoonists in Nazi Germany depicted Jews as gross and evil, and in World War I allied artists treated Germans in their posters in similarly unflattering ways. These are examples of art as propaganda and are considered acceptable, indeed patriotic, in times of war. Should the license to demean people in a racist or other hostile way be suspended after peace has been declared? Are there boundaries to artistic freedom? And finally, there is a legal constitutional issue here — how close does artistic freedom lie to the controversy caused by American Nazi or KKK groups who wish to parade on national holidays?
- If you examine the surface of the Washington monument, you will see that the color of the stone changes around a quarter of the way up. This is because some people were so enraged by its design that they dumped hundreds of slabs of stone into the Potomac River. The monument was completed some 40 years later when the furor subsided, but by then, it was impossible to match the original colors of the stone.
- In 1988 in San Diego, California, the city council voted down funds for a park that featured a sculpture composed of airplane fragments. Why is it that in Israel airplane fragments and other relics of war are accepted by the public as art while they are divided on the use of abstract sculpture in public spaces?
- In Grand Rapids, Michigan, a public sculpture is proposed to commemorate that city's role in fluoridation. The monument suggested is a 600-pound 18-foot-high molar, and its rejection is led by local dentists. Why?

These examples show how truly important aesthetics can be in practical matters. While it is helpful to have examined a primary source such as Plato's *Republic* or a commentary on Plato's ideas, this is not needed in order to get a good debate going. Censorship is a particularly effective topic to introduce problems of aesthetics because at some point all of us must deal with the conflict between reason and emotion. Iredell Jenkins states:

> It behooves the artistic community to accept the responsibility of exercising discrimination and selectivity in its own house. If it does not do this, then an extraneous censorship is sure to be imposed, which will at once touch off movements towards the two extremes of suppression and license.[16]

Is Jenkins suggesting that self-censorship is to be preferred to that of outsiders?

Aesthetics thus has a way of answering one question by posing another. If you can get students to accept this, then they are exercising that "tolerance of ambiguity" which is one characteristic of the sophisticated mind.

Aesthetics Controversy In Museums

The following example of real-life aesthetics is centered upon the nature of the art object. We'll call this example "The Question of the Missing Nose."

Situation:

> Go into any museum that collects classical art and you will find portrait busts minus their noses. This is understandable since protuberances from any basic form are vulnerable, especially when one considers the hazards of being buried for centuries under debris, dirt, and archaeological fragments.

Problem:

> As a curator of a museum, you have received a classical sculpture of a portrait bust from a donor. There is one condition attached to the gift, however. The donor insists that the missing nose be repaired so that viewers can see it exactly as did the Roman citizen at the beginning of the Christian era. Not all of your staff is overjoyed at the conditions under which the gift is offered. Some flatly reject it on the grounds that no person under any condition has the right to tamper with a work of art and there are others who say, "Why quibble? Don't look a gift horse in the mouth; our collection needs this work."

What does the class think?

This is a good situation for an adversary situation, and lends itself to a formal debate. One could also simulate a courtroom setting where two lawyers argue their case before a jury composed of their classmates. The curator, who has accepted the terms of the gift could also act as the defendant on trial for aesthetic misdemeanors. "The Question of the Broken Nose" has its counterpart in an incident that actually occurred.

A hammer-wielding vandal damaged Michelangelo's *Pietà*, destroying the Madonna's nose, breaking her arm, and chipping her eye and veil. There are several possibilities for restoration, and you, as museum director, must select one:

1. Do nothing to repair the damage other than clear away small amounts of rubble from the base of the statue.

2. Working from photographs and drawings of the *Pietà* made prior to the incident, restore the nose, arm, eye, and veil to their original contours, using a plaster material lighter in color than the original marble so that it is immediately obvious to any viewer which portions have been restored.

3. Using a technique which involves grinding of identical marble (including much of the rubble) to form a resin-bound plaster which will dry to a color and texture indistinguishable from the original, restore the nose and elbow to their original contours. The restoration will be undetectable to visual analysis.

4. Do number 3 above, but incorporate a tracer dye in the marble plaster to permit x-ray identification of the restored portions.[17]

"The Case of the Doubtful Picasso"—The Aesthetics of Forgery.   As one delves into the problems of choice, other questions begin to emerge which in turn lead to other quandaries, such as the relationship of forgeries to authentic art.

> You have recently come into an inheritance and have reached the conclusion that one of the safest ways to hold onto your money and ensure its growth is to invest in art. You decide to begin educating yourself rather than to rely exclusively on the advice of dealers. You begin to do some serious museum-going. You have decided to limit your collecting to European painters between World Wars I and II. You read books, journals, study catalogues, go to auctions, and talk to people who seem to know about art. One day you hear of a Picasso that another collector has to sell in a hurry. Despite the fact that Picasso is not one of your favorites, you go to the owner's home to see the painting, and to your surprise, you like it, and possessing the collector's mixture of greed and love, you buy it. Two years later, it comes to light that your painting may be a forgery. What should your reaction be?

1. Sell it as quickly as you can to another collector.
2. Keep it, because you still love it.
3. Sell it as an example of superb fakery.

What are the pros and cons of each of these solutions? Does the fact that someone else painted it lessen your enjoyment of it? Would you have purchased it if it had been painted by a relatively unknown artist? What is the relation between the intrinsic value of the work and its dollar value?

RIPPING OFF THE NAZIS

The most famous forger of all time was Dutch artist, Han Van Meegeren, who did more than copy, he created new works by old masters such as Vermeer and during World War II sold one of them, *Christ with the Adulteress*, to Nazi Hermann Goering. After the war Van Meegeren's sale was discovered by Dutch officials and he was brought to court. If Van Meegeren's sale to a German official is regarded as a form of collaboration with the enemy during the war, the sentence can be for life and if Meegeren admits he not only painted the work himself but did so as a way of pleasing (and fooling) the enemy, he is liable to only 4 years in prison. Should we feel more kindly toward him because he fooled a Nazi or should our attitude be one of outrage at his having besmirched the reputation of a master?

WAYS OF TEACHING: INQUIRY AND STRUCTURED DISCUSSION

Some form of inquiry lies at the heart of each of the art disciplines, including aesthetics. When any discussion goes beyond informal sharing of opinions, it begins to verge on what is called inquiry—the search for the best answers, through the questioning process. When we interpret art, when we study a work for its meaning by digging beneath the surface of some long-held assumption, we are practicing inquiry. If a student comments that abstract painting is "a put-on" or "I could do this stuff when I was in nursery school," then inquiry is in order. Every teacher of social studies who has heard students make unsupported generalizations about nationalities or ethnic groups knows that in such cases the rational examination of an idea should be encouraged. If inquiry is at the heart of philosophy in general, the ability to withhold opinions as we venture into uncharted waters lies at its heart. Underlying the inquiry process is an assumption that lecturing is the least effective way to discover meaning in art.

When inquiry is structured so that it follows certain accepted rules of logic, it is called a *dialectic* approach, a form of structured conversation. Plato's *Republic* is really a series of such student-teacher dialogues; succeeding philosophers have had their own ideas as to how such dialogues should be conducted.

Immanuel Kant, as an example, thought that the best way to begin is to make a false statement and invite the student to examine it for its logical weakness; for example, "Everyone is an artist" or "Art serves no practical use in society." The German philosopher Hegel believed that any premise or *thesis* will do as long as it is followed by an antithesis or counterargument. Both thesis and antithesis, however, must conclude with a *synthesis* which rejects the limitations of the two previous stages and preserves what is rational in both of them. These are Hegel's *triads* of discussion. Whether or not one wishes to follow an orderly structured approach, or a less structured one, there are some guidelines for discussion to consider. The following suggestions are not necessarily listed in order of importance.

1. Build your lesson around a few key questions that are embodied in the concepts you wish to teach. If you wish to stress the concept for third graders that "Art is man-made, not a creation of nature," show them a photo of a city scene and a painting by Edward Hopper and ask, "Which is the painting, which is the photograph, and what is the difference?" Try to stick to your key question and resist the temptation to go off into side issues in order to maintain your conceptual focus. (This is not always easy with imaginative primary graders.) Although informal brainstorming and free association do have their place, they are not to be confused with the process of inquiry.

2. Try to avoid yes/no questions since these have limited value and do not open further discussion.

3. Rote definitions repeated from text or dictionary can obscure understanding since they give the impression that there is only one correct answer. Since rote answers represent very little struggle on the student's part, they are also the most quickly forgotten.

4. Complex answers take time; obvious ones do not. Obvious answers do serve one purpose, however — they can get things rolling and involve the shy or reluctant participant. No one likes to keep saying, "I don't know."

5. Avoid asking questions that contain their own answers. For example, "Isn't Barbara Hepworth terrific in the way she simplifies natural forms?"

6. Encourage the role of devil's advocate by having students present counterarguments even when they go against their convictions.

7. Don't get carried away by the brilliance of your question. The longer and more involved the query, the quicker the point will be

lost. Be as clear and precise as you can in your questions since the nature of a question often determines the kind of answer you will receive.

8. Wait for the moment when it is the teacher's job to sum up — to clarify. The summation, a form of Hegel's third stage of *syntheses*, sets the stage for what is to follow.

9. Play off one student's answer to another's. ("Do you agree with Susan? No? Why?")

10. Move the discussion around the room instead of concentrating on a few bright lights. Above all, don't neglect those in the back row and never underestimate the role that seating plays. Proximity to windows, to friends, or to the teacher can all impact on attention of students.

11. There is no point in asking a question if you don't take time to listen to the answer.

12. Try the "pair-share" method as part of your inquiry. Divide the class into teams and allow two or three minutes for participants to think about an answer, then have a representative of each group share their answers with the class.

13. Although the truth does not necessarily lie in consensus, try an occasional survey to see what kind of consensus exists. ("How many agree with Bruce? You seem to be in the minority. George, since you don't agree with Bruce can you come up to the picture and identify what you are referring to?")

14. Since inquiry cannot proceed without guidelines, get the class involved in setting down a few rules before you begin. These may range from the general ("Try to be open to a point of view that's different from yours.") to the more specific ("When possible, give some clear evidence, such as pointing to a flaw in an argument to support your statement.")

15. Although aesthetics focuses upon what is said rather than what is seen, the ideas selected for discussion should, whenever possible, relate to artworks. Can you imagine how much would be lost in a discussion of formalist or expressionist philosophies of art without referring to the work of Mondrian or Kokoschka?

16. The general goal of any program of aesthetic inquiry is to develop in students the ability to deal with disagreement and uncertainty; to value ways of viewing a problem that differ from their own.

Never underestimate the desire of children to talk about art, particularly in primary grades. The fact is, the younger the child, the more eagerly discussion will be welcome. Any idea presented as a puzzle, a quandary, or that uses a case history has immediate appeal as a means of provoking discussion.

May Lin, Vietnam Memorial, 1982. What *thesis* and *antithesis* can be developed for a discussion of this memorial? Is it a work of art? What function does it serve for its society? Does it speak to some group within our society more than to others? Develop your own approaches to discussing the role of an artwork within its culture, and outside of it as well. Compare it to the figure below, a nearby monument representing the military in Vietnam.

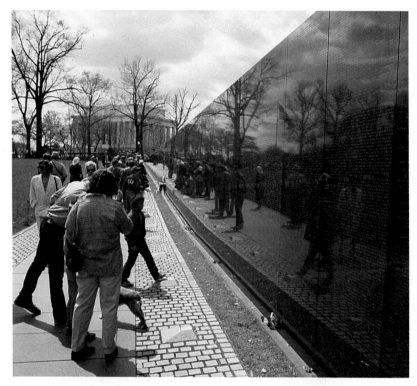

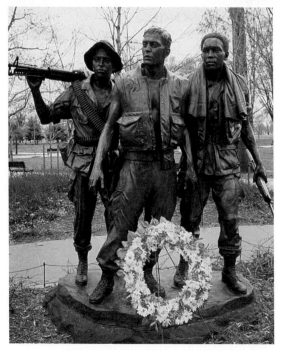

◆ NOTES TO THE TEXT

1. Kaufmann, Walter, ed., *Existentialism from Dostoevsky to Sartre* (New York: Meridian Books, 1956), p. 132.

2. Tolstoy, Leo, *What Is Art?* (Philadelphia: Henry Altemus, 1898), p. 281.

3. Ibid.

4. Ibid.

5. Sharer, Jon, "Children's Inquiry into Aesthetics," Paper presented at the National Art Education Association Convention, New Orleans, 1986.

6. Russell, Robert, "The Aesthetician as a Model in Learning About Art," *Studies in Art Education*, Vol. 27, No. 4 (1986).

7. Saunders, Robert, "The Socratic Dialogue: A Scenario for Talking About Art," Connecticut State Department of Education: Division of Curriculum and Professional Development, 1978.

8. *The American Heritage Dictionary* (Boston: Houghton-Mifflin, 1971).

9. An excellent sourcebook for aesthetics discussions is Margaret Battin, John Fisher, Ronald Moore, and Anita Silvers, *Puzzles about Art: An Aesthetics Casebook* (New York: St. Martin's Press, 1989).

10. For a videotape of this lesson write to: Lee Weaver, Director of Art, Hagerstown Public Schools, Hagerstown, Maryland 21740.

11. Louis Untermeyer, ed., *Modern American Poetry, Modern British Poetry: A Critical Approach* (New York: Harcourt Brace, 1936), p. 391.

12. Richard Foster and Pamela Tudor-Craig, *The Secret Life of Paintings* (New York: St. Martin's Press, 1986), p. 41.

13. Ibid.

14. Tolstoy, op. cit.

15. Iredell Jenkins, Smithsonian Magazine, October 1989, p. 2.

16. Iredell Jenkins, "Aesthetic Education and Moral Refinement," *The Journal of Aesthetic Education*, Vol. 2 No. 3 (July 1968), p. 35.

17. Margaret Battin, John Fisher, Ronald Moore, and Anita Silvers, *Puzzles about Art: An Aesthetics Casebook* (New York: St. Martin's Press, 1989), pp. vi-viii.

◆ SUGGESTED ACTIVITIES

1. Conduct a survey by asking six people, "What does the word 'aesthetics' mean?" Choose from a wide variety of occupations, such as teachers, nurses, lawyers, waitresses, truck drivers, bankers, etc.

2. A painting of a black circle could be interpreted as the artist's mood, the black hole of Calcutta, or just leftover black paint. Apply multiple meanings to Wyeth's *Christina's World* as you try to account for the subject's relation to her house. Is your interpretation as valid as Wyeth's?

3. Select a common object and endow it with meaning beyond itself. (Warhol did this with his Brillo boxes.) What can you do to transpose the object of your choice? Consider its environment, the lighting. How would you use written material?

4. Select a well-known artwork such as Picasso's *Guernica* and write reactions to it from the following points of view: a historian, an art historian, an art critic of the last century, and a survivor of the bombing.

5. In *Principles of Art*, R. G. Collingwood makes a distinction between fine art (or art proper) and craft, stating "the craftsman knows what he wants to make before he makes it." This suggests that the potter or jeweler's relation to their raw materials places a limitation upon the process of creation.

To examine the idea, create a clay vessel with some very clear specifications in mind, such as height, thickness, and shape. As these conditions are met, begin taking some freedom with your vessel by giving it a human reference, adding form, working the surface, etc. When you do this, have you passed over from craft to art?

6. Review the discussion about artist's intent in this chapter. Discuss the following case with a friend or colleague. Vincent Van Gogh's *Starry Night* is widely appreciated and highly regarded by professionals in the art field. It is considered to be one of his masterworks and, according to the current art market, is worth many millions of dollars. What if an art historian uncovered a lost letter by Van Gogh to his brother Theo, indicating his dissatisfaction with his recently completed painting entitled *Starry Night*. He wrote in the letter that it just didn't turn out the way he *intended* and he considered it to be a failure. Would such a revelation of the artist's intent and his negative evaluation of the painting change the way we respond to it and regard it?

7. Prepare a bulletin board for an ongoing display entitled "Big Questions about Art." When a question comes up through class discussion or studio activities, such as "Is a pot art?" (or a chair, car, building, African mask), bring in pictures of examples under discussion. Place each picture on the bulletin board under YES, NO, or MAYBE. Students might bring items such as a postcard from a natural history museum that pictures embroidered fishskin boots made by Nanai people in Siberia, a *National Geographic* picture showing jewelry and body scarification in an African tribe, or a picture of a beautifully designed modern toaster. Move pictures from one category to another as more information is gathered. A beautifully shaped piece of driftwood might be moved from the YES category to the NO category after it has been decided that natural objects are not considered art. The driftwood, however, may remain in the NO category until someone discovers Marcel Duchamp's "readymades."

8. Refer to Tolstoy's definition of art presented at the beginning of this chapter. Make a list of what he says art will not be and a list of what it will be. Then look at a range of artworks by artists such as de Kooning, Rembrandt, Kieffer, Clemente, Cassatt, Rodin, Nevelson, and so on, and decide which works you think fit Tolstoy's definition.

◆ SUGGESTED READINGS

Battin, Margaret, John Fisher, Ronald Moore, and Anita Silvers. *Puzzles about Art: An Aesthetics Casebook.* New York: St. Martin's Press, 1989. A collection of aesthetics issues with helpful suggestions for use in teaching. This book introduced the use of "quandaries" in teaching aesthetics.

Best, David. *Feeling and Reason in the Arts.* London: Allen and Unwin, 1985. Of particular interest to teachers are the chapters on "Questioning," "Art and Life," and "Creativity." The author is a British philosopher with an interest in art education.

Kern, Evan, ed. *Collected Papers: Pennsylvania's Symposium on Art Education, Aesthetics, and Criticism,* (Harrisburg, PA: Pennsylvania Department of Education, 1986). Report of a symposium on the teaching of aesthetics and art criticism in the schools.

Mathews, Gareth B. *Dialogues* (Cambridge, MA: Harvard University Press, 1984). Valuable insight into how children think and talk about philosophical problems.

Osborne, Harold. *Aesthetics and Art Theory.* (New York: E. P. Dutton and Co., 1970). Aesthetics treated within historic and cultural contexts.

Parsons, Michael. *How We Understand Art: A Cognitive Developmental Account of Aesthetic Experience* (New York: Cambridge University Press, 1987). Insightful book that offers a theory of different levels of aesthetic experience and response.

Read, Herbert. *The Meaning of Art* (London: Faber and Faber, 1931). While not current in much of its content, this little classic is a very good place to begin one's investigation of the nature of art because of its clarity.

Redfern, H. B. *Questions in Aesthetic Education.* (London: Allen and Unwin, 1986). Another British philosopher with a special interest in art education. Addresses five major issues arising from the place of aesthetics in education.

Russell, Robert. "Children's Philosophical Inquiry into Defining Art: A Quasi-Experimental Study of Aesthetics in the Elementary Classroom." *Studies in Art Education*, Vol. 29 No. 3 (1988). Report of actual classroom research on the teaching of aesthetics to elementary age children.

Smith, Ralph. *Aesthetics and Art Criticism in Art Education* (Chicago: Rand McNally and Co., 1966). Valuable basic anthology of articles dealing with defining, explaining and evaluating art.

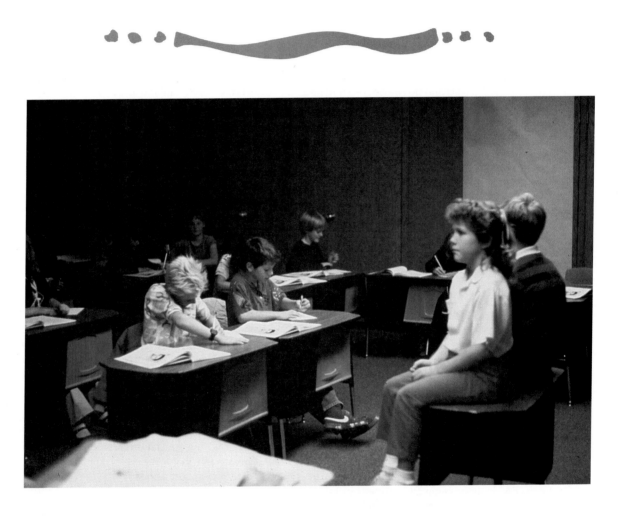

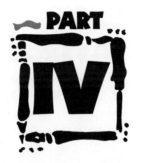

PART IV

INSTRUCTION

METHODS FOR TEACHING ART: CLASSROOM PRACTICE

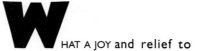

WHAT A JOY and relief to hear art discussed in terms of qualities and values instead of fashion, personalities, or auction sales records! To see it analyzed as a human activity involving the full range of mankind's passions and delights. To have it acknowledged not so much as something beautiful or valuable to own, but as an infinitely varied mode of expression, as one of humanity's finest and most effective ways of communicating and sharing.[1]

Theodore Wolff

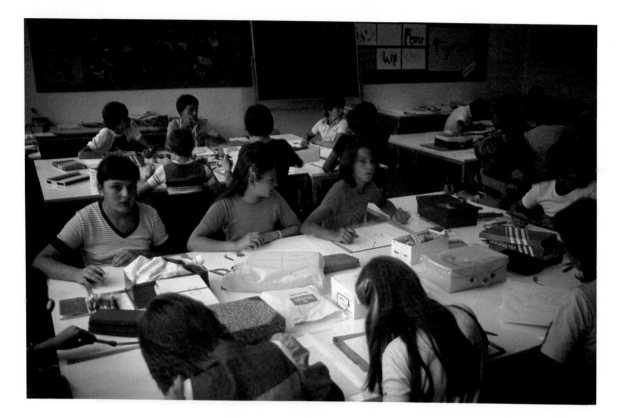

We noted in Part II that all children are unique individuals, and that we encounter a wide range of learning styles and abilities among the children in our schools. We discussed at considerable length in Part III the wide range of content for instruction within a balanced, comprehensive art program. Given the diversity of learners and the breadth and depth of the subject, art teachers need to develop and employ a repertoire of teaching methods. Indeed, the type of art program that has been outlined in previous chapters requires a variety of teaching methods for implementation. For example, art teachers demonstrate skills for art production, show slides or prints of artworks, and lead discussions about the works of adult artists and children's artwork. In this chapter we will discuss some of the issues and practices for teaching art in elementary and middle school classrooms, and will review the range of teaching methods that might be appropriate for different teaching situations.

METHODOLOGY

Methodology as dealt with in this chapter is not a rigidly prescriptive series of step-by-step directions on the "how" of teaching. Certainly there are a multitude of methods that can be used by any one teacher. If curriculum deals with the content of instruction, methodology concerns itself with the most effective means of moving students toward realization of curriculum goals. A program can be well planned and resources plentiful, but if a teacher is unaware of processes for getting children to move in a productive way, then the art program that the teacher (and students) envision will probably never materialize.

There are some factors, such as intelligence and personality of students, over which the teacher has little control, but methodology does bring to mind certain principles and techniques of motivation and control that can be studied, observed, and reflected upon. If we concede that methods are determined by the varying nature of the children and the task, then methodology invites an eclectic approach. Here are three general styles of instruction:

1. The *directive* method, appropriate for transmitting skills, techniques, or processes.

2. The *Socratic* or questioning method, employed with groups or individuals, is used to *guide* students in finding answers. This method requires certain skills of the teacher and takes more time, but it is particularly appropriate for aesthetics or any realm of instruction that deals with ideas, theories, interpretation, and analysis.

3. *Discovery*, the method in which the teacher sets the stage for lessons that are open ended, speculative, and problem-solving.

Not all students are ready for all styles of instruction; moreover, the teacher may use several modes in the same unit if not in the same lesson. The three general approaches mentioned above suggest different problems and therefore different methods of presentation, motivation, and styles of pupil-teacher relationships. The problem the teacher faces is to determine appropriate times to use each approach. The introduction of a new media can be either directive or discovery centered, a discussion of the meaning of an artwork can be Socratic, and calling attention to safety factors should be directive. The approach recommended is flexibility: a teaching style that draws on a number of strategies or methods of instruction suitable for a particular child, material, or idea.

The approaches discussed thus far are general. Another level of methodology deals with the specific aspects of instruction. When teachers suggest a particular way of developing a painting ("Begin large, then work small and choose your brushes to match the problem," or "Before you mix a color, think of the amount of paint you will need to cover the space"), they are working at the most immediate level of methodology. When two teachers discuss the most effective way of teaching lettering, or when a teacher plans to introduce a new tool in such a way as to minimize waste or accidents, this is methodology operating at both immediate and practical levels. In a broad sense, discussions of teaching methods might include questions such as: How does a teacher assist students to become more aware of forms or colors in nature as they create paintings? What do teachers say or do to open students' eyes, to heighten their perceptions of the aesthetic dimensions of their environment? How do teaching methods relate to motivation and discipline problems? Before dealing with the specifics of such questions, we must turn our attentions to more general contexts for instruction.

Contexts for Art Teaching. Art, like any subject, no matter how intrinsically interesting and attractive, can be poorly taught. Instruction in any subject is inadequate when students learn to dislike the subject and avoid contact with it in later life. Teachers must never become so concerned with emphasis on subject content that they ignore students' attitudes and feelings about the subject. In general, students will respond positively to art instruction when teachers are well prepared, have learning goals clearly in mind, and are able to explain the goals to children at their levels of understanding. When art is taught well, children are enthusiastic about learning and when such is the case, art can influence the whole atmosphere of a school, and other fields of study seem to benefit by its good effects. Thinking becomes livelier, and children take a greater interest and pride both in their school and in themselves. School halls, classrooms, and the principal's office are changed from drab areas into places of real visual interest. Children proudly bring their parents to school to see exhibitions of work. Principals report a greater degree of cooperation not only among the children themselves, but also among members of the teaching staff and between the public and the school. Most of all, successful teachers bring the student to believe that art counts. They also help parents understand why art is worth the time and money required; that it occupies a justifiable position in general education.

Who Should Teach Art? This question is a controversial one. The National Art Education Association understandably takes the position that "art instruction shall be conducted by qualified teachers of art."[2] Advocates for art instruction by specialists at the elementary level argue that most classroom teachers have not had the benefit of a fundamental art education and therefore are not qualified to teach art. Art teachers are specially prepared to implement art instruction and can do this much better than classroom generalists. They point out that classroom teachers already carry a heavy burden of instructional responsibilities, and do not need another subject to concern them. In some states, especially in the eastern region of the United States, art is taught by art specialists as part of the educational tradition.

On the other side of the controversy, and from a different tradition, we find some states that, through school funding patterns, discourage the employment of art and other subject specialists at the elementary level. Advocates of both sides of the issue appear to agree that art specialists, as a rule, can teach art better than classroom generalists, but some point out that other factors must be considered. In some cases the objection to specialists is a financial one; in other instances the argument is philosophical. Some educators argue that, for art to be integrated with the rest of the curriculum, for art to become part of the basic curriculum, it must be taught by classroom teachers. They point to art programs where art teachers move from school to school with hundreds of pupil contacts, preventing them from learning the names of children or developing meaningful relationships with them as individuals. And, in some cases, art programs are limited by what art specialists can bring to classrooms on a cart.

The number of variations on each of these arguments is great. Because school districts within states have significant autonomy, and principals of schools often have considerably autonomy within districts, the issue of who teaches art to elementary children becomes a local decision. In some districts part of the elementary schools employ art specialists, and others do not. There are districts in which art instruction is accomplished cooperatively by art teachers and classroom teachers. Although estimates vary, it is generally agreed that the majority of elementary school children attend classrooms in which art instruction is the responsibility of regular classroom teachers.[3]

Regardless of who is given the responsibility to teach art, effective teachers in all subjects are expected to demonstrate the following abilities:

1. Know the content of the curriculum and be able to identify and generate instructional materials, tasks, and activities suited to specific teaching-learning situations.
2. Be able to create an environment conducive to learning.
3. Accurately observe and record selected aspects of performance to enable the diagnosis of individual and group learning needs.
4. Be able to work effectively and harmoniously with colleagues, parents, and others in the community.
5. Be able to carry out administrative tasks appropriate to the level of appointment.
6. Adopt methodologies consistent with the goals of the curriculum and the intellectual and social backgrounds of students.

Most countries do not have trained art specialists in the elementary grades. (Israel, Canada, and the United States are a few exceptions.) In most countries it is assumed that art will be taught by the classroom

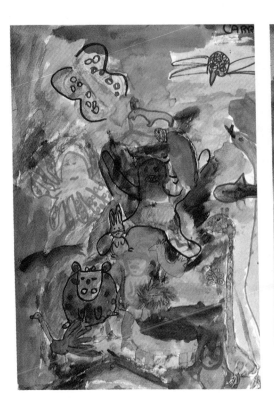

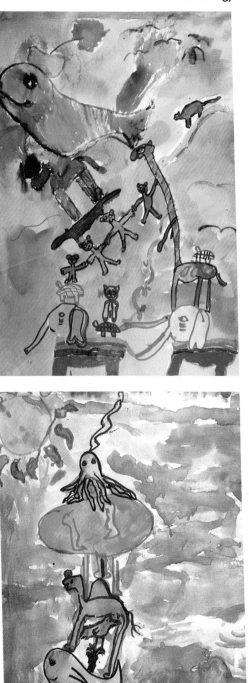

"Animal Tower," line drawings, grade 5. When children feel that art cannot be taught, a teacher may want to change their views on the nature of teaching. Here, the teacher gave the class a problem involving memory and imagination. Chidren were asked to "draw a tower of animals." No motivation, assistance, or criticism was offered. In the following session, the same topic was assigned, but only after a lively discussion was held on the problems that might attend a group of animals attempting to form a tower. (The story of "The Musicians of Bremen" was referred to.) Ideas then were developed from the first pencil sketch, which was enlarged and transferred to 12-by-18-inch paper with colored felt pens. In the third session, watercolor was added. The combination of exciting art media, motivational dialog, and assistance when needed convinced the children that art could indeed by "taught," and in the process, the art of teaching was redefined.

teacher. (Great Britain, Korea, Australia, New Zealand, and Japan have very active art programs conducted by non-art specialists.)

The teacher who has sufficient ability, tact, and liking for children to teach language, arithmetic, or social studies can probably teach art. Like any other subject, art requires of the teacher some specific knowledge and skills—such as a knowledge of design, an acquaintance with professional artwork, and some ability to use materials such as paint and clay. With the support of a well-written art curriculum, a competent teacher may gain the knowledge and master the skills associated with art education. The problems in teaching art, including classroom management and control, discipline, presentation of lessons, assistance of pupils, and appraisal of the success of the program are, broadly speaking, similar to those in the general school program. One may assert, therefore, that it is possible for a proficient teacher in an elementary school to be a capable teacher of art.

Generalist teachers can master basic art processes such as papier-mâché, clay, and printmaking, and can learn how to lead discussions of artworks using art concepts and terms. Teachers do not have to be accomplished artists, critics, or historians in order to know how to initiate classroom art activities. If they can handle basic materials and have the aid of a sound art curriculum, classroom teachers can provide children with an art program of value, if not of the same quality as art specialists.

There are basically three types of teachers who can offer some degree of art instruction:

1. The classroom teacher with limited preparation who encourages children to use art by assigning problems and conducting what has been called a laissez-faire program.

2. The classroom teacher who has taken the time for an inservice course, to study on his or her own, and who is able to begin art activities that go beyond making art into studying about art.

3. The professional art teacher who has the knowledge to advance the child's work through a trained critical mind.

One of the purposes of this book is to serve all three of these types of teachers.

The taped discussions of classroom teachers at work in Manuel Barkan's *Through Art to Creativity*[4] demonstrates a teacher's ability to communicate with children can compensate for a lack of professional art training, at least in the lower elementary grades. In a policy statement for the Commission on Art Education, Barkan wrote as follows:

> At the kindergarten and early elementary grade levels almost any truly good classroom teacher who accepts the commitments of the basic components of general education for young children can learn to teach art well. At the middle and upper elementary grade levels, however, special background and knowledge about the nature of art is essential.[5]

Even if every elementary school were suddenly to be allotted its own art teacher there would still be the problem of finding hours in the week for each child to be reached by the art specialist. Under ideal conditions, the classroom teacher should serve as a partner to trained art personnel in planning, and should take on a significant share of the program.

Since most elementary schools in the United States still do not have an art teacher, we must assume that the average classroom teacher with the will to conduct an art program is capable of providing art activities of value.

SOME SOUND TEACHING PRACTICES IN ART

The following discussion of teaching methods is based on tried and proven practices. Almost anyone who has taken a course in methods of teaching will be familiar with the ideas presented below. They are outlined merely as a reminder of certain facts about pedagogy that any teacher, whether in service or in training, would do well to keep in mind. The contemporary art program rests on the strong belief in the need for both positive guidance and methodologies that are consistent yet flexible.

A good teacher begins where the child's natural interests and abilities end. During the progressive era of the early 1930s teachers were apt to accept everything children did as evidence of their optimal potential. We now recognize that much of what children do on their own without guidance, motivation, or special material is repetitive and not a clear indication of the children's true capabilities. If children are to be challenged, their levels of development should be regarded as plateaus from which the child must advance rather than rest. The teacher, weary of seeing the same array of rainbows, cartoon characters, and other stereotypes, obviously must teach for the capability of the child. A good teacher realizes that one does not take away without giving something in return; that it is possible to build on stereotypes, so that even second-hand images can provide a basis for original thinking.

Setting the Stage

Methodology begins before the students enter the art room. Classroom teachers send out cues by the way they prepare their rooms. They should *avoid commercial giveaways* from product manufacturers and instead display reproductions of artworks and natural objects such as flowers, driftwood, or plants. Art teachers with their own rooms can create an environment rich in visual stimulation, well organized, and reasonably clean and orderly. When students first enter the room, they should receive cues about the possible delight that the room can hold. The teacher who stands at the door and greets the children, who does not begin the class until order is established, who has a pleasant expression, is teaching. The questions that all teachers must ask themselves are quite simple: "If I were a child, what set of circumstances in this room would direct my thinking and my attitudes? What will a child feel like in this space?"

The Sources of Art

Children can be motivated by their experiences to produce and respond to art. As children live from day to day, they have many experiences that arise from life at home, at play, at school, and in the community in general. They bring to each new experience the insight they have acquired from previous experiences. If, on the one hand, the new experience arouses their interest, and if it is sufficiently reminiscent of former experiences, learning should occur. If, on the other hand, children are not interested in the new experience, they will probably not profit from it. The majority of experiences that children enjoy, however, do arouse their intellect and stimulate their feelings, and so may be considered suitable subject matter for artistic expression. Indeed, no other kind of subject matter is worthy of a place in art education.

When a teacher respects the memories, the imagination and the life experiences of children, they not only set the stage for studio activities, but for an awareness of history and criticism as well. To cite an example, when a 7-year-old wants to draw his or her family, the family pictures and sculptures of Mary Cassatt, Picasso, or Romare Bearden might be of special interest to the child. Themes in art based on everyday life and universal human experiences, such as family, love, conflict, fantasy, and fear are evident in art from many cultures. The most powerful art often relates directly to the experiences we share as human beings. This is no less true of children.

A major source of motivation, then, is the life of the child, both internal and external. The teacher who can regard students as thinking, feeling organisms who function intimately with both the world of the senses and that of fantasy, imagination, and dreams, will have greater insight into the possibilities of motivation. Because the *total* makeup of the child provides sources for motivation, the teacher can go beyond lived experience and probe for what might be called the *inner landscape*; that is, the dream worlds, fears, desires, and reveries. A very real function of the art program is to provide visual objectification for what is felt and imagined as well as what is observed and directly experienced.

Motivation

In general, the teacher makes a distinction between *extrinsic* motivation, which consists of forces external to the child (such as contests and grades) that influence the child's level of motivation, and *intrinsic* motivation, which capitalizes on internal standards and goals that the

An example of a method of art history as motivation. Fourth graders create their own sun faces after a slide show on the sun image in the history of art.

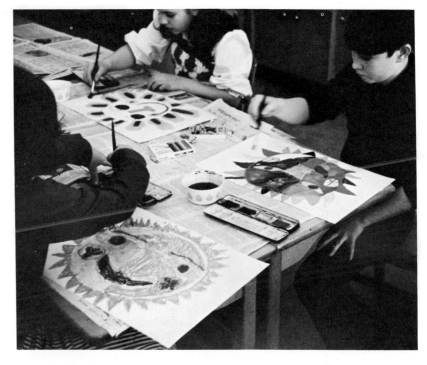

child recognizes as having value (such as the desire to perform well). The teacher should avoid striving for the short-term gain of the former, and work to bring out the latter kind of motivation, which is far more valuable in the long run to the child's development.

The teacher, having decided on the source of motivation, must consider this question: "What are the most effective means of getting the children to use their experiences with the materials I have provided?" At this point the teacher must be sensitive to the variables of the situation, linking subject to materials with techniques capable of capturing the attention of the class. The teacher may decide to focus on the excitement of untried materials, introduce the lesson with a new film, or set up a bulletin board using materials from outside the classroom. The teacher may engage the class in a lively discussion or bring in an animal or unusual still life, plan a field trip, invite a guest speaker, demonstrate how a particular skill might be used, or use an artwork to build their art vocabulary. In some instances, several such ideas may be combined in the same lesson.

When a discussion is planned to provide the basis of motivation, the teacher should involve more children than the usual bright extroverts. She or he should know when to let the class members do most of the talking until *they* have come up with the points to be emphasized.[6] The teacher may find it wise to increase interaction by seating the children close together or by dividing the class into small groups, each with their own reproduction of an artwork. In this kind of instruction, the teacher's personality, enthusiasm for the task, acceptance of unusual ideas, and flair for communication all play an important role. When the energy level is low and the class has to be brought up to a productive level, the motivational phase can be enhanced by a touch of showmanship. This is where creativity and imagination come into play.

It is important to remember that children do not normally connect their experiences with artistic acts. If a teacher tells children to paint a picture of an experience that appeals to them, or to do whatever they like, the results are usually disappointing. Under such circumstances, the children are often at a loss about where to begin. A well-known cartoon of children looking up at a teacher and asking with rueful expressions, ''Do we have to do anything we want to?'' illustrates the point. It is not that children are incapable of expression, but rather that they have not connected total freedom with expressive acts.

A Range of Teaching Methods

It is difficult to discuss teaching methods without referring at the same time to educational goals, curriculum, and evaluation, because they are all interrelated and each influences all of the others. The broad range of art content that we have suggested for the art curriculum suggests that a range of instructional methods should be used. Evaluation, if it is not to be considered as an afterthought, must be considered

In an example of media as motivation, pulling the first print provides a special excitement that is never quite achieved in other stages of the print process. When the print is completed, the student must decide on the size of the edition, the choice of paper, the ground or support — shall it be white or colored, collage or montage? — and the color of the ink itself. In each of these stages, the teacher should try to lead the child toward solving the problem independently.

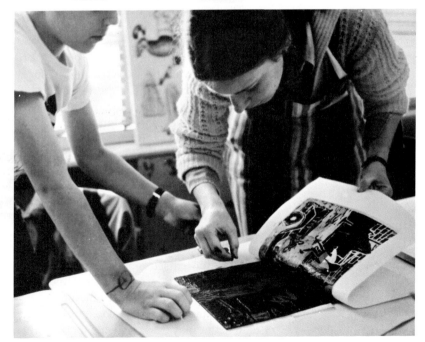

during the curriculum development process. As teachers conduct instruction in their classrooms, they are aware of curriculum goals, content for instruction, activities that are intended to foster learning, and evaluation processes that will assist teachers to assess student progress and program success. With this point in mind, we will focus attention here specifically on teaching methods, with occasional references to these other interrelated topics. By the same token, the chapters on curriculum organization and evaluation will refer back to some of the ideas in this discussion.

The Art in Teaching

Teaching can be considered as an art form; although much progress has been made toward improving teaching and learning in the schools, it certainly is not a science with specified actions that guarantee certain responses or reactions. When we observe a great teacher in action, it is not uncommon for us to remark, "She is an artist in the classroom!" or "He handled that situation beautifully," or "What a creative teacher!"[7] These comments are always meant as compliments for a person who has developed into a great teacher. Like artists (actors, poets, dancers, composers, and visual artists), teachers develop a repertoire of meaningful behaviors and apply them as they see fit according to their experience and goals. One of the differences that marks novices in art or in teaching from those who are masters is their limited repertoires. For this discussion we will review a range of teaching methods that many very good teachers are able to use fluently and flexibly, according to their teaching purposes and the needs of their students.

Following are twelve different methods that good teachers use with varying degrees of emphasis.

demonstrations	assignments
audiovisual presentations	lectures
individual work	group activities
student reports	games
field trips	guest speakers
dramatizations	visual displays

Many of these methods have been mentioned in previous chapters in conjunction with suggested activities for teaching art history, criticism, aesthetics, or any of the different modes of art production. They are not listed in any order of effectiveness, and the list is not exhaustive. It is not unusual to observe a good art teacher using several methods during a single class period.

Demonstrations.   When the children are prepared to paint, with brushes, tempera paints, water containers, paper towels, and old shirts worn backwards for smocks, the teacher demonstrates how to dip the brush into a color, brush color on the painting surface, rinse the brush in water, blot on a paper towel, and dip into another color.

Outside of the studio classroom, the teacher can show students how to use the resource books in the library to find information on the art history topics that they have selected to study. The teacher can ask for a student to share his or her topic, and can show students how to look up the topic in an encyclopedia, a dictionary of art terms, and a handbook on art and artists.

Assignments. After many discussions of puzzles about art over their years of art instruction, the sixth grade students are ready to write a paragraph on their own.[8] The teacher gives them a description of a difficult art situation and assigns them to write their response to the puzzle, stating reasons for their decision. This is the situation:

> There is a famous painting by a master artist from the seventeenth century that has hung in a great museum for many years where it has been seen by thousands of art lovers. The painting has been photographed and reproduced as beautiful art prints that are sold in the museum shop. Thousands of people have these prints hanging in their homes. During a routine cleaning of the painting, the art conservator discovered by means of an X-ray that the famous painting was painted over another painting by the artist. This happened when the artist was poor and could not afford a new canvas. Experts agree that the newly discovered painting is probably as good as the famous familiar work. Should the museum director:
>
> **(a)** Authorize the removal of the famous work in order to uncover the one never seen before? This would destroy the famous painting, but would provide the world with another great painting by the master.
>
> **(b)** Keep the famous work as is and leave the underpainting where it is, never to be seen?

For homework, children can be asked to bring a clipping about art from a magazine or newspaper. The clippings can then be placed on the bulletin board and used for discussions of what is happening in the world of art.

Audiovisual Presentations. Children often become bored watching instructional movies, videos, and sound filmstrips, or lengthy slide lectures. Audio and visual presentations need not be uninteresting to children if teachers adapt them to children's capacities for instruction and attention. Rather than showing an entire video, for example, accomplished teachers often preview and select only one relevant segment that focuses on the concept, skill, or understanding relevant to the art lesson. Brief A/V presentations interspersed with studio activities are often effective.

Interrupting their work on a collage assignment, the teacher can show six slides of surrealist paintings to the students, then turn the

In an English school the students were asked to select an artwork they would like to hang in their room. This girl's painting reflects a close study of a Modigliani portriat; the written section is part of the assignment.

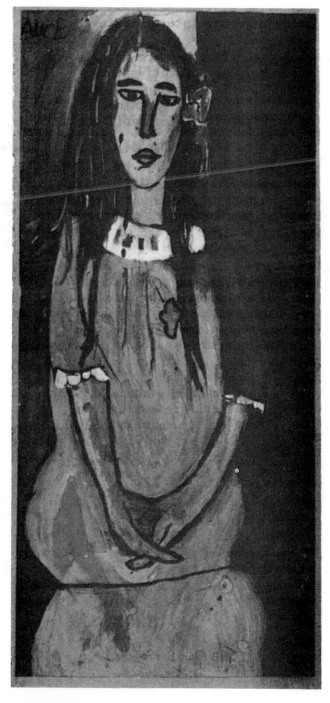

Alice   Modigliani

I think Alice is sad. I think
She has got a Sad look on
her face. Her eyes are Slanted
and they are brown. Her dress
is pale blue and if I had
this picture I would put it in
My bedroom. My bedroom is
White. I think she looks sad
because she has a pursed up
Mouth. She is thinking Very hard
about Something.
                Dunstan Ferris Age 8

lights back on so children can resume their work. This need not take more than five minutes.

Or, children can watch a ten minute segment of a videotape on the stained glass windows in Gothic cathedrals. After the video presentation, the teacher can hand out worksheets asking questions about the topic.

Lectures. Before starting the class on a ceramics project, the teacher can give the students a brief lecture about handling clay, including the health hazards and safety precautions that need to be understood when working with clay, glazes, and clay tools. The kiln in the artroom should be discussed and the teacher should preview the firing process, explaining the high temperatures inside the kiln. Lectures can also be combined with demonstrations.

In another lecture, the teacher may show slides of African masks and tell the children about the uses of masks in African societies. While lectures are often associated with higher education, this method can also be effective with all age groups if teachers will control duration, content, and use visual aids in conjunction with their lectures.

Individual Work: Studio Activity. As with other school subjects, most art learning activities involve individual work by students. When children

A docent uses the museum's studio area to present an activity which relates to a gallery tour. The children are fulfilling tasks based upon museum postcards. Such an activity may precede or follow the viewing.

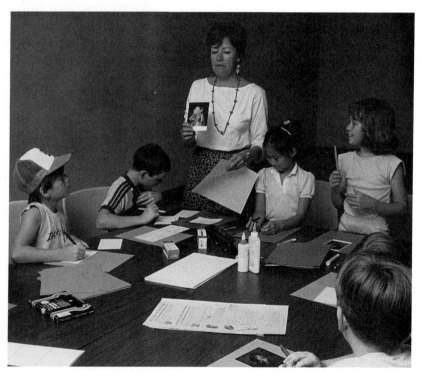

are involved in their own art expression, when they are working on individual reading or writing assignments, and when they are using learning centers during spare time in class, they usually work as individuals. Good teachers often try to vary the amount of individual work with group activities, providing variety for children in the class. Individual work will always be primary, however, because one person cannot learn for another, and because each child needs opportunities for individual artistic expression as well as individual response to the artworks of others.

After receiving a demonstration of art criticism as described in Chapter 11 and participating in a group discussion of an artwork, each student is given a worksheet with several questions about a Van Gogh painting that is displayed at the front of the room and asked to discuss their personal response to the painting. Each student completes the worksheet and hands it in to the teacher, who may share some comments worth noting after the papers have been read.

During a visit to an art museum children may be given a tour by a museum guide. After they have completed the tour and asked questions, the art teacher can ask each child to take ten minutes to select his or her favorite work (in a large museum this assignment might be restricted to one or two galleries), suggesting that the children copy the information from the label by the work, take brief notes describing the work, and be prepared to tell why they chose it.

Group Activities.   Children can be organized into groups to work on a mural that will be designed and painted on a wall in the school neighborhood. A delegation of children and the teacher will need to identify the wall and obtain the necessary permission from the owner and the city to paint on the wall. Each group has a task. One group will do library research on murals, especially contemporary murals in community settings. (The teacher can direct attention to the tradition of mural-making by the Mexican muralists Rivera and Orozco, and by some Hispanic artists in the United States). Another group can be assigned to plan the background, another to work on the buildings, another to work on the vehicles (cars, buses, trucks, etc.), and another group to draw and paint the figures.

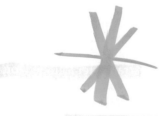

In the art museum, children can be divided into groups of three or four assigned to particular works of art. The task for each group is to discuss the work using strategies that they have learned in class, and to report on the work to the rest of the class when they are back at school. The teacher can show the slide of the work while each group reports.

Reports.   The method of fostering learning by assigning reports has been mentioned above in conjunction with other methods. Teaching methods are often integrated, although they might also be used separately as well. The same is true of learning activities that integrate content from art history and art production or other combinations of the art disciplines.

In preparation for a unit about architecture, the teacher may ask the children to notice some things about the buildings in which they live. Each child is to notice if their home is in a one-story, two-story, or more than two-story building. Each child should be given the opportunity to report this information at the next class meeting.

A fifth or sixth grade class can be given a library research assignment, in which they select an artist's name from the list provided by the teacher, spend a period in the library, and write a two-paragraph report about the artist. This assignment is in conjunction with a unit in language arts.

Games. If a fourth grade class has been learning about color — primary and secondary colors — the class can be divided into four groups and assigned to four locations in the classroom. In each location an assortment of art postcards from museums should be provided. The first group to select works of art that match each color category on their worksheet receives a reward (e.g., first group out for lunch).

Field Trips. Most teachers are convinced of the value of field trips, but many are faced with limited financial support from the districts in which they teach. Busing students to distant locations and sometimes paying for food can be expensive. Whenever possible, however, students should have opportunities to learn about the world away from school. For the art program, field trips to art galleries or museums are especially beneficial because children are able to experience original works of art of high quality and obtain a needed frame of reference that will help them better understand what the slides and prints they see in school actually represent.

There are many pointers about supervising children on trips that teachers learn through experience and share with one another. Books about visits to museums are also available.[9] Following are a few brief suggestions that might fall under the category of teaching methods in relation to field trips (other suggestions are listed in the section on using museums in Chapter 11).

1. Visit the museum or gallery ahead of time in preparation for the planned field trip. Take notes of possible problems that you can anticipate, such as parking, limited space for your purposes, etc. Contact the education staff if there is one. Arrange for a guided tour if one is available for your grade level, and if you prefer one. Learn of the services offered to school groups. *Schedule your visit!*

2. Select several artworks that you want all children to see. One of the problems with museums is that there is too much to see unless the

teacher can provide some focus for the children. You can discuss works seen after you return to school.

3. If possible, obtain slides of selected works, or take your own if permission is granted by the museum or gallery. Flash photography is almost always banned. You can show slides of some of the works to the children prior to the trip. This establishes an anticipatory mood and provides the works with "celebrity status."

4. Note such things as where the bus will stop, where students will enter, where they will place their coats, where the bathrooms are located, and so forth. Decide where the group will meet before and after the museum visit. Are there clocks in evidence so that everyone will know what time it is?

5. Draw a map (some museums provide maps) and show these items to the children in the classroom prior to leaving on the trip. Talk the class through the entire trip using the map to show where everything is, what the time schedule is, and how they should handle any problems that might arise, such as becoming separated from the group (this should never happen of course, but sometimes does, regardless of precautions).

6. Children may "act up" much more when they are nervous and uneasy because of strange surroundings and situations. By providing all of this information you will place the children more at ease and help them to enjoy the experience and learn from it.

7. Follow up the museum visit with discussion and sharing back in the classroom. Try to consolidate learning that has taken place. Help children to realize what they have learned. Report the successful trips to parents.

Field trips can also be taken in the neighborhood with little or no expense. The art teacher may take the class for a walking architecture tour in the neighborhood, noting some basic features of buildings that relate to the study of architecture, such as how the buildings relate to each other and to the environment, what materials they are constructed with, how old they appear to be, and for what purposes they were evidently built.

Guest Speakers.   There is a strong tradition in art education of inviting artists into schools. This tradition has been supported for many years by the National Endowment for the Arts' Artists in Schools Program. When the goal of the art program is for children to learn more about the world of art, this makes a great deal of sense. Children have opportunities to see a professional artist at work, talk with the artist and ask questions, and observe the materials and methods used to create works of art. It also makes good educational sense to invite other art professionals into the classroom, such as art historians, art critics, and aestheticians (probably more difficult to locate). There is often a parent or community figure who is happy to help, if asked.

The first grade teacher wants his students to see what oil paints are like, to smell the paint, linseed oil, and turpentine, and to see an artist's palette and easel. He asks his class if any of them knows of a person who paints. One little girl says her mother's friend is a painter. The teacher contacts the mother, learns the artist's name, and invites the woman to visit the class and demonstrate with her oil paints on a stretched canvas. Although the artist is not a professional, her tools and materials are authentic and the children learn a great deal from the artist's visit and enjoy it very much.

Several teachers can plan together to invite a local art critic to visit the elementary school and discuss his approach to writing about artworks. If students prepare a list of questions for the critic, the visit can result in a lively discussion. The critic is likely to be pleased that the children are so aware of art and that they can ask such good questions.

Dramatizations. This teaching method can make experience more vivid for children, who often remember dramatizations for many years. This does not mean that the teacher has to be an actor and dramatize classroom presentations, although some teachers have abilities in dramatics and use their talents effectively with children. Rather, this is a method whereby teachers assist children to act out, or dramatize, situations that are educationally meaningful with respect to the art curriculum.

For example, a third grade teacher has displayed on the bulletin board a large reproduction of Renoir's *Girl With a Watering Can*, which depicts a beautiful little blonde girl dressed in a lovely dress, and holding a watering can. A pretty little blonde girl in the class, Suzy, tells the teacher that her grandmother made a dress for her just like the one in the picture. The teacher follows up with a phone call to Suzy's mother and learns that the grandmother made a dress patterned after the one in Renoir's painting. Granny loved the painting and thought that her granddaughter looked just like the girl in the picture. Arrangements are made, the teacher finds the right type of watering can, and little Suzy comes to school wearing her dress and the same color ribbon in her hair as the girl in the picture. The teacher arranges for Suzy to visit every class in the school, accompanied by the Renoir print. She receives applause from every class. The teacher puts up a display in the hallway with the Renoir print, a photograph of Suzy, and some historical background about the artist and the impressionist style of painting.

In another example, a teacher asks for a volunteer from the class each month, alternating between boys and girls, to dress up as their favorite artist. One boy chooses Mondrian and, with help from the teacher and from home, develops a costume with primary colors and black vertical and horizontal lines. Another boy chooses Jackson Pollock and has a great time splattering some old clothes with multi-colored tempera paints to create his costume. A girl chooses Georgia O'Keeffe. She dresses like a photograph of the artist and somehow finds a bleached cow skull. Another girl chooses Whistler and dresses and poses like the painting known as *"Whistler's Mother"* (entitled *Arrangement in Gray and Black* by the artist). As each new month begins, students are asked to guess the name of the artist being dramatized. The child doing the dramatization, having studied the artist's life and works, answers questions that classmates ask as they try to get clues. Some of the artists are more difficult to guess than others. In every case, students are more interested to learn about the artist after the dramatic presentation.

In one further example, two teachers collaborate to dramatize a painting.[10] After rigging up a simple sound system, the art teacher projects a slide of a painting by American fantastic realist Ivan Albright, entitled *Ida*. Ida is an obviously aging woman sitting before a mirror. During his discussion of the painting, the art teacher asks the class, "I wonder what Ida could tell us if she could speak?" He asks the class, "What would you like to ask Ida?" Then he starts asking questions, facing the painting. The students are startled when Ida answers! The other teacher, a woman, is concealed outside the open door of the classroom where she can hear the questions. She is familiar with the life of Albright and answers questions through the sound system with the type of pith and humor that we might expect from Ida herself. Needless to say the students learn a great deal and probably will never forget the time they were able to ask questions of a person in a painting.

Visual Displays. One of the advantages that art teachers have is the visual nature of the subject. Many children learn visually, and art teachers can see visual evidence of the effectiveness of their instruction in students' art products. We can accomplish much instruction and foster learning without taking any class time, simply through the means of visual displays.

One teacher always includes didactic material as a component of exhibitions of students' artwork. When she teaches a unit about color, or composition, or an art style such as cubism, this teacher displays material about the concepts, skills, and instruction that children have received, along with examples of their work. As other teachers, parents, administrators, and students pass the room they learn that art content is being taught and learned by students in this teacher's class.

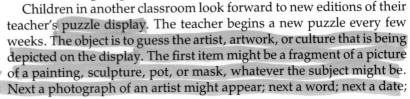

Children in another classroom look forward to new editions of their teacher's puzzle display. The teacher begins a new puzzle every few weeks. The object is to guess the artist, artwork, or culture that is being depicted on the display. The first item might be a fragment of a picture of a painting, sculpture, pot, or mask, whatever the subject might be. Next a photograph of an artist might appear; next a word; next a date;

next the name of a country, and so on. The student who guesses the answer wins extra credit points or some other reward.

This brief review of teaching methods is not complete. For example, the idea of organizing children into teams for the purpose of debating an art issue has not been mentioned. The reader might wish to add to and extend this list of teaching methods. In any single classroom there are children who learn in a variety of styles. By varying teaching methods and learning activities, as appropriate for the range of content in a balanced art program, teachers can sustain students' interest in art and accommodate the various learning styles of children.

ORGANIZING FOR INSTRUCTION

A large proportion of time during the art period will be spent by children in the process of making their own art. Teachers can increase the amount of time available for productive activities by organizing tools and materials for efficient use. Effective teachers often devise ways to organize and store art tools, such as brushes, water containers, clay tools, and so forth. Drawers and cupboards are labeled and sometimes color coded so everyone knows where things go and where things are. Children are taught to assist with the distribution of art tools and materials, clean up, and collection and careful storage of students' drawings, paintings, and other artwork. Children often enjoy helping and can become very efficient in performing these tasks. (Organization of a room for art instruction is discussed in Chapter 17.)

Selecting Art Materials and Tools

Media are the materials that a pupil employs in art activities. Their proper use in class depends on the teacher's knowledge of how children will use them.

Different types of media suit various stages of physical development of the pupils. At certain stages, for example, children have difficulty using soft chalk and require instead a harder substance such as wax crayon. Too hard a medium, however, makes it difficult for children to cover paper readily and will interfere with their expression. Very young children, who have not learned to use their smaller muscles with dexterity, require large surfaces for painting or assembling large objects. Yet children of all ages periodically have a desire to render detail, and there should be occasions when pencils are permitted for small-scale work, in which case the lead should be soft and the paper not too large. As children mature and gain greater muscular control, they can work with smaller surfaces and objects. Others, however, may wish to work on a large scale no matter what stage of muscular development they have reached.

Children often show marked preferences for a particular medium. One child may find greater satisfaction in using clay than in using cardboard; another may prefer watercolor to tempera paint. Unless these children are given reasonable, although of course not exclusive, opportunities to employ the media of their choice, their lack of enthusiasm may be reflected in their work.

Children may also have preferences as to tools. A certain size and type of brush may suit one child but not another. A fine penpoint may appeal to some, while broader nibs may be right for others. Teachers should be sensitive to the relationship between tools and paper size, bearing in mind that small tools (pencils and crayons) inhibit design on paper larger than 12 by 18 inches, and that large brushes limit detail and observation on smaller sizes of paper.

The teacher who makes an effort to provide a variety of materials and tools is following an accepted practice in art. Nearly every artist develops preferences among the many media and tools available, but this does not prevent exploration of further choices of favorite materials or testing of new materials.

Teacher Talk

One of the most important factors in instruction is student-teacher dialog, or, to put it more simply, "teacher talk." Attending any exhibition of children's work, we are struck by either shared characteristics or the lack of common attributes within groups of children's artworks of different teachers. These group differences are caused not only by materials and subject matter (one teacher prefers clay to other materials, while another may stress observational drawing) but also by the kind of language each teacher uses. *And it is through language that teachers convey much of their philosophy about art.* While teachers communicate much to their students through their way of dressing, their attitudes, and their personalities (little is missed by even the youngest child), their language probably has the most direct influence on how the work of their students develops.

The quality and level of student discussion is determined by the art vocabulary that the teacher has been able to develop with each lesson. Every new experience should include new words derived from both studio and critical experiences. Design terminology such as *contrast*, *proportion*, and *composition* reinforce both realms of experience.

Based on classroom observations, the following dialogs are typical of teachers who attempted to tread a fine line between direct and indirect teaching.

Six Levels of Art Talk

First Grade: Flower problem in tempera

TEACHER: I like your shapes, they move all over in so many ways. Tell me about this—it isn't a flower, is it?

STUDENT: It's a bug, yes, a bug.

TEACHER: Does it have a name?

STUDENT: A grasshopper.

TEACHER: Grasshoppers are long and skinny, aren't they? How about a different-shaped bug? Can you think of one?

STUDENT: I can paint a snake—

TEACHER: Well, a snake isn't a bug, but a snake is very nice.

Second Grade: "My Pet," drawing in felt-tip pen

TEACHER: That's a good rabbit, but he looks awfully small.

STUDENT: It's a girl rabbit.

TEACHER: Yes, well, it looks kind of lonely by itself. What can we add to keep it company—you know, to make the picture bigger?

STUDENT: It has a cage.

TEACHER: Cages are good; where do you keep your cage?

STUDENT: Outside, on the porch.

TEACHER: Well, if it's outside, there are other things to draw, aren't there? You put them in and let me see if I can tell you what they are.

Third Grade: Clay animal

STUDENT: It doesn't look like a dog, it's all lumpy.

TEACHER: I think you are going to have to decide what kind of a dog—

STUDENT: A German shepherd. I like German shepherds. My uncle has one.

TEACHER: What makes a German shepherd different from, say, a beagle?

STUDENT: The ears stick up.

TEACHER: Okay. Then let's begin there. Pull its ears up and I think you can smooth out some of those lumps.

Fourth Grade: Box sculpture

TEACHER: Having trouble, Chuck? You don't seem very happy.

STUDENT: I hate it, it's not turning out.

TEACHER: What seems to be wrong?

STUDENT: I don't know, it's a mess. Nothing seems to go together; I wanted this neat truck—

TEACHER: Well, I think you've been a little careless in joining the sections together (demonstrates joining process with tape). See what I mean?

STUDENT: Yeah, I don't know. It still won't look like a truck.

TEACHER: Look, Chuck, try to think ahead. You have a cereal box and a medicine carton and they both have pieces of letters and different colors showing. Why don't you join it, then paint it; I think you'll like it better.

Fifth Grade: Linoleum print

STUDENT: It won't work.

TEACHER: What won't work?

STUDENT: The tool, it keeps sliding and slipping.

TEACHER: Let me try. No, the blade's okay. Here, try standing and let your weight press the blade, and for goodness' sake, keep your left hand out of the way of the blade or your mother will be calling me tonight about an accident, okay?

STUDENT: Okay.

TEACHER: Say, I haven't checked your drawing, can I see it before you continue?

Sixth Grade: Landscape painting

TEACHER: Very nice, John, very nice.

STUDENT: It all looks the same.

TEACHER: What do you mean?

STUDENT: Well, there was more color—

TEACHER: You mean more kinds of green in the trees—?

STUDENT: Yeah, that's right.

TEACHER: Look, you keep using the same color green. Come on, you know how to change a color.

STUDENT: It will be messier.

TEACHER: You've got your palette set up; try out some mixtures, add yellow, try a touch of black—

STUDENT: Black?

TEACHER: Why not? Try it, it won't bite you. You can always paint over it.

Each teacher in these dialogs had to be sensitive to the range of vocabulary, the nature of the assistance needed, and the tone of address. The role of language is complex and plays a vital role in art education. The best way to learn how to use language more effectively is to observe good teachers in action, either in an art or general classroom situation.

The above lessons would have been improved had the teachers included somewhere in the discussion a reference to the work of an artist who dealt with the problem under discussion.

Questionable Methods for Teaching Art

In the absence of sound programs of art education, such as we have discussed throughout this book, some teachers have devised activities that might superficially resemble art instruction, but which have little or no educational substance. We mention these questionable practices here because they have been so pervasive in some locations, and because we believe that they are harmful to the extent that they, like junk food, take the place of something much better.

Mechanistic Production.   Every year when spring approaches, Miss L, a conscientious second grade teacher, provides the class with yellow and green construction paper. She has designed a pretty pattern of a daffodil in which the leaves are green and the flower yellow. She demonstrates first how to cut the petals and then shows how to make the leaves. "The children," says Miss L, "love to make a daffodil. It provides a most effective art lesson."

Miss L is correct in saying that the children love to make a daffodil. Spring is in the air and the bright new paper is fascinating. Motivation of the children is not difficult for Miss L, a friendly, likable, sympathetic person, who has timed her activity well. Miss L is incorrect, however, in saying that her assignment constitutes an effective art lesson. The activity is not art: it is "busy work." In producing the flower, no one but Miss L has done any planning. She has not only solved all the problems, but any expression of feelings about the flower is hers alone. The children may have developed some skill, but they have done so without thought and feeling. The children have been subjected to a mechanistic form of teaching.

The children's liking for a particular activity does not necessarily mean that the work is art or even an educationally sound pursuit. Miss L has wasted precious educational time and materials in this work. She has taught dictatorially, and not according to the children's potential. She has successfully avoided the use of the children's memories of flowers or their ability to discern differences among real flowers or flowers as painted by Monet, Dutch painters, or Asian still life artists.

Tidy Art.   Mr. W. is a tidy person; he presents a neat appearance and his classroom is a model of order. "I like things to look right," says Mr. W, as he goes about his duties in a fourth grade classroom. "I have no use for sloppy work," he asserts, "in drawing, painting, or any other subject, for that matter." Mr. W encourages neatness so vigorously that his pupils have grown afraid to experiment. Those who first tried to experiment with ideas and media ran into difficulties with both the media and Mr. W. Now they hold fast to thoroughly familiar materials and well-tried clichés in artistic thought, which pleases their teacher.

Sometimes even under these conditions Mr. W is not altogether satisfied with the neatness of the children's work. In these cases, he is not above "touching up" the youngster's work. He is so clever at this that the output of his class occasionally wins prizes. Only an expert in children's art could tell where the work had been doctored, and very few such experts judge children's artwork on a competitive basis, because well-informed art educators are skeptical about competition of this kind.

The children's mural work must also be neat. Sometimes in this activity, too, the children do not meet Mr. W's standards of neatness, and this embarrasses him, particularly when the principal visits the classroom.

Although no one would advocate untidiness for its own sake in a classroom, children must be allowed to experiment freely with ideas and media. Children's lack of skill in organizing both subject matter and materials makes it inevitable that their art production is often untidy. Tidiness in executing artistic activities will occur only after the children master the skills associated with the activities. To demand extreme neatness at all times is to handicap children in producing creative work. Among the basic principles of teaching neglected by Mr. W are that the products of expression must be the children's own and that teaching must be built on the children's interests. Exploration, even if it leads to blind alleys of thought, can be valuable.

When Freedom Is Misunderstood.   Down the hall from Mr. W's classroom is Mrs. deP, who spends each summer studying with painters and is a supporter of all forms of avant-garde art.

Mrs. deP says she is a lover of freedom to the extent that she is reluctant to interfere with any form of childlike expression in art. "Art is the free-expression of an untrammeled spirit," she says. The output of her pupils is messy, ill-conceived, and lusterless. The principal claims that the pupils are noisy and inattentive and inclined to be rude to Mrs. deP. Quite often, when not obstreperous, the pupils are listless. They say that they often do not know what to do. The situation is unfortunate, for Mrs. deP has much to offer. Her feeling for art is apparently deep, but she has failed to understand the meaning of teaching. She would have more success as a teacher if she recognized the following basic teaching principles: the pupils must be assisted in establishing personal themes for expression; teaching is most effective when the situation deals with some need; and the teaching of art should not be used as a vehicle for frustrated artists to satisfy their own egos.

Formula Art.   Miss Z, the teacher of a third grade class, is clever at mathematics. One of her favorite art lessons consists of having the children resolve objects into triangles, squares, oblongs, and circles. She admires the precision resulting from this activity. "The children are learning to handle basic forms," she explains. Thus, the children are taught to draw houses by means of a triangle supported by a rectangular oblong; a chicken by using two circles; a young girl, strangely enough, by resorting to triangles and squares.

Miss Z is another example of a teacher who prevents children from any sort of personal expression. Moreover, the designs she insists on are inaccurate in relation to the objects depicted. The forms of houses, chickens, and girls cannot be successfully arrived at through geometric shapes supplied by the teacher. They can be depicted adequately only by means of personal experience and observation on the part of the children. Miss Z's system is convenient for her, but asks woefully little of her students.

We find that these questionable practices seldom occur within art programs with clear educational objectives, well-articulated art content, adequate art materials and visual resources, and teachers who understand the essential role of art in general education. This does not mean that teachers never engage students in activities that relate to holidays or seasons. As we have discussed in other chapters, holidays and seasons are legitimate themes for the study of art and they have been used by many great artists.

TEACHING IN ACTION: PLANNING FOR THE FIRST SESSION

All teachers must plan for the first meeting with their pupils. The taped dialogs transcribed here represent two approaches to this first meeting. The first conversation depicts a teacher's attempt to deal with a basic question of aesthetics: a grass roots definition of art from disadvantaged children in the third grade; the second demonstrates how a first planning session with middle-class children sounds.

First Dialog

TEACHER: Do any of you know who I am? (*pause*)

TOMMY: You an art teacher?

TEACHER: That's right. I am your art teacher. Now, can anyone tell me what an artist does?

SARAH: He paints you pictures.

TEACHER: Very good. What other kinds of artists are there? (*longer pause*)

FLORENCE: Are you going to let us paint pictures?

TEACHER: Certainly, we'll paint pictures, but we'll do things that other kinds of artists do, too. Can you think of other things we can do that other artists do? (*pause*) Well, think of going shopping with your mother. Can you think of the work of artists in a shopping center?

TOMMY: (*suddenly*) I know! He can paint you a sign . . .

TEACHER: (*enthusiastically*) Yes, yes, sign painters are artists, too — what else?

TOMMY: (*picking up the enthusiasm*) And if you had a butcher shop and you had a good — I mean a *good* artist, he could paint you a pork chop on the window. . . .

The above conversation is a fragment of a discussion held during the first meeting with a group of third graders in an inner-city school.

The purposes of the teacher's discussion were to (1) learn the children's concept of art; (2) establish the kind of rapport that comes only through a relaxed exchange of ideas; and (3) prepare the children for the program she had planned for the year. As a result of her discussion, the teacher set aside quite a few activities she had planned because she realized they were inappropriate for the children. A skilled and experienced teacher would be sensitive to the range of differences among children and would understand that they all come to the art class with their own ideas of what constitutes an artist. To some, art represents part of social studies; to others it means carrying out school services. For one child it is the high point of the week, while to another it is a traumatic period during which the student is constantly cautioned against making a mess.

Second Dialog

Let us examine a planning session taking place at a meeting of the author and some pupils. These pupils are fifth graders in a middle-class neighborhood. A content analysis of the pupils' comments is provided in the outer column.

Teacher-Pupil Dialog

CONSULTANT: Good morning. My name is Mr. H. I'm an art teacher as well as your art supervisor, and I'd like to talk with you about some of the things you're going to be doing this year with Miss G, your regular art teacher.

SUSAN: You mean you're not going to be our art teacher?

CONSULTANT: No, but I hope I'll be coming in now and then to see what Miss G is doing, and perhaps later on I'll take a few classes myself.

MARK: What are we going to do today?

CONSULTANT: Well, as I said earlier, I'd like to take this time to talk about what you'd like to do this year.

SUSAN: Will Mr. S be back?

CONSULTANT: I don't know. Who is Mr. S? (*great commotion*) One at a time—could we please use our hands? Deirdre? (*The children had prepared name tags.*)

DEIRDRE: Mr. S illustrated books and he showed us how he did his pictures.

OTHERS: Yeah—he was cool. Boy, could he draw!

CONSULTANT: (*going to the blackboard*) Well, we have our first request. You'd like to meet a real artist. (*Writes this on board.*) Anything else?

MARCIA: The raccoon—the raccoon?

CONSULTANT: The raccoon?

Analysis of Pupil Comments

This remark may be interpreted as a sign of disappointment that Mr. H will not be their regular art teacher.

Mark is ready to go to work. In his eyes the art period (there are so few of them) is not a place to talk, but to make things.

"Mr. S" was a participant in the Creative Arts Council's program designed to bring performing artists of all kinds into the schools. The children's interest in observing professionals at work thus opens the door for potters, printmakers, painters, and the like to step into the art curriculum.

OTHERS: Yes—Miss G brought in this raccoon. We petted him. It climbed up the bookcase.

CONSULTANT: All right—let me see—how shall I put it? How about "Drawing from Live Subjects"—that way we can use live fifth graders as well as other kinds of animals. (*laughter*) Very good. I think drawing from nature is a great idea—it would be even better if we could get a baby elephant in here—(*laughter—other animals are suggested that are equally unrealistic*)—All right, now, keep going—yes, Barbara?

BARBARA: I liked the field trip to the Museum of Fine Arts.

CONSULTANT: Oh, what did you see?

BARBARA: It was Rembrandt.

PAUL: No it wasn't. (*others join in quick argument*)

CONSULTANT: Does anyone remember the exact title of the show?

PAUL: I know! "The Age of Rembrandt," that's what it was.

CONSULTANT: O.K. Let's put in "Field Trips." I'll write it under "Visiting Artists," rather than "Drawing." What else?

SUSAN: Are we going to paint?

CONSULTANT: Certainly—what's an art class without painting?

DAVID: I don't like to paint.

CONSULTANT: Why not?

DAVID: I don't know. I like making jewelry.

CONSULTANT: Well—we can't like everything can we? You must feel about painting the way I feel about lettering. Let me put down "Crafts," David. That'll hold the door open to other materials. Who'd like to name some?

POLLY: Clay.

PAUL: Clay is sculpture.

POLLY: Bowls are clay and . . .

PAUL: Clay is more sculpture.

CONSULTANT: Actually, clay can be either. If it is something we use, we generally refer to it as "craft"; if it's something we admire in the way that we admire a painting, we usually call it "fine arts." In any case we can put down "Sculpture" as long as you mentioned it. Can you name some other crafts?

EMMA: Batiks. We did batiks once.

PAUL: Weaving. That's crafts.

SUSAN: Are we going to do all these?

CONSULTANT: I'm afraid not—but let's get them down anyway so we'll see what we've done. Say—I've got one for you. How about movies? We can make a movie.

OTHERS: Movies? How?

PAUL: I took pictures with my father's camera. It's an 8mm.

CONSULTANT: Well, I had in mind another kind, something we could all do together. We can scratch designs right on the raw film, *ground) and design ("making a picture"). Sculpture was also broken down into several media, and printmaking was added.*

put all the pieces together, and put it to music. How does that sound?

The important thing to note in the above dialog is that the teacher knew in advance what the rough content of the year's work would be. In communicating with the pupils he could have:

1. Doled out the projects on a piecemeal basis as the year progressed without attempting to communicate the overall structure. This would be an *improvised*, teacher-directed approach.

2. Described the entire year's activities to the class, providing a *planned*, directed program.

Instead the teacher chose a third approach, in that he:

3. Involved the class in the planning. In so doing, many of the teacher's own ideas were made to seem to originate in the class. By engaging the students' participation, he ensured a climate of acceptance for new ideas that normally might not be well received.

Analyzing the Teacher: Five Phases of Instruction

Teaching art is far more complex than many new teachers realize. The following list is composed of significant factors that could bear on the success of a teacher. It is an evaluation instrument with which teachers can get a "profile" of their own style. Note that this form is not judgmental; it merely asks whether any of the factors listed were present, not present, or present in some exemplary way. Description of any one item could be elaborated if desired. The lesson is divided into five segments: preparation, presentation, the class in action, evaluation, and teaching style. Obviously no one lesson could possibly encompass all the items listed. The list also provides some indication of the possible variables in teaching.

Preparation for Instruction and Classroom Management
1. Display areas:
    a. Display pupils' work
    b. Relate materials to studio activity
    c. Relate materials to current events in art, school, community
    d. Show design awareness in the arrangement of pupils' work

2. Supplies and materials:
    a. Organized so that the room is orderly and functional
    b. Organized so that the room is orderly but inhibiting
    c. Organized so that the room is disorderly but functional
    d. Organized so that the room is disorderly and nonfunctional
    e. Distributed systematically

3. Resource materials (aids, art books, art magazines, file materials, live art, videos, and other audiovisual support):

    a. Provided by school system and school

    b. Not provided by school system and school

    c. Derived from teacher's reference file

    d. Not provided by teacher

4. Nonobservable data:

    a. (Pupil's work) Kept in portfolio for reference

    b. (Reference file) Made available for student use

Presentation of Lesson

1. Objectives clearly stated

2. Objectives arrived at through dialog

3. Discussion related to topic or objective

4. Discussion related to levels within group

5. Interaction between pupils and teacher:

    a. Teacher interrupts pupils

    b. Teacher welcomes disagreement

6. Demonstrations oriented toward multiple solutions

7. Demonstrations convergent on single solution

8. Class is flexible:

    a. Chairs easily reorganized for viewing demonstrations

    b. Children can come to teacher freely for additional material

    c. Several projects in operation at same time

    d. Children can move freely from project to project

The Class in Action

1. Teacher:

    a. Listens to pupils

    b. Asks open questions

    c. Asks closed questions

    d. Praises work of pupils in general terms

    e. Praises work in specific terms that are relevant to the problem

    f. Uses other forms of verbal reinforcement

    g. Is able to reach pupils who request consultation

    h. Talks at length to some pupils

    i. Relates comments not only to objectives but to pupils' frame of reference

    j. Motivates those who have become discouraged

    k. Remotivates those with short attention span

    l. Is flexible in permitting deviation from assignments

    m. Uses art vocabulary

    n. Is competent in handling discipline problems

2. Pupils:

    a. Are self-directive in organizing for work

    b. Are self-directive in organizing for cleanup

    c. Use art vocabulary

Evaluation Period (For final group evaluation)
1. Evaluation relates to goals of lesson
2. Pupils encouraged to participate
3. Pupils do participate as a group
4. Only one work is evaluated
5. Several works evaluated
6. Range of evaluation devices used
7. There is no final evaluation
8. Pupils do not feel embarrassed or threatened by public evaluation
9. Pupils generally negative to evaluation process

Teaching Style (Personality)
1. Teacher takes positive attitude toward instruction
2. Teacher shows rapport with pupils' age group
3. Teacher demonstrates sense of humor
4. Teacher has sense of pace: controls flow of lesson
5. Teacher is innovative in following respects:
   a.   c.
   b.   d.
6. Teacher is aware of language (vivid phrasing, imagistic speech, clarity of expression)

If a teacher wishes to have an objective profile of her/his performance, an administrator could be requested to use the instrument during an observation period. This may hold some surprises for the teacher, as well as educate the administrator regarding what is involved in conducting an art program.

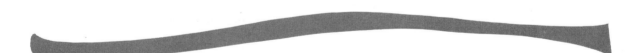

◆ NOTES TO THE TEXT

1. This statement by New York art critic Theodore Wolff was made after his association with a group of art educators who were involved with a curriculum development project. See Theodore Wolff, "Encounter with Committed Teachers Renews Faith in the Value of Art," *The Christian Science Monitor*, September 8, 1989.

2. See the NAEA's brochure, *Quality Art Education* (Reston, VA: National Art Education Association, 1984).

3. See, for example, statistics in *Toward Civilization: A Report on Arts Education* (Washington, D.C.: National

Endowment for the Arts, 1988).

4. Manuel Barkan, *Through Art to Creativity* (Boston: Allyn and Bacon, 1960).

5. In Jerome J. Hausman, ed., *Report of the Commission on Art Education* (Washington, D.C.: National Art Education Association, 1965), p. 84.

6. For some good examples of classroom dialog, see the seven case studies of art programs in Michael Day, Elliot Eisner, Robert Stake, Brent Wilson, and Marjorie Wilson, *Art History, Art Criticism, and Art Production*, Vol. II (Los Angeles: Rand Corporation, 1984).

7. For a discussion of teaching as an art form, see Elliot Eisner, *The Educational Imagination*, 2nd ed. (New York: Macmillan, 1985), Chapter 9, "On the Art of Teaching."

8. For the most useful resource for teaching about aesthetics, see Margaret Battin, John Fisher, Ronald Moore, and Anita Silvers, *Puzzles About Art: An Aesthetics Casebook* (New York: St. Martin's Press, 1989).

9. For example, see David Finn, *How to Visit a Museum* (New York: Harry N. Abrams, 1985).

10. Thanks to Laine Raty, Brigham Young University, for this example.

◆ ACTIVITIES FOR THE READER

1. Describe any situation you have experienced in which children disliked art. Explain how the dislike arose and indicate the means you might use to alter the children's attitude.
2. Describe the traits of a personal acquaintance whom you consider to be an effective teacher of art.
3. Observe some art lessons given by expert teachers and note especially (a) the motivational devices employed; (b) the manner in which themes are defined; (c) the way in which goals are established; (d) the problems that arise and the means by which a solution to them is found. Can you add any items to the analysis instrument at the end of this chapter?
4. Describe how you would motivate a class for a lesson in increased sensitivity to color based on fall colors in nature.
5. Take a close look at your personality and try to project your teaching "style" from it. Apply your style to a specific teaching situation—demonstration, evaluation, or selection of topic.
6. Describe the steps you might take to improve the following situations: (a) a third grade art class whose members are outrageously untidy and waste-ful of materials; (b) a class of fifth graders who have always been taught to copy during their art sessions and feel they are unable to create; (c) a group of sixth grade boys who think art is 'sissy''; (d) a group of children whose parents or older brothers and sisters have given them formulas for the drawing of objects.
7. Observe an art teacher in action and document the methods used by the teacher. How many methods mentioned in this chapter did you observe? Was the teaching effective? Did you observe ways that instruction might be improved through the use of a wider variety of teaching methods?
8. Review the list of teaching methods in this chapter. Add to the list other methods that you can think of or have observed.
9. Select two of the teaching methods listed in this chapter. Develop lessons that utilize each of these, and try them out in a classroom situation with students. Repeat this process with one or two more methods until you have developed a repertoire of teaching methods upon which you can rely as situations arise in your teaching position.

◆ SUGGESTED READINGS

Arends, Richard I. *Learning to Teach* (New York: Random House, 1988). A general textbook.

Brittain, Lambert W. *Creativity, Art and the Young Child* (New York: Macmillan, 1979), Chapter 7, "Role of the Teacher."

Chapman, Laura. *Approaches to Art in Education* (New York: Harcourt Brace Jovanovich, 1978). This comprehensive text presents a consistent view of a balanced art program.

Michael Day, Elliot Eisner, Robert Stake, Brent Wilson, Marjorie Wilson. *Art History, Art Criticism, and Art Production*, Vol. II (Los Angeles: Rand Corporation, 1984). Case studies of art programs in seven school districts around the United States are detailed in this volume. There are numerous accounts of classroom teaching practices.

Eisner, Elliot. *The Educational Imagination*, 2nd ed. (New York: Macmillan, 1985). For an excellent discussion on the design and evaluation of school programs.

Hubbard, Guy. *Art for Elementary Classrooms* (Englewood Cliffs, NJ: Prentice-Hall, 1982), Chapter 8, "Strategies for Teaching."

Lowenfield, Viktor. *Creative and Mental Growth*, rev. ed. (New York: Macmillan, 1952). See the discussion on "Proper Art Stimulation" in Chapter 7.

Robertson, Seonid. *Rosegarden and Labyrinth* (London: Routledge and Kegan Paul, 1963). A unique journal of introspection of an English art teacher.

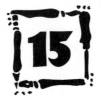

THE SOCIAL DIMENSION: GROUP ART AND INSTRUCTIONAL GAMES

A GROUP OF children around a conference table setting up goals, making plans, assuming responsibilities, or evaluating achievements represents an essential prelude to intelligent, responsible citizenship. Children learn from one another through sharing ideas; group action is more effective when several individuals have shared in the planning; individuals find a place in group projects for making contributions in line with special talents; and morale is higher when children work together cooperatively on group projects.[1]

William Ragan and C. B. Stendler

A school child, as well as an adult in society, is often an individual interacting within groups. Children belong to a class assigned to a teacher, they belong to a grade level, and they are associated with their particular school. Within the classroom, children are often grouped for various reasons. The girls compete against the boys in a contest, reading groups are formed, interest groups are organized, and children develop their own groupings according to friendships. Although much of their learning must be accomplished individually, learning and interacting within groups is also very important and beneficial. As they participate in groups children can learn social skills, enjoy making a contribution, share in the excitement of the group, and learn in a cooperative manner about the subject or topic that is the focus of the activity.

In his book *Democracy as a Way of Life*, Boyd H. Bode stated that "teaching democracy in the abstract is on a par with teaching swimming by correspondence."[2] In a democratic community, Bode says, there is provision for all people to share in the common life according to their interests and capacities. A democratic school promotes the doctrine that people are free and equal by taking proper account of individual differences and by reliance on the principle of community living.

In this chapter we discuss the expanded role that art education can play in giving children some understanding of social processes as they increase their understanding of art. We shall describe some art activities that are especially suitable for the development of children's social insights. We will discuss concepts of art that have emerged in recent years, as well as more traditional forms, such as puppetry and mural making. We will provide examples of children learning about art through participation in a variety of educational games.

THE ROLE OF THE TEACHER IN GROUP ACTIVITY

While realizing the desirability of including group activities in an art program, the teacher may have certain questions concerning the mechanics of this technique. How does group activity work? How should the activity be chosen? What should be its scope? What is the role of the teacher?

A number of years ago, Kilpatrick outlined the steps in what he called a "purposeful activity." These steps, which have stood the test of time, he called *purposing, planning, executing,* and *judging.*[3] Kilpatrick's steps were to be verified much later in the many descriptions of the creative process that came to light as a result of research into creativity. Creative minds in both the sciences and the arts were found to work in a progression of thought and action similar to Kilpatrick's steps.

Group activities, like those of an individual, must begin with some end in mind. This sense of purpose, Kilpatrick says, supplies the drive necessary to complete the project. Moreover, it is the children who should share a role in the "purposing." The teacher, of course, may make suggestions, but before these suggestions can be effected, the children must accept them wholeheartedly. Both the "planning" and the "executing," which are outcomes of the purposing, must also be controlled by members of the working group. Finally, the children themselves must ask the general and the specific questions concerning the outcome of the activity. Did they do what they planned? What was learned in the doing? What mistakes were made? How could the activity be done better next time? Children, in other words, should also be involved in evaluating the experience.

The functions of the teacher in a group activity in art are parallel to those associated with individual learning. The methods of motivation,

Public mural painting is a popular activity in Mexico, where group activities are often part of neighborhood festivals.

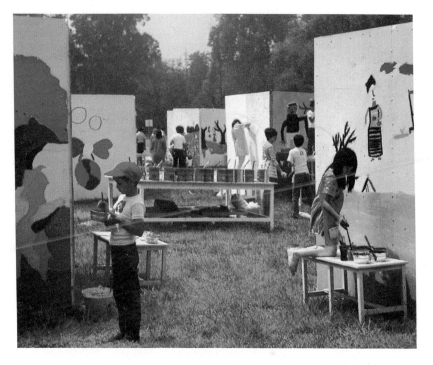

the definition of tasks, establishing artistic goals, and selecting media and tools of expression now must be applied to those pupils, whether few or many, who make up the art group.

In the collective life of the school or classroom, occasions requiring group effort in art invariably arise if goals are to be reached. "Let's have a play," the children say, "Let's run a puppet show. . . . Let's make a big picture to go in the hallway." Very little suggestion need come from the teacher to set in motion a desirable group project. The children themselves are often the first to suggest to a teacher that a group activity be considered.

It is in this area that the classroom teacher has an advantage over the art teacher who may see a class for only fifty minutes a week. Children quickly learn that some activities are inappropriate for the typical art schedule and do not even suggest time-consuming group activities. If art teachers are skillful, however, they can sustain interest from one week to the next so that a class is able to paint a wall, build a miniature city, or convert a section of the art room into an art "environment." There will always be some children who want to continue working on such a project after school, and there may even be release time for others to come to the art room as a large project nears completion.

Before encouraging children to proceed with a group project, the teacher must judge not only whether it is sufficiently challenging to occupy the attention of several people, but also whether it may be too large for successful completion by a group. In their enthusiasm for art, children are sometimes willing to plunge into a task that they could never complete. Once fired with the idea of a mural, for example, a group of fifth graders might cheerfully embark on the enormous task of designing murals for all four walls of a school gymnasium. One or even two murals might be made successfully, but production of many more would exhaust the pupils. A group activity in art that comes to a wavering halt because the children have lost interest or lack competence to complete it reflects not only on the group techniques but also on the teacher's judgment. When failure looms, the teacher must help the pupils alter their plans so that they can achieve success.

Having a greater maturity and insight into group processes, the teacher must fill the role of counselor with tact, sympathy, and skill. As soon as the need for group work in art is apparent, the children must be urged to elect leaders and establish committees necessary for "purposing, planning, executing, and judging" to take place. As stated earlier, the teacher should see that, as far as is practical, the children control these steps. Although teachers have the power of veto, they should be reluctant to use it. If at times the children's decisions seem to be wrong, the teacher should nevertheless allow them to proceed, unless, of course, their chosen course of action would only lead to overwhelmingly disastrous results. It is part of the learning process for people to make mistakes and, profiting from them, subsequently to rectify them.

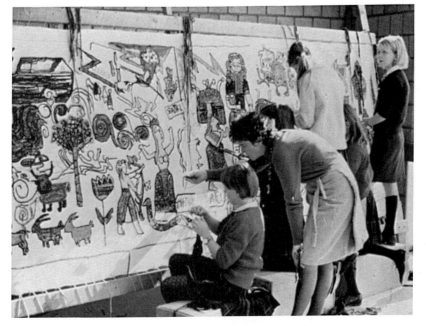

The teacher supervises pupils working on a rag tapestry. Although this sort of group craft activity takes considerable preparation, the results are uniqe in their richness of texture and color; they make an unusual contribution to the school or classroom.

To one aspect of counseling the teacher must give special attention. Since group procedures depend for success largely on the maximum contribution of each participant, the teacher must see that every child in the group is given a fair opportunity to make a suitable contribution to the project. A good group project should include a wide enough range of tasks to elicit participation from every member of the class.

GROUP ACTIVITIES: SIMPLER FORMS

Media and Techniques.   A group activity for primary grades may be based on any theme that interests the pupils and may make use of any medium and technique that the children are capable of handling. If a kindergarten class happens to be talking about the subject of spring, for example, each child who has reached the symbol stage may select one item of the season to illustrate. The children may draw and paint symbols of flowers, birds, trees, and other springlike objects. After drawing or painting each item, the children cut away the unused paper around the symbol. Then the drawings and paintings are assembled on a tackboard.

Many other suitable topics could be treated in a similar fashion. Among them might be the following:

1. Shopping with Mother: Various stores may be drawn and painted, together with people and automobiles. This subject could also be handled as an interior scene showing the articles on display in a supermarket.

2. Our House: Pictures of houses are eventually assembled to form a street.

3. My Friends: The outlines of boys and girls are assembled to form a crowd of children.

4. Spring in the Garden: Gathering associated forms such as bugs, butterflies, and flowers.

5. Above and Below: Including sky shapes (clouds and birds), trees and flowers, and imaginative treatment of what lies below the earth's surface.

Three-dimensional output also lends itself to early group activity. For example, the children can assemble modeling and paper constructions on a table to depict scenes such as "The Farm" with barns, cows, and so forth, and "The Circus" with clowns, elephants, and the like.

One of the simplest and most effective group projects is the "chalk-in," which can be executed on a sidewalk or parking lot. This can be done randomly or with sections marked off in a grid, with each section touching an adjacent one at some point.

In the primary grades, children like to work simultaneously on four sides of the paper. Later, they will be disturbed by the lack of a baseline and will prefer to work from one side. If they choose to paint in a nonobjective mode, a common realistic reference point is not as crucial.

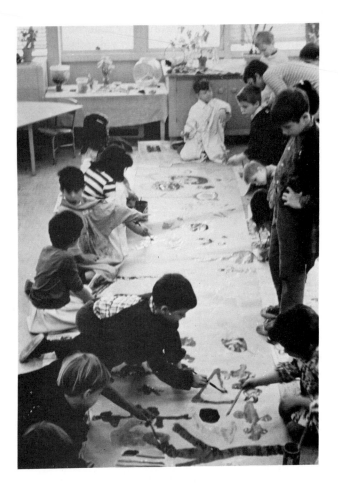

Teaching. The teacher begins the group activity in the same way as individual picture-making or three-dimensional work, supplying motivation and teaching as required. Eventually, when the children have produced their work, the teacher, who has reserved a display space in the room, asks each child to bring a piece of work to the board and pin it in place. At first, a rather disorganized arrangement may result. A short discussion with the class, however, will elicit a few suggestions for improving the placement of the individual drawings. Some of the largest and brightest work can be located near the center of the panel, while smaller drawings of the same symbol drawn by several children might be grouped or arranged in a rhythmic line. When the "mural" is made with cut-out shapes, even a first grader can begin to think of subject matter in relation to organization of masses in space. In such cases, it may facilitate matters to do the initial planning on the floor, where shapes may be more easily adjusted than on the wall.

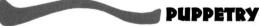

The finished composition will, of course, have many small areas of interest reminiscent of some of the output of Grandma Moses and other so-called primitive artists. Teachers should not attempt to improve the layout by adding any of their own work. If they are tempted to provide a fence or road in perspective, or even a horizon line, they should not, first, because the children should learn to depend only on themselves in developing a group activity and, second, because only a muddle could result if adult work (however naive) and children's work were assembled on the same panel. Children should not be used as surrogate artists for the teacher.

The main aim of conducting the master group activity is to lead children to the point at which they can master Kilpatrick's four steps. Therefore, even in this beginning stage, all the teacher's actions must be governed by this aim. The teacher should solicit themes from the children so that "purposing" may develop. Later, the children should be urged to decide as a group which items of any class of objects each child should draw. For example, at first all the children might draw lambs for the spring picture, but later the group might decide that certain children should draw chickens, ducklings, and so on. This would lead to better "planning." Then group decisions about, say, media or subject might begin to improve design. Finally, such a simple question as "Could we have made the picture better?" could begin the evaluation process even in these early years.

A "group" may be defined as a team ranging from three students to a complete class, depending on the nature of the project. Small groups work very well on dioramas, middle-sized groups can work in the sandbox, and larger groups can take on constructions like model shopping centers and housing communities. Other projects could include decorative maps or a mural that transforms the entire classroom into a medieval environment, complete with mullioned windows and stone walls.

PUPPETRY

Although puppetry is generally not taken seriously as an art form in the U.S. and Canada, it occupies a very high position in many other cultures. In Moscow, the National Puppet Theater is intended for adults rather than children and in Spain and Italy no public park is complete without an adult puppet theatre. In Indonesia and other Asian cultures, puppeteers begin their careers in childhood as apprentices, learning not only the intricate processes of construction and operation, but the roles to be enacted, many of which date back many generations. These plays recount the myths of creation and the battles between good and evil carried on by warriors and figures of royalty.

This shadow puppet from Java, Indonesia, while intended to be viewed lit from behind on a screen, can be enjoyed for the richness of its decorative detail when not in use. It is constructed of leather which is gilded, painted, and perforated. The continuous line beginning with the forehead and moving over the full profile has the flowing grace of Javanese calligraphy.

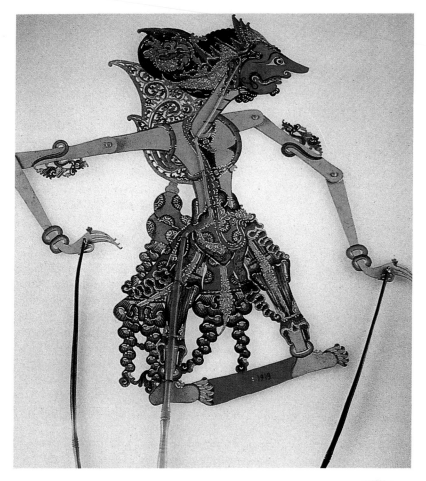

Like the so-called fine arts, puppetry has its own history and its unique function as an educational and socializing factor in both third world and European societies. Puppetry, from hand puppets to marionettes, has a legitimate place in a balanced art program. Perhaps some of the most effective group activities lie within this art form.

Because it is more complex than most art activities, puppetry is often seen as a threat to other priorities in the curriculum. It is therefore neglected in favor of art experiences that require less time and planning and fewer materials. This is to be regretted because, properly conducted, puppetry can carry the children into language arts and history as they go about gathering information, preparing scenarios, and planning and constructing a theater and sets. Work in puppetry is a natural focal point for the various learning styles.

To produce a successful puppet play the group as a whole must reach decisions, and each member of the group, although maintaining personal identity, must give full cooperation if the enterprise is to succeed. Puppets range in technical complexity from the very simple to the very intricate, so that groups of children at any particular stage of development may select techniques compatible with their capabilities. The two major types of puppets that elementary school children in one stage or another may select are fist puppets and shadow puppets.

Fist Puppets

Media and Techniques. Simple stick puppets — the type operated directly with one hand — may be produced in a variety of ways. The beginner can draw a figure on cardboard and later cut away the excess background. The cut-out figure is then attached to a stick. In place of a cut-out figure, the pupil may use a bag stuffed with paper or absorbent cotton, decorated with paint or cut paper, and tied to the stick.

A paper bag may also be used for a puppet that moves its head. A string is tied around the middle of a paper bag, leaving just enough room for inserting the index finger above the middle. A face is painted on the closed upper portion of the bag. To operate the puppet, the hand is thrust into the bag up to the neck and the index finger pushed through the neck to articulate the head.

An old stocking, appropriately decorated with buttons for eyes and pieces of cloth or paper for hair, ears, and other features, also makes an effective puppet when slipped over the hand and arm. Animals such as snakes or dragons may be formed by this means. They become especially fearsome if a mouth is cut into the toe of a sock and cloth is stitched to form a lining to the throat so formed. Both top and bottom jaws should be stuffed with a material like absorbent cotton. The jaws are worked by inserting the fingers in the upper section and the thumb

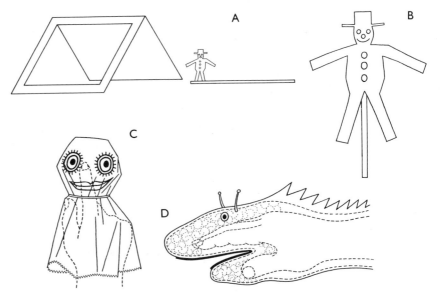

Diagrams of stick puppets (A and B), a puppet made from a paper bag (C), and a puppet made from an old stocking (D).

in the lower. The attractiveness of this creation can be enhanced by making a lining of a color contrasting with the sock, or by adding teeth or a tongue made from bright materials.

A fist puppet may be constructed from a wide variety of materials. Some of the modeling media mentioned in earlier chapters, including papier-mâché, are suitable for the construction of heads; plastic wood may also be used. The bodies of the puppets may be made from remnants of most textiles. These more advanced fist puppets should be capable of articulation in both the head and arms. The thumb and little finger are usually employed to create movements in the arms, while the index finger moves a modeled head.

To model a head, children should first cut and glue together a stiff cylinder of cardboard (preferably light bristol board) large enough in diameter to fit their index finger loosely. The modeling medium, which tends to shrink the cylinder slightly, is then worked directly around the cardboard until the head, including all features, and neck are formed. The neck of the puppet modeled over the lower part of the cylinder, or "fingerstall," should be increased slightly in diameter at its base to hold in place the clothes, which are attached by a drawstring. When the modeling medium is dry, it should be smoothed with sandpaper and then decorated with poster paint. An attractive sparkle can be added to eyes, lips, or teeth by coating them with shellac or, better still, clear nail polish. In character dolls, attention can be drawn to outstanding features by the same means. Most puppets tend to be more appealing if the eyes are considerably enlarged and made conspicuous with a shiny coating. Hair, eyebrows, and beards made from absorbent cotton, yarn, cut paper, or scraps of fur can be pasted or glued in place.

The clothing covers the child's hand and arm and forms the body of the puppet. The outside dimensions of the clothing are determined by the size of the child's hand. The hand should be laid flat on a desk with the thumb and index and little fingers extended. The approximate length of the puppet's arms will be indicated by the distance from the tip of the thumb to the tip of the little finger, and the neckline should come halfway up the index finger. To make clothing, fold a single piece of cloth in two, make a cut in the center of the fold for the neck, and then sew the sides, leaving openings for the fingers. Small mitts may be attached to the openings to cover the fingertips. If children wish their puppets to have interchangeable costumes, a drawstring can be used to tie the clothing to the neck. If they plan on designing only one costume for their puppets, the pupils can glue it into place, as well as tying it for extra security.

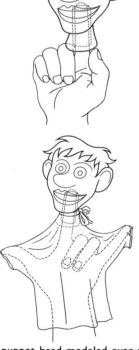

A puppet head modeled over a cardboard fingerstall. The puppet can be manipulated by placing the fingers as shown.

Lively puppet costumes can be made with bright textiles; men's old ties are valuable for this purpose. The lining of the ties should first be removed and the material ironed flat before being folded over and sewn to make a garment. Buttons and other decorations may be added, of course, as required.

When children make puppets, they expect to use them in a stage production. In presenting a fist-puppet show, the operators work beneath the set. This means that the stage must be elevated so that the puppeteers can stand or crouch under it while the show goes on. A simple stage can be constructed from a large topless cardboard carton with two sides removed and an opening for the stage cut in its base. The carton is then placed on a table with the opening facing the audience. The puppeteers stand or crouch behind the table and are concealed from the audience by a curtain around the table legs. Teachers can capitalize on the popularity of television's Muppets, but should avoid using commercially manufactured hand puppets, since children may see these as competing with their own efforts.

The stage settings should be simple. In most cases they may be approached as large paintings, but they should have strong "carrying" power and be rich in a decorative sense. The costumes and backdrops should be designed to provide a visual contrast with each other. Because the stage has no floor, the background is held or fixed in position from below or hung from a frame above. On it may be pinned significant items such as windows and doors. Separate backdrops may be prepared for each scene. Likewise, stage properties—tables, chairs, and the like—must be designed in two dimensions. Spotlights create striking effects and bring out the features of the presentation. Occasionally it may be worthwhile to experiment with projected materials like slides.

The manipulation of fist puppets is not difficult; the pupils can teach themselves the technique merely by practice. They should remember, however, that when more than one puppet is on stage, the puppet that is "speaking" should be in a continual movement, so that the audience may know exactly which puppet is the speaker. The other puppets should be still.

Shadow Puppets

Although shadow puppets are not difficult to make, successful operation of them demands some finesse. In this technique a silk or nylon screen is set up between the operators and the audience. Strong spotlights on the operators' side are then beamed on the screen. The puppets, consisting of cardboard figures attached to a thin control stick, are held close to the screen in the direct path of the light, thus casting a shadow on the screen. Because the puppet appears to the audience only as a shadow silhouette, the figure needs no painting or decorating. The technique of operating is similar to that used with fist puppets, so that the stage for the latter may also be used for shadow puppets.

An authentic Javanese puppet, manipulated by a fifth grade boy. Since the construction principle is simple, children can create a Western version of the same puppet; a sheet and two light sources will be needed to create the performance. Javanese puppetry can provide an introduction to Asian art, mythology, religion, and entertainment.

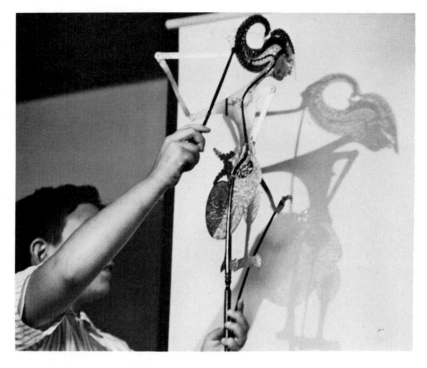

Children in the earliest phases of the symbol stage can be taught to make shadow puppets. The child simply cuts out a figure drawn on thin cardboard and glues it to a stick. As the children develop their ability to produce symbols and as their skill in using cutting tools improves, they can make much more elaborate puppets. Outlines will become more subtle so that such features as shaggy hair, heavy eyebrows, or turned-up noses can be suggested in the silhouette. By punching holes or cutting inside the puppet, the pupil can depict, say, buttons, eyes, and frilly clothing.

Still more experienced pupils can make shadow puppets with moving parts. To make a dragon, for example, a number of small sections of cardboard are joined with paper fasteners. Two sticks are attached to the assembly. With practice, a child can make the creature wiggle in a highly satisfactory manner. All properties, from tables to houses, must be cut from cardboard, placed on sticks, and also shown in silhouette.

Teaching All Types of Puppetry.   As indicated earlier, it is not difficult for a teacher to arouse pupils' interest in puppetry to the point where they desire to produce a play. Most children today are familiar with puppets; some puppets have even gained national interest and affection. Short educational films that show puppets in action are available. The screening of such a film in the classroom is often enough to launch a puppetry project.

Cooperative planning of the project is more difficult. Many teachers begin by holding a general discussion of the problems involved. After viewing a film, children are asked to list the various tasks that must be done before a show can be successfully produced. Eventually the main items of work are listed: selecting or writing the play; making the puppets; making the stage scenery; lighting the stage; and practicing manipulation.

Next, committees should be listed to carry out the various tasks. Such committees might include a selecting committee to recommend suitable plays to the general group and a production committee to recommend suitable stage properties and backdrops for each scene, the general size of the puppets, and the costumes.

Often the chairmen of the committees are elected with the understanding that they will form a "cabinet" with the duty of overall coordination of the project. Either the members of the cabinet or all the children elect a chairperson, or president, of puppeteers from among the cabinet members, whose duty is to report from time to time to the children about progress and to seek suggestions for improvement.

The teacher's task during these proceedings is to see that the organization of the project takes place smoothly. The work intensifies when the "executing" stage is reached. Often demonstrations, short lessons, and informal advice are needed. The teacher must be particularly careful to keep in constant touch with the chairperson, often through the president, to see that they are successful in their efforts. Exactly what a teacher does at this stage, however, would be difficult to define for all cases. Each situation brings its own problems and suggests its own procedures.

Puppetry, like any theatrical activity, culminates in the inevitable presentation of a performance for an audience. The teacher should help the class as a whole to decide who will review the performance — the PTA? the class next door? all the sixth grade classes? and so on. Once the audience has been decided on, publicity must begin; this may involve preparing posters for bulletin boards, a story for the school paper or PTA bulletin, and mimeographed programs, that final testimonial to all who have had a hand in the production.

It is most important that group evaluation or judging take place as the production proceeds, and after the show is finished the time-honored question is raised: "How can we improve the show next time?"

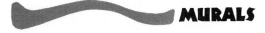 **MURALS**

Murals and Art History

The tradition of making murals, or very large paintings on walls, is an art form dating back to Egypt, Greece, and other early cultures. One might even claim that the prehistoric cave paintings are murals. During the Renaissance, murals in fresco were very popular, and two of the world's most famous works are murals in churches done during that period: Michelangelo's ceiling of the Sistine Chapel, and Leonardo da Vinci's *Last Supper*. Marc Chagall painted magnificent murals on the ceiling of the Paris Opera House, and American artists such as Thomas Hart Benton painted murals for the federal government as part of an assistance program during the Great Depression. Diego Rivera is perhaps as well known for his murals as any artist; the great Mexican artist painted numerous murals, many of them on highly charged social and political themes, in the United States and Mexico. Hispanic-American artists in contemporary communities such as Los Angeles have continued Rivera's influence with striking public murals on building exteriors.

Although elementary school children cannot use oil paints or do frescoes, they can gain familiarity with the terms used in discussing these media. They can also observe how mural materials have changed with advancements of technology: muralists now use such materials as welded metals, fired enamel plates, ceramics, and concrete. David Siqueiros, for example, has used automotive lacquers as well as other industrial materials in his murals. Gyorgy Kepes has produced murals using illuminated glass, and John Mason has used clay. Muralists today are more likely to be sculptors than painters; children who are exposed to their work may want to make a relief mural rather than a painting for their class activity. Children involved in mural-making

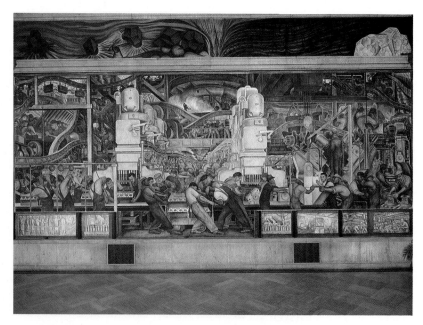

Diego Rivera, *Detroit Industry*, 1932–1933. © The Detroit Institute of Arts, Founders Society Purchase, Edsel B. Ford Fund and Gift of Edsel B. Ford. This is one panel of a very large fresco mural by the great Mexican artist, depicting the automobile industry in Detroit during the first decades of the century. Murals, because of their large size, provide an excellent format for telling complicated stories or expressing magnificent themes. A mural usually includes many details such as the figures in Rivera's work, each figure involved in some operation of the automobile factory.

activities will benefit from learning about these traditions, and teachers will note that children often demonstrate greater interest, have more ideas, and create better murals when they have been taught about the great traditions associated with murals.

Mural Making

While the term mural in its strictest sense refers to a painting made directly on a wall, in many schools it has come to denote any large picture. We have adopted that meaning for this discussion. Murals can be painted or constructed on exterior or interior walls, and we can find examples of both done by children in their schools and neighborhoods. For example, a school in an industrial part of town may be near an abandoned factory surrounded by concrete walls that are an eyesore for the community. With proper permissions, the school art classes could transform the ugly wall into an object of beauty and community pride.

Media and Techniques. When a school group decides to paint a mural inside the school it should be considered as part of a scheme of interior decoration and should be integrated with it. The color relationships already established in the interior in which the mural is placed should be echoed in the new work. Furthermore, since door and window openings create a design in a room, the mural should be placed so that it does not violate the architectural arrangement of these elements but rather tends to maintain the existing plan or even to improve on it. The

These fifth and sixth graders are painting the walls that connect the art and music rooms. The theme is animals making music. The medium is acrylic, and each student was required to submit several suggestions before beginning to paint his or her own subject. The teacher made the final decision on the grouping of the subjects.

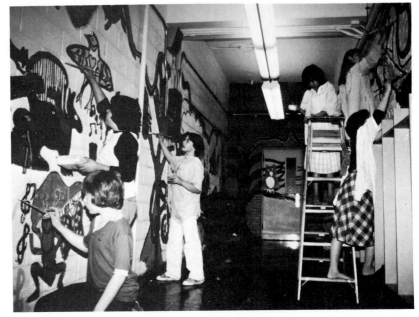

architectural limitations of classrooms are so consistently severe that most murals will probably be no larger than 4 by 8 feet—a size convenient for resting on the ledge of the blackboard. Homosote or composition board backing, which can be purchased at lumberyards or building supply stores, may be used as a light, portable background for direct painting or as a backing for mural paper.

Despite the technicalities involved in the successful production of a mural, most children find that the activity is generally within their capabilities, and the experience of mural making is a happy and rewarding one for them. Children in the primary grades will have difficulty in preplanning their work and will probably see mural making as an activity that allows them to paint large pictures on vertical surfaces. But those who have reached a stage of social maturity that allows them to work with a degree of cooperation and preplanning should find little difficulty in making a mural.

The subject matter for murals may be similar to that used in individual picture making, or it may derive from a broader frame of reference such as social studies. The most successful murals reflect the children's own experiences and interests. A subject such as "The Western Movement," though not a part of the child's personal background, can still be worthwhile if due attention is given to motivation by creating the environment of the early settlers with folk music, old prints, posters, and films. Whatever subject is chosen must be sufficiently broad in scope to allow several pupils to elaborate on it. A still-life composition, for example, would not be an appropriate subject for a mural.

The distinction between a painting with a limited focus of attention and a mural with multiple focuses must be made. A subject in which there are many objects of related but differing appearance, such as houses, factory buildings, or crowds of people, would be most suited to group activity. An example of a subject that offers a great variety of shapes is "At the Circus." Members of a third grade class included both circus performers and spectators in the mural. The following are examples of themes that elementary school pupils have successfully developed:

From the Experience of the Child	From Other Areas of the Curriculum
Our School Playground	The Year 3000
A Trip to the Supermarket	The Western Movement
Playing Outside in Winter	Books I Have Liked
Shopping	Our Town (Neighborhood)
The Seasons Change	Acting My Age in Ancient Greece

Most of the picture-making media can be used in mural production. The paper should be sufficiently heavy and tough to support the

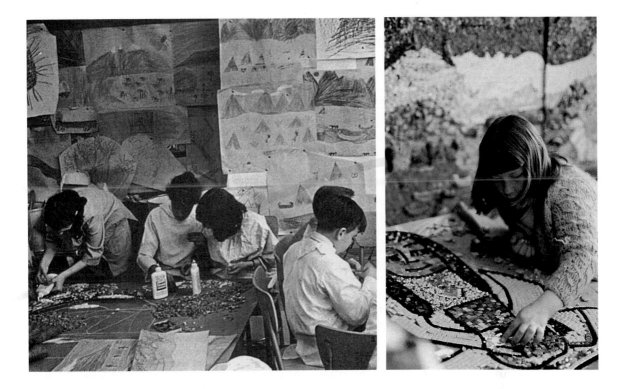

Lili Ann Rosenberg is an artist who divides her time between studio and community. The processes she uses to create her ceramic murals are illustrated in these photographs from her work with children. The students generate ideas that are mounted as they work, then the students and leader organize the ideas into an overall composition. They convert these into flat forms such as tiles or slabs, then color, fire, and glaze them. The "ground is prepared by fastening chicken wire to plywood, and the various sections are separated by "walls" of clay so that individual sections composed of tiles, sand, shells, etc. can be pressed into sections of wet, colored cement.

weight of the finished product. Kraft paper, the heavy brown wrapping paper that comes in large rolls, is suitable. Many school-supply houses offer a gray mural paper that is pleasant to use. When ordering paper, a 4-foot width is recommended. The most effective coloring medium for young children is tempera paint. This should be applied with the same wide range of the brushes suggested for picture making. Some especially wide brushes should be available for painting the large areas of the mural. In applying tempera paint excessive thickness should be avoided, since the paint will flake off when the mural is rolled up for storage. Chalk may be used, but it tends to be dusty and to smudge badly when several children are working at one time. Colored cut paper also yields effective results from the first grade on; the cut paper can also be combined with paper collage. Wax crayons are not suitable because they require too much effort to cover large areas, but crayons may be used in some areas as a resist with thin tempera.

The technique of planning and executing the mural varies with the nature of the group. The kindergarten child may begin by working side by side with classmates on the same long strip of paper. Beginners all paint on the same topic suggested by the teacher and use the same medium, but each child actually creates an individual composition without much reference to the work of the others. Not until they reach the third or fourth grade are some children able to plan the mural cooperatively. When they develop this ability they may begin by making sketches lightly in chalk on the area allotted for the mural. Considerable discussion and many alterations may occur before the design satisfies all the participants. By the time they reach the fifth or sixth grade, many pupils are ready to plan a mural on a reduced scale before beginning the work itself. They prepare sketches on paper with dimensions proportionate to those of the mural. These sketches are made in outline and in color. Later, when the mural paper has been laid over a large table or pinned to tackboard, the final sketch is enlarged on the mural surface. Usually this is done freehand, but sometimes teachers suggest that the squaring method of enlargement be used. By this method the sketch and the mural surface are divided into corresponding squares. A pupil redraws in the corresponding area of the mural what is in a specific area of the sketch. Such a procedure, while common practice with professional muralists, may easily inhibit elementary school children and should be used with caution. Only the most mature children are capable of benefiting from this technique.

After the drawing (or "cartoon," as it is sometimes called) has been satisfactorily transferred to the mural surface, the colors are applied. If tempera paint is to be used, it is usually mixed in advance in a relatively limited number of hues. Tints and shades are also mixed in advance. All colors should be prepared in sufficient quantity to complete all areas in the mural where they are to be used. In this way time and paint are saved, and the unity of the mural created in the sketch is preserved in the larger work. If colored chalk or cut paper is used, of course, the class is not likely to run out of a color. Acrylic paint, which is now comparable in price to tempera, is advisable for murals since it is waterproof, does not flake off if rolled up, and allows sand, paper, and other objects to be embedded in it while the paint is still wet.

When pupils use cut paper, the technique for producing a mural is less formal than when paint or chalk is used. The pupils can push areas of the colored paper around on the mural to find the most satisfying effects. Thus plans may undergo even major revision up to the final moment when the colored paper is stuck to the surface. Colored construction paper is recommended for the main body of the mural because it gives the background areas added interest.

In carrying out the plan of a mural the pupils quickly discover that they must solve other problems of design peculiar to this work. Because the length of a mural in relation to its height is usually much greater than in paintings, the technical problem arises of establishing a satisfactory center of interest. Although only one center of interest may be developed, it must not be so strong that the observer finds it necessary to ignore portions of the work at the extremities of the composition. On the other hand, if a series of centers of interest are placed along the full length of the composition, the observer may consider the result too jumpy and spotty. In general, the composition should be dispersed, the pupils being particularly careful about connecting the rhythms they establish so that no part of the mural is either neglected or unduly emphasized. The balances in a mural made by children, furthermore, have a tendency to get out of hand. Not infrequently children become intrigued with subject matter in one section of the work, with the result that they may give it too much attention and neglect other sections. Profuse detail may overload a favored part, while other areas are overlooked.

One problem of design that rarely occurs in mural making is lack of variety. Indeed, with many people working on the same surface the problem is usually too much variety. Once they become aware of this difficulty, however, children are usually able to remedy the defect.[4]

Teaching. As with puppetry, it is not difficult to interest children in making murals. Showing a film and slides or going to see a mural in a public building are two fairly practical ways of arousing their interest. Pictures of the recently restored ceiling of the Sistine Chapel, for example, show the tremendous scale of Michelangelo's masterpiece and the complicated foreshortening that the artist had to accomplish in the figures so they would look natural when viewed from the floor.[5] Before and after photographs show the remarkable effects of cleaning in restoring the vivid colors that Michelangelo applied, but which had been dimmed by dirt and deterioration over the centuries. Students can gain some idea of the tremendous size and scope of the artist's accomplishment, the value that is placed on the work by experts, and the care with which the restoration has been accomplished through the use of computers and other modern devices. Children are also motivated by seeing the murals that other children have made. Perhaps the most effective method is to discuss with the class the needs and benefits of making murals as decorations for specified areas of the school, such as the classroom, the halls, the cafeteria, or the auditorium.

Although in puppetry there is often enough work to be done to permit every member of the class to participate in the endeavor, this is not so in mural making. The pupils may all discuss the making of murals, including the various media, the most suitable subjects, and the probable locations in which the work might be placed, but eventually the pupils must divide into small groups, probably not to reunite until the final evaluation period. In the elementary school, the small groups may comprise from three to ten pupils each, depending on the size of the mural.

Preadolescents should be able to organize their own mural making. First, all the pupils in a class interested in mural making assemble to

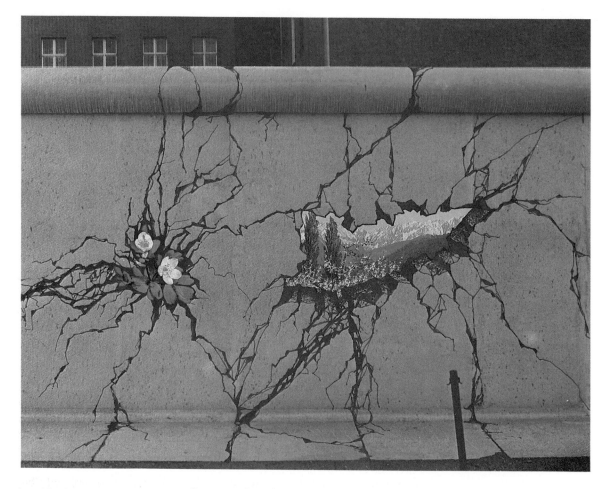

Lew Nussberg executed this plan for what was possibly the greatest mural opportunity in the world — the Berlin Wall. The hundreds of drawings, paintings, and graffiti filled its cold gray surfaces; it serves as an example of the artist acting as social critic. This is one section among dozens.

discuss what the theme should be. After the pupils' suggestions for the main theme have been written on the blackboard, each pupil selects some aspect to work on. Those pupils interested in the same aspect form a team to work on that particular mural. If too many pupils elect one aspect, two teams can be created, each to work separately on the same subject. The teams are finally arranged and each elects its chairperson.

Discussion then takes place within each team concerning the size and shape of its particular mural, the medium, and possible techniques. Sketches are then prepared, either cooperatively or individually. The teams can either choose the individual sketch most liked by all or prepare a composite picture, using the best ideas from the several sketches. The cartoon is then drawn, usually with the chairperson supervising to see that the chosen sketch is reproduced with reasonable accuracy. Next the color is added. From time to time the chairperson may find it necessary to hold a team consultation to appraise the work, so that some of the pitfalls of design in mural making are avoided. This process goes on until each team's mural is completed. Finally, under a general chairperson, all the mural-makers meet to review their work and to discuss the usual topics that arise in the "judging" stage.

During these proceedings the teacher acts as a consultant. If the pupils have previously made individual pictures, the teacher need give few demonstrations. The teacher's tasks consist for the most part in seeing that a working area and suitable materials are available, providing the initial motivation, outlining some of the technical requirements of a mural, and demonstrating the "squaring" method of enlarging, if it is to be used.

A completely different approach allows the children to develop the mural spontaneously. In this approach the children choose only the colors beforehand in order to assure some harmony. The group then gathers around all four sides of the paper that is placed on the floor and begins to paint. If the group is too large to do this comfortably, it is divided into smaller units. The first children paint whatever comes into their minds and succeeding groups try to relate their shapes and colors to those that have preceded them. The entire experience should be as open, and the children as immediately responsive, as possible.

Tableau Projects

In the late Middle Ages and into the Renaissance, many artists were called upon to provide or design entertainments for their patrons. Even Leonardo da Vinci designed many such projects for the Duke of Milan. Included among the entertainments were the production of tableaux vivants (living pictures) in which participant-actors dressed and posed in legendary or historical depictions. Such tableaux could provide an unusual assembly program.

Students working in teams should choose a work of art and "become" the work of art through the creation of a setting, costumes, and posing figures. They should be encouraged to use the simplest materials, the emphasis of the project being the understanding of the visual aspect of the work that they have chosen to portray.

As well as the tableau itself, the members of the group can include an oral presentation of background information on the artist, the work itself, or the historical context. At the time of the presentation, a slide of the original work can be shown so that the spectators can compare the original with the tableau.

Blowups

"Blowups" are another simple way to begin a mural, and the most manageable way as well, since each child works on his own section in his own space. First, select an interesting image. (Photographs of the facades of older buildings, group portraits, and city views are good subjects.) Then cut the master photo into as many squares as there are students and give each class member his or her own section of the photo to enlarge according to scale (a 1-by-1-inch square equals a 1-by-1-foot square, and so on.) They then transfer the small segments to the larger space, heeding whatever problem or technique the class has selected for attention. This is an excellent way to apply a particular skill in color, collage, or pencil. In studying color, children can work in flat tones, blend the tones, or try to match the original color purely as an exercise in color control. When the segments are assembled according to the original, nothing quite goes together; the viewer must accomplish the process of making things "fit"—of perceptual reconstruction—and that makes the viewer a more active participant when studying the final image.

When making blowups, randomness moves closer to control. In this situation students work strictly on their own but within certain limitations, knowing that a surprise awaits them. For example, a junior high school art teacher wanted to celebrate Washington's birthday in an unusual and memorable way. He cut up a reproduction of Leutze's *Washington Crossing the Delaware* into 1-inch squares. Each student received a square and a large sheet of paper cut to a proportionate size. The class then "blew up," or enlarged to scale, the small segments and transferred them to the large paper. No attempt was made to match colors, since Day-Glo paint was used instead of the standard tempera, watercolor, or chalk. Hence individual students used whatever colors they wanted to without regard for Leutze's painting or the choice of other students. A wall was selected for mounting the project. When the completed pieces were assembled in proper order and fixed in place, a black light was turned on the wall and the effect was overwhelming. The teacher's behavioral goal was reached: "Neither teacher nor students will ever forget Washington's birthday."

This blowup was created when two children drew the outline of the monster, then each child in the group filled in a section of the work. A reproduction of a painting can be created by dividing it into as many parts as there are students. Each student enlarges his or her segment with some medium such as paint, chalk, collage, pencil, or a single color, for the study of value.

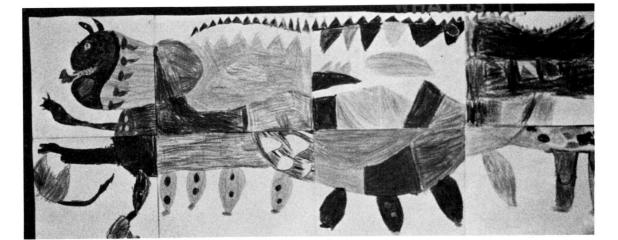

INSTRUCTIONAL ART GAMES

All group art activities are not centered on the making of art objects such as puppets or murals. Art games can be very effective as a means to teach children about art and engage them in enjoyable learning activities. Art games should relate to knowledge about the content of aesthetics, art criticism, and art history. Many of the approaches discussed in the following pages can be integrated with art production activities to lend additional interest and variety. Many of the games can be played with small groups or by individuals.

Art Images for Games

Art games usually require the use of art images; that is, reproductions of artworks. As mentioned earlier, teachers can obtain a wide selection of small, good quality art reproductions by purchasing art magazines such as *ARTnews, Art in America, American Artist, Connoisseur, Portfolio,* and others, and clipping the reproductions from the pages. We recommend that you record all of the pertinent information about each artwork, mount the picture, and place the information on the back. You can collect pictures of paintings, sculpture, prints, architecture, product design, and all modes of art. Another excellent source for small, manipulable art images is the postcards sold in art museums. One of the sources of income for art museums is in the sale of reproductions of the works in their collections. Most of these postcards sell for very reasonable prices, and some museums sell postcard portfolios, which result in even lower costs per card. Some games can be played with larger prints, such as those available from companies that sell reproductions (see the appendix "Art Teaching and Learning Resources" for addresses).

Artists Names and Styles. An elementary art teacher can organize and involve students in learning by using names of artists, styles, or cultures. For example, when students enter the room and sit down, the teacher directs them to look beneath their seats where a card is taped. Each child finds a card that has an artist's name, and possibly biographical information or a picture of a work by the artist. In preparing the cards, the teacher can create any type of categories, such as impressionist painters, cubist painters, abstract expressionist painters, and so on. Or the categories might be related to art modes such as drawing, painting, sculpture, ceramics, or architecture.

The teacher can use the card designators in a variety of ways. "Now students, look at your card and make sure you know who you are. Where is Pablo Picasso? Where is Mary Cassatt? Where is Helen Frankenthaler? I see you notice that your name can be a man's or a woman's; you can trade around later if you want to. The important thing to know is what style of painter you are. I would like all of the cubists to sit at this table, the impressionists over at that table, the fauvists here, and the abstract expressionists at the table by the door."

The teacher can use these categories for cleanup and monitor assignments, for dividing groups for games or studio projects, and for dismissing at the end of class period, or whatever reason group divisions are useful. The teacher can also reshuffle the groups at any time by using other information on the cards. "Will all of you artists please look one more time at the painting on your card. If you used mostly warm colors, sit here; mostly cool colors, sit there . . ." and so forth using categories such as color selection, dates of birth or death, or the subject matter of paintings, such as still-life, figure, or landscape.

The teacher can also use these card designators to encourage class participation. The teacher displays one of Monet's water lily paintings and addresses the class, "Everyone please look at this large print I am showing. Now which one of you painted this?" A boy raises his hand. "Please tell us a little about yourself. What is your name, where are you from, and how did you come to paint this?" The level of these questions and the student's responses will depend on how much instruction has been given and what information is included on the cards. Questions and answers can be very simple at early grades (even using only the visual properties of works for children who can't yet read), and can become very sophisticated with older students who have had the benefit of a regular program of art instruction.

Art Collector. Simple children's card games such as Animal Rummy and Old Maid can be altered to use art images instead of the traditional pictures. One teacher has devised card games using postcard-sized art images. The goal of one of the games is for the players to obtain entire "art collections" of four matching artworks, such as four by Degas, four portraits, four sculptures, and so on. The cards are shuffled, dealt, and the deck is placed face down for drawing. Each card in a collection has the titles and artists' names of the other three in the collection. Children then ask each other for cards that they need for a collection. "Do you have *Waves at Matsushima*, by Sotatsu? If the child who is asked has the card, he or she gives it to the asker, who then gets another turn. If not, the child draws a card. The next child asks, "Do you have *The Letter*, by Mary Cassatt?" or "Do you have *The False Mirror*, by Rene Magritte?" As with most of the games, children become increasingly familiar with art images, styles, modes, subjects, and names of artists.

Similar games are available for purchase in some museums and bookstores. For example, *Art Rummy* consists of 32 cards of quality artworks from the Metropolitan Museum of Art, *Quartet* is a card game with four art images by each of thirteen artists from the collection of the Tate Gallery in London, and *Masterpiece* is an art game of bidding and selling using artworks from the collection of the Chicago Art Institute.

Token Response.   This is one of a number of instructional art games developed by two art educators, Mary Erickson and Eldon Katter.[6] In one variation of the game, the teacher displays several large art prints side by side on the floor along a wall in the classroom or hallway. As always, the selection of artworks is important and can be controlled by the teacher according to the age group, curriculum, and students' familiarity with the artworks. The students are given cards that have certain responses written on them or portrayed with symbols or art images. For example, a card might say "I like it" next to the symbol of a heart or a depiction of a well-liked artwork such as Van Gogh's *Starry Night*. The card that represents "the oldest" might have an image of an Egyptian sculpture; the "best idea" might show Rodin's *Thinker*; and "took the most time" might show a drawing of the soft clock in Dali's *Persistence of Memory*. Other responses might be "I'd like this in my house," "worth the most money," and, "I don't like it." Teachers can make up responses that relate to concepts taught in the curriculum.

For the game, each student is given a set of cards (about eight responses) and is directed to place the cards next to the paintings according to their personal preferences. This often works better if you have a small box next to each painting with a slot for the cards. This eliminates the problem of a child being unduly influenced by others' responses. The rules of the game can be varied also according to the teacher's instructional purposes and the age levels of the children. They are usually told that they can "spend" more than one card on a painting, and that they do not have to use all of the cards if they don't find a painting for which the response fits. This part of the game stimulates a great deal of thinking, conversation, close observation, laughter, and sometimes indecision.

The discussion phase of the game is probably the most educational, as interesting questions about responses are raised. For example, the teacher might comment, "We can see from looking at the cards by each painting that some of us placed 'I don't like it' next to the Picasso, and others placed 'I like it' cards. Which group is right?" Or the question for discussion might be, "I saw one person place an 'I don't like it' card and a 'best in show' card next to the same painting. Is that inconsistent?" These questions and others raise aesthetics issues that are very stimulating for children to discuss. Children are encouraged to support their decisions with reasonable statements and arguments. Through all of the discussions children will begin to see that there are different points of view about these issues, that there is often not one simple right or wrong answer, and that more than one point of view might seem logical and persuasive. This is a wonderful opportunity to discuss with children the differences between preference and judgment.

Link Up. This game was developed at the S.L.O. Curriculum Institute in the Netherlands and is printed in several langauges.[7] The idea of the game centers on four artworks (postcard size) that come with the game, but which could be substituted with other images by the teacher. Students playing the game place the four art images where they can be seen together, then select a set of game cards identified with the same number. The number 1 set of cards consists of five pictures of objects: a tree, a scissors, a horizon line, a purse, and a ladder. Children match these cards with the four artworks, leaving out the incorrect extra card. The number 5 set has cards with dots that correspond to the organization of main objects in each artwork. They range from one to twenty-seven dots, and four of the cards correspond nicely to the compositions of the four artworks. Other cards have words describing materials of objects depicted in the paintings, materials out of which the paintings might be constructed, words describing moods of the artworks, and so on. Children can play the game individually or in groups. They can play for a few minutes or go through all of the cards in a longer period of time. When children become familiar with all of the items and responses, the teacher can make new sets of cards with different items, and can make changes in the selection of the four art images. The following games were devised by the authors and have been used with great success in classroom situations. Some will appeal more to older elementary students, but each game can be adapted by teachers to meet the levels of their students.

Guess the Theme. Using small reproductions or postcard art images, organize five or six artworks according to some theme or idea. For very young children this might be very simple, such as five paintings of babies, or five sculptures of horses. For older children themes can be more difficult to detect, such as six works from different cultures, in different art media, all representing some form of violence (which is, unfortunately, very common in history and in art).[8] A theme such as this might also raise questions about what art should depict, and what artists should create about the world around them. The number of themes is almost limitless. Some interesting examples might be: people at work (using different cultures); mother and child; people with authority; flowers in art; relationships between two people; hats; cityscapes; and so on. Themes can relate to topics in the grade level curriculum, such as The Sea, or The Westward Movement.

Compare and Contrast. For this game select two artworks that are similar in some ways, the more obvious for the younger children. Give the two reproductions to a group of three or four children and ask them to discuss (to list if they can write) ways that the two artworks are similar and ways that they are different. In making the comparisons, children should be encouraged to look at information on the back of the cards that will give them more of a basis for deciding on similarities and differences. For example, comparing the portraits of two American presidents, George Washington and Richard Nixon, students can point to both paintings as portraits of men who held the same office, both have dark suits and white shirts, both are looking at the viewer, and both have similar neutral brown backgrounds. From the back of the postcards students will learn that both artists, Gilbert Stuart and Norman Rockwell, are male Americans, but lived in different times, as did the presidents depicted. They will learn that both paintings are in galleries in Washington, D.C. and are owned by the people of the United States, both are oil paintings on canvas, and are approximately the same size, but one is vertical, the other horizontal in format.

Older children might be able to make comparisons of the two men and their records as president. The contrasting styles of the artists and the difference in level of formality of pose might be related to the different times that these men served as president. These paintings would provide teachers with opportunities to relate art to history and social studies as well as politics.

The comparisons that teachers can organize are limitless, including ideas from architecture, applied design, art materials, and cultures. For example: an ivory carving from the Congo of an African mother and child compared with a Raphael madonna; a gold Egyptian statue of *The God Amun* compared with the Roman marble sculpture of *The Apollo Belvedere*; and the geometric nonobjective colored squares painted by Frank Stella compared with the colored splashes and drips in a print by Sam Francis, both created in the 1970s and both hanging in the National Gallery of Art.

How Are These the Same?   In this game the group of children is given a series of art images that have something in common, either obvious or devious depending on the teacher's goals and the children's abilities. For example, the six or seven artworks given to a group might all be made of bronze, they might all be utilitarian art objects, they might all be watercolors, or they might all be nonobjective art. This activity can be used to push children beyond observation into other means of investigation. For example, a series of seven cards seems to have almost nothing in common upon observation of the artworks. One is a traditional portrait painting, another is a nonobjective wood sculpture, another is a floral abstract, another is a watercolor of the sea, and so on. Only by investigating the information on the back of the cards will the students be able to make the connection that all of the works were done by women artists. Other categories might include all religious objects, all in the same museum, or all created by a Dutch artist.

Blind Date. Art teachers have access to hundreds of depictions of men and women in art. We have very formal portraits of men like Napoleon, Giacometti's lonely, thin figures, Warhol's garish film stars, ideal Greek athletes, graceful Japanese figures, and many, many more. The teacher selects ten or twelve art objects depicting figures of men and the same number of images of women from various times and cultures. The task for students (more interesting perhaps for middle school ages) is to match pairs of men and women with the premise of a blind date. Then they are asked to justify their selections. Beyond light-hearted fun comments, students can make a case for selections according to style, period, social class, culture, medium, or by stating reasons that have to do with the personalities of the figures expressed in the works. Why are these two compatible for a blind date? In all discussions encourage students to use the correct titles and names of artists.

Is This Art? Postcard images are arranged in small packets of six or seven. The teacher selects these images to raise questions about definitions of art; what objects can be counted as art, and why? This game works best with small groups of children discussing the question and reporting what they decide and why to the entire class. For example, one packet might contain a photograph of an ordinary chair, a picture of a tree, a painting of a tree, a picture of an animal, a picture of a building, and a photograph of a sculpture. The primary question about art in this packet asks if natural objects are works of art, or if they have to be made by humans. If they have to be made by humans, which objects should be considered art and which objects should not?

Another packet contains art images that are suspect in the minds of some people. Among images that are generally acceptable, such as a Rembrandt painting or Greek sculpture, the teacher places one of the graffiti paintings of Keith Haring, a photograph by Man Ray, and an interior environment by Sandy Skoglund. The variety possible for this game is unlimited and can be directed by the teacher to correlate with curriculum goals and objectives.

Where and When? The teacher displays (maybe permanently) a large world map and a large time line on the wall or bulletin board. On the game table or in a box are several packets of postcards pasted on envelopes (the more substantial envelopes wear better). The information usually found on the back of the postcard, including when and where the works were created, is typed on a card inside each envelope. The task for children is to try to place each art object on the correct continent or island group and/or to place it approximately on the time line. One image is that of an African mask, another is a native American eagle feather bonnet, another is an Egyptian sculpture, another is a Gothic cathedral, and so on. Children can look on the card inside the envelope to see if they were correct. The packets of postcard images are arranged according to difficulty.

Connoisseur. As discussed in Chapter 12, teachers can organize bulletin board displays that include games. For example, for very young children the teacher might display three landscapes and a still life and ask, "Which painting doesn't belong?" Consistent with the notion of connoisseurship, the task can become more difficult as children progress. The image of the connoisseur is a person who can make very fine distinctions, such as art historians, when they give expert opinions of attribution and authenticity of artworks.

In one example of the connoisseur game for upper elementary children (or adults), the teacher displays twelve postcard images of artworks on the bulletin board, each with a number beside it. Six of the postcards show paintings of buildings by Edward Hopper, three show paintings of buildings by Charles Sheeler, Hopper's contemporary, and three show paintings of buildings by other artists such as de Chirico, Wood, Demuth, or Estes. By selecting works that are either very similar to Hopper, or very different, the teacher controls the difficulty of the game.

To play this game students might be asked to

1. list the numbers of the paintings that they think were done by the featured artist (the one with most works displayed)
2. name the featured artist
3. list the numbers of paintings by other artists
4. name as many of these artists as possible
5. list titles of paintings

Students might work individually or in teams. Points can be tallied for every correct response and individual and team champions recognized. To follow up, teachers might ask students to explain how they knew that the six paintings by Hopper belonged together (stylistic characteristics, subject matter, mood, etc.), and how they knew that the other paintings were done by other artists.

In another variation of this game the teacher displays landscapes by Van Gogh along with landscapes by the artist's contemporaries, such as Monet, Gauguin, and others. A few of Van Gogh's landscapes are very impressionistic and are difficult to distinguish from some of Monet's works, making this game a difficult one. Children can learn that artist's styles change with time, that artists are influenced by other artists, and that artist's styles can be very similar during some periods in their careers. They might also see examples of the same scene painted at the same time by two different artists, as is the case with a number of Monet-Renoir pairs. Children might be interested to know that artists sometimes work closely together and associate in social groups, such as the impressionists, cubists, and abstract expressionists did.

Art games can be fun for children and teachers; they can provide variety in teaching and learning; they can motivate and stimulate interest; and they can provide for a great deal of learning. Teachers can use games to raise issues of aesthetics and teach about history and criticism. In the hands (and minds) of good teachers, art games become another component in their instructional repertoire.

◆ NOTES TO THE TEXT

1. From William Ragan and C. B. Stendler, *Modern Elementary Curriculum* (New York: Holt, Rinehart and Winston, 1966), p. 192.

2. Boyd H. Bode, *Democracy as a Way of Life* (New York: Macmillan, 1937), p. 75.

3. W. H. Kilpatrick, *Foundations of Method* (New York: Macmillan, 1925).

4. See Lily Ann Rosenberg, *Children Make Murals and Sculpture* (New York: Reinhold, 1968).

5. For a fascinating article about the restoration of the Sistine Chapel ceiling with excellent pictures, see David Jeffery, "A Renaissance for Michelangelo," *National Geographic*, Vol. 176, No. 6 (December 1989).

6. See their address in the appendix "Art Teaching and Learning Resources" under MELD.

7. Ben Schasfoort, *Link Up* (Enshede, The Netherlands: Instituut voor Leerplanontwikkeling [S.L.O.], 1987).

8. For example, this set might include artworks such as: *The Burning of the Sanjo Palace*, thirteenth-century Japanese; *Battle Between Zanga and Awkhast*, fifteenth-century Iran; *The Martyrdom of St. Hippolytes*, fifteenth-century Flemish; *The Crucifixion*, Tiepolo, 1700; *Echo of a Scream*, Siqueiros, Mexican, 1937; and an untitled drawing showing two men in business suits struggling, by Robert Longo, contemporary American, 1986.

◆ ACTIVITIES FOR THE READER

1. Study a group activity in a classroom and analyze it according to Kilpatrick's four stages.
2. Describe three group activities not mentioned in this chapter.
3. Make three fist puppets: a simple stick puppet, a more complicated paper bag puppet, and, finally, a cloth puppet of an animal whose jaws will move. Improvise dialog around a situation with a fellow student's puppets.
4. Practice manipulating each of your puppets. When skillful, give a short performance for some of your younger friends and see how they react.
5. Study any professional murals in you locality. Make a note of their subject matter in relation to their location, their design, and the media used.
6. Design a small-scale mural suitable for the interior of your local post office, the foyer of a local theater,

or the entrance of the local high school. Choose subject matter of local interest.

7. Try some of the art games described in the chapter. Look for art games in museums and bookstores. Begin your own collection of art games.

8. Collect a large number of art postcards or art magazine cutouts and invent art games using the images. Make games that will be useful for teaching art concepts, skills, and knowledge.

9. Create a game that involves using the following elements:
   a. advancing an object, such as a checker or a chess piece, to reach a destination: a museum, a gallery, or a collection
   b. element of chance, such as rolling dice
   c. moves that are determined by color-coded cards that relate to the numbers on the dice

◆ SUGGESTED READINGS

"Art as Celebration," a special issue of *The Structurist*, No. 19–20 (1979–80). Published by the University of Saskatchewan, Saskatoon, Canada.

Barthelmeh, Volker. *Street Murals: The Most Exciting Art of the Cities of America, Britain and Western Europe*. New York: Alfred A. Knopf, 1982.

Jeffrey, David. "A Renaissance for Michelangelo," *National Geographic*, Vol. 176, No. 6 (December 1989).

Hurwitz, Al. *Programs of Promise: Art in the Schools*. New York: Harcourt Brace Jovanovich, 1972. The chapter "Art for Social Planning" describes environmental planning as a basis for learning in a group.

Hurwitz, Al, and Stanley Madeja. *The Joyous Vision: A Source Book for Elementary Art Appreciation*. Englewood Cliffs, NJ: Prentice-Hall, 1977. Chapter 2, "Teaching for Appreciation," describes several group-centered approaches.

Pavey, Don. *Art Based Games*. London: Love Publishing, 1979.

Rosenberg, Lili Ann Killen. *Children Make Murals and Sculpture: Experiences in Community Art Projects*. New York: Reinhold Book Corp., 1968.

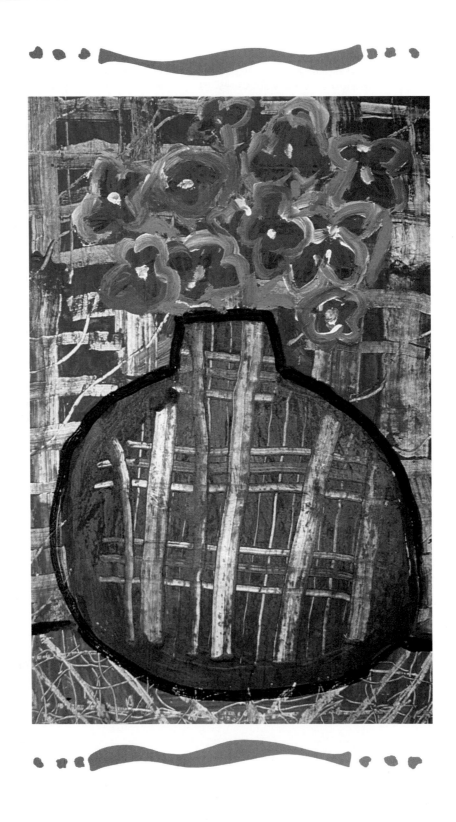

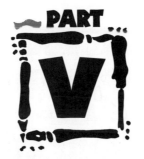

PART V

CURRICULUM AND EVALUATION

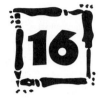

CURRICULUM: BACKGROUND, PLANNING, AND ORGANIZATION

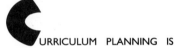URRICULUM PLANNING IS
not thought of as a series of distinct and fixed steps. No single
pattern, beginning, for instance, with stating objectives, will
suffice in solving all curriculum problems. The dynamics of
given school situations and the resources provided by interdisciplinary study and practical experience in curriculum
planning determine the ways in which problems should be
attacked.[1]

Ronald C. Doll

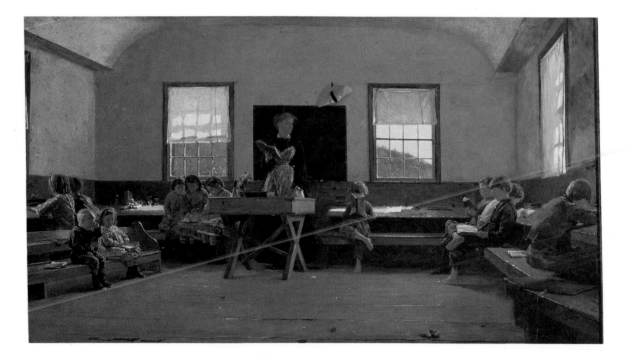

The term curriculum is used to refer to several aspects of the educational enterprise, depending on who is using the term and in what context. For some the curriculum is the organized content that is planned for students to learn; for others curriculum refers not to the written plans for learning, but to actual instruction as it takes place in the classroom. Other educators might indicate that curriculum refers not to what teachers teach, but to what students learn. Still others see the curriculum as the entire experience of children in and out of school. All of these connotations are worth considering whenever we set out to plan a program of art education for children and youth.

This chapter will focus upon organizing art content and planning art activities to promote learning about art. Ronald Doll's definition of curriculum seems appropriate for the emphasis taken here:

> The curriculum of a school is the formal and informal content and process by which learners gain knowledge and understanding, develop skills, and alter attitudes, appreciations, and values under the auspices of that school.[2]

As we discussed in Chapter 1, the art curriculum planning process requires that we pay attention to the dynamic nature of art, appropriate conceptions of children and their abilities to learn, and the values of society.[3] Curriculum planners in different states or provinces will be influenced and guided by the values set forth by the respective state frameworks. Within a particular state, different school districts will shape their state's framework to meet local values, needs, and resources. Within school districts individual schools will apply their own guidelines according to their perceived needs and, finally, each teacher will adapt all of the above educational guidance, as he or she sees fit, in the context of the needs and interests of children in the classroom.

It is difficult, if not inappropriate, to discuss curriculum without referring at the same time to instruction and evaluation. The planned curriculum is intended to be implemented through the teacher's direction and instruction. Art curriculum planners must be aware of the realities of the classroom, including the age levels and abilities of children, requirements and duties placed on the teacher by the school, and relationships between the art curriculum and the rest of the school curriculum. Curriculum developers must also consider relationships among the written curriculum with its goals and objectives, instruction and learning in the classroom, and evaluation of students' progress in relation to the stated goals and objectives. If the role of evaluation is to confirm the state of children's progress and provide information crucial to program improvement, then it must be considered concurrently with curriculum planning.

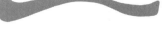

INFLUENCES ON CURRICULUM DECISION MAKING

Children's Characteristics and Needs

One item often mentioned in relation to curriculum development at all levels is "the characteristics and needs" of children. As educators we know that we are supposed to be sensitive to children, but how do we ascertain children's characteristics? How do we learn of their needs, and what needs are we supposed to respond to? How will these needs and characteristics influence the planning of art curricula? Much of what we need to know here is discussed in Chapters 3, 4, and 5 and numerous examples are provided that illustrate how teachers adapt their intentions and classroom activities according to what they know about their students. One authority on curriculum has provided an explicit illustration of what we mean when we refer to general characteristics and needs of children. The following lists were developed by a committee of teachers after close observations of kindergarten and first grade children.[4]

CHARACTERISTICS

1. Children begin to lose baby teeth, causing lisping, etc.
2. Right- or left-handedness is established. No change should be made without expert advice.

3. Bone structure growth is slower than in previous years.
4. Heart growth is rapid. The child should not be overtaxed physically.
5. Eyes are increasing in size. Watch reading and writing habits.
6. Feelings of tension may be evident in thumb-sucking, nail-biting, and mistakes in toilet habits.
7. Motor skills begin to develop; coordination may be awkward and uneven.
8. Large muscles are much more developed than smaller ones.
9. The child responds to rhythm-skips, beats time, etc.
10. The average child of these ages is full of vitality. He has good facial color, and can stand and sit erect.
11. Children are interested in an activity rather than in its outcome.
12. Self-dependence and a desire to help others are developing.
13. Children prefer activity — climbing, jumping, running — but they tire easily.

NEEDS

1. Short periods of activity.
2. Twelve hours of sleep.
3. Vigorous and noisy games essential to growth.
4. Many opportunities to do things for oneself.
5. Frequent participation in organized groups — games, dramatics, puppetry, etc.
6. Chances for the shy child to join in the routine and be important.

The characteristics and needs listed are general rather than specific to art education, but they follow closely many of the observations made about children of these ages in previous chapters. For example, children are encouraged to express their own ideas and feelings in their artwork rather than copying what other children are creating; children are given opportunities to release tension through expressive activities; and children are given art materials that are appropriate for their physical coordination. Reviewing this list gives us many ideas about teaching art activities to children in kindergarten and first grade. Similar lists can be made for older age groups as well.

Readiness of Learners

So broad is the subject content of a balanced art program that it can accommodate learners of any age, personality type, or experience. Curriculum writers as well as teachers must realize that just as no two children are exactly alike, so also classes or groups of children differ. The written curriculum should provide for differences, allowing teachers to adapt activities to the differences in individuals and groups. The capacities of the children to learn will obviously influence the art program and variations in intelligence may affect art production as well as general learning about art. Slow learners in other subjects are often also slow to profit from art activities, and the art curriculum must be flexible enough to accommodate such differences. Fast learners must also be considered by curriculum planners, and extensions of the regular activities should be provided for those who are ready to move ahead or work more in depth. The needs, capacities, and dispositions of the children demand diversification of the basic ingredients of every art program—materials to be used, problems to be solved, and concepts to be introduced and reinforced.

Values of Society

The values of the larger society, along with local community values and those expressed within school systems influence what curriculum planners select for art content and learning activities. As noted in Chapter 1, art education in the United States was initiated for the purpose of improving this country's ability to compete internationally in business and industry. Since that time we have seen national and international events and trends assert their influence on American education. Current examples of society's values often mentioned in discussions of education are

1. the success of Japanese business in competition with American business and industry

2. the need for cultural literacy among persons educated in this democratic society

3. renewed emphasis on the so-called basics of education: reading, writing, mathematics, and science

4. concern that American education aims too low and does not teach students to develop higher levels of thinking

Critics and educational reformers often mention one or more of these large issues as well as others when they present recommendations for improvement. Issues such as these influence federal support of education, state and local funding, professional meetings and publications, and even the local voting public when school issues are placed on the ballot. Sometimes the complexity of issues that impinge upon education is ignored and simplistic slogans or panaceas are offered to the lay public by reformers in place of sound proposals with sufficient financial support for implementation.

Educators in general, and curriculum planners specifically, need to be up-to-date with respect to educational trends and value issues in society. Curriculum writers can contribute significantly toward educational improvement through the content and activities they place in the curriculum. For example, art curriculum planners currently are very aware of the need to provide children with knowledge and understanding of world art as well as art from the Western tradition. Curriculum planners can also encourage art activities that engage children in higher levels of thinking.

Thinking Skills in the Art Curriculum

Although there is considerable variation in what different psychologists and educators mean when they refer to higher levels of thinking, Resnick has developed a brief set of characteristics that we can apply to art curriculum and instruction:[5]

1. Higher order thinking is *nonalgorithmic;* that is, the path of action is not fully specified in advance.

2. Higher order thinking tends to be *complex.* The total path is not "visible" (mentally speaking) from any single vantage point.

3. Higher order thinking often yields *multiple solutions*, each with costs and benefits, rather than unique solutions.

4. Higher order thinking involves *nuanced judgment* and interpretation.

5. Higher order thinking involves the application of *multiple criteria,* which sometimes conflict with each other.

6. Higher order thinking often involves *uncertainty.* Not everything that bears on the task at hand is known.

7. Higher order thinking involves *self-regulation* of the thinking process. We do not recognize higher order thinking in an individual when someone else "calls the plays" at every step.

8. Higher order thinking involves *imposing meaning,* finding structure in apparent disorder.

9. Higher order thinking is *effortful.* There is considerable mental work involved in the kinds of elaborations and judgments required.

When we consider the range of activities that children participate in with a balanced, comprehensive art curriculum, we can recognize art as a school subject that encourages higher levels of thinking. For example, when children apply a phased approach to art criticism, involving description, analysis, interpretation, and informed preference, they are involved in *complex* mental activity with *multiple potential solutions* requiring *nuanced judgment.*[6] When children apply what they have learned about color, composition, proportion, and distortion to the creation of a landscape painting that expresses a mood, they are involved in a *nonalgorithmic* activity with *multiple criteria* requiring *self-regulation.* When children are old enough to discuss and debate basic questions about art, such as the puzzles described in Chapter 13 on aesthetics, they might be engaged in several types of higher order thinking, including *effortful* thinking involving a good deal of *uncertainty.*

Much of the discussion of higher order thinking in general education is focused on subjects such as language arts, science, and mathematics with relatively little attention paid to the potentials in the art curriculum.[7] Although art is not generally associated with higher order thinking, the comprehensive art curriculum derived from the disciplines of art production, aesthetics, art history, and art criticism can provide many such opportunities. Those who encourage thinking skills in the curriculum do not often mention the notion of creativity, yet their descriptions of higher order thinking would surely include many of the activities that art educators have recommended for many years. A balanced art curriculum can provide all students with opportunities to express their ideas and feelings creatively through art media, and such expression requires application of high levels of mental functioning.

The Community Setting

The local community often provides the strongest influence on the school curriculum, regardless of the quality or value of state guidelines for education. Local control of education is one of the hallmarks of the American system. This principle is at once one of the most progressive values in education throughout the world and one of the most difficult practices. According to Doll:

> The great majority of American citizens live in communities of fewer than 10,000 people. Many such communities are quite isolated despite improvements in transportation and communication, and where they are not isolated physically, the people in them are isolated psychologically, often by their own choice. Both the traditions and the planning that touch people are grounded in local communities, so it seems unlikely that the power and influence of the community in educational decision making will be lost.[8]

When we consider that the many thousands of school districts across North America have the authority to establish the curriculum that will be implemented within their own boundaries, we can understand the great strength in such diversity and the likelihood that local programs can respond effectively to local conditions, resources, and needs. On the other hand, the task of moving progressive ideas in education into the schools is multiplied almost by the number of school districts across the land and at times it seems that needed changes move very slowly to the level of the classroom.

Nevertheless, there are a number of factors that encourage similarities among widely diverse school populations. One factor is the use of textbook series by large publishing companies by most of the school districts in the country, which tends to lend some degree of uniformity among the local curricula. Other factors that tend to bring uniformity in school curricula in many states are the establishment of graduation requirements for high school, college and university entrance requirements, and the use of standardized national aptitude and achievement tests. Even though some of these practices apply only to secondary schooling, the effects are seen in elementary schools as well.

Curriculum planners must respect local social issues and values. For example, an art curriculum developed within a school district that serves a primarily Hispanic community in west Los Angeles might differ significantly from an art curriculum tailored to the needs and interests of students in rural Kansas, northern Minnesota, or urban Philadelphia. Teachers, administrators, and curriculum planners should be aware of local issues that might be sensitive, such as sex education, religious issues, ethnic values, and such specific topics as nudity in art. Michelangelo's *David* and Botticelli's *Venus* are not welcome in all communities, for example, and curriculum planners should be aware of community mores and standards. Although these two artworks are considered by many experts to be masterworks of Western culture, and might be counted essential for cultural literacy in some schools, because of their nudity they might be rejected in other communities. Knowledgeable curriculum planners realize that the tremendous range and amount of art content for instruction makes the omission of particular artworks or classes of artworks from consideration a minor problem. There is much more of value to teach than class time available, and excellent art curricula can be developed without nude figures or other problematic issues when there is a need to work around local standards.

Knowing what to include and develop in the art curriculum is at least as important as knowing what to avoid. Locally developed art curricula can take advantage of local resources, such as architecture, museums and galleries, art-related industries and businesses, and local experts in the many occupations related to the fine, folk, and applied arts.

Sometimes the general character of the community will influence the materials used in an art program. In Oregon, the authors observed a far greater use of wood in the art program than in Miami, where sand casting was popular. Communities such as New Orleans, in which there is a well-defined interest in local history, might again influence some of the activities in the art program. In some communities, ethnic groups still maintain traditional arts and crafts of which they are proud.

The teacher and students will do well also to study physical aspects of the community, noting distinguishing characteristics of trees, buildings, public plazas, and places of recreation. Perhaps the class can go on a field trip to observe the community. Is the area hilly or flat, old or contemporary, cluttered or open? Answers to such questions can provide rich material for the art curriculum.

Perhaps the greatest resource of a community is its people. Some teachers have inventoried the careers of their students' parents and sent out form letters requesting volunteers to serve as aids on field trips, to give demonstrations in class, or to speak about their artwork or their careers. Other teachers have made arrangements with local institutions such as libraries or banks for exhibition space. Others have worked closely with their Parent-Teacher Associations and received financial support for the art program. The art curriculum can reflect the nature of the community and at the same time use it as a valuable resource.

The School Setting

The art program is greatly affected by the school setting. In most school districts the board of education, or school board, is elected to serve for a set term of years. The board is responsible for setting school policy, designating the curriculum, and overseeing the expenditure of funds to run the district. The board hires a superintendent as an educational professional to carry out board policy and administer the school program. The superintendent usually hires central office staff and selects principals for individual schools in the district. In this way the community is actually responsible for the school curriculum, but often relies on education professionals such as the superintendent for counsel and advice in decision making. It should be noted, however, that the superintendent serves at the pleasure of the board of education, so that the real power resides with the elected representatives of the community. The relationship of principals to superintendent is important for art educators to note. Most often the principals serve at the pleasure of the superintendent and take cues from their superior with respect to the relative value of various components of the curriculum.

What this established system means in practice varies, of course, from one district to the next, but certain facts are worth the attention of those who wish to see the art curriculum implemented. First, whether or not the state curriculum framework recommends art as a regular subject, art usually will not find a significant place in the curriculum unless the board of education formally indicates that it shall be taught. Second, even if the board of education formally establishes art as a regular subject in the curriculum, the superintendent can choose to neglect its implementation. If this occurs, it is up to the board to insist that their policy of art education be carried out by the superintendent. This requires careful attention by the board, who might not realize that the art curriculum is not being well implemented. Third, even if the superintendent indicates that art is to be implemented as directed by the school board, this will not occur in all schools if some principals are not convinced that regular instructional time should be spent on art education. Full implementation will usually occur only when the superintendent implements, reviews, and evaluates art education with the same attention given to mathematics, language arts, social studies, and so on.

The place of art in the school setting is influenced as well by the facilities and teaching resources that are provided for art instruction. Is regular school time set aside for serious art instruction? Does the school have an art room with the necessary sinks, display and storage spaces? If art is taught in regular classrooms, what provisions are in place to accommodate a comprehensive art program? Are sinks available? Is there storage space so that student work can be set aside and worked on over several periods of instruction? Are adequate funds available for art supplies? Where are art materials stored? Are slide and filmstrip projectors readily available for art instruction? Does the library hold an adequate array of art books and magazines? Are art prints and other visual support materials available for art instruction? Is there a written art curriculum with suggested evaluation procedures and instruments? Do teachers and administrators accept and respect art as a regular subject in the curriculum, or do they view art as a "fun" activity to be reserved as a reward for children who have applied themselves well to the "real" curriculum?

When these factors in the local school setting are lined up in favor of art education for all of the children, we can observe the strong contribution that art can make in the lives of children, in their understanding of the aesthetic domain, and in support of the other subjects in the curriculum.

WHO DESIGNS THE ART CURRICULUM?

There are several strategies for planning and implementing art programs, with wide variations of these approaches from one school district to another. The major issue is one that has been discussed in other chapters,[9] that is: Who shall teach art?, and the extension of this question, Who shall plan the art curriculum? This issue refers basically to two alternatives — either the art program is planned and taught by regular classroom teachers or by certified art specialists. Other important roles in various districts include the district art consultant or art supervisor and community art volunteers.

The Art Consultant or Art Supervisor

This person is an art specialist with administrative responsibilities, usually on a district-wide basis. Some art consultants have administrative training and credentials. Responsibilities of art consultants, known in some districts as art supervisors, usually include overseeing implementation of the art curriculum across the district, managing district stores of art supplies, ordering resource materials for art instruction, providing in-service education for teachers of art, and periodically overseeing the review and revision of the district art curriculum. Art consultants often have more responsibility and authority with respect to the elementary art curriculum than for secondary art education. This person usually provides leadership regarding art curriculum issues, often in consultation with art teachers, classroom teachers, and interested community members.

The role of art consultants varies a great deal according to the configuration of personnel for art instruction within the district; that is, whether art is taught by art specialists or by classroom teachers. When art is taught by classroom teachers the art consultant has the challenging task of overseeing art curriculum implementation by nonspecialists. The written curriculum becomes more essential and in-service instruction by the coordinator is often focused on basic principles of art and art teaching. The coordinator will likely be able to demonstrate art instruction only in selected classrooms, and will of necessity rely on classroom teachers to teach art on a regular basis.

When art is taught by elementary art specialists the role of the art coordinator is changed to that of providing support for colleagues with art expertise. This also significantly changes the requirements for art curriculum. If art is taught by classroom teachers the art curriculum is addressed to the levels and needs of this group and the curriculum development process will involve classroom teachers to a large extent. An art curriculum developed for art specialists might be less prescriptive and more flexible, allowing for the subject expertise of the art specialists. The curriculum might also assume more knowledge and deal with sophisticated materials and processes not recommended for classroom teachers.

The Elementary Art Specialist

Many school districts employ certified art specialists to teach art in elementary classrooms. In some regions of the country, especially in several eastern states, most art instruction is provided by art specialists. In other regions, especially in some western states, art instruction is often the responsibility of regular classroom teachers, sometimes under the direction of an art consultant. The NAEA recommends that all children should receive art instruction from certified art teachers who, because of their education and training, are able to provide the highest quality art instruction. Art teachers are the key persons to involve in any curriculum decisions. They generally have a background of training in the fundamentals of curriculum planning and development and, due to their teaching experience, knowledge of art, and familiarity with children of different age levels, are most valuable participants in curriculum development undertakings.

The Classroom Teacher

When elementary art specialists are not available for whatever reason, the responsibility to teach art falls on classroom teachers. Most elementary classroom teachers are not certified as art specialists and many do not have an extensive background of learning and experience with art as a subject for study. In this situation the guidance provided by a sound written art curriculum is of great importance, along with professional in-service support from an art consultant whenever possible. A classroom teacher with little art background, no written curriculum, and no professional support from a certified art specialist has little chance to provide the children with the type of art program recommended in this book. However, when an art curriculum, instructional materials and resources, and professional support by an art consultant are available, many classroom teachers are able to teach art very well.

Classroom teachers can be valuable consultants for art curriculum planning because, regardless of their responsibility for art instruction, they know the general curriculum and the characteristics and needs of their students. They can give advice that will assist planners to correlate art curriculum with other subjects, themes, or periods to be studied in the general curriculum. When art is taught by art specialists, it is the classroom teachers who are able to reinforce, support, and correlate art learning with other subjects.

Community Art Volunteers

In many communities, parents and other interested adults are willing to serve as volunteers in the schools. Some of these volunteers are well educated in the visual arts and have a great deal to offer children under the direction of professional teachers. Volunteers fulfill different roles in different school districts according to the type of art program that is in place. For example, some districts have developed brief critical and historical presentations using large, good-quality art reproductions. The art volunteer is trained to show an art print to children, make a brief presentation to them, and engage them in discussion and questions. The volunteer is scheduled into regular classrooms or the art room as a sort of art curriculum enrichment.

In other instances art volunteers work with art specialists, helping with tools and materials, working individually with children, and generally providing an additional set of hands to assist the art teacher. Art volunteers also assist with organizing and supervising field trips to art museums or other locations. They can schedule and organize a series of classroom visits by art professionals such as critics, art historians, or artists. Art volunteers often work in museums where they are known as *docents*, or guides. Here they train to guide tours of the museum collection or exhibit. Some large art museums have a corps of hundreds of art docents who volunteer their time and expertise on a regular, part-time basis for periods of years. In all situations, and there are many that have not been mentioned here, art volunteers are a significant resource for quality art education, and the persons who serve also can be consulted profitably for the process of curriculum planning.

School District Administrators

Most mid to large school districts employ administrators who are responsible for curriculum development and instruction across all subjects. As has been mentioned, the board of education makes curriculum policy and the superintendent is hired to carry out policy. The superintendent often appoints an assistant superintendent for curriculum and instruction, and sometimes a director of curriculum. The director of curriculum for the district works with subject area curriculum specialists, such as the art coordinator or art supervisor, when these positions are available.

Many districts have a regular cycle for curriculum evaluation, revision, and implementation. This means that the mathematics curriculum will be reviewed every so many years and changes in the program will be implemented through regular in-service education of teachers. When art is considered as a regular part of the school curriculum it should have a place in this cycle and should be the focus for in-service education. If the art program is not part of the regular review and implementation process, it cannot be considered as a basic subject in the school curriculum.

Who should design the art curriculum? We can say that all of the above should be involved. Certainly art curriculum review should be part of the regular cycle supervised by top-level district administrators. Art specialists, such as the art coordinator and art teachers, should play primary roles on the basis of their specialized expertise and experience. Committees are often formed to conduct curriculum reviews and recommend improvements. Art teachers, classroom teachers, art volunteers, specialists from local colleges and universities, and interested community members can serve profitably on such committees, providing curriculum planners with their own perspective.

Strategies for Art Curriculum Implementation

As if issues of art curriculum and instruction were not sufficiently complex, school districts around the country have developed a wide variety of means for delivering art instruction to children. Each of these strategies for implementation of the art curriculum has implications for curriculum development. The following list reviews a few of these implementation strategies:

The art teacher in an art room. The ideal situation for many elementary art teachers is to work in their own art room and meet the various grade level classes one at a time according to a regular schedule. This means that the art teacher can meet each child for an art lesson once each week, allowing for curriculum sequence and articulation between grade levels. Regular scheduling means that in-depth activities can be undertaken; working in an art classroom means that adequate storage, tools, materials, audiovisual equipment, art prints and slides, and items such as ceramics kilns are available. This implementation strategy allows for a full, balanced art curriculum written for use by art specialists. If the elementary schools are small the art teacher might work in two schools. Assuming that the art teacher teaches twenty-five art periods each week and classes average twenty-five students, the art teacher would have 625 pupil contacts.

The itinerant art teacher. Many school districts employ itinerant, or traveling, art teachers. Working within regular classrooms rather than in an art room limits these art teachers significantly, especially if classrooms are not equipped with sinks. This "art on a cart" approach means that the art teacher will move from room to room, bringing the needed art materials and teaching resources on a cart or other conveyance. Art projects that are to be worked on over several art periods will be stored in the classroom. Scheduling and numbers of pupil contacts can be identical to the strategy with an art room. The major limitations for curriculum are imposed by the lack of a fully equipped art room and the amount of materials that the teacher can move from room to room.

Unfortunately, in some school districts this strategy is badly misused in the name of providing art instruction for all students. Sometimes itinerant art teachers are asked to travel by automobile to two or more schools, further limiting the program that can be offered to children. In some situations art is offered twice a month or less, and the number of pupil contacts increases beyond the boundaries within which any meaningful teacher-student relationships might be established. When instructional time for art falls below the baseline of one lesson a week, the possibility of implementing a comprehensive, balanced program diminishes significantly. It is very difficult, because of the length of time between art lessons, for teachers to engage students in art activities that require more than one class period. All of these limitations restrict the type of art curriculum that can be reasonably implemented.

Art teachers and classroom teachers. Some school districts, operating on the principle of local curriculum decision making within each elementary school, employ more than one strategy. In some cases elementary principals and faculties are given the option of having two curriculum area specialists visit their schools. They are asked to choose among physical education, music, and art specialists and the classroom teacher will be responsible for teaching the remaining subject. In such districts we find some schools in which art is taught by art specialists and other schools in which art is taught by classroom teachers. Given the variations within each of these implementation strategies, this situation significantly challenges art curriculum planners.

Cooperative art teaching. Another strategy for implementing art curriculum attempts to utilize the expertise of both art teachers and classroom teachers. Under the reasonable assumptions that art specialists are better prepared with respect to art knowledge and techniques, and that classroom teachers know their students best and have opportunities to integrate art with other subjects, some districts engage art teachers and classroom teachers in a cooperative strategy. To initiate an art activity the art specialist visits the classroom and teaches a lesson. The art teacher provides all of the art expertise required for introduction of the lesson and leaves a clearly expressed assignment for students to complete under the direction of the classroom teacher. The classroom teacher remains in the classroom and assists the art teacher with the lesson, at the same time noting the direction of the lesson and observing the assignment that is given to students.

The classroom teacher is then responsible for conducting the art lesson the following week and to follow up on what the art teacher initiated. The classroom teacher can also innovate and enrich what has been started according to their own background and interests in art, and they can integrate and relate the art content with other subjects as opportunities arise. This strategy, if it can be smoothly implemented, allows for a broad and deep art curriculum that might be integrated in significant ways with themes and topics from the general curriculum.

Classroom teachers with supervision. This strategy involves classroom teachers teaching the art curriculum under the direction of and with support from a certified art specialist, the art coordinator. Classroom teachers teach art on a regular basis to their own students and integrate art with the rest of the curriculum. This strategy works best when teachers have access to a clearly written basic art curriculum with support materials that minimize the time required for lesson preparation. When the district employs an art coordinator to support the classroom teachers, this strategy becomes much more effective. The art coordinator orders art supplies and teaching support materials, demonstrates particular art lessons by request in various teachers' classrooms, provides in-service training in art education, and supervises the implementation of the art curriculum.

Art curriculum leaders and district administrators will be wise to assess their strategies for art curriculum implementation as they make decisions about curriculum development. They will be much more likely to develop or adopt an art curriculum with a good chance of actually reaching children in the district's elementary classrooms.

KEY DECISIONS IN PLANNING AN ART PROGRAM

District-level curriculum planners have a number of important decisions to make prior to actually formulating an art curriculum. They need to discuss and decide upon issues related to the philosophy of art education, organizational schemes, scope and sequence of art content, balance of art learning, student participation in curriculum development, and integration of art education with other subjects in the curriculum.

Philosophy of Art Education

Most school districts have produced documents that indicate, however briefly, what the goals of education are for their schools and their children. State departments of education usually have similar documents with broad statements of values and worth of education. Individual subject curricula should relate to and support the state or district statements of educational philosophy. The field of art education has developed such statements as well, referring specifically to the contributions that art learning can make in the lives of children. Chapters 1 and 2 discuss rationales and philosophical values of art education.

A statement of philosophy is an essential and helpful beginning for development of a district art curriculum. It can provide a very general type of guidance and can be referred to when difficult issues arise and resist resolution. The role of art education in the general curriculum can be established by relating the art rationale to the district goals. This relationship can assist board members and administrators who are not entirely sure of the values of art education.

Balanced Art Content

The rationale for art education upon which this book is based recognizes art as one of the major domains of human learning and accomplishment. It holds that a balanced general education requires fundamental understanding of art as part of the aesthetic domain of human experience. Study of the visual arts includes several unique perspectives, each of which sheds light on and increases our understanding of art. This view recommends a balanced curriculum that derives its content from the art disciplines. This position is widely held among art educators and other art professionals as well as many leaders in general education. For example, The College Board recommends the following skills and kinds of knowledge associated with education in the visual arts:

- the ability to identify and describe — using the appropriate vocabulary — various visual art forms from different historical periods
- the ability to analyze the structure of a work of visual art

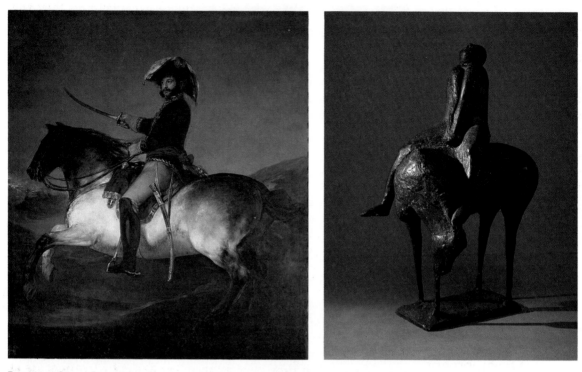

Francisco Goya, *General Jose de Palafox*, 1814. Utilizing paintings like this, children can study other subjects through artworks. The painting (above) of a general on his horse might be used as a starting point to discuss Spanish culture, military history, or the view of war depicted by the artist in this painting. Works of art can be used as subject for writing activities in conjunction with the language arts curriculum. (The Prado, Madrid.)

- the ability to evaluate a work of visual art
- the ability to know how to express themselves in one or more of the visual art forms, such as drawing, painting, photography, weaving, ceramics, and sculpture.[10]

Although this statement was intended for secondary education rather than for elementary levels, the basic ideas are similar. A curriculum that attends significantly to historical knowledge, analysis and evaluation of artworks, art concepts and vocabulary, and accomplishment in the production of art in several media is a balanced art curriculum. Art curriculum planners need to decide if the art curriculum will be balanced or if it will emphasize a narrower range of art learning.

Scope and Sequence

According to one curriculum professional, the term *scope* "refers to the extent and depth of content coverage," and *sequence* refers to "decisions about the order in which learners encounter content."[11] Scope and sequence documents address questions such as "Will the children learn about African art? If so, during what grade level?" A comprehensive, balanced art curriculum requires extensive planning so that children will learn as widely and deeply about art as instructional time allows. Decisions of scope will determine what historical periods children will study during their elementary school years, what different

Marino Marini, *Horseman*, 1947. By comparing and contrasting works of art, children can learn a great deal. The mood, level of detail, and art media of this painting (page 486) and Goya's portrait of General Jose de Palafox are very different, but both depict a horse and rider. Children can write insightful interpretations of mood and meaning in artworks. (National Gallery of Art, Washington, D.C. Gift of Enid A. Haupt.)

art modes and media they will experience, what cultures they will learn about, and what vocabulary of terms and concepts they will master.

Sequence becomes important in promoting cumulative learning. Learning activities organized in sequences that build upon previous learning help children develop from naive understandings to sophisticated knowledge. Curriculum sequences can occur within a single lesson, can develop from lesson to lesson in a single unit, and can be written across entire terms or grade levels. For example, as children learn about color their curriculum activities will progress from identifying the primary colors to mixing secondary and tertiary colors to use of complementary colors to decrease intensities for expressive purposes. Sequences of activities can be written and placed within a grade level that will take children from simple beginnings in their use of color to more and more complex understandings and applications in their own art production. Curriculum developers will need to deal with issues of content scope and sequence and decide how they will utilize these ideas in the art curriculum.

Student Participation in Curriculum Development

Although research indicates that students often have very little to say about curriculum development, this need not be the case.[12] Students are the ultimate recipients of the art curriculum and their participation at some levels can provide assurance that curriculum writers are at least on the right track. This does not mean that first and second grade students are able to tell professional educators what ought to be taught and how it ought to be organized. Rather, it means that students of various age levels can be consulted profitably at several stages of the curriculum development process. For example, children can be asked to try curriculum sequences and express their opinions. Children can be polled for their interests in current events, personalities, music, and other parts of the popular culture and these interests can be considered as starting points for art instruction. Children can view proposed art reproductions, can give their responses to particular artworks, and can provide curriculum writers with a running assessment of the activities they are planning. In brief, children can provide a reality check for curriculum developers who might be tempted to become pedantic, grandiose, and too academic in their writing and planning. This process can also serve as a form of evaluation.

Commercial Art Curricula

As the field has moved in the direction of discipline-based art education, or balanced, comprehensive art programs, the role of planned, written art curricula has gained in significance. Publishers of educational materials have developed a wide range of excellent art resource materials, including several series of elementary art curricula, such as *Discover Art*, the *SWRL Art Program*, *Art in Action*, and *SPECTRA*.

These art curricula and others that are available provide local curriculum planners with some options. School districts now can choose to *adopt* a commercially available art curriculum and *adapt* it to local goals and resources. This process requires an assessment of the available curricula, trial teaching in classrooms, analysis of content and activities, and determination of the match between commercial curricula and state or district art guidelines. It usually involves a committee that reviews, tries, and selects a curriculum that is then recommended to the board of education for adoption. When adoption is accomplished materials are developed to assist teachers to adapt the commercial curriculum to the specific goals of the local schools. This might mean suggested sequences of lessons, addition of lessons written locally, development of supplementary teaching materials, and designation of vocabulary and lists of artworks to be studied at each grade level. Prepared curricula, in other words, should be adapted for local needs.

Many districts choose to develop their own art curricula, sometimes based on the belief that teachers are more likely to enthusiastically teach what they have a stake in through their own efforts. In fact, researchers indicate that:

> . . . most school districts prefer homegrown curriculums developed by committees of teachers and administrators. Local control, however, requires long-term teacher participation that budget-watching school boards may be unwilling to pay for.[13]

The issue of cost is an important one. District leaders who believe that commercial art curriculum materials are too costly, and for that reason choose to develop their own, are apt to be disappointed. The process of developing an art curriculum, as is the case with other subjects, is a lengthy, time- and energy-consuming task. And when the curriculum is ready for implementation, released time in-service support is always required for adequate results. This requires long-term administrative and financial support.

The good news is that now these options for development and implementation of excellent programs of art education are available, and more school districts each year are making the commitments required for quality art education.

CORRELATING ART WITH OTHER SUBJECTS

Two major choices are reflected in many new programs now being developed. These are (1) integration within the various arts, and (2) the integration of art with academic subjects. The conscious seeking of relationships between separate disciplines is assumed to be educationally desirable in any discussion of art beyond its customary function. If one examines the "grass roots of art," to borrow Sir Herbert Read's phrase, the distinctive qualities of visual art become less apparent as one compares the formal characteristics of art to those of its neighbors. As an example, design features such as line, rhythm, and pattern have their counterparts in music, drama, and dance. For this reason, design components are used as the basis for some related art programs. The visual arts all involve perception, emotion, and the creative processes: a love of manipulation (of both forms and materials), a delight in sensations, and considerable pleasure in the contemplation as well as creation of structured experiences.

It is precisely because of these shared characteristics that art is so suitable as an adjunct of other activities. The major interest in the correlation of art with the general curriculum lies in its integration with academic subjects. Before we examine this direction, however, let us look at a few examples of the way art is employed in the first two areas mentioned above.

Relationships Within The Arts

In a situation in which the arts relate in a broad context, some principle or concept is selected because it is a part of the artistic experience, while at the same time existing separately from a particular art category. Let us take one concept that many artists face at various times in their careers—*improvisation*—and examine its possibilities as a "connector" between several art forms. Improvisation is borrowed from the professional training of actors and works well with students of any age.

As a rule, improvisations do not allow any preplanning. They are spontaneous acts that are created from moment to moment, using

These simulated Egyptian fresco paintings on low, carved relief were done by drawing the faces on slabs of plaster of Paris. The lines were incised with a sharp tool and the faces painted in tempera. Sandpaper was then lightly applied to contribute to the appearance of age. The thinner the paint, the more delicate the colors. This activity was part of a class unit on ancient Egypt.

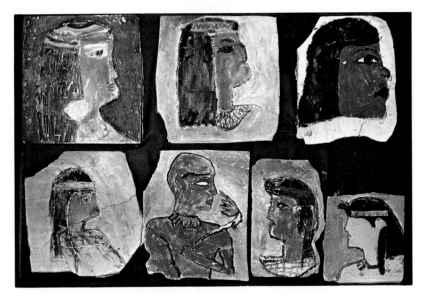

some stimulus in the immediate situation as a point of departure. Improvisations always call on the inventiveness of the participants, thus developing such attributes as flexibility, fluency, and imagination. Participants in improvisational situations learn to respond to the moment at hand and to trust in their ability to embellish, expand, and develop an idea. Below are several suggested improvisational activities organized by category.

VISUAL ARTS

1. *Graphic Improvisation:* Pupil A draws a line, B counters with another, and C follows suit. The idea is to work from the previous image, relating new images as intimately as possible to the preceding ones, thus provoking each pupil to respond immediately to the partners' work. Have each pupil use individual colors, or have them all use one color as a means of gaining cohesiveness. The criterion for success is the sense of unity that is attained. When divided into teams, students can also improvise stories and create a series of narratives and events.

2. *Musical Improvisation:* Select two or three violently contrasting musical pieces (such as Mozart's *Eine kleine Nachtmusik* and Ravel's *Bolero*). While listening to each, pupils can allow their crayons to roam freely over sheets of paper. They should allow themselves to respond completely to the suggestiveness of the music, especially in terms of color and rhythm. When the music has ended, set up a section of the wall on which to hang the pictures for class criticism and discuss differences and similarities in structure, choice of colors, and the like.

3. *Word Images:* The teacher calls out words that have strong emotional overtones, and the pupils improvise drawings suggested by the words. As an alternative, pupils can respond with their bodies, reacting either physically or pictorially to onomotopoetic words such as *explosion, piston,* and *eggbeater.*

MOVEMENT AND MUSIC

Sculpture Machines: The class is divided into four groups. A leader is selected for each group and creates a "living sculpture," designing the team for visual interest as well as for the possibility of movement. Each member of the team should adopt a frozen posture showing movement of the torso, arms, or legs. Working to the music of a Sousa march, for instance, the sculpture should activate itself in time to the musical beat. The basic form of the sculpture (the position of the pupils) remains in place while the separate parts (their bodies) move.

Connections and Sequences. Although the arts lend themselves to many styles of related instruction, teachers must learn to distinguish between forced and natural ways of connecting one experience to another. If the planning for sequences of activities can be shared by two or more arts specialists, the pooling of ideas can lead to rich possibilities for arts experiences. One arts area can provide motivation for another and so on, creating a sequential flow of activities. *Exercises* can free the body and attune it to *movement* to music, which in turn can set the stage for a more *formalized dance experience*. Since there is no dance without *rhythm*, exploration and creation of rhythmic patterns can lead to *creating sound-making instruments*. Rhythm can also be translated visually into *large-scale drawings* based on principles of conducting (imagine holding a brush instead of a baton). Making a spontaneous *graphic* record of a musical experience can then provide the basis for more thoughtful works, developed with care at the student's own pace rather than that of the music.

Experiences in related arts can also be connected through the grouping of activities around some common element. For example, *observation* is a skill that actors use in studying characteristics of various kinds of people (babies and very old people have their own way of walking, for example—hesitant, halting, insecure). Such observation

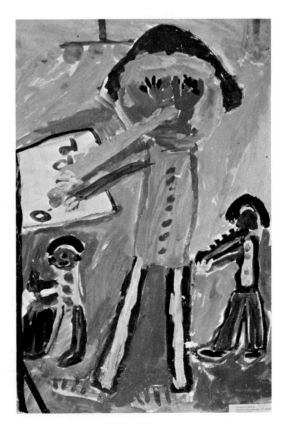

Musical Lesson, tempera by a six-year-old boy, South Africa. The human figure involved with a musical instrument is an excellent subject because of its positive associations with creating music and because it transforms the figure from symbol to active element.

helps in the actor's creation of a character. Artists use their powers of observation as a means of memory development and analysis of form. *Memory* can be developed, as can visual acuity; many kinds of artists store and call upon recollected experience. The actor must learn the lines of *King Lear*, the pianist commits musical scores to memory before a concert, the dancer must recall dozens of minute bodily movements within fixed time frames, and the artist develops a mental storehouse of shapes. *Improvisation* is part of every actor's training; and the painter who develops an image from each preceding stage without any preplanning or the jazz trombonist who picks up cues from what the clarinetist is playing, also is improvising. These are three of the many shared characteristics of the arts that suggest groupings of activities.

Overlapping Goals: Social Studies as an Example

Many of the claims art teachers make for their subject are parallel to goals in other subject areas. A group of social studies specialists specified the goals for which they teach. Their choices indicate some very obvious analogies to art. Listed below are eight points they felt were vital for any current social studies program. These assumptions may be similar to those made for an art program, but the teacher should be cognizant of the art program's unique features, as the comments in parentheses indicate.[14]

1. Humanity in relation to the natural environment and the cultural environment is a proper subject for the elementary school social studies curriculum. (This is also proper subject matter for art activities.)

2. Contrast is a powerful pedagogical tool: look at unfamiliar cultures to understand one's own; look at animal behavior to understand what characteristics man and animals have in common and what differentiates them. (The art teacher utilizes the contrasts found in works of art to reinforce learnings in criticism and appreciation. Polarities of style and technique are stressed to heighten the child's perceptions of likenesses and differences in artworks.)

3. "Ways of knowing" are important, such as the way of the anthropologist, the archeologist, and others. ("Ways of knowing" in art implies understanding not only the functions of critic, historian, and artist, but also of the kinds of "knowing," perceiving, and experiencing that differentiate the painter from the sculptor, the architect from the potter.)

4. Studies in depth provide a thorough foundation and a point of reference around which later learnings may cluster. (An art program that included in-depth studies would give a great deal of time to a few selected concepts deemed important, such as drawing, color, and painting, rather than skipping to a different activity each week without making any connections among the activities.)

5. Discovering how things are related and discovering how to discover are the ends of learning; the end should not be just mastery of the subject matter. (Discovery is a part of the process in art as well. Sensitive teachers are aware of the importance of the changes that may occur when children are taught for discovery as well as for adult-inspired goals.)

6. The students are participants; they can be self-motivated inquirers rather than just passive receivers. (The taped dialogs transcribed in this book testify to the value of interactions between teacher and pupil in discussions of art activities.)

7. Students should find their own meaning in the material, some of which should be "raw data." (Raw data have always been at the heart of the art program. The raw data the art student should encounter are creative studio experiences and original works of art, be they buildings, paintings, or craft objects.)

8. The gap between current research in curriculum and methodology in social studies should be narrowed. (No one has yet assessed the effects of research on art education in the classroom. The results obtained from doctoral dissertations are rarely read by classroom teachers, and much research is unfortunately too limited in nature to be of use. Art teachers need the kinds of broad curriculum investigation that have taken place in mathematics and physics; these are slow in coming to the humanities. This gap must be narrowed if the teacher is to reflect the findings of the researcher.)

The eight points have been included here to emphasize the need for art teachers to define the special nature of art, even when art appears to be close to other subjects in its ultimate objectives.

PROBLEMS OF CORRELATION

The teaching of art has, of course, been affected by both the correlation of subjects and their fusion in the unit curriculum. In certain circumstances art education has benefited from the grouping of areas of learning; in other circumstances, however, it has suffered.

Many educators feel that art is often abused in the process of integration—that in serving the rest of the curriculum, the creative drive necessary to art becomes diluted, and means are often confused with ends. Many activities, such as copying maps and model construction, are labeled "art" simply because art media are used. In these instances, the art teacher should say to the colleague in the classroom, "It is your right to have them color in maps of the Western movement, but let's not call it art."

Correlation or integration need not debase an authentic art experience. In two pilot programs, both dealing with language development, the resulting artworks reflected as much original thinking as those produced in the regular art program.[15] In Group A, children of Italian parents worked on mosaics, simulated frescoes, and travel posters. They studied Venice and created a city of islands in clay. In Group B, children of Cambodian, Vietnamese, and Laotian parents made paintings and drawings of their personal histories. In both cases, language developed out of labeling, naming, and using new language in the art activities. Both programs were conducted by art teachers who felt that, far from being an inhibiting factor, the thematic use of Italian and Asian cultures actually stimulated art activity.

Language Arts

Generally, stories and poems may encourage children in the symbol or later stages of expression to make two- and three-dimensional illustrations. The media associated with picture making or paper work serve best in this type of work, although modeling materials may also be useful. Either the stories and poems the children read and study in class, or in some cases those they write themselves, may be used as the basis for pictorial or three-dimensional expression.

One very natural way to relate language, art, and imagination is to ask children to write about what they have drawn. If the subject is selected with care (such as "Machines Designed to Perform Unusual Tasks"), then the interplay between idea and image grows dramatically. Children can speak and write about things they may not draw, and vice versa. Combining the two can enhance the development of both linguistic and graphic forms.

One study demonstrated that higher levels of achievement in reading and writing in the middle grades could be obtained when narrative drawing was used on a sustained basis.[16] The writer began by asking her students to draw the answers to such questions as, "How many kinds of people can you draw?" and "How many kinds of movement and emotions can you draw?" using these activities before creating a plot for the characters drawn. Such experiences made writing about sequences of events come more easily. As writing is increasingly stressed on all levels of instruction, children, particularly in the upper grades, should be encouraged, once familiarized with the critical process, to write on the descriptive and interpretive stages (see Chapter 11 on Art Criticism).

Social Studies

For children, social studies begin in their immediate environment. The geography, history, and civics they first consider are found close to home. Because children are naturally interested in what goes on around them, few problems arise when they base their art on this area of learning. Their paintings, murals, and three-dimensional work may depict such themes as "Our Neighborhood," "Our Waterfront," "Fam-

The environment studied through art experiences can range from the classroom to the home, neighborhood town, and city. Using the city as a core subject, a combined fifth and sixth grade studied everything from legal institutions to the metric system. After learning about the city as a topic in art history, the class prepared posters and other graphics and painted the background mural for the city they "designed."

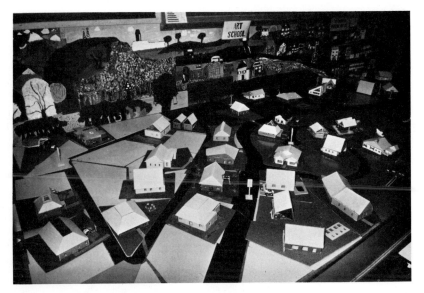

ilies Who Have Lived Longest in Our District," "What Our Firemen Do," "How We Travel in Our City."

In the lower grades, a topic frequently related to social studies is "Our Friends and Neighbors in Other Lands." Here the subject takes the children away from the environment they know, and as a result their artwork often deteriorates. The chief reason for this deterioration is that the children frequently do not know enough about the remote region to express much about it, with the consequence that the teacher may substitute stereotyped symbols for true information. National stereotypes can give so restricted an idea of a country that they interfere with the child's understanding of the true character of the foreign land. Granted that the Netherlands has tulips, that Mexicans build with adobe, and that Canada maintains the Royal Canadian Mounted Police, such images do not represent the heart of these lands.

Before children can be expected to give expression in art to a theme based on remote regions, they must gain a wide knowledge of them, and they must be stirred by some aspects of this knowledge. By reading books and looking at moving pictures, by singing songs of the countries, by studying the work of their artists, and so forth, in course of time they may gain a body of knowledge and a sense of the true character of distant places that will allow them to express something worthwhile.

Ethnic Awareness Through Art. To satisfy the desire of ethnic minority groups for improved recognition of their cultural histories, teachers can easily incorporate relevant information into both art-work and appreciation activities.[17] Collage, murals, and mask-making—which

Children can learn from other children through the growing number of exchange programs. These examples of the Bo Train Circle game are from Sierra Leone and are part of an exhibition organized by the Foster Parents Plan Program on understanding the Third World through art.

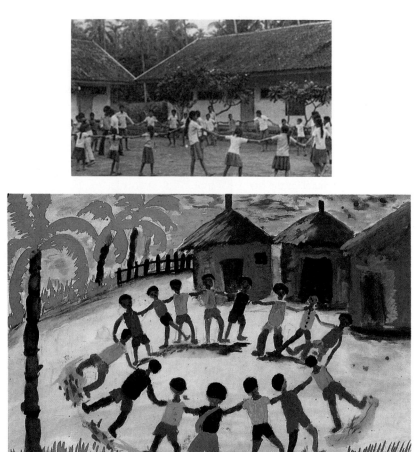

most teachers already include in their programs — can make clear references to Afro-American art and crafts. Activities such as jewelry and basket-making, weaving, and dyeing can also refer to cultures other than Western culture. However, this will mean shifting some of the usual historical references. When the class is involved in a problem of collage, the work of Romare Bearden may be of even greater use than that of Picasso of Schwitters. In showing the work of muralists, the Mexican School and the walls of a barrio in Los Angeles are exciting examples of the social role that art can play in a community.

Every urban area has artists from minority cultures to draw upon as possible visiting artists. Children need models for emulation and for improving their self-image — there is no reason that children cannot admire artists as well as athletes.

Masks provide one example of how ethnic sources can be utilized. Mask making is a perennially popular art activity. It combines a wide variety of techniques, transformation, imagination, even magic. A mask can be used for Halloween or it can be practical. Its effects are achieved quickly—as if simply adding paint and paper to a paper bag—or can be painstaking, such as careful modeling in clay. The mask-maker can add feathers, buttons, beads, hemp, and any number of objects to enhance the mask's visual appeal. Rarely, however, is the mask presented in any cultural context, such as the "Day of the Dead" in Mexico.

Yet the mask can convey information about the wearer: it can identify a scuba diver, a welder, an astronaut, and so on. Many African folktales, for example, involve masks, and mask styles differ from one African tribe or culture to another. All masks use local materials, serve different purposes, and possess their own visual styles. Studying these elements helps acquaint students with an important phase of another culture.[18]

Art and Nature

Although artists like Audubon and da Vinci have been able to bring art and science into close proximity, scientific drawings and artistic expressions differ in intent. A scientific drawing is an exact statement of fact, allowing no deviation from the natural appearance of an object.

For children, natural objects evoke feelings and hold meanings that go beyond a scientific statement. However, the objects in the science corner of the classroom, such as fossils, shells, and rocks can provide the basis for invention, as well as for the study of form. Studying the natural world satisfies the curiosity of both artist and scientist (see da Vinci's notebooks, for instance). The studios of many artists, Henry Moore as an example, are filled with specimens of rocks, bones, and fossils. A middle school art teacher describes his room as follows:

> My art classroom could be mistaken for an extension of the Smithsonian Institution's National History Museum. Along with children's art expressions on animal themes, there are continuous displays of real and pictured butterflies, seashells, wasps' nests, rocks, and peacock feathers. The children are constantly exposed to color slides, films, posters, photographs, and books about wild animals, tropical fish, beautiful and bizarre insects, various plant forms, and of course—dinosaurs.[19]

Art teachers should also avail themselves not only of films and specimens used for scientific study, but also of equipment such as microscopes and magnifying glasses to note the aesthetic character of natural structures and design. As one writer observed, "Microscopes reveal a strange world hidden to our normal eyes: giant telescopes study unknown areas of the universe and astronauts send us television pictures from space."[20] Technology that is available through science can provide us with sources of unique imagery.

Most elementary school children, of course, are incapable of drawing with scientific accuracy. This does not mean that they should not

The teacher in this school has provided an array of diverse materials which can be used in science and art. Most objects can be picked up, examined, and used at the student's desk.

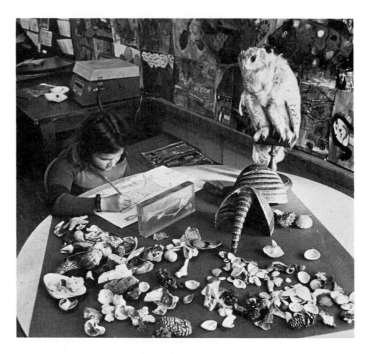

be exposed to natural objects or that they should not use them for expressive purposes. On the contrary, flowers, birds, seashells, fish, and animals, as stated previously, may be used with excellent effect in art. Any natural object may be employed as the basis of design, provided the children are also given freedom to depart from the scientific form they observe.

The fact that this freedom is allowed does not retard the children's growth in scientific knowledge. In looking at natural objects and experiencing them in other ways, they come close to nature. Later, should they be of a scientific turn of mind, their art experiences with the natural world will provide them with valuable insights that may lead to scientific inquiry.

A correlated art-science project could work as follows for the fifth and sixth grades. The first step would be an *observational phase*, in which students would be asked to draw as carefully as possible an object or specimen such as bones (skeleton segment); fossils embedded in plastic; flowers; or cellular forms viewed through a microscope. The second step, the *design phase*, would involve using the drawing in one of the following ways:

Fill in areas within outlines with flat tones based on a color theory.
Blow up the drawing to ten times the original size and turn it into a hard edge-style painting.

Move a piece of tracing paper over the original, allowing shapes to overlap. Fill in with textured pen-and-ink patterns, a color scheme, or a number of shades of one color.

Select a section for a small linoleum print and make a repeat pattern.

In such a sequence the student moves from observation to design judgment, and in making the print comes to understand how artists use natural forms as a basis for applied design. The entire sequence may take up to four or five class sessions, but it allows the student to "live with" one problem for an extended period of time.

The greatest care, of course, must be taken not to supply children with symbols, considered to be artistic, that tend to replace or interfere with a study of natural objects. The cutting of paper snowflakes, for example, could be practiced only after a careful study of these forms, and only if the activity were entirely creative. The drawing of evergreen trees in the well-known bisymmetrical zigzag design results more often from a teacher's demonstration than from a child's observation of a real tree.

Music

Music and art lend themselves to several types of correlation. As an indirect correlation, a background of music is often valuable to children while they are drawing, painting, or working in three dimensions. The music appears to influence the children's visual output in a subtle fashion.

The teacher may arrange direct correlations between music and art for children at any level in the elementary school. Music with a pronounced rhythmic beat and melodic line may be employed as a basis for drawing nonobjective patterns. The following are selections of classical music that lend themselves to correlations with art:

J. S. Bach, "Brandenburg" Concerto No. 1
     The Wise Virgins (ballet, arr. Walton)
Borodin, *Prince Igor:* "Polovetsian Dances"
Khachaturian, *Gayne Ballet*, Suite No. 1
Liszt, *Hungarian Rhapsodies*, Nos. 1–7
     Mephisto Waltzes
Prokofiev, *Peter and the Wolf*
Rossini, Overtures: *The Barber of Seville*
       William Tell
       Semiramide
Gershwin, *Rhapsody in Blue*
Electronic Music

Music depicting a definite mood may also lead to some interesting pictures, especially in the fifth and sixth grades. Before playing the record, the teacher usually discusses the mood of the selection. After hearing the music the class may discuss possible combinations of colors, lines, and other elements of design to express the mood pictorially. Work then begins, preferably in soft chalk or paint, with the music playing in the background. The following are selections expressing certain moods and are suitable for fifth and sixth grade pupils:

Britten, *Peter Grimes*, "Four Sea Interludes"
Copland, *El Salon Mexico*
Debussy, *Clair de Lune*
     La Mer
Mussorgsky, *Night on Bald Mountain*
Ravel, *Bolero*
Wagner, *Die Walküre*, "Ride of the Valkyries"

Music with a literary theme—*program music*, as it is sometimes called—may also assist in developing noteworthy picture making by pupils in the symbol or later stages of expression. The teacher gives the outline of the story, plays excerpts from the music, and from time to time draws attention to passages depicting specific events in the narrative. Examples of program music suitable mainly for pupils in the fourth or higher grades are as follows:

Bernstein, *West Side Story*, Overture
Bizet, *Carmen*, excerpts
Grofé, *Grand Canyon Suite*
Humperdinck, *Hänsel und Gretel*, excerpts
Respighi, *The Pines of Rome*
Rimsky-Korsakov, Scheherazade
Saint-Saëns, *Danse Macabre*

Varieties of pop and rock can be used with equal effectiveness. No listing of jazz or rock music is included because taste in these categories changes so quickly. Dixieland, Duke Ellington, the Beatles, electronic sound, synthesizers, etc. however, can always be used to motivate artwork. And record covers can be studied as a popular art form that links the mood and beat of music to visual experience. Musical selections from other cultures such as Spanish, African, West Indian, Scottish, or native American can add interest and variety to this type of experience.

Mathematics

As soon as a child is capable of using a measured line, mathematics may begin to enter into some of the child's art work. Activities such as building model houses, making costumes for puppets, or constructing puppet stages lend themselves to this correlation.

Some teachers have attempted to combine the two fields by having the children work during art sessions with mechanical drawing tools, such as compasses, triangles, and T-squares, to devise geometric designs. If this type of work is largely mechanical and hence not particularly expressive, there is little to recommend it. However, since children do enjoy the clarity and precision that designing with draftsmen's tools provide, in many situations the teacher may establish creative and aesthetic standards to make the design activities worthwhile. These tools might be combined with work in any number of techniques — crayon and pencil drawing, painting, crayon resist, and etching, among others.

ORGANIZING AND WRITING ART CURRICULUM

Goals and Objectives

The shaping of any curriculum must begin by establishing a direction. Although curriculum planners may bring to this problem some knowledge of art, of children, and of sound educational practice, the content of the curriculum begins to take form when they use all their knowledge and experience as a basis for setting down what they hope to accomplish in terms of art goals and objectives.

Ralph Tyler, in his brief but classic essay on curriculum planning, cites four questions that are generally accepted as a reasonable if not inevitable place to begin. These are as follows:[21]

1. What educational purposes should the school seek to attain?
2. What educational experiences can be provided that are likely to attain these purposes?
3. How can these educational experiences be effectively organized?
4. How can we determine whether these purposes are being attained?

The "purposes" that Tyler alludes to may also be viewed as goals, and his "experiences," the vehicles by which goals or purposes are attained. Lansing refers to the problem of goal definition when he states:

> Another thing that makes the formulation of goals difficult is the fact that some of them must be cognitive, while others must be affective and psychomotor. In other words, youngsters must know and understand certain things about art; they must have relevant attitudes and values; and they must possess certain skills. Their knowledge must cover life in general, artistic procedures, composition, art history, and aesthetics. Their attitudes must include an interest in the making and appreciating of art, confidence in their own ability to make and appraise art, tolerance of the various forms that art might take, and a willingness to work hard. And their skill must center around the efficient manipulation of art tools and materials.[22]

If we accept Lansing's statement, we can see that goals may exist in both broad and limited categories. An art program may be conceived of as having a design — that is, as being composed of a series of learning units, the components of which all contribute to the sense of wholeness. The teacher must discriminate between the broad goal and the subgoal or objective — and distinguishing between the two can be difficult. A lesson in color mixing, to cite one instance, does not fulfill the goal of "establishing color sensitivity" — an objective so inclusive that color mixing is obviously just one step in a sequence that might also include color matching from magazines, color identification in paintings, using color to express a mood, and finding color parallels to music and other sounds.

Objectives for a particular lesson will, of course, vary with the nature of the task. If the class is drawing pictures to send to a school in Europe or another part of the country, one objective might be to present as much specific information as possible, so that the recipients can determine from the drawings how Americans in Idaho, for example, dress and live. If the community has just experienced a hurricane, snowstorm, or torrential downpour, the objective could be to "create colors to show what it was like." Or, if sixth graders are having their first lesson in contour line drawing, the objective could relate to the amounts of variance in the line as evidence of clearly observed edges. Objectives should thus be presented in "manageable segments" and in clear, meaningful terms for the child.

Unless some sort of objective, however general, has been discussed in the early phase of the lesson, evaluation cannot be effective at the conclusion of the art period. The more specific the statement of the goal, however, the more effective the evaluation. The teacher who tells students, "Today we will concentrate on bright colors" does not help the students during the critique period as much as one who says, "Today let's see how much variety we can get out of a single color by changing it through the use of black, white, or its complement."

Goals are broad general aims, whereas objectives are more immediate ways of achieving a goal. Some statements of goals, however, are so vague as to have little meaning for student or teacher. The following examples of useful and nonuseful goals may help clarify these differences.

> *Art Appreciation:* Stated in lofty terms, a goal for this area might be: "To learn to appreciate art." This is a virtually meaningless statement, because no critic or aesthetician would claim that this achievement is totally possible for college students, much less for ten- or twelve-year-old children. It also gives no indication of the kinds of learning activities expected to take place. A more useful goal for the same topic would be: "To increase the enjoyment of artworks through discussion and studio experiences based on the work of professional artists."

Other useful objectives that might come under such a goal could provide the basis of lessons to follow. These could be:

To apply mental operations such as comparing, interpreting, describing, and arguing in response to artworks.

To demonstrate some connection between a studio exercise and the study of a style, a personality, or a period in art.

To employ newly acquired art vocabulary when discussing either professional or student artwork.

Objectives are intended to develop behaviors that students were not able to perform prior to some phase of instruction. It is hoped that if the children could not demonstrate the stated behavior in September, they should be able to do so in January. If they cannot, then either the teaching objective is unrealistic or the teacher lacks the skill to teach for the desired change.

The Competency Approach

Another approach to setting goals for the curriculum is *competency planning*. The following definitions are central to the competency approach to education. Since school systems often require such specificity in describing what the children will be able to do, it is well to note the meanings of these terms for possible future reference.

A *performance objective* is a positive goal, stated as a declarative sentence. Example: "The student will select, discuss, draw, center, and so on." In the case of a single activity, such as centering clay, the goal is specific; in the case of a sequence of activities, such as making a one-minute animated film, the goal is broad. It is also possible to set a goal for a group. Example: "The class will conduct the cleanup period without teacher intervention."

A *set* is a cluster of performance objectives that the student will have to accomplish in order to complete the task that leads to an end-product.

A *concept* precedes the choice of the carrier project and is a statement about art, such as, "Styles in painting vary with time." Concepts may ultimately be transformed into "overt" perceptual acts, such as asking the student to sort chronologically the work of a cave painter, Giotto, Manet, and Rauschenberg.[23]

Behaviorists in art education also recommend that the three major domains of learning be maintained. These domains, or classifications of learning, distinguish between the cognitive (knowledge, facts, intellectual abilities), affective (feelings and attitudes), and psychomotor (ability to handle specific processes involving physical coordination) skills.

A teacher, instead of suddenly deciding on Friday that drawing would be a good way to begin the week on Monday, will go through a considerable sequence of antecedent steps:

Think about the philosophy of art education.

Decide on the goals for the year for a particular age level. (This means considering what the art program can do to convert the philosophy into a realistic life process.)

Select both broad and specific strategies based on areas of art learnings to be covered.

Determine the sets for each activity.

State the performance objectives within sets.

State how the product will be evaluated.

Essential Elements. In developing performance objectives, program planners should also consider these elements.

1. *Identification of the individual or group* that will perform the desired behavior.

2. *Identification of the behavior* to be demonstrated through the product to be developed. The behavior should be described, as precisely as possible, in terms of an *action* that can be followed; or, similarly, the product should be described precisely as an *object* that can be observed.

3. The *primary conditions* under which the performance is expected to be measured: these might include restrictions placed on the project during the performance of specified tasks.

4. *Establishment of the minimum level of acceptable performance.* This step is the critical phase and the one that poses the most problems. What is the criterion for success? How will it function in evaluation?

5. *Establishment of the means of assessment*, which will be used to measure the expected performance or behavior. What forms will assessment take: checklists, informal observations, anecdotal records?

Criterion referenced objective [handwritten annotation]

Determining objectives within the behaviorist or competency approach is much easier in the psychomotor domain than in the emotional or affective domain, since the personal side of expression resists precise evaluation. Centering clay or sharpening a tool, on the other hand, is quite easy to note. There is also the problem of separating short-term from long-term objectives.

Many teachers have serious reservations about the competency approach because it defines results prior to process and does not deal adequately with experimentation or with learning through certain kinds of failure. Another argument some teachers have against this system is that it is not the way artists operate, since artists do not always know exactly how their work will turn out. Artists might even ask what the point is of creating art while already knowing exactly how it will turn out.

Organizational Categories for Art Curricula

There are several traditionally popular ways to organize art curricula and several notions that deserve the attention of curriculum writers. Many art curriculum guides and curricula have been organized on the basis of the elements and principles of design. Another traditional organizing scheme is according to modes of art production. The changing paradigm for art education, however, has caused art educators to consider additional categories suggested by art history, criticism, and aesthetics. Following is a brief list of topics or categories that might be considered for organizing art curriculum content:

Elements and principles of design. Units of instruction might be organized according to:

line	texture	harmony
shape	space	rhythm
color	unity	composition

Art modes and media. Units of instruction might be organized according to:

drawing	sculpture
painting	architecture
printmaking	ceramics

Periods of art history. Units of instruction might be organized according to:

prehistoric art	Roman art
Egyptian art	the Renaissance
Greek art	baroque art

Art from various cultures. Units of instruction might be organized according to:

the art of China	native American art
the art of Africa	contemporary American art
the art of Italy, Spain, or France	African-American art

Themes. Units of instruction might be organized according to:

the world of plants	mythology	images of women
the sea	the horse in art	art and worship
the westward movement	images of men	the artist as social critic

Aesthetics topics. Units of instruction might be organized according to:

purposes and functions of art	the artist's intent
beauty in art	art vs. nature
What is art?	the creative process

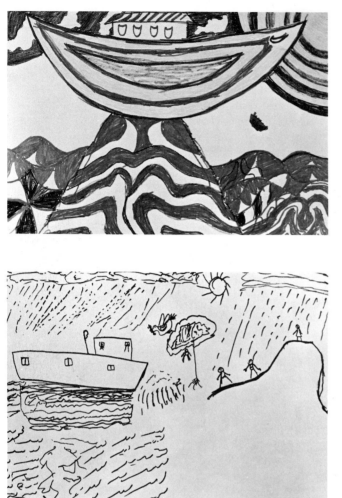

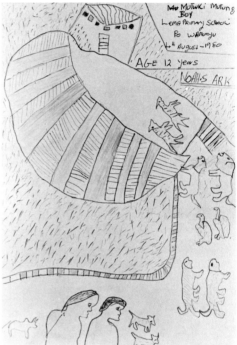

In a study by the author of art inspired by the story of Noah and the Ark, children from various nations produced work reflecting three major influences: cultural, educational, and personal. The children, ages ten to twelve, were told the same story, often through interpreters. Upper left: a Maori boy in New Zealand integrates designs from traditional Maori woodcarving into wave and sky patterns. Strong art program in the school. Lower left: a Bedouin child in the Negev area of Israel uses linear patterns from Arabic calligraphy to create the sea. The delicate broken lines of rain were also typical of his class. Art teacher not present. Right: a child in rural Kenya emphasizes the path to the ark because of the importance, in the child's homeland, of footpaths. The animals were traced, but the humans and ark were done freehand. No art instructor present. Opposite page, upper left: the orderly pattern of rain, waves, and wood distinguishes this rendering of the story by an Australian aboriginal child. Art teacher present. The watercolors at lower left and lower right are from two matched groups in separate schools in Seoul, South Korea. The two groups (like children in Taiwan, Hong Kong, and Japan, as well), shared a sensitivity to art media, drawing skills, and an ability to activate the human figure. But the tendency among the Korean children to depict the Noah story in human terms is unique. In the left-hand picture, animals dance in celebration at the end of the deluge; in the other picture, Noah and his family are busy at work. Upper right, a gypsy girl in a rural settlement in Hungary, considered gifted by her teacher, placed the dove inside another bird and combined olive branches. Mt. Ararat, and the ark in a forceful, coherent design. From an after-school art program in a special-interest center. Strong art teacher present.

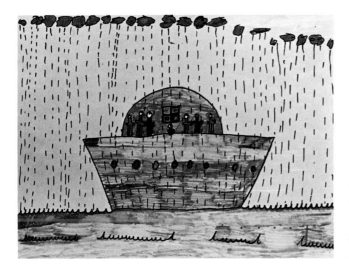

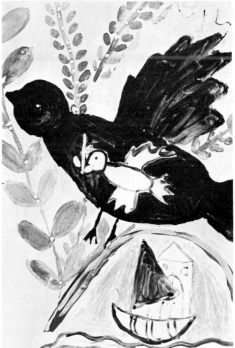

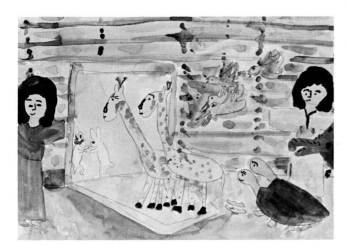

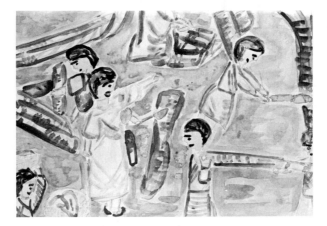

Landmark artworks. Units of instruction might be organized according to:

the Egyptian pyramids	Hokusai's *The Great Wave*	O'Keeffe's *Black Hollyhocks*
Michelangelo's Sistine Chapel ceiling	Rodin's *The Thinker* Van Gogh's *Starry Night*	Adam's *Yosemite* Notre Dame Cathedral
the Taj Mahal Marisol's *The Last Supper*	Picasso's *Les Demoiselles D'Avignon* and	Frank Lloyd Wright's Kaufman House (*Falling Water*)
Da Vinci's *Mona Lisa*	*Guernica*	

Art styles. Units of instruction might be organized according to:

Egyptian figures	cubism
Chinese figures	surrealism
baroque style	abstract expressionism
rococo style	pop art
impressionism	

Artists. Units of instruction might be organized about landmark artists as well as artworks, particularly if their work reflects periods of change or possess some element of personal history or artistic content that is interesting to children.

Picasso	Vincent Van Gogh
Georgia O'Keeffe	Frank Lloyd Wright
Romare Bearden	Francesco Goya

A balanced art curriculum can be organized on the basis of any of the organizational schemes listed above and the ways in which they interact. For example, if the elements of art are selected, works of art that exemplify different uses of line can be studied. Specific artists well known for their mastery of color can be studied. The history of color usage in Western art can be investigated and technological advances in the development of natural and artificial pigments noted. Color symbolism found in different cultures can be studied in relation to color meanings in contemporary American society. Students can develop skills in the use of line, shape, and color in their own artwork as a result of instruction and observation of the works of other artists. Likewise, any of the category systems listed above can be cross-referenced to art content from aesthetics, art history, art criticism, and art production. The organizational category usually assures emphasis on the topic of the category.

An example of a planning approach, recommended as an "organizing center" for the unit on color, is given in Table 16-1. This plan con-

⌇ **TABLE 16-1**

Unit on Color for Upper Grades*

A *unit* is a cluster of activities on one major theme. This is the simplest way to begin, and it can easily be extended into the vocabulary of competency planning by adding concepts, evaluation, and the division of activities (carrier projects) into sets or secondary groupings of objectives.

Expectancies in art: The student will be able to master art processes involving physical manipulation; sharply increase color perception; relate art vocabulary to art problems; recognize formal elements of design; and be able to organize a painting.

Content	Activities	Materials	Art References
1. *Color:* The distinction between primary and secondary colors	Creation of a design, based on a still life, that utilizes primary and secondary colors	Tempera	Expressionist paintings Fauve painters such as Andre Derain
2. The meaning of tints and shades	Creation of a design based on natural forms, using one color as a base and shades or tints of that color on top	Tempera	Cubist paintings Marie Laurencin
3. The emotive power of color	Creation of a nonobjective painting that reflects a mood or state of mind	Watercolor	Kandinsky, German Expressionists Film: *Fiddle-dee-dee* (National Film Board of Canada)
4. How color neighbors affect each other	Formation of a collage from samples of an assigned color chosen by each child	Colored paper, clippings from advertisements, fabrics, wallpaper	Josef Albers Victor Vasarely
5. Difference in function between mixing colors and selecting colors	Matching of colors in a painting, first with paint, then by pasting colors from magazine advertisements	Magazine advertisements, tempera, and construction paper	Collages of Romare Bearden

*"Color" is one of several units planned for the semester. Other areas of focus for art learning might be "Forms in Space" and "Printmaking." See also example of "Environment" unit.

(continued)

Content	Activities	Materials	Art References
6. Difference in effect between broken color,† mixed color, and flat, pure color	Painting of one tree in a painterly manner and another in a Hard Edge manner	Tempera	Impressionists such as Monet and Pissarro, and Hard Edge painters such as Stuart Davis, George Ortman and Frank Stella
7. How color behaves in relation to light	Experimentation on acetate or old slides	Tempera, hole punchers, nail polish, acetate, and slide projector	

†Broken color refers to the Impressionistic manner of painting an area in short, flickering strokes of different hues.

siders the character of the children and what can be expected of them in art before the content and activities of the program are decided on.

The unit outlined in Table 16-1 should take eight class sessions, so that if a class meets once a week, there would be two months of class contact. This may seem like an excessive amount of time to spend on color, but many kinds of learning are called into play: judgment, intuition, use of information, historical contexts, at least five kinds of media, and observation. The unit concept allows for an in-depth approach and permits sequencing of activities within a broader context. Needless to say, the classroom teacher's support in offering additional art activities can greatly enrich the value of this or any unit.

Matrix Systems for Curriculum Planning

One way for teachers to get their thoughts on paper is to use a matrix as a graphic guide for sorting ideas. The matrix is simply a grid that indicates where key issues intersect. Matrix A (Table 16-2) demonstrates how basic concerns can be related: What will be studied (art content)? To whom will it be taught (kinds of students)? In what order (sequence)? Before these questions are answered, the teacher should have given some thought to the two principal concerns that must precede the issues mentioned above: the philosophy of the teacher (What do I believe?) and its attendant goals (What do I hope to accomplish?).

Matrix A is the first stage of planning. The subdivisions of each content area must now be indicated so that more specific information can be accommodated.

The second stage shown in Table 16-3, Matrix B, moves to the heart of instruction and should also deal with concepts (statements about

~ **TABLE 16-2**

Matrix A — The First Stage

	Art Content Areas		
	Art history	Art Criticism	Studio Production
Upper Grades	Abstract Expressionism	Interpretation	Painting
Middle Grades	Impressionism	Analysis	Painting
Primary Grades	Cave Art	Description	Painting

~ **TABLE 16-3**

Matrix B — The Second Stage

	Art Criticism			
Concept Statements	Objectives	Activities	Media and Resources	Evaluation
"Styles vary with time and artist."	"The student will be able to recognize and distinguish between the works of surrealists, expressionists, and cubists."	Sorting postcard reproductions of works of artists	Slides Films Filmstrips Games Packages File material Postcard reproductions	After examining cubist paintings of Braque and Picasso, the pupils will be asked to separate works by the above artists painted during the period when their work was dissimilar.

art, which Eisner describes as "principles or generalizations to be used by the teacher as a focus for subsequent work with students").[24] The "Objectives" column translates the concept into a performance objective. The "Activities" column lists the major tasks that are designed to engage the child in learning the concept. The next column deals with materials, support, or resources that may be needed to fulfill the performance objectives that serve to realize the concept. The final column contains suggestions for evaluation, although this information could be reserved for the third, or lesson plan, stage.

Matrix C (Table 16-4) suggests another format; organizing thoughts for an entire semester. "Sources of Art" are listed in the first column. The other columns offer choices of how they can be given form — that is, through a choice of "Basic Modes of Expression" and "Media." The matrix assumes that the source of art is where to begin, and that media and modes are means to ends, rather than ends in themselves. As an example, students can exercise observation through drawing (pencil, ink), sculpture (clay), or painting (tempera). The source categories often overlap: a lesson on environmental awareness can involve drawing

∿∿ **TABLE 16-4**

Matrix C — Semester Planning

Grade _____
No. of
class sessions _____ Basic Modes of Expression/Media

Sources of Art	Drawing	Painting	Printmaking	Sculpture	Crafts	Mixed Media
	Pencil Ink Crayon, craypas	Watercolor Tempera Acrylic	Monoprints: linoleum calligraphy vegetable	Assemblage Clay Cardboard Wood scraps	Wood scraps Papier-mâché Clay	Collage-ink Crayon resist Craypas Crayon etching
Observation						
Problem-Solving						
Hidden Landscape (dreams, imagination, fantasy)						
Narrative Art (storytelling, illustration)						
Language of Art (design, line, form, color)						
Art History						
Art Criticism						
Aesthetics						

landscapes or discussing slides of local architectural styles (art history and art appreciation). When examining the concept of utopia through environmental improvement, the student is working from Source 2, Imagination and Fantasy. The Source category provides a focus of attention, a central core around which succeeding sessions may be planned. Most teachers, particularly those teaching on the secondary level, begin with the basic modes and then search for subject matter; but Matrix C is arranged to *begin* with subject matter, since this lies closer to the goals of art education.

Using Matrix C, teachers should try to achieve some balance between the sources and the different media used to deal with them, and to plan for some coverage of basic experiences that can be accommodated in the time allotted. For example, if there are fifteen class meetings in one semester, the teacher could accommodate three basic modes of expression that deal with four sources of art, or could deal with fewer sources and develop them through a wider range of media or modes. One plan for the first semester of a fifth grade environmental unit involved the following activities:

1. Viewing films of landscapes, including aerial views.
2. Studying painters who painted landscapes, from Constable (realistic) to Hundertwasser (abstract).
3. Making student self-portraits as skydivers, with views of the earth below.
4. Making a relief collage of an imaginary landscape viewed from above.
5. Direct painting from landscape, preceded by a study of broken color.

This is another example of a unit approach—a way of organizing the grouping or sequencing of art experiences that enables children to concentrate on a single artistic problem through a group of related tasks and materials.

Table 16-5 presents another plan for the fifth and sixth grades, in this case for an entire year—thirty-four class sessions. The number under each activity refers to the list of sources, some of which are brought into play when the students perform each of the sequences of activities.

The Lesson Plan

The creation of a lesson plan is the culminating exercise for student and beginning art teachers. Although most teachers stop using lesson plans after a few years of experience, it is a good exercise to analyze the final stage of curriculum planning—the point at which a new area of the curriculum is introduced. Lesson plans can cover a day or a longer period of time. A good lesson plan anticipates what can and should happen; it is a scenario for achieving an objective. Should the actual events not always go according to the plan, the value gained from writing lesson plans should not be minimized.

The sample plan that follows is the final stage of column 4, "Drawing," on Matrix A.

Art content area: Drawing.

Concept statement: "Contour or edge drawing is one way to become aware of the variety of edges of shapes of the overall structure of a form."

Time: Two sessions.

TABLE 16-5

A Program — 5th and 6th Grades

Sources from which activities are drawn:

1. Confronting the Exterior World
2. The Hidden Landscape: Fantasy, Imagination, Speculation, Dreams
3. Design: The Language and Structure of Art
4. Cultural Content: History, Criticism, and Ethnic Settings
5. Memory and Experience: Sports, Family, Vacations, Weekends, Personal History
6. Artist and Society: Practical Purposes, Commercial Art, Environmental Art, Industrial Design
7. Integrated Art: Art activity in relation to language arts, social studies, mathematics.
8. Public Rituals: Celebrations, Exhibits, Parties, Holidays, Events

Activity	Session	Sequences of Activities	Objectives
Drawing (may be used as a diagnostic instrument)	1	Memory drawing	
	2	Observational drawing: mechanical objects (bicycles, insides of watches, movie projectors, vehicles, toys, tools)	Ability to handle detail, to relate whole to parts, and to work with new visual structures
Mapping 2, 3, 4, 7	3	Introduction, planning, sketching of decorative maps	To develop imagination through maps. To create symbols and situations and to use design for embellishment. To relate all this to historical context of Portuguese cartography
	4	Development and drawing	
	5	Finishing	
Painting and Color 3, 6	6	Warm/Cool, Approach I: number/letter design	To see new possibilities of color. To deal with compositional problems in relating form and color to total space
	7	Warm/Cool, Approach II: still life selected for unusual shape	
	8	Complete still life	
Collage 1, 3	9	People collage, drawing, design	To develop design awareness through the collage technique (texture applied to surface). To use one activity (drawing) as a basis for subsequent activities
	10	Development	
	11	Complete collage	
Fish Mobile 1, 3, 6, 7	12	Developing drawing, working in tissue	To master a new craft process. To exploit the possibilities of transparency as a means of dealing with color
	13	Decorating and stuffing	
Clay: Dinosaurs, Mythological, etc. 1, 2, 3, 4, 5, 6, 7	14	Presentation, working	To deal with modeling and shaping techniques. To study and use mythological forms as a basis of art. To relate details (surfaces, anatomical structures) to large shapes
	15	Working, finishing	

(continued)

Activity	Session	Sequences of Activities	Objectives
Drawing: Crayon Engraving 1, 2, 3	16	Line drawing, animals	To learn how processes and stages of development can enrich and extend the possibilities of image development. To learn the values of extended concentration on a project. To learn a mixed-media technique
	17	Color phase	
	18	Paint phase	
	19	Engraving phase	
Linoleum Print 1, 2, 3, 5	20	Introduction, free choice of subject: animal, design, personal experiences	To learn how stages of processes can extend imagery. To acquire skill in using new tools. To use accident and pure design to achieve unexpected effects in printmaking. To use sources of design to generate ideas. To deal in balances of dark and light areas
	21	Introduction to tools; work on block	
	22	Work on block	
	23	Work on block	
	24	Work on block, start printing	
	25	Straight printing	
	26	Explorative printing	
Critical/Historical Study 4, 7		Selecting an artist whose work suggests some formal or conceptual problem (Klee, Matisse, Picasso); discussing meaning and intent as they relate to style and technique.	To learn about a new artist or painting. To discuss art: description and interpretation, analysis. To create a connection between art history and students' own creative decisions
Celebration: Masks, Headdresses, and Face-Painting 1, 2, 3, 4, 6, 8	27	Begin by modeling the form of the mask in clay	To see art as a social process that can enhance public rituals. To relate design to the human form. To discover imaginative solutions to paper sculpture used as body ornament. To establish relationships between costume and face-painting
	28	Begin covering with papier-mâché	
	29	Continuing papier-mâché	
	30	Finishing and planning surface treatment	
	31	Painting and decorating	
	32	Creating headdresses and decorating faces	
Evaluation of Program	33	Objective written examination to assess information retained.	To assess attitudes and knowledge as a basis for decision-making
	34	Celebration-eat, parade	

Objectives: The students will be able to make a continuous contour drawing of a group of simple objects selected from around the room or from their own pockets. (Several arrangements will be set up for those who prefer groups of large objects.) The students will demonstrate their handling of detail and edges of the subject, both characteristics of contour drawing.

Concepts and processes to be stressed at the introduction of the lesson: Drawing will be defined as "a record in line of forms in space." Contour drawing will be defined as "a record of the edges of shapes," as opposed to drawing that uses lines and tones to suggest volume or mass.

Materials to be used: Soft pencil or crayon on white paper.

Perceptual processes to be emphasized: The ability to focus on the edges of shapes and to see the shapes that are constituent parts of an object. The students may accomplish this by covering their hands with a sheet of paper so that they will not be tempted to compare object and drawing.

Group evaluation: The drawings of students and professional artists will be pinned up so that successful parts may be noted.
Questions for consideration in a group evaluation:
"How does contour drawing differ from other kinds we have done?"
"What did you notice in your subject that you had not seen before?"
"Let's take a look at some contour drawings by professional artists. How have they handled the edges of things?"

Art history: Picasso, Matisse, Ben Shahn.

The plan that covers the stages discussed above is an exercise in relating wholes to parts. If the teacher begins with a broad conceptual frame, then the art lesson has a clearly stated context. The novice teacher, however, too often begins at the other end of the scale, and as a result the students receive a potpourri of scattered experiences without any underlying logic.

Obviously, planning a program can be arduous and time-consuming if teachers feel they must do the entire job themselves rather than consult existing models. Most teachers, in any case, will not be expected to plan entire programs on their own. The suggestions described above are intended as a brief introduction for readers who suddenly find themselves on a team that is required to produce a total art program in depth and detail.

The idea of approaching art instruction in a disciplined manner may seem rather extreme to the teacher who feels that art lies beyond careful planning. But every teacher, regardless of philosophy or subject, must face the results of their instruction and planning for art simply requires that the instructor consider the end results before beginning to teach.

◆ NOTES TO THE TEXT

1. Ronald C. Doll, *Curriculum Improvement: Decision Making and Process*, 7th ed. (Boston: Allyn and Bacon, 1989), p. 26.

2. Doll, ibid., p. 8.

3. Ralph Tyler, *Basic Principles of Curriculum and Instruction* (Chicago: University of Chicago Press, 1950).

4. Doll, op. cit., p. 45.

5. Lauren B. Resnick, *Education and Learning to Think* (Washington, D.C.: National Academy Press, 1987), p. 3.

6. See Chapter 11, "Art Criticism."

7. See, for example, Barry K. Beyer, *Practical Strategies for the Teaching of Thinking* (Boston: Allyn and Bacon, 1987).

8. Doll, op. cit., p. 113.

9. See Chapter 14, "Methods for Teaching Art."

10. The College Board, *Academic Preparation in the Arts* (New York: College Board Publications, 1985), p. 27.

11. David G. Armstrong, *Developing and Documenting the Curriculum* (Boston: Allyn and Bacon, 1989), pp. 55, 56.

12. David Martin, Philip Saif and Linda Thiel, "Curriculum Development: Who Is Involved and How?" *Educational Leadership*, January 1987, p. 45.

13. Martin, ibid., p. 41.

14. The list of goals is taken from "Curriculum Study Group: Social Studies" (Newton, MA: Newton Public Schools).

15. "English as a Second Language" (Newton, MA: Newton Public Schools, n.d.).

16. Janet L. Olson, "Envisioning Writing: Toward an Integration of Drawing and Writing," Unpublished Doctoral Dissertation, Teachers College, Columbia University, 1989.

17. The concept of a minority is changing at a rapid pace. For example, the Hispanic population in California will be a majority by the year 2010.

18. See Eugene J. Grigsby, Jr., *Art and Ethnics: Background for Teaching Youth in a Pluralistic Society* (Dubuque: William C. Brown, 1977).

19. Frank J. Chetelat, "Art and Science: An Interdisciplinary Approach," *Art Teacher*, Fall 1979, p. 8.

20. Moy Keightley, *Investigating Art* (London: Elak Ltd., 1976), p. 146.

21. Ralph Tyler, *Basic Principles of Curriculum and Instruction*, see Chapter 1.

22. Quoted in Mary M. Packwood, ed., *Art Education in the Elementary School* (Washington, D.C.: National Art Education Association, 1967), p. 72.

23. These terms originated in several conferences organized by the National Art Education Association with the assistance of Professor Asahel Woodruff of the University of Utah.

24. Elliot Eisner, *Educating Artistic Vision* (New York: Macmillan, 1972), p. 174.

◆ ACTIVITIES FOR THE READER

1. Describe in some detail the significant planning decisions that must be made in an art program developed in the following situations: (a) a sixth grade classroom in a new, wealthy suburb of a large city; (b) a third grade classroom in a temporary school for the children of construction workers in an isolated part of North Carolina; (c) a mixed-grade classroom (first through fourth grades) in a mission school for Indians located in New Mexico.

2. Describe how you would constructively handle a situation in which your principal was more interested in having an art program based on a rigid program of outdated concepts than on a contemporary, creative approach. Choose a classmate and do some improvised role-playing on the subject.

3. You are elected chairman of an eight-person *ad hoc* committee in a city school system to submit ideas to a central authority for the improvement of the art program. You are expected, furthermore, to select the eight members of the committee. State the kinds of people you would choose. Describe the agenda you would draw up for the first hour-long meeting.

4. Because of negative associations with a previous art program, your fifth grade pupils do not seem interested in helping you develop an art program. Describe how you might improve matters.

5. A former teacher had for two years taught nothing to fourth, fifth, and sixth grade pupils except the copying of either comic strips or picture postcards. How would you proceed in developing an art program in your new teaching position?

6. Improvise the conversation you might have with a parent who thinks teaching art is a waste of taxpayer's money, which should be used for "more important fundamentals." Try this conversation with various types of parents: professionals, lower-middle-class factory workers, local shopkeepers.

7. Plan a sequence of six art activities for the middle grades, all based on a theme of your choice. Try one unit for a limited budget and one for a generous budget.

8. Divide the painting experience into "tight" (performance) objectives and "loose" objectives (more personal interpretations).

◆ SUGGESTED READINGS

Day, Michael, and Kay Alexander, eds., *Discipline-Based Art Education: A Curriculum Sampler*. Los Angeles: The Getty Center for Education in the Arts, 1990. Sample art curriculum units for elementary, middle school, and high school levels.

Chapman, Laura. *Approaches to Art Education*. New York: Harcourt Brace Jovanovich, 1978. Chapter 18, "Planning the Art Program." This is one of the best books for art curriculum development.

Doll, Ronald C. *Curriculum Improvement: Decision Making and Process*, 7th ed. Boston: Allyn and Bacon.

Grigsby, Eugene J., Jr. *Art and Ethnics: Background for Teaching Youth in A Pluralistic Society*. Dubuque: William C. Brown, 1977.

Hurwitz, Al. *Programs of Promise: Art in the Schools*. New York: Harcourt Brace Jovanovich, 1972.

See sections by Elliot Eisner, Ronald Silverman, Guy Hubbard, and Mary Rouse for structured approaches to art programming.

Resnick, Lauren B. *Education and Learning to Think*. Washington, D.C.: National Academy Press, 1987.

Tyler, Ralph. *Basic Principles of Curriculum and Instruction*. Chicago: University of Chicago Press, 1950.

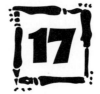

CLASSROOM ORGANIZATION AND DISPLAY OF STUDENT WORK

CHILDREN HAVE ENJOYED the creating of an art project and they also enjoy their completed work. They want to share with others a part of what is so vital to them. Realizing this need and desire for recognition, the teacher should plan to display the work of the children in whatever way best suits the particular art product.

Blanche Jefferson

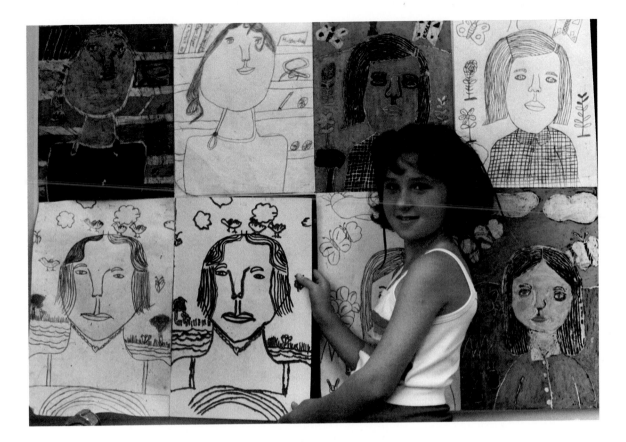

In order to conduct an art program successfully, the teacher must often plan alterations and additions to the basic classroom that is provided. In this chapter we will discuss some of the ways in which a general classroom may be modified to accommodate pupils engaged in art work. Some attention will be given also to the planning of an art room, if such a separate room is available. We will deal here only with the physical equipment and functional arrangements for art activities in different types of rooms. In the second half of the chapter, we will discuss the display of student artwork.

Many of the problems that arise from the task of reorganizing a room for art are unique to the particular situation. The size and shape of a room, the number of children in a class, and the type of activities in the program all will modify the arrangements to be made. The making of suitable physical arrangements for art, therefore, presents a challenge that in the long run only the teacher can satisfactorily meet.

PHYSICAL ARRANGEMENT OF THE CLASSROOM

A classroom in which art is taught requires physical provisions for the following operations: storing bulk equipment and supplies; preparing current supplies for the class; and setting out the supplies for current work. After children learn what to obtain and where to obtain it, and how to move so that they do not get in each other's way (all of which they learn through discussion with the teacher and subsequent practice), they must have suitable places to work. Drawing and painting are quiet activities; cutting and hammering are more active. Papers for drawing and painting are usually much larger than those for writing, so that surfaces to accommodate them must be larger than most school desks. Certain activities, such as wood sculpture or linoleum block printing, demand a special surface on which the materials may be cut. Through use this surface will roughen and become unsuitable for drawing, painting, and other activities. Two boards, a work board and a drawing board, are necessary. Drying unfinished or completed work, storing unfinished work, and displaying work also require their own spaces. These requirements suggest the following furniture:

1. A storage cupboard with some adjustable shelves, the latter at least 8 inches wide for small items and other shelves at least 18 inches wide for larger items. The outside dimensions of the cupboard will, of course, be determined by the floor and wall space available.

2. Two tables, preferably at least 5 feet long and 30 inches wide, one to be used largely by the teacher in arranging and displaying supplies and the other for children's group work.

3. A sink, or a stand for pails of water. The sink should have two faucets to hasten the clean-up activity.

4. A drying shelf or battery of shelves near a radiator or other source of heat. The shelf should be about 12 inches wide and as long as space permits.

5. Some display facilities such as cases and bulletin boards.

6. Some chalkboard space—but not so much as to displace needed display areas.

7. A screen for showing slides and films.

8. Storage for art prints, slides, and other art resource materials.

BASIC SUPPLIES AND EQUIPMENT

While each type of art activity demands particular tools and equipment, and sometimes special room arrangements, the following general list of tools and supplies seems basic to nearly any art program. Miscellaneous supplies and equipment such as scissors, thumbtacks, masking tape, and paper cutter (18-inch minimum) are not listed, since they are part of general equipment for other subjects. Crafts materials are not listed since they vary so much with each teacher.

1. *Brayers:* available in a variety of widths from 3 to 8 inches. Soft rubber rollers are recommended and a set for one class can service the entire school.
2. *Brushes:* for painting: flat, hog-bristle, ¼ inch to 1 inch wide. For painting: pointed, sable, large (size 6 or 7) paste brushes.
3. *Chalk:* soft; ten or twelve colors plus black and white; dustless preferred.
4. *Crayons:* wax; soft; ten or twelve colors plus black and white.
5. *Oil crayons:* often known as oil pastels.
6. *Pens:* felt-tip marking pens.
7. *Cutting tools:* sloyd knives, X-acto knives, single-edged razor blades, linoleum carving tools. (One set of linoleum tools can service several upper grades).
8. *Drawing boards:* about 18 by 24 inches; soft plywood at least "BC" grade (that is, clear of knots on at least one side); Masonite, composition board (optional).
9. *Erasers:* Artgum type.
10. *Inks:* black drawing ink; water-base printing inks in tubes for block printing.
11. *Linoleum:* minimum of 6 square inches per child; also available mounted on plywood blocks, but those are more expensive.
12. *Tempera paint:* liquid in pints or powder in pounds (white, black, orange, yellow, blue, green, and red as basic; magenta, purple, and turquoise as luxuries; probably twice the quantity of black, white, and yellow as of other colors chosen).

    Tempera paints have been the traditional mainstay of painting activity. Acrylic paint is now priced competitively with tempera and should be considered for its distinguishing properties: it is waterproof, and therefore ideal for interior and exterior wall murals; murals on paper can be rolled up without flaking. It will adhere to any surface — clay, wood, glass, and so on. When it is applied thickly, objects can be embedded into it; when thinned with water, it can serve as a substitute for watercolor. When applied with a soft foam brayer, it can also be used for linoleum printing. Purchase in quarts.
13. *Watercolor paint:* secondary colors selections are preferable.

14. *Paint tins:* muffin tins, with at least six depressions; baby food jars and frozen juice cans may also be used.

15. *Paper:* roll of kraft (brown wrapping), about 36 inches wide; or "project roll," 36 inches wide.
    Manila: 18 by 24 inches, cream and gray, 40 pound.
    Colored construction: 12 by 18 inches (red, yellow blue, light green, dark green, black, gray, and perhaps some in-between colors like blue-green and red-orange; about forty colors are available).
    Newsprint, colored tissue: size optional.

16. *Paste and glue:* school paste; in quarts.
    Powered wheat paste for papier-mâché.
    White glue for wood joining (thinned, it works well as an adhesive for colored tissue).

17. *Pencils:* drawing; black, soft.

18. *Printing plates:* glass trimmed with masking tape.

19. *Firing clay:* 3 pounds per child minimum.

20. Slide and filmstrip projectors should be available.

21. A collection of art prints and postcards is very desirable.

22. Art books and magazines should be available in the art room or the library.

CLASSROOM ARRANGEMENTS

A Primary Grade Classroom

The problems in arranging the room for the primary grades (K-2) arise largely from the stage of physiological development of the pupils, who use the large muscles in art work and require relatively large tools and bulky media, which create storage problems. The teacher's preparation of art materials for young children is often quite different from that for the upper grades. Older children can usually select art materials for themselves, but the primary teachers must, at least at the beginning of the school term, arrange sets or groupings of materials. These vary greatly in the number of items they contain. For example, for crayon drawing, children need only six crayons and a sheet of manila paper. For painting, they require perhaps an apron or a parent's old shirt, a sheet of newspaper or oilcloth to protect the painting surface, two brushes, a sheet of newsprint, a paint cloth, and some liquid colors.

From a necessarily large and convenient storage space the teacher selects materials and places them on a long table, cafeteria-style. Crayons may be placed on a paper plate and set on the sheet of paper. The painting kit may be assembled in discarded "six-pack" cartons, on a metal or plastic tray, or on a wooden work board. The paint should not be included at this point because children could spill it as they transport the kit to the place where they will be painting. Paint and any other "dangerous" materials should be placed in the work area ahead of time.

The following suggestions may be helpful in storing tools and supplies so that they will be ready for distribution:

1. Brushes and pencils should be placed in glass jars, with bristles and points up. Blocks of wood with holes bored in them, each hole large enough to hold one item, provide another convenient way of arranging this type of tool. This manner of storage also allows the teacher to make a quick visual check for missing brushes.

2. Crayons should be separated according to colors. Each container, which might be a milk carton or a cigar box, should hold only one color.

3. Moistened clay should be rolled into balls and placed in a large lidded earthenware jar or plastic bags to keep in the moisture.

4. Paper should be cut to size and arranged on a shelf in piles according to size and color.

5. Paper scraps should be separated according to color and saved in small cartons.

6. Paste should be kept in covered glass jars. The teacher should place paste on disposable paper plates or simply on pieces of cardboard after it has been mixed for use.

It is fortunate that the furniture in most primary rooms is movable, since floors provide an excellent work area for art. If the floor is covered with heavy linoleum or linoleum tile, it is necessary to set down only a thin protective covering such as oilcloth, plastic sheets, or wrapping paper before work begins. If the floor is in any way rough, cardboard mats may be put over the areas where the activities are to take place. The type of work being done, whether flat or three-dimensional, often determines the kind of floor or table covering to be set down.

Some teachers like to hang paintings to dry on a clothesline with spring clothespins. Tables are often used for drying three-dimensional projects.

Because it is desirable for all children eventually to learn how to procure and replace equipment and supplies for themselves, the room should be so arranged that children can perform the task easily. In the primary grades, as elsewhere in the art program, the cafeteria system is useful. Children must develop the ability to obtain and replace art materials according to a plan that they themselves help to determine. The teacher should discuss with children the necessity of learning these skills. However, in the primary grades the children will usually follow plans willingly and treat the routine as a game. The game can even include a rehearsal or drill of the routine.

A General Classroom

Many contemporary school plans give considerable thought to suitable accommodation for art activities in general classrooms. A description of the special provisions for art in the general classroom is offered here primarily for those teachers who are provided with a reasonably liberal budget for the furnishing of their act facilities.

In most classrooms desks can be easily arranged to suit the studies in progress. Movable desks are a great convenience for drawing and painting, since they allow a pupil to use a drawing board without interfering with other children. Clusters of desks may be arranged so that large flat areas of working space are available for group activities.

In some contemporary classrooms an entire wall is provided with fixtures that facilitate the teaching of art. These can include a counter covered with formica or some other suitably processed material, built from wall to wall. This counter houses probably the most important single convenience for art activities—a large sink supplied with hot and cold water. Below the counter are several storage cupboards equipped with adjustable shelves and swinging doors where all expendable supplies may be stored. A second row of cupboards is suspended about twelve inches above the counter. These cupboards also have adjustable shelves, but the doors are of the sliding variety so that pupils will not bump their heads on them when open. Additional supplies or the pupils' unfinished work may be kept in this storage space. Electrical outlets are frequently provided at convenient intervals along the counter. The whole assemblage, which substantially resembles a work unit in a modern kitchen, occupies relatively little floor space. Sometimes an additional work counter is provided along part of the window wall; more cupboards may be built below this counter.

Because the teacher in a general classroom requires a relatively large expanse of chalkboard, it is sometimes difficult to find sufficient space to display art. This is often provided, however, on the side wall to the rear of the room, and on two walls above the chalkboards, where a wide strip of tackboard is fastened. But since even these areas are usually insufficient for display purposes, many new schools are being equipped with display boards and cases in the main halls of the building.

The Art Room

In today's educational world, budgets are not always large enough for accommodating a separate art room in a new school, and the wishes of art teachers cannot always be satisfied. If not all the ideas set forth in this section can be adopted, perhaps some of them may be employed as the teachers gradually improve the working conditions in their school.

A typical wall fixture for art activities in a general classroom.

A Sink
B Counter
C Adjustable shelves
D Sliding doors
E Swinging doors

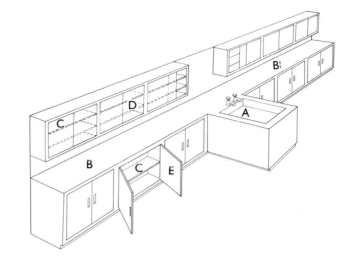

Design.   An art room should be placed near a service entrance on the main floor of a school building, for convenience in delivering supplies and equipment. In junior high schools it is preferable also to have the room situated reasonably close to home economics rooms and industrial arts shops so that pupils may conveniently move from one room to another to use special equipment.

The room should be large, with a minimum floor space of about 30 by 60 feet. A spacious floor can provide working centers in which many art activities may be carried out. The floor should be laid in heavy linoleum or tile.

Lighting in an art room is of the greatest importance. Natural north lighting is recommended whenever possible. Preferably the lights should be set flush with the ceiling, with the exception of spotlights for important displays. Unless the room has a daylight screen, blackout curtains for the windows should be provided so that films may be shown. In all matters pertaining to both artificial and natural lighting, architects and lighting engineers should be consulted. Many excellent materials and arrangements are available, including directional glass bricks, opaque louvers, clerestory lighting, and various types of blinds.

The efficient use of space around the walls should also be considered. Along one of the shorter walls, storage rooms jutting into the room might be planned. Two storage areas are desirable—one to house a stock of expendable art materials and the other to store the pupils' unfinished work. Each storage room should be fitted with as many adjustable shelves as convenient. Since the shelves may rise to a considerable height, it would be well to have at least one light stepladder available in either one of the rooms. The outside walls of these storage rooms, facing the classroom, can be faced with tackboard. The long wall area opposite the windows should for the most part be faced with tackboard running from about thirty inches above the floor up to the ceiling. An area of about twenty square feet, however, should be reserved for a chalkboard. Space might be provided for counters and cupboards.

The sink may be located on this long side of the room. Its position should be reasonably central, and it should be accessible from at least three directions (see illustration, p. 529). It may be placed in a separate cabinet so that the pupils can approach it from all directions, or it may be placed at the end of a counter running at right angles from the wall toward the center of the room. However arranged, the sink should be large, deep, acid-resistant, and equipped with hot- and cold-water taps. Clean-out traps should be fitted, and all plumbing leading from them should also be acid-resistant.

Along the entire wall at the end of the room opposite the storage rooms, storage cupboards might alternate with glass-enclosed display cases. These cases should be provided with adjustable glass shelves and illuminated with hidden or indirect lights.

Beneath the windows, a work counter might run almost the full length of the room. Below the counter storage cupboards could be constructed, or the space might be left open to house tools. Jutting out at right angles might be a series of small counters for delicate work. Each small counter, which might be collapsible, should be provided with a stool of convenient height. An area might be set aside for the teacher's desk and files.

The placement of electrical outlets is a problem for an expert who understands electrical loads, but the teacher must be sure that outlets are placed in correct locations. As well as outlets for ceramic and enameling kilns, and service outlets in general, there should be an outlet for an electric clock. The pupils should always be aware of how much time is available to begin certain phases of their work or to start cleaning up toward the end of the art period.

Furnishings.   Certain equipment should be placed in convenient relation to the arrangements around the walls. Such items might include an electric kiln with a firing area of not less than 3,000 cubic inches, a pull-out storage bin for clay, a storage box for keeping clay damp, and a spray booth. The clay-working area should be located near the sink. A filing cabinet for storing catalogs, folders containing information about the students, and miscellaneous items useful to the teacher should be placed near the teacher's desk.

Furniture for the art room must be chosen with care. Suitable art desks come in a variety of designs, but a desk with low shelves on which the pupils may place schoolbooks would have optimum utility. Desks with movable tops, by which the slope of the working surface may be regulated, are not proved particularly serviceable because they tend to get out of order. For seating, chairs, stools, and benches are all practical. One or two carpenter's benches as well as desks for drawing and painting should be provided. The benches should be supplied with vises and have storage space beneath them for tools and other equipment.

The colors used to decorate the art room must be carefully planned. Bright colors are generally to be avoided since they "rebound" and confuse a painter. Tints or neutral colors such as pale grays are recommended for the walls and ceiling. The ceiling should be lighter in tone than the walls. The floor should also be neutral, but mottled. Chalkboards come in pale greens or ivory as well as black. Natural or limed wood finishes on cupboards and doors are attractive and serviceable. In general, color in an art room must not interfere with the color work in progress, and it must serve as a background for the displays of the children's work.

Before an elaborate art room of the type described can be set up successfully, much study must be given to the problem and many experts consulted. Not only should plans of the room be drawn but a model also should be made. Particular attention should be given to the grouping of furniture and equipment to avoid overcrowding in any one part of the room and to locate in one area everything necessary for any one type of work. Obviously, an art room entails costly construction, and whatever arrangements are made, good or bad, are likely to be in use for a long time. One example to study is the comprehensive plan for an all-purpose art room provided here.

Creating a Learning Environment. Equipment, facilities, and storage have been considered thus far, but there are also functions other than purely practical ones. The art room can be an environment for learning

Comprehensive plans for an all-purpose art room.

A Tackboard and screen
B Sinks
C Work counters
D Heavy workbench
E Teacher's desk
F Cabinets and display cases
G Library corner
H Central space for tables and seats
I Clay-working area
J Storage area: expendable art materials
K Library corner
L Stepladder
M Area for 3-dimensional work
N Solid desks for 3-dimensional work and individual stool for each desk
O Windows (may not exist if room is air-conditioned): windows should be provided with blackout curtains for showing slides and films
P Area for easels, posing models, etc.
Q Filing cabinet

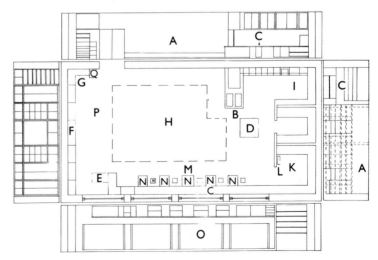

about art as well as an assembly of hardware. As a learning environment it must contain many stimuli; it must be a place for sensory excitement; it is also the child's link with the world outside the classroom. Here, before painting a favorite animal, a child may have access to slides, paintings, or photographs of animal life. One day the teacher may bring in a live puppy, kitten, or turkey to study. At times the art room may resemble a science laboratory as the teacher attempts to acquaint the children with intricate, hidden forms of nature. The room may contain inexpensive microscopes, aquariums, terrariums, bones, rock formations—anything that can direct the child's attention to visual cues that have bearing on the art experience.

A corner of the room might be reserved for research and supplied with art books, well-illustrated children's books, magazines on a suitable reading level, file material, slides, and filmstrips. Another part of the room might be set aside as a "serendipity corner"—a place for interesting and unusual things to draw. The more provocative these items are, the better. Each teacher creates a unique collection of objects chosen for their shapes, colors, and associations. This collection provides its own stimulus for any lesson that employs observation.

One way to create a learning environment in the art room is to have the children themselves design portions of the room. Orange crates painted in bright colors and units constructed of wallboard can provide flexibility even beyond purchased components. The teacher who thinks of the child as entering a laboratory of visual delight—a place for looking, feeling, shaping, and forming—will have some idea of what the art room or even a section of the classroom might be. Above all, an art room should have a special character. The moment a child enters should be one of happy anticipation. The art room is a space where creative things happen; it should be the most attractive place in the child's school life.

ART DISPLAYS

From the art program come tangible visual results of the learning experience; the art program in fact constitutes the only part of the school curriculum whose results are truly visible, because they can be exhibited over a prolonged period. As such, art lends itself to display, which serves as the final communicative stage of the creative process.

WHY DISPLAY CHILDREN'S ART?

Perhaps the most important reason for displaying art is simply that the results of children's artistic acts are usually worth observing for their aesthetic qualities. Children's art is often so attractive that it should be brought forth for people to see and enjoy. The production of any art form is not a casual event; it is an offering of heart and mind from one human being to another.

The display of children's art is an effective teaching device. One common method of display is to group the work according to topics or themes. When twenty-five or more pupils in a class present their re-actions to one theme, it is highly educative for all to observe those reactions. If art is suitably taught, no two children make identical state-ments about an experience. After viewing the various statements the children may gain a broader insight into the topic as a whole.

The display of children's art tends to develop in the pupils certain desirable attitudes toward the school. When young children see their artistic efforts on display among those of their fellows, they tend to sense a oneness with the group. Their participation brings out a feel-ing of belonging, which often increases the fullness of subsequent participation.

The display of children's art also has its decorative purposes. The classroom is usually a barren place when the teachers enters it, pre-paratory to the opening of school. Likewise, the halls of many schools are drab until suitable decorations have been arranged. Much of the artwork of children has highly decorative quality that will quickly change the character of a school building. Even the most delightful interior architecture of modern schools can be improved by a judicious display of children's production.

More and more, schools are serving as institutions of learning by day and as community centers by night. Parent-teacher groups, night school classes (in which, among other subjects, art may be studied), and other meetings of interest to the members of a community are

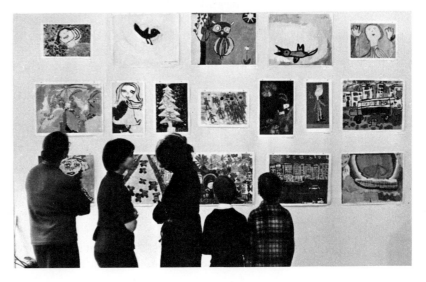

Russian teachers and students study an international exhibition of children's work. The arrange-ment is pleasing—simple and un-cluttered. The top rows, how-ever, are beyond the reach of the two boys.

causing greater numbers of adults to visit the schools than ever before. This is desirable since it provides the school with an opportunity to show the public what is being done with the taxpayer's money. Furthermore, it presents the opportunity of arousing or maintaining public interest in education in general and art education in particular. Art displays operate on three different levels: the classroom, the school, and the community. In the classroom or art room, display is linked closely to instruction and also enhances the environment. In the school and community, however, it should be used to alert viewers to the nature and goals of the art program. No work should be presented without a label conveying such information as the student's name, school, teacher, grade, title, and—most important—the concept, goal, or unit to which the work is related.

SELECTING WORK FOR DISPLAY

Probably the first question in the teacher's mind is how to choose the work for exhibition. The criteria for selection should be both pedagogical and aesthetic. Although children will find interest in the art output of others, they are also interested in their own work and are usually proud of it. This means that every child in a class sooner or later during the school term should have some work on display. Since space is limited in a classroom, pupils cannot expect their work to appear very often, but they will accept this fact if they feel that their chances to have work displayed are equal to those of others. Awareness of this tends to make them more active participants in all displays that appear on the classroom walls.

As children mature, they develop an ability to appraise the standards of both their behavior and their artistic output. They are capable of realizing when their output has not resulted in a success commensurate with their effort. An attempt at expression does not always result in success, as every creating person knows. When children realize that their output has not reached an accustomed standard, displaying their work would in all likelihood be an embarrassment to them. Before a particular child's work is displayed, therefore, a teacher would do well to compare it with previous performances.

If work for display is chosen with these ideas in mind, the child of exceptional ability will not create the problems of selection that might otherwise occur. It would be discouraging for the members of the class to see a more gifted child's work repeatedly occupying a major portion of the displays to the partial exclusion of the work of others. The gifted child exhibits a range of success just as everyone else does. This being the case, only the most significant items of that child's expression need appear on display.

The teacher will not have to save all the artwork of every pupil during the school year to summarize the general progress of each child. While some of the work may be kept in a folder for reference, the teacher will be able, for the most part, to remember each child's earlier performances. The art output of each child becomes unique in the eyes of an alert, interested, and sensitive teacher.

The selection of work for display is, then, a sensitive matter. It depends not only on the outward appearance of each piece but also on the intimate knowledge of every child responsible for it. The teacher must be fully aware of each child's potential and judge the work, not from some preconceived standard of attainment, but rather in relation to the pupil's personal abilities.

In general, it is suggested that the farther the display is removed from the classroom, the more selective should be the process of choosing the works to be displayed. When children's art goes to the front hall or to some location in the community, each piece should be selected for its ability to capture and hold the attention of the viewer. In the classroom, however, there may be times when the work of the entire class will be displayed.

ARRANGING DISPLAYS IN THE CLASSROOM

Media and Techniques for Displaying Two-Dimensional Work. The display areas should not be overcrowded. Each piece should be set apart and mounted in some way. Mounts should be chosen so that their color unifies the display but does not conflict with the colors used in the drawings and paintings themselves. Grays, browns, and sometimes black are usually suitable colors for mounts. White is also recommended, since it flatters the picture and gives a clean look to the exhibit. When the display panels are made of wood, cork, or celotex, both mount and picture may most conveniently be fastened to the display area by a gun-type wall stapler or clear-headed pushpins. Thumbtacks should be avoided because they distract the viewer's attention from the work.

Mounts or frames may be devised in a number of ways and with several materials. The simplest, cheapest, and, many think, most attractive method of mounting is to attach a sheet of newsprint, paper,

Some methods of mounting two-dimensional works

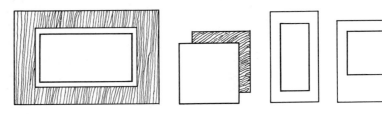

or cardboard to the display board and to fasten on this a drawing or painting having smaller dimensions. A variety of effects may be obtained with this method by altering the proportion of background to picture. Another method of framing a picture is to fix the picture to the board, cut a window the size of the picture in a sheet of paper or cardboard, and then, placing the frame over the picture, attach it to the board. Mounts need not be wide: even a 1-inch border with a 2-inch lower border can be effective, as long as it leaves room for a label.

In some displays no particular topical arrangement is required, but a certain aesthetic order is desired. Those arranging a display will find string convenient in establishing patterns. If various colors and types of string or yarn are strung from one place to another in a panel, some exceptionally interesting rhythms can be achieved throughout the display.

When a display is arranged, a title is usually required. Titles, of course, become part of the general design of a display. A title may be produced in two dimensions with lettering pens and India or colored inks and felt pens. Although they are beyond the ability of most elementary school children, three-dimensional titles can be made from cardboard cut-out letters. After it is cut out, each letter is stuck on a long pin that holds it away from the display board. Attractive background papers of contrasting color or texture help to make this type of title particularly arresting.

The simplest and most common arrangement of pictures on a display panel is one that follows the rectangular shape of the board. The pictures are hung so that their edges are parallel to those of the board. More often than not a formal balance is achieved, so that the viewer's attention will be attracted equally around imaginary central axes of the board. The margins established between the picture frames and the outside edges of a display panel that is horizontal should be such that the bottom margin is widest, the top narrowest, and the width of the sides in between. In a vertical panel, the traditional proportions to be observed reverse the proportions of sides and top: the bottom is widest, the top is second in size, and the sides are narrowest. A square panel calls for even margins at top and sides, with a wider margin at the bottom. These classic arrangements are safe, and by using them one may tastefully display any group of pictures.

If display panels are not available, it may prove difficult to exhibit works of art in the school hall. Curls of masking tape on the back of pictures are often used to attach flatwork to such surfaces, but this is far from ideal because of the expense involved and the tendency of pictures to slip. Two permanent solutions are strips of cork bolted to the wall and framed 4-by-8-foot sheets of composition board or any other material that takes staples and pins. Avoid Masonite for this reason. Masonite pegboard, however, is excellent because bent metal

The corner of a classroom has been temporarily converted into a gallery. Display units are dispersed to accommodate traffic and facilitate viewing.

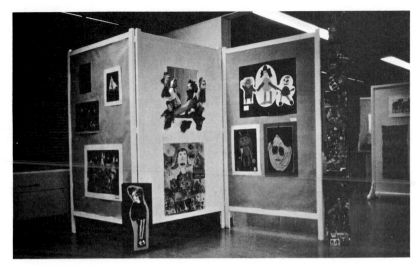

hooks can be inserted to hang shelves, puppets, and other three dimensional objects.

All exhibitions in a classroom must show an awareness of the display situation and should be considered as designs subject to the discipline of good taste. As each display is added, it must be considered in relation to whatever displays are already on view. In general, it is wise to restrict displays to those areas especially designed for them. A classroom can scarcely appear orderly if drawings and paintings are stuck to blackboards, pinned to chalk ledges, or plastered on windows. Blackboards, chalk ledges, and windows are functional parts of the classroom whose efficiency is impaired by displays of art.

Here are some other points the teacher might keep in mind when setting up bulletin board displays and exhibits:

1. A bulletin board has somewhat the same function as a poster. Both must capture attention, provide information, and present a unified design through pleasing relationships of textures, masses, subject matter, and lettering.

2. Pins with clear plastic heads are the best fasteners, metal pins next, and tacks last. Staples may be used if a staple remover is available.

3. Some areas of the background should be uncluttered, to give the eye a rest.

4. The eye level of the viewer should be respected. A good average height is 5 feet, 6 inches.

5. Extreme "artiness," such as complicated diagonal arrangements, should be avoided.

6. Bulletin board exhibits should seldom be on display for more than two weeks. There is no disgrace in occasionally having a blank display area.

7. If possible, a well-lighted area should be used for the display.

8. Usually tops or sides of pictures should be aligned for consistency and order, and vertical and diagonal lettering should be avoided.

9. A supply of materials such as solid-colored burlap and corduroy should be kept on hand. These make excellent background segments to unite a small group of pictures. Any material that distracts from the objects on display should not be used.

10. When "going public," avoid supermarkets and other busy environments.

11. Avoid large groups of objects that are too similar in either size or subject. Twenty drawings or paintings of different sizes can maintain variety within themselves.

12. Occasionally, break up displays with a sudden shift of scale. It can be quite exciting to have the usual 12-by-16- or 16-by-24-inch works set off against a life-size painting or mural.

13. Some works are "quieter" (lower key, smaller scale, less obtrusive) than others. A group of quiet paintings fares better than a row of loud ones, which tend to cancel out one another's effectiveness. Try alternating works of contrasting character.

14. When appropriate, statements by students or teachers, or Polaroid photographs of a class in action, can add diversity and a documentary effect.

15. Nothing is more barren than a blank wall when the public has become accustomed to a surface filled with art. Leave the walls empty for at least a week before putting up the next show. A never-ending exhibit ends up as pure decoration and after a while the public may take it for granted.

Media and Techniques for Displaying Three-Dimensional Work. Most classrooms are not equipped with display cases for three-dimensional output. It is frequently necessary, therefore, for the class to improvise other means of display. If space is available, a table may be placed directly in front of a display board. The three-dimensional objects may then be set on the table and descriptions of the work, or related two-dimensional work, may be pinned to the board. Should it be necessary to link a written description to any particular piece on the table, a colored string may be fixed from the description to the piece of work.

The objects should be arranged according to their bulk and height. Obviously the largest and tallest objects will have to be placed well in the background so that smaller objects will not be hidden. Some groups of objects, particularly modeled or carved forms and pottery, will demand the use of pedestals. The pedestals, which can be made from boxes or blocks of wood, may be painted or covered with textiles. By placing a sheet of glass over one or more of the pedestals, it is possible to arrange a convenient series of shelves of varying heights. Ceiling space can be utilized in many unusual ways, particularly for mobiles and kites. Caution should be used, however, in hanging objects from the ceiling, for certain ceiling surfaces and lighting fixtures must be treated with care. Custodians and principals can give information in this regard.

Display boards themselves may be used to exhibit three-dimensional work. Metal brackets fixed to the boards with screws are able to support glass shelves, which make attractive display space.

In arranging three-dimensional displays, the exhibitors must give the same attention to design that they would in displaying flat work. For example, brilliantly colored pieces or those having outstanding structural or textural qualities must be well placed with respect to the centers of interest, the balance, and the rhythm of the design. To bring unity to the three-dimensional display, it may be necessary to use the same background for the objects.

Teaching. Because the display of art is an art activity in itself, it is highly desirable for children to take part in it. Even a six-year-old can see how much better a drawing looks when it is mounted and displayed.

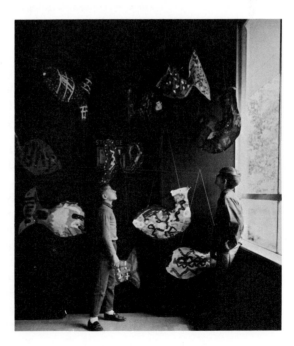

Paper fish stuffed with newspaper are hung in an arrangement that simulates a mobile. The strings are tacked to the soft celotex ceiling of the hallway. Many classrooms and other areas have high ceilings; the problem is to decide how to use the overhead space without damaging the ceiling or upsetting custodians or the fire department.

A simple act such as this can establish the connection between design and order in a young mind. Moreover, display techniques may lead to excellent group endeavors. The kindergarten is not too soon for children to begin this work. Kindergarten children may participate in quasi-group activities in which individuals bring their work to some central area for display.

The teacher should give every encouragement to the pupils to experiment with new ways of displaying their art. One method is to have members of the class report on any outstanding display techniques observed in store windows or elsewhere. Another method is to have the teacher from time to time arrange a display of children's work in which some new ideas for display are demonstrated.

ARRANGING DISPLAYS OUTSIDE THE CLASSROOM

The problems arising from displays arranged in the halls or elsewhere in a school are little different from those related to classroom exhibits. More people and examples of work are involved, of course, so that organizational problems are intensified.

Media and Techniques. School architects often give attention to display possibilities, so it is not unusual for some elementary schools to have gallery-type walls designed adjacent to the principal's office.

If no gallery space is available, school authorities may be expected to provide suitable panels and even display cases; the cost of these is a relatively minor item in most educational budgets. When the panels and cases are being installed, those responsible for the installations must remember to arrange suitable lighting for each one.

On occasion the school may need additional display facilities. Many extra panels might be required on Parents' Night, for example, when the school wishes to make an exceptional effort to interest the community. The design of panels for extra display facilities has become almost standard. The panels consist of sheets of building board, usually measuring from 4 by 4 feet to 4 by 8 feet, to either end of which legs are bolted. The legs are usually in the form of inverted T's, but other ingenious and attractive designs are to be seen. For three-dimensional displays a boxlike construction having shelves takes the place of a panel.

A second type of portable display board has been designed for space-saving and quick assembly. It consists of panels of building board and sturdy legs with slots cut into two adjacent sides. The panels are fitted into the slots to form a zigzag effect which is pleasing and practical. The panels are made secure by lashing the legs together with cord at the top and bottom of the panels.

A large zigzag display in a school gymnasium. Activities that normally take place in the gym must be rescheduled to accommodate the exhibit. Moreover, setting up such an exhibit may involve a good deal of the teacher's time and energy, even though the exhibit itself may be on display for only a short time.

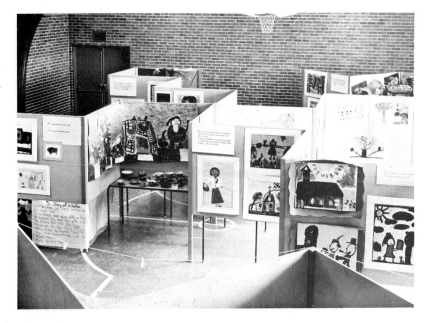

The illustration shows another portable display unit. The materials needed are 2-by-2-inch wooden rods slightly over 5 feet in length, with holes bored at approximately 30-inch intervals. These rods will receive 1-inch dowels, on which hang metal rings that are attached to the pictures. The placement of the holes on the 2-by-2-inch rods determines how the units may be angled, so that the flow of traffic can be controlled.

THE DISPLAY AS COMMUNITY EDUCATION

The subject matter of art displays for parent and community groups may be different from that of displays for children. Parents and other adults are interested not only in the work as such but also in the pedagogical principles supporting the art program. We should remember that for many adults, the comprehensive program of art in schools is completely different from the art education they received in their youth. Although ignorance of the contemporary program sometimes leads to disapproval, parents are generally quick to react favorably to present-day trends in art education, once they understand. For parents, subjects of exhibitions of children's art might emphasize the instructional implications of the art activities. It is now acceptable to display written commentary next to art works when a problem of critical reaction or art history is involved. Themes of exhibitions may dramatize the overall structure of the art program or a single aspect of it. The

Rarely has there been a more impressive place to set up a display of children's art than in one of the main galleries of the Hermitage Museum, Leningrad. The work comes from special children's art classes in the museum.

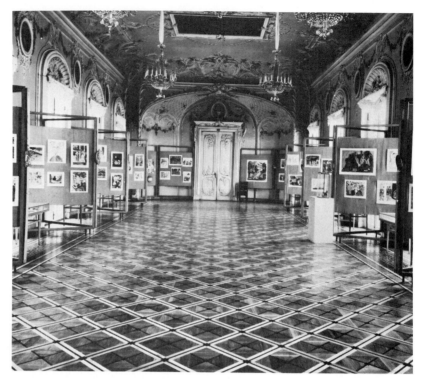

following are a few sample topics that have proved satisfactory for Parents' Night:

The Art Program: A Grade-Level Approach
Looking at Nature
Personal Development Through Art
Variety in Artistic Expression
Group Work in Art
Learning from Other Artists
Art from Other Cultures
Art Styles of Today

For each exhibition, brief but effective signs should be made to emphasize the points demonstrated by the children's work. Each show, moreover, should have a clearly marked beginning, a logical sequence of ideas throughout the body of the exhibition, and a short summary, either written or pictorial or both, at its close. The exhibit should be more than merely another chore. It is the most dramatic means of communicating the teacher's role in the school to the pubic, to the administration, and to other teachers.

◆ NOTES TO THE TEXT

1. Blanche Jefferson, *Teaching Art to Children* (Boston: Allyn and Bacon, 1959), p. 154.

◆ ACTIVITIES FOR THE READER

1. Describe the various criteria used by teachers you have observed to select children's art work for display. Appraise each criterion according to its educational effects on the children concerned.
2. Study and compare the display techniques you have observed in various classrooms.
3. Experiment with mounting and framing a picture on a surface such as a drawing board. Try some of the ways suggested in this chapter and then devise new ways to display the picture.
4. Sketch in pencil or crayon some plans for a display of five pictures. Select the plan you like best and use it in an actual panel display.
5. Repeat 4, this time including at least twelve pictures.
6. Make some plans for the display of three pieces of pottery. Carry out the plan you like best.
7. List some subjects for an art display to be used in the main entrance of a school on Parents' Night. The entrance hall is about 25 feet long and 12 feet wide. After selecting the subject that most appeals to you, indicate in detailed sketches (a) the type and position of the display panels; (b) the number and subject matter of the pictures or three-dimensional objects; (c) the captions to be used; and (d) the route that visitors should follow to view the exhibition.
8. Collect a number of boxes of varying sizes and arrange them so that when covered with one piece of cloth, they provide an attractive setting for ceramics, sculpture, or other three-dimensional objects.

◆ SUGGESTED READINGS

McFee, June King. *Preparation for Art*. San Francisco: Wadsworth, 1961. See Chapter 12, "Classroom Procedures for New Teachers."

Wachowiak, Frank, and David Hodge. *Art in Depth*, 3rd ed. Scranton, PA: International Textbook, 1977. See Chapter 9, "The Art Room," and Appendix C, "Art Supplies and Sources."

EVALUATION: ASSESSING STUDENT PROGRESS AND PROGRAM EFFECTIVENESS

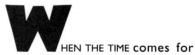HEN THE TIME comes for the teacher to make a summarized evaluation, he should base it on a consideration of the student's total experience. The appraisal should not appear as a final judgment of something that is finished, but should be stated and regarded as data for future direction of both the student and teacher. Thus it may be like the doctor's periodic check-up and prescription for healthy living.[1]

Elliot Eisner and David Ecker

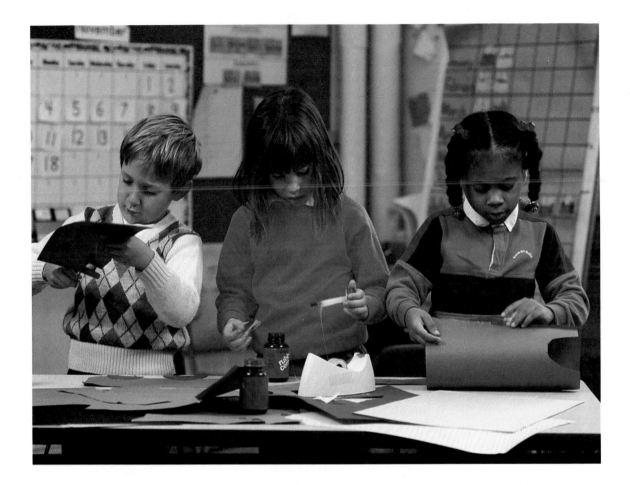

Evaluation, the topic for this final chapter, is interrelated with every other section in this book. It is not possible to conduct meaningful evaluation without considering the philosophy, goals, and objectives of the art program as discussed in Part I, *Foundations and Goals for Art Education*. We must understand the learners in our classrooms, as outlined in Part II, *Children as Learners*. Evaluation must be responsive to the content to be taught and learned, and a comprehensive program of art education ranges widely across the disciplines of art as outlined in Part III, *Content of Art*. The wide range of content requires that teachers employ a similar range of teaching styles, strategies, and methods, discussed in some detail in Part IV, *Instruction*. Methods of evaluation must be as diverse and particular as the art curriculum, and must be considered as part of the process of curriculum development, thus the grouping of *Curriculum and Evaluation* together in Part V of this book.

Although most art educators will probably agree that evaluation is a necessary component for responsible education, evaluation might be the least well-developed and most misunderstood part of art education. In this final chapter we will employ a broad definition of evaluation, provide examples of evaluation devices and applications with content from each of the four art disciplines, and we will attempt to dispel some of the potential misunderstandings about evaluation of art learning.

Evaluation in art education is a process of gaining information about some aspect of the educational enterprise and assigning value to it. We regularly make value judgments about many aspects of schooling, ranging from the quality of textbooks to the adequacy of school facilities or the behavior of individual students. Most of the evaluation that goes on is accomplished informally. On entering the classroom, for example, the teacher notices the room temperature, the lighting, and the arrangement of furniture. The teacher evaluates the situation and makes changes to suit his or her educational purposes. As the students enter the room and the class period progresses, the teacher makes numerous quick assessments of the students, noting who is engaged in activity and who is not, and adjusts teaching strategies accordingly. The teacher speaks quietly with a student, moves on quickly to a restless group, demonstrates a technique, offers words of encouragement, chastises mildly, and so on, as each situation warrants — all the while noticing in what ways students are encountering difficulties in their work and formulating changes in the plans for tomorrow's activity.

Numerous means for gaining information assist the educator in the evaluation process. Some of these are observation, interview, testing, viewing student work, and reading assigned papers. The results of evaluation are likewise numerous, ranging from the assignment of a grade to the development of new curriculum or a request for a change in school policy.

Evaluation of student learning is the concern of most formal assessment in schools, and since a report of student progress is usually required, this form of evaluation holds a high priority. The basis of appraisal of a pupil's progress in any area of learning can be found in the objectives of that area. If the objectives of a particular subject have been accurately stated, they will reflect not only the specific contributions that the subject has to offer, but also the philosophical purposes and educational practices of the school system. An appraisal of the progress of any pupil involves a judgment of the efficacy of the school system in general and of the teacher's endeavors in particular.

HOW THE OBJECTIVES OF ART EDUCATION INFLUENCE EVALUATION

Evaluation and instruction are both guided by the educational goals and objectives of those who educate (see Chapter 1). Evaluation must be made compatible with objectives, and the results of evaluation should be reported in ways that are meaningful to those who receive them.[2] Five basic questions can be asked about any system of evaluation:

Who will do the evaluation—teachers, pupils, some outside agency?
What is being evaluated—attitudes, or curriculum content such as skills, knowledge, or processes?
Who will be evaluated—elementary school children, high school art majors, retarded children?
What is the range of the evaluation—pupil, class, entire school program?

And finally, perhaps the most difficult:

What is the purpose or function of the evaluation?

Eisner states that evaluation in an art program can serve:

1. to diagnose
2. to revise curricula
3. to compare
4. to anticipate educational needs
5. to determine if objectives have been achieved[3]

For the purposes of this discussion we refer to evaluations conducted by teachers for their own students, classrooms, and curricula, and not to the work of professionals. This discussion is intended to assist teachers with the practical problems of assessing values both in their own work and that of their students.

Concerns About Evaluation in Art Education

The use of educational evaluation is perhaps the aspect that distinguishes most dramatically between what is traditional and what is contemporary in art education. Art educators in the past have expressed their concerns that formal assessment might discourage children from learning and progressing in their own creative production.[4] The evaluation process, of which assessment is a part, might place too much emphasis on children's art products and effectively censor their expressions of personal feelings and emotions. Art activities by children, they believe, should not be influenced by requirements to evaluate. These concerns have been expressed most prominently in relation to art programs that are nearly exclusively dedicated to children's work with art media.

Few educators would disagree with these concerns about evaluation, which must always serve to better education rather than detract from it. Evaluation should not be arbitrary, nor should it discourage children from learning and progressing in their understanding of art. Overemphasis on children's art products should be avoided, and the processes of learning and creating are of utmost importance. Few educators would advocate censorship of children's feelings and emotions in their artistic expression. Neither should evaluation devices such as tests dominate the art curriculum, influencing teachers to teach for test results. However, these negative aspects are not the inevitable results of educational evaluation and are certainly not related to the uses of evaluation within a responsible, comprehensive art program. As we will discuss with numerous examples, evaluation can be unobtrusive, interesting for students, and in some instances can be part of learning activities.

EVALUATION OF STUDENT PROGRESS IN ART

As with other school subjects many factors influence the progress of students as they study art. With a comprehensive program of art education, evaluation is essential as a means to improve student learning, assess effectiveness of the curriculum, and to assist teachers to improve their instruction. Following are a few of the general questions that evaluation might assist teachers to answer.

1. Are the students enjoying a positive experience in the class? Is the learning environment compatible with the goals for learning?

2. Are changes in the pace of learning needed? Is a shift in instructional strategy warranted? What about grouping of students versus individualized learning projects?

3. What are students learning? How does this relate to prior expectations for the class? How does this relate to prior performance by the students?

4. How can the teacher become more effective? How can sound judgments about student progress be made?

5. How can the teacher communicate with student about their strong and weak points in art? How can the teacher communicate the accomplishments of students to other teachers, school administrators, and parents?

A Balanced Program of Evaluation

Evaluation that is conducted as the school term unfolds can be used for two purposes: first, as feedback about the art class and how things are progressing; and second, as a basis for final assessments. Evaluation utilized to inform the teacher for in-process educational decision making is known as *formative evaluation*.[5] Flexible teachers are ready to respond to information obtained while curriculum implementation is in progress and are willing to revise their instructional approaches, or reteach areas of the curriculum that students did not understand.

Evaluation producing information about student learning that will assist teachers to reach summative statements about student accomplishments and the relative success of the class is known as *summative evaluation*. At the conclusion of the school term, often some type of final evaluation is conducted to certify student learning and to diagnose areas of the curriculum that might need extra emphasis in the future. This evaluation might include a wide range of assessment devices, including final examinations and personal interviews. Often, at this time teachers are required to report on each student's success in accomplishing the goals and objectives of the curriculum by assigning a letter grade or providing a more descriptive analysis of the students' work. The teacher can draw upon all of the information obtained during the school term as well as postinstructional assessments to prepare this report.

Within a balanced program of art education we expect children to learn about art from the perspectives of the four art disciplines.[6] As the curriculum content is organized, means to evaluate student learning need to be concurrently developed with the goal of improving learning and instruction as well as curriculum. When curriculum is developed on a systematic basis, more time and attention can be paid to concurrent development of appropriate evaluation methods, devices, and instruments. A balanced program of evaluation as an integral and ongoing component of the art program will provide teachers with appropriate and useful information that will assist in making sound decisions in relation to individual students, the curriculum, and the overall art program.

Evaluation of Children's Creative Work

The prospect of evaluating the creative artwork of children is a concern to many teachers, sometimes due to misunderstandings about evaluation. Before discussing this topic we offer several principles that will hopefully make the teacher's task easier and more acceptable.

1. As in all areas of art learning, evaluation should be closely related to instruction. This means that teachers can expect children to learn what is taught, and should focus evaluation on those skills and understandings that children have had a fair opportunity to learn. Evaluation of student progress then becomes more a measure of the teacher's abilities to foster learning than a means to distinguish students' strengths and weaknesses.

2. We do not attempt to evaluate students' creativity or expressiveness. Rather, evaluation is focused on what students have learned as a result of instruction. Students' creative and expressive efforts should always be encouraged despite difficulties of evaluation.

3. Evaluation in the area of students' art production is only a part of a balanced program of evaluation. Students who do not exhibit great natural ability in art production will still be able to succeed in art because of the diversity of a comprehensive art program. Students who appear to have natural abilities for making art will be rewarded for their efforts, but will need to make progress in the other areas of learning as well.

4. Part of instruction in art production deals with clear-cut skills, such as knowledge of color theory resulting in abilities to mix the hues, change color value and intensity, and identify cool and warm hues. There are technical skills and principles associated with every art mode that children can learn and apply. Appropriate evaluation methods can inform teachers about individual students' success in learning, allowing teachers to provide remedial instruction for those who need it.

When the art program focuses on the learning of art knowledge and skills, students soon realize that specific things are taught and can be learned, just as in other subjects in school. If children can learn and practice, they can make progress toward clearly defined, understandable goals. When finished art products reflect the intended learning, the reasons for their excellence can be pointed out, discussed, and related to classroom instruction. As in other subject areas in the curriculum, students in art can begin with whatever aptitude is given and can progress at faster or slower rates according to their individual motivation and application. The notion that art is only for the few "talented" stars will soon be dispelled and the idea that art learning is for everyone will be reinforced.

Many evaluation problems in the area of art production are alleviated when teachers realize that they have different instructional purposes at different times and that different evaluation procedures are appropriate according to the specific instructional purpose. For example, when instructional goals call for the learning of specific production skills evaluation can be equally specific. Teachers can readily learn if students are able to overlap objects to represent space, make a graded watercolor wash, or construct a coil clay pot that will hold water without leaking. Students' progress on such skills can be assessed, students and teachers can discuss results, and students can learn how to improve.

Not all learning in art production falls into this clear-cut relationship between instructional objectives and evaluation devices, however, and time in the curriculum should be maintained for art activities with no specified outcomes other than student participation in the process. For example, students are given access to water-soluble printing inks and brayers and a container of various objects that can be used to print and they are asked to explore the possibilities of the medium. The educational expectation is that the children will learn individually and from one another some of the properties and possibilities of the medium. The appropriate educational evaluation would be to note students' participation, the level of serious engagement, the sharing of discoveries, and the quality of the learning environment in terms of noise, activity, and attention to the task.

It would be inappropriate to evaluate this art activity by testing the children on specific information or skills that might have been discovered by some, but were not presented to all. It would be inappropriate to evaluate this activity by collecting the results of their experimentation and judging them for aesthetic quality.

Some instructional activities will foster individual expression, experimentation, and exploration; others will focus on precise technical skills; and still others will call for students to apply art concepts and skills to produce finished works appropriate to their age level and reflective of the art instruction that has taken place to that time. *A comprehensive art program will include a variety of instructional purposes and various evaluation devices.* When students are evaluated according to their participation, their successful completion of specific tasks of art production, and the quality of their completed art products, the teacher not only has a valid basis for assigning grades, but also has a basis for diagnosis and suggestions for improvement.

Evaluation of Learning in Art Criticism and Appreciation

As we discussed in Chapter 11, students in a balanced art program will view many artworks, respond to them in depth, and will discuss and write about artworks. They will learn approaches to art criticism such as the phased approach of description, analysis, interpretation, and informed preference, and will practice and apply these processes. As with art production, evaluation within some parts of the critical domain of art learning are obvious. For example, teachers can determine when students are able to apply concepts such as visual balance, distortion, and emphasis in their descriptions and analyses of artworks. Teachers can evaluate students' progress in analysis of artworks and their understanding of what they are doing and why. Teachers can assess students' progress in developing plausible interpretations of meaning in relation to particular works of art and their abilities to support their interpretations with good reasons. Teachers can ask if the children are able to see and understand how artists control and manipulate the principles and elements of design to achieve the effects and

Diego Rivera, *Agrarian Leader Zapata*, 1931. Teachers can gain insight into children's learned abilities to describe, analyze, and interpret artworks through their spoken and written comments. As children view this fresco, how do they explain the fallen man, his drawn sword, and the beautifully appointed, but riderless, white horse? How do they interpret the tool in the central figure's hand, his placement in front of the fallen figure, and his hold of the horse's rein? From their study of art history, what do children know about the white clothing of the men in the picture, their tools, hats, and the agricultural setting suggested on the right side of the painting? Who are these men and what is happening? What is the social theme of the painting? What do children know about Rivera, events in Mexico that he depicted, and the fresco process? (Collection, The Museum of Modern Art, New York. Abby Aldrich Rockefeller.)

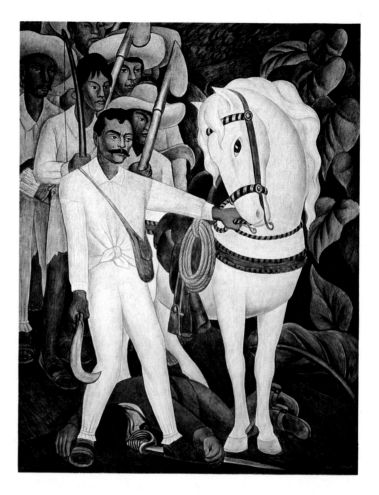

meanings that have been analyzed and interpreted, and teachers can devise ways to gain information that will help them to answer such questions. In all instances, the levels of instruction and the means of evaluation will be suited to the age levels and abilities of the children.

Conducting appropriate evaluation of children's critical understandings and skills can also challenge the teacher's ingenuity, as teachers strive to ask the most meaningful questions about students' progress and devise means to gather information in response to these questions. Teachers can ask questions and collect evidence in relation to children's understandings about purposes and functions of various modes of art, such as religious statuary, jewelry of many sorts, portraiture of royalty, furniture design, illustration, or landscape painting. They can seek to learn more about their students' knowledge of and recognition of psychological, religious, political, and social themes in art, such as in Michelangelo's *Pietà*, Picasso's *Guernica*, Rivera's *Agrar-*

James M. Flagg, "I Want You," recruiting poster. This classic recruiting poster has a firm place in American history. Children can learn about the events that led to the creation of this poster, its use during World Wars I and II, its place as an American icon, and how images become icons. They can interpret the emotional qualities of the image, what ideas it conveys, and they can debate whether this image should be considered art. Evaluation in a balanced art program will consider children's progress in art production, and their learning of concepts and skills from art history, art criticism, and aesthetics. (National Museum of American History, Smithsonian Institution.)

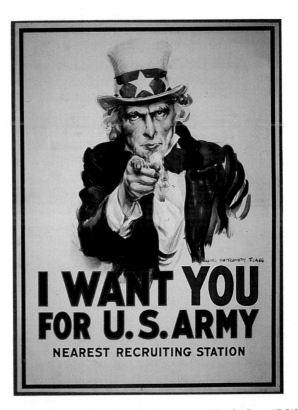

ian Leader Zapata, James Flagg's classic poster *Uncle Sam "I Want You,"* and Judy Chicago's *The Dinner Party*. Teachers will use various methods to gain information about students' understanding of these areas through class discussions, questionnaires, or interviews.

Concurrent with questions about children's technical skills, general knowledge, and critical skills in response to works of art, teachers need to attend to some large and very important questions about children's progress. Is the art program assisting students to respond more fully to works of art and to derive meaning and satisfaction in the process? What evidence can the teacher find that indicates the students are more ready to attend to art and derive meaning and satisfaction from the process? What evidence can the teacher find that indicates the students are more ready to attend to art and that they are developing positive attitudes toward art? Is instruction leading the children to richer and deeper encounters with art and to a broader and deeper understanding of the purposes and functions of art in the lives of human beings? Do the children use valid reasons to inform their art preferences? Do the children seem to enjoy these activities? Several of the methods for evaluation discussed later in this chapter might assist teachers to answer such questions.

Evaluation of Learning in Art History

Evaluation of art historical learning needs to be carefully conducted to correlate with instructional purposes, as in the other areas of the art curriculum. Learning in this domain includes a broad range of topics. Indeed, it would be possible to study much of the history of the world simply through the study of art history. The amount of information and the level of detail in which it is available is nearly overwhelming, making selection of curriculum content a major task. The mode of presentation in the field of art history is also of extreme importance.

As noted in Chapter 12, much teaching in art history can be done in a visual rather than in a verbal mode, with visual displays of the works of artists, styles of art, and art from various eras and cultures. Topics from art history can be related directly to the interests of children because the great themes of human experience are available in visual form in the art heritage from the past and present. Reproductions, pictures, slides, films, magazines, and books about art are readily available for use in schools.

Evaluation methods can be tailored to complement the teacher's instructional intentions and instructional approaches. If instruction is intended to assist children to recognize the characteristics of Chinese art, then the evaluation should be as general as the instructional goal. For example, children might be shown a series of slides of artworks from various cultures and asked to designate which works are from China. If the children are unable to do this, perhaps the instruction needs to be revised. When instruction in art history is precise in terms of specific information that is to be learned by students, then traditional objective tests might be appropriate, including identification of

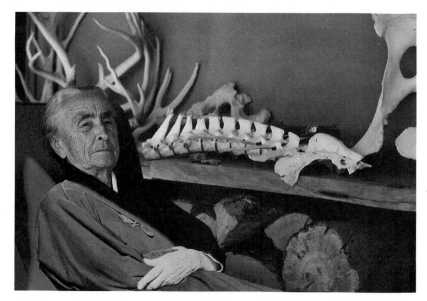

Malcolm Varon, *Georgia O'Keeffe.* Who is this person? What is her place in art history? Why is she portrayed with bleached animal bones? Evaluation of cultural and historical learning goes far beyond names, dates, and titles. Teachers can learn from their students how well they understand the roles of artists, how artworks are regarded by society and by art experts, and what artists have contributed to the world through their work. Study of the life of Georgia O'Keeffe will lead children from the bustle of her early career in New York City, her association with other, now famous artists, and her secluded and productive life in New Mexico.

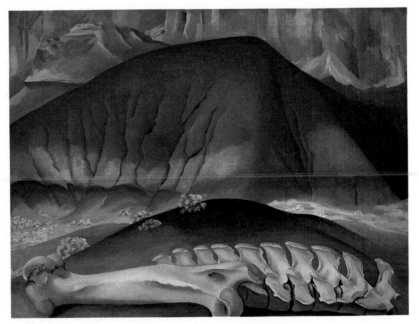

Georgia O'Keeffe, *Red Hills and Bones*, 1941. Historical background about the life of the artist, Georgia O'Keeffe can help students understand this painting. They can associate the painting of bleached animal bones and the barren red earth with the photograph of the artist on the previous page. Such learning and associations can be applied in students own art production as they select subjects or techniques suggested by the study of an artist's life and works. As an evaluation device, teachers might assign students to make a painting in homage to a particular artist, displaying their knowledge and understanding of the artist and works. (Philadelphia Museum of Art: The Alfred Stieghtz Collection.)

specific works of art by artist or style, period or country. When art history is taught to assist children to understand and appreciate the contributions of other cultures, other people in different parts of the world, and art from different times, evaluation must be responsive to those purposes. The use of attitude and preference measures are often as useful in this domain as objective measures.

Evaluation of Students' Progress in Aesthetics

In Chapter 13, we noted that a balanced art program includes instruction and learning derived from the discipline of aesthetics, or philosophy of art.[7] Aestheticians deal with many interesting questions that are raised whenever people begin to talk about art. Even young children ask such questions as, "Why is this object art and that object is not art?" Fundamental conceptions of art, beauty, quality in art, aesthetic experience, and bases upon which judgments about art can be made are examined by aestheticians, and the results of their thinking are available for educational applications.

Instructional approaches and methods for teaching about the questions to which aestheticians attend are probably the least developed among the four domains of art learning. It is certain that the levels of complexity in the study of aesthetics necessarily will vary greatly according to the ages of children, as with instruction in creative production, art history, and art criticism. Evaluation of student achievement in the domain of aesthetics will depend, as always, on instructional goals and strategies. Much of evaluation will evidently focus on the use of language by children as they read, discuss, and write about the basic questions identified with aesthetics. They will be asked to contemplate the nature of art and justify their conclusions at levels of sophistication appropriate for their ages. Children in middle grades, as an example, should be able to demonstrate the difference between art and nature by comparing a photograph of a tree to a painting of a tree, and upper grade students should be able to give three reasons for supporting or rejecting a philosophical position (e.g., "The purpose of art is to create works of beauty").

Methods for Evaluation of Student Progress in Art

Within the traditional creative self-expression approach to art education which emphasized art production, evaluation of student learning was not of central interest and therefore was not highly developed. With increasing acceptance of the broader conception of art education over the past 20 years by the National Art Education Association,[8] however, art educators have applied many of the standard approaches to educational evaluation in the classroom. Leading textbooks in the field by Eisner[9] and Chapman[10] have devoted entire chapters to evaluation. Levels of educational achievement in art have been assessed at the national level through the National Assessment of Educational Progress in Art in 1974-1975 and 1978-1979.[11] Issues of evaluation are attended to in the Getty national case studies of seven school districts that attempt to implement comprehensive art programs.[12] And assessment of learning in art is a major focus of the ARTS PROPEL project in the Pittsburgh schools.[13]

In his national study of school programs, Goodlad found that art teachers employ a greater variety of teaching methods in their classrooms than their colleagues who teach other subjects.[14] The same comparison might hold for methods of evaluation because art, unlike most other school subjects, involves much visual as well as verbal content and includes the creative production of students. Following are some examples of the use of the tools that might be used in the evaluation of a comprehensive discipline-based art program.

Observation. The task is for the students in the class to explore the properties of clay in preparation to learning some of the traditional forming techniques. The teacher observes that most of the students are engrossed in the task and seem to be experimenting with the clay: pinching, rolling, stamping, and marking the clay. Several students appear reticent and seem to need the teacher's attention and encouragement.

Interview. The teacher is interested to learn why a boy in the class consistently has trouble with drawing. The teacher talks to the boy privately in a corner of the room, trying to learn more about the apparent problem. Or the teacher wishes to learn more about what the students know about how the works of art are made, how artists work, and how they are educated.[15] The teacher talks with groups of five or six students, showing them a reproduction of a painting and asking them pertinent questions.

Discussion.   The teacher wishes to know more about the students' responses to art and their interpretations of what is acceptable as art. The teacher leads a class discussion of a series of reproductions of paintings that she shows to the students. Each painting shown is more abstract than the previous one.

Performance.   The teacher distributes tempera paints in the primary hues, black, and white, to the children along with the necessary brush and water. After distributing a sheet of paper divided into six rectangles, the teacher asks the children to mix and paint in the respective spaces: orange, green, violet, yellow-green, brown, and light blue. Or, the teacher gives each child a grease pencil and a reproduction of a still-life painting in a clear plastic envelope. The students are asked to circle the main centers of interest and to place a plus on the positive spaces and a minus on the negative spaces.

Check List.   As the teacher leads discussions of works of art from time to time in the classroom, he marks the class roster by the names of those students who participate. He encourages and invites responses from those who have not participated. In another example, the teacher keeps a list of the several drawing exercises for the drawing unit and checks off accordingly as each student completes the exercise satisfactorily.

Questionnaire.   The teacher administers a questionnaire that assesses student learning about architectural styles from various cultures and the reasons for the development of each style. Or, students are required to answer a questionnaire about the details of the copper enameling process. Each student must score 100 percent correct on the technical questionnaire, which includes items on hazards and safety precautions, in order to begin work with actual materials.

Test.   The teacher administers a multiple choice and short answer objective test with questions from several units of study completed during the school term, including items in the aesthetic, critical, historical, and productive domains of art learning.

Essay.   The teacher asks students to write about a painting, considering the appropriate level of writing ability for the grade level. Students are to use the skills of art criticism that they have practiced several times in class as a large group and in small discussion groups.

Carlos Almarez, *Greed*, 1982. What is the theme of this painting? How can you support your interpretation? How would you characterize the stance of the two animals? What feelings does the artist arouse through his choice of colors? Describe the colors in terms of hue, value, intensity, and relationship. How does this painting compare with Georgia O'Keeffe's painting of red hills and animal bones? How does the mood of Almarez's painting compare with the mood of O'Keeffe's? Which do you prefer, and why? Teachers can formulate questions such as these and engage children in response to them through various evaluation devices such as questionnaires, discussions, essays, interviews, and creative art production. (Collection of John and Lynne Pleshette.)

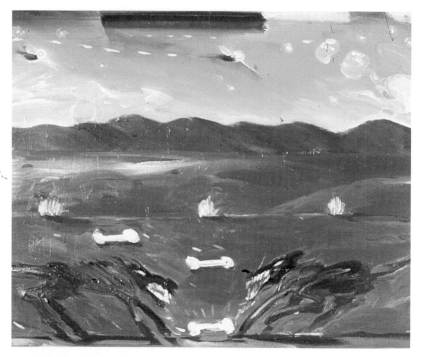

Visual Identification. Students are shown slides of works of art by artists that they have studied in class. They are asked to identify the work by artists, or by style, or according to other categories that they have practiced in class.

Attitude Measurement. The teacher is interested to know how students are responding to the new approach to art education that includes talking and writing about art as well as making art objects. In addition to talking to individual students and holding discussions with the entire class, the teacher develops and administers a questionnaire that asks for students' feelings about specific learning activities that have been completed.

Portfolio. Students' artwork, excercises, written assignments, notes, class handouts — virtually all of what they have produced as they study art — are saved in a folder. Periodically, the teacher reviews this work with each student, individually, and discusses the student's learning, progress, and aspirations in art.

Aesthetic Judgment. Within art programs dominated by studio production, many teachers have assumed that the basis for evaluation and grading is the teacher's judgment of the quality of students' art products. Many art teachers are aware of the biases and inconsistencies that are likely to occur as they attempt to render judgments, and under-

Name _____ Date _____

Art Vocabulary

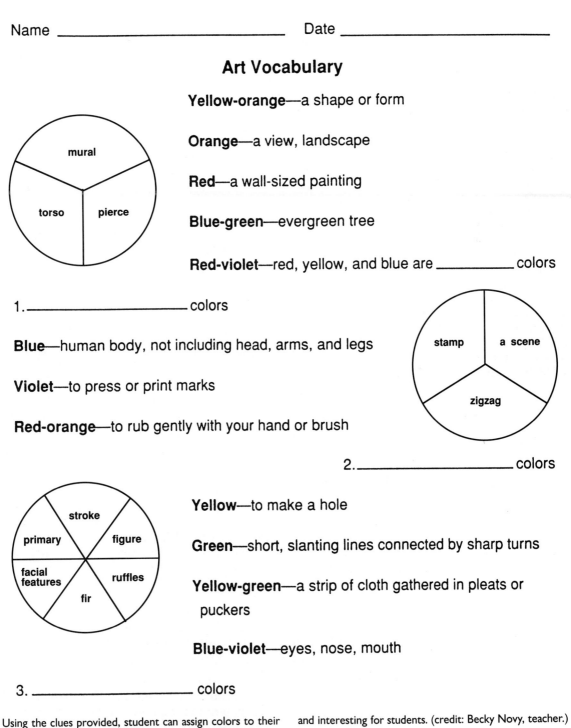

Yellow-orange—a shape or form

Orange—a view, landscape

Red—a wall-sized painting

Blue-green—evergreen tree

Red-violet—red, yellow, and blue are _____ colors

1. _____ colors

Blue—human body, not including head, arms, and legs

Violet—to press or print marks

Red-orange—to rub gently with your hand or brush

2. _____ colors

Yellow—to make a hole

Green—short, slanting lines connected by sharp turns

Yellow-green—a strip of cloth gathered in pleats or puckers

Blue-violet—eyes, nose, mouth

3. _____ colors

Using the clues provided, student can assign colors to their respective groups. Evaluation devices can also be instructional and interesting for students. (credit: Becky Novy, teacher.)

standably avoid evaluation. The making of judgments about art, however, is one of the major aspects of art criticism, which is integral to a balanced art program.

Art teachers, especially art specialists, will be able to make judgments of aesthetic quality with respect to their students' artworks in appropriate contexts. Teachers who have taught specific skills, principles, and understandings regarding art production, and who have implemented a balanced program of evaluation across the four domains of art learning using a variety of evaluation tools, will gain confidence in making judgments of students' culminating art products. As an example, the curriculum has taken students through a series of learning activities that have focused on the use of basic color theory, composition, and basic drawing skills including attention to proportion. The concept of unity in art has been explored in class. The completed paintings are judged by the teacher according to aesthetic criteria and evidence that students applied the concepts that they had studied.

Benefits of Evaluation in Art

For classroom teachers evaluation must be reasonably uncomplicated and the benefits must be obvious if it is to be worth the effort. The professional fields of educational evaluation and educational measurement have become very technical, and for many classroom teachers, intimidating. Questions of reliability, various types of validity, and statistical significance can require expert technical assistance. If such assistance is not available, if evaluation becomes too complex or too burdensome, or if the results are not sufficiently meaningful within the milieu of the classroom, teachers will not engage in it. When placed in a reasonable perspective and broadly defined, evaluation can aid teachers with their instructional responsibilities as well as provide essential information for vital educational decision making.

Within a balanced, comprehensive art program at the elementary and middle school levels, appropriate art evaluation can provide a sound basis for:

1. Validating student learning and progress in art
2. Diagnosis of each student's strengths and weaknesses in art learning and assistance for developing remedial instruction for children who need additional help
3. Assembling the necessary information to communicate to students regarding their progress in art; to teachers and administrators about the goals, content, and results of the art program; and to parents about their children's accomplishments and needed improvements
4. Changing and improving the art curriculum and instructional methods and strategies in order to improve student learning
5. Preparing reports of student progress, narrative reports, or letter grades

Student Self-Evaluation Form*16

Name _____

Date _____

Name of Project _____

Date Completed _____

1. I thought this project was: Boring   ____ ____ ____ ____ ____ Exciting

2. I found the work on it: Easy   ____ ____ ____ ____ ____ Difficult

3. I think I learned from this project: A Lot   ____ ____ ____ ____ ____ A Little

4. This project was my: Worst piece of work ____ ____ ____ ____ ____ Best piece of work

5. The most important things I got out of this project were: _____

_____

_____

_____

*Students can participate in the evaluation process through use of forms such as this self-evaluation form, personal interviews, portfolios, and essays written by students about their learning experiences in art.

Evaluation of student achievement is an essential aspect of a complete program of discipline-based art education. Subjects in the curriculum that are considered fundamental to the goals of general education are also considered to be worth evaluating. Evaluation need not thwart the educational process in any way, but when appropriately conducted can enhance and complement student learning by providing clear indicators of progress.

EVALUATION BASED ON A TAXONOMY OF OBJECTIVES

If the teaching objectives of the art program are given a *taxonomy*, or system of classification, the task of evaluation is made easier. A system of classification that is useful in establishing objectives as well as criteria was developed by Benjamin Bloom and his associates.[17] The classifications, or *domains*, that they chose for their taxonomy are the cognitive, the affective, and the psychomotor. The *cognitive domain* includes behaviors and goals having to do with knowledge and the development of intellectual abilities. The *affective* domain embraces objectives dealing with interests, values, attitudes, and appreciations. The *psychomotor* domain involves the manipulative and motor skills. Bloom states:

> It was the view of the group that educational objectives stated in behavioral form have their counterparts in the behavior of individuals. Such behavior can be observed and described and the descriptive statements can be classified. . . . The process of thinking about educational objectives, defining them, and relating them to teaching and testing procedures was regarded as a very important step on the part of teachers.[18]

A brief analysis of an art program using the first two categories of Bloom's taxonomy is offered in Table 18-1 to assist the teacher in planning. The levels into which the categories are subdivided are only sug-

～ TABLE 18-1

An Analysis of an Art Program in Terms of Bloom's Taxonomy

Content and Objectives of the Cognitive Domain

Knowledge Level:

Terminology
Art history: facts, names, dates, artistic schools.
Facts about the education and career possibilities of an artist.
Facts about processes, tools, and materials.
Knowledge of criteria for various kinds of art products.

Comprehension Level:

Recognition of styles and symbols of various periods.
Ability to understand key ideas in design (unity and variety) and in art history (the hierarchical art of Egypt, the educational and symbolic art of the medieval period, the stylistic breakthroughs of the twentieth century).
Ability to understand the various roles that the visual arts play and their concomitant satisfactions.
Ability to direct attention to specific visual references suggested by the teacher.
Ability to see analogies and to shift frames of reference.
Ability to summarize.

Application Level:

Capable of applying visual principles to studio activity: can carry ideas into practice.
Can function in situations that require assimilation of previous experience, information, and knowledge.

Analysis Level:

Can identify components of an art work (design).
Can point to relationships between elements in a particular composition.

(continued)

gestions. It is hoped that the teacher will add items appropriate for the grade being taught.

Bloom's taxonomy has provided theorists with much of the conceptual framework for the behavioral goals movement, particularly in art education.

Having sorted objectives according to various "levels," the teacher must select activities that will move pupils to the point where they might be evaluated. Obviously, in evaluating the activities some kinds of appraisal will be more appropriate than others. Will the work the children produce provide the point of reference, or will the teacher observe the children in action? Will the tests take a written or verbal form? The children might be asked to study slides and make judgments, provide information orally or write an essay, or they might keep a notebook, sketchbook, or scrapbook. Whatever the method of appraisal, it is the teacher's responsibility to see that the evaluation is consistent with the objectives and activities of the program.

The National Assessment of Educational Progress, operating under the sponsorship of the Educational Commission of the United States, provided one model for appraisal of achievement in learning. The Na-

---

Content and Objectives of the Cognitive Domain

Synthesis:

Ability to unite content, design, materials, and processes into a satisfactory whole.

Can distinguish between the relevant and irrelevant in solving a particular problem.

Can point to means-end relationships in discussing the formation of objects or the creation of a painting.

Receiving Level:

Accepts criticism from teacher.

Listens to comments of classmates in group evaluation.

Is open to varying points of views, styles, and philosophies of a wide range of professional artists, sculptors, and architects.

Responding Level:

Willing to participate in discussion and respond with expressed judgments: capable of an exchange of differing opinions.

Valuing Level:

Willing to pursue positive, constructive criticism and appreciation of the efforts of classmates and of the works of professional artists.

Can distinguish between kinds of values; product values, process values, and aesthetic values in a given work.

Capable of immediate valuing on an emotional level.

Able to make a judgment about an art problem or an art work within a defined context.

Capable of relating criteria to judgment and of developing a personal value system in accordance with mutually accepted standards developed in the art program.

---

tional Assessment project collected data that helped to describe the knowledge, attitudes, and skills gained by American students from age 9 to approximately age 24.[19] Planners who were involved in the initial phase had to state the goals for their subject area as well as the specific criteria for assessing how well the goals were being met. Brent Wilson, the major consultant to the project, appointed a committee composed of individuals with the highest professional qualifications to take the first step—the development of objectives. Feeling that this committee had produced only a summary of the educational ideas that had appeared during the previous quarter century, Wilson formed a second committee and broadened the conception of art they were to work with. The content of "art" was now to include the environmental arts, popular arts, and the informal art education that children receive at home, while traveling, or through the media, as well as the traditional art forms of painting, sculpture, ceramics, and the like. Wilson's committees jointly produced the following objectives of art education.

1. Perceive and respond to [different] aspects of art.
2. Value art as an important realm of human experience.
3. Produce works of art.
4. Know about art.
5. Make and justify judgments about the aesthetic merit . . . of works of art.[20]

As an example of how these objectives are treated, let us examine an outline of the first one:

I. Perceive and respond to aspects of art.

Clarifying Definition: Aspects of art are defined as: sensory qualities of color, line, shape, and texture; compositional elements such as structure, space . . . balance, movement, placement, closure, contrast, and pattern; expressive qualities such as mood, feeling, and emotion; subject matter, including (1) objects, themes (the general subject of a work, i.e., landscape or battle scene), events, and ideas (general presymbolic meanings) and (2) symbols and expressive content, which is a unique fusion of the foregoing aspects.

A. Recognize and describe the subject matter elements of works of art.

Age 9. Identify themes of specific works of art.
Identify events depicted in specific works of art.
Describe how the themes of two or more specific works of art are similar or different.

B. Go beyond the recognition of subject matter to the perception and description of formal qualities and expressive content (the combined effect of the subject matter and the specific visual form that characterizes a particular work of art).

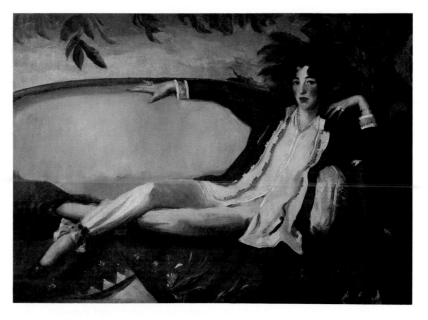

Robert Henri, *Gertrude Vanderbilt Whitney*, 1916. As an analysis task, ask the students to place tracing paper over this portrait and, using a pencil, indicate the major structural lines of the work. (Collection of Whitney Museum of American Art. Gift of Flora Whitney Miller.)

Age 9. Describe the characteristics of sensory qualities of works of art (that is, tell about colors, shapes, lines, and textures in a painting, building, photograph, etc.).
Describe the expressive character (feelings and moods) of works of art.

These behavioral objectives indicate the need for making reproductions part of the conceptual framework. Indeed, one of the National Assessment's unique contributions has been its imaginative use of visual materials (packaging and sculpture as well as reproductions) as part of the evaluation process.

Standardized Art Tests

Techniques for evaluation range from the most formal test to the most informal conversation with a child. A number of standardized art tests are available, dating back to the 1920s and 1930s and include the Meier-Seashore *Art Judgment Test*, the *McAdory Art Test*, and the *Bryan-Schwamm Test*. Although standardized art tests are interesting and provocative, often they are not very reliable and do not apply to the specific needs of classroom situations.[21]

Since the heyday of standardized testing several decades ago, the trend in testing for art ability has been directed toward specific ends — that is, tests have been designed by teachers or research workers to arrive at limited kinds of information. Tests may be designed for a number of purposes, but in all cases they represent "a judgment of the adequacy of behavior as compared to a set of educational objectives."[22] Any test is a reflection of what a teacher considers important in a student's behavior, studio processes, skills, and knowledge about art. The test may be formal or informal, and it may just as easily precede instruction in the form of a diagnostic device as it may follow the instructional period to measure a student's gain. In any case, the test is but one technique among many to gauge the kind and quality of change in the student.

Formal Tests Devised By The Teacher

In addition to the standardized tests devised by experts, there are tests composed by the classroom teacher. Such tests can often be useful, provided the teacher understands their significance. Sometimes the teacher may wish to use a test (usually cognitive) to discover whether or not the pupils have grasped some part of the art program. For example, it may be helpful to present a few questions based on the pupils' knowledge of a specific medium, or of facts surrounding an artist's life, or of techniques in using color.

The following completion-type problem could be used to test knowledge of color mixing:

> Fill in the blanks:
> 1. To obtain a *shade* of red tempera paint, add _____.
> 2. To obtain a *tint* of red watercolor, add _____.
> 3. To turn *blue* to gray, add _____.
> 4. To turn *green* into gray, add _____.

An essay-type answer might be obtained from the following:

> Describe two methods of mixing tempera paint to obtain gray.

Identification and multiple choice tests are useful for younger children, because they do not require written answers of any kind. For example, one item could be the following:

> Which pigment, when added to red tempera paint, will result in a *shade* of red?
> (a) green
> (b) white
> (c) black

Another recognition category might be based on slides and reproductions. After being shown a Rouault and a Rembrandt, a child may be asked the following items:

> An art form that had a great influence on Rouault is:
> (a) impressionist paintings
> (b) stained-glass windows
> (c) sculpture

> Which of the following methods did Rembrandt use to achieve his effects?
> (a) chiaroscuro
> (b) impasto
> (c) glazes
> (d) all of the above

It should be noted that the easiest test items to compose are often technical questions that tend to be trivial compared with the goals of developing personal expressiveness and artistic creativity. The most significant educational objectives are often the most complex and the most difficult to evaluate appropriately.

Informal Evaluations

The Anecdotal Method. Another evaluation device, known as the *anecdotal* method, is also valuable. With this method the teacher periodically jots down observations about each child, based on the questions in the three categories of criteria. A cumulative record of such specific reactions may become a reliable index of a pupil's progress. It at least furnishes the teacher and the pupil with some concrete evidence of strong and weak points in the pupil's art learning conduct.

As an example, opposite some of the items of the sample checklist previously outlined, the following remarks might be set down for a six-year-old in first grade:

The Student:	Comments:
1. Was able to use the concepts of line, shape, and texture in describing a painting by Mary Cassatt.	"Seemed to be very interested in looking at the painting. Good attention span."
2. Participated in class discussions of art reproductions.	"Indicated a special interest in African masks. Made very perceptive remarks about the feeling qualities of the masks. Referred to one of the library books on African art."
3. Participated in group activity of sorting art postcards according to warm and cool colors and primary colors.	"Had some difficulties with sharing and cooperating in group activities. Needs special help to work with group."
4. Completed line drawings done in response to Japanese print and Pollock painting.	"Was not clear about purpose for this activity at first. Was pleased when the drawings were displayed and discussed."

The teacher might also consider commenting from time to time after periodic examination of portfolios. A checklist might be used as a guide in writing these comments, but need not be referred to item by item. Such records give general, overall impressions of a large body of work. The following are examples of notes about children that a teacher might write for a personal file.

I like to draw.

a. I strongly agree.
b. I agree.
c. I am uncertain.
d. I disagree.
e. I strongly disagree.

I like to paint.

a. I strongly agree.
b. I agree.
c. I am uncertain.
d. I disagree.
e. I strongly disagree.

I enjoy learning about artists.

a. I strongly agree.
b. I agree.
c. I am uncertain.
d. I disagree.
e. I strongly disagree.

I like to look at paintings.

a. I strongly agree.
b. I agree.
c. I am uncertain.
d. I disagree.
e. I strongly disagree.

I enjoy talking about art.

a. I strongly agree.
b. I agree.
c. I am uncertain.
d. I disagree.
e. I strongly disagree.

I like to learn about art from other times and places.

a. I strongly agree.
b. I agree.
c. I am uncertain.
d. I disagree.
e. I strongly disagree.

This is a selection from an attitude assessment multiple choice questionnaire used to learn more about students' feelings about the art program and the various types of art activities.

John A (6 years, grade 1)
John uses a variety of personal experiences in his pictures, and he is certainly getting along well lately in trying to develop symbols of houses. It is strange, however, how his work seemed to deteriorate last week. He works hard, though, and participates well in a group.

Roberto L (11 years, grade 6)
He shows himself to be a sensitive child, and his writing about several sculptures from the museum field trip reflects his feelings. He seems to be fascinated by seeing actual sculptures and especially enjoys the painted wood sculptures of Louise Nevelson. His handwriting is improving, but sometimes is barely legible. His art vocabulary is excellent for his age group.

Betty McM (10 years, grade 5)
Betty continues to be careless and untidy; her paints are in a mess, her drawings all thumb-marks, her brushes unwashed. As stage manager of our play, nevertheless, she worked well. She seems to be more at home with sculpture than she is in drawing and painting. Her last sculpture in clay was quite vigorous. She likes to explore new materials and last week brought to school some wood for carving.

The data derived from checklists and other notations will greatly assist the teacher in arriving at an appraisal of a pupil's progress, but it is necessary also to keep a file of the child's actual art production for periodic study and comparison with the written notations. Usually lack of space prevents the teacher from keeping any but the flat work.

These methods of evaluation allow the teacher to summarize the child's progress in only the most general of terms. Once made, however, such a summary will prove valuable to the teacher in making progress reports to parents and others interested in the child's welfare. Such methods are difficult for the art teacher to follow, however, since their effectiveness rests on a day-to-day knowledge of the children being evaluated.

REPORTING PROGRESS IN ART

From time to time every school system reports to parents concerning their children's progress. This is one of the traditional and necessary functions of a school. Every aspect of the program of studies should be mentioned on a report form to parents, if only as a notice to parents that their children have been exposed to the subject. A teacher of art who has waited until report time to reach conclusions about a child's progress can scarcely have acted as an efficient and sympathetic counselor in art. Furthermore, if the pupils must depend on a report card to help them understand their progress, to improve their work, and to give them clues as to future action, communication in the classroom must have reached an extraordinarily low ebb.

Regarding the mechanics of reporting to the parents, several points must be kept in mind. First, the method of reporting must be easily understood by all parents. Any report that makes use of complicated symbols or what is considered by some to be highly professional language (and by others to be an undesirable "pedagese") will not be appreciated by most parents. Second, the report should reflect the objectives and practices of the art program and should attempt to comment on the child, both as an individual and as a member of a group. Third, any good report should, of course, be as accurate and fair as a teacher can make it. Fourth, from the teacher's point of view the system of reporting should not demand a disproportionate amount of clerical work.

Two of the best means of reporting available to teachers of art are *progress reports* and *narrative reports*. The progress report is based on the use of check marks, symbols, or letters. Often only two marks are used — S for satisfactory and U for unsatisfactory. Sometimes the letter O may be employed to signify outstanding progress. The teacher can make subheadings according to content categories (art history, art production), personal behaviors (initiative, social development), or other

～～ **TABLE 18-2**

Checklist for Art Production Activities

The Student:	Exceptional	Average	Below Average
1. Was able to use own experiences			
2. Progressed normally through manipulative symbol preadolescent } stage			
3. Work showed personal style			
4. Produced work that showed (a) respect for material (b) respect for function of object			
5. Used tools (a) appropriate to task (b) with dexterity			
6. Showed ability to use (a) line (b) shape (c) color (d) texture (e) space			
7. Work showed unity of design			
8. Work showed variety of design			
9. Work showed development over period of time			
10. Successfully related (a) art work to school experiences (b) other school experiences to artistic expression			
11. Responded positively to new situations in art			

topics. The parent would then expect to find either S, U, or O opposite each of these subheadings. This system appears to be theoretically sound for reporting art, in that it is based on each child's individual progress, rather than on progress in comparison with that of other pupils.

A teacher not thoroughly familiar with every child might, with the parents' consent, wish to make an initial report to them verbally during a short conference. This method tends to be time-consuming, but because of its flexibility it has some obvious advantages over written reports to parents. It demands, of course, that the teacher have some ability to report both good and bad aspects of a child's efforts without arousing the wrath of a parent. No teacher, furthermore, can afford to

Summary Report[23]

Name _____ Grade _____ Year ____

Personal Development in Art

Is learning to:

___ find own ideas for art

___ refine, modify ideas for art

___ use media effectively

___ perceive, respond to art forms

___ interpret art experience

___ judge the value of art experience

Learning About the Artistic Heritage

Is learning how and why:

___ artists find ideas for their work

___ artists refine, modify their ideas

___ artists use media

___ experts respond to art

___ experts interpret art

___ experts judge art

Learning About Art and Society

Is learning how and why:

___ people** create art

___ people change their art forms

___ people use media for expression

___ people respond to art forms

___ people interpret art forms

___ people judge art forms

Evaluation Key

* = See note on back for comment

G = Is making good progress

E = Is making excellent progress

N = Needs improvement in this area

** First term: (Eskimos, Native Americans) Second term: (People in community)

Reports such as this descriptive summary are useful for parent-teacher conferences about students' progress in art.

arrange an interview of this type without first being fully prepared. For the school's permanent records, a teacher must keep on file a complete written report of each pupil, even if this report is available to the parents only on request. Of course, if the child is gifted the teacher should make the parents aware of this, so that the child can gain support that might otherwise be lacking without this knowledge. Many parents are completely unaware of their children's creative abilities in art making as well as in the other domains of art.

1. Elliot Eisner and David Ecker, *Readings in Art Education* (Waltham, MA: Blaisdell Publishing Co., 1966), p. 400, "The Committee on the Function of Art in General Education."

2. Michael Day, "Evaluating Student Achievement in Discipline-Based Art Programs," *Studies in Art Education*, Vol. 26, No. 4 (1985), pp. 232–40.

3. Elliot Eisner, *The Educational Imagination: On the Design and Evaluation of School Programs*, 2nd ed. (New York: Macmillan, 1985), p. 192.

4. See any of the editions of Viktor Lowenfeld and Lambert Brittain, *Creative and Mental Growth*, 8th ed. (New York: Macmillan, 1988).

5. Michael Day, "The Use of Formative Evaluation in the Art Classroom," *Art Education*, Vol. 27, No. 2 (1974), pp. 3–7.

6. Portions of this chapter appeared originally in Michael Day, "Evaluating Student Achievement in Discipline-Based Art Programs," *Studies in Art Education*, Vol. 26, No. 4 (1985). Used here with permission.

7. See, for example, Monroe Beardsley, *Aesthetics: Problems in the Philosophy of Criticism* (New York: Harcourt, Brace and World, 1958); Stephen Pepper, *The Basis of Criticism in the Arts* (Cambridge, MA: Harvard University Press, 1945); Susanne Langer, *Mind: An Essay on Human Feeling*, Vol. 1 (Baltimore: Johns Hopkins University, 1967); and Eugene Kaelin, *An Aesthetics for Art Educators* (New York: Teachers College Press, 1989).

8. National Art Education Association, *Purposes, Principles, and Standards for School Art Programs* (Reston, VA: NAEA, 1980).

9. Elliot Eisner, *Educating Artistic Vision* (New York: Macmillan, 1972).

10. Laura Chapman, *Approaches to Art in Education* (New York: Harcourt Brace Jovanovich, 1978).

11. National Assessment of Educational Progress, *Art and Young Americans, 1974-79: Results from the Second National Art Assessment*, Report No. 10-A-01. (Denver, CO: NAEA, 1981). Eleanor Norris and Barbara Goodwin, editors.

12. Milbrey McLaughlin and Margaret Thomas, *Art History, Art Criticism, and Art Production: An Examination of Change Across Districts* (Los Angeles: Rand Corporation, 1985).

13. Dennie Wolf, "Opening Up Assessment," *Educational Leadership*, Vol. 45, No. 4 (1988).

14. John Goodlad, *A Place Called School* (New York: McGraw-Hill, 1984).

15. For an interesting study of this topic see Howard Gardner, Ellen Winner and M. Kircher, "Children's Conceptions of the Arts," *Journal of Aesthetic Education*, Vol. 9, No. 3 (1975).

16. Eisner, *op. cit.*, p. 203.

17. Benjamin Bloom, ed., *Taxonomy of Educational Objectives*, Handbook I: *Cognitive Domain* (New York: David McKay, 1956); David Krathwohl, Benjamin Bloom and Bertram Sasia, Handbook II: *Affective Domain* (New York: David McKay, 1964).

18. Ibid., p. 5.

19. National Assessment of Educational Progress, op. cit., p. 6.

20. Ibid.

21. For a thorough discussion of standardized art tests see Gilbert Clark, Enid Zimmerman, and Marilyn Zurmuehlen, *Understanding Art Testing* (Reston, VA: The National Art Education Association, 1987).

22. Elliot Eisner and David Ecker, eds., *Readings in Art Education* (Waltham, MA: Blaisdell, 1966), p. 384.

23. Chapman, *op. cit.*, p. 399.

◆ ACTIVITIES FOR THE READER

1. Describe some situations in which the art program reflects the educational outlook of (a) a school principal; (b) a school board; (c) a community.
2. Devise some test items in art as follows:
   a. A true-false type to test third grade pupils' knowledge of handling clay.
   b. A recall or completion type to test fourth grade pupils' knowledge of color mixing.
   c. A multiple choice type to test sixth grade pupils' knowledge of art history.
   d. A matching items type to test fifth grade pupils' ability to use a mixed media technique.
   e. A recognition type to test sixth grade pupils' knowledge of art terms.
3. Make checklists for (a) appreciation of sculpture by sixth grade pupils; (b) skills needed by fourth grade pupils when doing art criticism.
4. Over a period of two weeks, study the art output of a group of ten children and write a paragraph of

not more than fifty words for each child, summarizing their progress.

5. Describe any results, either good or bad, that you have observed as a result of competitive marking of children's art. How do those who have received a poor grade react?

6. Study the checklist in Table 18-2. Try to rework a portion of it to reflect part or all of Bloom's taxonomy of educational objectives.

7. Imagine yourself to be a parent. How would you want art to change your child? List the outcomes that, in your parental view, would demonstrate the effectiveness of art education. Pick a specific age level.

8. Make a checklist of items that would reflect the attitudinal change of the principal and faculty with respect to the art program.

9. Review the works by artists in this book and select three that would make good subjects for a pictorial analysis exercise involving the use of an overlay of tracing paper. Can these exercises be assigned according to grade level or experience of children?

◆ SUGGESTED READINGS

Bloom, Benjamin, ed. *Taxonomy of Educational Objectives*, Handbook I: *Cognitive Domain* (New York: David McKay, 1956); David Krathwohl, Benjamin Bloom, and Bertram Sasia. Handbook II: *Affective Domain* (New York: David McKay, 1964). See Chapter 17, "Evaluation of Learning in Art Education," by Brent Wilson.

Clark, Gilbert, Enid Zimmerman, and Marilyn Zurmuehlen. *Understanding Art Testing*. Reston, VA: The National Art Education Association, 1987.

Day, Michael. "The Use of Formative Evaluation in the Art Classroom." *Art Education*, Vol. 27, No. 2 (1974).

_____. "Evaluating Student Achievement in Discipline-Based Art Programs." *Studies in Art Education*, Vol. 26, No. 4 (1985).

Eisner, Elliot. *The Educational Imagination: On the Design and Evaluation of School Programs*, 2nd ed. New York: Macmillan, 1985. This book develops the notion of educational connoisseurship as a means for evaluation.

National Assessment of Educational Progress. *Art and Young Americans, 1974-79: Results from the Second National Art Assessment*, Report No. 10-A-01. Denver, CO: 1981. Report on results of national art testing.

Stake, Robert, ed., *Evaluating the Arts in Education: A Responsive Approach*. Columbus, OH: Charles E. Merrill, 1975. A discussion of evaluation based upon the author's "responsive" approach.

Worthen, Blaine, and James Sanders. *Educational Evaluation: Alternative Approaches and Practical Guidelines*. New York: Longman, 1987. This is a comprehensive and practical introduction to professional educational evaluation.

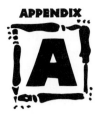

APPENDIX

A HISTORICAL FRAMEWORK FOR ART EDUCATION: DATES, PERSONALITIES, PUBLICATIONS, AND EVENTS

In the chronological listing of events and personalities in this appendix, there may be omissions which are inevitable and obvious to anyone familiar with the subject. What this listing does indicate are the antecedents of a content-based, balanced art program. The development of the child-centered program can also be traced, as can other directions. The authors suggest the following ways of using the chronology:

1. Updating the listing as the reader discovers personalities and events that have not been included.

2. Placing information from art history and other frames of reference in parallel columns.

1749 Benjamin Franklin advocates art instruction in the school curriculum for its use for utilitarian functions, thus establishing himself as a precursor of the Massachusetts drawing provision of 1870.

1827 A course in drawing is offered to students of Boston English High School.

1839 Horace Mann, while secretary of the Massachusetts Board of Education, visits Germany to study the teaching of drawing. He is particularly impressed by one teacher, Peter Schmidt, and publishes Schmidt's lessons. Mann viewed drawing as a source of pleasure, as well as leading to a vocation. G. Stanley Hall also visits Germany, but unlike Mann, he studies psychology instead of drawing. When Hall develops the idea that is to grow into the Child Study Movement (late 1800s), a marriage between psychology and art education is begun. The enduring nature of this partnership is reflected by the current research of Project Zero, which shares with Hall an association with Harvard University.

1849   William Minifie teaches drawing in the Boys High School in Baltimore, and like Benjamin Franklin, Walter Smith, and William Bentley Fowle, uses a "scientific" sequential approach to carry out his belief in drawing as a practical and useful skill.

Mid 1800s   Fowle publishes the *Common Schools Journal*, introducing the monitorial system—training students to teach other students. Fowle stresses the use of maps and blackboards and eliminates corporal punishment. Fowle writes over fifty books on all phases of education, and translates a European text on drawing.

By 1870   The Oswego Movement of the Oswego, New York Normal School, following the lead of the Kindergarten Movement, stresses the use of instructional "objects" such as charts, cards, picture sets, blocks, specimens in glass, textiles, and maps in the classroom. Although intended for general education, the implication of "objects" for art education becomes clearer over time. Related to this are the "type forms" or geometric models of spheres, cones, cubes, pyramids—those basic pure forms Cezanne referred to as the structural components of natural form. Type forms are formally introduced to art education students at the Pratt Institute in 1886. The dominant figure at Oswego is Herman Krusi, whose books on drawing influence classroom teachers.

1871   Walter Smith is invited to the Massachusetts Normal Art School by the state to help teachers fulfill a new state requirement for the teaching of drawing, to prepare students to function as draftsmen and designers.

1896   As head of the newly established department of pedagogy, John Dewey initiates the Laboratory School at the University of Chicago to test his theories in the classroom. Dewey sees education as an interactive process occurring between children and ideas. Using ideas as tools for learning, children literally create their own reality rather than study from a fixed, rational, ordered point of view, represented by the thinking of the philosopher Hegel. This utilitarian or pragmatic view of education is developed in Dewey's future writing.

1899   The NEA (National Education Association) appoints a committee to report on the teaching of drawing in the public schools. Their report stresses art appreciation, development of the creative impulse, the use of perceptual training for representational drawing, drawing as a vocational preparation, and the rejection of the use of public schools for the training of professional artists.

1899 *The Teacher's Manual (Part IV)* of the 8-volume Prang series of art instruction is designed to serve classroom teachers, using such consultants as Winslow Homer, Arthur Dow, and Frederick Church to develop curricula in aesthetic judgment, art history, nature drawing, perspective, decoration, design, and paper construction.

1899 *New Methods in Education* by J. Liberty Tadd is published. Tadd, the Director of the Public School of Industrial Arts in Philadelphia, is the first American art educator whose influence is felt in Europe. (He was invited to lecture in Great Britain.) His book is a marked departure from Walter Smith, stressing working directly from nature.

1901 The publication of *The Applied Arts Book* edited by James Hall promotes "projects and activities" that were to lead art teachers away from the "scientific" method of Walter Smith. A Massachusetts Normal Art School graduate, Henry Turner Bailey, is appointed editor of the newly titled *School Arts Book*.

1904 Franz Cizek, an Austrian artist/teacher begins his children's classes at the Vienna School of Applied Art. Cizek rejects the idea of realistic drawing and instead, draws upon the personal reaction, memories, and experiences of students. The pictorial results are so impressive that art educators from America come to study his methods. One observer (Thomas Munro of the Cleveland Museum) comes to the conclusion that the consistently high quality of student work is attributable to the structured nature of Cizek's teaching, a contradiction of which he (Cizek) may not have been aware.

1904–1922 Arthur Wesley Dow becomes the major spokesperson for the importance of composition or structure of art, what is now referred to as the elements and principles of art. Dow writes, teaches, and promotes his theories while teaching at Teacher's College, Columbia University. His first book (*Composition*, 1899) is centered around three concepts from the Japanese: line, color (notan), and value.

1911 The *Encyclopedia of Education* includes the first article on art education.

1912 Fifty art supervisors are working in New York City.

1912 Walter Sargent (University of Chicago), in his book *Fine and Industrial Art in the U.S.*, stresses the need to respect the child's needs, interests, and desire to create art, calling attention to the uneven course of progress in a child's ability to draw, and recommending the study of conventions established by artists as a means of developing ability in drawing. Some of Sargent's ideas have reemerged today, most recently in books and articles by Brent and Marjorie Wilson. (See chapter bibliographies)

1919 Pedro J. Lemos succeeds Henry Turner Baily as editor of *School Arts Book*, currently published as *School Arts Magazine*. Over time *School Arts* moves closer to serving art teachers as well as elementary classroom teachers.

1920s As Dewey's ideas begin to merge with other child-centered educators, the era of progressive education grows, lasting until the demise of the movement in the 1930s, during which time the public schools attempt to apply ideas that have had greater success in private schools. The progressives are committed to unit or project learning and integration of subjects. "Creative expression" becomes a catchword of the movement and continues to be used with less regularity. Since the teacher's responsibility is to provide materials and foster an environment conducive to freedom and exploration, the content of art is not deemed important. One consequence of emphasis upon the child rather that upon art is a decline in gains made by the Picture Study Movement. Many of the progressives' ideas will re-surface in the 1960s in the books of "radical" critics such as John Holt.

1920-1930 The Picture Study Movement thrives as an antecedent of the current discipline-based art education movement. Encouraged by advances in printing technology and the use of color reproductions, art appreciation is taken seriously as part of a balanced program. The goals of appreciation lie on the moralistic as well as the aesthetic side as sentimental narrative works take precedence over contemporary European exemplars. Pictorial images are regarded as natural vehicles for transmitting society's most dearly held values (patriotism, family, religion, etc.).

1924 Belle Boas publishes *Art in the Schools*, advocating art appreciation through an applied arts philosophy.

1925 The Carnegie Corporation supports a report on the role of art education prepared by the Federated Council in its call for greater content in art.

1927 The NEA, in its annual meeting in Dallas, Texas, recognizes art as fundamental in the education of children.

1932 *The Teaching of Art* by Margaret Mathias is published, contributing to the growth of serious literature in art education.

1933 The Owatonna Art Project in Minnesota creates an art program that falls not only within the responsibility of the school system, but responds to the needs of the citizenry, promoting and advising on home decoration, art in public places, landscaping, and even window display, thus demonstrating that art can be public as well as private, personal as well as utilitarian, and art teachers are capable of raising the general aesthetic level of an entire community. One of the teachers is Edwin Ziegfeld, later to become the first president in INSEA, head of the department of art education at Teacher's College, Columbia University, and author of *Today's Art*. The Owatonna Project loses its impact at the onset of WWII, but retains its importance as a historic landmark in art education.

1933 While Owatonna is getting underway, teachers from Germany's Bauhaus, an art academy that significantly influenced American art and art education, escape from Hitler and arrive at Black Mountain College in North Carolina, led by the painter Josef Albers. By the time the Bauhaus has to move to a more permanent setting at the Institute of Design in Chicago, the ideas begun in Germany begin to exert an influence in curricula of a growing number of American art programs. Chief among these is the growth of photography and photograms, a new attitude toward experimentation with materials, and an approach to design based more on the ideas of Johannes Itten than Arthur Dow. Architecture is accepted as a valid part of an art program.

1938 Leon Loyal Winslow, director of art for Baltimore City Schools publishes *The Integrated School Art Program* demonstrating a need and method for using art as a catalyst for learning academic subjects.

1940 Natalie Robinson Cole's *Art in the Classroom* reaffirms the importance of creative expression and is one of the few books to deal with the subject from a personal point of view. (Seonid Robertson's *Rose Garden and Labyrinth* is a good example of how an English art educator worked in this limited genre.)

1942 Victor D'Amico's *Creative Teaching in Art* states the case for the nature of creativity, moving closer to the artist as model. As director of the children's program for the Museum of Modern Art in N.Y.C., D'Amico creates a laboratory to carry out his ideas and exercise his power as a creative, charismatic teacher.

1943 Herbert Read, a British poet, philosopher, and critic publishes *Education Through Art*. Like Lowenfeld and Dewey, Read sees aesthetic education as the logical center for education in general. He inventories European and British developmental theories and endows his ideas with a wide frame of references from art, psychology, and philosophy.

1947 Viktor Lowenfeld's major work, *Creative and Mental Growth*, is published. Immensely influential, and still in use, Lowenfeld (another refugee from Germany) reorganizes the threads of developmental study of child art begun in Europe and relates these to the formation of personality. The authoritative and comprehensive nature of the book establishes it as a classic of enormous influence both here and abroad.

1947 The NAEA (National Art Education Association) is founded, adding three geographical regions to the existing Eastern Arts Association.

1950   Creativity is taken seriously by the psychological community and numerous research studies are conducted to study the creative personality. J. P. Guilford, president of the American Psychological Association, calls the attention of his colleagues to a hitherto neglected area embraced previously by art educators in the progressive era.

1951   The International Society for Education Through Art (INSEA) is founded by UNESCO in Bristol, England, with the guidance of Sir Herbert Read. The purpose of INSEA is to provide periodic forums for art educators interested in the philosophy, objectives, curricula, and methodology of art education within an international framework. Meetings are held on a national, regional, and tri-yearly basis. Americans who have served as presidents are Edwin Ziegfeld, Al Hurwitz, and Elliot Eisner.

1956   The publishing of Thomas Munro's *Art Education, Its Philosophy and Psychology,* is the first scholarly attempt by a museum-based educationalist and aesthetician to focus attention upon art education.

1957   The Soviets launch *Sputnik,* an event that establishes their lead over the U.S. in space technology, provoking a reevaluation of American education, beginning with science and mathematics, attempts at curricular reform, and eventually, reaching art education in later years.

1958   Congress passes the National Defense Education Act to encourage a reevaluation of curriculum, primarily in the "defense-related" subjects of math, science, and foreign languages. Art education receives limited funding along with other academic subjects.

1959   Blanche Jefferson's *Teaching Art to Children* is published.

1960   Viktor Lowenfeld dies.

1960–1970   The "greening" or consciousness-raising of America prior to the end of the Viet Nam War results in an awareness of the diversity of American ethnicity, environmental awareness, and an acceleration of interest in media technology.

1961   *Preparation for Art* by June King McFee is published, providing a significant shift towards the importance of perceptual and environmental issues in planning curriculum.

1962   Manual Barkan's article, "Transitions in Art Education: Changing Conceptions of Curriculum Content and Teaching," published in the *Art Education Journal of the NAEA,* marks the initial stage of a movement toward increased emphasis on art content in art education. This period is also a time of openness towards newer media, borrowed from the revolution of youth culture that was occurring in higher education. It parallels the more conservative rational methods of the accountability movement which represented mainstream thinking in all areas of education.

1965 The publication of *Art Education: The 64th Yearbook of the National Society for the Study of Education*, an anthology of essays by leaders in art education, serves as a status report on U.S. art educators. This book should be compared to the fortieth yearbook, published some 30 years earlier. A later, if somewhat briefer effort, is the *Report of the NAEA Commission on Art Education* (1977).

1965 The "Seminar in Art Education for Research and Curriculum Development," held at Penn State University, is the first conference to bring together artists, critics, historians, philosophers, and art educators in an attempt to reevaluate the nature of the curriculum in art education.

1968 Under the direction of Elliot Eisner, the Kettering Project at Stanford University develops a comprehensive elementary art curriculum based on art content.

1969 The National Assessment of Art is conducted at the request of the U.S. Office of Education. This study examines the knowledge, skills, and attitudes regarding art of 9, 13, and 17-year-olds using the objectives of art education as a basis of study. Brent Wilson is the major investigator. Mary Rouse and Guy Hubbard of Indiana University write *Meaning, Method, and Media*, the first commercially available elementary art curriculum.

1972 The Central Midwestern Regional Educational Laboratory (CEMREL) under the direction of Stanley Madeja is the first government-funded project to develop curriculum materials in aesthetic education, including art, music, dance, and drama. CEMREL utilized artists, historians, critics, and aestheticians as consultants.

1973 The Alliance for Arts Education is formed through a mandate of the John F. Kennedy Center and joins a growing family of support groups attempting to bring arts education closer to the mainstream of American educators. Art education is moving out of isolation and is included in all arts education deliberations. Other organizations which work for the arts as a whole are the JDR Fundamentals in Arts in Education Program, the State Arts Alliances programs, and the creation of the National Endowment for the Arts, with its support of numerous projects including the Artist-in-Schools program.

1981 A program on the gifted and talented in art is held at the NAEA convention in Chicago. This is to a large degree art education's response to a general interest in children with special needs and leads to a number of publications and conferences in art education as well as new programs for children and adolescents, such as the growth of magnet schools.

1982 The Getty Center for Education in the Arts is created as one of the trust's seven units. Headed by Lani Lattin Duke, the Getty Center offers support for discipline-based art education in the public schools through a program of research, publications, conferences, grants, and regional institutes. Laura Chapman publishes *Instant Art Instant Culture*, an independent view of art education policy that includes survey reports and recommendations for future practice.

1984 Dwaine Greer introduces the term "disciplined-based art education" in his article in *Studies in Art Education* entitled "A Discipline-Based Art Education: Approaching Art as a Subject Study."

1988 The National Endowment for the Arts publishes *Towards Civilization: A Report on Arts Education*, which attempts to reveal the status of the arts in education in the U.S.

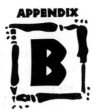

PROFESSIONAL RESPONSIBILITY AND PROFESSIONAL ASSOCIATIONS

We all agree that teaching is not just a job, and that preparing future generations of citizens for their place in society is the most important work that we can do. Dedicated teachers who view education as a career recognize their responsibilities as professionals. As citizens in our communities, as well as professional educators, we are often called upon to provide assistance and guidance in developing and maintaining sound programs of education for children and young people. Because of our education and experience as teachers, we have much to offer our communities and many insights about education that are not available to ordinary citizens from other walks of life.

We find that we face several responsibilities as professional teachers. First, we have an obligation to gain the best preparation for teaching by excelling in our undergraduate education so that we will have much to offer our students. As in-service teachers we should keep up with change and innovation in our subject areas, as well as with the issues and trends of education as a field and the place of education in our communities and in society. Like professionals in law, medicine, business, and other fields, we should be active in our professional associations, subscribe to our professional journals, and participate in the educational issues of the day to assure that the children receive the best education that we know how to provide.

If we, as teachers, are to model for our students the excitement of learning and the values and benefits of education, we must be active learners in our own right. We should collect, keep, and add to a professional library of important works in our field. We should be active learners by participating and enjoying the subject area of our teaching expertise. For teachers of art this means that we seek opportunities to visit art museums and galleries, read the current art books and periodicals, and take time to express our ideas and feelings through our own art production. The excitement and joy that we gain through our participation in and appreciation of art will be conveyed directly to our students. There is no substitute for our own enthusiasm and participation in the life of the mind. Students cannot be fooled; they seem to know which of their teachers are genuine in their advocacy of learning and education.

All too often teachers feel isolated from their colleagues, as they spend nearly their entire working days with their young students. Like professionals in other fields, teachers need time and opportunities to share ideas and values with their peers. Active membership in local, regional, and national professional associations provides many such opportunities. The following list is provided to encourage interested teachers to participate as professionals, to learn from their colleagues, and to become leaders in the advocacy of sound education for all children and young people.

The National Art Education Association
1916 Association Drive
Reston, VA 22091

NAEA publishes *Art Education*, the *NAEA Newsletter*, and *Studies in Art Education*, plus a list of professional publications. It sponsors an annual NAEA convention in a different city each year and provides insurance and other professional benefits of membership.

State Art Education Associations
Nearly all states have professional art education associations, many of which are affiliated with the NAEA. Most state associations hold annual conferences and other programs for teachers.

INSEA, the International Society for Education Through Art
For membership, write to:
Professor Kit Grauer
University of British Columbia
Department of Art Education
Vancouver, B.C. V6T 1Z5
Canada

This is the *UNESCO* international organization of art educators. World congresses are held every three years in different countries. Regional congresses are held annually in one or more of the six regions of the Society: Asia, Southeast Asia/Pacific, Latin America, Europe, Middle East and Africa, and North America. INSEA publishes *INSEA News* on a triannual basis.

National Endowment for the Arts
1100 Pennsylvania Avenue, NW
Washington, DC 20506

National Endowment for the Humanities
1100 Pennsylvania Avenue, NW
Washington, DC 20506

State Boards of Education

All of the states have state agencies that regulate, administer, and certify within that state. These are usually known as the state boards of education. Staffs of state boards of education often have a person who has responsibility for art education or for education in all of the arts. These state art coordinators or directors are excellent professional contacts and usually have very current contact with issues, educational materials, and resources for art education. Their jobs often include working with school district arts leaders within their respective states.

State Arts Agencies

Most states have state arts agencies that administer state arts funds, as well as monies that come to the states from the national endowments. These agencies are known by several titles, such as councils, commissions, boards, and foundations. State arts agencies administer arts in education programs and grants to artists and arts organizations.

Other Resource Organizations

American Arts Alliance
1319 F Street NW, Suite 307
Washington, DC 20004

American Council for the Arts
1285 Avenue of the Americas
New York, NY 10019

American Craft Council
40 W. 53rd Street
New York, NY 10019

College Art Association
275 Seventh Avenue
New York, NY 10001

Getty Center for Education
in the Arts
1875 Century Park East,
Suite 2300
Los Angeles, CA 90067

For 1300 pages of names, addresses, and descriptions of educational institutions and organizations in the United States, many of them dedicated to the arts, see *The Official Museum Directory*, published yearly by The American Association of Museums, Macmillan Directory Division. Contact:

National Register Publishing Company
3004 Glenview Road
Wilmette, IL 60091

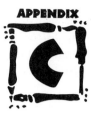

APPENDIX

ART TEACHING AND LEARNING RESOURCES

Following are some of the producers of art learning materials. We suggest that you write to these addresses for catalogs and lists of available materials.

Alarion Press
P.O. Box 1882
Boulder, CO 80306
Art learning programs

American Crafts Council
44 W. 53rd Street
New York, NY 10019
Slides and learning resources

American School Publishers
Box 408
Hightstown, NJ 08520
Filmstrips and learning
resources

Art Education, Inc.
28 E. Erie Street
Blauvelt, NY 10913
Art prints and learning resources

Art Extension Press
Box 389
Westport, CT 06880
Art prints

Binney & Smith, Inc.
1100 Church Lane
P.O. Box 451
Easton, PA 18044-0431
Dream-Makers support program
and art materials

Bower Studios
76 Main Street
Vergennes, VT 05491
ARCHIBLOCKS, architectural
building blocks

Corporation for Public
Broadcasting
The Annenberg/CPB Project
P.O. Box 1922
Santa Barbara, CA 93116-1922
Art of the Western World video
series

CRIZMAC
1647 Alvernon Way Suite #4
Tucson, AZ 85712
Art learning resources

Crystal Productions
Box 2159
Glenview, IL 60025
Filmstrips, videos, prints, slides

Dale Seymour Publications
P.O. Box 10888
Palo Alto, CA 94303
Prints, filmstrips, and learning
  resources

Davis Publications, Inc.
Box 15015
50 Portland Street
Worcester, MA 01615-0015
Art prints and learning
  resources

Educational Dimensions
Department 108, Box 126
Stamford, CT 06904
Filmstrips and learning
  resources

Encyclopaedia Britannica
  Educational Corporation
310 S. Michigan Avenue
Chicago, IL 60604
Films, videos, and learning
  resources

Film Associates
11559 Santa Monica Blvd.
Los Angeles, CA 90025
Films

Films Incorporated Video
5547 N. Ravenswood Avenue
Chicago, IL 60640-1199
Home vision

International Film Bureau, Inc.
332 South Michigan Avenue
Chicago, IL 60604-4382
Films and videos

Media for the Arts
P.O. Box 1011
Newport, RI 02840

MELD
464 E. Walnut Street
Kutztown, PA 19530
Art games and learning
  resources

Phoenix Films & Video, Inc.
468 Park Avenue South
New York, NY 10016
Films and videos

Reading & O'Reilly, Inc.
P.O. Box 302
2 Kensett Avenue
Wilton, CT 06897
Wilton filmstrips and videos

Roland Collection
3120 Pawtucket Road
Northbrook, IL 60062
Films and videos

Sandak, Inc.
70 Lincoln Street
Boston, MA 02111
Slides

Society for Visual Education,
  Inc.
Department BP
1345 Diversey Parkway
Chicago, IL 60614-1299
Prints, filmstrips, video and
  learning resources

Starry Night Distributors, Inc.
19 North Street
Rutland, VT 05701
Art prints and learning resources

University Prints
21 East Street, P.O. Box 485
Winchester, MA 01890
Art Prints

The Voyager Company
1351 Pacific Coast Highway
Santa Monica, CA 90401
Interactive laser videodiscs

Producers of art learning materials *(continued)*

Yellow Ball Workshop
62 Tarbell Avenue
Lexington, MA 02173
Films

Zephyr Press Learning Materials
P.O. Box 13488, Department F8
Tucson, AZ 85732-3448
Games and art learning
  resources

Art Curriculums

Art Image Publications, Inc.
P.O. Box 568
Champlain, NY 12919-0568
Art Image, grades 1–6

Crystal Productions
Box 2159
Glenview, IL 60025
Multicultural art prints

Dale Seymour Publications
P.O. Box 10888
Palo Alto, CA 94303
The SPECTRA Program, grades
  K–6

Davis Publications, Inc.
Box 15015
50 Portland Street
Worcester, MA 01615-0015
Discover Art and *Teaching Art*,
  grades 1–6

Holt, Rinehart and Winston
School Department
1627 Woodland Avenue
Austin, TX 78741
Art Works, grades 1–6

Phi Delta Kappa
8th and Union Streets,
P.O. Box 789
Bloomington, IN 47402-0789
SWRL Elementary Art Program,
  grades K–8

Prentice Hall
Route 59 at Brookhill Drive
West Nyack, NY 10995-9900
Art Smart, grades 3–9

Art Museum Education Resources

The museums listed below provide a variety of art education resource materials. This is a partial listing of the hundreds of museums in the U.S. For the sake of brevity, no university museums have been included. Contact your local college or university museums for information about their resources. For details of each museum's resources, write to the following addresses:

Albright-Knox Art Gallery
1285 Elmwood Avenue
Buffalo, NY 14222

American Art and Portrait
  Gallery
8th and F Streets, N.W.
Washington, DC 20560

American Craft Museum
40 West 53rd Street
New York, NY 10019

Amon Carter Museum of
  Western Art
3501 Camp Bowie Blvd.
P.O. Box 2365
Fort Worth, TX 76107

Art Institute of Chicago
S. Michigan and E. Adams
Chicago, IL 60603

Arthur M. Sackler Gallery
Asian and Near Eastern Art
1050 Independence Avenue,
   S.W.
Washington, DC 20560

Asian Art Museum of San
   Francisco
Gold Gate Park
San Francisco, CA 94118

Baltimore Museum of Art
Art Museum Drive
Baltimore, MD 21218

Buffalo Bill Historical Center
720 Sheridan Avenue
Cody, WY 82414

Carnegie Museum of Art
4400 Forbes Avenue
Pittsburgh, PA 15213

Contemporary Arts Museum
5216 Montrose at Bissonnet
Houston, TX 77006

Cincinnati Art Museum
Eden Park
Cincinnati, OH 45202-1596

Cleveland Museum of Art
11150 East Blvd.
Cleveland, OH 44106

Cooper-Hewitt Museum
National Museum of Design
2 East 91st Street
New York, NY 10128

Dallas Museum of Art
1717 N. Harwood
Dallas, TX 75203

Delaware Art Museum
2301 Kentmere Pkwy.
Wilmington, DE 19806

Denver Museum of Art
100 W. 14th Avenue Pkwy.
Denver, CO 80204

Detroit Institute of Arts
5200 Woodward Avenue
Detroit, MI 48202

Freer Gallery of Art
Jefferson Drive at 12th Street,
   S.W.
Washington, DC 20024

Frick Collection
1 E. 70th Street
New York, NY 10021

Greenville County Museum of
   Art
420 College Street
Greenville, SC 29601

High Museum of Art
133 Peachtree Street, N.E.
Atlanta, GA 30303

Hirshhorn Museum and
   Sculpture Garden
Independence Avenue at 8th
   Street, SW
Washington, DC 20560

Huntington Museum of Art
2033 McCoy Road
Huntington, WV 25701

Institute of American Indian
   Arts Museum
1369 Cerrillos Road
Santa Fe, NM 87504

J. Paul Getty Museum
17985 Pacific Coast Highway
Malibu, CA 90265
Mail: P.O. Box 2112
Santa Monica, CA 90406

Joslyn Art Museum
2200 Dodge Street
Omaha, NE 68102

Art Museum Education Resources *(continued)*

Kimbell Art Museum
3333 Camp Bowie Blvd.
Fort Worth, TX 76107

Los Angeles County Museum of
  Art
5905 Wilshire Blvd.
Los Angeles, CA 90036

Metropolitan Museum of Art
Fifth Avenue and 82nd Street
New York, NY 10028

Milwaukee Art Museum
750 N. Lincoln Memorial Drive
Milwaukee, WI 53202

Minneapolis Institute of Arts
2400 Third Avenue South
Minneapolis, MN 55404

Minnesota Museum of Art
Landmark Center—Fifth and
  Market
St. Paul, MN 55102-1486

Museum of Contemporary Art
237 E. Ontario Street
Chicago, IL 60611

Museum of Contemporary Art,
  Los Angeles
250 S. Grand Avenue, California
  Plaza
Los Angeles, CA 90012

Museum of the American
  Indian, Heye Foundation
Broadway at 155th Street
New York, NY 10032

Museum of Fine Arts
465 Huntington Avenue
Boston, MA 02115

Museum of Fine Arts, Houston
1001 Bissonnet
Houston, TX 77005

Museum of Fine Arts
107 W. Palace
Santa Fe, NM 87501

Museum of Modern Art
11 West 53rd Street
New York, NY 10019

National Gallery of Art
Sixth Street and Constitution
  Avenue, N.W.
Washington, DC 20565

National Museum of African Art
Smithsonian Institution
950 Independence Avenue, S.W.
Washington, DC 20560

Nelson-Atkins Museum of Art
4525 Oak Street
Kansas City, MO 64111

North Carolina Museum of Art
2110 Blue Ridge Blvd.
Raleigh, NC 27607

Oakland Museum
1000 Oak Street
Oakland, CA 94607

Oklahoma Museum of Art
7316 Nichols Road
Oklahoma City, OK 73120

Portland Art Museum
1219 S.W. Park Avenue
Portland, OR 97205

Saint Louis Art Museum
Forest Park
St. Louis, MO 63110

San Francisco Museum of
  Modern Art
401 Van Ness Avenue
San Francisco, CA 94102

Seattle Art Museum
Volunteer Park
Seattle, WA 98112

Solomon R. Guggenheim
  Museum of Art
1071 Fifth Avenue
New York, NY 10128

Southwest Museum
234 Museum Drive
Los Angeles, CA 90065

Virginia Museum of Fine Arts
2800 Grove Avenue
Richmond, VA 23221-2466

Walker Art Center
Vineland Place
Minneapolis, MN 55403

Whitney Museum of American
  Art
945 Madison Avenue
New York, NY 10021

Wichita Art Museum
619 Stackman Drive
Wichita, KS 67203

INDEX